6/05

Botswana

Okavango Delta • Chobe • Northern Kalahari

THE BRADT TRAVEL GUIDE

Chris McIntyre

Bradt Travel Guides Ltd, UK
The Globe Pequot Press Inc, USA

Reprinted February 2005

Bradt Travel Guides Ltd
19 High Street, Chalfont St Peter, Bucks SL9 9QE, England
www.bradtguides.com
Published in the USA by The Globe Pequot Press Inc, 246 Goose Lane,
PO Box 480, Guilford, Connecticut 06475-0480

British Library Cataloguing in Publication Data
A catalogue record for this book is available from the British Library

ISBN-10: 1 84162 024 6
ISBN-13: 978 184162 024 4

Photographs
Front cover Saddle-billed stork (Richard du Toit)
Text Chris McIntyre (CM), Rob McDowell (RM), David MacCallum-Price (DM),
Richard du Toit (RT), Ariadne Van Zandbergen (AZ)

Illustrations Annabel Milne, Carole Vincer
Maps Steve Munns

Typeset from the author's disc by Wakewing
Printed and bound in Italy by Legoprint SpA, Trento

Author and Contributors

AUTHOR

Chris McIntyre went to Africa in 1987, after reading physics at Queen's College, Oxford. He taught with VSO in Zimbabwe for almost three years and travelled around extensively. In 1990 he co-authored the UK's first *Guide to Namibia and Botswana*, published by Bradt, before spending three years as a shipbroker in London.

After that, Chris concentrated on what he enjoys: Africa. In 1996 he wrote the first guidebook to *Zambia* for Bradt, and later their acclaimed *Namibia* guide. Whilst keeping these updated, he is now managing director of Sunvil Africa – a specialist tour operator which organises a variety of high-quality trips throughout southern Africa, including Botswana.

He maintains a keen interest in development and conservation issues, is a Fellow of the Royal Geographical Society, and contributes photographs and articles to various publications, including *The Times, Wanderlust, BBC Wildlife* and *Travel Africa*. Based in west London, Chris spends two or three months each year researching in Africa, but can usually be contacted by email on africa@sunvil.co.uk.

MAJOR CONTRIBUTORS

Judi Helmholz counts travel consultant, entrepreneur, safari guide, chicken farmer and 'facilitator' among her occupations. She lives beside the Zambezi with her husband, Arthur, several rottweilers and 4,000 chickens. She is active in Livingstone's Tourism Association and conservation, and contributed much of the information for the Livingstone chapter.

Octavia Kenny studied Old English literature and archaeology at Oxford and York, before becoming a museum curator, with a particular interest in oral history. Octavia researched and wrote most of the history in the first chapter, and kept her cool during a long research trip to the Kalahari. She currently lives and writes in London, and travels as much as possible.

David MacCallum-Price spent eight years in southern Africa and travelled around Botswana extensively, often behind the wheel of his trusty old Series III Land Rover. More recently, he's visited many of the private reserves, helping with comments and additions on several sections of this book. David now works at Sunvil Africa, arranging trips for others around Africa.

Mike Unwin is a freelance natural history writer and illustrator, and author of Bradt's *Southern African Wildlife: A Visitor's Guide*. Mike contributed much expert natural history information, especially on the Kalahari's great salt pans. He now lives in England, having spent seven years in southern Africa pursuing wildlife around all corners of the region. In 2000, he won the *BBC Wildlife Magazine* Travel Writing competition.

THE BRADT STORY
Hilary Bradt

The first Bradt travel guide was written by Hilary and George Bradt in 1974 on a river barge floating down a tributary of the Amazon in Bolivia. From their base in Boston, Massachusetts, they went on to write and publish four other backpacking guides to the Americas and one to Africa.

In the 1980s Hilary continued to develop the Bradt list in England, and also established herself as a travel writer and tour leader. The company's publishing emphasis evolved towards broader-based guides to new destinations – usually the first to be published on those countries – complemented by hiking, rail and wildlife guides.

Since winning *The Sunday Times* Small Publisher of the Year Award in 1997, we have continued to fill the demand for detailed, well-written guides to unusual destinations, while maintaining the company's original ethos of low-impact travel.

Travel guides are by their nature continuously evolving. If you experience anything which you would like to share with us, or if you have any amendments to make to this guide, please write; all your letters are read and passed on to the author. Most importantly, do remember to travel with an open mind and to respect the customs of your hosts – it will add immeasurably to your enjoyment.

KEY TO STANDARD SYMBOLS

—·—·—	International boundary	🏛	Historic building
------	District boundary	✝	Church or cathedral
------	National park boundary	♟	Buddhist temple
✈	Airport (international)	🏠	Buddhist monastery
✈	Airport (other)	♠	Hindu temple
✈	Airstrip	☾	Mosque
🚁	Helicopter service	▶	Golf course
══	Railway	🏃	Stadium
----------	Footpath	▲	Summit
--🚢--	Car ferry	△	Boundary beacon
--🚢--	Passenger ferry	◉	Outpost
⛽	Petrol station or garage	⤬	Gate
🅿	Car park	🅐	Rock shelter
🚌	Bus station etc	⌐⟶	Cable car, funicular
🚲	Cycle hire	══	Mountain pass
M	Underground station	○	Waterhole
⌂	Hotel, inn, lodge etc	❄	Scenic viewpoint
Å	Campsite	❀	Botanical site
♦	Hut	♧	Specific woodland feature
♈	Wine bar	🔦	Lighthouse
✕	Restaurant, café etc	≔	Marsh
✉	Post office	♈	Mangrove
✆	Telephone	🦅	Bird nesting site
e	Internet café	🐢	Turtle nesting site
✚	Hospital, clinic etc	〰〰	Coral reef
♨	Museum	➤	Beach
🐘	Zoo	🤿	Scuba diving
i	Tourist information	🐟	Fishing sites
$	Bank	⊕	GPS point
♦	Statue or monument		
∴	Archaeological or historic site		

Other map symbols are sometimes shown in separate key boxes with individual explanations for their meanings.

Contents

LIST OF MAPS

NOTE ON DATUM FOR GPS COORDINATES

For all the GPS co-ordinates in this book, note that the datum used is WSG 84 – and you must set your receiver accordingly before copying in any of these co-ordinates.

All GPS co-ordinates in this book have been expressed as degrees, minutes, and decimal fractions of a minute. This is the same format as used by the 1998 edition of the Shell map, but differs from the 2001 *Contimap*, which uses degrees, minutes and seconds.

Acknowledgements

Writing this book has been a team effort; I'm indebted to many that have made researching a pleasure and this book possible.

Firstly thanks to African expert and fellow author, Phillip Briggs, for originally writing the text of the *Wildlife* appendix, and allowing me to build on it. Also to Janice Booth, for her box on *Women travellers* and, with Hilary Bradt, invaluable input on drafts of several chapters. I hope I've done justice to their inputs. Thanks also to Dr Felicity Nicholson and Dr Jane Wilson-Howarth for their knowledge and expertise on health matters. To Russel Friedman and Wilderness Safaris for kind permission to borrow from their diagrams for the illustrations of *Building islands* in *Chapter 3*.

Thanks to my patient colleagues at Sunvil Africa – Heather, David, Claire and Chantal – all veteran Africa travellers; Christos for keeping my computer running; and both Noel Josephides and John der Parthog for their good humour whilst I was away. Also to many of Sunvil Africa's travellers who have commented on drafts, and helped with feedback after their trips, but especially Peter & Julie Dodd, Martin Kendall, Peter & Sue Egan, and Sue Granger & Peter Dalby. I hope they'll forgive me when I wasn't able to incorporate all the information that they collected!

On a personal note, long-suffering travelling companions Purbs and Occy both proved superb during arduous research trips. Fritz, as ever, provided a solid sounding board on many things, whilst discussions with Duncan on development issues never failed to be a welcome challenge. Thanks has also long been due to Simon Atkins, who worked with me many years ago on Bradt's first *Guide to Namibia and Botswana*. Despite later hiccoughs, I know that without his encouragement and hard work then, I might never have started writing.

In the final stages, Colin Bell and Peter Sandenbergh kindly answered ever-more-detailed emails, and spent much time giving me invaluable insights. Dave van Smeerdijk not only read and commented on chapters, but also, at the end, provided the most amazing desert trip for R&R. Both that trip, and especially the company on it, meant a great deal to me.

On the road, thanks to Kiran Bhatarah and Daniel Bainbridge for making my travelling easier; Meregan Turner, Charles Norwood and Charlotte Chilcott for totally invaluable help with vehicles; and a special mention for Julie Brenner-Clifford, Rob Clifford and Tessa Bott who, with their long experience of Botswana, made research back home so much easier. Botswana Tourism, through Southern Skies, also helped make this book a lot more colourful in the process, sponsoring many of the pictures and the colour maps.

Others went far out of their way to help or guide me around Botswana, and I have appreciated them all. I hope that those who aren't mentioned here will forgive any accidental omissions. Some who spring to mind include: Annelies from Drumbeat; Bev & Guy from Guma; Dendy Barker; Willem & Sally Barnard;

Oreeditse Bojosi; Joyce Bestelink & Simon Paul; Rowan Calder; Lloyd & Sue Camp; Sarah Collins; Russell Crossey; Dany at AHS; Stephanie Drew; Elaine Dugmore; Roger & Sophie Dugmore; Beth Engelhart; Erica from Bushways; Tim Fincham; Carol-Ann Green; Doug & Sandi Groves; Adam & Brigitte Hedges; Heidi, Britt and team at Leroo-la-Tau; Caroline Helfer; Graham Hemson; Jan & Suzi from Huab; Map Ives; Nicky Keyes; Fiona Kimmins; Lorraine Kirk; Laura at Audi Camp; Louis at TRS; Alex Lugg; Guy Symons & Edurne Martinez; Ewan Masson; Matt & Lorna from Muchenje; Maureen at Landela; Glyn Maude; Suzy Lumsden & Ian Michler; Trust Mpotshane; Mike Myers; Craig Nesbitt, especially for double-checking some GPS points; Estelle Oosthuysen, for Tsodilo comments; Karl Parkinson; Mike & Angie Penman; Phil & Kay Potter; Phil & Nicky at Ker & Downey; Ryan Powell; Geoff & Nookie Randall; Richard Randall; Susan Rothbletz; Sarah & Steve at Phakwe; Robert Schaerer; Ishmael Sebosaha; Sharon at Kubu; Rosi Slogrove; Ian Tema; Vikki & Richard Threlfall; Redmond Walsh; Alwyn van der Watt; Win at Travel Wild; and Grant Woodrow, for help with the rhinos. Also Ralph, Paula, Bianca, Julie and especially Catherine from the Uncharted team; Diane Wright; Helen Simmans, Sally Brunning, Debra Fox, Shona Bagley from CCAfrica; Randall and, especially, Eliza Deacon at EBS; Karin, Kevin Leo-Smith, Mark Tennant and the Kwando team; PJ, Barney & Gogs from OHS; and also Connie, Kuda, Brian & Jan at Linyanti Explorations.

In writing this, I'm aware that there are many above who know much more about Botswana than I. However, three experts really stand out: Alec Campbell, Mike Main and Veronica Roodt. All have written amazing, scholarly works on Botswana which have been a real inspiration, and all kindly offered their help to me. Beside their erudite works (recommended in *Further Reading*), this book pales – but I hope that it may introduce Botswana, and their work, to a wider audience.

Finally, Bradt's team who've worked with me on this have been supremely patient and encouraging: Hilary Bradt, Adrian Phillips, Steve Munns, Sally Brock, Henry Stedman and, especially, Tricia Hayne – who contributed the sections on the economy and Francistown, and without whom this book would simply never have been finished. That which is good and correct owes much to their care and attention; errors and omissions are all my own.

Introduction

Botswana meant little to me at first; it was never in the news. Then, finding myself in Zimbabwe, I remembered an old friend's enthusiasm for the Okavango Delta. So, in April 1988, three of us set off from Victoria Falls and hitched a lift in an open pick-up into Chobe. We were badly prepared, but even our lack of food and close encounters with hyenas added to the magic. No fences here; everything was so wild.

From Maun we splashed out on a few days' camping trip on a mokoro. Whilst the boatman spoke little English, the Delta was magical, almost surreal – like floating on a tropical fish-tank with animals everywhere around. The Okavango's lush greenery contrasted with the harsh dryness in the rest of the subcontinent. Iridescent birds flashed past, whilst terrapins sunbathed and otters played. All added to the feeling of paradise; we left entranced.

Thus started my love affair with the country. Since then I've been lucky enough to return many times. I've been guided by some of the best, learning more about the bush, and its animals and plants. I've flown over the dry Kalahari and the verdant Delta, mesmerised by the ancient patterns of watercourses, islands and game trails. And I've walked and driven around, exploring for myself on the ground, exhilarated by the sense of freedom. Yet still I feel as if I've only scratched the surface of Botswana, and I always leave wanting to return.

It's tempting here, by way of introduction, to list the highlights of Botswana's main areas one-by-one, describing each to entice the reader. But to do this would be misleading, as Botswana has just three main attractions for me.

Firstly, it's the wildlife. Whether this is you first safari or your fiftieth, Botswana won't disappoint. The sheer variation of the country, from the arid Kalahari to lush, well-watered forest glades, ensures tremendous variety. Botswana is serious about its big game. It has spectacular herds of elephants and buffalo, and prolific populations of predators. Experienced safari enthusiasts can bounce across the bush following a pack of wild dogs; Botswana has probably the continent's best population of these highly endangered predators. Yet often it's the country's smaller residents that will keep you entertained, from tiny painted reed frogs and barking geckos, to troops of entertaining meerkats.

Secondly – and the underlying reason why many come here – is the feeling in Botswana that you're within an endless pristine wilderness, almost devoid of human imprint. For city-dwellers, such space seems to be the ultimate luxury.

In Botswana, animals wander freely across vast reserves which are measured in thousands of square kilometres, not hectares. Exploring these wilder corners is invariably deeply liberating.

Thirdly, and missed by some, is Botswana's rich history. It's often barely hinted at but, veiled and mysterious, it's all the more enticing. It reveals itself in the paintings at Tsodilo, and the magic that seems to surround those hills. You'll catch a glimpse of it as you search for Stone-Age arrowheads on the Makgadikgadi Pans.

And standing on an ancient river-bed, or the wave-washed hills around Savuti, it's hard not to think back and wonder what forces shaped this country, long before you, or any Europeans, first set eyes on it.

Back in the present, the world is changing fast. Most of the earth's great wilderness areas are under threat. The 21st century is an age when even the earth's wildest corners must earn their keep, adapt, or change irrevocably. Botswana's government has been a beacon of prosperity and stability amidst a troubled continent. Financed by diamonds, it has set many examples of how to run a country. Taking a long-term view, its thriving tourist industry is the envy of the continent: minimising impact by admitting only small numbers who pay handsomely to rejuvenate themselves in its pristine environments. Then it has channelled much of the revenue back to the poorer communities in the areas concerned. This first-rate approach has been a steady, growing strategy to increase responsible tourism to Botswana. It hasn't been a quick way for the country to get rich, but it has been a sustainable one.

However, as I write, economic storm-clouds threaten. Botswana's diamonds are predicted to run out in the next 10–15 years, leaving a black hole in the economy. Tourism is the obvious way to fill the gap, but exactly how is unclear. With only a sketchy understanding of Botswana's appeal for overseas visitors, large companies are tempted to build big new hotels in efforts to increase the number of visitors. But more tourists may not mean more revenue for Botswana; if the country's sense of wilderness is destroyed, then it'll rip the heart out of the experience that is found here today, leaving the country poorer in all respects.

So my plea to the reader is two-fold. First, go now and support Botswana's small-scale camps and responsible tourism; the country needs you. Second, having committed many of Botswana's secret corners to paper here, I ask you to use this guide with respect. Botswana's wild areas need great care to preserve them. Local people are easily offended, and their cultures eroded, by a visitor's lack of sensitivity. Enjoy - but be a thoughtful visitor, for the country's sake.

Part One

General Information

BOTSWANA FACTS AND FIGURES

Location Southern Africa, between 20° and 30° east, and between 18° and 27° south

Size 581,370km²

Climate Subtropical. Summer: 19–33°C; winter: 5–23°C

Time GMT +2

Electricity 220 volts

Weights and measures Metric

International telephone code + 267

Status Republic

GDP $6,600 per capita (2000)

Currency Pula (BWP)

Population 1,586,119 (2001 estimate)

Population growth per year 0.47% (2001 estimate)

Life expectancy at birth Male 36 years, female 37 years

Infant mortality 63.2/1,000 live births (2001 estimate)

Economy Major earners: diamonds, copper, nickel

Capital Gaborone; population 192,845 (1998)

Other main towns Francistown, Lobatse, Selebi-Phikwe, Orapa

Language English (official), Setswana (national), Shona, other local languages

Religion Christianity; traditional beliefs

Flag Broad, royal-blue horizontal stripes, divided by black central stripe bordered by narrow white stripes

National anthem *Fatshe leno la rona*, which translates to 'Blessed be this noble land'

Public holidays 1 January (New Year's Day), 2 January, Good Friday, Easter Monday, 1 May (Labour Day), 24 May (Ascension Day), 1 July (Sir Seretse Khama Day), 16 July (President Day), 17 July, 30 September (Botswana Day), 1 October, 25 December (Christmas Day)

History and Economy

We can learn a lot about Botswana today by looking back into its history. Its far distant past, explaining some of the main features of its landscapes, is covered as part of *The Natural Environment*, at the start of *Chapter 3*. A potted overview of Botswana's more recent human history is given here, casting some light on its current politics and economics.

EARLY PEOPLES

Read about the country's geological history and it's framed in terms of hundreds or at least tens of millions of year. Thus it's sobering to realise how relatively recent any human history is, and how much more compressed its timescales are.

Our knowledge about early human life in Botswana is derived from archaeology and from oral histories, which go back about 700 years. Written records only date from the arrival of Europeans in the 18th and 19th century. Most of these are personal accounts, which are interesting, but subjective. In many places the story is confused and incomplete, or even deliberately misleading (see *A note on 'tribes'* at the start of *Chapter 2*).

However, from the archaeology we know that the ancestors of the Khoisan (see pages 4–5) were once widely dispersed throughout the continent and probably had exclusive occupation of southern, central and eastern Africa from about 60,000 years ago up to the last 3,000 years. Skeletons of a Khoisan-type people, dating back 15,000 years and more, are found throughout southern and eastern Africa. It is believed to be these people who made the rock paintings of people and animals that are found all over eastern and southern Africa and even in the Sahara Desert. The earliest paintings have been found in Namibia (the 'Apollo 11' cave) and are thought to date back 26,000 years.

Rock paintings found in the Kalahari, at the Tsodilo Hills, are evidence that the living was good enough to allow the people to develop a vibrant artistic culture. Most experts believe that many of the paintings have deeper significance, probably connected with spiritual, religious or mythological beliefs. It is impossible to interpret them accurately without an in-depth knowledge of the culture and beliefs of those who created them. Unfortunately no group today claims historical responsibility. The local Zhu Bushmen claim that their god, Gaoxa, made the paintings.

The animals of Africa, such as antelope, eland, rhinos and giraffe, are the subject of many paintings. The images beautifully capture the form and the spirit of each animal. Humans also appear; one painting at the Tsodilo Hills shows a group of fifteen men exhibiting the permanent erection, or semi-erection, which is a distinctive feature of San men from birth to death. Later paintings, featuring black men and sometimes war, are thought to depict the arrival of the Bantu farmers.

The San

The San were perfectly adapted to their desert environment and had learnt to survive its harsh extremes of climate – drought and unrelenting heat and sun in the winter, and heavy rains and floods in the summer.

Predominantly hunter-gatherers, it is thought that at various times, when the climate was more favourable, the San may also have owned and grazed stock. Several times in past millennia the climate of Botswana has been much wetter, and at others much drier than it is at the moment. Periodically the huge pans that are a distinctive feature of the landscape, such as at Makgadikgadi and Nxai, became great lakes, full of water and supplied by several rivers. Probably some San groups took advantage of plentiful supplies of water to acquire stock. Now the rivers have dried up and the Okavango Delta has receded, the pans are full of water only during the rainy season and the San are herders no longer. There are also more recent records of them owning and trading copper from secret mines in the Kalahari, and bartering it for iron.

The Khoe

Around 3000BC, Late Stone Age hunter-gatherer groups in Ethiopia, and elsewhere in north and west Africa, started to keep domestic animals, sow seeds, and harvest the produce: they became the world's first farmers.

By around 1000BC these new pastoral practices had spread south into the equatorial forests of what is now the Democratic Republic of Congo, to around Lake Victoria, and into the northern area of the Great Rift Valley, in northern Tanzania. However, agriculture did not spread south into the rest of central/southern Africa immediately. Only when the technology, and the tools, of iron-working became known did these practices start their relentless expansion southwards.

It's thought that during the last centuries BC many Khoe-speaking peoples in northern Botswana converted their lifestyle to pastoralism – herding cattle and sheep on the rich pastures exposed by the retreating wetlands of the Okavango Delta and Lake Makgadikgadi.

It used to be thought that the Khoe acquired their stock during the (black) Iron Age, from Bantu-speaking farmers who are thought to have migrated into their area around 1,500 years ago. However, finds of sheep bone dating back 3,000 years now suggest that the Khoe had obtained stock long before the arrival of the Bantu, probably from East Africa where they had been herded for thousands of years. The Khoe spread, migrating with their livestock through central Namibia, as far south as the Cape of Good Hope, by about 70BC.

When the first Dutch settlers saw the Khoe in about AD1600 they lived in groups with a leader, but were split into smaller clans under their own headman. The clans came together only in times of stress or war. Because water was vital for the stock animals, the Khoe dug wells that were owned exclusively by the clan and group. In times of drought, when water was scarce, fights might erupt over these water-holes. Then each clan sent men to fight to protect the group's interests.

Each clan lived in a village, which was built inside a circular thorn hedge. In the centre were thorn enclosures to pen and protect the stock, surrounded by a circle of houses. Khoe houses are of a 'bender' or dome tent construction type; that is, long flexible poles are bent to form arches and the ends stuck into the ground. They are then covered with mats. When the clan needed to move to find more water or grazing these huts were simply taken down and strapped onto the back of their animals.

Tlou and Campbell describe one such village, which is known to have existed at Toromoja on the Boteti River around AD1200. A group of Khoe known as the

Bateti lived there and kept long-horned cattle, sheep and goats, but they lived mainly on fish, zebra and other animals which they caught in the pits they dug by the river. They also ate plants, particularly water-lily roots. They had San servants who hunted and collected wild food for them. Sometimes they traded skins and ivory for iron tools, copper and tobacco, with the people living at Maun in the northwest, or the Toutswe people to the southeast.

Archaeologically speaking the Khoisan peoples were examples of Late Stone Age cultures; that is, their tools and weapons are made of wood, bone and stone. The Late Stone Age refers not to a period of time, but to a method and style of tool construction. Human beings had made stone tools for millennia and the name Late Stone Age refers to stylistic refinements and to the manufacture of tools developed for specific uses.

Specifically, experts define the transition from Early to Middle Stone Age technology as indicated by a larger range of stone tools often adapted for particular uses, and signs that these people had a greater mastery of their environment. This was probably in progress around 125,000 years ago in Botswana.

They normally characterise the late Stone Age by the use of composite tools, those made of wood and/or bone and/or stone used together, and by the presence of a revolutionary invention: the bow and arrow. This first appeared in southern Africa, and throughout the world, about 15,000 years ago. Skeletons of some of these Late Stone Age hunters had a close physical resemblance to the modern Khoisan people.

The Bantu-speaking farmers

The next people to arrive in Botswana were the Bantu-speakers. This collective term refers to a number of different tribes, from a related linguistic group, who gradually migrated down into southern Africa, from north of the Equator, over the course of thousands of years. The date of their arrival in Botswana is hard to pinpoint.

The Bantu were grain farmers (agriculturalists) as opposed to pastoralists or hunter-gatherers and they brought Iron Age technology with them; that is their tools and weapons were made of iron. Physically these Iron Age farmers were much taller and heavier than the Khoisan, and they became the ancestors of the modern black Africans in southern Africa.

Crucial to the production of iron is a smelting furnace capable of reaching very high temperatures. Associated with the Iron Age is a new kind of pottery, which also had to be fired at high temperatures. Archaeologists use the finds of pottery and iron to date the arrival of the new people on the landscape of Botswana.

It is thought that the Bantu-speakers arrived in two main waves, bringing western and eastern Bantu languages. From West Africa, Late Stone Age farmers on the upper Zambezi were converted to the use of iron tools by about 300BC. From East Africa, Early Iron Age farming spread south along the east coast as far as the Zambezi by around 20BC.

By 200BC, in the Okavango-Makgadikgadi region, people were making a kind of pottery which archaeologists think was Khoe pottery influenced by western Iron Age (Bantu) styles, suggesting an initial contact between the two groups. The major Bantu influx probably occurred around the first few centuries AD, and the ancestors of the Khoisan people, with their simple Stone Age technology and hunter-gatherer existence, just could not compete. Since then the Khoisan have gradually been either assimilated into the migrant groups, or effectively pushed into the areas which could not be farmed. Thus the older Stone Age cultures persisted for much longer in the Kalahari (which is more difficult to cultivate) than in the rest of the country.

In theory, the stronger iron weapons of the Bantu should easily have made them the dominant culture. However, it took a very long time for Bantu language and culture to replace that of the Khoe – as late as the 19th century people were still speaking Khoe on the Boteti River. This supports a theory of communities living peacefully there, side by side, for a thousand years or more.

There is some evidence of inter-marriage or inter-breeding between the two groups and the Batswana today are a mixture of Bantu and Khoisan features and they are noticeably lighter in skin colour than Bantu-speakers further north. They also tend to have the almond eyes, high cheekbones and thin lips of the Khoisan.

More immigrants

There are numerous problems with compiling a historical record of Bantu history in Botswana. We are dependent on oral history and archaeological records, and the two sometimes conflict with each other. The situation is very complex because of the number and mobility of the tribes involved.

The earliest dated Iron Age site in Botswana is an iron-smelting furnace in the Tswapong Hills, which is dated to around AD190. There is evidence of an early farming settlement of beehive huts made of grass matting, dated to around AD420 by the Molepolole River and a similar one has been found coexisting with Khoisan sites in the Tsodilo Hills, dating to around AD550.

By the 4th or 5th century AD, Iron Age farmers had certainly settled throughout much of southern Africa. As well as iron-working technology, they brought with them pottery, the remains of which are used by archaeologists to work out the migrations of various different groups of these Bantu settlers. These migrations continued, and the distribution of pottery styles suggests that the groups moved around within the subcontinent: this was much more complex than a simple north-south influx. Many of the tribes roamed over the whole of southern Africa, before various colonial authorities imposed artificial country borders in order to carve out territories for themselves.

This situation was complicated more recently by the prolonged and horrifically bloody tribal wars of the 19th century, known to historians as the Difaquane Wars.

TSWANA HISTORY

The Tswana rose to domination from among a number of powerful dynasties that spread out from the western Transvaal, around AD1200–1400. During the period AD1500–1600 the Phofu dynasty in western Transvaal disintegrated with junior brothers forming breakaway, independent chiefdoms. Oral history traditions explain this as a response to drought. The archaeological record shows populations expanding into open country in small villages with cattle corrals, but by around AD1700 the settlements were often larger towns built of stone and situated on hills, reflecting the growth of hostile states, and the need for a strong defence.

The Difaquane Wars

The whole of southern Africa was subject to increasing disruption, migration and war from about 1750 onwards, as trading and raiding for ivory, cattle and slaves spread inland from the coasts of Mozambique, the Cape Colony and Angola. The tribes often captured opponents during battle and sold them to slave raiders. Some of the battles themselves may have been slave raids against an enemy tribe.

Paramount amongst the aggressors in these wars was an ambitious Zulu leader named Shaka, who controlled a large slice of Natal by around 1810. The Ngoni people, which includes the Zulu nation, refer to the wars which Shaka initiated as the Mfecane, or 'the crushing.' However, the Tswana people, who were amongst the victims of Shaka's wars of expansion, refer to them as the Difaquane, which means 'the scattering.' Because they scattered, so they dispersed others.

A good explanation of this period is covered in John Reader's excellent Africa (see *Further Reading*). He summarises the root causes:

> Thus they [the Zulus] were trapped in 'the trans-continental cross-fire of interrelated European plunder systems.' It was the unrelenting advance of settlers from the west, and the predacious demands of slavers in the east – exacerbated by intermittent drought – that set southern Africa in turmoil during the early eighteenth century. Not Shaka, not the Zulus, not the Mfecane.

Eventually, after the wars passed in the 1840s, the Tswana states of Ngwaketse, Kwena and the Ngwato rose to prosperity. They organised their people into wards with their own chiefs, but all paying tribute to the king. The states were in competition over trade benefits for ivory and ostrich feathers, down new roads, south to the Cape Colony. These roads also brought Boer trekkers and Christian missionaries to Botswana.

One of the Tswana kings, Sechele of the Kwena (1829–92), was baptised by David Livingstone, who passed through Botswana on his missionary travels. However it was the Ngwato, who superseded the Kwena in trading supremacy, who produced the most remarkable and famous dynasty – and upon whom the following pages will concentrate.

Ngwato dynasty

In *Serowe: Village of the Rain Wind* (see *Further Reading*), Bessie Head describes this remarkable dynasty, beginning with the reign of Khama the Great. He was king when the capital of the Bamangwato (Ngwato) moved to Serowe in 1902. Previously the capital had been 100 miles away at Shoshong, and then at Palapye, but each time the tribe was forced to move on when water sources dried up. In 1902 two rivers, the Sepane and the Manonnye, flowed through Serowe, although both have subsequently dried up.

Khama the Great

Khama was the eldest son of Segkoma I, who was the chief when David Livingstone, the missionary explorer, first moved northwards through Botswana in the 1840s. Whilst the capital had still been at Shoshong, Livingstone had converted Khama and his brothers to Christianity. Although their father, Segkoma I, had allowed the missionaries to stay with them, and was interested to talk to them, he had refused to give up the traditional ways.

Eventually this led to a war between father and son, which Khama won, becoming king of the Bamangwato. Khama was a poetic visionary who changed the customs of his people in line with his Christian beliefs, and who foresaw the need for strong protection in the colonial carve up of Africa, and campaigned strongly for the British Protectorate of Bechuanaland. (See also *People and Culture*.)

Segkoma II

In 1916 Khama was kicked on the knee by a horse. At this time he invited his son Segkoma II, who had been in exile for ten years governing his own branch of the Bamangwato, to come home and rule at Serowe. This he did, and subsequently ruled at Serowe for nine years, although for most of that time he remained in the shadow of King Khama. Most importantly Khama insisted that Segkoma marry a woman given to him by the Bamangwato, and the heir from this marriage was Seretse, who would later become the first president of Botswana.

Tshekedi Khama

Following the death of Khama, and shortly afterwards of Segkoma II, Tshekedi Khama, (Khama's son from a late second marriage) stepped in as regent until the four-year-old Seretse should come of age.

Where Khama was a visionary and politician, Tshekedi was full of pragmatic common sense and his rule, from 1926 to 1959, is marked by educational advances and self-help projects. When he first became leader there was only a primary school in Serowe. Then Tshekedi used his own money to send the young people of the village to South Africa for further education. From there they came home to teach in the village school. Later a secondary school and subsequently a college were built, using the voluntary labour of what were known as the age regiments (see page 35). Also known as the mephato, these were groups of young men of about the same age, usually formed from those who had graduated from the tribal initiation ceremony (known as bogwera) at the same time. They could be called upon to carry out services for the good of the community, ranging from routine community tasks to helping out with emergencies.

Moeng College of higher education is exciting for the principles on which it was founded, which gave equal weight to traditional knowledge and craft skills alongside academic instruction. As an experiment in social relations the houses built for the teaching staff were the equivalent of houses for white government officials. It was the only college in southern Africa at the time where houses for white and black teachers were equal and where they lived together in the same hostel.

Seretse Khama

During the reign of Tshekedi, a problem arose over the future of Seretse Khama. Seretse was educated abroad, in London, Fort Hare and Oxford. In 1948 Seretse wrote to inform his uncle that he wanted to marry an English woman, Ruth Williams. Tshekedi opposed the marriage on the grounds that a king or chief could not do as he pleased because he was the servant of the people, and an heir to the chieftaincy was at stake. Traditionally the chief's wife was chosen by the *morafe* or tribal group. Seretse insisted on his right to choose his own wife and married the Englishwoman.

They were still arguing when the British took matters into their own hands. In a case that created international scandal, the British government barred Seretse from the chieftaincy of the Bamangwato, and exiled him for six years. They invited him to Britain, where they forced him to stay. They also banned Tshekedi Khama from entering the Bamangwato reserve.

Secret documents have since confirmed that this British intervention was in order to satisfy the South African government, which objected to Seretse Khama's marriage to a white woman at a time when the policy of racial segregation, apartheid, was being enforced in South Africa.

Seretse, Tshekedi and their people fought against this banishment. The Bamangwato refused to pay taxes, sent delegations to the British and led protests. They refused to accept a British nominated chief and many people, including women, were flogged for this refusal.

Finally Tshekedi visited Seretse in London and the two resolved their differences. Seretse returned to Botswana with Ruth. Although a condition of his return was that he remained barred from the chieftancy, both he and Tshekedi continued to play an active role in the politics of Botswana, and were instrumental in the lead up to independence.

Traders

The earliest Europeans to come to Botswana were adventurers, explorers, hunters and missionaries. Travel in Botswana was very expensive, even then. A year's travel could cost up to £600 – equivalent to what a soldier of the period might earn during thirty years in the army. So early travellers came to trade for ivory, which made them huge profits with which to finance their expeditions. They travelled in wooden wagons, drawn by oxen or horses, and brought guns, beads, clothing and other, less valuable items, which they bartered for significant amounts of ivory.

One of the biggest problems on the journey was the lack of water. There were often stretches of 50km or more without any. Water would be carried on the wagons, but not enough for both men and beasts. Sometimes the oxen died of thirst. There are stories of the wagons being unhitched and the oxen led to the nearest water – which could be some kilometres distant – and then returning to pull the wagons further. Oxen often died from drinking bad water or from tsetse fly bite, while horses died of tick bite. A distance of 20km per day was thought to be a good rate of travel.

However, a wagon that did make it could return with about 200 elephant tusks – worth around £1,200 when sold in Cape Town. As they heard tales of huge profits, more traders began to venture into the region and gradually introduced money, which had been unknown until then. Previously barter and exchange systems functioned in the village – one goat equals one woven grass basket, and so on. Subsequently money became important in trade and people were forced to either sell something, or sell their labour, to get money. Little paid work could be found in Botswana, so large numbers of people were forced to emigrate to find work, often in the mines in South Africa.

Meanwhile the traders began to settle in Botswana at Shoshong, though the Bamangwato chiefs, Segkoma and Khama, were keen to prevent them from going further into the interior, so that they could maintain their trading supremacy.

DAVID LIVINGSTONE

David Livingstone's *Missionary Travels and Researches in South Africa* excited great interest in England. This account of his journeys across southern Africa in the 1840s and 50s had all the appeal that undersea or space exploration has for us now. Further, it captured the imagination of the British public, allowing them to take pride in their country's exploration of Africa, based on the exploits of an explorer who seemed to be the epitome of bravery and righteous religious zeal.

Livingstone had set out with the conviction that if Africans could see their material and physical well-being improved – probably by learning European ways, and earning a living from export crops – then they would be ripe for conversion to Christianity. He was strongly opposed to slavery, but sure that this would disappear when Africans became more self-sufficient through trade.

In fact Livingstone was almost totally unsuccessful in his own aims, failing to set up any successful trading missions, or even to convert many Africans permanently to Christianity. However, his travels opened up areas north of the Limpopo for later British missionaries, and by 1887 British mission stations were established in Zambia and southern Malawi.

The missions

Following the traders came the missionaries, and missionary societies, who were already active in South Africa. Robert Moffat of the London Missionary Society (LMS) established a station at Kudumane, which succeeded in bringing Christianity to the Batswana and in training African evangelists to spread the word. It was to Kudumane that David Livingstone came in 1841. In 1845 he married Moffat's daughter, Mary, and they settled among the Bakwena.

Although ostensibly a missionary, Livingstone's main interest was exploration and in 1849 Livingstone and his party became the first whites to see Lake Ngami. He died in 1873 while looking for the source of the Nile, in Zambia.

Khama and his Bamangwato family at Shoshong were converted by the missionaries of a German Lutheran society, although he later joined the London Missionary Society Church. Most missionaries tried to change local Setswana customs, which they considered heathen and inferior to European Christian customs. Most of all they fought against the medicine men, who defended the old traditional customs. However, despite leaders like Khama who abolished male and female initiations, rain-making and beer drinking, some customs still flourish because people like them.

The early missionaries affected disinterest in politics, although they inevitably supported Christians against non-Christians. Their position was always precarious because they needed to retain the goodwill of the chiefs to remain in their mission posts. However, during the Protectorate, missionaries who knew they had the backing of the British government became quite cavalier, demanding the removal of chiefs who resisted Christianity.

Although the missionaries tried to destroy local cultures, they also provided education and established the first schools. They introduced useful tools such as the plough and the wagon, taught gardening and crop irrigation. The missionaries' wives taught sewing and baking and helped to nurse the sick and deliver babies.

Botswana and the British

British foreign policy in southern Africa had always revolved around the Cape Colony, which was seen as vital to British interests in India and the Indian Ocean. Africa to the north of the Cape Colony had largely been ignored. The Boers were on the whole left to their farming in the Transvaal area, since they posed no threat to the Cape Colony.

However, from the 1850s to the 1870s the Batswana leaders appealed to the British for protection against the Boers, who had formed their own free state ruling the Transvaal, but were continually threatening to take over Tswana lands in Botswana.

When Germany annexed South West Africa (now Namibia) in 1884, the British finally began to take those threats seriously. They became afraid that the Boers might link up with the Germans and prevent British access to the 'north road', leading to the interior of Africa – now Zambia and Zimbabwe. It was really to safeguard this road that the British finally granted Botswana protection in 1885. Significantly, the German government was told about the British Protectorate of Bechuanaland before the chiefs in Botswana.

Cecil John Rhodes

Initially the British government had fully intended to hand the supervision of the Protectorate over to the government of the Cape Colony, but the Cape was unwilling to take on the responsibility and the potential expense.

In 1886, the Boers discovered large gold deposits in the Witwatersrand (around Johannesburg). The influx of money from this boosted the Boer farmers, who expanded their interests to the north, making a treaty with Khama's enemy to the east, the powerful Lobengula. This in turn prompted the British to look beyond the Limpopo, and to back the territorial aspirations of a millionaire British businessman and prominent Cape Colony politician, Cecil Rhodes. By 1888 Rhodes, a partner in the De Beers consortium, had control of the lucrative diamond-mining industry in Kimberley, South Africa. He was hungry for power, and dreamt of linking the Cape to Cairo with land under British control.

Rhodes was fuelled by the belief that other areas of Africa had great mineral wealth and he wanted to colonise them and reap that wealth. In order to do so he formed the British South Africa Company (BSAC) in 1889. At that time, if companies or individuals could obtain concessions to African land from the owners, they were able to colonise it for the Crown. The British government expected that these concessions would be obtained honestly. However they were often gained fraudulently, by persuading illiterate African chiefs to sign (or put their mark on) documents which were presented to them as treaties, but which actually appropriated their lands.

The immediate reason for forming the BSAC was in order to colonise the land of the Amandabele and the Mashona (now Zimbabwe). In 1888 Rhodes' men had obtained, by trickery, a treaty known as the Rudd Concession from the King of the Amandabele, Lobengula. This granted Rhodes all mineral rights on the king's land. Although the king rejected the treaty when he discovered its real intention, Rhodes was nevertheless granted a royal charter by the British government.

The British also promised to transfer the Bechuanaland Protectorate to the BSAC, on condition that Rhodes first obtained the agreement of the Batswana rulers. Rhodes wanted the Protectorate, because he needed the right to build a railway across Bechuanaland. He further wanted to annex the Protectorate to Rhodesia (now Zimbabwe), and from there attack the Boer state of Transvaal from the north.

Rhodes and other British businessmen had stakes in the highly profitable gold mines at Witwatersrand (Johannesburg), but the state was controlled politically by the Boers. Rhodes wanted British rule in the Transvaal, to protect his profits from the gold mines.

The three chiefs

In 1895 three Batswana chiefs, Khama, Bathoen and Sebele, travelled to London to plead a case against the British government handing over the Protectorate to Rhodes, whom they did not trust. Some Batswana chiefs had already signed concessions with the BSAC, but in nearly all cases they did not realise that they had given away their land. It was, in any case, against Setswana law to sell or give away land. Rhodes attempted to stop the kings in Cape Town and prevent them from going to Britain but he was unsuccessful.

In a meeting with Joseph Chamberlain, then the British Colonial Secretary, the three chiefs criticised the BSAC and asked that:

• Bechuanaland should remain a Protectorate directly under the Queen.
• Their independence should be preserved.
• Their lands should not be sold.
• Liquor drinking should be prohibited in their areas.

Chamberlain, told them that the British government could not go back on its promise to transfer the Protectorate to the BSAC. However, he also said that the company would obey the Queen, so it was the same as being governed by her. Hence the chiefs must reach an agreement with the BSAC. Then he went on holiday.

Instead the chiefs toured England, seeking the support of the British people against the company. Their campaign was organised by the London Missionary Society, and supported by temperance groups, anti-slavery and humanitarian groups and businesses that feared the effect of a costly war if the transfer went ahead. Chamberlain returned from holiday to find letters to this effect. Worried that the affair might become an election issue and lose the government votes, he agreed to the chiefs' demands, with the provisos that they must all cede the land which Rhodes required for the railway, and that taxation would be introduced to pay for the administration of the Protectorate.

The Jameson Raid

A month later, in October 1895, Rhodes found a pretext for attacking the Transvaal. The raid was led by Dr S Jameson on behalf of the non-Boer whites or 'Uitlanders' in the Transvaal, who had complained of unequal treatment by the Boers. This famous raid, which came to be known as the Jameson Raid, was carried out from within the Bechuanaland Protectorate. However, it failed. The anticipated uprising of the Uitlanders never happened, so the raiders soon surrendered to the Boers.

The fact that Britain had allowed the Protectorate to be used to attack another country caused an international scandal. The British government, angered at being brought into disrepute by Rhodes, refused to transfer the Protectorate to the BSAC, and removed control of the Tswana lands that had been obtained for the raid.

It was the failure of the Jameson Raid, and Rhodes' subsequent if temporary disgrace, which protected the independent future of Botswana. Rhodes did later receive land for a railway strip and some blocks of 'Crown Land' – the Gaborone, Lobatse, and Tuli blocks. These, together with the Tati Block and Ghanzi, which had been settled earlier, became the only European areas in Bechuanaland.

The Protectorate

Britain continued to administer the Protectorate for 70 years, through the Anglo-Boer War (1899–1902) and two world wars. However, Britain disliked spending money on her colonies, and from the time the Union of South Africa was formed in 1910 it was always intended to transfer the Protectorate to the Union. The Batswana continued to fight against it, especially as they witnessed the poor treatment of black Africans in that country.

By 1955, the policy of the British government had changed. This was due in part to the problems with Seretse and Tshekedi Khama and the Bamangwato (see page 8), and partly because of South Africa's gradual move towards apartheid and away from the more egalitarian values of the post-war society that was emerging in the UK and the rest of the West.

In 1956 Seretse, who was supported by many groups in Britain, including Members of Parliament, spoke strongly against the British government's intervention. Tshekedi also turned against the British, accepting Ruth as the rightful wife and demanding Seretse's return to Bechuanaland. He believed that the British wanted to use the problem to break his tribe, and as an excuse to transfer the Protectorate to South Africa.

However, by then the issue of transferring the protectorate to South Africa's control was dead in the minds of the British government. Clearly Botswana would have to be diplomatically protected from South Africa's ambitions, but the British didn't seem to have a plan for it beyond that.

MODERN HISTORY
The dangerous decade

Between 1955 and 1966 was a dangerous, formative decade in Botswana's history. For a detailed, insider's view of it read *Botswana: The Road to Independence*, by Peter Fawcus and Alan Tilbury. The authors were two of Britain's most senior administrators who were at the sharp end of steering relations between Britain and the Protectorate during this period.

Whilst the British government couldn't see into the future, supporters of Seretse Khama had organized political movements as early as 1952. Eventually a legislative council was set up in 1961, based on an interim constitution and limited national elections. Then Seretse Khama joined the legislative council, and the Protectorate's new executive council.

Meanwhile local politics was developing rapidly. The Bechuanaland People's Party (BPP) was founded in 1960, and later split into two factions, which were later to become the Botswana Independence Party (BIP) and the Botswana People's Party (BPP).

Both factions espoused a fairly radical agenda calling for immediate independence, the abolition of the chiefs, nationalisation of some lands and the removal of most whites from the civil service. With the material support of other nationalist movements in Ghana and Tanzania, 1960–61 saw support for the BPP grow rapidly in the townships of eastern Botswana.

From his position on the inside of government, Seretse Khama could see the danger that these parties posed to the constitution that was developing, and the smooth-running of the civil service after independence. Hence early in 1962, under a morula tree in Gaborone, he and five others (Ketumile Masire, A M Tsocbebe, Moutlakgola Nwako, Tsheko Tsheko and Goareng Mosinyi) formed the Botswana Democratic Party (BDP) to campaign for a more ordered transition to independence. All were experienced, educated men and between them had strong links throughout the country, in both the educated elites and the poorer rural communities.

In particular, Seretse Khama and Ketumile Masire, as president and general secretary of the party, formed a strong partnership, without any signs of the feuds and splits that had beset the opposition. One was from the north, the other from the south; one a chief, the other a commoner. Gradually their conservative message began to win over the electorate. This was helped by the fear that any radical new government could provoke problems with South Africa – which still apparently had an appetite for control of Bechuanaland.

Independence

From 1956 to 1966 Fawcus and Tilbury observe that 'constitutional and political development far outstripped economic and social advance. The thought that independence might be at the end of the road only emerged in the early 1960s and was discounted by Lord Hailey as late as 1963.'

Fortunately since about 1956 there had been a slow build-up in Britain's financial grants to the Protectorate. By 1963 a £10-million plan was in place for development that covered the transition period around independence. This included the immediate start to constructing a new administrative capital, at Gaborone – as previously Bechuanaland had been administered from Mafikeng, over the border in South Africa.

During this time, Sir Ketumile Maşire, Bechuanaland's first deputy Prime Minister and second president, commented that there was a high 'degree of consultation and co-operation between the local representatives of the British government and the people of Botswana' and that there was 'immense goodwill on both sides'. Perhaps this, more than anything else, explains how the transition was completed so peacefully.

On March 1 1965 a remarkably peaceful election was held, with voters placing coloured symbols in envelopes to allow for the largely illiterate electorate. This worked without problems. The Bechuanaland Democratic Party (BDP) won 28 out of the 31 seats, and on March 3 1965 Seretse Khama became the country's first Prime Minister. Within this new administration, a number of senior British public servants were kept on – including the minister of finance and the attorney-general, and a senior civil servant in each of the ministries.

This clear victory for the BDP, and stable administration, gave the new government the platform from which to amend the constitution. The new Setswana name of the Republic of Botswana was chosen for the country, and on September 30 1966, Sir Seretse Khama became the first president.

Politics since independence
1966–80: President Sir Seretse Khama

Seretse Khama inherited a poor country. In 1965 the population stood at about 550,000 with a low level of literacy, and the country was gripped by a bad drought. Fortunately Britain was sympathetic to continuing to cover substantial costs of the new nation's administration costs, although with the discovery of diamonds at Orapa in 1967 by geologists from De Beers, and the subsequent mining operations which began in 1971, this assistance was only needed for six years after independence.

Botswana had long been in the Southern African Customs Union – and in 1969 it succeeded in renegotiating the terms of this, to become more financially independent. (Previously it had received a fixed percentage of total customs union income, rather than the income that was due directly from its own territory.)

During the 1970s Botswana's economy grew steadily, typically by around 12–13%, as Botswana extended its basic infrastructure for both mining development and basic social services for its population. Despite threats from, amongst others, the Marxist-leaning Botswana National Front (BNF), Sir Seretse Khama steered the country on a fairly moderate line – and the BDP were consistently re-elected in generally fair elections.

With civil war in Rhodesia throughout the 1970s, and apartheid regimes in South Africa and South West Africa (Namibia), Botswana's position was tricky. It accepted refugees from neighbouring countries, but refused to be used as bases for resistance organisations. Such neutrality was often severely tried, not least when, in February 1978, the Rhodesian army crossed the border and massacred 15 Botswana soldiers at Leshoma.

Zimbabwe gained independence in 1980, and the same year saw the foundation of the Southern African Development Coordination Conference (SADCC) with the aim of co-ordinating the region's disparate economies in the face of the huge economic muscle wielded by South Africa's apartheid regime.

Sir Seretse Khama died in July 1980 and, as envisaged by the constitution, was succeeded by his deputy, Sir Ketumile Masire. He left behind him an impressive legacy of a stable, prosperous country amidst a changing subcontinent. He had skilfully steered Botswana, with foresight and prudence, during perhaps its most vulnerable period – leaving it with the firm foundations of a democratic tradition, and well-trained executive and administrative branches of government.

The 1980s: President Sir Ketumile Masire

Masire's succession was mandated by another victory for the BDP in a general election to the national assembly in 1984 – although at the same time they lost control of all the town councils except Selebi-Phikwe. This sign of discontent was widely ascribed to the high levels of unemployment.

Just as the 1970s had witnessed upheavals in Rhodesia, so the 1980s saw the intensification of pressure on the white regime in South Africa to give way to majority rule.

Botswana continued to welcome refugees, but refused to harbour bases for the ANC's war on apartheid in South Africa. During this period Botswana had a delicate balancing act to play. Like most countries it was calling for the end to apartheid, and geographically it was one of the 'front line' states in the battle against apartheid. However, Botswana's economy was so dependent on its southern neighbour that it couldn't afford to apply the sanctions which most countries were calling for.

In 1981 tensions arose with South Africa over the supply of military equipment from the USSR for the Botswana Defence Force (BDF), though by 1986 Britain and the USA were offering hardware to the BDF to deter South African incursions into Botswana.

Meanwhile on its eastern border, relations with Robert Mugabe's ZANU government were business-like rather then terribly friendly. The early 1980s saw Mugabe's notoriously ruthless Fifth Brigade terrorising Matabeleland – the province adjacent to Botswana. Zimbabwean refugees flooded into Botswana including, in March 1983, the leader of ZAPU, Mugabe's opposition in the elections, Joshua Nkomo.

Nkomo left for London rapidly, but later allegations that the refugee camps were harbouring armed dissidents caused problems, culminating in a border skirmish in 1983 between the BDF and 'armed men wearing Zimbabwean military uniforms.' It wasn't until April 1989 that Botswana felt able to revoke the 'refugee' status for Zimbabwean nationals and, soon after, the refugees left – although Botswana continued to have many illegal migrants from Zimbabwe.

Internally, political tensions between the BDP and the BNF peaked in early 1987 with a referendum on constitutional amendments to the electoral system, which was boycotted by the BNF. However, by October 1989, the BDP demonstrated its substantial support by winning 65% of the votes in an election. (The result of which was again challenged by the BNF in several constituencies.) In October the new national assembly returned Masire to the president's office for a third term.

During this time there were several incursions into Botswana by South African troops – including two raids on alleged ANC offices in Gaborone in 1985 and 1986. But a few years later, tensions began to ease as South Africa's President De Klerk started to set his country on a course for majority rule. One of his first steps was independence for Namibia in 1990.

1990–98: President Sir Ketumile Masire

The early 1990s saw several corruption scandals in which a number of ministers resigned – including, in March 1992 the vice-president, Peter Mmusi. (Contrast these with the paucity of resignations that occur during corruption scandals in most governments and you'll realise this is a good sign, not a bad one, for the integrity of Botswana's government!)

Another general election was held on October 15 1994, with the BNF triumphing in the urban areas, winning 13 seats (37.7% of the vote), while the

BDP continued to command the support of the rural constituencies, which elected it to 40 seats (53.1% of the vote). The elections had been peaceful, with around a 70% turnout, and at last Botswana had an opposition party capable of a serious challenge to the BDP.

There was some unrest in early 1995, with several days of violence between the BDF and demonstrators (mainly students and the unemployed) during which one person was killed. However, most of this was sporadic and short-lived.

During this time relations with Botswana's neighbours were generally good. However, in 1992 a border squabble arose between Botswana and Namibia over a tiny island (called Sedudu, or Kasikili, by Botswana, or Namibia, respectively) in the Chobe River. See page 195 for more details of this argument. A potentially much more serious issue arose in 1996 when Namibia announced plans to construct a pipeline to take water from the Okavango River at Rundu. Given that this would impact directly on the Okavango Delta, the possibility of such a pipeline remains a source of great concern for Botswana.

Then in 1998 an influx of refugees from Namibia's Caprivi Strip arrived, including Mishake Muyongo, who had been suspended as president of the Namibia's opposition party, the Democratic Turnhalle Alliance. He and other leading Caprivians had campaigned for independence for the province. By 1999, over 2,000 refugees were living near Gaborone. Namibia's extradition demands were refused, although eventually a settlement was brokered by the UNHCR whereby the most prominent refugees were granted asylum in Denmark, and the rest returned to Namibia under an amnesty.

Internal electoral reform had long been on the agenda in Botswana, with some consensus about the need for it from all the political parties. In 1997 various amendments to the constitution were passed, including a reduction in the voting age from 21 to 18 years old, the establishment of an electoral commission which is independent of the government, and a measure to restrict the president to a maximum of two terms in office.

Masire reshuffled the cabinet slightly in September 1997, and soon announced that he planned to retire in 1998.

1998–present: President Festus Mogae

On March 31 1998 Sir Ketumile Masire retired as president, and the next day the vice-president, Festus Mogae, was inaugurated. His new cabinet was virtually identical to the old one; the only new minister was Lt-General Seretse Ian Khama, son of Botswana's first president (the late Sir Seretse Khama). Ian Khama had been commander of the Botswana Defence Force, and soon became vice-president.

Meanwhile, the same year, infighting in the opposition, the BNF, led to a split with dissident members forming the Botswana Congress Party (BCP). After 11 of the BNF's 13 deputies joined this, the BCP was declared the official opposition in mid-July 1998.

Current politics

In October 1999 National Assembly Elections were again held, and the BDP were returned with 33 seats, the BNF won 6, and the Botswana Congress party (BCP) won one.

The next elections are scheduled for October 2004. There's every expectation that these will be on time, free and fair – like the previous elections. The main opposition, the Botswana National Front, has done little to spell out how it would change the running of the country, although its continued presence does help to hold the BDP to account, and maintain at least some democratic debate. Meanwhile the long experience of the ruling party, and the general success that they have made of the country and its economy, tend to suggest that the BDP will again retain power.

Into the future

Botswana is highly regarded by the world community. It has maintained one of the world's highest growth rates since independence, using its diamond revenues to change from one of the world's poorest countries into a prosperous 'middle-income' country.

President Festus Mogae was born in 1939 and trained at Oxford as an economist. He served as executive director at the IMF for Anglophone Africa, and later in various senior government posts including governor of the Bank of Botswana, before becoming vice-president in 1992. He has a thorough understanding of economics and although not one for high-profile media splashes on the world stage, he is likely to make a first-rate job of running the country. There is nothing to indicate that anyone on the domestic political scene will be able to mount an effective challenge to the BDP or President Mogae in the near future.

Looking to the next few years, Botswana will have some major challenges to face up to. Unemployment is becoming a problem: officially 19%, but unofficial estimates claim closer to 40%. HIV/AIDS infection rates are amongst the highest in the world, and it remains to be seen how the government will cope.

The relative instability of Zimbabwe, on Botswana's eastern border, is a cause for concern – although it seems unlikely that this will impact on Botswana significantly, except for a possible influx of refugees and economic migrants.

Perhaps the most interesting issue, and a litmus test of the government's foresight, will be their preparations for the gradual demise of the country's diamond industry. Diversification is essential, and tourism must surely be a crucial part of this mix, but replacing such a huge sector of the economy will be difficult.

ECONOMY
Overview

In economic terms, Botswana is very much one of Africa's success stories, reflecting both the country's natural mineral wealth and a political and social stability which far outweighs that of its neighbours. In the 30-year period following independence in 1966, the economic growth rate averaged just over 9% a year, marking the economy out as the fastest growing in the world, according to the World Bank. By the turn of the century, the growth rate had stabilised at around 7% a year, and the country had foreign reserves of some US$6.3 billion. The annual rate of inflation is between 7% and 8%.

Fundamental to this growth has been the exploitation of Botswana's diamond mines, although other growth sectors have been in telecommunications and financial services. Attempts to stimulate the manufacturing sector, however, have proved less successful, with the closure in 2000 of the Hyundai assembly plant, which exported vehicles to South Africa. Although manufacturing represents only 5% of the country's GDP, the closure represented a loss to the economy of US$144 million per year, or nearly half of the total manufacturing output.

The Botswanan government is all too conscious of the country's narrow revenue base and continues to seek means to diversify this. A recent initiative is the introduction in 2001 of value added tax (VAT), while privatisation of state-owned companies such as the Botswana Telecommunications Corporation (BTC) and Air Botswana could also bring significant income into the treasury coffers.

In recent years, this rosy picture has been heavily overshadowed by the threat of disease. Botswana has one of the highest HIV/AIDs levels in the world, currently affecting over a third of the population, and resulting in an average life expectancy of just 40 years.

Economic development

Prior to independence, Botswana's economy was primarily based on farming, particularly cattle. Even in 1993, some 46% of the country's land was permanent pasture, while a further 1% was given over to arable farming. Since the 1970s, however, the extraction of mineral resources, particularly diamonds, has become big business, and today the sector accounts for a significant proportion of the country's wealth. Other areas of importance include tourism and cattle raising.

Total exports in 2000 were valued at around US$2.6 billion, with the bulk of these, some 77% in 1998, going to European Union countries. Other markets included South Africa (18%), and Zimbabwe (3%). Diamonds account for about 75% of all exports, but other goods include agricultural products, foodstuffs, brewing, metal products, paper products and textiles. Export business is the responsibility of the Botswana Export Development and Investment Agency (Bedia).

In the same year, Botswana's imports were valued at around US$2.2 billion, with around three quarters of these coming from South Africa, which is also the source of most of the country's electricity. Goods imported range from foodstuffs and textiles to machinery and petroleum products. The country's other trading partners include Europe, where 10% of the country's total imports originate, and South Korea, at 5%.

Botswana is an associate member of the European Union, whereby products manufactured in the country enter EU markets free from duties and quotas. In the United States there are no restrictions on textile products from Botswana. Within Africa, Botswana is a member of the Southern Africa Customs Union (SACU), an economic bloc comprising South Africa, Botswana, Namibia, Lesotho and Swaziland. Goods produced in Botswana enter the markets of the other four member states free of duty or any other restrictions. Botswana is also an active member of the Southern African Development Community (SADC), a body which groups together 14 countries within the region.

Diamond mining

Botswana's economic success is founded on its natural resources, particularly diamonds. Today, it is the leading producer of gem-quality diamonds in the world, totalling 24.6 million carats per year, and representing one third of the country's GDP. Since mining began in 1971, the industry has catapulted the economy on to a course of sustained growth over most of the last quarter of the 20th century.

The majority of diamond mining is carried out by Debswana, a 50/50 partnership between De Beers and the Botswanan government. The company has three large, open-cast operations, responsible for almost the entire diamond yield of the country as a whole. The largest and richest of these mines is at Jwaneng, in the south of the country. Founded in 1973, but only in production since 1982, the mine is one of the largest in the world. Also founded in the same year was the mine at Letlhakane, which was in production by 1977. The third mine is at Orapa.

In addition to diamonds, the country is rich in copper and nickel, with salt, soda ash, potash, coal, iron ore and silver to be found as well. Although diamonds account for some 60% of the country's prospecting licences, the government is seeking to diversify its mineral output.

Tourism

Botswana's natural environment is a significant attraction for tourists, as highlighted in this guide. The government's policy of encouraging small numbers of upmarket visitors to its pristine wilderness areas is proving successful within the overall aim of protecting the environment. In the last couple of years, however, the tourist industry has been thrown off balance by the knock-on effect from unrest in neighbouring Zimbabwe. This is largely because countries within southern Africa have elected to promote the region as a whole, rather than the individual countries, as a result of which many tourists choose to combine several countries in the area in one trip. Unfortunately, therefore, the problems in that one country have caused a drop in visitors to the region as a whole.

According to the Botswana Tourist Board, Botswana welcomed nearly 750,000 overseas visitors in 1998, although in reality only a small proportion of these were tourists. Visitors from South Africa alone accounted for nearly half this total. Beyond Africa, the majority of visitors, 38,755 in total, originated from Europe, with a further 10,346 from North America. With income from tourism valued at around US$204 million per year, the sector represents an important source of revenue for the government, and employment within individual communities. In order to increase the benefits from tourism without adverse impact on the environment, attempts are being made to diversify into smaller 'ecotourism' projects that will benefit local communities at ground level, and to offset the negative effects of a clash between tourism projects and the needs of local people.

Workforce

In 1995, the total workforce in Botswana stood at 235,000. Industrial relations are good, with virtually no worker unrest or strikes. The overall rate of literacy in the country is 74%, a direct result of the financial success of the mining industry to the country's economy. In 2000, Botswana's GDP was some US$10.4 billion, representing a growth rate that year of 6%. At US$6,600, GDP per capita was the highest in Africa, with mining accounting for 36%. The minimum wage is P600 (about US$105) per month, with an average annual income of US$2,800. Nevertheless, while the rate of unemployment is officially said to be 19%, unofficial figures place it at nearer 40%, and in 2000 some 47% of the population was said to be below the poverty line.

Foreign investment

The combination of political stability, low rates of taxation and the lack of exchange controls, which were abolished in 1999, makes Botswana attractive to investors. Pursuit of the government's policy of privatisation is also significant in this area.

There are strict rules both for foreign ownership and for foreign investment in companies listed on Botswana's small stock exchange, which was established in 1995. Private investors hold less than a tenth of the total market capitalisation. No one foreigner may own more than 10% of the issued capital of a publicly quoted company, while foreign ownership of the free stock of a local company trading on the exchange may not exceed 55%. Repatriation of funds is regulated by law. For further information, contact the Administrator, PO Box 41015, Khama Crescent, 4th floor, Finance House, Gaborone; tel: 30 5190/3740; fax: 37 4079.

People and Culture

PEOPLE
The population

The most recent statistics (2001) put Botswana's population at around 1,586,000, with a population growth per year of 0.47%. This growth rate is low by African standards, and results from about 49% of fertile women using contraceptives. This is exceptional for sub-Saharan Africa and reflects the educated people with a prosperous and generally developed economy (Botswana's GDP is around US$6,600 per capita).

UNICEF's current statistics indicate that 95% of the population has access to safe water, 66% to adequate sanitation, and that well over 90% of children under one have been immunised with polio, diphtheria and the BCG triple vaccine shots. These are very good levels by the continent's standards, and are no doubt helped by the government's policy of paying the full cost of all these vaccines.

Primary school enrolment is around 98/99% for boys/girls, and secondary school enrolment is around 61/68%. Literacy is 74/80% for men/women. This pattern of the girls generally receiving more education is unusual in Africa, where sons are often favoured by their parents over daughters – but given women's pivotal role in bringing up children and running households in this traditional society, it bodes well for the future.

About 49.6% of the population is under 18, and the average life expectancy is about 47 years. It's sobering to note that this life expectancy has been going down recently, largely due to the impact of the high rate of AIDS infection in the country.

However, these statistics say nothing of what Botswana's people are like. If you venture into the more rural areas, take a local bus, or try to hitchhike with the locals; you will often find that people are curious about you. Chat to them openly, as fellow travellers, and you will find most to be delightful. They will be pleased to assist you where they can, and as keen to help you learn about them and their country as they are interested in your lifestyle and what brings you to Botswana.

That said, I find that it's not uncommon, especially in the towns, to find people surly and largely uninterested sometimes … just as they are in London, or New York, or many modern cities.

A note on 'tribes'

The people of Africa are often viewed, from abroad, as belonging to a multitude of culturally and linguistically distinct tribes – which are often portrayed as being at odds with each other. Whilst there is certainly an enormous variety of different ethnic groups in Africa, most are closely related to their neighbours in terms of language, beliefs and way of life. Modern historians eschew the simplistic tag of 'tribes', noting that such groupings change with time.

Sometimes the word tribe is used to describe a group of people who all speak the same language; it may be used to mean those who follow a particular leader or to refer to all the inhabitants of a certain area at a given time. In any case, tribe is a vague word that is used differently for different purposes. The term 'clan' (blood relations) is a smaller, more precisely defined, unit – though rather too precise for our broad discussions here.

Certainly, at any given time, groups of people or clans who share similar language and cultural beliefs do band together and often, in time, develop 'tribal' identities. However, it is wrong to then extrapolate and assume that their ancestors will have had the same groupings and allegiances centuries ago.

In Africa, as elsewhere in the world, history is recorded by the winners. Here the winners, the ruling class, may be the descendants of a small group of immigrants who achieved dominance over a larger, long-established community. Over the years, the history of that ruling class (the winners) usually becomes regarded as the history of the whole community, or tribe. Two 'tribes' have thus become one, with one history – which will reflect the origins of that small group of immigrants, and not the ancestors of the majority of the current tribe.

Botswana is typical of many African countries. Currently historians and linguistics experts can identify at least 26 different languages spoken here. As you will see, there are cultural differences between the people in different parts of the country. However, in many ways these are no more pronounced than those between the states of the USA, or the different regions of the (relatively tiny) UK.

There continues to be lots of inter-marriage and mixing of these peoples and cultures – perhaps more so than there has ever been, due to the efficiency of modern transport systems. Generally, there is very little friction between these communities (whose boundaries, as we have said, are indistinct) and Botswana's various peoples live peacefully together.

The San

There is not another social/language group on this planet which has been studied, written about, filmed and researched more than the San, or Bushmen, of the Kalahari. Despite this, or indeed because of it, popular conceptions about them, fed by their image in the media, are often strikingly out of step with the realities. Thus they warrant a separate section devoted to them here.

The aim of these next few pages is to try and explain some of the roots of the misconceptions, to look at some of the realities, and to make you think. Despite having spent a lot of time with San in the Kalahari, it is difficult to separate fact from oft-repeated, glossy fiction. If parts of this discussion seem disparate, it's a reflection of this difficulty.

Recent scientific observations on the Khoisan

Our view of the San is partly informed by some basic anthropological and linguistic research, mostly applying to the Khoisan, which is worth outlining to set the scene.

Anthropology

The first fossil records that we have of our human ancestors date back to at least about 60,000 years ago in East Africa. These are likely to have been the ancestors of everyone living today.

Archaeological finds from parts of the Kalahari show that human beings have lived here for at least 40,000 years. These are generally agreed to have been the ancestors of the modern Khoisan peoples living in Botswana today. (The various peoples of the Khoi and the San are known collectively as the Khoisan. All have relatively light golden brown skin, almond shaped eyes and high cheekbones. Their stature is generally small and slight, and they are now found across southern Africa.)

WHAT'S IN A NAME?

Historians, anthropologists and social scientists are divided, and often perplexed, about what name to use for the people known as 'Bushmen'. The confusion is compounded by the mix of different tribal tags used in historical texts, often for reasons of political correctness.

San, Bushmen, San/Bushmen, Khoisan, Khoi are all used, often apparently randomly. In Botswana you'll also hear RAD (Remote Area Dweller) or Masarwa/Basarwa used, but the former is exceedingly vague and the latter often considered insulting. Some avoid the term 'Bushmen', regarding it as debasing and sexist, often using 'San' in preference – which others claim to be a derogatory Nama word. Meanwhile 'Khoisan' is a language grouping, not a specific race or tribe, and encompasses the Khoi (or Khoe or Khoi-Khoi or Khoi-khoin), and hence also Namibia's Damara and Nama people. All have similar 'click' languages, but they live very differently from many of the people that we think of as the Bushmen.

Ideally, we would use the term by which these people use themselves, but there lies the rub. Ask villagers in the Kalahari and they will describe themselves as members of the Ju-/wasi, the !Kung, the Hai-//omn – or any one of a dozen other language groups. (See page 24 for an explanation of the ! and // in these names.) If we used these much more precise linguistic terms (see *Language classifications*, later in this chapter, for a few of the main ones), they would overly complicate our discussions and require an accuracy that is beyond me.

These people have no label for the broad racial category that we regard as 'the Bushmen'. They simply don't think of themselves as belonging to one race of people. Therefore, the concept of an overall grouping of people that we call 'Bushmen' must have originated from someone other than the people themselves. In truth, it is an invention of those who came to this corner of Africa later – a legacy of colonialism in its broadest sense.

Given the questionable validity of any term, I have used San throughout this book: not because I believe it to be more accurate than the alternatives, but simply because this is a term that is widely used in southern Africa, and widely understood elsewhere. It's also the term adopted by the Kalahari People's Fund, and agreed by various San communities in Namibia (see www.kalaharipeoples.org). That said, it's a vague term; just try to make it precise and you'll realise how inadequate it is. I apologise if it is, in any language, derogatory; it isn't meant to be!

Language research

Linguists have grouped all the world's languages into around 20 linguistic families. Of these, four are very different from the rest. All these four are African families – and they include the Khoisan and the Niger-Congo (Bantu) languages.

This is amongst the evidence that has led linguists to believe that human language evolved in Africa, and further analysis has suggested that this was probably amongst the ancestors of the Khoisan.

The Khoisan languages are distinguished by their wide repertoire of clicking sounds. Don't mistake these for simple: they are very sophisticated. It was observed by Dunbar (see *Further Reading*) that, 'From the phonetic point of view these [the Khoisan languages] are the world's most complex languages. To speak one of them fluently is to exploit human phonetic ability to the full.'

CULTURAL SENSITIVITY AND LANGUAGE

Cultural sensitivity isn't something that a guidebook can teach you, though reading the section on cultural guidelines, at the end of this chapter, may help. Being sensitive to the results of your actions and attitudes on others is especially important in this area.

The San are often a humble people, who regard arrogance as a vice. It is normal for them to be self-deprecating amongst themselves, to make sure that everyone is valued and nobody becomes too proud. So the less you are perceived as a loud, arrogant foreigner, the better.

Very few foreigners can pick up much of the local language without living here for a long time. (Readers may already realise that spellings of the same word can vary greatly.) However, if you want to try to pronounce the words then there are four main clicks to master. In the well-documented Ju/'hoansi language, these are:

/   a dental click, a sucking sound, made by putting the tongue just behind the front teeth.

//   a clucking sound, like that used in English to urge on a horse.

!   a sharp popping sound, like a cork coming out of a bottle, made by pulling the tongue down quickly from the roof of the mouth.

(a soft popping sound, made by putting your tongue just behind the ridge back of the front teeth (this is usually the hardest).

At some point the Khoisan languages diverged from a common ancestor, and today three distinct groups exist: the northern, central and southern groups. Languages gradually evolve and change as different groups of people split up and move to new areas, isolated from their old contacts. Thus the evolution of each language is specific to each group, and reflected in the classifications described later in this chapter.

According to Michael Main (see *Further Reading*), the northern group are San and today they live west of the Okavango and north of Ghanzi, with representatives found as far afield as Angola. The southern group are also San, who live in the area between Kang and Bokspits in Botswana. The central group is Khoe, living in central Botswana, and extending north to the eastern Okavango and Kasane, and west into Namibia, where they are known as the Nama.

Each of these three Khoisan language groups has many dialects. These have some similarities, but they are not closely related, and some are different to the point where there is no mutual understanding. Certain dialects are so restricted that only a small family group speaks them; it was reported recently that one San language died out completely with the death of the last speaker.

This huge number of dialects, and variation in languages, reflects the relative isolation of the various speakers, most of whom now live in small family groups as the Kalahari's arid environment cannot sustain large groups of people living together in one place as hunter-gatherers.

Genetic discoveries

Most genetically normal men have an X- and a Y-chromosome, whilst women have two X-chromosomes. Unlike the other 22 pairs of (non-sex) chromosomes that each human has, there is no opportunity for the Y-chromosome to 'swap' or 'share' its DNA with any other chromosome. Thus all the information in a man's Y chromosome will usually be passed on, without change, to all of his sons.

However, very rarely a single 'letter' in the Y-chromosome will be altered as it's being passed on, thus causing a permanent change in the chromosome's genetic sequence. This will then be the start of a new lineage of slightly different Y-chromosomes, which will be inherited by all future male descendants.

In November 2000, Professor Ronald Davis and a team of Stanford researchers (see *Further Reading*) claimed to have traced back this lineage to a single individual man, and that a small group of East Africans (Sudanese and Ethiopians) and Khoisan, are the closest present-day relatives of this original man. That is, their genetic make-up is closest to his. (It's a scientific 'proof' of the biblical Adam, if you like.)

This is still a very contentious finding, with subsequent researchers suggesting at least ten original male sources ('Adams') – and so although interesting, the jury remains out on the precise details of all these findings. If you're interested in the latest on this, then you'll find a lot about this on the web – start searching with keywords: 'Khoisan Y chromosome.'

Historical views of the San
Despite much evidence and research, our views of the San seem to have changed relatively little since both the Bantu groups and the first Europeans arrived in southern Africa.

The settlers' view
Since the first Bantu farmer started migrating south through East Africa, the range of territory occupied by the foragers, whose Stone Age technology had dominated the continent, began to condense. By the time the first white settlers appeared in the Cape, the Khoisan people were already restricted to Africa's southwestern corners and the Kalahari.

All over the world, farmers occupy clearly demarcated areas of land, whereas foragers will move more and often leave less trace of their presence. In Africa, this made it easier for farmers, first black then white, to ignore any traditional land rights that belonged to foraging people.

Faced with the loss of territory for hunting and gathering, the foragers – who, by this time were already being called 'Bushmen' – made enemies of the farmers by killing cattle. They waged a guerrilla war, shooting poison arrows at parties of men who set out to massacre them. They were feared and loathed by the settlers, who, however, captured and valued their children as servants.

Some of the Khoisan retreated north from the Cape – like the ancestors of Namibia's Nama people. Others were forced to labour on the settlers' farms, or were thrown into prison for hunting animals or birds which had been their traditional prey, but which were now designated property of the crown.

This story is told by Robert J Gordon in *The Bushman Myth: The Makings of a Namibian Underclass* (see *Further Reading*). He shows that throughout history the hunter-gathering San have been at odds with populations of settlers who divided up and 'owned' the land in the form of farms. The European settlers proved to be their most determined enemy, embarking on a programme of legislation and massacre. Many San died in prison, with many more shot as 'vermin'.

Thus the onslaught of farmers on the hunter-gatherers accelerated between the 1800s and the mid-1900s. This helped to ensure that hunter-gathering as a lifestyle only continued to be practical in marginal areas that couldn't be economically farmed – like the Kalahari. Archaeological evidence suggests that hunter-gatherer peoples have lived for about 60,000 years at sites like the Tsodilo Hills.

Western views of the San in the 1800s

Though settlers in the Cape interacted with Khoisan people, so did Europe and the US, in a very limited way. Throughout the 1800s and early 1900s a succession of Khoisan people were effectively enslaved and brought to Europe and the US for exhibition. Sometimes this was under the guise of anthropology, but usually it didn't claim to be anything more than entertainment.

One of the first was the 'Hottentot Venus' – a woman who was probably of Khoisan extraction who was exhibited around London and Paris from 1810 to 1815, as an erotic curiosity for aristocrats.

A string of others followed. For example, the six Khoisan people exhibited at the Coney Island Pleasure Resort, beside New York, and later in London in the 1880s and billed as the 'missing link between apes and men', or the 'wild dancing bushman' known as Franz brought to England around 1913 by Paddy Hepston (see Parsons' piece in *Botswana Notes & Records*, detailed in *Further Reading*).

Impressions of the San from the 1950s

In the 1950s a researcher from Harvard, John Marshall, came to the Kalahari to study the Kung! San. He described a peaceful people living in harmony with nature, amidst a land that provided all their needs. The groups had a deep spirituality and no real hierarchy: it seemed like the picture of a modern Eden. (Especially when viewed through post-war eyes.) Marshall was a natural cameraman and made a film that follows the hunt of a giraffe by four men over a five-day period. It swiftly became a classic, both in and outside of anthropological circles.

Further research agreed, with researchers noting a great surfeit of protein in the diet of the Kung! San and low birth rates akin to modern industrial societies.

Again the San were seen as photogenic and sources of good copy and good images. The lives were portrayed in romantic, spiritual terms in the book and film *The Lost World of the Kalahari* by Laurens van der Post (see *Further Reading*). This documentary really ignited the worldwide interest in the San and led to subsequent films such as *The Gods Must be Crazy*. All the images conveyed an idyllic view of the San as untainted by contact with the modern world.

The reality

The reality was much less rosy than the first researchers thought. Some of their major misconceptions have been outlined particularly clearly in chapter 13 of John Reader's *Africa: A Biography of the Continent* (see *Further Reading*). He points out that far from an ideal diet, the nutrition of the San was often critically limited, lacking vitamins and fatty acids associated with a lack of animal fat in their diet. Far from a stable population with a low birth rate, it seems likely that there had been a decline in the birth rate in the last few generations. The likely cause for this was periods of inadequate nourishment during the year when the San lost weight from lack of food, stress and the great exertions of their lifestyle.

In fact, it seems likely that the San, whom we now see as foragers, are people who, over the last two millennia, have become relegated to an underclass by the relentless advance of the black and white farmers who did not recognise their original rights to their traditional land.

San today and the media

Though scientific thought has moved on since the 1950s, much of the media has not. The San are still perceived to be hot news.

The outpost of Tsumkwe is the centre for many of the San communities in Namibia. It's a tiny crossroads with a school and a handful of buildings, in a remote corner of northeastern Namibia. Despite its isolation, in 2001 this desert outpost hosted no less than 22 film crews. Yes, really, that's an average of almost two each month – and I'm not counting a whole host of other print journalists and photographers.

Talk to virtually any of the directors and you'll realise that they arrive with very clear ideas about the images that they want to capture. They all think they're one of the first, they think they're original, and they want to return home with images which match their pre-conceived ideas about the San as 'the last primitive hunter-gatherers'.

As an example, you'll often see pictures in the media of San hunters in traditional dress walking across a hot, barren salt pan. When asked to do these shoots the San's usual comment is, 'Why, there's no point. We'd never go looking for anything there.' But the shots look spectacular and win prizes ... so the photographers keep asking for them. From the San's perspective, they get paid for the shots, so why not pose for the camera? I'd do the same!

Thus our current image of the San is really one that *we* are constantly re-creating. It's the one that we expect. But it's doesn't necessarily conform to any reality. So on reflection, popular thinking hasn't moved on much from Marshall's first film in the 1950s.

Current life for the San
Looking at the current lifestyle of the San who remain in the more remote areas of the Kalahari, it's difficult not to lapse into a romantic view of ignoring present realities. There are too many cultural aspects to cover here, so instead I've just picked out a few that you may encounter.

Nomads of the Kalahari
Perhaps the first idea to dispel is that the San are nomads. They're not. San family groups have clearly-defined territories within which they forage, called a n!ore (in the Ju/'hoansi language). This is usually centred on a place where there is water, and contains food resources sufficient for the basic subsistence of the group.

Groups recognise rights to the n!ore, which is passed on from father to first-born son. Any visiting people would ask permission to remain in these. Researchers have mapped these areas, even in places like the Central Kalahari.

Hunter-gatherers
Any hunter-gatherer lifestyle entails a dependence on, and extensive knowledge of, the environment and the resident fauna and flora found there. In the Kalahari, water is the greatest need and the San know which roots and tubers provide liquid to quench thirst. They create sip wells in the desert, digging a hole, filled with soft grass, then using a reed to suck water into the hole, and send it bubbling up the reed to fill an ostrich egg. Water-filled ostrich eggs are also buried at specific locations within the groups 'area'. When necessary the San will strain the liquid from the rumen of a herbivore and drink that.

Researchers have observed that any hunting is done by the men. When living a basic hunting and gathering lifestyle, with little external input, hunting provides only about 20% of their food. The remaining 80% is provided largely by the women, helped by the children, who forage and gather wild food from the bush. By age twelve a child might know about 200 plant species, and an adult more than 300.

Social system
The survival of the San in the harsh environment of the Kalahari is evidence of the supreme adaptability of humans. It reflects their detailed knowledge of their

environment, which provides them not only with food, but with materials for shelter and medicine in the form of plants.

Another very important factor in their survival is the social system by which the San live. Social interaction is governed by unwritten rules that bind the people in friendship and harmony, which must be maintained. One such mechanism is the obligation to distribute the meat from a large kill. Another is the obligation to lend such few things as are individually possessed, thereby incurring a debt of obligation from the borrower.

They also practise exogamy, which means they have an obligation to marry outside the group. This creates social bonds between groups. Such ties bind the society inextricably together, as does the system of gift exchange between separate groups.

Owing to the environmental constraints a group will consist of between 80 and 120 people, living and moving together. In times of shortage the groups will be much smaller, sometimes consisting of only immediate family – parents, grandparents and children. They must be able to carry everything they possess. Their huts are light constructions of grass, and they have few possessions.

Because no one owns property, no one is richer or has more status than another. A group of San has a nominal leader, who might be a senior member of the group, an expert hunter, or the person who owns the water rights. The whole group takes decisions affecting them, often after vociferous discussions.

Hunting

The San in the Kalahari are practised hunters, using many different techniques to capture the game. Their main weapons are a very light bow, and an arrow made of reed, in three sections. The arrowhead is usually poisoned, using one of a number of poisons obtained from specific plants, snakes and beetles. (Though most San know how to hunt with bows and arrows, the actual practice is increasingly uncommon when it's not done to earn money from observing visitors.)

All the hunters may be involved in the capture of large game, which carries with it certain obligations. The whole group shares in the kill and each member is entitled to a certain portion of the meat.

There are different methods for hunting small game, which only the hunter's family would usually share. One method for catching spring hares involves long, flexible poles (sometimes four metres long) made of thin sticks, with a duiker's horn (or more usually now a metal hook) fastened to the end. These are rammed into the hare's hole, impaling the animal, which is then pulled or dug out.

Trance dancing

Entertainment for the San, when things are good, usually involves dancing. During some dances, which may often have overtones of ritual or religion, the dancers may fall into a trance and collapse.

These trances are induced by a deliberate breathing technique, with a clear physiological explanation. Dances normally take place in the evening, around a fire. Then the women, children and old people will sit around and clap, whilst some of the younger men will dance around the circle in an energetic, rhythmic dance. Often this is all that happens, and after a while the excitement dies down and everyone goes to sleep.

However, on fairly rare occasions, the dancers will go into a trance. After several hours of constant exertion, they will shorten their breathing. This creates an oxygen deficiency, which leads to the heart pumping more strongly to compensate. Blood pressure to the brain increases; the dancer loses consciousness and collapses.

SURVIVAL AND THE 'BUSHMEN' OF THE CENTRAL KALAHARI GAME RESERVE

The following text has been contributed by Survival International.

> We know this land belonged to our great grandparents. But now, just because we are Bushmen, our land is being taken from us.
>
> Bushman woman, Central Kalahari Game Reserve

Survival International is a worldwide organisation supporting tribal peoples. It stands for their right to decide their own future and helps them protect their lives, lands and human rights.

Today there are more than 150 million tribal people worldwide, including at least 70 uncontacted tribes. Almost all are persecuted relentlessly – they are flooded by dams, wiped out by disease, driven from their homes by logging and mining, and evicted by settlers. However, with the support of people outside, these threats can be averted and tribal peoples can live healthy and secure lives: there is nothing inevitable about their demise.

Survival has been supporting the Gana and Gwi 'Bushmen' of the Central Kalahari Game Reserve (who are the indigenous people of this region) for over 15 years. For all this time the Botswana government has expressed its desire to relocate the Gana and Gwi, together with their neighbours the Bakgalagadi, out of the reserve, in spite of the fact that the reserve was actually created to provide a home for the Bushmen, and the wildlife they hunt. The Bushmen's life in the reserve was gradually made impossible, especially by heavily restricting the hunting on which the Bushmen depend for their food.

In two big operations, in 1997 and 2002, the authorities trucked out virtually all those Bushmen who had not previously succumbed to a combination of inducement and pressure. The government also destroyed the Bushmen's water supplies and borehole. Some observers believe that behind the evictions lurk the prospect of huge riches from the diamond deposits known to be in the reserve (Botswana's economy largely depends on diamonds). The government has now relocated these people to bleak 'resettlement' camps where they live on government handouts and are reduced to boredom, alcoholism and despair; many are desperately struggling to return to their homes in the reserve.

Until they were evicted from their land, the Gana and Gwi lived self-sufficient lives. Of the entire 'Bushmen' population, they are virtually unique in having maintained hunting as central to their way of life. In modern-day Botswana, however, this lifestyle is widely seen as 'primitive' and an embarrassment to a 'developing' country. The president, for example, has said, 'How can you have a Stone Age creature continue to exist in the age of computers? If the Bushmen want to survive, they must change or otherwise, like the dodo, they will perish.'

Survival is the only international organisation supporting tribal peoples worldwide which does not accept funding from any national government. For more information about our campaign with the Gana and Gwi, contact: Survival International, tel: + 44 (0) 207 687 8700; web: www.survival-international.org.

Issues for the future

As commented above, foragers throughout the world are perceived to have less valid claims on lands than the farmers, who usually occupy more clearly demarcated areas of land.

Firstly, as a matter of policy, Botswana doesn't allow any of its policies to favour one ethnic group or another. This is generally held to be a very sensible policy, framed to avoid creating ethnic divisions and strife. However, having such a disadvantaged position, it's much more difficult for the San to access their rights than most other groups.

Secondly, the San are not recognised within the power structure accorded to the various chiefs of Botswana's other tribal groups. There's no San representation in the House of Chiefs (Botswana's second legislative chamber), and no traditional land rights accorded to them. This puts them at a major political disadvantage.

Thirdly, under Botswana law hunting and gathering isn't recognised as a formal category of land use – so in local disputes the needs of the San are frequently subjugated to those of Botswana's farmers.

The resulting disenfranchisement has led many of the San into situations of extreme poverty. Alcoholism is a problem amongst some San populations. Today the government provides schools in villages where the supply of water and drought relief food encourages the people to stay. But with no recent farming tradition, self-sufficiency is difficult. Others work on cattle farms or game farms and reserves.

Central Kalahari Game Reserve

This is one of the most contentious issues facing Botswana today – with much rhetoric from all quarters.

The Central Kalahari Game Reserve (CKGR) was proclaimed in 1961 in the last days of the British Protectorate with the intention of placating international concern over the well being of the San, by safeguarding it for the San hunter-gatherers who were living there. Although for ease of administration it was designated as a game reserve, the needs of its people was a prime motivating factor in its declaration.

In the early 1960s the population here was estimated at around 5,000 people; by the 1996 it had reduced to an estimated 1,482. The largest settlement, a small village called Xade, had a borehole which supplied water, and a few basic buildings. As early as 1986 a government white paper spelled out that the policy was for the residents of the CKGR to be relocated outside the reserve. The story since then has been one of the government using carrots and sticks to attain this aim.

Supporters of the San's right to remain have alleged that since the mid-1990s the government and its servants, including the park's game scouts, have been applying more and more pressure on the local people, forcing them to resettle to new locations outside the reserve. The best known of these is named, with Orwellian flair, New Xade. They allege that San individuals have been beaten and otherwise coerced into moving, and that even the water supply has been stopped for those who stay.

In return, the government denies that they have ever used force. They say that water and other services have been withdrawn from Xade for reasons of practicality and cost, and that any relocations have been voluntary.

In conclusion it seems likely that the government has, at best, been a little 'over-zealous' in its resettlement policy, and at worst it may have committed serious injustices to the people in the reserve. For me, the most pertinent question is 'Why bother?' as the official line that it's to protect the game seems implausible given all the bad press that this generates for them throughout the world.

RELOCATION OF BASARWA FROM THE CENTRAL KALAHARI GAME RESERVE

The following is taken from a speech given by President Mogae on November 7 2002, in which he sought to refute a connection between diamond exploration in the CKGR and the relocation of the Basarwa. For the complete text of the speech, see www.gov.bw/government/relocation.html.

In view of the extended campaign of deception which has been waged by Survival International, it is necessary for me to set the record absolutely straight on a number of matters of fact which, fortunately, are easily verifiable by those, including Survival International, who care to do so. These facts are:

- Despite exploration over many years, beginning in the mid-1960s, no commercially mineable mineral deposit has been found inside the CKGR. There is neither any actual mining nor any plan for future mining inside the reserve.
- A diamond deposit was discovered at Gope, inside the CKGR, in 1980. After extensive testing, including the sinking of a trial shaft which still exists, it has been determined that the deposit cannot be economically mined. The area remains the subject of a retention licence, but all activity has ceased and there is no plan to resume.
- The activity associated with past mineral prospecting, including the sinking of a borehole at the location, attracted a small number of Basarwa to abandon a more nomadic lifestyle and adopt a settled existence in the area. The borehole has subsequently been disconnected because prospecting activity in the area has ceased. This was criticised by Survival International on the absurd notion that the government was terminating the 'traditional' water supply of the Basarwa.
- The programme of assisted relocation of Basarwa from areas of the CKGR, where it is virtually impossible to provide any kind of basic human infrastructure, began in 1997 after having been the subject of consultations since 1985. It was in no way related to any plan, real or fictitious, to commence diamond mining in the CKGR.
- The great majority of the Basarwa communities are anxious to seize the opportunity for an improvement in the quality of their lives and the lives of their children. Even some of those who are apparently resisting such opportunities have found the means to advance the lives and the future prospects of their own families, by tapping into the fruits of economic development which are already available to them outside the CKGR.

The relocation exercise, which is accepted as being in the best interests of the majority of the Basarwa and of the nation as a whole, has been carried out in the most sensitive and constructive manner possible. The government has devoted significant resources to assist the Basarwa in their new settlements. Funds have been allocated for infrastructural developments, such as schools, health posts, water reticulation and other social amenities. Apart from land for residential and commercial purposes, people have been given cattle and goats, and more than P30 million (US$5 million) has been expended on projects to improve the new settlements. In a world where governments stand accused of many terrible crimes, it does seem strange that the Botswana Government should have to defend itself against the charge of improving the lives of its citizens.

There are two obvious theories. One recognises that the government is putting an increasing emphasis on tourism, and is concerned that the presence of the San will detract from the tourist's experience. A second suggests that the government wants to clear the way for the possibility of exploiting mineral claims in the area – diamond prospectors have long been looking for another find like Orapa beneath the Kalahari.

Hope for the future?
Perhaps one of the few rays of hope is that as a consequence of the prevailing image of the San, visitors really are willing to pay to see something of their 'traditional culture'. Hence the springing up of various traditional villages and tourism projects in both Botswana and neighbouring Namibia.

These vary from really interesting, genuine insights into the people and their skills, to little more than curiosity shows put on for the benefit of visitors.

I'd probably argue that virtually all are worthwhile for the San – provided that they bring a substantial income into the community involved, and do so without actively harming the people's self-esteem. Meanwhile from experience of the best, I know they can be absolutely fascinating personal interactions for the visitor, as well as acting to reinforce the community's own self-esteem and value in their own skills, whilst bringing much-needed money into the community.

What's become very, very clear is that to make such a tourist-community interaction really successful for both parties needs the permanent commitment of someone on the ground who has been working with the community for a long period – and understands both the community, and the tourists. Without this, such projects invariably fail.

Other social groups
The Khoisan
The Khoisan group includes the San people, discussed at length in the previous sections, and the Khoe, covered here.

The Khoe
The San are often described as hunter-gatherers and the Khoe as pastoralists. The distinction is not quite so clear-cut, but it is generally useful. The Khoe, who live in central Botswana and Namibia, have herds of cattle, but continue to source some of their food from hunting and gathering, supplemented by milk products.

The ownership of animals is a mark of status in these groups, so laws are required to protect property and status. Because of the intrinsic value of the animals, the Khoe milk their herds but do not kill them for food; stock animals are only killed to mark special occasions.

The ownership of property (stock) has created a more rigid and complex social structure. Property creates wealth, which can be inherited after the death of the owner, and so laws of inheritance have been developed. Wealth brings with it the power to control others, thus creating leaders. It also leads to a wealth-based economy that depends on the exchange of goods and work that have an economic value. What must be freely given among the San must be bought and paid for among the Khoe.

Little is known about the religious beliefs of the Khoe, though they believe in a Supreme Being and it is thought that some beliefs are similar to the San and can be traced back to a common source.

Bantu-speaking peoples
After a complex history of conflict, a number of tribes of Bantu origin can now be found in Botswana. As discussed on pages 21–2, today the word 'tribe' has colonial

connotations, but unfortunately we do not have a suitable alternative. Likewise, definition by ethnic group is not considered politically correct in Botswana; all people are primarily Batswana, (the people of Botswana) and only secondarily Bayei, or Bakwena or European etc. Tribal names are frequently preceded by Ba – which means 'the people of ...'

Tswana

Although the same name applies to all the people of Botswana, the Batswana (or Tswana) are also the largest ethnic group in the country. As an aside, colonial partitioning led to three-quarters of the Tswana actually living in South Africa. The name embraces a number of different offshoots. The Tswana speak Setswana, which is the second language of Botswana, English being the official language.

The Basubiya, the Hambukushu and the Bayei

Around AD1600 these three groups of river-dwelling people all lived close together in the region to the south of the Chobe River. Their closeness is reflected in the similarity of their customs. Significantly, their system of inheritance meant that wealth and status were not passed to the first son, but through to the children of the father's eldest sister. So a man inherited the chieftancy if his mother was the eldest sister of the chief.

The Basubiya

According to tradition, after a fight over a lion skin the Bayei were defeated by the Basubiya. They moved away to the Linyanti River, but they still came under the rule of the Basubiya.

Meanwhile, the Hambukushu were driven from their homeland by the expansionist and tribute-seeking Chief of the Balozi, whose capital was at Katima Mulilo (now in western Zambia.) To avoid paying the tribute and escape his attentions, the Hambukushu left the Zambezi River and moved nearer to the Chobe and Linyanti rivers, into a region which was already occupied by the Bayei.

The Basubiya eventually grew very powerful and had a large state which stretched from Luchindo on the Chobe river, westwards towards the Okavango.

SEROWE, A TYPICAL TSWANA VILLAGE

Bessie Head's book, *Serowe: Village of the Rain Wind* (see *Further Reading*), offers an invaluable and very readable introduction to Tswana culture, Bamangwato style. (The Bamangwato tribe rose to ascendancy over the other tribes, following the Difaquane wars. This was due partly to their prime location for trading contacts and partly to visionary leadership.)

The book gives a wonderful insight into an African village and the lives, knowledge and skills of the inhabitants. Writing in 1981 Head describes Serowe as a typical traditional village. Most people had three homes; one in the village, one at the lands where they ploughed and one at the cattle post where they kept their cattle. The homes were all round, thatched mud huts and people moved from home to home all the time.

We learn how the homes are constructed – that the walls of the mud huts were built and externally decorated by the women, but were thatched by the men. The weaving of grass baskets was a woman's occupation, but tanning hide to make leather Tswana mats and blankets was a man's profession.

Eventually they were defeated by the Balozi and incorporated into the Lozi empire until its collapse in 1865. According to Campbell, the Basubiya were mainly agriculturalists who also kept some cattle, sheep and goats. They cultivated the flood plains, which they prepared by hoeing in the autumn before the winter floods and planting crops such as millet, sweet reeds and melon when the floods had receded. Today they still live in the northwest and Chobe Districts of the country.

Bayei (and Banoka)
In response to the Basubiya invasion, the Bayei moved away from the Chobe River, into the Okavango, and between 1750 and 1800 they firmly established themselves in the area of the delta around Lake Ngami. This shallower, southern section of the delta perfectly suited the Bayei, who lived mainly from fishing. They also kept cattle, but used them only as pack animals. In the Delta they encountered a group of Khoe, called the Banoka, (otherwise known as the River Bushmen), who had adapted their hunter-gatherer skills to the environment of the delta.

The two peoples seem to have coexisted peacefully and even swapped skills. For example the Bayei taught the Banoka to fish with nets where before they had only used baskets. The Bayei made nets from the twisted fibres of succulent plants, which they then trawled behind their boats, called mekoro. A mokoro (mekoro is the plural form) is a dug out canoe that is poled from the rear. In return the Banoka taught the Bayei how to dig pits, filled with sharp pointed sticks, in the middle of a game trail, to trap unsuspecting animals on their way to the river.

A prize catch for the Bayei was the hippo, which they sometimes hunted from their mekoro. Their method, like the old whale hunters, was to harpoon the hippo from the boat. Instantly the hippo would take flight, towing the mokoro in its wake. The hunters had to kill the hippo with their spears, before it either broke loose or killed them. This they did by attempting to reach the bank in their boats, tying the rope attached to the harpoon to a tree and waiting for the hippo to tire before approaching it with spears. Hippos are notoriously bad tempered and dangerous and are liable to attack if they are surprised in the water. Mekoro today are more likely to be transporting tourists for a spot of hippo watching, and may well be made of fibreglass instead of wood, but they are still often poled by a Bayei man.

Another favourite method of hippo hunting was to place a spear weighted with rocks suspended from a tree over a hippo trail. Hippos live in the water during the day, but come out at night to graze and they tend to keep to the same tracks.

The Hambukushu
Meanwhile the Hambukushu found that settling on the Chobe did not take them far enough from the Balozi tribute seekers, so they moved again and settled in the more northerly, upper reaches of the Okavango Delta. Being agriculturalists as well as hunters and fishermen, they preferred the deeper water there. Unlike the lower regions, this area did not flood when the rains came and so was more suitable for agriculture. They cleared the bush and planted crops along the river, such as millet, sugar cane, pumpkins and root crops.

Like the Bayei, the Hambukushu used mekoro boats, but instead of poling them standing up, they sat down and used paddles to propel them through the deeper water.

Campbell's *History of Botswana* (see *Further Reading*) describes how the Hambukushu hunted for elephants. 'They took the blade of a spear which had a barb in it and fixed this into a heavy piece of wood. They dug shallow holes on paths used by elephants and then set these spear blades facing upwards. The elephant stood on this, driving the blade deep into the bottom of its foot, after

TRADITIONAL CULTURE AND CHANGE

Because he was a deeply committed Christian convert, Khama, the leader of the Bamangwato, began to make changes to the traditional way of life. One of the most significant changes was the abolition of the initiation ceremonies for men and women. He reformed the *bogadi* tradition, which had meant that a woman's children belonged to her husband, even those children she had after he had died. Khama also laid down laws and regulations for his people to live by, including banning the consumption of alcohol.

One elderly man described the men's initiation ceremony or *bogwera*: 'Not only was the foreskin cut and the youths put through endurance tests, but one of us had to remain behind. He was killed in a painful way, in the secrecy of the bush. When we came home, it was made out that the youth had died because he could not stand up to the tests. Everyone knew the truth but it was treated as a deep secret. That was why Khama abolished bogwera.'

However, it was still important to mark the passing of boyhood into manhood, so Khama preserved the tradition of 'age regiments'. All young men had their coming of age marked by a gathering with prayers and lectures. Those who came of age at the same time formed an age regiment. From Khama's time on, the age regiments began to volunteer to work on community projects such as building schools or churches and many things were accomplished.

It was also largely due to the efforts of Khama that Botswana became a British Protectorate, known as the British Bechuanaland Protectorate. This probably saved Botswana from becoming another South Africa or Rhodesia (Zimbabwe) and resulted in Botswana's peaceful Independence in 1966.

When the Protectorate was finally granted, Khama expressed his gratitude and laid down the following principles of government, in a document which related primarily to the Bamangwato, but was later applied to the whole country.

'I am not baffled in the government of my town, or in deciding cases among my own people according to custom. I have to say that there are certain laws of my country which the Queen of England finds in operation, and which are advantageous to my people, and I wish these laws should be established and not taken away by the Government of England. I refer to our law concerning intoxicating drinks, that they should not enter the country of the Bamangwato, whether among black people or white people. I refer further to our law which declares that the lands of the Bamangwato are not saleable. I say this law is also good; let it be upheld and continue to be law among black people and white people.'

The system of traditional law to which Khama referred in this document was well established. It centered upon the chief, whose position of prestige and power carried with it the obligation that the good of the tribe must be placed above personal desire. The chief held property and land on behalf of the tribe and had always to be available to his people to settle disputes and business affairs.

There was also a tribal court, known as a *kgotla* to help him make decisions. This consisted of the headmen of the wards into which the village was divided, and of senior tribesmen. Disputes which could not be settled within the ward were brought to the *kgotla*. There was an obligation for people to be open in all their dealings with each other and to act in the best interests of the community.

which it couldn't walk. When it was weak, men came with axes and slashed the tendons in its back legs so that it fell down and could be speared.'

Today the Hambukushu are most famous for their beautiful hand-woven baskets, which are internationally recognised for their craftsmanship and design. The wide variety of basket types reflects the numerous purposes for which they were traditionally used, ranging from enormous grain storage baskets, to tightly woven beer baskets for holding the local brew. Unfortunately, the baskets are now being produced commercially, which enables the makers to earn a reasonable living, but has led to over-exploitation of the natural resources from which the baskets are made. The Hambukushu are also renowned as rain-makers, another skill which they have exploited commercially by selling their services to neighbouring tribes.

The Ovaherero and the Ovambanderu

The Ovaherero and their relatives the Ovambanderu are pastoralists, who keep large herds of sheep, goats, and especially cattle, which have a religious significance for them. According to their oral history tradition they seem to have moved southwest from central Africa, probably to escape the spread of the tsetse fly which spreads sleeping sickness and kills cattle and people.

The religious life of the tribe was of great importance. The tribe was divided into religious clans under a priest/chief. He owned the most cattle and he maintained a sacred herd on behalf of the tribe. On his death the priesthood and the care of the sacred herd passed to his son. The Ovaherero practised ancestor worship, and one of the priest's main religious duties was appeasing the dead relatives of the tribe.

As pastoralists the clans led their herds in search of grazing but each clan had a designated area. Within this area the women built round huts from a framework of branches covered with mud. The huts were built in a circle around corrals for the animals. As well as tending the herds, the men hunted with wooden spears, (their only iron came from trading with the Batswana). The women also collected wild food and made *omaere*, a kind of sour milk which was their staple food.

Most of the Ovaherero today live in Namibia, though some are also found in Botswana, where they fled following the German-Herero War at the beginning of the twentieth century. In the 19th century the Ovaherero were living in what is now northern Namibia, but were becoming increasingly unhappy about their loss of land to the German colonists. In January 1904 their leader, Samuel Maherero, ordered a Herero uprising against the colonial forces.

Initially the Hereros had success in taking many German farms and smaller outposts, and in severing the railway line between Swakopmund and Windhoek. However, later in 1904, the German General von Trotha led a large German force including heavy artillery against the Hereros. By August 1904 the Hereros were pushed back to their stronghold of Waterberg, with its permanent water-holes.

On August 11, the Germans attacked, and the battle raged all day. Though not decisive, the Hereros' spirit was beaten by the superior firepower and they fled east, into the Kalahari and towards Maun. Many perished; the rest settled in what is now northern Botswana.

They had lost their cattle and were forced to work as servants to another tribe, the Batawana. However they soon rebuilt their herds and also learnt agriculture from the Batawana, which they used to supplement their traditional diet of soured milk. The Ovaherero are recognisable today because the women continue to dress in the clothes they were taught to wear by Victorian Christian missionaries, including long bulky dresses and headdresses.

The Bakalanga

The Bakalanga are the second largest population group after the Tswana, despite having been divided by colonial boundaries. Today over 75% of them live in Zimbabwe. Those in Botswana live mainly in the area around Francistown, although they are scattered as far afield as Maun, Palapye, Serowe, Mahalapye and Mochudi. Their origins are unclear, though some of them have probably lived in the region of the upper Shashe River for at least a thousand years. For the last 600 years they have been ruled by other peoples, but interestingly their conquerors have always ended by inter-marrying with the Bakalanga and adopting their customs and language.

The Bakalanga are primarily agriculturalists and this is reflected in their religion and culture, but cattle and goats are also kept, usually by the chief on behalf of his tribe. The chief would give cattle to people who had performed services to the tribe, or those who needed them in order to get married or to sacrifice to the ancestors. The primary importance of agriculture is shown by the traditional marital gifts of specially forged iron hoes that were given to the bride's parents to symbolise the continuity of her livelihood.

The Kagalagari

This name is applied to different people of varied descent who currently live in the Kalahari Desert. There are five major groups who have settled in different areas of the Kalahari. They all have their own tribal names and customs and they speak a variety of languages – the combined form of which is a Sotho language, not a dialect of Tswana.

Of these five groups the Bakgwatheng remain in the east of the Kalahari on the fringes of the desert, which receives sufficient rainfall for their crops of sorghum, melons and beans. They also keep small herds of cattle, sheep and goats, and mine and work iron. As the iron ore was not available in the heart of the Kalahari these factors all restricted them to the desert's fringe.

The Bangologa and the Babolaongwe, on the other hand, are pastoralists with large herds of sheep and goats, and a few cattle. They obtain most of their food from hunting and gathering, so they are not reliant upon agriculture and they trade for iron, so they were able to live a nomadic existence within the desert.

Others

White Botswanans

The current white population of Botswana is much lower than that of her surrounding neighbours, and many of these are not permanent residents. This reflects the unusual history of Botswana; the fact that the country was a 'Protectorate' rather than a colony.

Note that this small numbers of white Botswanans are very different from the expat community (see below), who are often white but simply working in the country on a temporary basis. Many white Botswanans will trace their families back to colonial immigrants who came over during British rule, but most are citizens of Botswana rather than, say, British. This is generally an affluent group of people, a number of whom own and run their own businesses.

Expatriates

Totally distinct from the permanent population of citizens of Botswana who are white, there is also a significant 'expat' community in Botswana. These foreigners usually come to Botswana for two or three years, to work on short-term contracts, often for multi-national companies or aid agencies. Most are highly skilled individuals who come to share their knowledge with local colleagues – often teaching skills that are in short supply in Botswana.

There are also a significant number of foreigners working in the safari industry. These are often residents of other southern African nations who come to guide or manage camps for a few years, although as work permits become increasingly difficult to obtain, numbers of expats in the safari business are slowly starting to fall.

Religion

Officially Botswana is a Christian country, although the number of practising Christians is estimated at only around 20% of the population. These mostly belong to the Catholic, Anglican, Methodist, Lutheran and Zion Christian Church (where its members are noted for the khaki dress worn when attending). Services are usually in Tswana, though the larger churches in the main towns also have English services, and the smaller, rural ones will sometimes use the local languages. Faith healing is often incorporated into services.

Other religions, such as Islaam, are only represented in the larger towns; their following is small, mainly amongst expat workers.

As usual in the subcontinent, many Botswana's blend Christian beliefs with aspects of traditional beliefs. In times of crisis or ill health, most people are as likely to seek out a traditional healer as they are to visit a priest or a hospital. Though more often still, they will pursue both a traditional and a more western approach at the same time. (From a medical standpoint, the best practices of traditional healers are increasingly lauded throughout southern Africa as holistic approaches, which can complement Western medicine.)

People's traditional beliefs depend largely on ancestry, differing widely from tribe to tribe, but generally incorporating a great respect for ancestors, a belief in their continued existence in the spirit world, and a certainly that the spirits affect everyone's day-to-day lives.

LANGUAGE CLASSIFICATIONS

According to data from *Ethnalogue: Languages of the World* there are at least 26 languages spoken in Botswana. The official languages are English, and Tswana – 70% of the population speak Setswana. Many people are at least bilingual, speaking English and their mother tongue, and possibly Setswana, or Afrikaans, depending on what is locally required to get work.

It's interesting to note here that all the world's languages have been grouped into around 20 linguistic families. Of these, four are very different from the rest. All these four are African families – and they include the Khoisan and Niger-Congo (the Bantu languages). The Khoisan languages are amongst the world's most complex languages; this is part of the evidence that has led linguists to believe that human language evolved in Africa, and probably amongst the ancestors of the Khoisan.

For more scientifically minded readers, here's a list of most of Botswana's main language groups, with their linguistic family roots and a few brief notes on where they're spoken. This tells you the history of that language, starting with the main group to which it belongs, and defining it more specifically. Thus English and Afrikaans are both Indo-European languages, and more specifically Germanic and West. That means they both originally derive from one ancient language, West Germanic. The classification of the Khoisan and Bantu languages gives a similar view of their history and relationships. Obviously information below is best read in conjunction with the previous section on social groups.

Languages of the Bantu family

Tswana *Classification: Niger-Congo, Atlantic-Congo, Volta-Congo, Benue-Congo, Bantoid, Southern, Narrow Bantu, Central, S, Sotho-Tswana (S.30), Tswana.* Around 70% of the population speak Tswana (also known as Setswana). Some official business is conducted in Tswana, the media often use English and Tswana interchangeably, and it's a lingua franca between different citizens who don't speak English.

Tswapong *Classification: Niger-Congo, Atlantic-Congo, Volta-Congo, Benue-Congo, Bantoid, Southern, Narrow Bantu, Central, S, Sotho-Tswana (S.30), Tswapong.* Several thousand speakers, in the Central District and Mahalapye Sub-district.

Kagalagadi *Classification: Niger-Congo, Atlantic-Congo, Volta-Congo, Benue-Congo, Bantoid, Southern, Narrow Bantu, Central, S, Sotho-Tswana (S.30), Kgalagadi.* Estimated total of about 35,000 speakers in Botswana.

Birwa *Classification: Niger-Congo, Atlantic-Congo, Volta-Congo, Benue-Congo, Bantoid, Southern, Narrow Bantu, Central, S, Sotho-Tswana (S.30), Sotho.* Estimated total of about 10,000 speakers in Botswana.

Kalanga *Classification: Niger-Congo, Atlantic-Congo, Volta-Congo, Benue-Congo, Bantoid, Southern, Narrow Bantu, Central, S, Shona (S10).* Estimated total of about 160,000 speakers in Botswana.

Ndbele *Classification: Niger-Congo, Atlantic-Congo, Volta-Congo, Benue-Congo, Bantoid, Southern, Narrow Bantu, Central, S, Ngui.* Estimated total of about 10,000 speakers in the Northeast District, though this is the main language over the border in Zimbabwe's Matabele Province.

Herero *Classification: Niger-Congo, Atlantic-Congo, Volta-Congo, Benue-Congo, Bantoid, Southern, Narrow Bantu, Central, R, Herero.* Estimated total of about 31,000 speakers scattered among other ethnic groups, often having their own area in towns and villages. This is one of Namibia's major ethnic groups.

Yeyi *Classification: Niger-Congo, Atlantic-Congo, Volta-Congo, Benue-Congo, Bantoid, Southern, Narrow Bantu, Central, R, Yeye.* Estimated total of about 27,000 speakers in Botswana, with probably another 20,000 ethnic Bayeyi who do not actually speak Yeyi.

Mbukushu *Classification: Niger-Congo, Atlantic-Congo, Volta-Congo, Benue-Congo, Bantoid, Southern, Narrow Bantu, Central, K, Kwangwa.* Estimated total of about 12,000 speakers in Botswana, located in the Northwest District, especially in Gomare, and in the villages to the north of there, and in the Okavango Delta.

Subiya *Classification: Niger-Congo, Atlantic-Congo, Volta-Congo, Benue-Congo, Bantoid, Southern, Narrow Bantu, Central, K, Subia (L50).* Estimated total of about 12,000 speakers in Botswana, mostly living in the Northwest and Chobe Districts.

Languages of the Khoisan family

!Xoo *Classification: Khoisan,southern Africa, Southern, Hua.* There are between 3,000 and 4,000 speakers of this Khoisan language, and its related dialects, living in Botswana.

=/Hua *Classification: Khoisan,southern Africa, Southern, Hua.* Around 1,000–1,500 speakers, living mainly in the Southern Kalahari Desert and the Kweneng District.

//Gana *Classification: Khoisan, southern Africa, Central Tshu-Khwe, Northwest.* Around 1,000 speakers living around the Ghanzi District, in villages and farms, and in the Central Kalahari Game Reserve. Speakers are also found in the Central District (Boteti Sub-district) and the cattle-posts south and west of Rakops.

/Anda *Classification: Khoisan, southern Africa, Central Tshu-Khwe, Northwest.* About 1,000 speakers live in the Northwest District, mostly around the Khwai River and Mababe Village areas.

Ksoe *Classification: Khoisan, southern Africa, Central Tshu-Khwe, Northwest.* People speaking this language are also often known as the 'River Bushmen'. Speakers of this language number around 1,700–2,000, and live in and around the Northwest District, mainly in the villages: Gan, Cadikarauwe, Mohembo, Shakawe, Kaputura, /Ao-Kyao, Sikonkomboro, Ngarange, Sekanduko, Xongoa, Cauwe, Moxatce, Dungu, Seronga, Beyetca, Gudigoa, Sikokora, Geixa, /Qom-ca, Tobere, 0/Umbexa, Djaxo, Kangwara villages.

Deti *Classification: Khoisan, southern Africa, Central Tshu-Khwe, Central.* Spoken in the Central District, Boteti Sub-district, and in the villages which are strung out along the Boteti River.

Nama *Classification: Khoisan, southern Africa, Central Tshu-Khwe, Central.* In Botswana there are about 200–1,000 Nama speakers, mostly in the Kgalagadi District, around Tsabong, Makopong, Omaweneno, Tshane villages, and in the Ghanzi District, in the villages along the Ghanzi-Mamuno road. It's also spoken by a much larger population in Namibia.

Ganadi *Classification: Khoisan, southern Africa, Central Tshu-Khwe, North Central.* Spoken in the Northeastern area.

Shua *Classification: Khoisan, southern Africa, Central Tshu-Khwe, North Central.* There are around 19,000 Shua speakers in Botswana, counted together with the Tshwa group. Located in Central District and Tutumi Sub-district.

//Gwi There are around 800 speakers in villages in the Kweneng District and the Ghanzi District.

Naro *Classification: Khoisan, southern Africa, Central Tshu-Khwe, Southwest.* Botswana has an estimated 8,000 speakers of Naro.

Ju/'Hoansi *Classification: Khoisan, southern Africa, Northern.* This is one of the larger Khoisan languages, with 4,000–8,000 speakers in Botswana, and many more in Namibia – around the Tsumkwe area.

=/Kx'au//'ein *Classification: Khoisan, southern Africa, Northern.* There are about 3,000 speakers in Botswana, mostly in the Ghanzi District, in the villages and working on commercial farms.

Languages of the European family

English *Classification: Indo-European, Germanic, West, English.* English is the official language in Botswana, the language of government and schools, although official work is increasingly being carried out in Setswana (Tswana).

Afrikaans *Classification: Indo-European, Germanic, West; Low Saxon-Low Franconian, Low Franconian.* There are 20,000 people in Botswana whose native tongue is Afrikaans, mainly on the commercial farms in the Ghanzi District – however many of the white community who have close links with South Africa can communicate in Afrikaans.

CULTURAL GUIDELINES

Comments here are intended to be a general guide, just a few examples of how to travel more sensitively. They should not be viewed as blueprints for perfect Botswana etiquette. Cultural sensitivity is really a state of mind, not a checklist of behaviour – so here we can only hope to give the sensitive traveller a few pointers in the right direction.

When we travel, we are all in danger of leaving negative impressions with local people that we meet. It is easily done – by snapping that picture quickly, whilst the subject is not looking; by dressing scantily, offending local sensitivities; by just brushing aside the feelings of local people, with the high-handed superiority of a rich Westerner. These things are easy to do, in the click of a shutter, or flash of a dollar bill.

However, you will get the most representative view of Botswana if you cause as little disturbance to the local people as possible. You will never blend in perfectly when you travel – your mere presence there, as an observer, will always change the local events slightly. However, if you try to fit in and show respect for local culture and attitudes, then you may manage to leave positive feelings behind you.

One of the easiest, and most important, ways to do this is with **greetings**. African societies are rarely as rushed as Western ones. When you first talk to someone, you should greet them leisurely. So, for example, if you enter a bus station and want some help, do not just ask outright, 'Where is the bus to ...' That would be rude. Instead you will have a better reception (and a better chance of good advice) by saying:

Traveller:	'Good afternoon.'
Local:	'Good afternoon.'
Traveller:	'How are you?'
Local:	'I am fine, how are you?'
Traveller:	'I am fine, thank you. (pause) Do you know where the bus to ...'

This goes for approaching anyone – always greet them first. For a better reception still, learn these phrases of greeting in Setswana, or even the local language (see *Appendix 2: Languages*). English-speakers are often lazy about learning languages, and, whilst most people in Botswana understand English, a greeting given in an appropriate local language will be received with delight. It implies that you are making an effort to learn a little of their language and culture, which is always appreciated.

Very rarely in one of the towns you may be approached by someone who doesn't greet you. Instead s/he tries immediately to sell you something, or even hassle you in some way. These people have learned that foreigners aren't used to greetings, and so have adapted their approach accordingly. An effective way to dodge their attentions is to reply to their questions with a formal greeting, and then politely – but firmly – refuse their offer. This is surprisingly effective.

Another part of the normal greeting ritual is **handshaking**. As elsewhere, you would not normally shake a shop-owner's hand, but you would shake hands with someone to whom you are introduced. Get some practice when you arrive, as there is a gentle, three-part handshake used in southern Africa which is easily learnt.

It consists of taking each other's right hand, as for a normal handshake, but just shaking once, up and down. Then whilst leaving the thumbs linked, the grip is changed by both people raising their hands, until their arms make a right-angle. Each then grasps the other person's thumb and the top of their hand firmly. Then this is swiftly relaxed, with thumbs still interlinked, and the hands are dropped back into one last normal 'shake'.

Your **clothing** is an area that can easily give offence. Most people in Botswana frown upon skimpy or revealing clothing, especially when worn by women. Shorts are fine for walking safaris, otherwise dress conservatively and avoid short shorts, especially in the more rural areas. Respectable locals will wear long trousers (men) or long skirts (women).

Photography is a tricky business. Most people in Botswana will be only too happy to be photographed – provided you ask their permission first. Sign language is fine for this question: just point at your camera, shrug your shoulders, and look quizzical. The problem is that then everyone will smile for you, producing the type of 'posed' photograph that you may not want. However, stay around and chat for five or ten minutes more, and people will get used to your presence, stop posing and you will get more natural shots of them (a camera with a quiet shutter is a help).

Note that special care is needed with photography near government buildings, bridges, mines, and similar sites of strategic importance. You must ask permission before photographing anything here, or you risk people thinking that you are a spy.

(To be fair to the country, I've never come across such problems in Botswana, though I'd still exercise the same caution as in any other country.)

If you're travelling, and seeking directions to somewhere, don't be afraid of **asking questions**. Most people will be polite and keen to help – so keen that some will answer yes to questions if they think that this is what you want to hear. So try to avoid asking leading questions. For example, 'Yes' would often be the typical answer to the question, 'Does this road lead to...' And in a sense the respondent is probably correct – it will get you there. It's just that it may not be the quickest or shortest way.

To avoid misunderstandings, it is often better to ask open-ended questions like, 'Where does this road go to?' or 'How do I drive to ...'

The specific examples above can only be taken so far – they are general by their very nature. But wherever you find yourself, if you are polite and considerate to the people of Botswana that you meet, then you will rarely encounter any cultural problems. Watch how they behave and, if you have any doubts about how you should act, then ask someone quietly. They will seldom tell you outright that you are being rude, but they will usually give you good advice on how to make your behaviour more acceptable.

GIVING SOMETHING BACK

Botswana is one of the richer of the developing nations, but despite this you may see scenes of poverty when you are visiting the country, especially in more rural areas. Beggars are fairly rare in the towns, but often the least able are dependent on charity. Whilst giving a few coins to people is one way to put a sticking plaster over your feelings of guilt, this is not a long-term solution.

There *are* ways in which you can make a positive contribution, but they require more effort than giving to someone on the street, and perhaps this is the least you can do after an enjoyable trip to Botswana?

There is an established, trustworthy and reliable network of charities, churches and NGOs (non-government organisation). If you really want to help, then contact someone and make it happen!

Local charities working in Botswana

One good source of information on NGOs is the website of the Botswana Council of Non-Governmental Organisations (BOCONGO), at www.bocongo.bw. They can also be contacted on tel: 3911319; fax: 3912935; email: bocongo@bocongo.bw. Their website is a good reference site giving a brief synopsis of many of the country's groups doing valuable work. It doesn't include all charities, but is a good start to your research.

Helping poorer communities

Botswana has a whole range of good, small charities working at grassroots level to improve the lot of the poorest members of society here, and help them to develop economically. A few which concentrate on the north of the country, include:

Chobe Enclave Conservation Trust PO Box 91, Kavimba; tel: 3950486; fax: 3950746; email: gben@gov.bw. A village trust that aims to support the sustainable management of the Chobe enclave's natural resources for the benefit of the local community.
COCEPWA c/o Maun General Hospital, PO Box 12, Maun; tel: 6864758; fax: 6864758. This 'coping centre' provides support for people infected with HIV/AIDS.
Ditshwanelo (The Botswana Centre for Human Rights) P Bag 416, Gaborone; tel: 3906998; fax: 3907778; email: ditshwanelo@info.bw. Involved all over Botswana, including a base in Kasane, Ditshwanelo works with poorer communities on a range of issues

including access to water and the Chobe River.

Thuso Lutheran Rehabilitation Centre P Bag 40, Thitoyamoda, Maun; tel: 6864076; fax: 6860539; email: tlrc@botsnet.bw. Rehabilitation centre for disabled people in the community, providing vocational skills' training such as gardening, knitting, sewing and computing.

Helping the wildlife

The first thing to do if you want to help protect Botswana's wilder areas is to travel there, often; the income generated by tourism is the main hope to enable these areas to survive and thrive in the long-term.

The second thing to do is to support organisations like the Botswana Society, the Kalahari Conservation Society, the Okavango Wildlife Society, and the Chobe Society. (See *Societies* in *Botswana Today*, page 149) All of these do very good work in promoting knowledge of Botswana's wilder areas, and some work in campaigning for environmental and social issues.

In addition, helping the country's poorer communities (see above) will, ultimately, also help preserve the wildlife areas, as without sustainable economic development there's little long-term hope for the wildlife.

There are also several good small charities that we know which are working for different small-scale, but non the less important projects:

White rhino have been successfully re-introduced to Moremi Game Reserve (see page 253) and there are plans in hand to re-introduce the black rhino as well. However, this requires significant financial support. For details, contact Grant Woodrow at the Environmental Division of Okavango Wilderness Safaris, P/Bag 014, Maun, Botswana; tel: +267 660 086; fax: +267 660 632.

Botswana's only **animal orphanage** (see pages 456–7) is in Francistown, and is owned by the Uncharted Safari Company, PO Box 173, Francistown; tel: 241 2277; fax: 241 3458; email: office@unchartedafrica.co.bw; web: www.unchartedafrica.co.bw. In order to care for the animals in natural environment, the company is trying to raise sufficient money to move the orphanage to community land in the hills outside Francistown.

The Natural Environment

PHYSICAL ENVIRONMENT
Topography
Botswana lies landlocked in the heart of southern Africa, straddling the Tropic of Capricorn covering about 585,370km², of which about two-thirds is in the tropics. Most of Botswana is a gently undulating sandsheet with an altitude of between 900m and 1,300m. This is punctuated by occasional isolated rock outcrops, which are rarely more than 100m tall. Two major features stand out from this: the enormous Salt Pans and the huge inland delta of the Okavango River.

A relatively narrow corridor of land on the southeast side of Botswana is rockier and less flat than the rest, with sandstone and granite hills leading down to the Shashe, Limpopo and Marico rivers. This land is much more suitable for agriculture, and is where most of the country's population is concentrated.

Geological history
Looking back into Botswana's geological history gives us insights to explain how the Great Salt Pans and the Okavango Delta were formed. It's a long story though, of which I can give only a brief outline here. For a deeper and much more scholarly approach, seek out John Reader's *Africa: A Biography of a Continent* and especially Mike Main's *Kalahari: Life's Variety in Dene and Delta* (see *Further Reading*). Both are excellent, giving much more comprehensive discussions of the latest scientific thinking than I'm able to give here – the first in terms of Africa generally, and the second with immense detail specifically about Botswana.

Setting the scene
To put discussions in perspective, and give our history a sense of scale, let me start at the beginning… Around 4,600 million years ago the Earth's crust began to form and cool. A thousand-million years later, fossils from South Africa's Barberton Mountain Land give us evidence of the first recorded simple, single-celled bacteria.

By 3,300 million years ago more complex blue-green algae had appeared, though it took a further 2,300 million years for multi-cellular organisms to evolve. Palaeontologists say that around 600 million years ago there was an 'evolutionary explosion', when many different species evolved, including ancestors of most of the world's existing invertebrates.

About 230 million years ago the Earth saw the emergence of both dinosaurs and the first mammals. For the next 165 million years the dinosaurs dominated the earth and the largest mammals which evolved were probably no bigger than present-day rabbits. Only around 65 million years ago, when some great calamity killed off most of the dinosaurs, did the mammals begin to rise to dominance and inherit the earth.

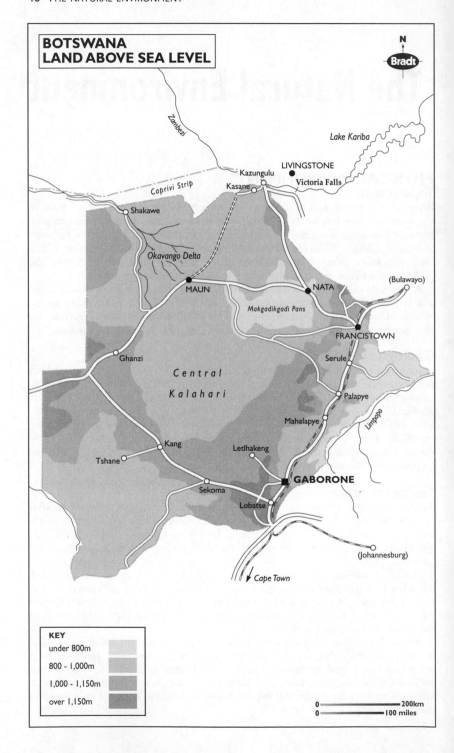

BOTSWANA LAND ABOVE SEA LEVEL

N

Bradt

Zambezi

Lake Kariba

Kazungulu
LIVINGSTONE
Victoria Falls
Kasane

Caprivi Strip

Shakawe

Okavango Delta

MAUN
NATA
(Bulawayo)

Makgadikgadi Pans

FRANCISTOWN

Ghanzi
Serule

Central Kalahari

Palapye

Mahalapye

Limpopo

Kang
Letlhakeng

Tshane

GABORONE

Sekoma
Lobatse

(Johannesburg)

Cape Town

KEY

under 800m

800 - 1,000m

1,000 - 1,150m

over 1,150m

0 _____ 200km
0 _____ 100 miles

KIMBERLITE PIPES

Diamond is a crystalline form of ordinary carbon formed under conditions of extreme pressure and temperature. In nature, such conditions are only found deep below the Earth's surface, in the lower crust or upper mantle. Under specific circumstances, the rock matrix in which diamonds occur was subjected to such great pressure that it became fluid and punched its way up to the earth's surface in a volcanic pipe of liquid rock. This situation is similar to a conventional volcanic eruption, except that instead of basaltic magma being erupted through fissures in the crust, the volcanic material is a peculiar rock called kimberlite. This contains a wide assortment of minerals (including diamonds), often in addition to large chunks of other rocks that have been caught up in the whole process.

Such kimberlite pipes occur throughout southern Africa from the Cape to Zaire. However, only a small proportion of those discovered contain enough diamonds to be profitably worked.

Botswana mines kimberlite pipes for diamonds at Orapa and at Jwaneng. It's interesting to note that Botswana's neighbour, Namibia, has diamond deposits along its Atlantic coast. These are 'secondary diamond deposits', because they do not come directly from kimberlite pipes. Instead, Namibia's diamonds are found in areas where ancient rivers have eroded kimberlite pipes in the interior, washing diamonds down to the sea, and depositing them in sediments there.

The Super-continent

Meanwhile somewhere between 135 and 10 million years ago the super-continent, Gondwanaland, broke up and the continents started to move away from each other.

By the time that the continents split from Gondwanaland, the basic rocks upon which southern Africa is built, the Karoo lavas, had been laid down. By about 65 million years ago – the end of the Cretaceous Period – most of the subcontinent's diamonds, gems and other mineral wealth had also been formed, and erosion was gradually wearing away at the land.

The world's earliest primate fossils are from Europe and North America, dating from around 65 million years ago, but it wasn't until about 4 million years ago that Australopithecus appeared in Africa – which is a prime candidate for being one of our earliest ancestors.

This period, as our first ancestors were evolving, is about the time when we start looking at how Botswana's landforms were created.

The Kalahari's superlake

During the Tertiary Period, which dates from about 65 million years ago, Botswana's climate was probably very arid, and as the region's rocks were gradually eroded, so the wind-blow sands accumulated and began to form what we now call the Kalahari.

Around four or five million years ago it's thought that the Okavango, Kwando and the Zambezi rivers had completely different courses than they do today – probably all flowing into one channel which headed south through the Kalahari and into the Orange River and/or the Limpopo. (Different theories suggest different courses for these.)

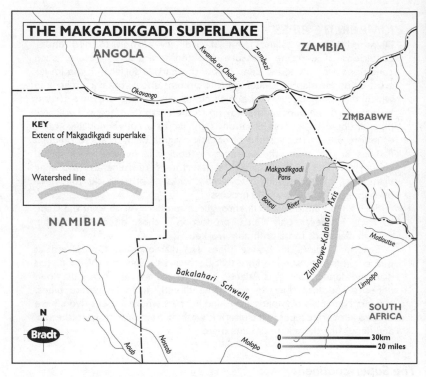

Then, around 2–4 million years ago, it's thought that seismic shifts forced parts of southern and central Botswana upwards. Geologists identify the areas raised as the 'Zimbabwe-Kalahari Axis' and the 'Bakalahari Schwelle' – both of which are now watersheds in the region.

The net effect of these upward movements was to block the flow southwards of the rivers, and to form a super-lake that had its deepest parts where the Makgadikgadi Pans are today. This greater Lake Makgadikgadi existed until very recently, though its extent varied greatly over the millennia, depending on the climate and inflows. It is thought that at its greatest, it covered an area of up to 80,000km², and that it probably only dried up in the last 10,000 years. At its largest it probably stretched as far as Lake Ngami in the west, what is now Chobe in the north, and beyond Nata to the edge of present-day Zimbabwe in the east.

Evidence suggesting the existence of this lake is dotted around its ancient shorelines. The great Magwikwe Sand Ridge that you cross as you drive between Savuti and North Gate, probably defined one of its northwestern shorelines. Similarly, another is thought to have been the less obvious Gidikwe Sand Ridge, which lies just to the west of the western border of the present Makgadikgadi National Park.

Look at the base of several of the Kalahari's isolated hills and you'll find rounded, water-washed pebbles and rocks worn smooth over the centuries by waves. The eastern side of the Gchoha Hills, north of Savuti, are a particularly clear example of this – though all of Savuti's hills show some of this history if you look carefully.

In some areas of the Makgadikgadi you can stroll around and pick up the flint arrowheads and other tools of Stone-Age encampments, which must have sat beside the shores of this lake within the last few thousand years.

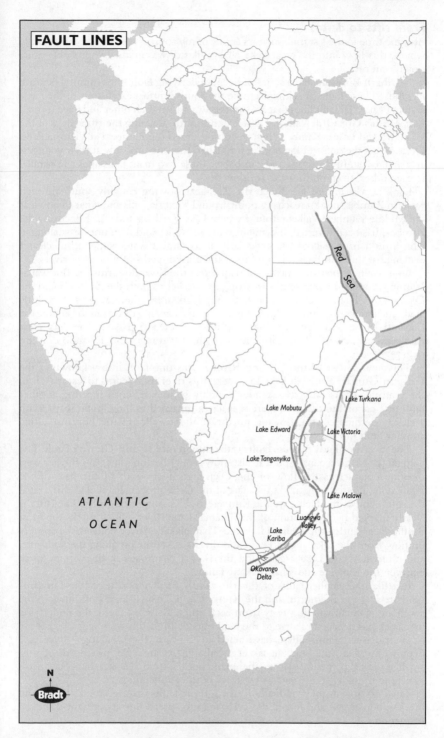

FAULT LINES

Red Sea

Lake Mobutu

Lake Turkana

Lake Edward

Lake Victoria

Lake Tanganyika

Lake Malawi

ATLANTIC
OCEAN

Luangwa
Valley

Lake
Kariba

Okavango
Delta

N

Bradt

From rifts to deltas

At some time in the last million years (none of my sources seems to be sure exactly when), this flow into the great Lake Makgadikgadi was gradually, probably quite slowly, cut off.

Northern Botswana has a series of deep, underlying fault lines running beneath its sands. These faults are thought to be the southernmost extensions of the same system of parallel fault lines that are pulling away from each other and have formed East Africa's Great Rift Valley. These extend south, forming the rift valleys of the Luangwa and Lower Zambezi, before cutting across the Zambezi at Victoria Falls. Here amidst the sands of the northern Kalahari they are probably at their youngest and shallowest. In Botswana and Zimbabwe these two main fault lines run parallel to each other, from northeast to southwest.

Look at a map and you'll see the Zambezi flowing roughly south through western Zambia, until it reaches a point around Victoria Falls and what's known as the Middle Zambezi Valley (around where Lake Kariba is today). Effectively the Zambezi has been diverted, flowing into the rift valley and then northeast along it. This would have starved the great lake of its largest water supply, but clearer evidence of the fault lines can be seen in the present paths of two other rivers.

Look again at the maps and you'll realise that the Kwando forms the Botswana-Namibia border flowing southeast (roughly parallel to both the Zambezi and the Okavango). Then it clearly passes through an area where there's very little gradient, and forms a mini-delta, before abruptly changing direction to become the Linyanti River, and starts to flow northeast. (Note, in passing, the very clear parallels between the delta formations of the Okavango and Kwando/Linyanti rivers.)

This new course of the Linyanti River marks one fault line – known as the Linyanti-Gumare Fault. At Lake Liambezi, this river then seems to 'escape' from the confines of its fault to meander roughly southeast, until meeting another fault line parallel to the first. Here it is again renamed as the Chobe River, with a clearly defined course, flowing northeast and parallel to the Linyanti, along another fault line.

The more northerly of these faults is the important Linyanti-Gumare Fault. The Selinda (or Magwegqana) Spillway also flows roughly along this, and further west the line cuts across the flow of the Okavango, just south of the base of the Panhandle. It effectively marks the start of the Delta proper. Parallel to this, but at the south end of the Delta, are the Kunyere and Thamalakane faults. The latter is clearly marked by the position of the Thamalakane River, which marks the most southerly extent of the Delta. Here the Thamalakane River collects the meagre outflow from the Okavango's Delta and diverts it southwest along the fault line, and ultimately into Lake Ngami and the Boteti. Maun sits in the narrow space between the Kunyere and Thamalakane faults.

Just like the parallel faults of the rift valleys further northeast, the Linyanti-Gumare Fault in the north, and the Kunyere and Thamalakane fault lines in the south are gradually pulling away from each other. Between them, the underlying base rock has dropped relative to the land outside the faults – some geologists say by as much as 300m. These have acted to 'capture' the Okavango River in a depression where the gradient is very shallow. (As an aside, just north of this, smaller faults, perpendicular to the main ones, act to restrict the Okavango's sweeping meander to the narrow confines of the Panhandle.)

Thus, in time as they gradually formed, these faults diverted the Zambezi and the Kwando rivers, and forced the Okavango to spread into its present-day delta formation.

KEY
Fault line
Permanent swamp
Seasonal swamp

OKAVANGO'S FAULTS

The Great Salt Pans

As its feeding rivers were diverted, the great Lake Makgadikgadi was starved of its sources. This would probably have happened over a very long period of time. We know that the climate in Botswana varied greatly, and during periods of heavier rainfalls the lake might have persisted. Geologists have identified at least five clearly different levels of the lake – each of which has its own identifying features that are still visible. And for each the size of the lake must have been totally different.

NW–SE SIMPLIFIED GEOLOGICAL CROSS–SECTION FROM MOHEMBO TO MAUN

KEY
Okavango sediments
Kalahari sands
Base rocks

But eventually, starved of inflow in a drier climate, the lake shrank. With no known outflows, it would probably have already been very brackish. Now its remaining salts were concentrated more and more, and eventually crystallised out where the last of its waters evaporated – at its lowest point, where the pans are now. Too saline for plants to grow, this residue formed the amazingly flat surface of the Great Salts Pans that are now such a distinctive feature of the northern Kalahari.

The formation of the Okavango Delta

The geological history outlined so far in this chapter explains how the Okavango has been constrained by faults, but it doesn't really help to explain how the Delta's strange and wonderful landscapes came about. That's really due to much more recent processes, of which I'll try to give you a brief summary here.

From the air

Firstly, if you're flying over the Delta, note what you see. There are man-made tracks, like the straight lines of the buffalo fence, which surrounds part of the Delta. Or the close, parallel lines of bush tracks made by vehicles, sometimes curving, sometimes perfectly straight.

You'll also see more erratic, single tracks, often radiating from pans or waterholes; these are clear animal tracks. (Yes – animals have favourite paths that they like to use too.) Deeper in the Delta you'll find more and more winding drainage lines, of water channels which glint in the sun. Catch the light right and you'll realise that areas which you thought were thick, green vegetation are floodplains, which reflect the sky.

Look carefully at the 'browner' areas between these and you'll start to distinguish the dry land and the islands from the floodplains and the water. Look out for the small, round islands that often have a ring of palms around the outside of them. Note that some, at their centre, have barren patches of what looks like white salt.

Many islands will be longer. A few of these may look like a number of the small islands joined together. But many are long and narrow – we'll call them ribbon islands. Note how parallel their sides are, and how the vegetation on the edges looks that much more lush than the vegetation in the middle.

Building islands

The Okavango's an amazing sight from the air – and all the more incredible if you understand a little of how its features were formed. Here are the basics of the main two methods:

Biological mechanism: round islands

The Okavango's floods are erratic and its water levels variable, sometimes giving the chance for small mounds to develop which, when flooding returns, are above the level of the flood. Often, but not always, these are termite mounds, made by the *Macroternes michaelseni* termite.

Obtruding above the water level of the subsequent flood, this allows the termites to survive, and makes a handy perch for birds. Eventually seeds take hold, and grow into shrubs and trees, fertilised by the guano from the birds that rest there. In some areas of the Delta (the Jao flats stand out in my mind) you'll see these small islands at the early stages of their formation everywhere. Often the dominant plants are wild date palms (*Phoenix reclinata*), though *Ficus* species and the usual broad-leafed trees of the Delta will follow.

Once started, the trees will transpire, sucking water up with their roots to fuel photosynthesis. This lowers the water table directly under the island, which then attracts inflows from the surrounding floodplains seeping under the island. However, the tree roots don't take up many salts, and gradually the ground water under the island becomes saturated with salts – especially silica and calcite. Eventually these crystallise out underneath the roots. As this precipitate increases, the level of the ground around the edge of the island is raised.

This gradually acts to enlarge the island, raising it above the surrounding floodplains. However, as the island enlarges the groundwater that moves toward the centre of the island becomes increasingly saline – and eventually toxic to plants. The wild date palms die off first in the centre, as they are the least salt-tolerant, then the broad-leaved trees, until finally the relatively salt-tolerant real fan palms (*Hyphaene petersiana*) will be the only trees in the centre. When the salt concentrations rise further they die, leaving salt-tolerant grasses like the spiky sporobolus (*Sporobolus spikatus*).

Capillary action and evaporation force the supersaturated water to the surface of the centre of the island, where salt deposits are now left and no plants can survive. This whole process is estimated to take at least a hundred years, and the remaining crystalline salt deposits are known as 'trona' deposits, and are clearly visible as a white crystalline powder from the air or the ground.

Channel mechanism: linear islands

The Okavango's water is at its richest in nutrients as it enters the Panhandle and the top of the Delta – as flowing over the nutrient-poor Kalahari sands of the Delta itself won't enrich it. In this Panhandle and upper Delta area, the deep waters are surrounded by the vigorous growth of papyrus (see box on *Papyrus* on page 274 for details).

These live and die fast, forming a mat of thick vegetal matter by the side of the channel. This builds up the sides of the channel, and gradually its deeper stems are compressed and start forming peat. Meanwhile, suspended sediments are deposited on the floor of the channel. Thus the whole channel, floor and papyrus surrounds, start to rise slightly above the surrounding floodplains.

Once this happens it only takes a hippo track, or some other leakage, for the water in the channel to cut through the peat sides of the channel and the papyrus beds find a completely alternative, lower path through the floodplains. This leaves behind a dry, slightly raised line of sandy deposits, lined on either side by high beds of peat. This higher land will encourage plants to grow – forming a

long, narrow island, which can be enlarged by the biological mechanisms mentioned above.

Once dry, the peat eventually burns down to a thin layer of nutrient-rich ash, which now lines this island, encouraging what biologists call 'sweet' floodplains, which support nutrient-rich grasses and other high-quality vegetation, and a rich growth of trees and bushes at the edge of these long islands.

Meandering mechanism: alluvial islands

Some islands in the Delta were probably built up first as sandy alluvial deposits during wetter periods in the Delta's history – as the banks beside meandering rivers. Then, when times became drier they were colonised by vegetation, and enlarged by the biological mechanisms mentioned above.

Geological mechanism: Chief's Island

Chief's Island, the largest island in the Delta, is thought to have geological origins. Note that its western edge traces out a line which, if continued northwest, would coincide perfectly with the eastern faultline that constrains the Panhandle. (See page 51 for a diagram showing this faultline).

Chief's Island was probably pushed up as higher land during the formative rifting/warping of the area, which fits with the observation that it is largely made up of uniform deposits of sand and clay.

Climate

Botswana is landlocked far from the coast and mostly in the tropics. It receives a lot of strong sunlight and most of the country is classed as either semi-arid or arid (the line being crossed from semi-arid to arid when evaporation exceeds rainfall). In many respects, most of central and northern Botswana has a sub-tropical 'desert' climate, characterised by a wide range in temperature (from day to night and from summer to winter), and by low rainfall and humidity.

Botswana's climate follows a similar pattern to that found in most of southern Africa, with rainfall when the sun is near its zenith from November to April. The precise timing and duration of this is determined by the interplay of three air-streams: the moist 'Congo' air-mass, the northeastern monsoon winds, and the southeastern trade winds. The water-bearing air is the Congo air-mass, which normally brings rain when it moves south into Botswana from Central Africa. Effectively a belt of rain works its way south across the continent, reaching its southernmost point around January or February. If you listen to any local weather forecasts, they'll probably refer to this as the Intertropical Convergence Zone, or simply the ITCZ. As the sun's intensity reduces, the Congo air-mass moves back north, leaving Botswana dry by around April. Most areas receive their heaviest rainfall in January and February. The rainfall is heavier in the north and east, and lighter in the south and, especially, the southwest.

Thus **January** and **February** are the wettest months, when many areas will have regular and often torrential downpours in the late afternoon. When there are no clouds, temperatures can peak as high as 40°C. However, it's much more usual for them to be moderated by afternoon cloud cover and to stay between about 20 and 30°C. Humidity fluctuates during the day, typically from about 50 to 80%.

By **March** the rainfall is decreasing, though still the afternoon clouds are around. Mornings and early afternoons will often be cloudless, and a few of the nights will go below 10°C even though the average of the nightly minimums is nearer 18°C.

April and **May** are lovely months. You may catch the odd afternoon shower in April, but these are gone by May – as are most of the clouds. The maximum day temperatures are around 33°C, and while the nightly minimum average is between 10–15°C, this hides the occasional chilly nights when areas of the Kalahari will record temperatures just below freezing.

June and **July** are the coolest months, with daytime average highs around 25°C concealing the occasional day when the mercury just reaches 30°C. You'll still need your shorts, T-shirt, sun-hat and sun-cream for the middle of the day, but as dusk approaches you'll quickly need warmer clothes. The average night goes down to about 6°C, but cold snaps of well below freezing (typically –5°C) are common – especially in the drier areas of the Kalahari. **August** is very similar, though not quite as cold. You'd be very unlucky for it to go below freezing, even at night, and the days will often creep over 30°C.

September and **October** are really the heart of the dry season, and the daytime heat gradually builds as these months wear on. Typical early afternoon temperatures are in the low 30s (°C), and nights will seldom fall below 10°C – and most will be nearer to 20°C. The humidity is usually very low, typically 20–40%.

November is always interesting and can be unpredictable. Often much of it will simply be a continuation of October's heat and dryness. But eventually the humidity will build and clouds start to appear in the afternoons. These will block the sun, cool the temperatures, and eventually produce some showers in the late afternoon. November mornings will generally remain fine and hot, with blue skies.

During **December** the temperatures will usually stay around 20–30°C, day and night, and rain will be an increasingly regular occurrence in the afternoon. Humidity is normally 50–60%. The hottest days may just reach 40°C, but even so the coolest nights won't go below about 10°C.

Maun's climate statistics

Typical of the pleasant climate in northern Botswana, here are the average maximum and minimum temperatures for Maun. Note that these are slightly less extreme than you might expect for somewhere in one of the Kalahari's drier environments. Similarly, expect the highs and lows of somewhere in the heart of the Delta to be more moderate than this (lower highs, and higher lows!):

| | Temp °C | | Temp °F | | Rainfall |
	max	min	max	min	mm
Jan	33	19	91	68	101
Feb	32	19	90	70	101
Mar	32	18	90	65	51
Apr	30	15	87	60	26
May	28	10	82	50	0
Jun	25	6	78	42	0
Jul	26	6	80	42	0
Aug	27	9	81	48	0
Sep	34	14	93	58	0
Oct	38	19	100	68	0
Nov	37	20	98	69	25
Dec	35	20	95	69	76

FLORA AND FAUNA
Flora

In many ways a brief description of some of the main habitats for plants is really a step through the various types of environment that you'll encounter in Botswana.

Vegetation types

As with animals, each species of plant has its favourite conditions. External factors determine where each species thrives, and where it will perish. These include temperature, light, water, soil type, nutrients, and what other species of plants and animals live in the same area. Species with similar needs are often found together, in communities which are characteristic of that particular environment. Botswana has a number of different such communities, or typical 'vegetation types', within its borders – each of which is distinct from the others. The more common include:

Mopane woodland

The dominant tree here is the remarkably adaptable mopane, *Colophospermum mopane*, which is sometimes known as the butterfly tree because of the shape of its leaves. It is very tolerant of poorly drained or alkaline soils, and those with a high clay content. However, it doesn't thrive on the Kalahari's sands. This tolerance results in the mopane having a wide range of distribution throughout southern Africa; in Botswana it occurs mainly in the Okavango-Linyanti region, and throughout the eastern side of the country.

Mopane trees can attain a maximum height of 25m when growing on rich, alluvial soils. These are then called cathedral mopane, for their height and the graceful arch of their branches. However, shorter trees are more common in areas that are poor in nutrients, or have suffered extensive fire damage. Stunted mopane will form a low scrub, perhaps only 5m tall. All mopane trees are deciduous, and the leaves turn beautiful shades of yellow and red before falling in September and October.

Ground cover in mopane woodland is usually sparse; just thin grasses, herbs and the occasional bush. The trees themselves are an important source of food for game, as the leaves have a high nutritional value – rich in protein and phosphorus – which is favoured by browsers and is retained even after they have fallen from the trees. Mopane forests support large populations of rodents, including tree squirrels, *Peraxerus cepapi*, which are so typical of these areas that they are known as 'mopane squirrels'.

Pan

Though not an environment for rich vegetation, a pan is a shallow, usually seasonal, pool of water without any permanent streams leading to or from it. Mopane woodlands are full of these small pans during and shortly after the rainy season, the water being held on the surface by the clay soils. They are very important to the game that will feed here during the summer, but will dry up soon after the rains cease.

Saltpan

A saltpan is, as its name implies, a pan that's salty. The huge Makgadikgadi Saltpans are the residues from ancient lakes. Because of the high concentrations of mineral salts found there – there are no plants there when they are dry. When they fill with water it's a slightly different story as algal blooms appear, sometimes attracting the attention of specialist filter-feeders like flamingoes.

Miombo woodland

Although this would be the natural vegetation across most of neighbouring Zambia, in Botswana miombo woodland, and its associated *dambos* (see below), are uncommon. There are patches in central Chobe and the northeast of the country. It is found in areas where the soils are acid and not particularly fertile. Often they have been leached of minerals by the water run-off.

Miombo woodland consists of a mosaic of large wooded areas and smaller, more open spaces dotted with clumps of trees and shrubs. The woodland is broad-leafed and deciduous (though just how deciduous depends on the available water), and the tree canopies generally don't interlock. The dominant trees are *Brachystegia*, *Julbernardia* and *Isoberlinia* species – most of which are at least partially fire-resistant. There is more variation of species in miombo than in mopane woodland, but despite this it is often known simply as 'Brachystegia woodland'. The ground cover is also generally less sparse here than in mopane areas.

Dambo

A *dambo* is a shallow grass depression, or small valley, that is either permanently or seasonally waterlogged. It corresponds closely to what is known as a *vlei* in other parts

BOTSWANA VEGETATION

KEY to vegetation

Miombo woodland

Wetland

Recent alluvium

Mopane dominated

Lake deposits

Kalahari sandveld

KEY
Main road
International boundary
National park

of the subcontinent. These open, verdant dips in the landscape often appear in the midst of miombo woodlands and support no bushes or trees. In higher valleys amongst hills, they will sometimes form the sources of streams and rivers. Because of their permanent dampness, they are rich in species of grasses, herbs and flowering plants, like orchids – and are excellent grazing (if a little exposed) for antelope. Their margins are usually thickly vegetated by grasses, herbs and smaller shrubs.

Teak forest
In a few areas of the far north of Botswana, including the northern side of Chobe National Park, the Zambezi teak, *Baikaea plurijuga*, (aka Rhodesian teak) forms dry semi-evergreen forests on Kalahari sand. Often these woodlands occur on fossil dune-crests. As this species is not fire-resistant, these stands are only found where fire is rare, and slash-and-burn type cultivation methods have never been used. Below the tall teak is normally a dense, deciduous thicket of vegetation, interspersed with sparse grasses and herbs in the shadier spots of the forest floor.

The teak is a lovely strong wood, with an even texture and deep red-brown colour. It is expensive, often exported, and widely used from furniture to expensive wooden floors.

Kalahari sandveld
A number of trees and bushes thrive on Chobe's extensive areas of Kalahari sand, including various *Acacias*, *Terminalias* and *Combertum* species. 'Kalahari sandveld' is a general term that I'll use to describe any of these plant communities based on sand.

In appearance they range from a very open savannah with a few tall trees separated only by low undergrowth, to quite dense tickets of (often thorny) shrubs which are difficult to even walk through. If you want to be a little more technical about this, then biologists will often divide this into distinctive sub-groups, including:

Terminalia sericea **sandveld** occurs where you find deep, loose sand – these are unfertile areas which cover large areas of the Kalahari. The main species found here are the silver terminalia, *Terminalia sericea*, or silver cluster-leaf as it's sometimes called, and the Kalahari apple-leaf, *Lonchocarpus nelsii*. These generally occur with wild seringa bushes, *Burkea africana*, and the bushwillow, *Combretum collinum*. Underneath these you'll often find the rather beautiful silky bushman grass, *Stipagrostis uniplumis*.

Acacia erioloba **woodlands** also occur on sand, but often where there are fossil river valleys that have an underground supply of water throughout the year. Camelthorn trees, *Acacia erioloba*, have exceedingly long taproots that reach this, sustaining large stands of these mature trees reaching an impressive 16–17m in height. They grow slowly but give good shade, so the bush cover beneath them is fairly sparse.

Acacia tortilis **woodlands** are not found on such deep sand; instead they prefer the fine alluvium soils, which water has deposited over time. Although it forms homogenous stands less often than the camelthorns, a number of the very distinctive, flat-topped umbrella thorns (*Acacia tortilis*) can often be seen together. Between these you'll find low grasses rather than much undergrowth. This results in a beautiful, quintessentially African, scene which fits many first-time visitors' picture of the continent as gleaned from the blockbuster film *Out of Africa*.

Moist evergreen forest

In the areas of higher rainfall and (as is more likely in Botswana) near rivers, streams, lakes and swamps, where a tree's roots will have permanent access to water, dense evergreen forests are found. Many species occur, and this lush vegetation is characterised by having three levels: a canopy of tall trees, a sub-level of smaller trees and bushes, and a variety of ground-level vegetation. In effect, the environment is so good for plants that they have adapted to exploit the light from every sunbeam.

This type of forest is prevalent in the Okavango and Linyanti areas, and beside the country's larger rivers. It's perhaps worth distinguishing here between two very different types of this forest:

Riverine forests (occasionally called riparian forests) are very common. They line many of Botswana's major rivers and are found throughout the Okavango-Linyanti area. Typical trees and shrubs here include the jackalberry (*Diospyros mespiliformis*), African mangosteen (*Garcinia livingstonei*), sausage tree (*Kigelia africana*), large feverberry (*Croton megalobotrys*), knobthorn (*Acacia nigrescens*), marula (*Sclerocarya birrea caffra*), raintree (*Lonchocarpus capassa*) and various species of figs. Move away from the river and you'll find riparian species thinning out rapidly.

Swamp forest – or something very akin to it – occurs in tiny patches on small islands in permanently flooded areas of the Okavango. These will occasionally be flooded, and might include a mixture of fig and waterberry species, plus lots of wild date palms (*Phoenix reclinata*) and a few tall real fan palms (*Hyphaenea petersiana*).

In the centre of slightly larger small islands, where the ground is salty from Trona deposits (see page 53) you will find only spiky sporobolus grassland (*Sporobolus spicatus*) – no trees at all!

Floodplain

Floodplains are the low-lying grasslands on the edges of rivers, streams, lakes and swamps that are seasonally inundated by floods. The Okavango and, to a lesser extent, the Linyanti-Chobe region has some huge areas of floodplain. These often contain no trees or bushes, just a low carpet of grass species that can tolerate being submerged for part of the year. In the midst of most of the floodplains in the Okavango, you'll find isolated small 'islands' slightly raised above the surrounding grasslands. These will often be fringed by swamp forest (see above).

Sometimes the communities of vegetation will be 'zoned' to reflect the extent and frequency of the flooding. In areas that become submerged for long periods you'll find species like wild rice, *Oryza longistaminata*, and the sedge *Cyperus articulatus*. Grasses, like *Imperata cylindrica*, often dominate places that generally spend less time under water.

Channels

Vegetation found in permanent channels includes the giant sedge, papyrus (*Cyperus papyrus*), that dominates large areas of the Okavango, plus species like the distinctive cylindrical hippo grass, *Vossia cuspidata*, the tall maize-like phragmites reed used for thatching, *Phragmites australis*, and the unmistakable bulrush, *Typha capensis*.

Lagoons

Where the water is more still, in deep lagoons and side-channels where the surface is open but the water doesn't flow much, the bottom will often be covered with fairly stable peat deposits. This gives a stable base for many species of aquatic plants. Some are strictly submerged whilst others have floating leaves. An obvious indicator of this type of environment is the presence of waterlilies.

Fauna
Mammals
Botswana's large mammals are typical of the savannah areas of southern Africa. The large predators are here: lion, leopard, cheetah, wild dog and spotted hyena. Cheetah are found in higher densities here than in most other areas of the subcontinent, and northern Botswana has one of Africa's three strong populations of wild dogs.

Elephant and buffalo occur in large herds that roam throughout the areas where they can find water. Rhino had largely been wiped out throughout the wilds of northern Botswana, though are now being slowly reintroduced into one of the private areas of Moremi. So far only white have been brought in, but there are plans to reintroduce black rhinos too.

Antelope are well represented, with impala, springbok, tsessebe and red lechwe all numerically dominant in different areas – depending on the environment. The sheer range of Botswana's ecosystems means that if you move about there is a really wide range of totally different species to be seen.

Because the Okavango area is so well watered, its natural vegetation is very lush and capable of supporting a high density of game in the dry season. This spreads out to the surrounding areas during the earlier months of the year – accounting for the sheer volume of big game to be found in northern Botswana's parks and private reserves.

Game migrations – historical factors
Like most of Africa's big game, some of Botswana's larger animals have major seasonal migrations – or at least used to have, until relatively recently. The 'big picture' was that large numbers of big herbivores put a great strain on the vegetation in any given locale, and so moving around gave the plants time to recover. Thus the basic patterns were for the game to move out into the Kalahari's drier areas during the rains, when they would have no difficulty finding small pools to drink from, and then to gradually migrate back to sources of permanent water as the dry season progressed.

The main species involved were elephant, buffalo, zebra, wildebeest and hartebeest. These migrations still occur, and do affect the game densities in many areas, although they're much reduced due to two main factors.

First, competition for land from humans and their domestic stock which has reduced the possible range of the wildlife, and caused particular problems by monopolising some of the few areas of permanent water in the Kalahari.

Second, the erection of long, game-proof, disease-control fences which have appeared across historical migration routes in the Kalahari. The first of these was in 1954, in response to the EU's insistence that to import Botswana's beef, the country must have an effective strategy for containing and dealing with outbreaks of foot and mouth disease.

The relative damage done by these two factors is still a hotly debated issue in Botswana, but the results are serious. In some years tens and possibly hundreds of thousands of animals, mostly wildebeest, died of thirst or starvation. (See pages 434–6 for further comments.) Many were in very close proximity to the fences. Some blame the fences directly; others regarded them as a scapegoat for the real cause – the scale of human encroachment on the Kalahari. Whatever the cause, Botswana no longer has migrations of this scale.

TRACKS

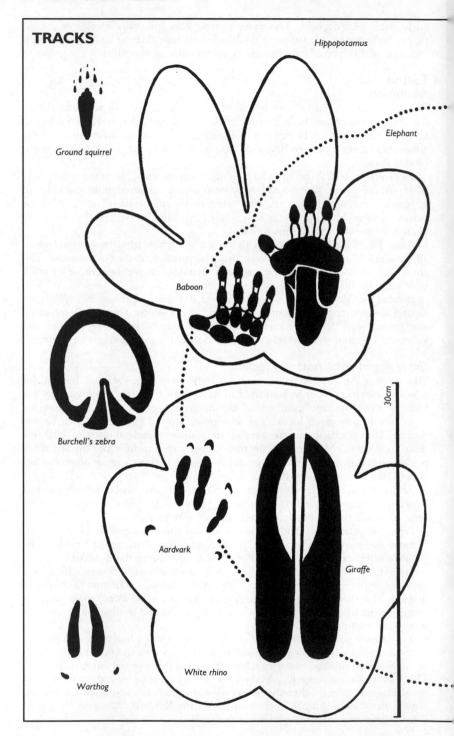

Hippopotamus

Ground squirrel

Elephant

Baboon

Burchell's zebra

Aardvark

30cm

Giraffe

White rhino

Warthog

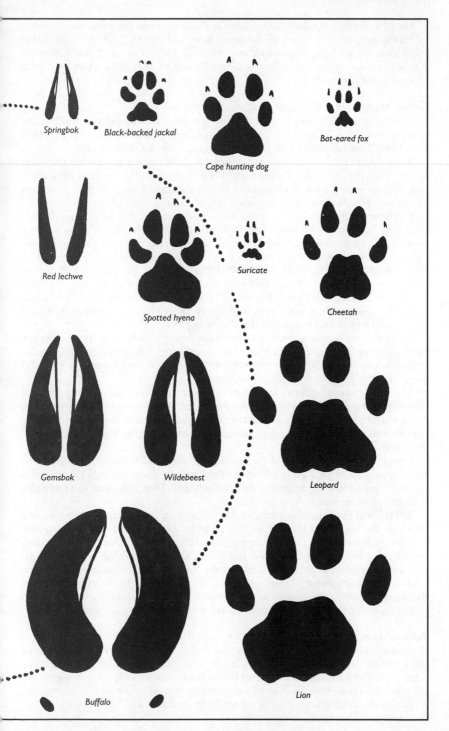

Springbok

Black-backed jackal

Cape hunting dog

Bat-eared fox

Red lechwe

Spotted hyena

Suricate

Cheetah

Gemsbok

Wildebeest

Leopard

Buffalo

Lion

See Mike Main's *Kalahari: Life's Variety in Dune and Delta* for a rational overview of this debate, various issues of *Botswana Notes and Records* (especially 1984) for more detailed partisan arguments, and Mark & Delia Owens' book *Cry of the Kalahari* for an impassioned but one-sided view of the story of people who observed it at firsthand.

Game migrations – the current story

Mention the word 'migration' and there's a tendency to picture millions of wildebeest in the Serengeti, fording rivers of waiting crocodiles and filling endless flat plains. That's not what you get in Botswana, so forget those images.

What you do find is a modest but noticeable drift of game away from the main water points of the Chobe, Linyanti and Okavango around the start of the rains – usually somewhere around November – and a gradual return as the dry season progresses. However, the precise details vary with the species of game.

Elephant and **buffalo** have broadly similar movements. As the rains come their large herds split into much smaller family groups, of which some move away from the Linyanti and Okavango systems. They spread out into the drier areas, especially the vast swathes of land dominated by mopane which lie between these areas (Wildlife Management Areas NG14/15/16/18/20; see pages 67–8 for an explanation of WMAs). Those from the Chobe Riverfront areas similarly split, heading into the Chobe Forest Reserve and the rest of Chobe National Park, while some move east of the Chobe Park into Zimbabwe's Hwange National Park, and the Matetsi area between that and the Zambezi.

From around May they start to head back, and gradually join up into larger herds, until by September and October the riverfronts of the Chobe and Kwando-Linyanti have some of the most amazing densities of buffalo and (especially) elephants that you'll find anywhere in Africa.

The migrations of **zebra** are somewhat more complex, and still the topic of research, but is seems that during the rains large herds of zebra congregate on Makgadikgadi Pans, forming an amazing spectacle (if you can find them). During the dry season these animals congregate in numbers beside the Boteti River, on the west of the game reserve.

Separate populations from the Okavango, Chobe and Linyanti areas move to more open areas of the Kalahari. Some of these groups always seem to pass through the sweet grass plains of the Savuti area around April-May, and often this coincides with their foaling season.

Wildebeest in the north of the country follow a similar pattern to the zebra, but those in the centre and south of the Kalahari are effectively now a separate population. It seems that numbers in the central area of the Kalahari have fluctuated wildly since records began; before the fences there was probably a big annual migration northeast in the dry season to Lake Xau – the nearest water point to the CKGR. Like **hartebeest** in the central Kalahari, they certainly move around with the season, but the complexities of their current migration patterns are unclear.

For more details on these and many smaller mammals, see *Appendix 1*, page 499.

Animal tracks

A good guide can make animal tracks come alive, helping you to make sense of what you see in the bush. Showing you, for example, that cats' tracks have three lobes at the bottom, whereas dog and hyena tracks feature only two; pointing out the cheetah's claws, usually absent from other cat tracks; or the direction in which an elephant's walking from small scuff marks around its track. The more you learn, the more you'll enjoy about the bush.

The tracks illustrated on pages 62–3 are shown in relation to each other, sizewise, and are intended as a simple introduction to the many signs of wildlife that may be seen around a waterhole, or in the sand.

Birdlife

Large areas of Botswana are still covered by relatively undisturbed natural vegetation, and hunting is not a significant factor for most of Botswana's 550 recorded species of birds. Thus, with a range of natural habitats, Botswana is a superb birding destination.

There are fairly clear distinctions between the birds that you're likely to find in areas of swamp or open water, those that frequent riverine forest, and those found in the drier areas. None are endemic, though several have very restricted distributions. These include the slaty egret, which is restricted to the Okavango, Linyanti and Chobe river systems, the brown firefinch, and the Natal nightjar.

The Okavango Delta is a particularly good place for birdwatching as the habitats change from dry, to flooded, to deep-water over very short distances.

In addition to its resident bird species, Botswana receives many migrants. In September and October the Palaearctic migrants appear (ie: those that come from the Northern Hemisphere – normally Europe), and they remain until around April or May. This is also the peak time to see the intra-African migrants, which come from further north in Africa.

The rains from December to around April see an explosion in the availability of most birds' food: seeds, fruits and insects. Hence this is the prime time for birds to nest, even if it is also the most difficult time to visit the more remote areas of the country.

Field guides

Finding good, detailed field guides to plants, animals and birds in Botswana is relatively easy within the country. There are now very comprehensive guides on the flora and fauna of southern Africa – which usually cover Botswana – and several guides dedicated just to Botswana.

See *Further Reading*, for recommendations and details, but top of your list should be Veronica Roodt's *Trees & Shrubs*, even if you're not that interested in trees or shrubs. I've always used Newman's *Birds of Southern Africa*, by Kenneth Newman, although the same author has a specific *Birds of Botswana* in print which may be more appropriate if you're confining your visit to Botswana.

Finally, if you have room and lots of time, then Richard Estes' *Safari Companion* is a great general book on mammalian behaviour.

CONSERVATION

A great deal has been written about the conservation of animals in Africa; much of it is over-simplistic and intentionally emotive. As an informed visitor you are in the unique position of being able to see some of the issues at firsthand, and to appreciate the perspectives of some of the local people. So abandon your preconceptions, and start by realising how complex the issues are.

Here I shall try to outline a few ideas common to current thinking on conservation, and to many areas in the region. Only then will I frame them in the context of Botswana.

Being pragmatic: conservation and development

Firstly, conservation must be taken within its widest sense if it is to have meaning. Saving animals is of minimal use if the whole environment is degraded, so we must consider conserving whole areas and ecosystems, not just the odd isolated species.

Observe that land is regarded as an asset by most societies, in Africa as it is elsewhere. (The San are a notable exception in this regard.) To 'save' the land for the animals, and use it merely for the recreation of a few privileged foreign tourists, is a recipe for huge social problems – especially if the local people remain excluded from benefit and in poverty. Local people have hunted animals for food for centuries. They have always killed game that threatened them or ruined their crops. If we now try to protect animals in populated areas without addressing the concerns of the people, then our efforts will fail.

The only pragmatic way to conserve Africa's wild areas is to see the *development* of the local people, and the *conservation* of the ecosystems, as inter-linked goals.

In the long term, one will not work without the other. Conservation without development leads to resentful local people who will happily, and frequently, shoot, trap and kill animals. Development without conservation will simply repeat the mistakes that most developed countries have already made: it will lay waste a beautiful land and kill off its natural heritage. Look at the tiny areas of undisturbed natural vegetation that survive in the UK, the USA, or Japan. See how unsuccessful we in the Northern Hemisphere have been at long-term conservation over the past 500 years.

As an aside, the local people in Africa are sometimes wrongly accused of being the only agents of degradation. Many would like to see 'poachers' shot on sight, and slash-and-burn agriculture banned. But observe the importation of tropical hardwoods by the West to see the problems that our demands place on the natural environment in the developing world.

In conserving some of Africa's natural areas and assisting the development of her people, the international community has a vital role to play. It could effectively encourage African governments to practise sustainable long-term strategies, rather than grasping for the short-term fixes which politicians seem universally to prefer. But such solutions must have the backing of the people themselves, or they will fall apart when the foreign aid budgets eventually wane.

In practice, to get this backing from the local communities it is not enough for a conservation strategy to be compatible with development. Most rural Africans are more concerned about where they live, what they can eat, and how they will survive, than they are about the lives of small, obscure species of antelope that taste good when roasted.

To succeed in Africa, conservation must not only be *compatible* with development, it must actually *promote* it. Conservation efforts must also actively help the local people to improve their own standard of living. If that situation can be reached, then local communities can be mobilised behind long-term conservation initiatives.

Governments are the same. As the famous Zambian conservationist, Norman Carr, once commented, 'governments won't conserve an impala just because it is pretty'. But they will work to save it *if* they can see that it is worth more to them alive than dead.

The continent's best current strategies involve trying to find lucrative and sustainable ways to use the land. They then plough much of the revenue back into the surrounding local communities. Once the local communities see revenue from conservation being used to help them improve their lives – to build houses, clinics and schools, and to offer paid employment – then such schemes rapidly get their backing and support.

Carefully planned, sustainable tourism is one solution that is working effectively. For success, the local communities must see that the visitors pay because they want the wildlife. Thus, they reason, the existence of wildlife directly improves their income, and they will strive to conserve it.

It isn't enough for people to see that the wildlife helps the government to get richer; that won't dissuade a local hunter from shooting a duiker for dinner. However, if he is directly benefiting from visitors, who come to see the animals, then he has a vested interest in saving that duiker.

It matters little to the average rural African, or ultimately to the wildlife, whether these visitors come to shoot the wildlife with a camera or with a gun. The vital issue is whether or not the hunting is done on a *sustainable* basis (ie: only a few of the oldest animals are shot each year, so that the size of the animal population remains largely unaffected).

Photographers may claim the moral high-ground, but should remember that hunters pay far more for their privileges. Hunting operations generate large revenues from few guests, who demand minimal infrastructure and so cause little impact on the land. Photographic operations need more visitors to generate the same revenue, and so generally cause greater negative effects on the country.

In theory: high revenue, low volume
In the late 1980s Botswana's parks, and especially the Chobe Riverfront area and Moremi, were being badly over-used. Many visitors were self-contained South Africans who would arrive with all their food and kit. They bought little in Botswana except their cheap park entry tickets, and contributed little to the nation's economy.

In an effort to reduce numbers, and stave off serious environmental (and aesthetic) problems due to too many visitors, it was decided to increase the park fees by a factor of ten. This worked miraculously – reducing the number of visitors and their impact, but retaining the same level of revenue for the parks authorities.

At the time this was revolutionary, even though now it seems obvious. Thus Botswana's policy of 'high revenue, low volume' tourism was born. Most of Botswana's wild areas are expensive to maximise revenues and keep environments pristine – and they're the envy of Africa for having a good, working system that is delivering increasing revenues as well as many local development initiatives.

In practice
For the last 15 years this basic policy has been in place, and it's extended way beyond the national parks, and evolved to embrace virtually the whole of northern Botswana, going beyond the official national parks and game reserves

National parks and reserves
The national parks, like Chobe, and the game reserves, like Moremi, work on a simple system. Nobody lives in these (the San in the CKGR being the exception). Anyone can visit, provide they pay the fees. These are scaled to be cheapest for citizens of Botswana, reasonable for residents, and more costly for visitors. (See *National parks* in *Chapter 8*, for these charges.)

Private concessions or reserves
Outside of the national parks and game reserves, northern Botswana has been divided up into a series of wildlife management areas (WMAs). See the maps on pages 284–5 and 232 for some of these. Those in northwestern Botswana, in Ngamiland, are numbered NG1, NG2, up to NG51. These areas are normally referred to in Botswana as 'concessions' although in this guide I have used this term virtually interchangeably with the phrase 'private reserve' or simply just 'reserve.'

Within each of these the government, via the local 'land board', has defined who owns the wildlife, and what can be done with it. In some hunting is forbidden, in most limited (controlled and sustainable) hunting is allowed.

Community concessions

In most of these concessions, the approach taken centres around Community Based Natural Resource Management (CBNRM) – a modern phrase for a strategy which tries to reconcile conflicts over resources between the people and the wildlife in it's broadest sense.

CBNRM is based on the premise that the people living next to a resource are the ones best suited to protecting that resource – as they would lose most if that resource is lost, and gain most if it's managed well. There is also an ethical consideration: for example, the people that pay the costs of living near wildlife (destruction of crops, livestock and loss of human life) benefit from its conservation. Local people need to be involved in the decision-making process and need to benefit from the areas around them, and CBNRM tries to make this possible.

Thus in most of Botswana's concessions, the local communities now make decisions about how they are run, and they reap the rewards if they are run well and successfully. See the box entitled: *The anatomy of a community partnership* about NG22 & 23 in *Chapter 13* for an example of one such arrangement.

Tourism

Botswana lies in the heart of sub-Saharan Africa – and its tourism is the envy of the continent in many ways. It's regarded, quite rightly, as having some of the continent's best wildlife areas, which are still in generally pristine condition.

What's more, the expansion of tourism from the nucleus of the national parks to the areas around them, has gradually increased the area effectively protected for wildlife since the 1980s. Areas that were devoted to hunting are now becoming solely photographic. This is enlarging the contiguous area in northern Botswana available for the wildlife, helping to ensure that the game populations increase in size, and become more viable.

A final word here goes to Peter Sandenberg, who has been running safari camps and tourism operations in this area for longer than most. He observes that 'one of the greatest changes since coming to this area in 1983 has been the remarkable increase in animal numbers and species' diversity.'

Changing economics of tourism

Tourism isn't yet as important to Botswana as diamonds or beef production. However, it is increasing every year, and is providing substantial employment and also bringing foreign exchange into the country, which gives the politicians a reason to support conservation.

When the diamonds run out – within the next few decades – Botswana needs to have an alternative, and renewable, source of income … and tourism is one of the most obvious contenders. The difficulty for the government will be trying to increase substantially tourism's revenues whilst still keeping tourism a premium product, and hence at a low density.

How you can help more

The visitor on an expensive safari is, by his or her mere presence, making a financial contribution to development and conservation in Botswana. See pages 42–3 for ways in which you can support small local charities which directly help the people of Botswana. When on safari, one very simple thing that you can do to help is to question your safari operator, in the most penetrating of terms:

- Besides employment, how do local people benefit from this camp?
- How much of this camp's revenue goes directly back to the local people?
- What are you doing to help the people living near this reserve?
- How much control do the local people have in what goes on in the area in which these safaris are operated?

If more visitors did this, it would make a huge difference. If safari operators felt that their clients wanted them to be involved with community development, then they would rapidly get more involved.

Hunting issues

Big-game hunting, where visiting hunters pay large amounts to kill trophy animals, is practised on a number of private reserves and concessions. Just like photographic tourism, this is a valuable source of revenue in the long term for people living in the country's concessions.

In practice, there is room for both types of visitors in Botswana: the photographer and the hunter. The national parks, and some of the private reserves nearest the parks (eg: NG23, NG27A and B), are designated for photographic visitors; here no hunting is allowed.

Around there, controlled sustainable hunting is allowed in many of the private reserves, although a few of these maintain a policy of no hunting (eg: the concessions run by Wilderness Safaris, like NG15 and NG26).

Most of the others have divided their concessions into areas where hunting is allowed, and places where it is not. Any photographic camps are usually built in the non-hunting areas.

Integral to this approach is that the concessions provide a buffer between the pristine national parks and the land around where sustainable hunting is allowed. This would protect the national park's animals from any incursions by poachers, whilst the park acts as a large gene pool and species reservoir for the private concessions.

Poaching

Having just mentioned 'poaching' it's perhaps worth commenting that Botswana has very, very little poaching. There is always a little small-scale poaching of game 'for the pot' by local people … but large-scale commercial poaching operations are virtually unknown here.

Occasionally there's a complaint about poachers coming across the river from Namibia – putting the blame on poachers from neighbouring countries is a very usual tactic in this part of the world. However, the Kwando, Linyanti and Chobe rivers, and the rest of the country's borders, are so well patrolled by the Botswana Defence Force (BDF) that this seems unlikely.

Planning and Preparation

GETTING THERE
By air

Air Botswana does not fly outside southern Africa, and there are relatively few other airline links to Botswana. The vast majority of visitors to northern Botswana fly via the gateways of Maun and Kasane, which is effectively serviced by the nearby airports at Victoria Falls (in Zimbabwe) and Livingstone (in Zambia).

Most common for many visitors to the region is to fly to Livingstone (three-letter airline code: LVI) via Johannesburg, and then leave from Maun (code: MUB), again routing via Jo'burg (code: JNB).

Botswana's capital, Gaborone (code: GBE), is relatively rarely visited if you're on your way to or from northern Botswana – although occasionally you might stop in Gaborone as you fly between Maun and Jo'burg.

Buying air tickets

However you arrange your flights, remember some basic tips. Firstly, make sure your purchase is protected. Always book through a company that is bonded for your protection – eg: in the UK this means holding an ATOL license (Air Travel Organiser's License) – or use a credit card.

Secondly, note that airlines seldom give the best deals direct. (The notable exception to this is some clever marketing by sophisticated airlines like the 'World Offers' periodically pushed by British Airways.) Generally you'll always do better through a discounted flight centre or a tour operator.

Thirdly, book the main internal flights at the same time – with the same company – that you book your flights to/from Johannesburg. Often the airline taking you to Africa will have cheap deals for add-on regional flights within Africa. You should be able to get Jo'burg–Livingstone flights, or Maun–Jo'burg flights, at discounted rates provided that you book them at the same time as your return flights to Jo'burg. Further, if you book all your flights together with the same company, then you'll be sure to get connecting flights, and so have the best schedule possible.

Never be talked into getting an apparently cheap return to Jo'burg on the basis that you'll be able to then get a separate ticket up to Maun; it'll cost you a lot more in the end.

From Europe

Johannesburg is invariably the best gateway as it's widely served by many carriers. From Europe, British Airways, South African Airways, Lufthansa and Air France (to name but a few) have regular flights to Jo'burg. Generally these are busy routes which fill up far in advance, so you're likely to get cheaper fares by booking well ahead rather than at the last minute; this is a virtual certainty during the busiest season from July to October, and in December–January around the Christmas period.

For a return from Jo'burg to London with a decent airline, expect to pay around £500/US$750 for most of the year, and around £600/US$900 in the busiest period from mid-July to the end of August; for flights departing after December 9, you'll be lucky to pay less than £800/US$1,200. Unless there's some major international upset, these flights become progressively more expensive as you get closer to the departure. So as with most long-haul destinations, book early for the cheapest flights.

One-way flights between Jo'burg and Maun, with Air Botswana, should cost around £220/US$330. One-way flights between Jo'burg and Livingstone (with the South Africa-based Nationwide Airlines) or Victoria Falls (with British Airways or South African Airways) should cost around £100/US$150.

Booking all your flights at once should save a lot of money as good add-on rates between Maun from Jo'burg of nearer £100/US$150 one-way are possible through good tour operators who have access to special add-on rates for Air Botswana's flights.

From North America
If you are coming from the US then you will certainly need to at least pass through Johannesburg. It's often easiest to also route via London or another European capital. There isn't much of a discounted long-haul flight market in the US, so booking all your flights in the US will not always save you money.

Investigate the flight prices between the US and Botswana bought in the US. Look especially closely at fares with Delta and South African Airways direct from the US to Jo'burg – and talk to 'consolidators' who are the nearest that the US gets to having discounted ticket agents.

Then compare these to buying a US-London return in the US, and London-Botswana tickets from a good source in London. London is Europe's capital for cheap flights, and increasingly visitors from the US are discovering that flights bought from the UK, as well as trips from UK tour operators, offer better value than those in America.

From Australasia
Both Quantas and British Airways fly between Jo'burg and Sydney or Perth, whilst South African Airways services routes to Asia, including Singapore.

From Windhoek or Lusaka
It is possible, although rarely either easier or cheaper, to approach Botswana from one of the region's other capitals, Lusaka and Windhoek.

Travel between Windhoek and Maun ought to be easy, as both Air Botswana and Air Namibia service this route about two or three times per week. However, in practice they both use small 19-seater planes, which are often full months in advance, and they both frequently change their schedules with relatively little regard to their passengers' pre-arranged plans. If you plan to use this route as part of a fixed itinerary, you have been warned.

Travel from Lusaka to Kasane is easier and more reliable, though slower. Think of it in two stages: between Lusaka and Livingstone, and Livingstone and Kasane. Lusaka to Livingstone is a long six-hour drive (though there is an efficient and cheap coach line for the more adventurous) or a short 90-minute flight. There are a handful of good, small Zambian charter companies that will organise a charter flight on this route, or seats on a scheduled charter two or three times a week. Expect a cost of around US$175 per person.

See below for options to get between Livingstone and Kasane, but note that now it's very, very easy to arrange to be transferred across by vehicle and boat for about US$55 per person one-way.

Overland

Most overland border posts open from about 06.00 or 08.00, to 16.00 or 18.00, although a few of the busier ones, on main routes connecting with South Africa, stay open a few hours later than this.

To/from Zimbabwe

Botswana has several border posts with Zimbabwe, of which the two most important are the one on the road between Kasane and Victoria Falls, at Kazungula (open 06.00–18.00) and the one on the main road from Francistown to Plumtree (and hence Bulawayo), at Ramokgwebane (open 06.00–18.00).

The third is a much smaller post at Pandametenga (open 08.00–16.00). This is 100km south of Kasane, and sometimes used by visitors as a neat short-cut into the back of Zimbabwe's Hwange National Park.

To/from Zambia

Despite their territories meeting only at a point, Botswana does have one border crossing to Zambia: a reliable ferry across the Zambezi linking Kazungula with its namesake village in Zambia. This ferry costs about US$25/£17 per vehicle, and runs from 06.00 to 18.00, weather permitting.

To/from Namibia

Despite the long length of its border with Namibia, Botswana has very few border posts.

The most important of these by far is the post on the Trans-Kalahari Highway, the route between the towns of Ghanzi and Gobabis. The Botswana side of this, Mamuno, is open 08.00 to 16.00, and so is the Namibian post at Buitepos on the other side.

There are two other main crossings. One is at Mohembo (north of Shakawe and at the south end of Namibia's Mahango National Park), that opens from 06.00 to 18.00. The other is across the Chobe River at Ngoma, which opens from 06.00 to 18.00.

There are two other possible crossings that you should know about. One is the option to cross the Kwando River by boat (only as part of an organised safari with these lodges), between the Botswana's Kwando concession, and Lianshulu Lodge in Namibia's Caprivi Strip. This obviously links two private areas, but the customs and immigration formalities are now in place to allow such a crossing.

The other is the road between Tsumkwe, in Namibia, and Nokaneng, on the west of the Delta, which is opening as an official border post. In doing so it will gradually, and probably radically, alter the options for routes in that whole area. Let's hope it has a positive effect on the Bushman communities in that region, and not the negative one that is widely feared.

To/from South Africa

South Africa has always been Botswana's most important neighbour politically and economically, and for many years (even before South Africa was welcome in the international fold!) it was in a 'customs union' with South Africa and Namibia. Thus it's no surprise to find a range of border posts with South Africa. In order from northeast to southwest these are:

- Pontdrift (open 08.00–16.00)
- Platjan (open 08.00–16.00)
- Zanzibar (open 08.00–16.00)

- Martin's Drift (open 08.00–18.00) to Groblersbrug
- Parr's Halt (open 08.00–16.00) to Stockpoort
- Sikwane (open 07.00–19.00) to Derdepoort
- Tlokweng, near Gaborone (open 08.00–16.00) to Kopfontein
- Ramotswa (open 07.00–19.00) to Swartkopfonteinhek
- Pioneer Gate, near Lobatse (open 07.00–19.00) to Skilpadshek
- Ramatlabama (open 07.00–20.00) to Ramatlabama
- Phitshane Molopo (open 07.30–16.30) to Makgobistad
- Bray (open 08.00–16.00)
- Makopong (open 08.00–16.00)
- Tshabong (open 08.00–16.00) to McCarthy's Rest
- Middlepits (open 08.00–16.00)
- Bokspits (open 08.00–16.00)

ENTRY REQUIREMENTS
Visas
If you need a visa for Botswana, then you must get one before you arrive. Contact your local Botswana embassy or high commission – who are also the best source to verify that the information here is still current.

Currently visitors holding passports from the following countries **do not need a visa**:

- All EC (European Community) countries
- USA, South Africa, Scandinavian countries, Uruguay, Western Samoa and countries from the former Yugoslavia
- All Commonwealth countries (except Ghana, India, Sri Lanka, Nigeria and Mauritius – whose citizens do need visas).

Citizens from these countries will be granted a one-month entry permit on arrival. Though Botswana hasn't changed these rules often in the past, it's always wisest to check with your local embassy before you depart – or on the government's website: www.gov.bw/tourism/entry_req/entry_req.html

The prevailing attitude amongst both Botswana's government and its people is that visitors are generally very good for the country as they spend valuable foreign currency – so if you look respectable then you will not find any difficulties in entering Botswana.

Given this logic, and the conservative nature of Botwana's local customs, the converse is also true. If you dress very untidily, looking as if you've no money when entering via an overland border, then you may be questioned as to how you will be funding your trip. Very rarely, you may even be asked for a return ticket as proof that you do intend to leave. Dressing respectably in Botswana is not only courteous, but will also make your life easier.

Visa extensions
Visitors can stay for a maximum of three months in a 12-month period, and it's a serious offence to stay longer without permission. If you want longer than a month, then you must renew your permit at the nearest immigration office. If you want to stay longer than three months, then apply to the Department of Immigration, PO Box 942, Gaborone; tel: 374545 – preferably before entering Botswana.

If you wish to work, then work permits can be obtained from the Department of Labour, Private Bag 002, Gaborone; tel: 360100. Note that Botswana is now quite strict about granting work permits only for jobs for which a suitably qualified Botswana citizen is not available.

Botswana's diplomatic missions abroad

For an up-to-date list of Botswana's diplomatic missions, see the useful government website: www.gov.bw. Currently the relevant page to look for is: www.gov.bw/tourism/embassies/embassies.html. A list of the current missions includes:

Belgium Embassy of the Republic of Botswana to the European Community, 169, Av de Tervuren, B1150 Brussels; tel: 02 735 2070 or 735 6110; fax: 02 735 6318

China Embassy of the Republic of Botswana, Unit 811 IBM Tower, Pacific Century Place, #2A Gong Ti Bellu, Cha Oyan District, Beijing 100027; tel: 6539 1616; fax: 6539 1199

Ethiopia Embassy of the Republic of Botswana, PO Box 22202, Code 1000, Addis Abbaba; tel: 01 715 422/23; fax: 01 717 215

Japan Embassy of the Republic of Botswana, Shiba Amerex Building No. 2, 4-5-10 Shiba Minato-Ku, Tokyo; tel: 03 5440-5676; fax: 03 5765-7581; web: www.botswanaembassy.or.jp

Namibia Botswana High Commission, 101 Klein Windhoek, PO Box 20359, Windhoek; tel: 061 221 941/2-7; fax: 061 236 034

South Africa Botswana High Commission, 24 Amos St, Colbyn, PO Box 57034, Arcadia 0007, Pretoria; tel: 012 342 4761/2/3/4; fax: 012 342 1845

South Africa Botswana Consulate General, 8 Riebeeck St, 4th Floor, Southern Life Centre, PO Box 3288, Cape Town 8000; tel: 021 211 045; fax: 021 211 046

South Africa Botswana Consulate General, 122 De Korte St, 2nd Floor, PO Box 32051, Braamfontein 201, Johannesburg 2017; tel: 011 403 3748; fax: 011 403 1286

Sweden Embassy of the Republic of Botswana, Tyrgatan 11, PO Box 26024, 10041 Stockholm; tel: 08 723 0035; fax: 08 723 0087

Switzerland Botswana Permanent Mission to the United Nations, 80 Rue de Lausanne, 1202 Geneva; tel: 022 906 1060; fax: 022 906 1061

UK Botswana High Commission, 6 Stratford Place, London W1C 1BA; tel: 020 7499 0031; fax: 020 7409 782

United Nations Permanent Mission of the Republic of Botswana, 103 East 37th St, New York, NY 10016, USA; tel: (212) 889 2277 or 889 2331 or 889 2772 or 889 2491; fax: (212) 725 5061

USA Embassy of the Republic of Botswana, 3400 International Drive NW, Suite 7M, Washington DC 2008; tel: (202) 244 4990: fax: (202) 244 4164

Zambia Botswana High Commission, 5201 Pandit Nehru Rd, Diplomatic Triangle, PO Box 31910, Lusaka; tel: 01 252 058; fax: 01 253 895

Zimbabwe Botswana High Commission, 22 Philips Av, Belgravia, PO Box 563, Harare; tel: 04 729 551/3; fax: 04 721 360

Botswana's national tourist board offices

Until relatively recently, Botswana had done little in the way of tourism promotion overseas. However, now that tourism is becoming increasingly recognised as Botswana's best base for a sustainable income after its diamonds run out, resources are being mobilised very effectively to raise Botswana's profile as a destination for tourists.

Currently these efforts are concentrating on four representatives, in four different countries:

Germany Karin Zwiers Interface International GmbH, Petersburger Str 94, D-10247, Berlin; tel: 030 4225 6027; fax: 030 4225 6286; email: 100762.3614@compuserve.com; web: www.interface-tourism.com

Japan Kinki Nippon Tourist Co Ltd, Club Tourism Division, Shikjuku Hand Wind, 6-3-1 Nishi-Shinjuku, Shinjuku-Ku, Tokyo 160-8308

UK Southern Skies Marketing, Index House, St George's Lane, Ascot, Berkshire, SL5
7EU; tel: 01344 636430; fax: 01344 873737; email: botswanatourism@southern-skies.co.uk;
web: www.southern-skies.co.uk
US Henry Kartagener, Kartagener Associates Inc, 631 Commack Rd, Suite 1A, Commack,
NY 11725; tel: 631 858 1270; fax: 631 858 1279; email: kainyc@att.net

WHEN TO GO

See the section on *Climate*, pages 54–6, for a detailed description of the weather that
can be expected, and note that Botswana's rainy season occurs between around
December and April, with January and February usually being the wettest months.

The **dry season** (May to November) is the easiest time to travel, as then you are
unlikely to meet rain and can expect clear blue skies. This is ideal if this is your first
trip to Africa, or if seeing lots of big game is top of your wish-list.

Within this, you'll find June-August the coolest, when night temperatures in
the Kalahari can drop below freezing. Then from September onwards the heat
gradually builds up. The interior areas of the Kalahari, including central Chobe
and the Great Salt Pans, get very hot towards the end of October. Occasions
when it reaches over 40°C in the shade have earned this the tag of 'suicide
month'.

That said, note that in the Okavango, where there are large areas of water and
green vegetation, the extremes of temperature are much more pleasant and
moderated: the nights in August never reaching freezing, and the days in October
are never unbearable.

Everywhere November is a variable month. Some days will be hot. Some will
be cooler, as gathering clouds shield the country from the sun. Sometimes these
bring welcome showers; sometimes they simply build, and with them come
tension and humidity.

The **wet season**, December to March, is totally different, although the days can
still vary enormously from one to the next. Even within a day, skies can change
from sunny to cloudy within minutes and then back again. Downpours are usually
heavy and short – and usually late in the afternoon – although there are often a few
days when the sky remains grey and overcast. You will need a good waterproof for
the rainy season, but it seldom rains for long enough to really stop you doing
anything.

There simply isn't one 'best time' to visit Botswana, or any of its wild areas.
Here is some guidance on various issues to help you decide what the best time for
your visit would be…

Travelling

Travelling around Botswana in the dry season often has its challenges, but in some
places in the wet season it's a totally different game. Then the areas of pure sand
are still fine to drive on, and even a bit firmer than they are when it's hot and dry.

Driving yourself

In some areas where the soil has a high clay content, the bush tracks become
quagmires – the track from Rakops to the Central Kalahari's scout camp near Kuke
Corner is a fine example, as are most of the Makgadikgadi Pans. Some tracks,
especially those in the Delta-Linyanti region, like the route between Xakanaxa and
North Gate, become submerged completely. Thus travel in Botswana during the
wet season requires careful research, and scrupulous attention to your emergency
precautions. If you're heading for somewhere remote in the wet season, then
travelling with two or more vehicles is wise.

Flying around

In contrast, the weather is seldom a problem if you're flying into one of Botswana's safari camps. All are used to the vagaries of the weather and the water levels, although it may affect your activities. Similarly, if you're heading out on a budget mokoro trip or safari, it shouldn't affect your trip significantly – though your vehicle may need the occasional push!

Although there are less visitors around during this period, Botswana's flight schedules don't change much, and only a few of its camps will close. (Many will close during this period for a few weeks of planned maintenance or any building work that's needed. Those that remain open are often very quiet – so if you've often been to Africa in the dry season, then this is a fascinating time to visit – like being introduced to a different side of an old friend.)

Vegetation

During the wet season, the foliage runs wild. The Kalahari springs into life as the bush turns many shades of green. Open clay pans become small pools in the bush and it's a time of renewal, when a gentler light dapples Botswana's bush.

When the rains end, the leaves in the Kalahari gradually dry and many eventually drop. More greys and browns appear, and good shade becomes harder to find. Eventually, by late September and October, most plants look dry and parched, coloured from straw yellow to shrivelled brown.

However, note that large areas of the Okavango have their own permanent water supply – regulated more by the annual floods than the rainfall – and so don't follow this pattern so clearly. See the comment below on *The Okavango's flood*.

Game

From the point of view of most herbivores, the wet season is much more pleasant than the dry season. During the wet, most animals live in enormous salad bowls, with convenient pools of water nearby. It's a good time to have their young and eat themselves into good condition.

Visitors who have been to Africa before will often find something special about seeing all the animals when they aren't struggling with thirst and a lack of vegetation. It gives a sense of luxuriance and plenty, which isn't there in the dry season.

Before people started to have a big impact on Botswana's landscape (which, arguably, has only been in the last 150 years or so), many of the animals here used to follow regular seasonal migration patterns, often over very large distances. It was the same throughout Africa originally; many species, and especially the herding species of plains game, would move around to where the best food sources were to be found.

Despite the changes wreaked by man since then, the remnants of these migrations still happen. Understanding them will help you to work out what the best times are to visit the various parks – so first read the section on *Game migrations* in *Chapter 3* for detailed comments.

The finer details of each area are covered under sections entitled *When to go* which are spread throughout the book, but in very general terms:

Chobe Areas with riverfront are at their best July–October; the Savuti Marsh area is totally different, with some good game all year. Savuti Marsh is probably at its best around March–April–May and (if the rains have arrived) November – when herds of zebra and plains game are passing through.

Kwando/Linyanti Follows the same basic pattern as Chobe's riverfronts – so is best in the late dry season, when it's the only source of water for miles around.

Okavango/Moremi The central areas of the Delta have permanent water all year, and equally permanent populations of animals all year round. Thus many game species stay here all year, and densities of animals (excluding elephant and buffalo) don't change that much. However, in the dry season the permanent populations of game found on the edges of the Delta are swelled by an influx of animals from the parched Kalahari. Thus, the game densities on the accessible edges of the Delta often rise significantly as the dry season progresses.

Nxai Pan Can be erratic, but always used to be at its best when wet, from December to March – though often still very good into May and June. However, the artificial pumping of a waterhole a couple of kilometres north of the gate has changed this pattern. During the rest of the year, you'll find plains game staying here in numbers, often accompanied by a few lion.

Makgadikgadi Pans The pans themselves can be superb when wet, December to April; large herds of zebra and other plains grazers appear. On their western border, the Boteti River (or at least its channel, as the river seldom flows!) follows the opposite pattern, attracting game at the end of the dry season, around August to early November.

Central Kalahari Game congregates in the huge grassy valleys here, most famously in Deception Valley, when the vegetation is lush during and shortly after the rains, from about December to May.

The bottom line is probably that if game viewing is your over-riding priority, or this is one of your first trips to Africa, then you'll be better visiting during the dry season. Then the animals are much easier to spot, as no thick vegetation obscures the view, and they are forced to congregate at well-known water points, like rivers, where they can be observed.

However, more experienced African travellers are missing out if they never travel during the rains – as it's completely different and can be superb. A few specific highlights of Botswana's animal calendar would include:

Feb–Apr Most of the herbivores are in their best condition, having fed well on the lush vegetation. It's a perfect time to catch huge concentrations of springbok and oryx on the short grass plains of the Central Kalahari's fossil river valleys.

May–Jun Probably my favourite time to be in Botswana (and most of southern Africa!). It's a great time to visit Savuti Marsh, and in the Okavango the floodwater moves down the Delta.

Jul–Aug Leopard are generally easier to see, as they come out more during the twilight hours. Later in the year, they often wait until it is cool, only appearing later in the evening.

Sep–Oct Elephant and buffalo tend to amalgamate into larger, more spectacular herds. (They splinter again just before the rains.) Lion sights become more frequent, as they spend more time near the limited remaining water sources.

Nov Can be a great month as often the rains haven't arrived, leaving amazing game densities in the riverfront areas (yet visitors are thin on the ground and prices are low). However, too many cloudless days can mean high midday temperatures.

Dec–Jan Crocodiles are nesting, and so found on or near exposed sandbanks. Various baby animals start to appear in November, followed by most of the mammals that calve sometime during the rainy season.

The Okavango's annual flood

This very complex variable is really a minor point for most visitors – who will find the Okavango Delta enchanting whenever they visit! However, the flooding levels will have some influence on some of your activities, and may even influence your choice of where you want to visit in the Delta.

Firstly, note that the water levels at any point in the Okavango Delta depend mainly on three variables: firstly, the local rainfall in your location; secondly, the height of the seasonal flood of the Okavango; thirdly, your location within the Delta – as the further north you are in the Okavango, the more water you're likely to have.

The local summer rains and the arrival of the seasonal floods are generally out of sync by around two to six months, depending on exactly where you are within the Delta. This represents the time taken for the peak of the rains in the Okavango River's main catchment area – the Angolan highlands – to make it down the Okavango River and into the various different areas of the Delta.

These annual floods are very variable. They have been monitored very carefully for years at Mohembo, where the river enters Botswana – see the graph below. From this we know that the peak of the flood at Mohembo generally occurs between mid-March and mid-May – just after the local summer rains in the region of the Delta have come to an end. Given the tiny gradient and very slow flow rate, this surge of water from Angola can take up to six months to work its way from the Panhandle to the far extremities of the Delta's waterways.

Hence expect the highest water levels in most areas of the Delta to occur after the rains – from about May to August. After that, levels will generally fall until around February, when the local rains start to slowly raise water levels prior to the main flood.

OKAVANGO FLOOD LEVELS

KEY
1984
1992
1999
1994
1995
2001
2000
2002

The Okavango River's flow rate, measured at Mohembo, in thousands of m³ per second

Birdlife

The birdlife in Botswana is certainly best when the foliage is most dense, and the insects are thriving, ie: in the wet season. Then many resident birds are nesting and in their bright, breeding plumage. This coincides to a large extent with the 'summer' period, from around October to March, when the Palaearctic migrants from the Northern Hemisphere are seen.

To give you an idea of the richness of the avifauna here, in the Okavango-Linyanti-Chobe areas during the rainy season it isn't difficult for competent ornithologists to record a hundred different species between dawn and midday. Really energetic bird-watchers can notch up as many as 200 different species in a 24-hour period in somewhere as rich as the northern Chobe Riverfront area. A real enthusiast might count about 320 species (out of the 550 or so which occur) during a two-week trip here.

The highlights of Botswana's birding calendar includes:

Mar–Jul Wattled cranes and other opportunists follow the floods in the Okavango, snapping up drowning insects and reptiles.

Aug–Oct 'Fishing parties' of herons, egrets and storks will arrive at pools as they dry up, to feed on the stranded fish.

Sep–Nov Nesting carmine bee-eaters colonise soft vertical riverbanks, skimmers nest on exposed sandbanks, and large breeding colonies of storks and herons gather at places like Gcodikwe Lagoon. Migrant waders appear beside the edge of most pans and lagoons.

Nov–Apr Most of the weavers are in breeding plumage.

Feb–Apr Red bishop birds, yellow-billed storks and the spectacular paradise whydahs have their breeding plumage on display. If the rains have been good then the flamingos may be nesting on Sua Pan; ostriches gather in numbers on the pans of the Central Kalahari.

Apr–Jun Juvenile birds of many species abound as this season's young are fledged and leave their nests.

Photography

I find the light clearest and most spectacular during the rainy season. Then the rains have washed the dust from the air, and the bright sunlight can contrast wonderfully with dark storm clouds. The vegetation's also greener and brighter, and the animals and birds often in better condition.

However, it will rain occasionally when you're trying to take shots, and the long periods of flat, grey light through clouds can be very disappointing; you'll get few good shots then. Sometimes it can seem as if you're waiting for the gods to grant you just a few minutes of stunning light, between the clouds. A much more practical time is just after the rains, around April to June, when at least you are less likely to be interrupted by a shower. (This is one of my reasons for being a fan of May as a great time to travel!)

The dry season's light is reliably good, if not quite as inspirational as that found during the rains. You are unlikely to encounter any clouds, and will get better sightings of game to photograph. Do try to shoot in the first and last few hours of the day, when the sun is low in the sky. During the rest of the day use a filter (perhaps a polariser) to guard against the sheer strength of the light leaving you with a film full of washed-out shots.

During the hotter months around October, you're also likely to encounter more bush fires than normal, which can leave a thin pall of smoke covering a large area. (This was especially a problem last time I was up in the Linyanti area, as smoke from the many man-made fires in Namibia seemed to blanket the area.)

General ambience
One of the biggest reasons for coming to the Okavango – and you may only realise this once you've visited – is not the game or the birds. It's simply the whole general ambience of being able to float over lily-covered lagoons with the sun on your back and a gentle breeze in your hair. This is certainly best when the skies are fairly clear of clouds – from April to November.

Other visitors
Most tourists to Botswana visit during the dry season, from around May to November. Within that season, the period from mid-July to mid-October is definitely the busiest – although Botswana's small camps/lodges and private reserves ensure that it never feels busy, even when everywhere is full. (In fact, the country's capacity for tourism remains tiny compared with that of South Africa, Kenya or Tanzania.)

Most of those visiting outside of this season are cognoscenti, who visit early or late in the season – May to July or late-October to November – when the camps are quieter and often costs are lower.

A much smaller number of visitors come during the rains, from December to April, when camps will often be quiet for days. This often means that they will give visitors a much more personal experience, with private drives; their rates are often lower too, and they're usually far more flexible about bringing children on safari.

Much of the blame for this 'glut or famine' of visitors lies with overseas tour operators. Many who advertise trips here just don't know Botswana well enough to plan trips which work during the rainy season. It's much easier for them to make blanket generalisations, telling enquirers who don't know any better that it's 'not interesting' or that 'you won't see any game' if you visit in the wet season. None of this is true, as long as you choose your destinations carefully, but of course most people don't know this in advance.

While the rains are not the ideal time for everybody's trip, they are a fascinating time to visit and should not be dismissed without serious thought.

Costs of trips
Aside from the airfares to get here, which vary in their own way (see *Getting there*, at the start of this chapter), some safari operators also lower their rates when business in quieter. Generally July to October is the peak season when prices are highest; January and February is the green season when prices are lowest, and the rest of the year falls somewhere in between.

Walking safaris
For safe and interesting walking, you need the foliage to be low so that you can see through the surrounding bush as easily as possible. This means that the dry season is certainly the best time for walking – and even then I'd counsel you to choose where you visit very, very carefully as standards of walking guides can be highly variable. (See my comments on the safety of walking safaris on pages 127–8.)

I wouldn't advise anyone looking for a serious walking trip to visit Botswana in the wet season. Walking through shoulder-high grass is nerve-racking with the best of walking guides, and only two or three operations in Botswana are really likely to have anything like that calibre of guide. The best months for walking are

May to October, though away from the moderating influence of the Okavango's waters, October can be very hot for longer walks.

MONEY

Botswana has probably Africa's strongest and most stable currency, underpinned by the huge annual earnings of its diamond industry. See the section on *Cost of living* in *Chapter 8*, for comments on inflation and exchange rates.

There is no 'black market' in foreign currency in Botswana, as the Pula floats freely on the international money markets. Thus don't expect to see any shady characters on the street hissing 'change money' as you pass; I never have. (If you do, then assume they're con-men trying to dupe visitors who don't know any better!)

Budgeting for safaris

Botswana isn't a cheap country to visit. This is due to a combination of the high costs of the logistics needed to operate in remote areas, plus the deliberate policy of the government to maximise revenues from tourism, whilst preserving the pristine nature of the country by using high costs to limit the number of visitors. That said, different kinds of trips need very different budgeting...

For backpackers

Camping at organised sites is by far your cheapest way to stay in most areas of Botswana, and always a good bet if you're relatively self-sufficient and have the equipment with you. If you do then expect to pay around US$2.50–3/£1.50–2.50 per person camping per night.

Restaurant meals in the towns are cheap compared with Europe or America: expect to pay US$6–10/£4–6 for a good evening meal, including a local beer or two. Imported drinks are always more expensive than those from southern Africa – but as southern Africa has some first-class breweries and wineries, this really is seldom an issue. European wines and spirits, as you might expect, are ridiculously priced (and so make excellent gifts if you are visiting someone here). You will pay well over US$100/£65 for a bottle of decent French champagne!

For self-drivers

If you have your own rugged 4WD with equipment *and* the experience to use it and survive safely in the bush, then you will be able to camp and cook for yourself. This is then an affordable way to travel and see those remote areas of Botswana which are open to the public.

Your largest expense will be the hire of a decent and well-equipped vehicle. (Taking anything less into remote areas of wild bush is really very foolish.) See page 119 for more comments on this, but expect it to cost around US$195–240/£130–160 per day, including all your camping kit.

Your next largest expense will probably be park and camping fees in the national parks. These can be substantial: expect a total of about P175 (US$29/£19) per person per day for both park entry and camping fees. Note, however, that there are still many interesting areas outside of the national parks – including parts of Makgadikgadi, the Tsodilo Hills, Aha Hills, Gcwihaba Caves and various offbeat areas of the Kalahari.

The cost of food depends heavily on where you buy it, as well as what you buy – but most people will probably do one large shop in Maun or Kasane at the start of their trip, topping up on perishables as they progress. If you are sensible then US$10–16/£7–10 per day would provide the supplies for a good, varied diet without having to be at all stingy.

For mobile safaris

The question 'how much are mobile safaris?' is as tricky to answer as 'how long is a piece of string?' It depends on where your trip is visiting, what the equipment, staff and guides are like, and how big the group is. In short, these trips vary greatly. To choose you must carefully prioritise what you want, what will suit you, and what you can afford to pay. Note also that prices for higher-end trips are heavily dependent upon the time of year that you travel.

On a bargain-basement trip for backpackers you will put up your tent, do the camp chores and even supply your own sleeping bag and drinks. On this you can expect to visit the parks, but not to have your time there maximised (parks are costly relative to staying outside them!). This would cost you around US$120–150/£80–100 per day per person sharing.

By contrast, a luxurious mobile safari, visiting pristine areas in the company of a small group with a top professional guide might cost up to US$350–450/£200–300 per person per day, including superb meals and all your drinks.

Between these two extremes, you ought to be able to get a trip of a decent quality for something around US$200–250/£140–170 per person per night sharing. Then expect to be camping in comfortable tents, with a small camp staff who will organise them, cook your meals and do all the chores.

As a final thought, if you value having a really comfortable bed at night, but still want the continuity of a good professional guide to stay with your group throughout the trip; if you like the idea of putting in a lot of time and energy game viewing in the parks, and don't mind a lot of time in a vehicle, then look at a mobile trip which moves between the lodges. These cost around US$400–500/£270–330 per person per day, including superb meals and all your drinks.

For fly-in safaris to lodges and camps

Again, the prices for fly-in trips vary considerably – though they're never cheap, and there's relatively little difference between the few bottom-end camps, and the vast majority of middle-market camps that provide good experiences in good areas.

Expect the most basic camp which offers only mokoro activities (which are cheaper to run than vehicles or boats) to cost around US$180/£120 per person per night sharing.

Otherwise a mid-range camp in a good area will usually be around US$350–450/£230–300 per person per night sharing, all-inclusive. By going off-season, or to slightly more offbeat, marginal areas, this can be reduced. However, note that quality of accommodation is only one factor in the price: some of the smallest, simplest bushcamps are amongst the most expensive places to stay.

If money really is no object, then there are a few really top-end places that cost a lot more than this. Abu and Mombo spring to mind. For these, you'll pay double this or more. But then, some would argue, you're getting the pinnacle of what Africa has to offer.

Having said this, there are two obvious caveats. Firstly, none of the prices here include flight transfers. These probably average out at about US$90/£60 per person per transfer, though working them out precisely is a complex business.

Secondly, you will almost always be quoted a rate for a 'package' of camps and flights; that's normal and often cannot be broken into its components.

Thirdly, note that although the prices for camps given in this guide indicate what you can expect to pay (in 2002 though, the figures in US$/£ don't change much from year to year) if you book directly, this really should be a maximum figure. You will usually be able to get them a little cheaper – and this is especially applicable to the more costly lodges – if you book through a good tour operator.

See the section on *Organising a fly-in safari*, at the end of this chapter, and note that, like airline tickets, the better rates for lodges are usually available indirectly.

How to take your money

If you are changing money at one of the main banks, then there is minimal difference in the rates between presenting a travellers' cheque, or presenting pounds sterling or US dollars in cash. This perhaps makes travellers' cheques preferable from a security point of view, as they are refundable if stolen. (AMEX travellers' cheques are probably the most widely recognised.)

However, outside of the banks you really need to have Pula to use, especially for smaller transactions and anything bought by the roadside. In the more rural locations, nobody will accept anything else. Petrol stations only accept cash in Pula; they do not usually accept credit cards.

In the towns you'll find people who, if pressed, will accept small denominations of US dollars. Because of the risk of forgeries, people are suspicious of larger denomination notes. US$100 and even US$50 bills are often rejected in shops and even banks. So always bring a mixture of US$5, US$10 and US$20 notes. US$1 notes make useful (generous) tips for porters.

South African rand are sometimes accepted, though not as widely as dollars or pounds – and they're not very popular. Most hotels, restaurants and safari camps will accept credit cards, pounds sterling, US dollars, or travellers' cheques.

WHAT TO TAKE

This is an impossible question to answer fully, as it depends on how you intend to travel and exactly where you are going. If you are flying in for a short safari holiday then you need not pack too ruthlessly – provided that you stay within your weight allowance. However, note that smaller, privately chartered planes may specify a maximum weight of 10–12kg for hold luggage, which must be packed in a soft, squashable bag. Once you see the stowage spaces in a small charter plane, you'll understand the importance of not bringing along large or solid suitcases.

If you are backpacking then weight becomes much more important, and minimising it becomes an art form. Each extra item must be questioned: is its benefit worth its weight?

If you have your own vehicle then neither weight nor bulk will be so vital, and you will have a lot more freedom to bring what you like. Here are some general guidelines:

Clothing

For most days all you will want is light, loose-fitting cotton clothing. Pure cotton, or at least a cotton-rich mix, is cooler and more absorbent than synthetic materials, making it more comfortable in the heat.

For men shorts (not too short) are fine in the bush, but long trousers are more socially acceptable in the towns and rural villages. (You will rarely see a respectable black man in Botswana wearing shorts outside a safari camp.) For women a knee-length skirt or culottes is ideal. Botswana's dress code is generally conservative: a woman wearing revealing clothing in town implies that she is a woman of ill repute, whilst untidy clothing suggests a poor person, of low social standing.

These rules are redundant at safari camps, where dress is casual, and designed to keep you cool and protect skin from the sun. Green, khaki and dust-brown cotton is de rigueur amongst visitors at the more serious camps. Wardrobes full of shiny, new safari gear will generally earn less respect than battered old green shirts and khaki shorts.

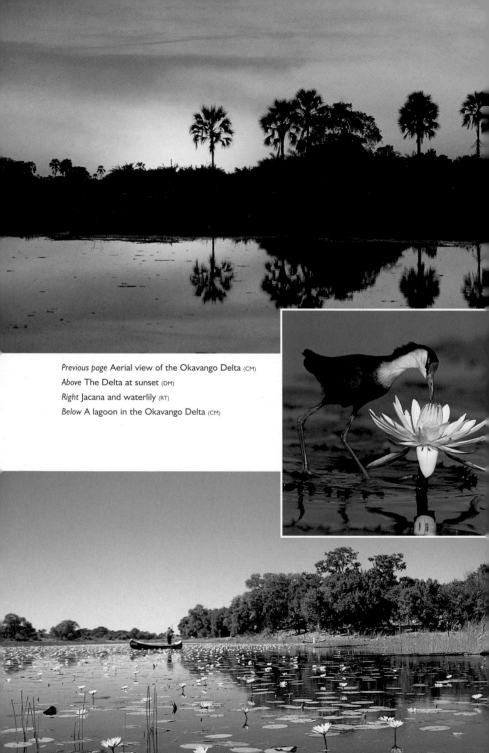

Previous page Aerial view of the Okavango Delta (CM)
Above The Delta at sunset (DM)
Right Jacana and waterlily (RT)
Below A lagoon in the Okavango Delta (CM)

At the less serious camps you'll see a smattering of brighter coloured clothes amongst many dull bush colours, the former usually worn by first-time visitors who are less familiar with the bush. Note that washing is done daily at virtually all camps, so few changes of clothes are necessary. A squashable hat and a robust pair of sunglasses with a high UV-absorption are essential.

Finally avoid anything which looks military. Leave all your camouflage patterns at home. Wearing camouflage is asking for trouble anywhere in Africa. You are very likely to be stopped and questioned by the genuine military, or at least the police, who will assume that you are a member of some militia – and question exactly what you are doing in Botswana. Few will believe that this is a fashion statement elsewhere in the world.

Footwear

If you plan to do much walking, either on safari or with a backpack, then lightweight walking boots (with ankle support if possible) are sensible. This is mainly because the bush is not always smooth and even, and anything that minimises the chance of a twisted ankle is worthwhile. Secondly, for the nervous, it will reduce still further the minute chance of being bitten by a snake, scorpion or other creepy-crawly, whilst walking.

Because of the heat, bring the lightest pair of boots you can find – preferably go for canvas, or a breathable Gore-tex-type material. Leather boots are too hot for wearing in October, but thin single-skin leather is bearable for walking in July and August. Never bring a new pair, or boots that aren't completely worn in. Always bring several pairs of thin socks – two thin pairs of socks are more comfortable than one thick pair, and will help to prevent blisters.

For mokoro trips, or generally relaxing at camp during the day, rafting sandals are ideal. These are sandals with a strong sole and firmly fitting straps which are waterproof. At night around camp you'll need to cover your feet/ankles against mosquitoes, and so lightweight boots of some sort are ideal.

Camping equipment

If you are coming on an organised safari, then even the most simple bushcamp will mean tents with linen, mosquito nets and probably an en-suite shower and toilet. However, if you're planning on doing any camping, then note that equipment is easier to buy in Europe or North America, and see *Camping equipment for backpackers* on pages 125–6 of *Chapter 6* for ideas of what you should bring.

Other useful items

Obviously no list is comprehensive, and only travelling can teach you what you need, and what you can do without. Here are a few of my own favourites and essentials, just to jog your memory. For visitors embarking on an organised safari, camps will have most things but useful items include:

- Sunblock and lipsalve – for vital protection from the sun
- Binoculars – totally essential for game viewing
- A small pocket torch (see page 126)
- 'Leatherman' tool – never go into the bush without one
- A small water bottle, especially on flights (see *Camping equipment*)
- Electrical insulating tape – remarkably useful for general repairs
- Camera – long lenses are vital for good shots of animals
- Basic sewing kit – with some really strong thread for repairs
- Cheap waterproof watch (leave expensive ones, and jewellery, at home)

- Couple of paperback novels
- Large plastic 'bin-liner' (garbage) bags, for protecting luggage from dust
- Simple medical kit and insect repellent

And for those driving or backpacking, useful extras are:

- Concentrated, biodegradable washing powder
- Long-life candles – African candles are often soft, and burn quickly
- Nylon 'paracord' – bring at least 20m for emergencies and washing lines
- Hand-held GPS navigation system, for expeditions to remote areas
- Good compass and a whistle
- More comprehensive medical kit

Maps and navigation
Finding the right map
Botswana has an excellent range of detailed 'Ordnance Survey' type maps available cheaply in Maun and Gaborone. See *Maun*, page 155, for details. However, many were made many years ago, and tracks have changed since. Thus unless you have a lot of time to interpret them, and can afford to carry around lots of maps, they're of limited use.

There are several very good maps designed specifically for visitors, but unfortunately these are very rarely available outside southern Africa. The ones that you're most likely to find in bookshops and map-stores outside Africa are generally fine if you're visiting the towns and simply want to know roughly where the parks are.

Amongst these is the **Botswana Traveller's Map** (by Macmillan Education Ltd, ISBN: 0333492641). This is certainly easy on the eye, with colour photographs, descriptions, mini street plans, and even a list of lodges and hotels, places of interest, a wildlife identification chart and a calendar of festivals.

In a similar vein is the **Globetrotter Travel Map of Botswana** (by New Holland Publishers UK, ISBN: 1853686468). Again this has clear colouring, showing all the tarred roads and parks beautifully, and includes town plans of Francistown, Gaborone and Maun, and even distance and climate charts.

Similarly, the ITMB map of **Botswana** (aka the *International Traveller Map*) includes sections on the history, geography and people of Botswana, plus a small street plan of Gaborone and paragraphs on each of the main national parks.

Lonely Planet's **Zimbabwe, Botswana and Namibia Travel Atlas** (ISBN: 0-86442-274-1) – which has its vague travel information translated into five languages – gives a similarly general overview.

However, I view all the above as useless – or worse – if you actually plan to head anywhere remote in the bush. The locations of their tracks and camps are mostly out of date, and the idea of using them to navigate anywhere off the tar is completely fanciful.

The alternatives, which stand head-and-shoulders above the rest, are the Shell maps and the ContiMap. The first of the these was the ground-breaking **Shell Tourist Guide to Botswana**, which incorporated a short but very informative 60-page booklet on the country – effectively an impressive mini guidebook – and a serious, well-researched, original map. These were produced by Veronica Roodt, an expert on the flora and fauna of the area (see *Further Reading* for her excellent books on the flora).

Originally this was published in 1998, and what really made the difference was that, on the reverse, were smaller, inset maps of all the main parks, complete with a number of GPS waypoints. It was this information which revolutionised independent trips around Botswana, and effectively opened the doors for more travellers into some of the country's less-known areas like the Central Kalahari. (Note that by 2003 a new edition of the main map, considerably enhanced, should be in publication.)

Since then Shell have also published more detailed **Chobe** and **Moremi** maps. These have much more detailed coverage of the game-viewing tracks in the park – utilising satellite images, and including bird and animal checklists. Both are worth having, in addition to the main Botswana map, if you're visiting these parks.

The **ContiMap** (so-called because of its sponsorship from Continental tyres) is the second map that you ought to consider getting. It covers half of the country on each of its sides, with no insets. It's been researched primarily by Mike Main – a very knowledgeable and experienced Botswana traveller (see *Further Reading*) – and has an extensive range of reliable GPS points. These include some of the more offbeat roads outside the parks, and are especially good on areas like the Makgadikgadi Pans and south of Ghanzi.

So if you're going into the bush in Botswana, best to take both the Shell maps, and the ContiMap. Between them you'll have the best information available.

In the UK

Because of the general lack of availability of the Shell and ContiMaps in the UK, Sunvil Africa (see page 98 for contact details) has brought stocks of all three Shell maps and also the ContiMap to the UK. These are available to anyone with a UK postal address – even if you're not travelling with Sunvil Africa to Botswana. Just send a cheque payable to Sunvil Africa and your address to them, and they will send you the maps that you want, normally by return. Currently the costs are:

- £10 for the Shell Guide to Botswana (map and booklet)
- £5 each for the Shell maps to Moremi and Chobe
- £5 for the ContiMap map of Botswana

See their website page www.sunvil.co.uk/africa/botswana/maps for more details of this offer, and please add £2 per order for postage and packing.

GPS systems

If you are heading into one of the more remote parks in your own vehicle, then you really should invest in a hand-held GPS: a Global Positioning System. Under an open, unobstructed sky, these can fix your latitude, longitude and elevation to within about 100m, using 24 American military satellites that constantly pass in the skies overhead. They will work anywhere on the globe.

What to buy

Commercial GPS units now cost from around US$160/£100 in Europe or the USA. As is usual with high-tech equipment, their prices are falling and their features are expanding as time progresses.

I used one of the older, less expensive models, the Garmin GPS 38, for many years. It was invaluable, but ate batteries at a great rate and sometimes took ages to 'fix' my position. More recently I've bought as new model, a Garmin II+, and the difference is startling. It uses far fewer batteries, fixes positions much more quickly, and even works when sitting on the car's dashboard.

Whatever make you buy, you don't need a top-of-the-range machine. Pre-loaded maps are a waste of time in Africa, as none of them have the detail that you need.

What a GPS can do

A GPS should enable you to store 'waypoints' and build a simple electronic picture of an area, as well as working out basic latitude, longitude and elevation. So, for example, you can store the position of your campsite and the nearest road, making it much easier to be reasonably sure of navigating back without simply re-tracing your steps.

It will also enable you to programme in points, using the co-ordinates given throughout this book and by the Shell and ContiMaps, and use these for navigation. See page viii for important comment on datums. Thus you should be able to get an idea of whether or not you're going in the right direction, and how far away your destination is.

What a GPS can't do

A GPS isn't a compass, and when you're standing still, it can't tell you which direction is which. It can only tell you a direction if you're moving.

Secondly, it can give you a distance and a bearing for where you might want to go … but it can't tell you how to get there. You'll still need to find a track. You should NEVER just set out across the bush following a bearing; that's a recipe for disaster.

Thirdly, it can't replace a good navigator. You still need to be able to navigate and think to use a GPS effectively. If you're clueless on navigation then driving around the bush in Botswana will get you into a mess with or without a GPS.

Accessories

Most GPS units use quite a lot of battery power, so bring plenty of spare batteries with you. Also get hold of a cigarette lighter adapter for your GPS when you buy it. This will enable you to power it from the car whilst you're driving, and thus save batteries.

Finally, if you want to use the information in any way when you're back home, or store logs of various trips, then I can recommend Fugawi's moving map software (see www.Fugawi.com) – which I found invaluable whilst compiling this book. This allows you to exchange information between your GPS and computer, and plot points on top of scanned-in maps – or indeed to make your own maps.

Warning

Although a GPS may help you to recognise your minor errors before they are amplified into major problems, note that such a gadget is no substitute for good map work and navigation. They're great fun to use, but shouldn't be relied upon as a sole means of navigation. You MUST always have a back-up plan – and an understanding of where you are – or you will be unable to cope if your GPS fails.

Photography and optics

Outside of Gaborone, optical equipment isn't widely available in Botswana – so bring everything that you will need with you.

Cameras

As a rule, 35mm SLR cameras with interchangeable lenses offer you the greatest flexibility. For general photography, a mid-range zoom lens (eg: 28–70mm) is best – much more useful than the standard (50mm) lens. For wildlife photography you will need at least a 200mm zoom lens, otherwise most animals and birds will look like mere dots on the horizon.

Compact cameras are fine for shots of people and landscapes, but of little use for pictures of wildlife.

Autofocus zoom lenses are a godsend for capturing animals and birds that move in the time that it takes to focus manually, but they need extra care to ensure that they remain dust-free. A few grains of sand or dust in the wrong place will render some such lenses useless.

Binoculars

For a safari holiday, a good pair of binoculars is essential. They will bring you far more enjoyment than a camera, as they make the difference between merely seeing an animal or bird at a distance, and being able to observe its markings, movements and moods closely. Do bring one pair per person; one between two is just not enough.

There are two styles: the small 'pocket' binoculars, perhaps 10–12cm long, which account for most popular modern sales – and have only been in production since the 1980s. These were popularised by the makers of compact and autofocus cameras, and are now often made in the Far East. Then there are the larger, heavier styles, double or triple that size, which have been manufactured for years. Many of the remaining manufacturers of these are in the CIS, Germany or Austria.

The small ones are now mass-produced at around US$160/£100, whilst the larger ones vary widely in cost and quality. If you are buying a pair, then consider getting the larger style. The smaller ones are fine for spotting animals; but are difficult to hold steady, and very tiring to use for extensive periods. You will only realise this when you are out on safari, by which time it is too late.

Around 8 x 30 is an ideal size for field observations, as most people need some form of rest, or tripod, to hold the larger 10 x 50 models steady. Get the best-quality ones you can for your money. The cheapest will be about US$60/£40, but to get a decent level of quality spend at least US$300/£200. You will be able to see the difference when you use them.

Accessories

The bush is very dusty, so bring plenty of lens-cleaning cloths, and a blow-brush. Take great care not to get dust into the back of any camera, as a single grain on the back-plate can be enough to make a long scratch which ruins every frame taken.

Tripods are very useful if you're serious, though they are inconvenient to lug around. A small bean-bag is very useful for resting the camera on the window-sill of a vehicle.

Film

Film is widely available in Botswana, but slightly more expensive than in Europe and the USA. Outside of the main centres, supplies are very limited – and you'll have much less choice than in Europe or the Americas. If you have a specific film that you want to use, bring a large stock with you.

The range of film speeds should be dependent upon the type of photography that most interests you. For most landscape shots, where you will have plenty of light, a slow film (100ASA or less) will give the highest quality of results. For wildlife photography, you will probably need a faster film – 200 or even 400ASA – unless you're using very fast lenses.

Pictures taken around dawn and dusk will have the richest, deepest colours, whilst those taken in the middle of the day, when the sun is high, will seem pale and washed-out by comparison. Beware of the very deep shadows and high contrast which are typical of tropical countries – film just cannot capture the range of colours and shades that our eyes can. If you want to take pictures in full daylight, and capture details in the shadows, then you will need a good camera, and to spend some time learning how to use it fully. By restricting your photography to mornings, evenings and simple shots you will get better pictures and encounter fewer problems.

Especially after exposure, film deteriorates rapidly in the heat. Aim to keep all your film somewhere shady and cool, and away from heat sources like sunlight.

ORGANISING AND BOOKING YOUR TRIP

How you organise your holiday depends on what kind of a trip you're taking. Generally the more expensive the trip, the more organisation it needs.

Organising a budget or backpacking trip

If you're backpacking then usually you're more restricted by money than by time. Many of the side-trips and safaris that you take will be organised at the time, on the ground – and trying to do too much in advance might be counter-productive.

So, read the book, and head off. Start by heading towards Maun or Kasane, keeping your eyes open and talking to people you meet to see what's going on. And enjoy! Much of the joy is the unpredictability of these trips; if you want everything fixed and arranged then backpacking isn't really for you!

Organising a self-drive trip

Describing the roads in Botswana is like describing Dr Jekyll and Mr Hyde. The tarred main routes, and most of the roads in the towns, are beautifully smooth roads with excellent signposts. They're often delightfully free of traffic; a dream to drive on. They're eminently suitable to potter around in a normal 2WD Toyota Corolla or Citi Golf.

However, by contrast the tracks through the national parks and more remote areas can become nightmares. Inexperienced or badly prepared drivers will find deep sand in the dry season, and glutinous mud when it's wet – often compounded by a complete lack of signposts or directions.

If you want to hire a self-drive vehicle for the trip, then you must treat Botswana's two personas very differently. Your biggest decision is your vehicle, as this will make or break your trip.

Hiring a 2WD

If you are sticking to the towns and tar roads then hire a 2WD from one of the normal hire companies – Avis, Budget or Imperial would be the obvious three. Contacting them directly, a small saloon (Group A) for about two weeks will cost you around P220 (US$37/£25) per day, including comprehensive CDW (Collision Damage Waiver; see page 92) insurance cover. This includes a free mileage allowance of 120km per day, but outside that you'll pay an extra P1.21 per kilometre – and if you're travelling around then you'll find the mileage will add up! See *Car hire* in the chapters on Kasane and Maun for the relevant contact details.

Hiring a 4WD

If you want to explore Botswana in your own 4WD, then the obvious solution would appear to be to hire one locally. Again, contacting them directly you'll find a twin-cab 4WD hired for about two weeks will cost you around P450 (US$75/£50) per day, including comprehensive CDW insurance cover. Again, this includes a free mileage allowance of 120km per day, but outside that you'll pay an extra P2.17 per kilometre.

However, think carefully. What you need to drive into the bush in Botswana is a serious, fully equipped vehicle – and what you'd be hiring off-the-peg isn't, in my view, up to the job. You need a vehicle that you can rely on, with long-range tanks, a high-lift jack, a spade and decent tow-rope, extra fuel cans if necessary and all the other bits and pieces that make all the difference. Perhaps most vitally, you need to have confidence that if anything goes wrong, there's a system in place to help you swiftly.

South African 4WDs
One South African company to consider is Britz; it has offices in Australia, New Zealand and Johannesburg (PO Box 4300, Kempton Park 1620, Jo'burg, South Africa; tel: (2711) 396 1860; fax: (2711) 396 1937; email: info@britz.co.za; web: www.britz.co.za). They offer five different types of vehicles, including their 'Nomad' Land Rovers and their 'Safari 4WD' which is basically a twin-cab Toyota Hilux. The Land Rovers cost about R1,225 per day (US$153/£102), the Toyota R1,115 (US$139/£93) per day, including unlimited mileage. These come with stoves, fridges and roof tents.

As with many apparently cheaper car deals, expect there to be various additions – in this case start with R220 per day (US$28/£18) for their full CDW cover, and R500 for their '4WD recovery kit' (tow-ropes, tyre repair, radiator repair, torch, safety triangle, spanners, and screwdrivers).

The main drawbacks are that they don't have an office in Botswana, and the drive from Maun to Jo'burg is well over 1,000km – realistically that's a two- to three-day drive in a Land Rover. This lack of back-up is also reflected in the small print of their hire agreement – which means that you would pay a heavy price for serious accidents (see below).

Backed-up 4WDs
The companies mentioned above simply deal with hiring out vehicles; they don't get involved with helping you plan your trip or give you any advice. A step up from this, in both price and completeness, are a few companies that provide not only a vehicle, but also put their expertise at your disposal. They cost more, but if you're not living in southern Africa then it's probably what you need.

Africa Explorer, Safari Drive and Sunvil Africa are all specialist African operators (see pages 97–9) based in the UK. They're the only overseas companies that I know of who regularly send self-driving clients to Botswana. All can advise you on self-drive trips from personal experience.

Safari Drive and Sunvil Africa use probably the region's best fleet of bush-equipped Land Rovers, and their support team has bases in Maun, Kasane, Victoria Falls and Windhoek. I've used these for all my research trips to Botswana, and they come fully equipped with everything that you'll need for comfortable bush camping, from long-range fuel tanks, roof (or ground) tents and fridges to the washing up bowls, condiments and crockery that really make a trip comfortable.

Probably more important than the kit is that they provide you with a service before you leave, planning your trip based on their detailed local knowledge. Their team in Maun makes the tricky campsite bookings with the National Parks office. Most importantly, they offer first-rate back-up in Botswana – based around a well-connected team on the ground who know all the local operators, and have the contacts and know-how to help you speedily if any problems occur.

Expect these Land Rovers and the service to cost around US$220/£145 per day, including all the equipment and full insurance cover. The only added extras might be an optional satellite phone, for which they charge around £10 per day (plus call charges).

Africa Explorer offers a similarly expert level of first-rate local knowledge – but use much larger, converted six-wheeled vehicles. These cost around US$300/£200 per day, plus US$48/£32 per day for vehicle insurance and CDW. Because of the sheer size of these vehicles, these trips often use a driver/guide, who costs a further US$150/£100 per day.

Checking the fine print
The devil's in the detail, especially if you're looking at any of the cheaper options. You should check any rental agreement very carefully, so that you know your position. Preferably also discuss any questions or queries with someone within the company that is supplying you with the vehicle. A few specific pointers may help:

CDW Insurance
The insurance and the Collision Damage Waiver (CDW) clauses are worth studying particularly closely. These spell out the 'excess' that you will pay in the event of an accident. These CDW excesses vary widely, and often explain the difference between cheap rental deals and better, but more costly, options.

Some hire companies have very high excesses (ie: the amounts that you pay if you have a major accident). An 80% CDW is normal – which means that you will always pay 20% of the cost of any damage. However, look around and you should be able to reduce this to zero – although most hiring companies will still want a deposit, in case you damage or lose any of their vehicle's equipment.

Other fine print
Though accidents are fortunately uncommon, they do happen. Then it's very important to get the situation resolved swiftly and carry on with your trip. Some of the companies have quite onerous terms – so be aware of these before you agree to take the vehicle. For example, Britz state that if you have a single-vehicle accident, then a replacement vehicle can be collected from the closest branch – which is likely to be at least two days' drive away from most of Botswana's parks.

However, you are responsible for the costs of getting there, and also for the costs of returning the damaged vehicle to the original rental station (usually Jo'burg). There's no refund if you can't reach a replacement vehicle – and if you do take a replacement, then a new rental contract and insurance conditions will apply.

Suggested self-drive itineraries
If you're driving yourself outside the national parks, and have lots of time, then you can afford to have total flexibility in your route, and plan very little. However, if you're coming for a shorter time, and want to use any of the campsites in the national parks, then you would be wise to arrange your trip carefully in advance. Note that campsite bookings in the national parks can be quite difficult to get, and are fixed when you have them. Effectively, this commits you to a specific route and schedule.

Perhaps the most obvious and instantly rewarding trip for your first self-drive trip across Botswana would be between Livingstone and Maun. This is best done in the dry season.

Livingstone, Chobe, Moremi and Maun: 11 nights/12 days
- 2n Livingstone – hotel/lodge (or campsite)
- 2n Ihaha Campsite, Chobe
- 2n Savuti Campsite, Chobe
- 2n North Gate Campsite, Moremi

- 2n Xakanaxa or Third Bridge Campsite, Moremi
- 1n Maun – hotel/lodge (or campsite)

This really is the fastest trip that you should consider through this area if you want to have time to enjoy the parks. Allowing more time would be better, and another 3–4 nights camping in the parks (including both Third Bridge and Xakanaxa for a few nights each) would improve it enormously.

Of course it can easily be reversed. Some prefer Livingstone at the start, to relax after the flight. Others prefer to leave it until the end, with the highlight of seeing Victoria Falls (and buying curios) at the end. If you do start at Livingstone, then consider picking up your vehicle on the day that you leave for Ihaha, as this could save you a few days of vehicle hire.

I recommend that you use a hotel or lodge, rather than camp, for your first and last few days – I find that this makes my trips much easier and gives me time to get organised more easily at the start and end.

To visit the hills of the northwest Kalahari, ideally consider a trip based out of Maun:

The Panhandle plus Tsodilo, Aha & Gcwihaba Hills: 14 nights/15 days
- 1n Maun – hotel/lodge (or campsite)
- 2n Drotsky's Cabins, Shakawe
- 3n Tsodilo Hills – camping (spend longer here if possible)
- 3n Nxamaseri Lodge or Guma Lagoon Camp, Panhandle
- 2n Aha Hills – camping
- 2n Gcwihaba Hills – camping
- 1n Maun – campsite or hotel/lodge

If you plan to do this trip during the rains then I'd reduce the time at Drotsky's and Nxamaseri (or Guma) and increase my time in the hills of the Kalahari. I love the Tsodilo Hills – and could spend a lot longer there than three days – but you might not feel the same!

If done in the dry season, August or after, then you might tag on a few days after Maun to visit the Boteti River area, where the game concentrations should then be good. Certainly whenever you go, I'd visit Tsodilo before Aha; it's that little bit more accessible. Do remember to fill up with fuel at Etsha 6 between your time in Tsodilo and the Aha/ Gcwihaba area.

If you're experienced in the African bush, feel a lot more adventurous, and don't mind the idea of spending hours digging yourself out of mud, then consider a trip to Nxai and the northern part of the Central Kalahari Game Reserve. This would probably be at its best between February and May, though going later in that period will make the travelling much easier.

Nxai Pan and the Central Kalahari Game Reserve: 20 nights/21 days
- 1n Maun – hotel/lodge (or campsite)
- 2n South Camp, Nxai Pan
- 2n North Camp, Nxai Pan
- 3n Nata Lodge – lodge (or campsite)
- 1n Leroo-La-Tau – campsite (or lodge)
- 1n Deception Valley, CKGR – campsite at north end, CKD1-6
- 2n Sunday Pan, CKGR – campsite
- 1n Tau Pan, CKGR – campsite
- 1n Phokoje Pan, CKGR – campsite
- 2n Piper Pans, CKGR – campsite

- 2n Deception Valley, CKGR – campsite towards the south side, CKL2 or 3
- 1n Leroo-La-Tau – lodge (or campsite)
- 1n Maun – hotel/lodge (or campsite)

As with any rainy-season trip, or excursion into the Central Kalahari Game Reserve, you should be doing this with a minimum of two vehicles, and safety precautions like taking a satellite phone might be a good idea.

Making bookings

If you're driving a 2WD on the tar, then you can afford to find a campsite in Maun or Kasane when you get there. If you need a room, then you only need to book one in advance during the busy season. For the rest of the year you shouldn't have a problem finding one.

Generally, finding a campsite outside the national parks is not a problem. Even at places like Tsodilo and Gcwihaba Hills, there are currently no regulations. There you can just turn up and camp.

However, campsites within the national parks **must** be booked in advance – or you simply will not be allowed to stay there. See the section on *Organising and booking* in *Chapter 8* for the finer details of this – and do it as early in your trip-planning as possible. Any lodges at which you plan to stay should also be reserved in advance.

Organising a mobile safari

Mobile trips in Botswana range from cheap-and-cheerful budget safaris to absolutely top-class operations running privately guided trips for small family groups. Thus generalising amongst them is difficult.

That said, as a general rule, the more they cost, the further in advance they should be booked. The cheaper ones often survive on last-minute bookings from people who turn up; the more costly private ones can be booked-up years in advance.

Ideally, talk to someone who has been on safari with the mobile operator that you're considering before booking with them. If this isn't possible then don't hesitate to ask a lot of questions before you decide which trip is right for you. You'll be stuck with your guide and group for a week or more, so it's vital to make the right choice.

You'll find most of these companies are based in Maun, with only a few elsewhere – like Kasane. The best often have overseas tour operators who know them well, and will sell their trips at around the same price (or even cheaper) than they do directly.

Organising a fly-in trip

Most tourists who come to Botswana for a few weeks' safari fly between a series of remote safari camps; this is by far the easiest and most popular way to visit the country. Combinations of the Okavango Delta, and the Kwando-Linyanti and Chobe areas are most common, with relatively few people venturing further south or west into the Kalahari.

When to book?

These trips are not cheap, but they are not difficult to arrange for a knowledgeable tour operator who knows Botswana. If you have a favourite camp or operation, or will be running to a tight schedule, then book as far ahead as you can. Eight to ten months in advance is perfect. Bear in mind that most camps are small, and thus easily filled. They organise their logistics with military precision and so finding space at specific camps at short notice, especially in the busier months, can be tricky.

Unless you're lucky, or book very early, expect one or two of your chosen camps to be full. Usually there will be good alternatives available. That said, it's fairly rare for visitors to have a really bad time in any of the upmarket camps in Botswana, as standards are generally high – so don't be put off just because your first choice isn't immediately available.

The exception to this is usually the rainy season – when camps often close for maintenance for a few weeks; those that do stay open, however, are seldom full.

How much?

Fly-in safaris in Botswana are not cheap. Expect to pay an average of around US$375–600/£250–400 per person sharing per night, for a trip starting from Maun between about July and October. This will include light aircraft transfers and all meals, laundry, activities and local drinks.

Depending on the particular trip, April, May, June and November should cost less. Expect something nearer US$340–500/£225–325, again, including internal flights and everything.

Prices in the wet season are generally lower (except the camps in the Kalahari); then a rough cost of US$225–375/£150–250 per person sharing per night should be quite realistic.

If you spend more than two or three nights at each camp you visit, then these rates will drop; if you fly between camps every day or two, only spending one or two nights at each camp (not recommended) then they'll rise.

None of these trips are cheap, so you should expect a good level of service and knowledge from the operator who is arranging it for you. If you don't get it, go elsewhere.

How to book?

It's best to arrange everything at the same time, using a reliable, independent tour operator. Many operators sell trips to Botswana, but few know the country and the camps. Insist on dealing directly with someone who does. If the person you're dealing with hasn't visited most of the places that you're thinking of going to, or many of the camps, then find someone who has.

Botswana's areas, camps and lodges do change, so up-to-date local knowledge is vital in putting together a trip that runs smoothly and suits you. Make sure that whoever you book with is bonded, so your money is protected if they go broke. If you're unsure, pay with a credit card. Never book a trip from someone who hasn't spent time there – you are asking for problems.

Booking directly with the Botswana companies is possible, but piecing together a jigsaw of complex transfers and flights can be tricky. All the operators in Botswana are primarily interested in selling space at their own camps and lodges – regardless of whether these are the best camps for you or not. It's wise to seek out an independent operator.

European, US and other overseas operators usually work on commission for the trips that they sell, which is deducted from the basic cost that the visitor pays. Hence you should end up paying the same whether you book through an overseas operator or with a company in Botswana.

Perhaps because of the UK's historical links, or the high number of British safari-goers, there seems to be more competition amongst UK tour operators than elsewhere. Hence they've a reputation for being generally cheaper than US operators for the same trips – and the best usually work out much cheaper than similar trips booked directly.

Botswana's larger safari groups

Most of the larger groups of camps have offices outside of Botswana who hold their booking sheets and take reservations. These usually work largely with the overseas travel trade, which has special contracts with them. So, paradoxically, booking a fly-in safari through one of these offices below in southern Africa is usually more expensive than arranging it through a specialist tour operator based outside Africa.

Illustrating this clearly, Botswana's largest operator, Okavango Wilderness Safaris (which runs about 19 camps in Botswana), comments on their website that they have deliberately not included any of their contact details on their site. They add that they

> believe that bookings should be done in your home country through a
> specialist travel agent or tour operator. There are a number of superb
> Africa specialist travel agencies and tour operators who love Africa – and
> 'talk, breathe, eat and sleep' the continent. These people have created
> businesses in their home countries specialising in selling quality safaris in
> Africa. We suggest you book your safari through one of these companies.

However, if you want a direct contact, then the booking offices of some of the larger groups are outside Botswana (most started off based in Johannesburg, South Africa, for ease of communications):

CC Africa (including AfroVentures) See page 170 for details; their main booking office is in Johannesburg: PBag X27, Benmore 2010, South Africa; tel: (27) 11 809 4300; fax: (27) 809 4400; email: bookings@ccafrica.com; web: www.ccafrica.com

Desert & Delta See page 171 for details; their main booking office is in Johannesburg: PO Box 130555, Bryanston 20201, South Africa; tel: (27) 11 706 0861/2; fax: (27) 11 706 0863; email: reservations@desertanddelta.com; web: www.desertdelta.com

Orient-Express Safaris See page 174 for details; their main booking office is in Johannesburg: PO Box 786432, Sandton 2146, South Africa; tel: (27) 11 481 6052; fax: (27) 11 481 6065; email: reservations@gametrackers.co.za; web: www.gametrackers.orient-express.com

Ker & Downey See page 172 for details, Trips can be booked through their Maun office, or through their US booking office at 2825 Wilcrest Drive, Suite 600, Houston, Texas 77042-6007; tel: (713) 917 0048; fax: (713) 917 0123; email: info@kerdowney.com; web: www.kerdowney.com

Landela Safaris Landela House, 29 Mazowe St, PO Box 66293 Kopje, Harare, Zimbabwe; tel: (263) 4 734043-6 or 706532 or 708377 or 708388; fax: (263) 4 708119; email: bookings@landela.co.zw; web: www.landela.co.zw. Landela started in 1990 and is based in Zimbabwe. Landela Lodge, near Harare, was its first property but it soon expanded to run a string of camps including Chokomella near Hwange, Gache Cache on Lake Kariba and Sekuti's Drift, near Victoria Falls. As above, their head office is still in Harare – the range of phone numbers given illustrating the problems of getting telephone lines, and getting them working, in that city today! In 1998 they branched out into Botswana, taking on Ranns Camp and Xudum in NG29, which had been hunting camps, and shortly after that Gubanare in NG30. More recently they have taken over Chobe Valley Lodge, in an unusual spot near the Zimbabwean border, outside Kasane. Neither Landela's operations, nor their locations, are top-of-the-range – but then neither are their prices. A typical 7-day/6-night itinerary costs US$2,060/2,860 per person sharing/single from July to October, or US$1,360 per person sharing or single during the rest of the year.

Wilderness Safaris (aka Okavango Wilderness Safaris) See page 174 for details; their main booking office is in Johannesburg: PO Box 5219, Rivonia 2128, Johannesburg, South Africa; tel: (27) 11 807 1800; fax: (27) 11 807 2110; email: enquiry@wilderness.za; web: www.wilderness-safaris.com

Sanctuary Lodges See page 176 for details; their main booking office is in Johannesburg: PO Box 782607, Sandton 2146, Johannesburg, South Africa; tel: (27) 11 781 1497; fax: (27) 11 787 7658; email: southernafrica@sanctuarylodges.com; web: www.sanctuarylodges.com

Note that the above is only a list of the companies with booking offices outside Botswana; see pages 167–77 for the companies in Maun – where most of the rest of Botswana's major safari companies are located.

Which tour operator?

Botswana looks on the surface like an easy country to sell, and you'll find scores of brochures that feature a trip or two there. The vast majority will include only camps from one local operator – perhaps using only Wilderness Safaris, or only Gametrackers' camps, or visiting nothing but Desert & Delta places. This is a really bad sign, as no one operator in Botswana has a monopoly of the best camps.

However, start asking detailed questions about the alternatives and you'll rapidly sort the best from the rest. Don't let anyone convince you that there are only half a dozen decent safari camps in Botswana; that's rubbish. If your operator doesn't know most of the camps in this book – and offer a wide choice to suit you – then find one that does. Booking a fly-in trip with one of the top overseas tour operators will usually cost you the same or less than if you contacted Botswana's camps directly – plus you should have independent advice, full financial protection, and experts to make all the arrangements for you.

Here I must, as the author, admit a personal interest in the tour operating business. I organise and personally run the southern African operations of the UK operator Sunvil Africa (tel: 020 8232 9777; fax: 020 8568 8330; email: africa@sunvil.co.uk; web: www.sunvil.co.uk/africa). We are currently one of the leading tour operators from the UK to Botswana – based on my team's detailed personal knowledge of the country. We organise trips for travellers to Africa from all over the world, especially the UK and America.

Our fly-in trips start at about US$3,375/£2,250 per person for a 12-night/13-day safari, including flights from London, accommodation, meals, drinks, laundry and game activities. Call us for a free, detailed colour brochure, or you can download one directly from our website.

For a fair comparison, I recommend that you contact the best tour operators to Botswana, who include:

UK

Aardvark Safaris RBL House, Ordnance Rd, Tidworth, Hants SP9 7QD; tel: (01980) 849160; fax: (01980) 849161; email: mail@aardvarksafaris.com; web: www.aardvarksafaris.com. Recently founded, small upmarket operator featuring much of Africa including Madagascar, with good knowledge of Botswana.

Abercrombie & Kent Sloane Square House, Holbein Place, London SW1W 8NS; tel: 0845 0700 610; fax: 0845 0700 607; email: info@abercrombiekent.co.uk; web: www.abercrombiekent.co.uk. Long-established, large, posh operator worldwide, with a wide choice of Africa trips. (Note that Botswana's Sanctuary Lodges are owned by A&K's owner.)

Africa Explorer 5 Strand on the Green, Chiswick, London W4 3PQ; tel: 020 8987 8742; email: africa.explorer@easynet.co.uk; web: www.africa-explorer.co.uk. Tiny but knowledgeable company that has unusual, large six-wheeled self-contained vehicles for hire across northern Botswana.

Cazenove & Loyd 9 Imperial Studios, 3–11 Imperial Rd, London SW6 2AG; tel: 020 7384 2332; fax: 020 7384 2399; email: safaris@caz-loyd.com; web: www.caz-loyd.com. Bespoke posh operator with tailor-made trips to East/southern Africa and South America. Good local knowledge and service with a high price tag.

Cox & Kings Gordon House, 10 Greencoat Place, London SW1P 1PH; tel: 020 7873 5000; fax: 020 7630 6038; email: cox.kings@coxandkings.co.uk; web: www.coxandkings.co.uk. Long-established operator famed for its Indian trips. Also features more recent programmes to the Middle and Far East, Latin America and Africa, including fly-in trips to Botswana.

Hartley Safaris The Old Chapel, Chapel Lane, Hackthorn, Lincs LN2 3PN; tel: 01673 861600; fax: 01673 861666; web: www.hartleys-safaris.co.uk. Old-school, established tailor-made specialists to East/southern Africa, and Indian Ocean Islands – with close historical connections to Botswana.

Nomad Africa Travel Smugglers Cottage, Church Rd, Westbourne, Emsworth, Hants PO10 8UA; tel/fax: 01243 373929; email: info@nomadafricantravel.co.uk; web: www.nomadafraicantravel.co.uk. Small operator concentrating mainly on set-departure tours to southern Africa, including camping trips around Botswana.

Okavango Tours and Safaris Marlborough House, 298 Regents Park Rd, London N3 2TJ; tel: 020 8343 3283; fax: 020 8343 3287. Established specialists to East/southern Africa, and Indian Ocean. Not part of the Maun company of the same name, but linked indirectly to Delta Camp and Oddballs.

Rainbow Tours 64 Essex Rd, London N1 8LR; tel: 020 7226 1004; fax: 020 7226 2621; email: info@rainbowtours.co.uk; web: www.rainbowtours.co.uk. Established specialists to southern Africa and Madagascar with a strong ethical streak and a varied Botswana programme.

Safari Consultants Orchard House, Upper Rd, Little Cornard, Suffolk CO10 0NZ; tel: 01787 228494; fax: 01787 228096; web: www.safari-consultants.co.uk. Very 'old school' tailor-made specialists to East/southern Africa and Indian Ocean with a competent Botswana programme.

Safari Drive Wessex House, 127 High St, Hungerford, Berks RG17 0DL; tel: 01488 681611; fax: 01488 685055; email: safari_drive@compuserve.com; web: www.safaridrive.com. Specialist African operator with first-class knowledge of Botswana. They concentrate on self-drive trips using well-equipped Land Rovers.

Steppes Africa The Travel House, 51 Castle St, Cirencester, Glos GL7 1QD; tel: 01285 650011; fax: 01285 885888; email: safari@steppesafrica.co.uk; web: www.artoftravel.co.uk. Originally founded as 'Art of Travel', this posh tailor-made specialist features most of East, central and southern Africa, plus Mauritius and the Seychelles.

Sunvil Africa Upper Square, Old Isleworth, Middx TW7 7BJ; tel: 020 8232 9777; fax: 020 8568 8330; email: africa@sunvil.co.uk; web: www.sunvil.co.uk/africa. This is a team of enthusiastic Africa experts run by Chris McIntyre – this book's author. I like to think they have the best fly-in and self-drive trips to Botswana!

Tim Best Travel 68 Old Brompton Rd, London SW7 3LQ; tel: 020 7591 0300; fax: 020 7591 0301; email: info@timbesttravel.com; web: www.timbesttravel.co.uk. Bespoke operator concentrating on South America, the Indian Ocean and Africa, including upmarket fly-in lodges in Botswana.

Tribes Travel 12 The Business Centre, Earl Soham, Woodbridge, Suffolk IP13 7SA; tel: 01728 685971; fax: 01728 685973; email: bradt@tribes.co.uk; web: www.tribes.co.uk. Not a Botswana specialist, though an interesting selection of trips worldwide, based on fair-trade principles, include some innovative Botswana options.

Worldwide Journeys & Expeditions 27 Vanston Place, London SW6 1AZ; tel: 020 7386 4646; fax: 020 7381 0836; email: enquiry@worldwidejourneys.co.uk; web: www.worldwidejourneys.co.uk. Wide-ranging operator with programmes to Asia, Central and South America and Africa from the Nile to fly-in lodges in Botswana.

Whoever you book through, make sure first that the company has in place a 'bond' to protect your money in case they go bust. The most usual form of this in the UK is the ATOL licence; if a company doesn't have one of these then question them very carefully indeed. All the companies above have good track records, and currently have ATOL bonds for your protection.

Other tour operators who feature Botswana include:

UK

African Odyssey 1 St Margaret's Terrace, Cheltenham GL50 4DT; tel: 01242 224482; fax: 01242 253078; email: tca@africanodyssey.co.uk; web: www.africanodyssey.co.uk

Africa Travel Centre Leigh St, London WC1H 9EW; tel: 020 7387 1211; fax: 020 7383 7512; email: sales@africatravel.co.uk; web: www.africatravel.co.uk

Gane & Marshall 98 Crescent Rd, New Barnet, Herts EN4 9RJ; tel: 020 8441 9592; fax: 020 8441 7376; email: holidays@ganeandmarshall.co.uk; web: www.ganeandmarshall.co.uk

Oasis Safaris PO Box 26905, London SE21 8WE; tel: 020 8766 6405; fax: 020 8670 6105; email: judith@oasis-safari.com; web: www.oasis-safari.com. *In Botswana:* P Bag BO59, Maun; tel: 00 267 686 3011; fax: 00 267 686 3011; email: oasis.safaris@info.bw

Somerville Wood (Drive Africa) The Nightingale Centre, 8 Balham Hill, London SW12 9EA; tel: 020 8675 3974; fax: 020 8675 3913; email: info@somervillewood.com; web: www.driveafrica.com or www.somervillewood.com

Wildlife Worldwide Chameleon House, 162 Selsdon Rd, South Croydon, Surrey CR2 6PJ; tel: 020 8667 9158; fax: 020 8667 1960; email: sales@wildlifeworldwide.com; web: www.wildlifeworldwide.com

World Odyssey Ltd 1a St Martins House, St Martin's Gate, Worcester WR1 2DT; tel: 01905 731373; fax: 01905 726872; email: info@world-odyssey.com; web: www.world-odyssey.com

USA

Adventure Center 1311 63rd St, Suite 200, Emeryville, California 94608; tel: 510 654 1879; fax: 510 654 4200

Adventure Travel Desk (ATD) 308 Commonwealth Rd, Wayland, MA 01778; tel: 800 552 0300 or 508 653 4600; fax: 508 655 5672

David Anderson Safaris 4635 Via Vistosa, Santa Barbara, CA 93110; tel: 800 733 1789 or 805 967 1712; fax: 805 964 8285

Australia

The Classic Safari Company Town Hall House, Level 11/456 Kent St, Sydney NSW 2000; tel: 01 800 351 088 or 02 9264 5710; fax 02 9267 3047

African Wildlife Safaris 1st Floor, 259 Coventry St, South Melbourne, Victoria 3205; tel: 03 9696 2899; fax: 03 9696 4937

Tricks of the trade

If you're looking for a company who knows what they're doing, then look very carefully at their brochure. Start with the text: is it factually correct? If not, that's a really bad sign. Is it free of clichés? If so that's a rare but very positive sign. A more subtle check is to look at their pictures. Notice if they have used pictures which are 'standard', which you've seen in a dozen other brochures, or if they're one-off shots that you don't see anywhere else.

Companies with the best local knowledge have staff who spend a lot of time visiting Africa. They do this because they love it, and not just because it's their work. Most will enjoy taking their own pictures, even if they're sometimes not quite as professional as they might be. Thus in their brochures the pictures will usually be originals, and the company's team will usually be able to tell you where and when most of them were taken.

Companies who don't visit so often will use pictures taken for them by people in Botswana. These same pictures are usually copied to many overseas operators and agents – who then reproduce them in their own brochures and promotional work. That's why you'll often see these same 'standard' pictures in half a dozen totally different brochures. Usually this indicates that the company producing the brochure hasn't visited the place for themselves – and so won't be able to advise you from firsthand experience.

Finally, when discussing trips, don't hesitate to ask the person helping you if they have been to this area/lodge – and if so, when. You'll always get the best advice (and the best chance of problem-free trips) from people who know the places that you're thinking of going to personally. Make sure you insist on this.

Suggested fly-in itineraries

Most fly-in trips to Botswana last between ten days and three weeks, and are often limited more by travellers' available budgets than anything else. The Okavango Delta, Kwando-Linyanti and Chobe areas are the most common destinations, but Deception Valley Lodge, beside the Central Kalahari, and Jack's Camp, in Makgadikgadi, also have their own landing strips and are sometimes added on to the start or end of trips.

Less commonly, it's quite possible to plan a trip that's part mobile or self-drive, followed by a few days of relative luxury at a fly-in camp or two (usually in the Delta).

Concentrating on the fly-in element, the key to an interesting fly-in trip is variation: making sure that the different camps that you visit really are different. For me this means that they're in different environments and have different activities. So mix deep-water camps with shallow-water ones, and forested areas with open ones. That way you'll not only have the greatest variety of scenery, of which there's a lot in the Delta, but also see the widest variety of game.

I also prefer to mix camps run by different companies – one from Wilderness, one from CC Africa and one from Kwando for example. I find that this makes a more interesting trip than staying at camps which are all run by the same company (sometimes in predictably similar styles).

When flying in, the costs of visiting the camps in the parks are very similar to the costs of those in the private concessions. Because of the ability to do night drives, to drive off-road, and (sometimes) to go walking, I generally prefer to use camps in private areas. Hence I've included relatively few of the camps which are inside the parks here.

For most trips, if you work on spending around three nights at each camp that you visit, that's ideal. Four would be lovely, though often visitors haven't got that much time (or money), whereas two nights is OK for some camps, but a fraction too short for most.

Here I'll give you a few ideas for combinations of areas that I think work well together, giving a real variation to trips. These are **not** lists of my all-time favourite camps; I have deliberately chosen not to pick out just my favourites. (Simply because the type of camps that I love – the simpler, smaller ones with their emphasis on guiding and wildlife – may not be so ideal for you.)

Instead, these are trips in which I think the various areas, camps and experiences go well together – and demonstrate what I mean about varying the areas that you stay in and the companies that you use.

Livingstone, Kwando-Linyanti and Okavango Delta: 11 nights/12 days
- 2n Livingstone, a hotel or lodge
- 3n Selinda, NG16 – mostly open, permanently dry areas best for game viewing
- 3n Kwara, NG20 – for deep-water motor-boat trips plus some game viewing in areas of denser vegetation
- 3n Kwetsani, NG25 – for picturesque shallow-water *mokoro* trips, plus some game viewing in open floodplains

Livingstone, Kwando-Linyanti, Okavango and the Pans: 15 nights/16 days
- 2n Livingstone, a hotel or lodge
- 3n Lagoon, NG15 – dry-land game viewing in mostly riverine forest
- 4n Vumbura, NG20 – for some deep-water, some shallow-water mokoro trips, and some game viewing in an open floodplain environment.
- 3n Sandibe, NG31 – for shallow-water trips and game viewing in a more forested environment
- 3n Jack's Camp – something totally different on the great salt pans

Just the Okavango Delta: 11 nights/12 days
- 3n Xakanaxa Camp, Moremi – for dry-land game viewing
- 2n Xugana, NG21 – transfer here from Xakanaxa by boat for deep-water trips
- 3n Nxabega, NG31 – for shallow-water trips and game viewing
- 3n Deception Valley Lodge – something totally different in the Kalahari

After reading this book you'll realise there are so many possibilities that you'd be wise to talk through your wishes with someone who knows the camps and can work out what's best for you.

Health and Safety

There is always great danger in writing about health and safety for the uninitiated visitor. It is all too easy to become paranoid about exotic diseases that you may catch, and all too easy to start distrusting everybody you meet as a potential thief – falling into an unfounded us-and-them attitude toward the people of the country you are visiting.

As a comparison, imagine an equivalent section in a guidebook to a Western country – there would be a list of possible diseases and advice on the risk of theft and mugging. Many Western cities are very dangerous, but with time we learn how to assess the risks, accepting almost subconsciously what we can and cannot do.

It is important to strike the right balance: to avoid being excessively cautious or too relaxed about your health and your safety. With experience, you will find the balance that best fits you and the country you are visiting.

BEFORE YOU GO
Travel insurance
Visitors to Botswana should always take out a comprehensive medical insurance policy to cover them for emergencies, including the cost of evacuation to another country within the region. Such policies come with an emergency number (often on a reverse-charge/call-collect basis). You would be wise to memorise this, or indelibly tattoo it in as many places as possible on your baggage.

Personal effects insurance is also a sensible precaution, but check the policy's fine print before you leave home. Often, in even the best policies, you will find a limit per item, or per claim – which can be well below the cost of replacement. If you need to list your valuables separately, then do so comprehensively. Check that receipts are not required for claims if you do not have them, and that the excess which you have to pay on a claim is reasonable.

Annual travel policies can be excellent value if you travel a lot, and some of the larger credit-card companies offer excellent policies. However, it can often be better to get your valuables named and insured for travel using your home contents insurance. These year-round policies will try harder to settle your claim fairly as they want your business in the long term.

Immunisations
Having a full set of immunisations takes time, normally at least six weeks, although some protection can be had by visiting your doctor as late as a few days before you travel. Ideally, see your doctor or travel clinic (see below) early on to establish an inoculation timetable.

Legal requirements
No immunisations are required by law for entry into Botswana, unless you are coming from an area where **yellow fever** is endemic. In that case, a vaccination

certificate may be required. To be valid the vaccination must be obtained at least ten days before entering the country.

Recommended precautions

Preparations to ensure a healthy trip to Botswana include checking on your immunisation status: it is wise to be up-to-date on **tetanus** (ten-yearly), **polio** (ten-yearly) and **diphtheria** (ten-yearly). Regular travellers are advised to have **hepatitis A** immunisation with Havrix Monodose or Avaxim. The course comprises two injections given about a year apart (total cost about £100) and lasts for ten years.

The newer **typhoid** vaccines (eg: Typhim Vi) last for three years and are about 85% effective. They should be encouraged unless the traveller is leaving within a few days for a trip of a week or less when the vaccine would not be effective in time.

Immunisation against cholera is considered ineffective and is not required for trips to Botswana.

Vaccination against rabies is unnecessary for most visitors, but would be wise for those who travel for extended periods (four weeks or longer), or stay in rural areas. Ideally three injections taken over a four-week period prior to travel are advised. But there is some benefit to be gained from even one injection if time is short.

Hepatitis B vaccination should be considered for longer trips (two months or more) or for those working with children or in situations where contact with blood is likely. Three injections are needed for the best protection and can be given over a four-week period if time is short. Longer schedules give more sustained protection and are therefore preferred if time allows. A BCG vaccination against **tuberculosis** (TB) is also advised for trips of two months or more.

Malaria prophylaxis

Malaria is the most dangerous disease in Africa, and the greatest risk to the traveller. It occurs in most of Botswana (predominantly from November to June), and is most common in the north, so it is essential that you take all possible precautions against it.

Prophylaxis regimes aim to infuse your bloodstream with drugs that inhibit and kill the malaria parasites that are injected into you by a biting mosquito. This is why you must start to take the drugs before you arrive in a malarial area – so that they are established in your bloodstream from day one. Unfortunately, the malaria parasites continually adapt to the drugs used to combat them, so the recommended regimes must also adapt and change in order to remain effective. None is 100% effective, and all require time to kill the parasites – so, unless there is a medical indication for stopping, it is important to complete the course as directed after leaving the area (usually one to four weeks, depending on the regime).

It is vital that you seek current advice on the best anti-malarials to take. If mefloquine (Lariam) is suggested, start this two weeks before departure to check that it suits you; stop it immediately if it seems to cause depression or anxiety, visual or hearing disturbances, severe headaches, fits or changes in heart rhythm. Side effects such as nightmares or dizziness are not medical reasons for stopping unless they are sufficiently debilitating or annoying. Anyone who is pregnant, has been treated for psychiatric problems, is epileptic, has suffered fits in the past, or who has a close blood relative who is epileptic, should avoid mefloquine. The usual alternative is chloroquine (Nivaquine) weekly plus proguanil (Paludrine) daily. The latter is the most likely regime to be offered for Botswana at the time of writing. However, if your trip includes visits to other

African countries where there is a higher prevalence of more resistant falciparum malaria then other prophylactic drugs may be suggested. These include mefloquine (as described above), doxycycline (a daily antibiotic) or Malarone (also taken once daily, but needing to be continued for only one week after leaving the area).

Prophylaxis does not stop you catching malaria, however, although it significantly reduces your chances of fully developing the disease and will lessen its severity. Falciparum (cerebral) malaria is the most common in Africa, and usually fatal if untreated, so it is worth your while trying to avoid it.

It is unwise to travel in malarial parts of Africa, including most of Botswana, whilst pregnant or with young children: the risk of malaria in many areas is considerable and such travellers are likely to succumb rapidly.

Because the strains of malaria, and the drugs used to combat them, change frequently, it is important to get the latest advice before you travel. Normally it is better to obtain this from a specialist travel clinic than from your local doctor, who may not be up-to-date with the latest drugs and developments. For details of relevant clinics, see below.

Travel clinics and health information

A full list of current travel clinic websites worldwide is available on www.istm.org/. For other journey preparation information, consult ftp://ftp.shoreland.com/pub/shorecg.rtf or www.tripprep.com.

UK

British Airways Travel Clinic and Immunisation Service There are now only three BA clinics, all in London: 156 Regent St, W1B 5LB (no appointments); 101 Cheapside, EC1V 6DT (tel: 020 7606 2977); 115 Buckingham Palace Rd, SW1W 9SJ (Victoria Station; tel: 020 7233 6661); see also www.britishairways.com/travelclinics. Also sell a variety of health-related goods.

Fleet Street Travel Clinic 29 Fleet St, London EC4Y 1AA; tel: 020 7353 5678

Hospital for Tropical Diseases Travel Clinic Mortimer Market Centre, 2nd Floor, Capper St (off Tottenham Ct Rd), London WC1E 6AU; tel: 020 7388 9600; web: www.thhtd.org. Offers consultations and advice, and is able to provide all necessary drugs and vaccines for travellers. Runs a healthline (tel: 09061 337733) for country-specific information and health hazards. Also stocks nets, water purification equipment and personal protection meaures.

MASTA (Medical Advisory Service for Travellers Abroad) Keppel St, London WC1 7HT; tel: 09068 224100. This is a premium-line number, charged at 50p per minute.

NHS Travel Website, www.fitfortravel.scot.nhs.uk, provides country-by-country advice on immunisation and malaria, plus details of recent developments, and a list of relevant health organisations.

Nomad Travel Pharmacy and Vaccination Centre 3–4 Wellington Terrace, Turnpike Lane, London N8 0PX; tel: 020 8889 7014; email: sales@nomadtravel.co.uk; web: www.nomadtravel.co.uk. As well as dispensing health advice, Nomad stocks mosquito nets and other anti-bug devices, and an excellent range of adventure travel gear.

Thames Medical 157 Waterloo Rd, London SE1 8US; tel: 020 7902 9000. Competitively priced, one-stop travel health service. All profits go to their affiliated company, InterHealth, which provides health care for overseas workers on Christian projects.

Trailfinders Immunisation Centre 194 Kensington High St, London W8 7RG; tel: 020 7938 3999.

Travelpharm The Travelpharm website, www.travelpharm.com, offers up-to-date guidance on travel-related health and has a range of medications available through their online mini-pharmacy.

Irish Republic

Tropical Medical Bureau Grafton Street Medical Centre, Grafton Buildings, 34 Grafton St, Dublin 2; tel: 1 671 9200. Has a useful website specific to tropical destinations: www.tmb.ie

USA

Centers for Disease Control 1600 Clifton Rd, Atlanta, GA 30333; tel: 877 FYI TRIP; 800 311 3435; web: www.cdc.gov/travel. The central source of travel information in the USA. Each summer they publish the invaluable *Health Information for International Travel*, available from the Division of Quarantine at the above address.

Connaught Laboratories PO Box 187, Swiftwater, PA 18370; tel: 800 822 2463. They will send a free list of specialist tropical-medicine physicians in your state.

IAMAT (International Association for Medical Assistance to Travelers) 736 Center St, Lewiston, NY 14092; tel: 716 754 4883. A non-profit organisation that provides lists of English-speaking doctors abroad.

Canada

IAMAT (International Association for Medical Assistance to Travellers) Suite 1, 1287 St Clair Av W, Toronto, Ontario M6E 1B8; tel: 416 652 0137; web: www.sentex.net/~iamat

TMVC (Travel Doctors Group) Sulphur Springs Rd, Ancaster, Ontario; tel: 905 648 1112; web: www.tmvc.com.au

Australia, New Zealand, Thailand

TMVC Tel: 1300 65 88 44; web: www.tmvc.com.au. 20 clinics in Australia, New Zealand and Thailand, including:

Auckland Canterbury Arcade, 170 Queen Street, Auckland City; tel: 373 3531

Brisbane Dr Deborah Mills, Qantas Domestic Building, 6th floor, 247 Adelaide St, Brisbane, QLD 4000; tel: 7 3221 9066; fax: 7 3321 7076

Melbourne Dr Sonny Lau, 393 Little Bourke St, 2nd floor, Melbourne, VIC 3000; tel: 3 9602 5788; fax: 3 9670 8394

Sydney Dr Mandy Hu, Dymocks Building, 7th Floor, 428 George St, Sydney, NSW2000; tel: 2 221 7133; fax: 2 221 8401

South Africa

SAA-Netcare Travel Clinics PO Box 786692, Sandton 2146; fax: 011 883 6152; web: www.travelclinic.co.za or www.malaria.co.za. Clinics throughout South Africa.

TMVC (Travel Doctor Group) 113 DF Malan Drive, Roosevelt Park, Johannesburg; tel: 011 888 7488; web: www.tmvc.com.au. Consult the website for details of clinics in South Africa.

Switzerland

IAMAT (International Association for Medical Assistance to Travellers) 57 Voirets, 1212 Grand Lancy, Geneva; web: www.sentex.net/~iamat

Medical kit

Pharmacies in the main towns in Botswana generally have very good supplies of medicines, but away from these you will find very little. If you're venturing deep into the wilds, then you should take with you anything that you expect to need. If you are on an organised trip, an overland truck, or staying at hotels, lodges or safari camps, then you will not need much, as these establishments normally have comprehensive emergency kits. In that case, just a small personal medical kit might include:

- antihistamine tablets
- antiseptic
- aspirins or paracetamol
- blister plasters (if you plan any serious walking)
- condoms and contraceptive pills
- insect repellent
- lipsalve (ideally containing a sunscreen)
- malaria prophylaxis
- Micropore tape (for closing small cuts – and invaluable for blisters)
- moisturising cream
- sticking plaster (a roll is more versatile than pre-shaped plasters)
- sunscreen

However, if you are likely to end up in very remote situations, then you should also consider taking the following – and know how to use them:

- burn dressings (burns are a common problem for campers)
- injection swabs, sterile needles and syringes
- lint, sterile bandage and safety pins
- oral rehydration sachets
- Steristrips or butterfly closures
- strong painkiller (eg: codeine phosphate – also useful for bad diarrhoea)
- tweezers (perhaps those on a Swiss army knife)
- water purification equipment (2% tincture of iodine with dropper is ideal)
- several different malaria treatment courses and a broad-spectrum antibiotic – plus a good medical manual (see *Further Reading*, page 521).

If you wear glasses, bring a spare pair. Similarly those who wear contact lenses should bring spare ones, also a pair of glasses in case the dust proves too much for the lenses. If you take regular medication (including contraceptive pills) then bring a large supply with you – much easier than hunting for your usual brand in Botswana. Equally, it's worth having a dental check-up before you go, as you could be several painful days from the nearest dentist.

Hospitals, dentists and pharmacies in Botswana

Should you need one, Botswana's main hospitals are good and will treat you first and ask for money later. However, with comprehensive medical insurance as part of your travel cover, it is probably better go to one of the private clinics. The main ones are in Maun and Francistown, and these are capable of serious surgery and a good quality of care.

If you've a serious problem, then MediRescue (MRI) organise medical evacuations from anywhere, and can be contacted by dialling 911 from a normal 'land line', or as follows:

Maun Tel: 6861831; mobile: 713 04426
Francistown Tel: 203666; mobile: 713 04425
Gaborone Tel: 301610 (this is certainly manned 24 hours per day)

MediRescue do insure individual travellers, but many lodges are members, covering you whilst you are staying there; it may be that your insurers overseas would ultimately pick up the MediRescue bills if their services were needed.

LONG-HAUL FLIGHTS

There is growing evidence, albeit circumstantial, that long-haul air travel increases the risk of developing deep vein thrombosis. This condition is potentially life threatening, but it should be stressed that the danger to the average traveller is slight.

Certain risk factors specific to air travel have been identified. These include immobility, compression of the veins at the back of the knee by the edge of the seat, the decreased air pressure and slightly reduced oxygen in the cabin, and dehydration. Consuming alcohol may exacerbate the situation by increasing fluid loss and encouraging immobility.

In theory everyone is at risk, but those at highest risk are shown below:

- Passengers on journeys of longer than eight hours duration
- People over 40
- People with heart disease
- People with cancer
- People with clotting disorders
- People who have had recent surgery, especially on the legs
- Women on the pill or other oestrogen therapy
- Pregnancy
- People who are very tall (over 6ft/1.8m) or short (under 5ft/1.5m)

A deep vein thrombosis (DVT) is a clot of blood that forms in the leg veins. Symptoms include swelling and pain in the calf or thigh. The skin may feel hot

Pharmacies in the main towns stock a good range of medicine, though often not in familiar brands. Bring with you a repeat prescription for anything you may lose or run out of.

STAYING HEALTHY

Botswana is one of the healthiest countries in sub-Saharan Africa. It has a generally low population density, who are affluent by the region's standards, and a very dry climate, which means there are comparatively few problems likely to affect visitors. The risks are further minimised if you are staying in good hotels, lodges, camps and guest farms, where standards of hygiene are generally at least as good as you will find at home.

The major dangers in Botswana are car accidents (caused by driving too fast, or at night, on gravel roads) and sunburn. Both can be very serious, yet both are within the power of the visitor to avoid.

It's interesting to note that the most frequent medical reason for air evacuations from the Okavango Delta, and surrounds, is the unexpected side-effects of the anti-malarial drug Lariam.

The following is general advice, applicable to travelling anywhere, including Botswana:

Food and storage

Throughout the world, most health problems encountered by travellers are contracted by eating contaminated food or drinking unclean water. If you are staying in safari camps or lodges, or eating in restaurants, then you are unlikely to have problems in Botswana.

However, if you are backpacking and cooking for yourself, or relying on local to touch and becomes discoloured (light blue-red). A DVT is not dangerous in itself, but if a clot breaks down then it may travel to the lungs (pulmonary embolus). Symptoms of a pulmonary embolus (PE) include chest pain, shortness of breath and coughing up small amounts of blood.

Symptoms of a DVT rarely occur during the flight, and typically occur within three days of arrival, although symptoms of a DVT or PE have been reported up to two weeks later.

Anyone who suspects that they have these symptoms should see a doctor immediately as anticoagulation (blood thinning) treatment can be given.

Prevention of DVT
General measures to reduce the risk of thrombosis are shown below. This advice also applies to long train or bus journeys.

- Whilst waiting to board the plane, try to walk around rather than sit.
- During the flight drink plenty of water (at least two small glasses every hour).
- Avoid excessive tea, coffee and alcohol.
- Perform leg-stretching exercises, such as pointing the toes up and down.
- Move around the cabin when practicable.

If you fit into the high-risk category (see above) ask your doctor if it is safe to travel. Additional protective measures such as graded compression stockings, aspirin or low molecular weight heparin can be given. No matter how tall you are, where possible request a seat with extra legroom.

food, then you need to take more care. Tins, packets, and fresh green vegetables (when you can find them) are least likely to cause problems – provided that clean water has been used in preparing the meal. In Botswana's hot climate, keeping meat or animal products unrefrigerated for more than a few hours is asking for trouble.

Water and purification
Tap water in Botswana's major towns and borehole water, which is used in most of the more remote locations, is perfectly safe to drink. However, even the mildest of the local microbes may cause a slightly upset stomach for an overseas visitor. Two-litre bottles of mineral water are available from most supermarkets; these are perfect if you're in a car. Bottled water is also available at most safari camps – though think about the resources used to get it to you, and you might reflect that the local borehole water is likely to be just as good. (It's mineral water too!)

If you need to purify water for yourself in the bush, then first filter out any suspended solids, perhaps by passing the water through a piece of closely woven cloth or something similar. Then bring it to the boil, or sterilise it chemically. Boiling is much more effective, provided that you have the fuel available.

Tablets sold for purification are based on either chlorine, iodine or silver, and are normally adequate. Just follow the manufacturer's instructions carefully. Iodine is the most effective, especially against the resilient amoebic cysts which cause amoebic dysentery and other prolonged forms of diarrhoea.

A cheaper alternative to tablets sold over the counter is to travel with a small bottle of medical-quality tincture of iodine (2% solution) and an eye dropper. Add four drops to one litre of water, shake well, and leave to stand for ten minutes. If the water is very cloudy (even after filtering) or very cold, then either double the iodine dose, or leave to stand for twice as long.

HEAT AND SUN

Heatstroke, heat exhaustion and sunburn are often problems for travellers to Botswana, despite being easy to prevent. To avoid them, you need to remember that your body is under stress and make allowances for it. First, take things gently; you are on holiday, after all. Next, keep your fluid and salt levels high: lots of water and soft drinks, but go easy on the caffeine and alcohol. Thirdly, dress to keep cool with loose-fitting, thin garments – preferably of cotton, linen or silk. Finally, beware of the sun. Hats and long-sleeved shirts are essential. If you must expose your skin to the sun, then use sunblocks and high factor sunscreens (the sun is so strong that you will still get a tan).

This tincture of iodine can also be used as a general external antiseptic, but it will stain things deep brown if spilt – so seal and pack its container exceedingly well.

Avoiding insect bites

The most dangerous biting insects in parts of Botswana are mosquitoes, because they can transmit malaria, yellow fever, dengue fever and a host of other diseases. Research has shown that using a mosquito net over your bed, and covering up exposed skin (by wearing long-sleeved shirts, and tucking trousers into socks) in the evening, are the most effective steps towards preventing bites. Bed-net treatment kits are available from travel clinics; these prevent mosquitoes biting through a net if you roll against it in your sleep, and also make old and holey nets protective. Mosquito coils and chemical insect repellents will help, and sleeping in a stream of moving air, such as under a fan, or in an air-conditioned room, will help to reduce your chances of being bitten.

DEET (diethyltoluamide) is the active ingredient in many repellents, so the greater the percentage of DEET, the stronger the effect. However, DEET is a strong chemical. Just 30% is regarded as an effective, non-toxic concentration. It will dissolve some plastics and synthetic materials, and may irritate sensitive skin. Because of this, many people use concentrated DEET to impregnate materials, rather than applying it to themselves. An alternative to this is to use Bug Guards – wrist and ankle bands containing 100% DEET in capsule form. The capsules break on movement, but the chemical never touches the skin. One pack contains four bands, which when opened, last for two weeks. Mosquito nets, socks, and even cravats can be impregnated and used to deter insects from biting. Eating large quantities of garlic, or cream of tartar, or taking yeast tablets, are said to deter some biting insects, although the evidence is anecdotal – and the garlic may affect your social life.

Dengue fever

This mosquito-borne disease may mimic malaria but there is no prophylactic medication available to deal with it. The mosquitoes that carry this virus bite during the daytime, so it is worth applying repellent if you see any mosquitoes around. Symptoms include strong headaches, rashes and excruciating joint and muscle pains and high fever. Dengue fever only lasts for a week or so and is not usually fatal. Complete rest and paracetamol are the usual treatment. Plenty of fluids also help. Some patients are given an intravenous drip to keep them from dehydrating. It is especially important to protect yourself if you have had dengue fever before. A second infection with a different strain can result in the potentially fatal dengue haemorrhagic fever.

Snakes, spiders and scorpions...

Encounters with aggressive snakes, angry spiders or vindictive scorpions are more common in horror films than in Botswana. Most snakes will flee at the mere vibrations of a human footstep whilst spiders are far more interested in flies than people. You will have to seek out scorpions if you wish to see one. If you are careful about where you place your hands and feet, especially after dark, then there should be no problems. You are less likely to get bitten or stung if you wear stout shoes and long trousers. Simple precautions include not putting on boots without shaking them empty first, and always checking the back of your backpack before putting it on.

Snakes do bite occasionally, and you ought to know the standard first-aid treatment. First, and most importantly, don't panic. Most snakes are harmless and even venomous species will only dispense venom in about half of their bites. If bitten, you are unlikely to have received venom; keeping this fact in mind may help you to stay calm.

Even in the worst of these cases, the victim has hours or days to get help, and not a matter of minutes. He/she should be kept calm, with no exertions to pump venom around the blood system, whilst being taken rapidly to the nearest medical help. The area of the bite should be washed to remove any venom from the skin, and the bitten limb should be immobilised. Paracetamol may be used as a painkiller, but never use aspirin because it may cause internal bleeding.

Most first-aid techniques do more harm than good; cutting into the wound is harmful and tourniquets are dangerous; suction and electrical inactivation devices do not work. The only effective treatment is antivenom. In case of a bite which you fear may be both serious and venomous:

- Try to keep calm. It is likely that no venom has been dispensed.
- Stop movement of the bitten limb by applying a splint.
- If you have a crepe bandage, firmly bind up as much of the bitten limb as you can. Release the bandage for a few minutes every half-hour.
- Keep the bitten limb below heart height to slow the spread of any venom.
- Evacuate the victim to a hospital that has antivenom.
- Never give aspirin. You may offer paracetamol, which is safe.
- Do not apply ice packs.
- Do not apply potassium permanganate.

If the offending snake can be captured without any risk of someone else being bitten, take it to show the doctor. But beware, since even a decapitated head is able to dispense venom in a reflex bite.

When deep in the bush, heading for the nearest large farm or camp may be quicker than going to a town: it may have a supply of antivenom, or facilities to radio for help by plane.

DISEASES AND WHEN TO SEE A DOCTOR
Travellers' diarrhoea

There are almost as many names for this as there are travellers' tales on the subject. Firstly, do resist the temptation to reach for the medical kit as soon as your stomach turns a little fluid. Most cases of travellers' diarrhoea will resolve themselves within 24–48 hours with no treatment at all. To speed up this process of acclimatisation, eat well but simply: avoid fats in favour of starches, and keep your fluid intake high. Bananas and papaya fruit are often claimed to be helpful.

If you urgently need to stop the symptoms, for a long journey for example, then Lomotil, Imodium or another of the commercial anti-diarrhoea preparations will do the trick. They stop the symptoms by paralysing the bowel, but will not cure the problem. They should only be used as a last resort and never if you have bad abdominal cramps with the diarrhoea.

If the diarrhoea persists for more than two days, or the stools contain blood, pus or slime, or it lasts for more than three or four days and/or you have a fever, you must seek medical advice. There are as many possible treatments as there are causes, and a proper diagnosis involves microscopic analysis of a stool sample, so go straight to your nearest hospital. The most important thing, especially in Botswana's climate, is to keep your fluid intake up. If it is not possible to reach medical help quickly then take 500mg of ciprofloxacin repeating the dose six to twelve hours later if you still haven't reached help. If the diarrhoea is greasy and bulky and is accompanied by sulphurous (eggy) burps the likely cause is Giardia. This is best treated with tinidazole (four x 500mg in one dose repeated seven days later if symptoms persist).

The body's absorption of fluids is assisted by adding small amounts of dissolved sugars, salts and minerals to the water. Sachets of oral rehydration salts give the perfect biochemical mix necessary to replace what is pouring out of your bottom but they do not taste so nice. Any dilute mixture of sugar and salt in water will do you good so, if you like Coke or orange squash, drink that with a three-finger pinch of salt added to each glass. The ideal ratio is eight level teaspoons of sugar and one level teaspoon of salt dissolved in one litre of water. Palm syrup or honey make good substitutes for sugar, and including fresh citrus juice will not only improve the taste of these solutions, but also add valuable potassium.

Drink two large glasses after every bowel action, and more if you are thirsty. If you are not eating you need to drink three litres a day plus whatever you are sweating and the equivalent of what's going into the toilet. If you feel like eating, take a bland diet; heavy greasy foods will give you cramps.

If you are likely to be more than a few days from qualified medical help, then come equipped with a good health manual and the selection of antibiotics which it recommends. *Bugs, Bites & Bowels* by Dr Jane Wilson-Howarth (see *Further Reading*, page 523) is excellent for this purpose.

Malaria

You can still catch malaria even if you are taking anti-malarial drugs. Classic symptoms include headaches, chills and sweating, abdominal pains, aching joints and fever – some or all of which may come in waves. It varies tremendously, but often starts like a bad case of flu. If anything like this happens, you should first suspect malaria and seek immediate medical help. A definite diagnosis of malaria is normally only possible by examining a blood sample under the microscope. It is best to get the problem properly diagnosed if possible, so don't treat yourself if you can easily reach a hospital first.

If (and only if) medical help is unavailable, then self-treatment is fairly safe, except for people who are pregnant or under 12 years of age. There are a number of treatments available that can be obtained before you leave. Currently the most likely to be prescribed are quinine and fansidar or Malarone. It is always best to ask a doctor at a travel clinic for the most up-to-date advice. In Botswana you should always be able to get experienced local advice to tell you which will be the most effective.

Quinine is very strong, but often proves to be an effective last defence against malaria. Include it in your medical kit, as occasionally rural clinics will have the expertise to treat you, but not the drugs. Quinine's side effects are disorientating and unpleasant (nausea and a constant buzzing in the ears), so administering this whilst on your own is not advisable.

Sexually transmitted diseases

AIDS is spread in exactly the same way in Africa as it is at home, through body secretions, blood, and blood products. The same goes for the dangerous Hepatitis B. Both can be spread through sex.

Remember that the risks of sexually transmitted disease are high, whether you sleep with fellow travellers or locals. About 40% of HIV infections in British people are acquired abroad. Use condoms or femidoms. If you notice any genital ulcers or discharge, get treatment promptly.

Hepatitis

This is a group of viral diseases that generally start with Coca-Cola-coloured urine and light-coloured stools. It progresses to fevers, weakness, jaundice (yellow skin and eyeballs) and abdominal pains caused by a severe inflammation of the liver. There are several forms, of which the two most common are typical of the rest: hepatitis A (or infectious hepatitis) and hepatitis B (or serum hepatitis).

Hepatitis A, and the newly discovered hepatitis E, are spread by the faecal-oral route, that is by ingesting food or drink contaminated by excrement. They are avoided in the same ways you normally avoid stomach problems: by careful preparation of food and by drinking only clean water. There are now excellent vaccines against hepatitis A (Havrix Monodose or Avaxim) and it is certainly worth getting one of these before you travel. See *Recommended precautions* on page 104.

In contrast, the more serious but rarer hepatitis B is spread in the same way as HIV (by blood or body secretions), and is avoided the same way as one avoids HIV. There is a vaccine which protects against hepatitis B, but three doses are needed over a minimum of four weeks. It is usually only considered necessary for medical workers, people working closely with children or if you intend to travel for eight weeks or longer. There are no cures for hepatitis, but with lots of bed rest and a good low-fat, no-alcohol diet most people recover within six months. If you are unlucky enough to contract hepatitis of any form, use your travel insurance to fly straight home.

Rabies

Rabies is contracted when broken skin comes into contact with saliva from an infected animal. The disease is almost always fatal when fully developed, but fortunately there are excellent post-exposure vaccines. It is possible, albeit expensive, to be immunised against rabies before you travel. You are advised to take this if you intend working with animals or you are travelling for four weeks or more to remote areas.

Rabies is rarely a problem for visitors, but the small risk is further minimised by avoiding small mammals. This is especially true of any animals acting strangely. Both mad dogs in town and friendly jackals in the bush should be given a very wide berth.

If you are bitten, scratched or licked over an open wound, clean and disinfect the wound thoroughly by scrubbing it with soap under running water for five minutes, and then flood it with local spirit or diluted iodine. Then seek medical advice.

At least two post-exposure rabies injections are needed even in immunised people. But for those who are unimmunised even more injections are needed together with rabies immunoglobulin (RIG). RIG is expensive (around US$900 a dose) and is also in very short supply – another good reason for taking pre-exposure vaccine.

You should always seek help immediately, ideally within 24 hours, but since the incubation period for rabies can be very long it is never too late to bother. The later stages of the disease are horrendous – spasms, personality changes and hydrophobia (fear of water). Death from rabies is probably one of the worst ways to go.

Bilharzia or schistosomiasis

Though a low risk in Botswana, bilharzia is an insidious disease, contracted by coming into contact with contaminated water. It is caused by parasitic worms which live part of their lives in freshwater snails, and part of their lives in human bladders or intestines. A common indication of an infection is a localised itchy rash – where the parasites have burrowed through the skin – and later symptoms of a more advanced infection may include passing bloody urine. Bilharzia is readily treated by medication, and only serious if it remains untreated.

The only way to avoid infection completely is to stay away from any bodies of fresh water. Obviously this is restrictive, and would make your trip less enjoyable. More pragmatic advice is to avoid slow-moving or sluggish water, and ask local opinion on the bilharzia risk, as not all water is contaminated. It's generally thought that that the Okavango Delta is not infected with bilharzia.

Generally bilharzia snails do not inhabit fast-flowing water, and hence rivers are free of it. However, dams and standing water, especially in populated areas, are usually heavily contaminated. If you think you have been infected, don't worry about it – just get a test done on your return at least six weeks after your last possible exposure.

Sleeping sickness or trypanosomiasis

This is really a cattle disease, which is rarely caught by people. It is spread by bites from the distinctive tsetse fly – which is slightly larger than a housefly, and has pointed mouthparts designed for sucking blood. The bite is painful. These flies are easily spotted as they bite during the day, and have distinctive wings that cross into a scissor-shape when they are resting. They are not common in Botswana, and a very low proportion of tsetses carry the disease, so a bite is not generally a cause for panic or worry.

Prevention is easier than cure, so avoid being bitten by covering up. Chemical insect repellents are also helpful. Dark colours, especially blue, are favoured by the flies, so avoid wearing these if possible.

Tsetse bites are nasty, so expect them to swell up and turn red – that is a normal allergic reaction to any bite. The vast majority of tsetse bites will do only this. However, if the bite develops into a boil-like swelling after five or more days, and a fever starts two or three weeks later, then seek immediate medical treatment to avert permanent damage to your central nervous system. The name 'sleeping sickness' refers to a daytime drowsiness which is characteristic of the later stages of the disease.

Because this is a rare complaint, most doctors in the West are unfamiliar with it. If you think that you may have been infected, draw their attention to the possibility. Treatment is straightforward, once a correct diagnosis has been made.

RETURNING HOME

Many tropical diseases have a long incubation period, and it is possible to develop symptoms weeks after returning home (this is why it is important to keep taking anti-malaria prophylaxis for the prescribed duration after you leave a malarial zone). If you do get ill after you return home, be certain to tell your doctor where you have been. Alert him/her to any diseases that you may have been exposed to. Several people die from malaria in the UK every year because victims do not seek medical help promptly or their doctors are not familiar with the symptoms, and so are slow to make a correct diagnosis. Milder forms of malaria may take up to a year to reveal themselves, but serious (falciparum) malaria will usually become apparent within four months.

If problems persist, get a check-up at one of the hospitals that specialise in tropical diseases. Note that to visit such a hospital in the UK, you need a letter of referral from your doctor.

For further advice or help in the UK, ask your local doctor to refer you to the Hospital for Tropical Diseases, Mortimer Market Centre, 2nd Floor, Capper St (off Tottenham Ct Rd), London WC1E 6AU; tel: 020 7388 9600; web: www.thhtd.org, or in the US to the Centers for Disease Control at 1600 Clifton Rd, Atlanta, GA 30333; tel: 877 FYI TRIP; 800 311 3435; web: www.cdc.gov/travel.

SAFETY

Botswana is not a dangerous country. If you are travelling on an all-inclusive trip and staying at lodges and hotels, then problems of personal safety are exceedingly rare. There will always be someone on hand to help you. Even if you are travelling on local transport, perhaps on a low budget, you will generally be perfectly safe if you are careful.

Outside of rougher parts of the main cities, crime against visitors, however minor, is rare. Even if you are travelling on local transport on a low budget, you are likely to experience numerous acts of random kindness, but not crime. It is certainly safer for visitors than the UK, USA, or most of Europe.

To get into a difficult situation, you'll usually have to try hard. You need to make yourself an obvious target for thieves, perhaps by walking around at night, with showy valuables, in a less affluent area of the city. Provided you are sensible, you are most unlikely to ever see any crime here.

For women travellers, especially those travelling alone, it is doubly important to learn the local attitudes, and how to behave acceptably. This takes some practice, and a certain confidence. You will often be the centre of attention but, by developing conversational techniques to avert over-enthusiastic male attention, you should be perfectly safe. Making friends of the local women is one way to help avoid such problems.

Theft

Theft is not a problem in Botswana – which is surprising given the poverty levels amongst much of the population. The only real exception to this rule is theft from unattended vehicles, which is becoming less unusual in the larger towns. If you leave a vehicle with anything valuable on view there, then you may return to find a window smashed and items stolen. Aside from this, theft is really very rare.

When staying at safari camps in the bush, you'll often find that there are no locks and keys on the doors and there is a tremendous amount of trust. Regardless of this, leaving cash or valuables lying around or easily accessible is both stupid and very unfair to the camp's staff. Your watch could easily be worth a year's salary to them; make sure you keep such items out of sight and out of the way of temptation.

Should you experience a theft in a camp, report it to the management immediately; but bear in mind that most such reports are solved with the realisation that the property's owner mislaid it themselves!

SAFETY FOR WOMEN TRAVELLERS
Janice Booth

When attention becomes intrusive, it can help if you are wearing a wedding ring and have photos of 'your' husband and children, even if they are someone else's. A good reason to give for not being with them is that you have to travel in connection with your job – biology, zoology, geography, or whatever. (But not journalism – that's risky.)

Pay attention to local etiquette, and to speaking, dressing and moving reasonably decorously. Look at how the local women dress, and try not to expose parts of yourself that they keep covered. Think about body language. In much of southern Africa direct eye-contact with a man will be seen as a 'come-on'; sunglasses are helpful here.

Don't be afraid to explain clearly – but pleasantly rather than as a put-down – that you aren't in the market for whatever distractions are on offer. Remember that you are probably as much of a novelty to the local people as they are to you; and the fact that you are travelling abroad alone gives them the message that you are free and adventurous. But don't imagine that a Lothario lurks under every bush: many approaches stem from genuine friendliness or curiosity, and a brush-off in such cases doesn't do much for the image of travellers in general.

Take sensible precautions against theft and attack – try to cover all the risks before you encounter them – and then relax and enjoy your trip. You'll meet far more kindness than villainy.

How to avoid it

Like anywhere, thieves in the bigger cities here work in groups and choose their targets carefully. These targets will be people who look vulnerable and who have items worth stealing. To avoid being robbed, try not to look too vulnerable or too rich – and certainly not both. Observing a few basic rules, especially during your first few weeks in Botswana's cities, will drastically reduce your chances of becoming a target. After that you should have learnt your own way of assessing the risks, and avoiding thefts. Until then:

- Try not to carry anything of value around with you.
- If you must carry cash, then use a concealed money-belt for your main supply – keeping smaller change separately and to hand.
- Try not to look too foreign. Blend in to the local scene as well as you can. Act like a streetwise expat rather than a tourist, if possible. (Conspicuously carrying a local newspaper may help with this.)
- Rucksacks and large, new bags are bad. If you must carry a bag, choose an old battered one. Around town, a local plastic carrier bag is ideal.
- Move confidently and look as if you know exactly what you are doing, and where you are going. Lost foreigners make the easiest targets.
- Never walk around at night – that is asking for trouble.
- If you have a vehicle then don't leave anything in it, and avoid leaving it parked outside in a city.

Reporting thefts to the police

If you are the victim of a theft then report it to the police – they ought to know. Also try to get a copy of the report, or at least a reference number on an official-looking piece of paper, as this will help you to claim on your insurance policy when you return home. Some insurance companies won't act without it. But remember that reporting anything in a police station can take a long time, and do not expect any speedy arrests for a small case of pickpocketing.

Arrest

To get arrested in Botswana, a foreigner will normally have to try quite hard. There's no paranoia about foreigners, who are now generally seen as welcome tourists who bring money into the economy.

One simple precaution to avoid trouble is to ask for permission to photograph near bridges or military installations. This simple courtesy costs you nothing, and may avoid a problem later.

One excellent way to get arrested in Botswana is to try to smuggle drugs across its borders, or to try to buy them from 'pushers'. Drug offences carry penalties at least as stiff as those you will find at home – and the jails are a lot less pleasant. Botswana's police are not forbidden to use entrapment techniques or 'sting' operations to catch criminals. Buying, selling or using drugs in Botswana is just not worth the risk.

Failing this, arguing with any policeman or army official – and getting angry into the bargain – is a sure way to get arrested. It is essential to control your temper and stay relaxed when dealing with Botswana's officials. Not only will you gain respect, and hence help your cause, but you will also avoid being forced to cool off for a night in the cells.

If you are careless enough to be arrested, you will often be asked only a few questions. If the police are suspicious of you, then how you handle the situation will determine whether you are kept for a matter of hours or for days. Be patient, helpful, good-humoured, and as truthful as possible. Never lose your temper; it will only aggravate the situation. Avoid any hint of arrogance. If things are going badly after half a day or so, then start firmly, but politely, to insist on seeing someone in higher authority. As a last resort you do, at least in theory, have the right to contact your embassy or consulate, though the finer points of your civil liberties may be overlooked by an irate local police chief.

Bribery

Bribery is not at all common in Botswana, and the government takes a very strict anti-corruption stance. Certainly no normal visitor should ever be asked for, or offer, a bribe. It would be just as illegal as offering someone a bribe back home. Forget it.

SAFARI DRIVE

Polly Loxton

IF YOU PLAN TO DRIVE ACROSS AFRICA YOU HAD BETTER BE PREPARED FOR THE BUSH

Safari Drive have 10 years experience of operating self drive safari's in Botswana and offer you the freedom and security to explore the amazing Deserts, Deltas and Game Parks in safety. Discover Moremi game reserve in the Okavango Delta drive to Savuti and on through Chobe National Park to Victoria Falls. Follow the migrating game herds out to the Central Kalahari Game Reserve and the vast Makgadikgadi Pans. Our experience on the ground means that we can tailor your trip to suit your needs and importantly we have a comprehensive network of back up representatives that will ensure you have a safe and rewarding safari.

THE CLASSIC SELF DRIVE EXPEDITION-VICTORIA FALLS TO MAUN

We can offer this classic self drive expedition with regular departure dates including National Parks Bookings. You will cross the game rich areas of Savuti & Chobe National Park. Here there are poor roads and plenty of dust. By night you will be joined by hyena's around your camp fire. Make no mistake, although this is a short journey it is still one of the great driving experiences and if the discomforts get too great you can always schedule in a couple of days at one of the superb lodges along the way. You will have achieved more than most people will have done on their holidays and you will have earned your sundowners ! Please Call us to discuss your plans.

 Self Drive Safaris

 Guided Mobile Safaris

 National Park bookings

 Fully Equipped Land Rovers

Call for a brochure UK 0870 2406305

AiTO
THE ASSOCIATION
OF INDEPENDENT
TOUR OPERATORS

Into the Wilds

DRIVING
Driving around Botswana is exceeding easy if you stick to the network of first-class tarred roads between the towns, but heading into the bush is a completely different proposition, which usually requires a small expedition.

Botswana's bush tracks are maintained only by the passage of vehicles, and aren't for the novice, or the unprepared. However, if you've been to Africa at least once or twice before, perhaps including a driving trip around South Africa or Namibia, then such trips can be a lot of fun provided that you realise that you're embarking on an adventure as much as a holiday.

To explore the more rural areas and remote parks on your own you'll need a fully equipped 4WD vehicle, stocked with food and water for your trip. Depending on where you are going, some form of back-up is often wise. This might be a reliable satellite phone, a radio (and the know-how to use it), someone tracking your schedule – with frequent call-in points so they can look for you if you don't turn up on time, or the security of travelling in convoy with at least one other vehicle.

Having pointed out all the dangers, those who do this kind of trip often get addicted to the space and the freedom; it can be really rewarding and tremendous fun!

Equipment and preparations
Fuel
Petrol and diesel are available in all of the larger towns. However, for travel into the bush you will need long-range fuel tanks, and/or a large stock of filled jerrycans. (Only use metal jerrycans for fuel; plastic containers are highly dangerous.)

It is essential to plan your fuel requirements well in advance, and to carry more than you expect to need. Remember that using the vehicle's 4WD capability, especially in low ratio gears, will significantly increase your fuel consumption. Similarly, the cool comfort of a vehicle's air conditioning will burn your fuel reserves swiftly. In late 2002 the price in Maun for diesel was P2.50 per litre, and for petrol P3.00 per litre. The further you go away from the major centres, the more these prices will increase.

Spares
Botswana's garages generally have a comprehensive stock of vehicle spares – though bush mechanics can effect the most amazing short-term repairs, with remarkably basic tools and raw materials. Spares for the more common makes are easiest to find; most basic Land Rover and Toyota 4WD parts are available. If you are arriving in Botswana with an unusual foreign vehicle, it is best to bring as many spares as you can.

Navigation

See the section on *Maps and navigation* in *Chapter 4* for detailed comments, but there are two good maps designed for visitors widely available – and offices of the Surveyor General in Maun and Gaborone. It's wise to take a GPS, though learn how to use it before you arrive and never switch your brain off and rely on it totally.

Coping with Botswana's roads
Tar roads
Botswana's tar roads are excellent, and a programme of tarring is gradually extending the network of roads. Note that the police do operate radar traps, especially near the towns. A speeding ticket will usually mean that you have to turn up at the nearest police station within 48 hours and pay a fine – which can be particularly inconvenient if you were just rushing out of the town and into the bush. Botswana's police are efficient; it'd be foolhardy not to obey such a summons.

Gravel roads
There aren't many good gravel roads in Botswana – most are either good tar, or basic bush tracks. However, the few gravel sections can be very deceiving. Even when they appear smooth, flat and fast (which is not often), they still do not give vehicles much traction. You will frequently put the car into small skids, but with practice at slower speeds you will learn how to deal with them. Gravel is a less forgiving surface on which to drive than tar. The rules and techniques for driving well are the same for both, but on tar you can get away with sloppy braking and cornering which would prove fatal on gravel.

Further, in Botswana you must always be prepared for the unexpected: an animal wandering on to the road, a pot-hole, a sand-trap, or an unexpected corner. So it is verging on insane to drive over about 80km/h on any of Botswana's gravel roads. Other basic driving hints include:

- **Slowing down** If in any doubt about what lies ahead, always slow down. Road surfaces can vary enormously, so keep a constant lookout for pot-holes, ruts or patches of soft sand that could put you into an unexpected slide.
- **Passing vehicles** When passing other vehicles travelling in the opposite direction, always slow down to minimise both the damage that stone chippings will do to your windscreen, and the danger in driving through the other vehicle's dust cloud.
- **Using your gears** In normal driving, a lower gear will give you more control over the car – so keep out of high 'cruising' gears. Rather stick with third or fourth, and accept that your revs will be slightly higher than they normally are.
- **Cornering and braking** Under ideal conditions, the brakes should only be applied when the car is travelling in a straight line. Braking whilst negotiating a corner is dangerous, so it is vital to slow down before you reach corners. Equally, it is better to slow down gradually, using a combination of gears and brakes, than to use the brakes alone. You are less likely to skid.

Driving at night
Outside of the main towns, **never** drive at night unless it's a matter of life and death. Both wild and domestic animals frequently spend the night by the side of busy roads, and will actually sleep on quieter ones. Tar roads are especially bad as the surface absorbs all the sun's heat by day, and then radiates it at night – making

it a warm bed for passing animals. A high-speed collision with any animal, even a small one like a goat, will not only kill the animal, but will cause very severe damage to a vehicle, with potentially fatal consequences. And in the bush the danger of startling elephants is very real.

Driving techniques for 4WD

You want a high-clearance 4WD to get anywhere in Botswana that's away from the main arteries. However, no vehicle can make up for an inexperienced driver – so ensure that you are confident of your vehicle's capabilities before you venture into the wilds with it. You really need extensive practice, with an expert on hand to advise you, before you'll have the first idea how to handle such a vehicle in difficult terrain. Finally, driving in convoy is an essential precaution in the more remote areas, in case one vehicle gets stuck or breaks down. Some of the more relevant ideas and techniques include:

When and how to use 4WD

Firstly, read your vehicle's manual. All makes are different, and have their quirks, and so you must read the manual before you set off. Note especially that you should **never** drive in 4WD mode with fixed (or 'locked') differentials on tar roads. Doing this will cause permanent damage to the mechanics of your vehicle.

When you do encounter traction difficulties, stop when you can and put the vehicle into 4WD – usually setting the second 'small' gear-stick to '4WD high' is fine for most situations.

Now get out of the vehicle and check if the front two hubs of your vehicle have, at their centre, knobs to turn. (This is the case with many Toyotas, though some newer vehicles have 'automatic' hubs.) If so, you'll need to turn these to the 'lock' position – a fact forgotten by many novices that causes untold trouble for them, and endless smug amusement for old Africa hands.

When you're past the problem, using 2WD will lower your fuel consumption, though many will use 4WD the whole time that they're in the bush. Remember to re-set your hubs to 'free' before you drive on tar again.

Driving in sand

If you're in 4WD and are really struggling in deep sand, then stop on the next fairly solid area that you come to. Lower your tyre pressure until there is a small bulge in the tyre walls (having first made sure that you have the means to re-inflate them when you reach solid roads again). A lower pressure will help your traction greatly, but increase the wear on your tyres. Pump them up again before you drive on a hard surface at speed, or the tyres will be badly damaged.

Where there are clear, deep-rutted tracks in the sand, don't fight the steering wheel – just relax and let your vehicle steer itself. Driving in the cool of the morning is easier than later in the day because when sand is cool it compacts better and is firmer. (When hot, the pockets of air between the sand grains expand and the sand becomes looser.)

If you do get stuck, despite these precautions, don't panic. Don't just rev the engine and spin the wheels – you'll only dig deeper. Instead stop. Relax and assess the situation. Now dig shallow ramps in front of all the wheels, reinforcing them with pieces of wood, vegetation, stones, material or anything else which will give the wheels better traction. Lighten the vehicle load (passengers out) and push. Don't let the engine revs die as you engage your lowest ratio gear. That probably means using '4WD low' rather than '4WD high.' Use the clutch to ensure that the wheels don't spin wildly and dig themselves further into the sand.

Sometimes rocking the vehicle backwards and forwards will build up momentum to break you free. This can be done by the driver intermittently applying the clutch and/or by getting helpers who can push and pull the vehicle at the same frequency. Once the vehicle is moving, the golden rule of sand driving is to keep up the momentum: if you pause, you will sink and stop.

Grass seeds in the Kalahari

After the rains, the Kalahari's tracks are often knee-high in seeding grass. As your vehicle drives through, stems and especially seeds can build up in front of and inside the radiator, and get trapped in crevices underneath the chassis. This is a major problem in the less-visited areas of the Kalahari. It's at its worst March to June, after the rains, and in the areas of the Great Salt Pans, the CKGR, and the tracks around Tsodilo and the Aha Hills. The main tracks around Chobe and Moremi are used relatively frequently, and so have less dangerous.

This causes a real danger of overheating (see below) and fire. Firstly, the build-up of seeds and stems over the radiator insulates it. Thus, if you aren't watching your gauges, the engine's temperature can rocket. It will swiftly seize up and catch fire. Secondly, the grass build-up itself, if allowed to become too big, can catch fire due to its contact with the hot exhaust system underneath the vehicle.

There are several strategies to minimise these dangers; best apply them all. Firstly, before you set out, buy a few square metres of the tightly woven window-meshing gauze material used in the windows of safari tents. Fix one large panel of this on the vehicle's bull-bars, well in front of the radiator grill. Fix another much closer to it, but still outside of the engine compartment. Hopefully this will reduce vastly the number of seeds reaching your radiator.

Secondly, watch your vehicle's engine-temperature gauge like a hawk when you're travelling through areas of grassland.

Thirdly, stop every 10km or so (yes, really, that often) and check the radiator and the undercarriage for pockets of stems and seeds. Pay special attention to the hot areas of the exhaust pipe; you should not allow a build-up of flammable material there. Use a stick or piece of wire to clean these seeds and stems out before you set off.

Overheating

If the engine has overheated then the only option is to stop and turn it off. Stop, have a drink under a tree, and let it cool. Don't open the radiator cap to refill it until the radiator is no longer hot to the touch. Even then, keep the engine running and the water circulating while you refill the radiator – otherwise you run the risk of cracking the hot metal by suddenly cooling it. Flicking droplets of water on to the outside of a running engine will cool it.

When driving away, switch off any air-con (as it puts more strain on the engine). Open your windows and turn your heater and fan full on. This may not seem pleasant in the midday heat – but it'll help to cool the engine. Keep watching that engine-temperature gauge.

Driving in mud

This is difficult, though the theory is the same as for sand: keep going and don't stop. That said, even the most experienced drivers get stuck. A few areas of Botswana (the road from Rakops to the CKGR's main gate is legendary in this respect) have very fine soil known as 'black-cotton' soil, which becomes impassable when wet.

Push-starting when stuck
If you are unlucky enough to need to push-start your vehicle whilst it is stuck in sand or mud, there is a remedy. Raise up the drive wheels, and take off one of the tyres. You should have a hi-lift jack with you, and know how to use it.

Then wrap a length of rope around the hub and treat it like a spinning top: one person (or more) pulls the rope to make the axle spin, whilst the driver lifts the clutch, turns the ignition on, and engages a low gear to turn the engine over. This is a very difficult equivalent of a push start, but it may be your only option.

Rocky terrain
There's not much of this in northern Botswana – but you will find some in the southeast. Have your tyre pressure higher than normal and move very slowly. If necessary, passengers should get out and guide you along the track to avoid scraping the undercarriage on the ground. This can be a very slow business.

Crossing rivers and stretches of water
The first thing to do is to stop and check the river. You must assess its depth, the type of riverbed and its current flow; and determine the best route to drive across it. This is best done by wading across the river (though in an area frequented by hippos and crocodiles this is not advisable). Beware of water that's too deep for your vehicle, or the very real possibility of being swept away by a fast current and a slippery riverbed.

If everything is OK then select your lowest gear ratio and drive through the water at a slow but steady rate. Your vehicle's air intake must be above the level of the water to avoid your engine filling with water. It's not worth taking risks, so remember that a flooded river may subside to safer levels by the next morning.

Driving near big game
The only animals which are likely to pose a threat to vehicles are elephants – and generally only elephants which are familiar with vehicles. So, treat them with the greatest respect and don't 'push' them by trying to move ever closer. Letting them approach you is much safer, and they will feel far less threatened and more relaxed. Then, if the animals are calm, you can safely turn the engine off, sit quietly, and watch as they pass you by.

If you are unlucky, or foolish, enough to unexpectedly drive into the middle of a herd, then don't panic. Keep your movements, and those of the vehicle, slow and measured. Back off steadily. Don't be panicked, or overly intimidated, by a mock charge – this is just their way of frightening you away. For detailed comments, see the boxes on *Driving near elephants* in *Chapter 10*.

BUSH CAMPING
Many 'boy scout' type manuals have been written on survival in the bush, usually by military veterans. If you are stranded with a convenient multi-purpose knife, then these useful tomes will describe how you can build a shelter from branches, catch passing animals for food, and signal to the inevitable rescue planes which are combing the globe looking for you – whilst avoiding the attentions of hostile forces.

In Africa, bush camping is usually less about survival than comfort. You're likely to have much more than the knife: probably at least a bulging backpack, if not a loaded 4WD. Thus the challenge is not to camp and survive, it is to camp and be as comfortable as possible. With practice you'll learn how, but a few hints might be useful for the less experienced:

Where you can camp

In national parks, there are strictly designated campsites that you should use, as directed by the local game scouts. These must be pre-booked or you are unlikely to be allowed entrance.

Outside of the parks, you should ask the local landowner, or village head, if they are happy for you to camp on their property. If you explain patiently and politely what you want, then you are unlikely to meet anything but hospitality in most areas of rural Botswana.

Choosing a site

Only experience will teach you how to choose a good site for pitching a tent, but a few general points, applicable to any wild areas of Africa, may help you avoid problems:

- Avoid camping on what looks like a path through the bush, however indistinct. It may be a well-used game trail.
- Beware of camping in dry riverbeds: dangerous flash floods can arrive with little or no warning.
- In marshy areas camp on higher ground to avoid cold, damp mists in the morning and evening.
- Camp a reasonable distance from water: near enough to walk to it, but far enough to avoid animals which arrive to drink.
- If a lightning storm is likely, make sure that your tent is not the highest thing around.
- Finally, choose a site which is as flat as possible – you will find sleeping much easier.

Camp fires

Camp fires can create a great atmosphere and warm you on a cold evening, but they can also be damaging to the environment and leave unsightly piles of ash and blackened stones. Deforestation is a major concern in much of the developing world, including parts of Botswana, so if you do light a fire then use wood as the locals do: sparingly. If you have a vehicle, consider buying firewood in advance from people who sell it at the roadside – or collect it in areas where there's more wood around.

If you collect it yourself, then take only dead wood, nothing living. Never just pick up a log: always roll it over first, checking carefully for snakes or scorpions.

Experienced campers build small, highly efficient fires by using a few large stones to absorb, contain and reflect the heat, and gradually feeding just a few thick logs into the centre to burn. Cooking pots can be balanced on the stones, or the point where the logs meet and burn. Others will use a small trench, lined with rocks, to similar effect. Either technique takes practice, but is worth perfecting. Whichever you do, bury the ashes, take any rubbish with you when you leave, and make the site look as if you had never been there. (See *Further Reading* for details of Christina Dodwell's excellent *Travel, Survival and Bush Cookery*.)

Don't expect an unattended fire to frighten away wild animals – that works in Hollywood, but not in Africa. A campfire may help your feelings of insecurity, but lion and hyena will disregard it with stupefying nonchalance.

Finally, do be hospitable to any locals who appear – despite your efforts to seek permission for your camp, you may effectively be staying in their back gardens.

Using a tent

Whether to use a tent or to sleep in the open is a personal choice, dependent upon where you are. In an area where there are predators around (specifically lion and hyena) then you must use a tent – and sleep completely inside it, as a protruding leg may seem like a tasty take-away to a hungry hyena. This is especially true at organised campsites, where the local animals are so used to humans that they have lost much of their inherent fear of man.

Outside game areas, you will usually be fine sleeping in the open, or preferably under a mosquito net, with just the stars of the African sky above you. On the practical side, sleeping under a tree will reduce the morning dew that settles on your sleeping bag. If your vehicle has a large, flat roof then sleeping on this will provide you with peace of mind, and a star-filled outlook. Hiring a vehicle with a built-in roof-tent is a perfect solution for many, though it can take time to pack when wanting to rush off on an early-morning game drive.

Camping equipment for backpackers

If you are taking an organised safari, you will not need any camping equipment at all. If you're hiring a 4WD, then it's best to hire one here with all the kit. However, for those backpacking, there is very little lightweight kit available in Botswana. Most of the equipment is designed to be sturdy, long-lasting and carried around in vehicles. So buy any lightweight kit before you leave home, as it will save you a lot of time and trouble once you arrive. Here are a few comments on various essentials:

Tent During the rains a good tent is essential in order to stay dry. Even during the dry season one is useful if there are lion or hyena around. If backpacking, invest in a high-quality, lightweight tent. Mosquito-netting ventilation panels, allowing a good flow of air, are essential. (Just a corner of mesh at the top of the tent is *not* enough for comfort.) Don't go for a tent that's small; it may feel cosy at home, but will be hot and claustrophobic in the heat.

I have been using the same 'Spacepacker' tent (manufactured by Robert Saunders Ltd, Five Oaks Lane, Chigwell, Essex IG7 4QP, UK) for almost ten years. It's a dome tent with fine mesh doors on either side which allow a through draught, making all the difference when temperatures are high. The alternative to a good tent is a mosquito net, which is fine unless it is raining or you are in a big game area.

Sleeping bag A lightweight, 'three-season' sleeping bag is ideal for Botswana most of the time, though probably not quite warm enough for the very coldest nights in the Kalahari. Down is preferable to synthetic fillings for most of the year, as it packs smaller, is lighter, and feels more luxurious to sleep in. That said, when down gets wet it loses its efficiency, so bring a good synthetic bag if you are likely to encounter much rain.

Ground mat A ground mat of some sort is essential. It keeps you warm and comfortable, and it protects the tent's ground sheet from rough or stony ground. (Do put it underneath the tent!) Closed cell foam mats are widely available outside Botswana, so buy one before you arrive. The better mats cost double or treble the cheaper ones, but are stronger, thicker and warmer – well worth the investment.

Therm-a-Rests, the combination air-mattress and foam mat, are strong, durable and also worth the investment – but take a puncture repair kit with you just in case of problems.

Do watch carefully where you site your tent, and try to make camp before dark. My trusty Therm-a-Rests deflated badly one night in the Kalahari, sleeping near the Mamuno-Buitepos border. Breaking camp the next morning, I lifted the mat to find a large scorpion in its burrow immediately beneath the mat.

Sheet sleeping bag Thin pure-cotton sheet sleeping bags (eg: YHA design) are small, light and very useful. They are easily washed and so are normally used like a sheet, inside a sleeping bag, to keep it clean. They can, of course, be used on their own when your main sleeping bag is too hot.

Stove 'Trangia'-type stoves, which burn methylated spirits, are simple to use, light, and cheap to run. They come complete with a set of light aluminium pans and a very useful all-purpose handle. Often you'll be able to cook on a fire with the pans, but it's nice to have the option of making a brew in a few minutes while you set up camp. Methylated spirits are cheap and widely available, even in the rural areas, but bring a tough (purpose made) fuel container with you as the bottles in which it is sold will soon crack and spill all over your belongings.

Petrol- and kerosene-burning stoves are undoubtedly efficient on fuel and powerful – but invariably temperamental and messy. Gas stoves use pressurised canisters, which are not allowed on aircraft.

Torch (flashlight) This should be on every visitor's packing list – whether you're staying in upmarket camps or backpacking. Find one that's small and tough, and preferably water- and dust-proof. Head-mounted torches leave your hands free (useful when cooking or mending the car) but some people find them bulky and uncomfortable to wear. The strong and super-bright torches (such as Maglites) are excellent. Bring several spare bulbs with you; they are expensive in Maun.

Those with vehicles will find a strong spotlight, powered by the car's battery (perhaps through the socket for the cigarette lighter), is invaluable for impromptu lighting.

Water containers For everyday use, a small two-litre water bottle is invaluable, however you are travelling. If you're thinking of camping, you should also consider a strong, collapsible water-bag – perhaps 5-10 litres in size – which will reduce the number of trips that you need to make from your camp to the water source. (Ten litres of water weighs 10kg.)

Drivers will want to be self-sufficient for water when venturing into the bush, and so carry several large, sturdy containers of water.

See *Planning and preparations*, pages 85–6, for a memory-jogging list of other useful items to pack.

Animal dangers for campers

Camping in Africa is really very safe, though you may not think so from reading this. If you have a major problem whilst camping, it will probably be because you did something stupid, or because you forgot to take a few simple precautions. Here are a few general basics, applicable to anywhere in Africa and not just Botswana.

Large animals

Big game will not bother you if you are in a tent – provided that you do not attract its attention, or panic it. Elephants will gently tip-toe through your guy ropes whilst you sleep, without even nudging your tent. However, if you wake up and make a noise, startling them, they are far more likely to panic and step on your tent. Similarly, scavengers will quietly wander round, smelling your evening meal in the air, without any intention of harming you.

- Remember to use the toilet before going to bed, and avoid getting up in the night if possible.
- Scrupulously clean everything used for food that might smell good to scavengers. Put these utensils in a vehicle if possible, suspend them from a tree, or pack them away in a rucksack inside the tent.
- Do not keep any smelly foodstuffs, like meat or citrus fruit, in your tent. Their smells may attract unwanted attention.
- Do not leave anything outside that could be picked up – like bags, pots, pans, etc. Hyenas, amongst others, will take anything. (They have been known to crunch a camera's lens, and eat it.)
- If you are likely to wake in the night, then leave the tent's zips a few centimetres open at the top, enabling you to take a quiet peek outside.

Creepy crawlies

As you set up camp, clear stones or logs out of your way with great caution: they make great hiding places for snakes and scorpions. Long moist grass is ideal territory for snakes, and dry, dusty, rocky places are classic sites for scorpions.

If you are sleeping in the open, it is not unknown to wake and find a snake lying next to you in the morning. Don't panic, your warmth has just attracted it to you. You will not be bitten if you gently edge away without making any sudden movements. (This is one good argument for using at least a mosquito net!)

Before you put on your shoes, shake them out. Similarly, check the back of your backpack before you slip it on. Just a curious spider, in either, could inflict a painful bite.

WALKING IN THE BUSH

Walking in the African bush is a totally different sensation to driving through it. You may start off a little unready – perhaps even sleepy for an early morning walk – but swiftly your mind will wake. There are no noises except the wildlife, and you. So every noise that isn't caused by you must be an animal; or a bird; or an insect. Every smell and every rustle has a story to tell, if you can understand it.

With time, patience, and a good guide you can learn to smell the presence of elephants, and hear when a predator alarms impala. You can use ox-peckers to lead you to buffalo, or vultures to help you locate a kill. Tracks will record the passage of animals in the sand, telling what passed by, how long ago, and in which direction.

Eventually your gaze becomes alert to the slightest movement; your ears aware of every sound. This is safari at its best: a live, sharp, spine-tingling experience that's hard to beat and very addictive. Be careful: watching game from a vehicle will never be the same again for you.

Walking trails and safaris

One of Africa's biggest attractions is its walking safaris – which attract people back year after year. However, because of the danger involved, the calibre and experience of guides when walking is far more important than when driving. Anyone with a little experience can drive you around fairly safely in a large metal vehicle, but when you're faced with a charging elephant you need to be standing behind a real expert to have much chance of survival.

Walking guides

I am not confident that Botswana has progressed well towards the implementation of rigorous minimum standards for guides who lead walking safaris. Zimbabwe has for many years led the field, with a really tough training course leading to the exalted status of 'pro guide' – in many ways this is Africa's 'gold standard' of guiding.

Zambia has adopted an alternative, but also very safe, system requiring an armed scout and an experienced walking guide to accompany every walk. The scout controls the problem animal, the guide controls the group of people. It's rarely necessary to even fire a warning shot, and injuries are exceedingly rare,

However, Botswana, like South Africa, has minimum standards which I think are too low for walking guides. Thus, in my opinion, the term 'qualified guide' in Botswana doesn't mean that I should necessarily feel safe going walking with them. Thus it's mostly up to the individual safari operation to make sure its guides are experienced.

One or two operations (the Selinda Reserve, and the Footsteps operation near Shinde, both spring to mind) really concentrate on walking safaris. These take their walking very seriously, employ top walking guides, and put safety at the top of their agenda. I'm confident to go walking with such operations.

The rest are a mixed bag; some use good guides, others I've been out with I felt were actually dangerous. One good rule of thumb is the presence of a rifle. If your guide *doesn't* carry one, then I certainly wouldn't walk with them to anywhere where we were likely to see any dangerous game. (The converse doesn't apply though; carrying a rifle does not make an inexperienced guide safe.)

Often you'll see adverting for camps in the Okavango with comments along the lines that your guide is '... a man of the swamps, completely at one with his environment.' This is doubtless true, but doesn't imply that this same guide automatically has the foresight, command and communication skills to look after frightened foreigners whilst avoiding game in a dangerous situation. Knowing how to save himself is different from controlling a small group, and saving *them* from a nasty end.

Thus my advice is that if you want to do much walking in Botswana, go to one of the places that really concentrate on walking safaris. The rest of the time, stick to canoes, boats and driving. Only go walking with guides who are armed, know how to use their guns, and you have discussed the issues with and satisfied yourself that they have sufficient experience for you to be safe.

Etiquette for walking safaris

If you plan to walk then avoid wearing any bright, unnatural colours, especially white. Dark, muted shades are best; greens, browns and khaki are ideal. Dark blue tends to attract tsetse flies, so best to avoid that if you can. Hats are essential, as is sun-block. Even a short walk will last for two hours, and there's no vehicle to which you can retreat if you get too hot.

Binoculars should be immediately accessible – one pair per person – ideally in dust-proof cases strapped to your belt. Cameras too, if you decide to bring any, as they are of little use buried at the bottom of a camera bag. Heavy tripods or long lenses are a nightmare to lug around, so leave them behind if you can (and accept, philosophically, that you may miss shots).

Walkers see the most when walking in silent single file. This doesn't mean that you can't stop to whisper a question to the guide; just that idle chatter will reduce your powers of observation, and make you even more visible to the animals (who will usually flee when they sense you).

With regard to safety, your guide will always brief you in detail before you set off. S/he will outline possible dangers, and what to do in the unlikely event of them materialising. Listen carefully: this is vital.

Face-to-face animal encounters

Whether you are on an organised walking safari, on your own hike, or just walking from the car to your tent in the bush, it is not unlikely that you will come across some of Africa's larger animals at close quarters. Invariably, the danger is much less than you imagine, and a few basic guidelines will enable you to cope effectively with most situations.

Firstly, don't panic. Console yourself with the fact that animals are not normally interested in people. You are not their normal food, or their predator. If you do not annoy or threaten them, you will be left alone. No matter how frightened you are, you'll probably run slower than whatever is worrying you. So don't try to run; think your way out of the tight spot.

If you are walking to look for animals, then remember that this is their environment, not yours. Animals have been designed for the bush, and their senses are far better attuned to it than yours. To be on less unequal terms, remain alert and try to spot them from a distance. This gives you the option of approaching carefully, or staying well clear.

Animals, like people, are all different. So whilst we can generalise here and say how the 'average' animal will behave, the one that's glaring at you over a small bush may have had a really bad day, and be feeling much grumpier than normal.

Finally, the advice of a good guide is far more valuable than the simplistic comments noted here – though a few general comments on some potentially dangerous situations might be of use:

Buffalo

This is probably the continent's most dangerous animal to hikers, but there is a difference between the old males, often encountered on their own or in small groups, and large breeding herds.

The former are easily surprised. If they hear or smell something amiss, they will charge without provocation – motivated by a fear that something is sneaking up on them. Buffalo have an excellent sense of smell, but their eyesight is not so good. Avoid a charge by quickly climbing the nearest tree, or by side-stepping at the last minute. If adopting the latter, more risky, technique then stand motionless until the last possible moment, as the buffalo may well miss you anyhow.

The large breeding herds can be treated in a totally different manner. If you approach them in the open, they will often flee. Sometimes though, in areas often used for walking safaris, they will stand and watch, moving aside to allow you to pass through the middle of the herd.

Neither encounter is for the faint-hearted or inexperienced, so steer clear of these dangerous animals wherever possible.

Black rhino

There are no black rhino left in Botswana, though there are plans to reintroduce them to the heart of Moremi. If you are both exceptionally lucky enough to find one, and then unlucky enough to be charged by it, use the same tactics as you would for a buffalo: tree climbing or dodging at the last second. (It is amazing how even the least athletic walker will swiftly scale the nearest tree when faced with a charging rhino.)

Elephant

Normally elephants are only a problem if you disturb a mother with a calf, or approach a male in musth (state of arousal), so keep well away from these. Lone bulls can usually be approached quite closely when feeding. If you get too close to any elephant it will scare you off with a 'mock charge': head up, perhaps shaking – ears flapping – and trumpeting. Lots of sound and fury. This is intended to be frightening, and it is. But it is just a warning and no cause for panic. You should just freeze to assess the elephant's intentions. When it's stopped making a fuss, back off slowly. Don't run. There is no easy way to avoid the charge of an angry elephant, so take a hint from this warning and move away.

When an elephant really means business, it will put its ears back, lower its head, and charge directly at you. This is known as a 'full charge' and they don't stop. It is one of the most dangerous situations in Africa. Then you probably have to run – but elephants are much faster than you, so think while you run. Aim to get behind an anthill, up a tall tree, or out of the way somehow.

See also the boxes on *Driving near elephants*, in *Chapter 10*, for more details of this behaviour with reference to vehicles.

Lion

Tracking lion can be one of the most exhilarating parts of a walking safari. Sadly, they will normally flee before you even get close to them. However, it can be a problem if you come across a large pride unexpectedly. Lion are well camouflaged; it is easy to find yourself next to one before you realise it. If you had been listening, you would probably have heard a warning growl about 20m ago. Now it is too late.

The best plan is to stop, and back off slowly, but confidently. If you are in a small group, then stick together. *Never* run from a big cat. First, they are always faster than you are. Secondly, running will just convince them that you are frightened prey, and worth chasing. As a last resort, if they seem too inquisitive and follow as you back off, then stop. Call their bluff. Pretend that you are not afraid and make loud, deep, confident noises: shout at them, bang something. But do not run.

John Coppinger, one of Africa's most experienced guides, adds that every single compromising experience that he has had with lion on foot has been either with a female with cubs, or with a mating pair, when the males can get very aggressive. You have been warned.

Leopard

Leopard are very seldom seen, and would normally flee from the most timid of lone hikers. However, if injured, or surprised, then they are very powerful, dangerous cats. Conventional wisdom is scarce, but never stare straight into the leopard's eyes, or it will regard this as a threat display. (The same is said, by some, to be true with lion.) Better to look away slightly, at a nearby bush, or even at its tail. Then back off slowly, facing the direction of the cat and showing as little terror as you can. As with lion – loud, deep, confident noises are a last line of defence. Never run from a leopard.

Hippo

Hippo are fabled to account for more deaths in Africa than any other animal (ignoring the mosquito). Having been attacked and capsized by a hippo whilst in a mokoro, I finds this very easy to believe. Visitors are most likely to encounter hippo in the water, when in a boat or mokoro. (See the other section on *hippo*, below.)

However, as hippos spend half their time grazing on land, they will sometimes be encountered out of the water. Away from the water, out of their comforting lagoons, hippos are even more dangerous. If they see you, they will flee towards the water – so the golden rule is never to get between a hippo and its escape route to deep water. Given that a hippo will outrun you on land, standing motionless is probably your best line of defence.

Snakes

These are really not the great danger that people imagine. Most flee when they feel the vibrations of footsteps; only a few will stay still. The puff adder is probably responsible for more cases of snake bite than any other venomous snake in Boswana because, when approached, it will simply puff itself up and hiss as a warning, rather than slither away. This makes it essential to always watch where you place your feet when walking in the bush.

Similarly, there are a couple of arboreal (tree dwelling) species which may be taken by surprise if you carelessly grab vegetation as you walk. So don't.

Spitting cobras are also encountered occasionally, which will aim for your eyes and spit with accuracy. If one of these rears up in front of you, then turn away and avert your eyes. If the spittle reaches your eyes, you must wash them out *immediately* and thoroughly with whatever liquid comes to hand: water, milk or even urine if that's the only liquid that can be quickly produced.

BOATING

Trips on motor boats and mekoro are very much an integral part of a safari trip to northern Botswana – they're both very different, and both a lot of fun. Almost no operators use the paddle-yourself Canadian-style canoes that are popular elsewhere in Africa (Linyanti Tented Camp is perhaps the exception which proves this rule).

By mokoro

In *Lake Ngami* (see *Further Reading*), the explorer Andersson describes a mokoro used by him on Lake Ngami in the early 1850s:

> The canoe in which I embarked (and they are all somewhat similarly
> constructed) was but a miserable craft. It consisted of the trunk of a tree,
> about 20 feet long, pointed at both ends, and hollowed out by means of
> fire and a small hatchet. The natives are not at all particular as to the shape
> of the canoe. The after part of some that have come to my notice, would
> form an angle of near forty-five degrees with their stem! Nevertheless,
> they were propelled through the water by the Bayeye (my boatmen were
> of that nation) with considerable speed and skill.
>
> The 'appointments' of the canoe, consist of a paddle and a pole, ten to
> twelve feet in length. The paddle-man sits well in the stern, and attends
> mostly to the steering; whilst his comrade, posted at the head of the
> canoe, sends her along, by means of the pole, with great force and skill.
>
> The natives, however, rarely venture any distance from the shore in
> their frail Skiffs.

Local inhabitants of the Okavango still use mekoro like this, but for visitors it's more usual to have simply a single poler standing up at the stern and propelling the craft with a long pole. It's very like the punting done at some universities in Britain; a gentle form of locomotion best suited to shallow waters.

Only certain trees are suitable for making mekoro; they must usually be old, straight and strong. Jackalberries (*Diospyros mespiliformis*), sausage trees (*Kigelia africana*) and kiats (*Pterocarpus angolensis*) are favourites, whilst occasionally African mangosteens (*Garcenia livingstonei*) and rain trees (*Lonchocarpus capassa*) are also used. The wood used to make the poles to propel them is less crucial, though these are often made from silver-leaf terminalia trees (*Terminalia sericea*).

The last few decades have seen a mushrooming demand for mekoro, which began to deplete the older specimens of these species in some areas. Fortunately, fibreglass mekoro, that look very similar, are now being made. Most safari camps use these now. This is worth encouraging, so if you are given a wooden craft, check with your camp that when it's no longer useable, they intend to replace it with a fiberglass version. The Delta can't afford to lose more of its oldest trees!

By motor boat

Motor boats are used on the rivers, and in the deeper channels and lagoons of the Okavango. They can be a lot of fun although, used carelessly, their noise and (especially) their wake can do a lot of damage; so be sensitive to the dangers and don't encourage your guide to speed. You'll often see much more by going slowly anyhow.

Interesting variations on this theme include the stately, almost silent electric boat that's been introduced at Sandibe and the small, double-decker boat used at Kwara which affords views out over the top of the papyrus beds.

The main dangers

It's tempting to become concerned about dangerous animals in Africa, but it's foolish to get paranoid. With common sense and a little knowledge, boat and mokoro trips are very safe – certainly no more dangerous than going on a game drive or walking safari. And if these worry you, maybe you shouldn't be heading out into the bush at all!

On motor boat trips, you'd have to try hard indeed to get into difficulties. Mekoro are also safe, though these craft are smaller and more vulnerable, so you should be aware of the dangers posed to you by hippos and crocodiles:

Hippo

Hippopotami are strictly vegetarians, and will usually only attack a mokoro if they feel threatened. Your poler is usually standing up, so he has the best vantage-point for spotting potential dangers ahead. It's helpful if you're either silent, or making so much noise that every animal in the bush can hear you approaching!

During the day, hippopotami will usually congregate in deeper water. The odd ones in shallow water, where they feel less secure, will head for the deeper places as soon as they are aware of a nearby mokoro. Avoiding hippos then becomes a fairly simple case of steering around the deeper areas, and sticking to the shallows. This is where the poler's experience, knowing every waterway in the area, becomes valuable.

Really large and deep channels and waterways are seldom a problem, as the hippos can avoid you provided that you make enough noise so that they know you are around. Shallow floodplains are also fairly safe, as you'll see the hippo in advance, and avoid them.

Problems usually occur when mekoro use relatively small and narrow 'hippo trails' where hippos can submerge but can't get away. Then there's a danger of accidentally approaching too close. A mokoro inadvertently surprises a hippo, and/or cuts it off from its path of retreat to deeper water. Then the hippo feels cornered and threatened, and may even attack. Some camps now send mekoro out in small groups, with an armed guide in the lead mokoro – though others maintain that this isn't necessary.

An angry hippo could overturn a mokoro without a second thought, biting at it and/or its occupants. Once in this situation, there are no easy remedies. So avoid it in the first place.

Above Exploring the heart of the Delta
near Xigera by mokoro (CM)

Right Reed frog (CM)

Below Dragonfly on waterlily leaf (RM)

Above Thatched lodges, like Kwetsani, lie hidden among the trees (CM)

Right Dining at Xakanaxa Campsite, under the stars (CM)

Below Luxury rooms give a new slant on tented accommodation (CM)

Crocodiles

Crocodiles may have sharp teeth and look prehistoric, but are of little danger to you ... unless you are in the water. Then the more you struggle and the more waves you create, the more you will attract their unwelcome attentions. They sometimes become an issue when a mokoro is overturned by a hippo; you must get out of the water as soon as possible, either into another canoe or on to the bank.

When a crocodile attacks an animal, it will try to disable it, normally by getting a firm, biting grip, submerging, and performing a long, fast barrel-roll. This will disorient the prey, drown it, and probably twist off the limb that has been bitten. In this dire situation, your best line of defence is probably to stab the reptile in its eyes with anything sharp that you have. Alternatively, if you can lift up its tongue and let the water into its lungs whilst it is underwater, then a crocodile will start to drown and will release its prey.

I have had reliable reports of a man surviving an attack in the Zambezi recently when a crocodile grabbed his arm and started to spin backwards into deep water. The man wrapped his legs around the crocodile, to spin with it and avoid having his arm twisted off. As this happened, he tried to poke his thumb into its eyes, but with no effect. Finally he put his free arm into the crocodile's mouth, and opened up the beast's throat. This worked. The crocodile left him and he survived with only a damaged arm. Understandably, anecdotes about tried and tested methods of escape are rare.

MINIMUM IMPACT

When you visit, drive through, or camp in an area and have 'minimum impact' upon it, this means that that area is left in the same condition as – or better than – when you entered it. Whilst most visitors view minimum impact as being desirable, spend time to consider the ways in which we contribute to environmental degradation, and how these can be avoided. Most of these points apply to any areas of rural Africa.

Driving

Use your vehicle responsibly. If there's a road, or a track, then don't go off it – the environment will suffer. Driving off-road can leave a multitude of tracks that detract from the 'wilderness' feeling for subsequent visitors. Equally, don't speed through towns or villages: remember the danger to local children, and the amount of dust you'll cause.

Hygiene

Use toilets if they are provided, even if they are basic long-drop loos with questionable cleanliness. If there are no toilets, then human excrement should always be buried well away from paths, or groundwater, and any tissue used should be burnt and then buried with it.

If you use rivers or lakes to wash, then soap yourself near the bank, using a pan for scooping water from the river – making sure that no soap finds its way back into the water. Use biodegradable soap. Sand makes an excellent pan-scrub, even if you have no water to spare.

Rubbish

Biodegradable rubbish can be burnt and buried with the campfire ashes. Don't leave it lying around: it will look very unsightly and spoil the place for those who come after you.

Bring along some plastic bags with which to remove the rest of your rubbish, and dump it at the next large town. Items that will not burn, like tin cans, are best cleaned and squashed for easy carrying. If there are bins, then use them, but also consider when they will next be emptied, and whether local animals will rummage through them first. For this reason, it's probably best not to use the bins at most National Parks' campsites; better to carry out all your own rubbish to the nearest town.

Host communities

Whilst the rules for reducing impact on the environment have been understood and followed by responsible travellers for years, the effects of tourism on local people have only recently been considered. Many tourists believe it is their right, for example, to take intrusive photos of local people – and even become angry if the local people object. They refer to higher prices being charged to tourists as a rip-off, without considering the hand-to-mouth existence of those selling these products or services. They deplore child beggars, then hand out sweets or pens to local children with outstretched hands.

Our behaviour towards 'the locals' needs to be considered in terms of their culture, with the knowledge that we are the uninvited visitors. We visit to enjoy ourselves, but this should not be at the expense of local people. Read *Cultural guidelines*, pages 40–2, and aim to leave the local communities better off after your visit.

Local payments

If you spend time with any of Botswana's more rural communities, perhaps camping in the bush or getting involved with one of the community-run projects, then take great care with any payments that you make.

Firstly, note that most people like to spend their earnings on what they choose. This means that trying to pay for services with beads, food, old clothes or anything else instead of money isn't appreciated. Ask yourself how you'd like to be paid, and you'll understand this point.

Secondly, find out the normal cost of what you are buying. For example, most community campsites will have a standard price for a pitch. Find this price out before you sleep there. It is then important that you pay about that amount for the pitch – not less, and not too much more.

As most people realise, if you try to pay less you'll get into trouble – as you would at home. However, many do not realise that if they generously pay a lot *more*, this can be equally damaging. Local rates of pay in rural areas can be very low, and a careless visitor can easily pay disproportionately large sums. Where this happens, local jobs can lose their value overnight. (Imagine working hard to become a game scout, only to learn that a tourist has given your friend the equivalent of your whole month's wages for just a few hours guiding. What incentive is there for you to carry on with your regular job?)

If you want to give more – for good service, a super guide, or just because you want to help – then either buy some locally made produce (at the going rate), or donate money to one of the organisations working to improve the lot of Botswana's most disadvantaged. See pages 42–3 for ideas, but also consider asking around locally and you'll often find projects that need your support.

Many lodges and camps will assist with community projects, and be able to suggest a good use for donations. Increasingly they're becoming more involved in the welfare of the local communities near them, which is something in which you can encourage them.

Botswana Today

Tourists come to Botswana in relatively small numbers. Many pass through the airports and towns briefly, spending the vast majority of their time in the bush – trips for which they have already paid. They will probably find most of this chapter useless, except for the *Cost of living* comments towards the start. However, if you're planning to venture into any of the towns, or are wondering how life really ticks in Botswana, then read on ...

COST OF LIVING

Like anywhere else, the cost of visiting Botswana varies with the style in which you travel, and the places where you spend your time. However, as covered under *Planning and preparations*, in *Chapter 5*, Botswana's costs are usually relatively high.

If you plan to get the most from what Botswana has to offer, you will probably need an average of US$450/£300 per day. This is high by African standards, but what you get for it is high quality, and includes everything: your activities, food, drinks, accommodation, and even the odd charter flight between camps. You'll then be staying at a handful of small safari camps, each of which is situated in a different, but often stunning, corner of a pristine wilderness. This is one of the world's top wildlife experiences – the kind of magical trip at which Botswana excels.

At the other end of the spectrum, if you travel through Botswana on local buses, camping and staying near the towns, then the country isn't too expensive. A budget of US$60–90/£40–60 per day for food, accommodation and transport would suffice. However, most backpackers who undertake such trips won't be able to afford to visit any of the camps or more remote wildlife locations – which I think means that it's scarcely worth visiting Botswana.

Between these two extremes, at around US$120–180/£80–120, you'll find some relatively basic budget-style safaris run out of Maun which will give you a real experience of the national parks and the Okavango Delta. They won't match what you'd find in the private concession areas, or further into the Delta, but they will make you glad you came to Botswana and probably harden your determination to return when you've a lot more money!

One of these mid-range options, though only one for those with substantial African experience, is to hire a fully equipped 4WD. Such a choice enables you to camp, buy food, and drive yourself around. This requires driving ability and planning, and isn't something to undertake lightly. But then four people in a decent vehicle (a slight squash, unless you're very well organised) would cost around US$120/£80 per person per day, including the vehicle, camping kit, equipment, park fees and food. Such trips are really much better for two people per vehicle, but in that case the daily costs would work out nearer US$180/£120 each.

Currency and inflation

Botswana's unit of currency is the pula – a word that also means 'rain' in Setswana, and hence tells you something about the importance of water in this country. Theoretically each pula is divided into 100 thebe, although one thebe isn't worth that much, so most prices are rounded to the nearest ten thebe. The pula's exchange rate is free-floating on the world market, so there is no black market for the currency.

As a result, US dollars, euros and UK pounds sterling are easily changed – and most of the more international businesses in the tourism sector set their prices in US dollars.

On October 22 2002 the **exchange rates** were £1=P9.50; US$1=P6.33; €1=P6. I've used roughly about this level (US$1=P6) as a convenient round-number value for converting prices in this book between pula and US dollars – when helpful for ease of reference. I've assumed an average £/US$ rate of 1:1.5.

Inflation has generally been relatively modest in Botswana. Between 1993 and 1998 the rate of inflation averaged 10.2%, but since then it has subsided and in June 2002 the rate (based on a Consumer Price Index) was 5.9%. More up-to-date statistics can be found on the Bank of Botswana's website: http://bankofbotswana.bw/.

The rough trends (showing the lowest/highest interbank rates during each period) have been as follows:

| | Rate of exchange/pula | | |
Date	To US$	To British £	To SA rand
1998 Jan–Jun	3.64/4.49	6.22/7.35	0.72/0.78
1998 Jul–Dec	4.21/4.93	7.18/8.21	0.79/0.79
1999 Jan–Jun	4.30/4.75	7.27/7.68	0.74/0.78
1999 Jul–Dec	4.50/4.73	7.26/7.70	0.74/0.78
2000 Jan–Jun	4.55/5.33	7.50/8.04	0.74/0.76
2000 Jul–Dec	5.04/5.56	7.34/8.04	0.68/0.76
2001 Jan–Jun	5.13/5.80	7.31/8.28	0.69/0.71
2001 Jul–Dec	5.61/6.31	7.96/9.20	0.47/0.71
2002 Jan–Jun	5.93/6.94	8.66/10.07	0.51/0.63

As can be seen from the table of historical exchange rates, Botswana's currency has gradually declined in value against the US dollar and the British pound over the last four years. By comparison, it broadly held its value against the South African rand in the late 1990s, and then strengthened against it in the early years of the new century (as the rand declined quite abruptly).

Given the strength of Botswana's economy, this pattern seems likely to continue in the foreseeable future: with the pula strengthening relative to the rand, but gently declining relative to the world's major currencies.

Banks

If you need to change foreign currency, receive bank drafts, or do any other relatively complex financial transactions, then the banks here are perfectly capable and efficient. Their opening times vary, but expect them to start around 08.00 and finish by 14.30 during the week. Some may close a few hours earlier than this on Wednesday. On Saturday, only the bigger banks open, typically 08.00–11.00.

Cashpoint (ATM) machines can be found in most large towns, including Maun and Kasane – and they work with foreign credit cards.

GETTING AROUND
By air
There are two ways to fly within Botswana: on scheduled airlines or using small charter flights. The national carrier, Air Botswana, operates the scheduled network. This is limited in scope, but generally very efficient and reliable.

Air Botswana links Maun directly with Kasane, Gaborone, Windhoek and Johannesburg. In addition, Kasane is linked to Victoria Falls and there is a new service to Johannesburg, which also stops in the Tuli Block area, in the east of the country.

The small charter flights operate out of the hub of Maun, with Kasane as a secondary focus, and ferry travellers around all the camps of northern Botswana like a fleet of taxis. They use 6- to 12-seater planes which criss-cross the region between a plethora of small bush runways. Flights are usually organised by the operator who arranges your camps as an integral part of your trip; there's no other way to reach most camps, and you'll never need to worry about arranging these flights for yourself.

Several people usually end up sharing these small flights, and the flight companies schedule the timings a few days beforehand. Expect them to take under about an hour, during which you may stop at one or two other airstrips before reaching your destination. See my comments in From the air (in *The Natural Environment* chapter, page 52 to help you understand a little about the patterns that you'll be able to see in the landscapes below.

By rail
There is a railway that links South Africa with Lobatse, Gaborone, Palapye, Francistown and Bulawayo (in Zimbabwe) – but that's the only railway in the country. It's reliable, but rarely used by travellers coming to northern Botswana.

By bus
Botswana has a variety of local buses which link the main towns together along the tarred roads. They're cheap, frequent and a good way to meet local people, although they can also be crowded, uncomfortable and noisy. In short, they are similar to any other local buses in Africa, and travel on them has both its joys and its frustrations.

There are two different kinds: the smaller minibuses, often VW combies, and the longer, larger, 'normal' buses. Both will serve the same destinations, but the smaller ones go faster and stop less. Their larger relatives will take longer to fill up before they leave the bus station (because few buses ever leave before they are full), and then go slower and stop at more places. For the smaller, faster buses there is a premium of about 20% on top of the price.

Driving
Driving in Botswana is on the left, based on the UK's model. The standard of driving is reasonably good. Most roads in the towns, and the major arteries connecting these, are tarred and are usually in superb condition. Note that Botswana's police have radar equipment, and do actively set up radar traps, especially just outside the towns.

Away from the main arteries, and throughout virtually all of the wild areas covered by this guide, the roads are simply tracks through the bush made by whatever vehicles have passed that way. They are almost never maintained, and usually require at least a high-clearance vehicle – although often a 4WD is essential. During the wet season some of these tracks can be less forgiving, and become virtually impassable.

Travelling on these bush tracks at any time of year is slow and time consuming – but very much one of the joys of an adventurous trip to Botswana.

Hitchhiking

Hitchhiking around Botswana is a practical way to get around the main towns – but very, very difficult as a means of getting around the national parks.

Hitching on the tarred roads has the great advantage of allowing you to talk one-to-one with a whole variety of people, from local business-people and expats, to truck-drivers and farmers. Sometimes you will be crammed in the back of a windy pick-up with a dozen people and as many animals. Occasionally you will be comfortably seated in the back of a plush Mercedes, satisfying the driver's curiosity as to why you were standing beside a road in Botswana at all. It can be a great way to get to know the country, through the eyes of its people, though it is not for the lazy or those pressed for time.

Waiting times can be long, even on the main routes, and getting a good lift can take many hours. If you are in a hurry then combining hitchhiking with taking the odd bus can be a quicker and more pragmatic way to travel.

The essentials for successful hitching in Botswana include a relatively neat set of clothes, without which you will be ignored by some of the more comfortable lifts available. A good ear for listening and a relaxed line in conversation are also assets, which spring naturally from taking an interest in the lives of the people that you meet. Finally, you must always carry a few litres of water and some food with you, both for standing beside the road and for lifts where you can't stop to eat.

Dangers of drunk driving

Unfortunately, drinking and driving is relatively common in Botswana. It is more frequent in the afternoon/evening, and towards the end of the month when people are paid. Accepting a lift with someone who is drunk, or drinking and (simultaneously) driving, is foolish. Occasionally your driver will start drinking on the way, in which case you would be wise to start working out how to disembark politely.

An excuse for an exit, which I used on one occasion, was to claim that some close family member was killed whilst being driven by someone who had been drinking. Thus I had a real problem with the whole idea, and had even promised a surviving relative that I would never do the same... hence my overriding need to leave at the next reasonable town/village/stop. This gave me an opportunity to encourage the driver not to drink any more, and when that failed (which it did), it provided an excuse for me to disembark swiftly. Putting the blame on my own psychological problems avoided blaming the driver too much, which might have caused a difficult scene.

Safety of hitchhiking

Not withstanding the occasional drunk driver, Botswana is generally a safe place to hitchhike for a robust male traveller, or a couple travelling together. Dressing neatly and conservatively is a very good idea. Although safer than in the UK, and considerably safer than in the USA, hitchhiking still cannot be recommended for single women, or even two women travelling together. This is not because of any known horror stories, but because women from outside of Botswana, and especially white women hitching, would evoke great curiosity amongst the local people, who might view their hitching as asking for trouble, whilst some would associate them with the 'promiscuous' behaviour of white women seen on imported films and TV programmes. The risk seems too high. Stick to buses.

ACCOMMODATION
Hotels
Hotels in Botswana's towns tend to be aimed at visiting business-people, in which case they're functional but boring, regardless of price level. That said, they're also generally clean and rarely unpleasant. Expect costs to be around P180–240 (US$30–40/£20–27) per person sharing per night.

Guesthouses
In the last few years a few guesthouses have sprung up in Botswana's larger towns, including Maun, but these are still very limited, and often so suburban that they're only practical if you've got your own vehicle.

Lodges and camps
Botswana's lodges and camps vary from palatial residences crafted by top designers to simple spots with a few small tents, and a table in the shade. Given that range, the vast majority have rooms which are at least as comfortable as a good hotel room.

When the words 'tented camp' are mentioned, forget your memories of cramped scout tents and think instead of canvas designer chic. En-suite flushing toilets, running hot and cold water and battery-powered lights are standard, while many have electric fans. A few (eg: Gametracker's camps) have air conditioning. Only the odd old stalwarts, like the delightfully simple walking trails camps at Selinda, still use traditional long-drop loos.

Note that expensive does not always mean luxurious. Some of the top camps are very simply constructed. As a quid pro quo, looking for basic, simple camps won't make your trip any cheaper. You're usually paying for virtually exclusive use of pristine wilderness areas, and will find little cost difference between a tiny bush-camp and the largest lodge. In fact, if anything there's increasingly a premium on space in the smaller camps. These need booking earlier as many find these friendlier than the larger ones.

FOOD AND DRINK
Food
Talking of any one 'native cuisine' in Botswana is misleading, as what a person eats is dependent on where they live and what ethnic group they belong to. In the Kalahari and Okavango there was relatively little agriculture until recently; there, gathering and fishing, supplemented by hunting, provided subsistence for the various groups.

In the kinder climes east of the Kalahari, where there is enough rain for crops, sorghum is probably the main crop. This is first pounded into meal before being mixed with boiling water or sour milk. It's then made into a paste *bogobe* – which is thin, perhaps with sugar like porridge, for breakfast, then eaten thicker, the consistency of mashed potatoes, for lunch and dinner. For these main meals it will normally be accompanied by some tasty relish, perhaps made of meat and tomatoes, or dried fish. Maize meal (often imported as it doesn't tolerate Botswana's dry climate that well) is now often used in place of this. (In Zimbabwe this same staple is known as *sadza*, in Zambia it's *nshima* and in South Africa *mealie-pap*.) You should taste this at some stage when visiting. Safari camps will often prepare it if requested, and it is always available in small restaurants in the towns.

Camps, hotels and lodges that cater for overseas visitors will serve a very international fare, and the quality of food prepared in the most remote camps is usually amazingly high. When coming to Botswana on safari your biggest problem with food is likely to be the very real danger of putting on weight.

If you are driving yourself around and plan to cook, then get most of your supplies in Maun or Kasane. Both have large supermarkets which are well stocked – though Maun's Shoprite is by far the best.

Alcohol

Like most countries in the region, Botswana has two distinct beer types: clear and opaque. Most visitors and more affluent people in Botswana drink the **clear beers**, which are similar to European lagers and always served chilled. Castle and Lion are the lagers brewed by South African Breweries' subsidiary here. They are widely available and usually good. You'll also sometimes find the Zimbabwean Zambezi beer, and Windhoek Lager, from Namibia – which are similar and also excellent.

The less affluent residents will usually opt for some form of the **opaque beer** (sometimes called Chibuku, after the market-leading brand) – though as a visitor you'll have to really make an effort to seek this out. Most bars that tourists visit don't sell it. This is a commercial version of traditional beer, usually brewed from maize and/or sorghum. It's a sour, porridge-like brew; an acquired taste. Locals will sometimes buy a bucket of it, and then pass it around a circle of drinkers. It would be unusual for a visitor to drink this, so try some and amuse your companions.

Remember that this changes flavour as it ferments: you can often ask for 'fresh beer' or 'strong beer'. If you aren't sure about the bar's hygiene standards, stick to the pre-packaged brands of opaque beer like Chibuku.

Soft drinks

Soft drinks are available everywhere, which is fortunate when the temperatures are high. Choices are often limited, though the ubiquitous Coca-Cola is usually there, along with southern African specialities like Grapetize. Diet drinks are available in the towns, but rarely seen in the small bottle stores which pepper the rural areas – which is no surprise for a country where the rural population are poor and need all the energy their food can give them.

Water

Water in the main towns is usually purified, provided there are no shortages of chlorine, breakdowns, or other mishaps. It's generally fine to drink.

Out in the bush, most of the camps and lodges use water from bore-holes. These underground sources vary in quality, but are normally free from bugs and so perfectly safe to drink. Sometimes it is sweet, at other times the water is a little alkaline or salty. Ask the locals if it is suitable for an unacclimatised visitor to drink, then take their advice.

The water in the Okavango Delta is generally fine to drink. You'll be expected to do so during most budget *mokoro* trips, which is fine for most backpackers who are in Africa for long trips. There are relatively few people living in the communities in the Delta; contamination levels are very low. However, if you've a sensitive stomach, or are visiting for a short trip, then you'd be best to avoid it and stick to borehole water. (I'd recommend that you do not insist on bottled water as the costs/waste involved in transporting it to you are high, and borehole water is generally fine.)

Tipping

Tipping is a very difficult and contentious topic – worth thinking about carefully. Read the section on *Local payments*, page 134, and realise that thoughtlessly tipping too much is just as bad as tipping too little.

Ask locally what's appropriate; here I can only give rough guidance. Helpers with baggage might expect four or five pula for their help, whilst sorting out a problem with a reservation would be P12–18 (US$2–3/£1–2). Restaurants will often add an automatic service charge to the bill, in which case an additional tip is not usually given. If they do not do this, then 10% would certainly be appreciated if the service was good.

At safari camps, tipping is not obligatory – despite the destructive assumption from some visitors that it is. If a guide has given you really good service then a tip of about P30 (US$5/£2–3) per day per person would be a generous reflection of this. A similar bonus for a *mokoro* poler might be around P20 (US$3/£2) per day per person. If the service hasn't been that good, then don't tip.

Always tip at the end of your stay – not at the end of each day/activity. Do not tip after every game drive. This leads to the guides only trying hard when they know there's a tip at the end of the morning. Such camps aren't pleasant to visit and this isn't the way to encourage top-quality guiding. It's best to wait until the end of your stay, and then give what you feel is appropriate in one lump sum.

However, before you do this find out if tips go into one box for all of the camp staff, or if the guides are treated differently. Then ensure that your tip reflects this – with perhaps as much again divided between the rest of the staff.

WHAT TO BUY
Curios
Botswana's best bargains are handicrafts, and you'll find a variety. Look especially for hand-woven baskets made from the fronds of the real fan palm, *Hyphaene petersiana*, and the many different handicrafts of the San, like jewellery made from ostrich eggshells.

There's usually a divide between the simpler outlets, perhaps direct from the producers, and the more stylish, well-located shops which often have the best pieces, but invariably charge the highest prices.

If you're starting or ending your trip in Livingstone, then don't miss the curio stalls near the border post to Victoria Falls. This is one of the region's best places for carvings (though expect to bargain hard here). Other places to include would be the Babomoso Basketry Co-op in Shorobe, for excellent baskets direct from the makers, and the smaller shop in Gumare. Ghanzi has a superb shop, Ghanzi Craft, for bushman crafts – although it was closed for some time, it is highly likely that it will reopen.

There are plenty of shops at the more stylish end of the spectrum, especially in Maun, and many lodges have small shops selling curios. (Ask them if the staff or a local village makes these – and if they do, then buy some to support the initiative!)

Supplies
In the main towns, notably Maun, Kasane and Francistown, there are large supermarkets with extensive ranges of high-quality, mostly imported foods. Of these, the Shoprite store in Maun (part of a large southern African chain) is probably the best example in the area. Here you'll find most everyday foodstuffs that you'd want, and a lot more besides. If they have weaknesses compared to the supermarket back home, it's probably in the fresh food and vegetable section, where the logistics of transport can often make for a smaller selection than you might expect.

It's usually best to stock up with food at these main centres, as away from them the range will become sparser. Expect villages to have just a bottle stall, selling the most popular cool drinks (often this excludes 'diet' drinks), and a small shop selling bread, staples like rice, and perhaps a few tinned and packet foods. Don't expect anything refrigerated.

ORGANISING AND BOOKING
Public holidays
Botswana's public holidays are as follows:

New Year's Day	January 1
Public holiday	January 2
Good Friday & Easter Monday	
Labour Day	May 1 (variable)
Ascension Day	May 16 (variable)
Sir Sereste Khama Day	July 1
President's Day	third Monday and Tuesday in July
Independence Day	September 30
Christmas Day	December 25
Boxing Day	December 26

National parks
Until the late 1980s you could just arrive, pay your park fees, and visit any national park. Now things are different and the 'high-revenue, low-volume' policy (see page 67) has led to a constriction in the numbers of campsites available at each location: they are very limited. Sites must be pre-booked in Maun or Gabarone; once they're full, you'll be turned away.

This makes it *essential* to book as early as you can for a trip through the national parks – though they don't usually take bookings for more than a year in advance. Hence booking 11–12 months before you plan to visit is usually ideal.

Where to book
There are two booking offices for the national parks, which divide the country's park in half. They both have very extensive opening hours: 07.30–12.30 and 13.45–16.30 Monday to Saturday, and on most public holidays; 07.30–12.00 on Sundays. They close only on Christmas Day.

The northern parks
For bookings to Chobe, Moremi, Nxai and Makgadikgadi, contact:

Parks and Reserves Reservations Office PO Box 20364, Boseja, Maun; tel: 6861265; fax: 6861264. This is found behind and to the right of Maun's police station, east of Sir Seretse Khama Road, and close to the roundabout with Sekgoma Road.

The southern parks
For bookings to the Central Kalahari, Khutse, and Botswana's side of the Kgalagadi Transfrontier Park, contact:

Parks and Reserves Reservations Office PO Box 131, Gaborone; tel: 3180774; fax: 3180775; email: dwnp@gov.bw. This is in the Department of Wildlife and National Parks offices, in Gaborone's 'government enclave', opposite the end of Queen's Road.

Entry fees and permits
Most organised trips will include park entry fees in their costs, but if you are travelling on your own then you must pay these directly. There are usually three sets of park fees: entry fees for the people, entry fees for your vehicle, and camping fees. These depend on your nationality/immigration status, and where your vehicle is registered.

Usually the camping fees are paid when the sites are booked in advance, through the office in Maun (or the one in Gaborone). Sites in the national parks are very,

very limited and often booked out almost a year in advance – so it's only rarely possible to get any space by just turning up. Everybody books their trips in advance; it's the only way.

By far the best way here is to go into the office in Maun in person – or have someone do this for you. Then if what you ask for is full, you'll be able to look at the availability sheets and make an alternative plan. If you try to accomplish this by phone, fax or email then it can be a lot more difficult, and is often less successful. Currently the various fees are:

Park entry fees

per person per day	Bots citizen	Bots resident	Non-resident
Adult (18+)	P10	P30	P120
Child (age 8-17)	P5	P15	P60
Infant (7 & under)	free	free	free

Camping fees

per person per night	Bots citizen	Bots resident	Non-resident
Adult (18+)	P5	P20	P30
Child (age 8-17)	P2.50	P10	P15
Infant (7 & under)	free	free	free

Vehicle fees (per day)

Foreign-registered vehicle:	P50
Botswana-registered vehicle:	P10

To give you some idea of the total costs here, the following are based on a foreign-registered vehicle with two adult visitors coming to Moremi for seven days and camping. Their total costs for the parks would be:

Park entry fees	P1,680	=	2 x 7 x P120
Camping fees	P420	=	2 x 7 x P30
Vehicle entry fees	P350	=	7 x P50
Total costs	**P2,450**	(=	US$408/£272)

That's an average cost of P175 (US$29/£19) per person per day.

Note that until recently, any camping fees paid to the Maun office, or parks fees paid at the scout camps at park gates, had to be in Pula; they would not accept foreign currency, travellers' cheques or credit cards. This strict approach is meant to have been relaxed – they should now also accept cash in pula, British pounds or US dollars. However, I strongly recommend that you take pula for this, as you'll find it a lot easier and simpler to pay.

COMMUNICATIONS AND MEDIA
Post

BotswanaPost, the government-owned postal service, is reliable, but often slow. They have post offices in all the larger towns, and then a network of many agencies in some of the larger villages. You'll find a brief listing of these on www.botspost.co.bw and also details under 'Postal Services' in the yellow pages section at the back of the telephone directory. These include offices or agencies in Francistown, Ghanzi, Gumare, Gweta, Kasane, Maun, Nata, Nokaneng, Rakops, Sepopa and Seronga.

Currently letters are classified by size, with a 'standard' size being up to 120mm x 235mm x 20mm, and a 'large' one up to 229mm x 324mm x 20mm. Provided they weigh under 200g, postal rates are:

in pula	Botswana	SADC region *surface/air*	Europe *surface/air*	Elsewhere *surface/air*
postcards	0.55	0.90/1.95	0.90/1.95	0.90/1.95
standard	0.55	1.10/1.95	1.45/2.75	1.65/3.30
large	1.45	4.20/5.50	4.95/9.35	5.50/11.00
over-sized	2.35	8.15/11.00	9.90/16.50	11.00/19.80

SADC – the Southern Africa Development Community – is a regional grouping of states and includes Angola, the Democratic Republic of Congo (DRC), Lesotho, Malawi, Mauritius, Mozambique, Namibia, Seychelles, South Africa, Swaziland, Tanzania, Zambia and Zimbabwe.

There is a post restante service at all the major post offices.

Telephone

Botswana's telephone system is generally very good, and you can access some remarkably offbeat places by just dialling from overseas. There's very rarely a need to redial repeatedly to get a line, as happens in so many countries in the region.

To dial into the country from abroad, the international access code for Botswana is 267. From inside Botswana, you dial 00 to get an international line, then the country's access code (eg: 44 for the UK, or 1 for the USA), then omit the first 0 of the number you are calling.

Number changes

From 2001 to 2003 there's been a rolling programme of number changes which, when complete, will ensure that the number for every land line in Botswana has seven digits, rather than the previous six. Normally the old and new numbers have both worked in parallel for two to four months, during a 'change-over' period, and the transitions have been run efficiently and smoothly.

So if you're looking at any old literature and see a six-digit number in Botswana, then it's likely to be out of date. The main ones that you're likely to come across include:

Kasane	changed from	65xxxx to 625xxxx
Nata	changed from	61xxxx to 621xxxx
Maun	changed from	66xxxx to 686xxxx
Francistown	changed from	21xxxx to 241xxxx

With more numbers overall, Gaborone's changes are much more complex. For example, to illustrate just a few of the main ones:

30xxxx changed to 390xxxx   35xxxx changed to 395xxxx
31xxxx changed to 391xxxx   37xxxx changed to 397xxxx
32xxxx changed to 392xxxx   39xxxx changed to 310xxxx
34xxxx changed to 394xxxx   5xxxxx changed to 31xxxxx

If you've got web access then there's a particularly useful website site run by Botswana Telecommunications Corporation, www.btc.bw, which includes a residential directory, the white pages, at www.btc.bw/dirwhite.htm, and a business directory, the yellow pages, at www.btc.bw/yellow.asp. This is a service to find out a number for any person, or business, in Botswana – but you can also input an old number to find out how it has been changed. It's excellent when it works, but note that fax numbers, or anything else not in the usual directories, don't seem to be covered.

Public phones
Dotted around the main towns you'll find public phone boxes, some of which take coins and others phonecards. A recent innovation are the 'scratch and dial' cards, available from post offices, fuel stations and some shops. These are available in three denominations – P20, P40 and P100 – and incur the same call charges as a normal payphone. The cards have a number on the back, only revealed when you scratch it. With this you dial 1351 (a free call) from any phone, and following the voice prompts to enter the card number and then the number you wish to call. The cost of this call is then deducted from the card's balance. You can use this repeatedly until your card's balance reaches zero.

Fax
If you are trying to send a fax to, or within, Botswana then it's often wise to use a manual setting to dial the number. Then listen for a fax tone on the line yourself, and only when you finally hear one should you press the 'start' button on your machine to send the fax. You'll find a directory of fax numbers at the start of the telephone directory.

Telex
Telex machines are still used in some places, but are becoming less and less common. Where they do exist, they provide communication that you can instantly verify. You need not worry if your message has arrived, as the answer-back code will confirm that for you. Again, you'll find a list of these near the start of the telephone directory.

Email and the internet
Like most places, Botswana is rapidly adopting email and you'll now find that most people are on email, and a lot of businesses have websites. That said, outside of the main towns, email is often limited to a radio-based service known as 'bushmail', which has a tiny bandwidth and so is only practical for simple text messages. (Never send attachments to a bushmail address!)

The media
With a small population, many in rural locations, the press here is equally small, and partly relies on the larger South African media companies. However, Botswana has several newspapers, radio and TV stations.

Independence issues
Botswana's small media is generally fairly free and expresses its opinions, even when they disagree with government policy. Even media which are owned by the government are obliged by law to give basic coverage of opposition views as well as the official versions. That said, disagreements do occur on a fairly regular basis, and clearly the independent press here fights a continuing battle to remain independent.

In May 2001, all government offices were instructed to stop using the two independent weekly papers, *The Guardian* and *The Midweek Sun*, following their criticism of Vice-President Ian Khama. Given that the government is the largest advertiser in these papers, this had significant commercial impact. Shortly after this, the papers' editors began proceedings against the government and, in late September, a High Court judge ruled that the advertising ban was unconstitutional as the authorities were deemed to be applying unfair financial pressure on the papers in order to curtail their right to freedom of expression.

Subsequently, the government has looked into bringing out a 'Mass Media Communications Bill' which would establish a 'press council', though critics have decried this as state censorship by another name – and it's not yet been passed through parliament.

Occasionally the press also comes into the firing line for sensationalism, which is claimed to be fuelling ethnic tensions, and once recently a High Court judge started proceedings against *Mmegi* for defamation.

In late April 2001, the head of news and current affairs at the official Botswana Television (BTV) station quit his job in protest about government interference in the station's editorial policy and programming. He alleged that officials had threatened him, and that the authorities had blocked the broadcast of a documentary on a South African woman who had been convicted of murder by a Botswana court and subsequently executed.

The press

Botswana's most widely read newspapers are the *Botswana Guardian* and *Mmegi: The Reporter*; both are weekly. *Mmegi* has the largest circulation (about 27,000 copies) and comes out every Friday; it's a fairly weighty tome. Recently this has spawned a sister-publication, the *Mmegi Monitor*, which comes out on a Tuesday. Other papers include the *Botswana Gazette*, the *Midweek Sun* and the government's free weekday newspaper, the *Daily News*. For newspapers on the web, see page 523.

Radio

Botswana has a couple of radio stations that broadcast around the main towns, but there's generally nothing but long-distance shortwave services away from these.

The state-run Radio Botswana has two stations, both mixing Setswana and English in their schedules, and often their programmes. The non-commercial Radio Botswana One (RB1) has no advertising and majors on news and current affairs, whilst the commercial station Radio Botswana Two (RB2) features mainly popular music from ballads, R&B, house, reggae, fusion and jazz to pop and disco. Within this you'll find the usual inane banter, as well as full news bulletins at 07.00, 13.00, 18.00 and 21.00 every weekday.

Alternative independent stations include Yarona FM (106.6MHz) and GabzFM (96.2MHz). See www.advertiser.bw/gabzfm.htm for the schedules of the latter.

TV

Botswana launched its first national television service on July 31 2000. Based in new headquarters on the outskirts of Gaborone, this is part of the Department of Information and Broadcasting (which also runs Radio Botswana's two stations). This broadcasts for just a few hours in the evening, usually 17.00–21.00, and originally aimed to carry at least 60% local content.

Apparently in the months preceding the launch there was some doubt about it being on schedule, so a consultancy team from Britain's BBC was brought in. They observed that, 'Ten days before the launch, the general manager and his colleagues laughed at the idea that the launch would take place on time. The government even cancelled plans for a lavish ceremony and speech by the president at the national stadium on launch day. So we booked the stadium and arranged a charity shield football match between the country's two best teams, which attracted a bigger television audience on July 31 than the abandoned show would have done.' This charity shield match has now become a regular fixture.

In Gaborone there is a private channel, Gaborone Television, which is owned by Gaborone Broadcasting Company (GBC) and funded by advertising. Throughout Botswana most people with televisions are connected to one of the large South African networks – like the MultiChoice satellite service. There is no cable TV.

MISCELLANEOUS
Electricity
The local voltage is 220V, delivered at 50Hz. Sockets usually fit plugs with three square pins, like the current design in the UK, though plugs with three large round pins, like those in South Africa, are also widely in use. Ideally bring adapters for both.

When staying in bush lodges and the more upmarket camps, you are relatively unlikely to have sockets in your room/tent. However, it's usually easy to arrange for items to be plugged in for you (eg: to charge the batteries in video cameras), as behind the scenes most camps run generators in order to power their kitchens and communications equipment.

Embassies and consulates
There's often a list of Gaborone's diplomatic missions, including those in neighbouring countries when necessary, in the front of the telephone directory. Alternatively see the government website page: www.gov.bw/tourism/embassies/embassies.html

Angolan Embassy 5131 Kopanyo House, Nelson Mandela Road, P Bag BR 11, Gaborone; tel: 3900204 or 3905453; fax: 3975089 or 3181876

British High Commission P Bag 0023, Gaborone; tel: 3952841; fax: 3956105

Canadian Consulate PO Box 882, Gaborone; tel: 3904411

Chinese Embassy 3096 North Ring Rd, PO Box 1031, Gaborone; tel: 3952209; fax: 3900156

Cuban Embassy Plot No 5198, The Village, PO Box 40261, Gaborone; tel: 3911484 or 3911485; fax: 3951750

Danish Consulate Plot 10227, Mopororo Rd, PO Box 1973, Gaborone; tel: 3953505; fax: 3953473; email: rohlig@info.bw

French Embassy 761 Robinson Rd, PO Box 1424, Gaborone; tel: 3973863; fax: 397173

German Embassy 3rd Floor Professional House, Segoditshane Way, Broadhurst, PO Box 315, Gaborone.

Indian High Commission 5375 President's Drive, P Bag 249, Gaborone; tel: 3972676; fax: 3974636

Kenyan High Commission 5373 President's Drive, P Bag BO 297, Gaborone; tel: 3951408; fax: 3951409

Libyan Embassy (aka the People's Bureau of the Great Socialist People's Libyan Arab Jamairiya) Plot 8851 (Government Enclave), PO Box 180, Gaborone; tel: 3952481; fax: 3956928

Namibian High Commission PO Box 987, Gaborone; tel: 3902181; fax: 3902248

Nigerian High Commission PO Box 274, The Mall, Gaborone; tel: 3913561; fax: 3913738

Norwegian Consulate Plot No. 3284, Bontleng Close, Extension 12, P Bag 242, Gaborone; tel: 3908648/9; fax: 3908648

Russian Embassy Plot 4711, Tawana Close, PO Box 81, Gaborone; tel: 3953389; fax: 3952930; email: embrus@info.bw

South African High Commission P Bag 00402, Gaborone; tel: 3904800/1/2/3; fax: 3905502

Swedish Embassy 4th Floor Development House, The Mall, P Bag 0017, Gaborone; tel: 3953912; fax: 3953942; email: ambassaden.gaborone@foreign.ministry.se

United States Embassy PO Box 90, Gaborone; tel: 3953982; fax: 3956947

Zambian High Commission PO Box 362, Gaborone; tel: 3951951; fax: 3953952

Zimbabwean High Commission Plot 8850, PO Box 1232, Gaborone; tel: 3914495; fax: 3905863

Honorary consuls in Botswana

There are many countries that don't maintain a full embassy in Botswana, but do have honorary consuls who can help their citizens in case of need. Their contacts can be found on www.gov.bw. Currently they are as follows:

Austria Doreen Khama Attorney, PO Box 335, Gaborone; tel: 3952638; fax: 3953876

Belgium Mr M C Tibone, PO Box 821, Gaborone; tel: 3957438; fax: 3957476

Finland Mr S A Mphuchane, Trade World, PO Box 1904, Gaborone; tel: 3901500; fax: 3901966

Ghana Mrs Helfer, PO Box 906, Gaborone

Guyana Mr T H Pariang; tel: 3912655

Ireland Mr J M Walking, 1st Floor Standard House, P Bag 00347, Gaborone; tel: 3903333; fax: 3903400

Israel Mr Richard Lyons, PO Box 160, Gaborone.

Italy Mr G R Grach, 4th Floor Tirelo House, PO Box 451, Gaborone; tel: 3952882; fax: 3975045

Netherlands Mr P L Steenkamp/Mrs Vink (asst.), 2535 Nyerere Drive, PO Box 457, Gaborone; tel: 3902194; fax: 3951200

Spain Mr Guido Renato Giachetti, Plot No. 5624, Real Estate Office Park, Lejara Rd, Broadhurst Industrial, Gaborone; tel: 3912641; fax: 3973441

Thailand Mrs Vonna Hermans, 22358 Semowane Rd, Gaborone West Phase IV, PO Box 60945, Gaborone; tel: 3906818; fax: 3906811; email: hermans@info.bw

International organisations in Botswana

Contact details for a few of the larger international organisations who have offices in Botswana include:

European Commission Delegation Plot 68, North Ring Rd, PO Box 1253, Gaborone; tel: 3941155; fax: 3913626; email: eudelbwa@info.bw

Southern African Development Community (SADC) P Bag 0095, Gaborone; tel: 3951863; fax: 3972848

United Nations Children's Fund PO Box 20678, Gaborone; tel: 3952752 or 3951909; fax: 3951233

United Nations Development Programme PO Box 54, Gaborone; tel: 3952121; fax: 3956093

World Health Organisation Rizka House, 1st Floor, PO Box 1355, Gaborone; tel: 3971505/6; fax: 3959483

World Conservation Plot 2403, P Bag 003000, Gaborone; fax: 3971584; email: iucn@iucnbot.bw

Hospitals and dentists

Should you need one, there are good hospitals in Botswana. However, the public health system is over-stretched and under-funded – so unless your illness is critical, it will take time for you to be attended to and treated at the public hospitals.

Also a large number of patients in the public hospitals have serious infectious diseases, so there's a risk of coming away from these with something worse than you had when you arrived.

In the main towns – Gaborone, Maun, Francistown – there are better-funded private clinics that cater for both affluent citizens of Botswana and expats/diplomatic staff/travellers. These will accept payment from genuine travel health insurance schemes.

Pharmacies in these towns generally have a good range of medicines, though specific brands are often unavailable. So bring with you all that you will need, as well as a repeat prescription for anything that you might run out of. Outside of the larger towns you probably won't be able to find anything other than very basic medical supplies. Thus you should carry a very comprehensive medical kit if you are planning to head off into the wilds.

The best way to find details of the nearest private clinics is to look up 'medical – private clinics/practitioners' in the yellow pages at the back of the phone book or, in an emergency call MediRescue on 911, or an ambulance from a public hospital on 997.

Imports and exports

There is no problem in exporting normal curios, but you will need an official export permit from the Department of National Parks to take out any game trophies. Visitors are urged to support both the letter and the spirit of the CITES bans on endangered species. In any case, without such permits you will probably have big problems when you try to import items back into your home country.

Maps

The best maps of northern Botswana for most visitors are the Shell series, and the Contimap – see the section on *Finding the right map*, page 86, for more details.

However, if you want more detailed, Ordnance Survey-type maps, then by far the best plan is to go directly to the offices of the Department for Surveys and Mapping, in either Maun (see page 155) or Gaborone (P Bag 37, Gaborone; tel: 3953251).

Each of these two offices has roughly the same variety of excellent maps on offer, although some are always out of print. A particular favourite is the 1:350,000 map of the Okavango Delta that covers the whole of the Okavango area in detail – although don't expect its safari camps to be up to date.

Societies
The Botswana Society

The Botswana Society is the learned society of Botswana. It publishes the excellent annual journal *Botswana Notes and Records* (see *Further Reading* for just a few examples of the many papers that have appeared in this over the years) and various books, including the proceedings of a series of conferences held under the Society's auspices.

You'll find its current webpage on the site of the University of Botswana's History Department: http://ubh.tripod.com/bsoc/botsoc.htm.

The Kalahari Conservation Society

Plot 112, Independence Avenue, PO Box 859, Gaborone; tel: 3974557; fax: 3914259

The Kalahari Conservation Society (KCS) aims to conserve Botswana's natural heritage by promoting knowledge of Botswana's wildlife and environment, to encourage and finance research into issues affecting Botswana's resources, and to promote and support policies of conservation. In recent years it seems to have taken a conciliatory approach to government-sponsored developments, and now it doesn't generally get involved in any aggressive campaigning.

The Okavango Wildlife Society

PO Box 2137, Cresta 2118, South Africa; tel: (2712) 365 1625; fax: (2712) 365 1622; email: owls@global.co.za; web: www.sintef.no/units/chem/chemengr/staff/paals/owls
Formed in 1964, Okavango Wildlife Society was initially concerned just with the Okavango Delta's survival, though now its aims have widened to encompass conservation throughout Botswana. Its newsletters, stretching back as far as 1996, are available for download (in .pdf format) on its website – and there's also a useful (if incomplete) archive of pieces on various topics relating to conservation in Botswana, including the controversial veterinary fences. The OWS adopts a generally more pro-active campaigning stance, and clearly isn't the least bit afraid to tackle awkward subjects.

The Chobe Society

PO Box 55, Kasane; tel: 6250516; fax: 6250223; email: cwt@info.bw;
web: www.chobewildlifetrust.com or (at time of press)
www.envngo.co.bw/pages/cwt.html.
The Chobe Wildlife Trust aims to assist with the conservation of natural resources of the Chobe National Park and the region as a whole, co-operating with the government, various NGOs and community-based organisations. It has several projects supporting conservation and fostering awareness of projects to care for Botswana's wildlife – and especially that of Chobe.

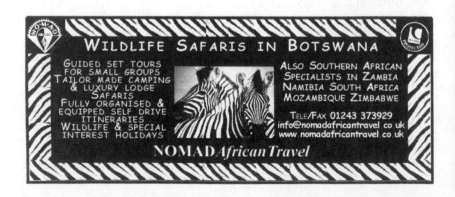

Part Two

The Guide

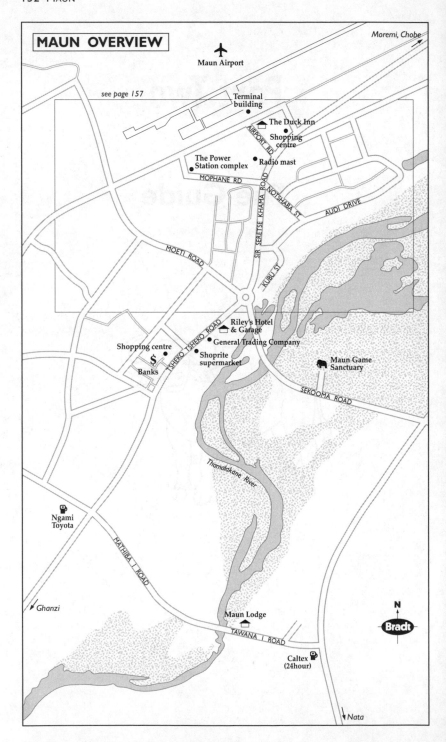

MAUN OVERVIEW

Moremi, Chobe

Maun Airport

see page 157

Terminal
building

The Duck Inn

Shopping
centre

The Power
Station complex

Radio mast

AIRPORT RD

MOPHANE RD

SIR SERETSE KHAMA ROAD

NTSHABA ST

AUDI DRIVE

MOETI ROAD

KUBU ST

Riley's Hotel
& Garage

TSHEKO TSHEKO ROAD

General Trading Company

Shopping centre

Shoprite
supermarket

Banks

Maun Game
Sanctuary

SEKOOMA ROAD

Thamalakane River

Ngami
Toyota

MATHIBA ROAD

Ghanzi

Maun Lodge

TAWANA ROAD

Caltex
(24hour)

N

Bradt

Nata

Maun

This dusty, sprawling town has been the start of expeditions into the wilds since the turn of the century, and it is now the safari capital of the country. Maun's elongated centre is dotted with modern shops and offices, while its suburbs are mainly traditionally built, thatched rondavels. Look carefully amongst these and you'll find quite a lot which incorporate old tin cans from drinks into their mud walls.

In the 1980s everywhere and everything here seemed geared towards the tourism bonanza. Maun had a rough-and-ready frontier feel, as contemporary cowboys rode into town from the bush in battered 4WDs. Its focal point were the camps north of town – Island Safari Lodge, Crocodile Camp, Okavango River Lodge and, of course, the Duck Inn opposite the airport.

However since then Maun has changed. Government departments moved here en masse, as Maun became the administrative centre for the northern and western parts of Botswana. The town's roads became sealed tar, rather than pot-holed gravel tracks, which opened the door to an influx of normal saloon cars from the rest of the country.

Finally the tourism product itself changed. The pendulum swung away from last-minute budget trips bought in Maun, to upmarket safaris bought in advance from overseas. The new breed of visitors just change planes here; they seldom spend more than a few hours at Maun Airport. The town is no longer the place to book a top safari; that's usually done before you arrive.

However, for those who are driving themselves, Maun remains a centre to get organised, and perhaps a place to look at what cheaper safari options are available. Thus the aim of this chapter is to help you find your way about, with the basics of where to stay and eat, and to get organised. There are banks, including a Barclays, First National and Standard Chartered, garages, well-stocked supermarkets and a number of travel agents and operators.

GETTING THERE AND AWAY

Maun is 950m (3,100ft) above sea level, and fairly easy to reach, however you are travelling.

By air

Maun is well connected by scheduled Air Botswana flights. These connect with Gaborone and Johannesburg every day, and with Kasane on Monday, Wednesdays, Fridays and Sundays.

For more detail contact Air Botswana at their stylish office near the airport (tel: 6860391). Maun also has a number of air charter companies, where you can hire light aircraft for private flights and transfers – see pages 178–9. These can sometimes be economic if you have four or five people travelling together.

Air Namibia runs regular flights between Windhoek and Maun on Wednesdays, Fridays and Sundays, though using fairly small aircraft so these flights are frequently sold out far in advance. Note also that there are inherent risks in relying on these flights to fit in with a complex, 'fixed' trip itinerary in both countries – as the schedules for them can, and do, change relatively regularly. (There are moves to run a regular charter service on this route, but nothing's materialised yet.)

Maun Airport

On the north side of town, Maun's airport has always been a focal point of the safari industry here. Inside you'll find it's fairly small, with a few relaxed check-in desks and toilets downstairs, and a café with places to sit upstairs. There's no 'hassle' as such, as you find at some airports, though there are often a lot of reps from safari companies waiting with name-boards for travellers to arrive.

The airport itself has no left luggage facility, though if you're passing through to visit camps in the region by light aircraft, then most safari companies will collect any spare baggage from you, and return it to you as you leave.

By bus
Local buses

The fairly chaotic local bus station is around Tsaro Street, where the local market is. Here you'll find frequent departures for Francistown (P45), which take about seven hours; Ghanzi (P30), which takes about four hours; and Shakawe (P35), which takes about seven hours and stops at most of the larger towns on the way. To reach Kasane, hop on a bus towards Francistown and change at Nata.

Others
Kasane shuttle

Until recently, Audi Camp Safaris ran a 2-night/3-day 'shuttle' between Maun and Kasane, camping one night in Moremi and one in Chobe, for US$200 per person – given a minimum of four people, with everyone bringing their own tents, sleeping bags and mattresses. This is no longer on offer, though organising a very, very swift mobile like this might be an option for a group wanting to get to Kasane and have a swift glance at Moremi and Chobe as they pass. Talk to any of Maun's budget operators; you may find one who needs to reposition a vehicle and will be happy to do this for you for a good rate.

Windhoek shuttle

Audi Camp Safaris (tel: 6860599; see page 168) still have a scheduled shuttle service (usually a 16-seater air-con bus) between Maun and Windhoek costing US$50 per person. It takes about nine hours on the road and leaves Maun on Mondays and Fridays at 08.00; departing Windhoek on Saturdays and Wednesdays at 08.00. The best place to book this in Windhoek is at Africa Tourist Info (tel: (264) 61 247668; email: infotour@iafrica.com.na), though any of the backpackers' lodges there will book it for you.

By road

Ignoring the odd tiny bush track, there are only three significant roads linking Maun with the rest of the country.

Northeast towards Kasane

Routing right through Chobe National Park, it's about 360km of bush and thick sand (accessible only by 4WD) to Kasane. For details of the track northeast of

Maun, through Shorobe to Moremi and Chobe, see the separate section, *The road north of Maun*, at the end of this chapter.

Southwest towards Ghanzi

It's about 286km of good tar road to Ghanzi. About 2.5km past the old T-junction and Engen garage, you'll pass the Maun Sports Complex on your left – a huge, modern floodlit stadium and sports area. If you're hitch-hiking then consider catching a bus, or taxi, or walking this far out as it'll get you beyond most of the local traffic.

East towards Nata

Nata is about 305km due east, again along a good tar road which crosses between the Nxai Pan and Makgadikgadi national parks. If you're hitching, then at least cross to the south side of the Thamalakane River as far as the 24-hour Caltex service station. If you prefer, continue for a few kilometres south until the road starts to bend west and you're beyond the outskirts and the local traffic.

ORIENTATION

Finding your way around Maun used to be simple. Now it's more complex, though perhaps part of this is that on any one trip, one never quite spends enough time there to really get an intuitive understanding of it.

Though the town stands astride the (often-dry) Thamalakane River, the main places of interest are all on the north bank. Here there are two focal points: the old Duck Inn/airport area, and main banks/Riley's Hotel area.

Maps

Though it's grown a lot in recent years, there aren't any really good maps of Maun apart from the detailed town planners' survey maps, which are too detailed for most purposes, and the sketch maps in this book.

However, whilst you are in Maun if you really want to head anywhere 'off-piste' in Botswana's bush, then consider a visit to:

Dept of Survey & Mapping PO Box 74, Maun; tel: 6860272; fax: 6860993. Proper survey maps may be useful if you are driving yourself into more offbeat parts – although the Shell maps, by Veronica Roodt, and the new Contimap (see *Further Reading*), have become the standard references for most travellers. Open: Monday to Friday. Closed on Saturday

If you want to track down some more traditional survey maps in Maun, then seek out the Surveyor General's Office. This is cunningly disguised as an unused building, just to the right of the stylish Air Botswana office on the road to the airport. Despite its appearance, at the back you'll find an office where a very helpful team will arrange any number of maps for you for about P10 each. These survey maps are only otherwise available in Gaborone, so make the most of this convenient office.

Even if you're not exploring, the large 1:350,000 map of the Okavango Delta makes a great souvenir – though many of the camps on it are long gone.

WHERE TO STAY

Just as Maun has changed in the last decade or two, so have the places to stay. In the 1980s the few camps on the edge of town felt like outposts in the wilderness. Places like Crocodile Camp, Island Safari Lodge and Okavango River Lodge had the atmosphere of oases of comfort. They seemed like remote lodges and often, when the water was high enough, mokoro trips would start from the banks of the river beside the lodge, to pole adventurers into the Delta along the Thamalakane River.

Now times have changed. Better roads and more neighbours have made these camps feel less isolated and more a part of Maun. Less water in the river has put an end to mokoro trips starting in Maun. Whereas most visitors used to stop for at least a night in Maun (especially the backpackers who came), now most visitors simply transit briefly through Maun Airport to fly in to a safari camp (and there are far less backpackers).

Hence these fine old camps have lost much of their atmosphere – though still there's a feeling that they're more interesting than the hotels and B&Bs which are the alternative.

Hotels

Maun Lodge (30 rooms) Plot No 459, Boseja, PO Box 376, Maun; tel: 6863939; fax: 6863969; email: maun.lodge@info.bw

Maun Lodge is a small efficient, modern hotel on the south bank of the Thamalakane River, next to the Tawana Road Bridge. Entering you'll find a high lobby with a locally produced rug on the wall together with a trendy metal sculpture of pelicans.

The lodge's rooms all have twin beds with ethnic-print covers, tea/coffee-making facilities, and a jug of water. The en-suite bathroom usually has a bath with fixed shower above it, a large mirror, a washbasin and a flush toilet. The floors are tiled and you'll find pictures on the walls, but otherwise the decor is bland. That said, they have efficient air conditioning, decent sized TVs, direct-dial telephones, and everything feels very clean and well maintained. Maun Lodge also has an outside swimming pool and a conference centre. If you need a fairly standard business-like hotel, this could be for you.

At the back you'll find ample parking patrolled by security guards (a big bonus for drivers), and the Pygmy Goose Pub and Restaurant. Whilst this isn't the town's hottest party venue, it does serve a good continental breakfast for P20, and will do an à la carte dinner if you don't have the energy to venture further.

Rates: P390/495 for a double room/suite, P330/440 for a single room/suite. Open all year.

Riley's Hotel PO Box 1, Maun; tel: 6860204 or 6860320; fax: 6860580; email: reservations@cresta.co.bw or rileys@info.bw

Riley's has always been more of an institution than a hotel. It was founded when Harry Riley arrived in Maun, in 1910. Initially he simply built an extra rondavel next to his own, suitable for one visitor. It had no bed, just reed matting on the floor. A few years later he joined the two rondavels together, building a simple dining room between them, and soon he was running Maun's first hotel. In his book *The Lost World of the Kalahari*, Laurens van der Post described Riley's in the 1950s as a: '... remarkable little hotel which he [Harry Riley] had founded for the odd, intrepid traveller who had been determined enough to cross the desert, as well as for the score or so of Europeans patient and courageous enough to make Maun the unique outpost of life that it is today.'

Now those first buildings form part of the manager's house, and Riley's is a luxury hotel owned by Cresta, a group who run excellent hotels and lodges across the subcontinent.

For the visitor, Riley's has a very central location, on the eastern side of the main street, and the added benefits of a good restaurant, bar, lovely outdoor swimming pool, well-appointed rooms and, for business-people, good communications. Almost every time that I've tried to 'drop in' here, it's been full; so if you want to stay I'd recommend that you reserve your space in advance.

Rates: P232/361 per person sharing/single for a standard room, P432/760 for a suite. Open: all year.

Sedia Hotel (25 rooms and campsite) PO Box 29, Maun; tel/fax: 6860177; email: sedia@info.bw; web: www.sedia-hotel.com

Originally called the ' Sedi Motel', the Sedia is just off the main road, on the right as you head north, a few kilometres north of Maun. It has been around since the early 1990s and

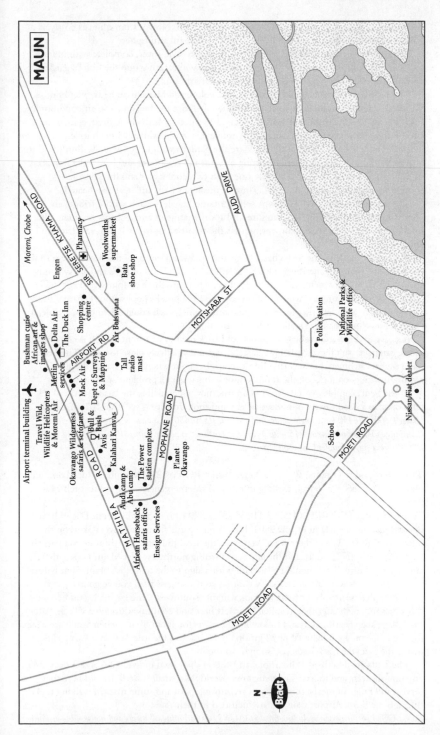

MAUN

Moremi; Chobe →

Airport terminal building ✈
Travel Wild, Wildlife Helicopters & Moremi Air
Okavango Wilderness safaris & sefofane
Audi camp & Abu camp
African Horseback safaris office
Ensign Services

Bushman curio African art & images shop
Merlin services
Mack Air
Bull & Bush
Avis
Kalahari Kanvas
The Power station complex

Engen
Pharmacy
Delta Air
The Duck Inn
Shopping centre
Air Botswana
AIRPORT RD
Dept of Surveys & Mapping
Tall radio mast
Planet Okavango

SIR SERETSE KHAMA ROAD
Woolworths supermarket
Bata shoe shop

MATHIBA ROAD
MOPHANE ROAD

AUDI DRIVE
MOTSHABA ST

Police station
National Parks & Wildlife office
School
MOETI ROAD
Nissan/Fiat dealer

MOETI ROAD

N
Bradt

has gradually moved upmarket and expanded since then. Now it's not quite as costly as Riley's or Maun Lodge, and has a livelier, more colourful atmosphere.

Guests entering the Sedia are greeted by a Grecian-style foyer, complete with indoor fountain. Most of the rooms are laid out along two wings facing into the hotel's gardens, and there are a few larger chalets built in the hotel's grounds.

The rooms are furnished with bright ethnic colours and have twin beds, telephone, a TV (with satellite and local channels), a ceiling fan above the bed and also air conditioning. Each has an en-suite bathroom, which when last visited looked a little tired, containing a bath with a shower (with erratic pressure) above it, a washbasin and a flush toilet.

In the middle of the hotel at the back are the gardens with large lawns. Within these are a large swimming pool, an open-air sitting area for the restaurant and bar, and a fine array of poinsettia bushes. The bar is a lively one with two pool tables and the restaurant sometimes organises braais; the pool is one of the area's best, and it's solar-heated.

There are one- and two-bedroom self-contained chalets, each with a fridge, air conditioning, lounge with TV (satellite and local channels) and a shady veranda. The one-bedroom chalets have a shower, whilst the two-bedroom chalets have a bath and a shower.

Behind the gardens, the Sedia has a large and sprawling campsite that leads down to the banks of the Thamalakane River. Dotted around this are plenty of trees and a few handy shade-cloths, under which tents can be pitched. There are three or four well-kept showers and toilets for the campers, who are allowed to use the hotel's pool without charge. In the campsite there are a few simple, pre-erected tents which each contain two beds, a table, a chair, a power point and a small, shaded veranda.

It's easy to drive your vehicle into this, and park next to your tent, which is convenient, as the campsite isn't fenced terribly securely, and it is relatively close to town. The Sedia has a night watchman, but security didn't seem that tight when I last stayed there – although with good locks on the room's doors, this wasn't a problem at all.

In the Sedia complex you'll also find an internet café which is the base for Afro Trek, who operate a good variety of budget safaris and mokoro trips – see page 167 for details. *Rates: P360/420/450 for a single/double/twin room, P550/650 for a one- or two-bedroom chalet. Camping is P7 per person, or P15 with a caravan (includes a power point). Pre-erected tents cost P50/90 for a single/double. Open: all year.*

The Tree Lodge (7 tents) Book via Travel Wild: PO Box 236, Mathiba I Rd, Maun; tel: 6860822; fax: 6860493; email: t.wild@info.bw. (For emergencies, lodge direct tel: 7170 0331)
This new lodge (✪ TREELO 20°03.110'S; 23°22.329'E) is owned by Brent Dacomb, and opened just outside Maun in July 2002. It's set on a game farm that covers 3km² on the outskirts of town. To get there leave Maun on the road to Nata. Shortly after you pass the Caltex 24-hour fuel station, and the adjacent turning northwest past Maun Lodge, there's another right turn. This should be labelled with a sign to the lodge; it's about 50m before you reach the 'Auto Pedigree' car showroom – so if you pass that, you've gone too far.

Taking this turning right (which heads roughly southwest), the tar road soon becomes a dirt track and, 50m after that, it splits. Bear left here and continue through a village. After the village keep bearing left, and following the signs for about 8km – when you'll see a sign for the lodge on your right. After 500m this track leads to the gate of Game Farm. Once inside the gate, the track leads you straight to the lodge.

The tents are described as luxurious and set on their own individual wooden decks, with en-suite showers and toilets. The main area overlooks a small waterhole, and here they serve a full range of meals; there's also a swimming pool and some marked walking trails through the bush. Airport transfers are included in their rates.
Rates: US$115 per person including breakfast; US$145 including all meals and house wine at dinner.

Guesthouses and B&Bs

In recent years a couple of small B&B's have sprung up, usually run by Maun residents as a way of earning a few extra Pula. Expect them to be basic and functional, with no frills at all.

Kagiso Guest House (3 rooms) Tel/fax: 6863466; email: kagiso@info.bw
About 8km from Maun's radio mast, on the way to Shorobe, this is signposted on the left just before the turning to Island Safari Lodge. It's a tiny local guesthouse with very basic en-suite rooms, each with just two beds, a shower and a toilet.
Rates: P140/160 for a double/single room. Breakfast is P25 per person, and dinner may be possible if you ask early in the day.

Maduo Guest House (7 rooms) PO Box 210, Maun; tel: 6860846; fax: 6862161
About 6km from Maun's radio mast, on the way to Shorobe, this small guest house is almost opposite the Hotel Sedia on the left hand side of the road. It's plain and simple, with basic en-suite rooms, though friendly enough, and there's a swimming pool to cool off in.
Rates: P200/150 for a double/single room. Breakfast/dinner is P20/35 per person.

Camps and camping

Most of these are north from the main centre of Maun, on the road to Shorobe. They're the obvious places to stay if you arrive in your own vehicle, and will usually provide a pick-up/drop-off service into town at a price.

If you are backpacking, then it's cheaper to hitch from the main road near any of these camps into town by catching a lift (P1) with one of the small combies that come past every few minutes. To get from town to these camps, a taxi will cost you around P20 or you can take one of the combies for P1 – though you'll need to ask around to find the right one. (These may be marked as 'Sedie' or 'Route 1'.)

Audi Camp (campsite and pre-erected tents) P Bag 28, Maun; tel: 6860599; fax: 6860581; email: audicamp@info.bw; web: www.audicamp.bizland.com
The turn-off for Audi Camp is well signposted barely 300m south of Crocodile Camp's turning, about 12km from the centre of Maun on the road to Shorobe, Moremi and Chobe.

This is the base for Audi Camp Safaris (see page 168), whilst also having a shady campsite with some pre-erected tents on solid bases, which is securely fenced and patrolled at night by security guards. The tents are either bare dome tents with camp beds and no linen, for P44/66 per person sharing/single, or small Meru tents with linen included for P72/110. Camping costs P22 per person (half price for children under 12), plus P22 if you want a power point. All share clean ablutions including hot open-air showers. There a swimming pool for cooling dips, and a laundry service if you need one.

The camp has a large thatched bar and restaurant area, which serves meals and snacks all day from a bar menu, though there's also a camper's kitchen and braai stands if you prefer to cook for yourself. The camp's been working on its food, and now organises 'themed' food evenings. There's a caged parrot here if you need conversation – though the ethics of keeping such an endangered bird caged would also provide a challenging conversation with the management. Firewood can be supplied, as can ice for cool-boxes.

Audi Camp has a limited amount of camping kit for hire, and some canoes (P55 per half-day) if you want to splash around on the relatively innocuous stretch of river next to camp.
Open: all year.

Crocodile Camp (9 chalets) PO Box 46, Maun; tel: 6860265; fax: 6860793; email: crocamp@info.bw; web: www.botswana.com
Now a base for the operations of Crocodile Camp Safaris (see page 170 for alternative contact details), 'Croc Camp' as it's universally known is one of the old institutions of

Maun. It jealously guarded a reputation for the best food in town, and used to station its own mekoro on the river beside the camp for trips into the Delta. (This used to require days of poling just to get to the buffalo fence!)

Now the camp has nine chalets of which six are brick with thatched roofs, 24-hour electricity, a fan, and slatted glass windows screened by mosquito gauze. These are quite simple, with basic locks and no frills, but they do have an en-suite shower, toilet and washbasin. All have twin beds except for the 'family' chalet that has four beds in two separate bedrooms.

The camp is often full, so you'd be wise to reserve space in advance. If necessary, there are also two older, much more basic chalets constructed of reeds, which are cheaper than the brick ones.

Croc Camp's restaurant works on a 'set menu' basis for a fixed price (P50 per person). If you want to eat here then you should let them know in advance, by either dropping in or phoning. The bar stands on decking over the river, shaded by thatch.

If you need to spend some time here then there's a pleasant, small kidney-shaped swimming pool surrounded by a grassy area with seats, ideal for kids, and shady gardens where the tree species have been thoughtfully labelled. All this overlooks the Thamalakane River, which normally first flows around July, and then dries up again around December. *Rates: US$35/60 per person sharing/single. Breakfast/dinner costs US$10/22. Open: all year.*

Crocodile Camp Campsite PO Box 46, Maun; tel: 6860796; fax: 6860793; email: sales@botswana.com; web: www.botswana.com
A short walk from the main camp is a separate campsite, set under a few shady *Acacia erioloba* trees. There's a separate area within this for groups with overland trucks. It was all a bit dusty and dry when I visited, but that was in October. The site has three showers each for men and women, complete with hot and cold water and hand-basins with mirrors. *Rates: P20 per person per night. Open: all year.*

Island Safari Lodge (12 chalets and camping) PO Box 116, Maun; tel: 6860330; fax: 6862932; email: island@info.bw
Island Safari Lodge was a well-established hub when I first visited Maun in 1988. It's now run by the helpful Phil and Kay Potter and still stands in the same place, beside the Thamalakane River about 12km north of Maun, under a forest canopy dominated by tall sycamore figs (*Ficus sycomorus*). Coming from Maun you take a well signposted left turn just before the river. Then the drive (a kilometre or so) is corrugated and bumpy in places, but is a really lovely stretch of track through old riverine forest (and perfectly navigable for 2WD vehicles).

Accommodation here is in one of twelve thatched bungalows, which are widely spaced in indigenous vegetation and lawns beside the river. All have twin beds with mosquito nets, ceiling fans, tea and coffee facilities, and en-suite toilet and shower – and a bench outside on which to sit and contemplate the sunset!

The bar/restaurant can be lively when there are large groups in, but it's normally a more gentle, sedate spot which serves breakfast (a full one costs an extra P16.50 per person), bar snacks and light meals from 10.00 to 21.30, and à la carte dinners from 19.00 to 21.00. *Rates: P303 per chalet including light breakfast, P22 per person camping. Open all year.*

Maun Rest Camp (campsite) PO Box 250, Maun; tel: 6862623; tel/fax: 6863472 (with answerphone); email: simonjoyce@info.bw
This nice, quiet campsite is also the base for a small mobile safari operation (see page 173) run by the owners, Simon and Joyce. Find it by heading north from Maun on the road to Shorobe, Chobe and Moremi. They are about 7km past the Engen Filling Station.

Maun Rest Camp's campsite has good clean ablutions (four separate showers, loos and basins plus laundry tubs and sinks for dishes – all with copious hot water from a gas geyser) under some large shady trees. Ask the owners to show you the birdplum tree here, *Berchemia discolour*, which is indigenous but a little uncommon, with its thick foliage and small, edible fruits.

There's no bar or restaurant at the camp, though the Sports Bar and Restaurant is barely two minutes' walk away – so finding somewhere for a drink or dinner isn't a problem. If you don't have a tent then existing ones with bedding can be arranged for about P66 per person, or P30 for just the use of the tent's shell with no bedding.
Rates: P20 per person per night camping.

New Moon Campsite PO Box 210, Maun; tel/fax: 6861665; email: newmoon@info.bw
About 3km from the radio mast, on the road to Moremi, New Moon organises budget mokoro trips and has a small campsite. A short walk from the main camp is a separate campsite.
Open: April to December; can be difficult to contact at other times.

Okavango River Lodge (campsite and 4 bungalows) P Bag 28, Maun; tel/fax: 6863707; email: freewind@info.bw
Okavango River Lodge first opened in the late 1980s and stands on the opposite side of the Thamalakane River to Island Safari Lodge, about 15km north of Maun on the road to Shorobe, Chobe and Moremi.

It has a campsite beside the river, under shady acacias, with a volleyball court and swimming pool nearby.The rustic little lodge has a lively bar at its centre, and an efficient kitchen that will rustle up a variety of tasty bites from the bar menu, from toasted sandwiches to T-bone steaks. There's a wholesome set meal on offer every night. There are also four simple twin-bedded bungalows with showers and en-suite toilets.

Although not to everybody's taste, Okavango River Lodge does claim to have the only golf course in Maun – set in the open floodplain opposite camp. Whilst perhaps not very conventional, it's easy to play when the river is dry, and even more fun when it's in flood. This is a favourite with various local characters, especially on Sundays.

As well as booking activities for you, Okavango River Lodge have their own flexible mobile camping trips to Moremi, Nxai and Makgadikgadi, the Central Kalahari, or anywhere else in Botswana. All are tailor-made. If you take all your own camping equipment and food supplies, then expect a day-trip to Moremi to cost around P1,200 for the vehicle and driver; a one-night/two-day trip for P2,600 per person sharing, or a two-night/three-day trip for P4,000. Alternatively, Okavango River Lodge can supply all your food and camping equipment, though they'd have to make special arrangements for this.

Okavango River Lodge also organises various mokoro trips of varying lengths, based from the poling station at the Boro River in NG32. These range from day-trips, typically costing around US$60 per person sharing, to longer camping trips. A one-night/two-day trip costs US$90/100 per person sharing/single, or a two-night/three-day trip costs US$120/140 per person sharing/single. Note that even if you're paying the single supplement for your own mokoro, the transfers to/from the mokoro area need at least two people.
Rates: Camping costs P15 per person; the bungalows are P200 per bungalow, including breakfast.

Sitatunga Camp PO Box 66, Maun; tel: 6864539; email: sitatunga@info.bw
To reach Sitatunga Camp you head southwest from Maun, towards Toteng and Ghanzi, before turning off the main road about 10.8km past the old left turn to Francistown and the Engen Garage. The lodge is about 2km off the main road down a sandy track. Because of this distance, and the fact that all of Maun's other camps are on the road northwest of town, Sitatunga always feels something of an 'outsider'. However, situated next to the crocodile farm, it remains a good place for campers with vehicles who want a peaceful spot to stay for a few days. (Though Sunday can be busy, as it's a popular outing for Maun's residents.)

The campsites are spread out under trees. A shaded patio and adjacent bar (with braai facilities) stand beside a small pool nearby. The ablutions are basic but clean, and hot water is heated by (wood-burning) donkey-boiler. A simple laundry service is available: about P30 for a large pillowcase full, and P10 for a small one!

There is a small, but very busy, shop here selling a few very basic foodstuffs, cool drinks, wine, beer and an extensive range of ice cream. There's also a curio shop with T-shirts, hats and simple souvenirs. Many are branded with the logo of 'Penduka', reflecting that Sitatunga was bought by Penduka Safaris (see page 175) a few years ago, and is now used as their base. *Rates: P15 per person camping for overland trucks, P20 for private individuals, including firewood and entry to the crocodile farm.*

WHERE TO EAT

Maun's not really a town for fine dining, but there are a few reasonable venues, including some of the hotels and camps. There are also numerous fast-food places in town, including Nandos, Steers, Chicken Licken and many more. Expect a decent burger to cost around P10 – and remember that you're in a country which counts beef as one of its main exports.

Of the hotels, **Riley's** and **Maun Lodge** both have competent restaurants, though neither is really inspired and prices are relatively high. The **Sedia Hotel's** open-air restaurant beside its pool at the back can be fun with a good atmosphere, but the food isn't anything special.

Crocodile Camp always used to have the reputation for the best food. Whilst their set meals remain very competent, I don't think that they are now worthy of a special journey unless you're staying north of town – and they do need booking in advance early in the day. When full, **Island Safari Lodge's** bar can have a great mix of people. Again the food here is fine, but nothing amazing.

A few places are worth singling out that you might not otherwise find:

Bull & Bush Mathiba I Rd; tel: 6864250
On the road beside the airstrip, and within a short walk of the airport building, this is a lively spit-and-sawdust bar that is a fun place to eat and drink. It serves (often slowly) substantial bar meals at reasonable prices; expect steak-and-chips (P35), ribs with sauce (P35) and pizzas (P30). As this goes to press the news is that the Bull & Bush has been taken over by a chef of local renown with a reputation for trendy dishes, so it's certainly a place that's worth trying.

The locals know it as the 'Bullet & Ambush' – after its opening night, which was something of a gala event in Maun. Lots of the people in the safari industry turned up from all corners of the bush and, towards the end of the evening, someone was shot. Its nickname is a little unfair, as it's not by any means an unsafe place; quite the opposite, I'd recommend it.

The Power Station Mophane Rd; tel: 6862037
Round the corner from the Bull & Bush, the Power Station is a modern complex of quite radical design, incorporating a small theatre, various offices (including Okavango Tours & Safaris), a craft centre, Maun's first beauty salon and a fairly trendy small restaurant. In the evening there's also a lively bar which may continue late into the evening; it can be a busy spot. The restaurant here serves inventive salads (P25) and a good range of modern, light dishes (around P30–40) and juices; it's especially good for lunch.

Hillary's Coffee Shop Tel: 6861610
Located behind the offices of Okavango Wilderness Safaris, Hillary's is reached by taking a small side turning off Mathiba I Road, just before the Avis office. It's on the left as you walk from the airport's entrance gate towards the Bull & Bush.

Hillary's has been serving since about 1995, and is one of the more interesting and reliable places to eat in Maun.

Seating is either outside amongst mopane trees and pot plants, and the owner, Hillary, makes everything herself, from the mayonnaise and salad dressing to the bran muffins. Expect the best home-cooked breakfasts in Maun and tasty wholesome lunches all day long. Breakfast is P15–30, sandwiches and salads around P10–20, and amazing desserts and cakes for P10–20. Hillary's home-baked wholewheat bread is to die for, and with a little advance notice she can make this to order for a camping trip if you ask nicely...

The Sports Bar Shorobe Rd, Sedie, P Bag 272, Maun; tel: 6862676
This is a long-standing favourite, though a little out of town, to the north, and so you'll need transport to get here. Just head towards Chobe and turn right to it just before you cross the Thamalakane River. It's about 7km past the Engen Filling Station.

The Sports Bar serves food in the evening only, for dinner, but it's now probably *the* restaurant in the area – helped by speedy service and the frequent presence of the owners. The whole complex is spread over two levels, but the restaurant is downstairs and separate from the bar and pool tables.

The menu is fairly extensive, but it's known for great pizzas (P28–32), the best spare ribs in northern Botswana (P35), and a fine line in specials (around P35) and steaks (from P42). As you'd expect, the 'bar' area is well-stocked. Come here on a Friday night when the place rocks; there's usually a live DJ and no cover charge. It's here that Maun's younger and more affluent residents (including lots from the safari industry) and expats dance the night away.

The French Connection
This new café/restaurant has just opened next to BGI Liquor – around the corner from the power station. It's run by a couple of French/Dutch origin who used to run Crocodile Camp, and promises a modern and stylish range of sandwiches, baguettes and croissants. Expect smoked salmon and rocket on the menu, with costs around P20-30. It is licensed and has seating indoors or out.

Rendezvous
Is a new restaurant that opened in early 2002, near the Ngami Toyota garage. The author would welcome detailed reports, but I believe that it serves Indian and Chinese meals, at around P35–40 for a main course, and that they often have karaoke shows.

GETTING AROUND
A vehicle is useful in town, though taxis can be hailed from the street and are relatively inexpensive. If you're around the centre, between the banks and the airport, then walking is hot but feasible. Heading further out you'll need to either hitchhike or use a taxi.

Taxis
Maun's only taxis that you can pre-book and order by phone are **Atol Taxis**; tel: 6864770.

Minibuses
Small combies which frequent ply between the centre of town to the outlying suburbs and areas are used by most of the residents of Maun – at least those who don't have their own cars – most of the time. These routes aren't often clearly marked; you really need to ask someone and then hop on. Costs are very low though, typically just a couple of pula for a ten-minute ride.

GETTING ORGANISED
These days Maun is, above all for most visitors, a place to restock, refuel and get organised.

Banks and money

Many places in town will accept credit cards; some will take travellers' cheques. The main banks all have ATM machines that will deliver cash with most international cards, including Visa and MasterCard – which is usually the easiest, quickest and cheapest way to get Pula if you have a credit card.

Alternatively, with your passport and a little time spent in queues, you can cash travellers' cheques or obtain a manual cash advance on a credit card. The best place for this is one of the two main banks: **Barclays Bank** (PO Box 126, Maun; tel: 6860210; fax: 6860274) or **Standard Chartered Bank** (PO Box 112, Maun; tel: 6860209). Both are within sight of each other, virtually opposite Shoprite, slightly west of Riley's. These should certainly be your first stop if you need to arrange any more complex transactions.

There are a couple of **bureaux de change** dotted around town – Sunny's Bureau de Change being an obvious one, upstairs from Steers Restaurant. These generally charge more commission than the banks, though can be quicker to use and stay open longer. There won't be any difference in the effective exchange rates.

Shopping
Food and drink

Maun's original supermarket, 'Maun Fresh Produce' was taken over around 1997 by the giant South African supermarket chain of **Shoprite** (Tsheko Tsheko Road, Maun; tel: 6860497 or 6860015; fax: 6860342). In the same location, just west of Riley's, but much expanded, Shoprite is by far the town's largest supermarket now, and your first stop to buy food for an expedition. (Open 08.00–19.00 during the week, 08.00–17.00 on Saturday and 08.00–13.00 on Sunday, but closes for public holidays.)

More recently, two good new Spar shops have opened. The Delta Spar has opened opposite Shoprite (behind Nandos, opposite the taxi rank) and the other nearer the airport (in what's known as the 'New Mall', with Steers, the new Woolworths and a First National Bank).

With a combination of these (and often by just visiting one of the three!), you can buy most things here that you'll find in a supermarket in Europe or North America. However, often the brand names are different and the choice (especially of fresh fruit and vegetables) won't be as varied.

Local markets

The main local market is on Tsaro Street, virtually opposite Shoprite. Here you'll find lots of small stalls and local sellers; it's certainly worth checking out for the odd pile of fruit and vegetables. Also expect more offbeat foods, like mopane worms in season, and an assorted range of bootleg tapes and second-hand items.

Souvenirs and curios

There's no shortage of places that sell curios in Maun, and virtually every camp in Botswana has a small curio shop. However, there are still only a few really good places in Maun, including:

The General Trading Company PO Box 39, Maun; tel: 6860025. This shop has been established for years, next to Delta Sports, almost beside Riley's Garage. It has a comprehensive range of books on the region, endless T-shirts and souvenir and safari clothing, torches, knives and all sorts of useful stuff. Plus a good range of various carvings and crafts, some locally produced, others sourced from far away in Africa. Don't expect the prices here to be cheap, but do expect to find some high-quality souvenirs and probably what you want.

Bushman Curio Shop Tel: 6860220. Inside the gates of the airport, immediately opposite the steps to the main terminal building, this convenient little shop sells books, postcards, crafts and curios. Barely two-minutes' walk from the check-in desks, it's perfectly situated to dash out to whilst you're waiting for a plane! (Note this has close commercial links with the General Trading Company, above.)

The Craft Centre Mophane Road. PO Box 39, Maun; tel: 6863391. In the Power Station complex, on Mophane Road just off Mathiba I Road, this small shop sells local crafts including pottery, textiles, paper products and paintings. There's a workshop here with a kiln in which pottery is fired most days, having been glazed and made on the premises. Paper is also hand-made here, from a mixture of recycled paper and elephant dung (yes, really), and it's a place for various workshops and small exhibitions.

African Art & Images PO Box 236, Maun; tel: 6863584; fax: 6863594; email: african.art.images@botsnet.bw. Immediately across the road from the airport, beside the Bushman Curio Shop, this is owned by the well-known wildlife film-makers, Tim and June Liversage. In atmosphere it's reminiscent of a private art gallery, and it sells high-quality African art, carvings and photographs/prints – with correspondingly high price tags.

Garages and motor spares

If you're passing through and heading off into the bush then Maun is your best place to make sure your 4WD is in tip-top condition with plenty of spares. Some places that may be able to help include:

Ngami Toyota Tsheko–Tsheko Rd, PO Box 101, Maun; tel: 6860252; fax: 6860525. At the junction of Tsheko-Tsheko Road and Mathiba I Road, this is Maun's main Toyota dealer which has a bodyshop, spares and does repairs. They will repair all makes, not just Toyotas.

Motovac Plot 1196, New Mall, P Bag 202, Maun; tel: 6860872; fax: 6860008. This isn't a garage, but does sell spares and accessories.

Riley's Garage (Shell) P Bag 19, Maun; tel: 6860203; fax: 6860556; email: rg@info.bw. In the centre of town, next to the famous old hotel, this has 24-hour petrol, plus a workshop. It carries various spares including tyres and batteries.

Trans-world Motors Industrial Sites Box 20092, Maun; tel: 6862137; fax: 6860656. Offers mechanical repairs, panel beating and spray painting.

Tyre Services PO Box 130, Maun; tel: 6860860; fax: 6862108. Specialist supplier of tyres.

Tyre Vision PO Box 149, Maun; tel: 6860107. Specialist supplier of new tyres, tubes and rims – but mainly wholesale.

Vehicle hire

Avis PO Box 130, Maun; tel: 6860039 or 6860258; fax: 6861596
Holiday Safari 4x4 Hire P Bag 35, Maun; tel/fax: 6862429

Equipment hire

Most visitors either bring their own camping equipment, or arrive for trips which include it. If you don't, then some of the tour operators who run budget trips have their own schemes for you to hire their kit for the duration of the trip. However, if you need to buy some, or you need some of your own kit repaired, then the first place to try is:

Kalahari Kanvas Co PO Box 689, Maun; tel: 6860568; fax: 6860035; email: kal.kanvas@info.bw
On Mathiba I Road, next to Avis, Kalahari Kanvas started as a tiny tent repair company in 1986, and now employs about 45 people as a major manufacturer of tents and equipment for the safari industry. They also hire out an amazing range of such kit and offer a tent repair service.

For the forgetful traveller, or one that doesn't have the kit at home, you can hire just about anything that you need here, from a knife, fork and spoon set for P0.50 per day, to a 5.9m x 10.2m marquee/mess tent for P165 per day. A two-person canvas 2.4m x 2.4m bow tent costs about P37 per day; an intriguing two-person tree-hanging tent (which 'needs no poles but a tree is very necessary') costs P25 per day; and a double-canvas bedroll with 75mm-thick mattress, a blanket, two pillows and two sheets costs P30 per day. Deposits are required, proportional to the items hired, and credit cards are accepted. Best to book stuff in advance if you want it, and note that it must be returned here to the office in Maun.

National Parks and Wildlife Service Office

Set back from Sir Seretse Khama Road, and down a little passageway, this important office is set in a very unassuming complex of prefabricated government buildings. This is the place to book your campsites for all the national parks in northern Botswana, and if possible it's much, much better to come in person than to ring up or fax. See pages 142–3 for more details.

Open: Mon–Sat 07.00–12.30 and 13.45–16.30; Sun 07.30–12.00.

WHAT TO SEE AND DO

Maun is really much more of a place to get organised than it is a destination in its own right; so few visitors are really looking for activities here. That said, if you have half a day to kill, here are a few suggestions:

Birding walks

Richard Randall leads birding walks in the Maun area. Allow between two hours and a whole day, and you can cover any area from parts of the Thamalakane Riverbed as it passes through Maun, to the Game Sanctuary (see below) or the Boteti River bed, south of town. Expect this to cost about US$10 per person per hour, for a minimum of two people. (Contact Richard at Afro Trek on tel/fax: 6862574; tel: 686510; email: info@afrotrek.com; web: www.afrotrek.com)

Maun Game Sanctuary (Tel: 6861390)

Found on the northeast side of the Sekgoma Road, barely 2km from the centre of town, this small, fenced park is only about 3km long by 1km wide. However, it's a good, easy option for those who want to walk in a scenic area amongst non-dangerous game species and an impressive variety of birds.

The sanctuary preserves the last of the natural habitat that used to be found in and around Maun – before goats and people wreaked havoc on its vegetation. Here you'll find some some fine stands of real fan palms (*Hyphaene petersiana*), various acacia thickets and some lovely riverine woodland. It's bordered by the Thamalakane River, which attracts many aquatic bird species, whilst there are also a few open, grassy areas where you'll often find zebras, wildebeest and warthogs grazing.

Other animal species found here include blue wildebeest, red lechwe, kudu, impala, giraffe, chacma baboon, vervet monkey and a variety of smaller mammals. Most of the larger mammals are very relaxed and it's often possible to walk up close to them.

In summer here a keen bird-watcher should be able to count 80 to 100 species of birds here in three hours, although in winter it is more likely to be 50 to 80. Ones to look out for specially include red-necked falcon, bronze-winged courser, giant eagle-owl, lesser jacana, spotted dikkop, pied and Hartlaub's babblers, yellow-bellied eremomeia, and swamp boubou. Fish eagles and crimson-breasted boubous are fairly easily seen residents, whilst bat hawks are sometimes spotted hawking in the early morning or evening.

You can wander through here yourself – and cover most of the area in two to four hours, but better would be to come for a few hours of serious 'birding' with Richard Randall (see *Birding walks*, above) who knows the sanctuary well. *Admission: free. Open 07.30–12.30 and 13.45–16.40 most days.*

Maun Sports Complex
About 2.5km southwest of the Engen Garage and the old turn-off to Francistown, this large and impressive new sports arena stand beside the road to Ghanzi and is used for political rallies as well as sports matches. It's worth going just to marvel at the stadium, but check with the *Ngami Times* for what's on there.

Crocodile Farm PO Box 66, Maun; tel: 6864539; email: sitatunga@info.bw
On the same site as Sitautunga Camp (see pages 161–2), the turn-off for this is on the road to Toteng and Ghanzi, about 10.8km past the old left turn to Francistown and the Engen Garage.

Follow the signs to the camp and farm about 2km down a sandy track, and you'll find tours of the farm starting on the hour 09.00–16.00. You'll get to see crocodiles from hatchlings to fully-grown adults, and learn much about the morphology of these amazing reptiles.
Rates: P10 per person for the tour.

INFORMATION AND ADDRESSES
Safari companies
Looking at the length of this list, you'll realise that Maun is the safari capital of Botswana. Listed alphabetically, these range from large safari companies with many camps through to tiny operators which are little more than a guide and a vehicle.

Note that for most of the larger operators, the contact details listed here are simply their base for logistics and operations in Maun. Many do not have booking offices here, preferring to take all reservations, and answer all queries from visitors, from dedicated reservation offices elsewhere (usually Johannesburg in South Africa).

In contrast the smaller operations will often take days, or even weeks, to answer communications – sometimes because the whole team is out of the office and on safari. This kind of tiny outfit has both its advantages and disadvantages, as you'll realise.

African Horseback Safaris PO Box 20538, Maun; tel/Fax: 663154; email: sjhorses@info.bw; web: www.africanhorseback.com
Specialist horse-riding safaris based out of Macatoo Camp on the western side of the Delta, in NG26. See page 310–11 for details.

Afro Trek P Bag 58, Maun; tel/fax: 6862574; tel: 686510; email: info@afrotrek.com; web: www.afrotrek.com
Run by Richard Randall, Allan Bimson and Janet Maruza, this relatively new company is based next to the internet café in the Sedia Hotel complex. (It has sprung up as Quadrum Safaris has been phased out.) They offer a variety of options, including some original short trips in and around Maun.

Afro Trek's shortest trip is a two-hour guided birding walk from the Sedia Hotel led by Richard Randall, who has been a keen birdwatcher in the area for many years, some of them spent guiding and running camps in the Delta. With more time, Richard's three-hour trip usually takes in the birds of the Maun Game Sanctuary, while his four-hour trip is long enough to reach the reedbeds and pools of the Boteti River, south of Maun. These cost about US$10 per person per hour, for a minimum of two people.

Afro Trek also offers budget mokoro trips in NG32 (see page 339). These involve road transfers to/from Ditshipi Village on the Santantadibe River, and then taking a poler and mokoro from there. (Alternatively, going from a launch on the Boro River is also possible.) These cost around US$55 per person sharing for a day-trip, US$85/130 per person sharing/single for a two-day/one-night trip, and US$110/170 per person sharing/single for a three-day/two-night trip. Travellers supply all their own camping kit, food and drinks.

They've a range of good value mobile trips which cost around US$120 per person (based on a minimum of four people) per day. Trips typically last between three and five days (two and four nights), and camping kit is supplied. All the usual areas are offered – Chobe/Moremi, Makgadikgadi/Nxai, and even the Central Kalahari Game Reserve.

Afroventures see CC Africa, below.

Audi Camp Safaris P Bag 28 Maun, Botswana; tel: 6860599; fax: 6860581; email: audicamp@info.bw; web: www.audicamp.bizland.com
Based out of Audi camp (see page 159) north of Maun, Audi Camp Safaris have their town office next to the Bull & Bush, on Mathiba I Road. From here they organise shuttle transfers between Maun and Windhoek (see page 154) – and also run fully-fledged budget mobile trips, and drive-in mokoro trips in the Delta, in conjunction with the local polers of the Ditshipi area in NG32 (see page 339).

Their simple mobile trips run with a minimum of two people and include meals, park fees, vehicle, guide and camping equipment – but travellers are expected to bring their own drinks and sleeping bags, and muck in with all the camp chores. Typical prices would be US$725 per person for a four-night Moremi/Chobe trip, scheduled to start every Thursday; US$395 per person for a two-night Moremi trip; and US$755 per person for a four-night trip to the Central Kalahari.

Mokoro trips depart from Audi Camp around 07.45 and return around 17.00. You're driven by 4WD for about two hours to the poling station at Morutsa or Ditshipi, on the lower reaches of the Santantadibe River. There you meet your poler and head off up the river for your trip – later returning downstream, and being driven back to Maun the same way. (See my comments on budget trips in the section on NG32.)

If you take all your own camping equipment and food supplies, then this costs US$65 for a one-day trip – though this is hardly worth the effort for the minimal time that you get on the water. Better to take a one-night/two-day trip for US$110 per person sharing, or a two-night/three-day trip for US$145. Alternatively, Audi Camp can provide all the food and camping equipment – but then the two-night/three-day trip costs US$220 per person sharing.

Botswana Safaris & Tours P Bag BO46, Boseja, Maun; tel/fax: 6864845; home: 6862656; cell: 0721518; email: botswanasafaris@botsnet.bw or edurne@info.bw
Run by Guy Symons (a guide trained in South Africa) and Edurne Martinez (who is also a partner in Africa Pride (see page 177), Botswana Tours & Safaris has been running mobile trips to all the parks and areas of interest in northern Botswana since about 1989.

They have a number of fixed departure dates and their standard 10-day/9-night camping trip from Maun to Victoria Falls costs US$2,000 per person. They will also organise private mobile trips, usually concentrating on Chobe, Moremi, the Central Kalahari and the great salt pans area.

Bush Ways Safaris P Bag 342, Maun; tel/fax: 6863685; email: reservations@bushways.com; web: www.bushways.com
Established in 1996, Bush Ways Safaris operates small-group mobile trips with guaranteed departures, as well as tailor-made trips. Their scheduled trips cover Chobe, Moremi, Nxai, Makgadikgadi and the Central Kalahari, whilst their tailor-made mobile trips go anywhere. Their custom-built vehicles have canvas tops, open sides (with covered sides for wet or wind), and take a maximum of twelve passengers.

A typical guided trip like their 6-night/7-day 'Buffalo' itinerary spends three nights in Moremi, two in Chobe and one in Livingstone, and costs around US$825 per person sharing. It has the advantage of being on fixed dates and will run even if there's only one person booked onto it.

Bush Ways' scheduled trips are 'semi-participation' – where travellers pitch their own tents and assist with catering duties 'if they wish'. The costs include accommodation in two-man tents with mattresses, all meals and park entry fees. It doesn't include drinks or some of your meals at the lodge in Livingstone, and you should bring your own sleeping bag and pillow.

Their private mobile trips can be more luxurious, though the cost of these will be significantly more, as you'd expect. Note that they have guides who can speak French, German, Spanish, English and Afrikaans, and if you're organising a private safari then specify that you want a guide who speaks your language.

Butler & Lindstrom Safaris PO Box 236, Maun; tel: 6860994; fax: 6860995; cell: 716 56455; email: sls@info.bw
This company has been run since the early 1980s as Soren Lindstrom Safaris – owned by the eponymous, well-known professional guide. In the last few years it's been renamed, as Soren has been joined by Greg Butler – another top professional guide – and his wife, Kelly. Soren has now retired from most of the guiding, which is these days usually led by Greg.

This is a top-end company offering expert-guided tailor-made private safaris in both the national parks and a few of the region's private concession areas (where they can offer walking and night drives). Expect very comfortable camping: the large walk-in tents have en-suite showers and flush toilets; the cuisine is impressive and served in style by candlelight; the guiding is amongst the best around.

Vehicles are custom-built Toyota 4WDs (some open and some fitted with roof hatches), which take a maximum of five people. Expect costs of around US$350 per person per day, regardless of group size – including all meals, activities, drinks and park fees.

Capricorn Safaris P Bag 21, Maun; tel: 6861165; fax: 6862991; email: capsaf@info.bw
Run by Adam and Brigette Hedges, who have a long pedigree from running safaris in Kenya and Tanzania with Dick Hedges' Safaris (Adam's father), Capricorn is a reliable operator with fixed-date trips across northern Botswana. They can also organise private mobile trips anywhere you want to go.

Capricorn's most popular trip is a 13-night/14-day mobile that usually starts with a night in Maun at Riley's Hotel or Crocodile Camp. Typically this continues with two nights in a mobile tented camp either in Nxai Pan or the Okavango (depending on the season); then four nights in Moremi, including a boat trip and a night fly-camping on an island; then five nights split between two different areas in Chobe; before ending with a night at Victoria Falls.

Transport is by custom built Toyota LandCruisers (maximum of six travellers plus a driver/guide in each) which have large roof hatches for photography, a drinks fridge and a small reference library. The camp is erected by the back-up team, so visitors have no chores to do. Tents are Meru-style in which you can stand. They have twin beds (with duvets, pillows and towels) and bedside battery lights. Hot bucket showers and long-drop toilets are shared. Food includes full three-course dinners, which are wholesome but not fancy, served at a candlelit table in the dining tent. All wine, drinks and bottled water are included.

Capricorn offers good-value, fairly traditional mobile safaris without too many frills, and with the emphasis firmly on game viewing. Travellers from the UK often come through the large, world-wide British operator, Kuoni – and this is often their first taste of southern Africa.

Rates: from March to June and October this costs US$3,200/3,400 per person sharing/single; during July, August and September the price increases to US$3,560/3,760 per person sharing/single. Between November and February there are no scheduled trips, only private mobile safaris for small groups.

Crocodile Camp Safaris PO Box 46, Maun; tel: 6860796 or 6860265; fax: 6860793; email: sales@botswana.com; web: www.botswana.com
From its base in the Bull & Bush building, near the airport, CCS run Semetsi Camp and Gunn's camps (see page 322) in NG27B, on the southwest side of Chief's Island. They also manage Swamp Air. Until about 2001, they ran Gomoti, in NG32, but this has since been closed. They have some of the best, or at least the most visible, marketing of any of the smaller Maun-based safari operators – with a large variety of possibilities on offer.

CCS have their own infrastructure and guides for mobile camping trips around Botswana, and these they build into a variety of small low/mid-budget packages. They also market mid-budget fly-in trips, often combining their own camps with other mid-range options like Okuti at Xakanaxa, or Chobe Safari Lodge.

If you're in Maun and looking for something relatively inexpensive and last-minute, then CCS should certainly be high on your list.

CC Africa Sir Seretse Khama Rd, DDS Complex; tel: 661979; fax: 661972; email: ccabotswana@info.bw; web: www.ccafrica.com
Originally called 'The Conservation Corporation', CC Africa made its name with a vision for conservation through super-luxurious lodges like Londolozi and Ngala, based on private land adjoining the Kruger National Park, in South Africa's Eastern Transvaal (the area now called Mpumalanga). Their prices were high, but they promised top-class levels of food, service and guiding at a time when most of their competition had only just discovered en-suite toilets. Now they have lodges throughout east and southern Africa, including Nxabega and Sandibe in the Okavango – two very high-quality lodges in private photographic reserves.

In 1999, the Conservation Corporation merged with AfroVentures, a large established company which focused on mobile guided trips around the subcontinent. Under the AfroVentures name, they still run high-quality mobile trips in northern Botswana, including some innovative, original itineraries.

CC Africa's Maun office doesn't usually take bookings; see page 96 for details of where to make reservations.

Desert & Delta Safaris Lot 851, Opposite Nhabe Museum, Desert & Delta Complex, P Bag 310, Maun; tel: 6861234/6862246; fax: 6861791; email: reservations@desertdelta.com; web: www.desertdelta.com
Operating only in Botswana (plus Lianshulu, just over the Kwando in Namibia), Desert & Delta was originally started by Jessie Neil, in 1982. Now it runs Chobe Game Lodge, Chobe Savanna Lodge, Lianshulu Bush Lodge (actually just over the Kwando River in Namibia!), Savute Safari Lodge, Camp Moremi, Camp Okavango and Xugana Island Lodge.

A typical six-night package, including two nights in each of six lodges starting and ending in Maun costs around US$2,760/3,540 per person sharing/single from July to October; US$2,400 per person sharing or single for the rest of the year.

Drumbeat Safaris PO Box 20228, Maun; tel/fax: 6863096; email: drumbeat@info.bw
Run by Johan Knols and Annelies Zonjee, who are of Dutch origin and ran camps for Ker & Downey for many years, Drumbeat started in 1995. It offers high-quality mobile safaris for individuals and small groups throughout northern Botswana. Trips are usually guided personally by Johan (who speaks English, Dutch and German), whilst Annelies manages the camps with a small team of staff. The vehicles used are open 'safari outfitted' Toyota Landcruisers, with extensive radio communications. These take a maximum of seven

visitors plus the guide, so the camp's equipment and staff accompany the tour in a separate DAF 4WD truck.

Safari accommodation is in large Meru-style walk-in tents with two proper beds, a private bush shower and private long-drop toilets. There's also a separate dinner tent used in these camps, where impressive three-course meals are prepared and served. Camps are usually set up on private 'Mobile Operator' campsites within the parks and the trips include park fees, activities, all meals, all drinks and laundry – and welcome children as part of a safari party.

As all trips are private safaris, costs depend on how many people are travelling together. A typical six-night/seven-day safari into Moremi and Chobe would cost around US$2,595/1,665/1,345 per person for each of 2/4/6 people from January to mid-June, or mid-October to December. During the busier season, from mid-June to mid-October the same trip would cost US$3,115/1,995/1,615 per person for each of 2/4/6 people.

Eco Africa Botswana (PTY) Ltd P Bag 371, Maun; tel: 6862427; email: rogersafaris@info.bw
Run by Roger and Sophie Dugmore, Eco Africa Botswana specialises in small mobile safaris and specialised photographic expeditions around all of Botswana's national parks and wilder areas. Typical ball-park costs for fully-inclusive trips would be around US$620 per night for an individual travelling alone, US$550 per person per night for two people, US$495 for three, or US$450 for four or more people.

Elephant Back Safaris P Bag 332, Maun; tel: 6861260; fax: 6861005; email: ebs@info.bw; web: www.elephantbacksafaris.com
The booking and logistical office in Maun runs the ultra-upmarket Abu camp, on the west of the Delta in NG26. See pages 307–10 for more details, and don't even think about asking for any cheap last-minute deals. They don't exist!

Game Trails Safaris P Bag BO13, Maun; tel: 6862405; fax: 6862405; email: gametrails@botsnet.bw
Game Trails operates exclusive, tailor-made mobile safaris throughout Botswana's main parks and wilderness areas. Some are more basic, others less so. Typical costs for their three levels of trips are around US$120 per person per night for their adventure safaris, US$200 for their serviced safaris and US$260 for their semi-luxury safari.

Gunn's Camp Safaris see Crocodile Camp Safaris, above.

Island Safari Lodge PO Box 116, Maun; tel: 6860330; fax: 6862932; email: island@info.bw
Based out of the lodge (see page 160), north of Maun, are a variety of budget mokoro trips and participation safaris – all of which can often be booked at short notice when you're in Maun.

Island Safari have been very supportive of the Okavango Polers' Trust, and their trips based out of Mbiroba Camp (see page 352), and so usually have packages which include flights there and back, and time in the Delta. You'll need to take all your food and equipment, yet stay within a modest 10kg luggage allowance.

They also run their own trips on the Boro River in conjunction with the local polers in NG32 (see pages 339–40). These trips start from Island Safari Lodge at around 08.00 and normally return around 17.00. You're driven by 4WD for about two hours to the poling station at Morutsa, on the lower reaches of the Boro River, where you meet your poler and head off up the river. After your trip you'll return downstream, and be driven back to Maun the same way. (See my comments on budget trips in the section on NG32.)

For these you need to bring all your own food and camping kit. Costs are around US$70 per person for a one-day trip – though this is hardly worth the effort for the minimal time that you get on the water. Better take a one-night/two-day trip for US$150 per person sharing, or a two-night/three-day trip for US$210. A trip very like this, from Island Safari Lodge, was my first view of the Okavango, about 15 years ago – and whilst it has its limitation, I'd still regard four or five days in the Delta like this as remarkably good value.

Island Safari's participation safaris are squarely aimed at backpackers who haven't got the transport or the kit, but want to see something of the parks on an inexpensive trip. They'll supply an open-topped 4WD (usually with optional canvas sun shade) which takes up to six passengers and a professional guide. Also dome tents, mattresses, cooking equipment, crockery, gas lamps, cooler boxes and ice, and basically all the rest of the usual paraphernalia that goes with a trip to the bush. Food is included, but soft drinks and alcohol are not.

The costs for these trips varies with the destination and group size. To hire just the 4WD and driver/guide is around US$300 per day (from experience, they won't let you drive their vehicles yourself!). Budget safaris around the parks of northern Botswana, including camping equipment, food and park fees cost around US$210/130/100 per person for two/four/six people. If you're booking any of their trips during the green season, from December to March, then sometimes there's a discount available of up to 20%.

Ker & Downey Airport Box 27, Maun; tel: 6860375 / 6861226; fax: 6861282; email: safari@kerdowney.bw; web: www.kerdowney.com
Now based out of offices near the airport, behind the Duck Inn, Ker and Downey are two of the oldest names in the Delta. As far back as 1945, Donald Ker and Syd Downey founded a hunting safari company in Kenya, only to be joined in the mid-1950s by Harry Selby – who started their Botswana operations in 1962. Around 1979 they bought Khwai River Lodge, as a photographic camp, and in 1985 the photographic company 'Ker, Downey Selby' was split off from the hunting company, Safari South.

Today it's known simply as Ker & Downey, and they run Camp Okuti, Kanana, Machaba, Shinde and its neighbouring walking trails, known as 'Footsteps across Africa'. These are all quite different camps and experiences, and the costs vary too. Reservations for Ker & Downey camps can be made through their Maun office, above, or their Houston office in the US (see page 96).

Expect a 6-night/7-day trip, visiting two of their camps to cost around US$2,950/4,150 per person sharing/single from July to October, or about US$2,500/2,800 for the same trip in the rest of the year. Including all internal transfers, activities, meals, laundry and local drinks.

Kgori Safaris P Bag 146, Maun; tel: 6862049 or 6861073; fax: 6862048; mobile: 72152596; email: kgorisaf@info.bw; web: www.mankwe.com
A relatively new company on Botswana's scene, they own and run Mankwe Bush Lodge, in NG45, just south of Chobe and east of Moremi, and also manage the boat station on the northwest tip of Mboma Island in Moremi. Their reservations are administered from South Africa at tel: (27) 12 3617464; fax: (27) 12 3617464; email: tourism@mankwe.com.

Kwando Safaris PO Box 550, Maun; tel: 6861449; fax: 6861457; email: reservations@kwando.co.za; web: www.kwando.co.za
Based here in Maun, Kwando is a small, independent operator running three first-class camps in Botswana, as well as Songwe Village, a small camp in Zambia near Livingstone which overlooks the Zambezi's gorge, just below Victoria Falls.

Lagoon and Lebala are primarily dry-land camps beside the Kwando River in NG14, and Kwara has a full range of dry and wet activities, on the north side of the Delta. All are different, but all three operate game drives with both a tracker and a driver – a real advantage when it comes to tracking the predators. Their focus is on enthusiastic wildlife spotting rather than excessive frills in camp, although their camps are of a very good standard.

Expect a 6-night/7-day trip, visiting two of their camps to cost around US$3,450/4,890 per person sharing/single from July to October, or about US$2,490/3,510 for the same trip in the rest of the year. Including all internal transfers, activities, meals, laundry and local drinks.

Linyanti Explorations Based in Kasane, from where they run Selinda and Zibalianja camps adjacent to the Zibadianja Lagoon on the Kwando/Linyanti system. See pages 192–3 for details.

Lodges of Botswana The Power Station Building, PO Box 39, Maun; tel: 6861154; fax: 6860589; email: lodges@okavango.bw; web: www.okavango.bw
This Maun-based company is run by irrepressible Peter Sandenbergh, who was one of the first to see the area's potential for backpacking tourism as well as the more usual up-market variety. Today they own and run Delta Camp and Oddballs, in NG27B. They are based in the Power Station Building and have particularly close links with the General Trading Company, the Power Station, the airline Delta Air and the Maun-based travel agent, Okavango Tours and Safaris.

Masson Safaris P Bag 257, Maun; tel/fax: 6862442; email: sallie@masson-safaris.com; web: www.masson-safaris.com
Physically located at Plot 855, Tsanokana Ward, Masson Safaris runs mobile photographic safaris which concentrate on game and bird life, with a general appreciation of Botswana's more remote areas. (Especially keen on the more offbeat bits of the Kalahari – the Great Salt Pans, Tsodilo, and the Central Kalahari.) They're a small, family operation. Ewan Masson, who has been guiding in Botswana for 15 years, leads most trips. The mobile camps have walk-in dome tents, complete with linen, washstand, reading light and a private chemical flush loo. Game drives are taken in extended Land Rovers, taking a maximum of eight guests.

The costs for private tailor-made safaris vary depending on the itinerary and the number of travellers. Expect a trip across Moremi and Chobe, with seven-days and six nights spent in the parks to cost around US$250/200/150 per day per person sharing between July and October for a group of 2/4/6 people. For the rest of the year this would be nearer US$200/150/125 per day per person sharing

They also run several scheduled safaris every year, with some details of these posted on their website (but few prices). Prices vary, but a typical 14-day trip costs around US$150 per person sharing per day.

Maun Rest Camp Safaris PO Box 250, Maun; tel: 6862623; tel/fax: 6863472 (with answerphone); email: simonjoyce@info.bw
Based from Maun Rest Camp (see pages 160–1), owners Simon & Joyce run fairly small, low-budget mobile safaris. Their mobiles use adapted Toyota Landcruisers and are led by either Simon or Joyce – both of whom are qualified guides. A staff member comes along with each trip to help with the camp chores. For accommodation they use bedrolls inside dome tents (in which you can stand), and make an effort with the catering to provide good, wholesome meals. Don't expect glossy brochures or silver service here, but do expect a swift and efficient response to any queries and a budget safari at a very fair price.

They cover the Moremi and Chobe areas as well as the Central Kalahari, Nxai Pan, Baines' Baobabs, Makgadikgadi, Tsodilo Hills and even Drotsky's Caves. Costs depend on the number of participants – but a larger group means lower prices. Expect a typical 2-night/3-day trip to Moremi to work out at about US$525/350/300 per person when there are 2/4/6 people travelling together, or US$1,000/625/500 per person for a swift 4-night/5-day trip across Chobe and Moremi (in either direction). Their costs include all guiding, fuel, park fees, camping kit, food, wine, beer and cold drinks. You'd be wise to make arrangements in advance if you can, simply so they can secure bookings for your trip with the National Park's campsites.

Moremi Safaris P Bag 26, Maun; tel: 6860222
Runs: Xakanaxa Camp.

New Moon Safaris P Bag 210, Maun; tel/fax: 6861665; email: newmoon@info.bw

Okavango Polers' Trust PO Box 24, Seronga; tel: 6876861.
Based on the northern edge of the Delta, at Seronga (a village of about 3,000 people), this is
a village co-operative of mokoro polers who have joined together to offer budget trips in
the north of the Delta. You can get to Serong yourself, or book flights and a package there
with the local operators in Maun. See page 352 for more details and costs.

Okavango Wilderness Safaris Mathiba I Road, P.Bag 14, Maun; tel: 6860086; fax:
6860632. Note that to make reservations or enquiries you should call their Johannesburg
office (see pages 96–7).
Started by safari guides Colin Bell, Chris MacIntyre (not the author!) and Russel Friedman
in Botswana in 1983, this has since grown into one of the subcontinent's leading safari
organisers – with operations in Botswana, South Africa, Namibia, Zimbabwe, Zambia (The
River Club in Livingstone) and, most recently, on the North Island in the Seychelles. They
have close business links with Sefofane, the flight company.
   In Botswana, their operations office is virtually opposite the airport, slightly set back
on Mathiba I Road. From there they run Botswana's largest selection of safari camps.
These are mostly in private reserves and include: DumaTau, King's Pool, Linyanti
Tented Camp and Savuti Camp in NG15; Kaparota, Vumbura and Little Vumbura in
NG22; Duba Plains in NG23; Kwetsani, Jacana, Jao and Tubu in NG25; Pom Pom in
NG27A; Chitabe and Chitabe Trails in NG31; and Mombo, Little Mombo, Xigera and
Zepa in the Moremi Game Reserve. The style and standard of these do vary, and
recently have been marketed as either 'platinum', 'classic' or 'vintage' camps – with
prices which vary slightly accordingly. However, despite this, Wilderness effectively set
the 'base-line' standard for the high-quality camps in Botswana, by which other
operators tend to be measured.
   Expect a 6-night/7-day trip, visiting three of their rustic 'vintage' camps to cost around
US$2,335/3,485 per person sharing/single from January to June or in November and
December. From July to October the same trip would cost about US$3,300/4,4450 per
person sharing/single. A similar trip using the 'classic' camps would be US$3,880/5,352
from July to October, whilst 6 nights at the two 'platinum' camps (Mombo and Jao) would
cost around US$5,758/7,606 from July to October.
   The Maun office doesn't usually take bookings; see pages 96–7 for contact details of
where to make reservations. Note that Wilderness actively advises travellers to book
through their local tour operator rather than making direct bookings.

Orient-Express Safaris (formerly **Gametrackers**) PO Box 100, Maun; tel: 6860302; fax:
6860153; email: gtb.mngr@info.bw; web: www.gametrackers.orient-express.com
Originally an old safari company run by a couple in Maun, Gametrackers was bought in
the early 1990s by the Orient Express Group. They not only own the famous Venice-
Simplon Orient Express train, but also a string of top hotels around the world including
the Mount Nelson in Cape Town, Hotel Splendido in Portofino (Italy), and Le Manoir
aux Quat'Saisons in the UK.
   In Botswana, their office is situated very close to the airport, on Airport Road,
between the Department or Surveys and Mapping and Merlin Air Service. Gametrackers
now have Savute Elephant Camp (which used to be two camps, Savuti South and
Allen's Camp), Khwai River Lodge and Eagle Island Camp. Their roots in the hotel
trade show through in a very similar style for all of their camps, and virtually identical
room designs: basically very high specification hotel rooms built on wooden platforms
with canvas walls.

Expect a 6-night/7-day trip, visiting all of their camps for three nights each, to cost around US$2,740/3,460 per person sharing/single from January to June or in November and December. From July to October the same trip would cost about US$3,370/4,090 per person sharing/single. See page 96 for contact details to make reservations.

Penduka Safaris PO Box 66, Maun; tel: 6864539; fax: 6864540; email: sitatunga@info.bw
Based at Sitatunga Camp (see pages 161–2), Penduka Safaris was started as long ago as 1963 by Izak Barnard, and has been run by his son, Willem, for the past ten years. Penduka operates fully inclusive safaris throughout Botswana; all camp duties are taken care of by permanent staff. Excellent meals with fresh fruit and vegetables are served daily, and they provide large spacious tents with camp beds and mattresses. Vehicles are specially-adapted 4WDs with pop-top roofhatches.

Expect costs of around US$200 per person per day to join a trip with 6-8 passengers. Trips to vary in length, and some are tailor-made, but 8–12 nights would be typical.

Penstone Safaris PO Box 370, Maun; tel: 6861721; fax: 6861722; email: penelope@info.bw
Penstone have an office opposite Audi's (on left of power station). They used to do mobiles, though rarely do now – but will lead the occasional drive-between-camp trip for travellers who know them well and have been on safari with them in previous years.

Phakawe Safaris Shorobe Rd, P.Bag 385, Maun; tel/fax: 6864377; email: sarah@phakawe.demon.co.uk; web: www.phakawe.demon.co.uk
Run by Sarah and Steve, Phakawe Safaris is based about 3km north of the centre of Maun, in the Sedia area. It's clearly visible on the left as you drive towards Moremi or Chobe. It is a very successful operation offering some of the cheapest budget safaris around; some with scheduled departure dates, others tailor-made to suit groups of four people or more. Costs for either are usually US$120 per day. This includes transfers and transport (usually a maximum of six people per trip), parks fees, ingredients for all meals and use of simple tents, mattresses and camping kit. It doesn't include sleeping bags, drinks or any 'optional activities'.

Their website covers a lot of information, and their trips are long – typically eleven days. However, if you want to really understand where they go, you'll have to quiz them carefully. Find out exactly what is, and what is not, included – and where their trips stay each night.

Looking carefully at their eleven-day 'Northern Parks' trip, you'll find the first night is spent camping in Maun. Then three days/two nights on a budget mokoro trip in NG32 – the type of trip that's offered by many budget operators at an average daily rate that's lower than US$120. Then you return to Maun, for another night camping before heading into Moremi (again, camping at South Gate would have been better – but is more costly.) The next night heads you north again for five nights through Moremi and Chobe. Then there's a night at Ngoma and one camping at Kasane – both of which would be more interesting spent at Ihaha campsite, in the park ... although the park fees would make that option more expensive.

So whilst US$1,320 is quite good value for the whole trip, when you look carefully at the finer details, with even a modicum of local knowledge, they are not *amazing* value. It's not only the luxuries that have been cut to make these trips cheap, it's also the time spent in prime game areas.

Planet Okavango Mophane Rd, PO Box 236, Maun; tel: 6864575; email: planet.okavango@info.bw
Run by the helpful and efficient Sarah Collins, Planet Okavango don't run any lodges – but they do oversee and co-ordinate all of the budget poling trips in NG32. See my comments on pages 239–40 and you'll realise that they're useful people to talk to first about these budget mokoro trips.

They also run their own mokoro trips into NG32, though these are a slight cut above the rest. Their day-trip to mokoro here includes a picnic lunch, and costs US$45 per person sharing. For overnight trips they pre-arrange small bushcamps, complete with a cook and a camp attendant, dome tents, bed-rolls, linen and blankets. These are set for you in advance, before you arrive, near the river along which you're being poled. Their 2-day/1-night trip costs US$190 per person sharing, while a 3-day/2-night trip is US$285 per person sharing. These costs are good value for what they offer, as they include transfers, food, soft drinks, equipment (and staff help!) and mokoro trips, but exclude any alcohol.

With very close connections to the communities in NG32, Planet Okavango has also been running some simple camping mobiles in that area in the past – though it's uncertain if they will continue to do this. Contact them if you're interested.

Quadrum Expeditions – now seems to have been 'phased out' in favour of Afro Trek, see above.

Sanctuary Lodges P Bag 45, Maun; tel: 6862688; fax: 6863526
Abercombie & Kent's lodges in Botswana and East Africa – including Chobe Chilwero and Chief's Camp – are now being marketed by this apparently new company. However, the style of the lodges remains firmly that of A&K, and as Geoffrey Kent (A&K's founder and owner) also owns Sanctuary Lodges, this has left some people alleging that this is simply an exercise in 'rebranding'. Observers note that in the past there has been a reluctance amongst other tour operators to book visitors into A&K's lodges; they were perceived as belonging to a competitor. It remains to be seen if this change of name will make a difference.

Whatever the company background, expect a 6-night/7-day trip, visiting their lodges to cost around US$2,850 per person sharing or single from January to June or in November and December. From July to October the same trip would cost about US$3,750/4,650 per person sharing/single. The Maun office doesn't take bookings; see page 97 for details of where to make reservations.

Wilderness Dawning P Bag B017, Maun; tel/fax: 6862962; email: wd@info.bw
Wilderness Dawning is a reliable small mobile operator that boasts that its guides all have a minimum of ten years' guiding experience in Botswana. They offer a mix of scheduled and tailor-made safaris, some aimed at mid-level budgets, and others more luxuriously accommodated trips, taking in all the usual wildlife areas of northern Botswana.

Costs start at about U$170–200 per person per day for comfortable camping trips, where back-up crews do all the work (and all the food, activities and equipment are included.) The tents on these trips are walk-in dome tents about 2.4m x 2.4m, and 1.8m high, with proper beds and all linen including sheets, blankets, pillows and sleeping bags. Toilets and hot bucket showers are shared; one between three tents.

They also have an innovative range of luxury mobile safaris where you sleep at lodges, but you drive between them, and go on game drives, with the same experienced guide for the whole trip. This offers the best of both worlds in some ways – comfort of accommodation and continuity of guiding – but costs from about U$390 per person per day.

Wilderness Dawning use custom-made Toyota LandCruisers, which take a maximum of eight guests in individual bucket seats. The vehicles have roll-down canvas sides and tops.

Wilderness Safaris See Okavango Wilderness Safaris, page 174.

Wild Lifestyles PO Box 66, Maun; tel: 6863664; fax: 6861045; email: mikepenman@info.bw; web: www.wildlifestyles.com
Mike Penman isn't a guy that shrinks into the background easily, but when on good form he can be exactly the kind of large, slightly wild, old-style guide that you'd want to have between you and a charging buffalo. He's been guiding in Botswana for many years, and knows northern Botswana well. His trips range from the normal Maun-Chobe routes,

through to more esoteric options of the Bushmen at Xai Xai and some of the private concessions. These are usually a mixture of luxury mobile trips, and also specialist trips for film-makers and photographers. Recently Mike has collaborated on several trips with another guide who is well-known locally, Mark Tennant (from Kwando Safaris).

Mike's wife, Anglie, runs most of the logistics and keeps the camp standards very high. Accommodation is usually in dome tents with beds, mattresses, high-quality linens, and down duvets and pillows. These have private bucket showers and long-drop toilets. The vehicles used are Toyota HiLuxes with raised seats on the back, beneath a canvas sunshade, usually accompanied by a back-up vehicle carrying the camp. Meals are a highlight, with excellent food and wine; expect crystal glasses and china on white tablecloths served by lantern-light.

Trips cost around US$475/625 per person per night sharing/single between May and October, when a trip can be confirmed with a minimum of two people. From November to April expect around US$375/500 per person per night sharing/single, although then a minimum of four people is required to confirm a trip. This excludes park fees, campsite fees, recommended tips and any boat or mokoro hire in the Delta.

Travel agents and others

Glancing superficially, Maun may seem to the uninitiated to be full of travel agents. However, many of the companies you see are tour operators who own and run camps and safari companies. However, if you look hard there are a handful of normal travel agents who (generally) know the local safari industry well, and can help you choose a trip. They are especially useful if you arrive in Maun without any arrangements and want to book a budget trip immediately. In such cases, booking through one of these agents will cost you exactly the same as booking directly with the camp or safari company.

The caveats to this are that none are well prepared for booking a range of the top-end lodges at short notice; there's very little demand for this. Secondly, some will have their own favourite camps or operators – so do ask them to be exhaustive about researching the options for you before you make a decision. Also ask them to make very clear if anyone associated with their travel agent has any links with the camps/trips that they're suggesting to you. (This shouldn't necessarily put you off booking – but you ought to know!)

Africa Pride P Bag BO 46, Boseja, Maun; tel/fax: 6864845; email: africapride@botsnet.bw; web: www.africapridebotswana.com. Based in Maun and run by owners, Edurne Martinez and Carol-Ann Green, Africa Pride is a booking agent/tour operator for lodges throughout southern Africa and the Indian Ocean islands. They can arrange for Spanish, French, German and Italian interpreters to accompany trips, and note that this company is closely linked with Botswana Safaris & Tours (see *Tour operators*, above).

Bathusi Travel & Safaris P Bag 44, Maun; tel/fax: 6860647; email: bathusi@info.bw. Situated immediately next to Riley's garage, the team here seemed friendly and helpful when I last visited. They're probably one of the better agents to walk into if you want to book an immediate short safari or trip into the Delta, and they don't have any direct financial links (of which I'm aware) with any of the operators.

The Booking Company P Bag 198, Maun; tel: 6860022 or 6860654; fax: 6860037; email: book@info.bw. On the south side of the main Sir Seretse Khama Road, opposite the Nhabi Museum, just west of Airport Road, this small and independent travel agency was started by Derek Flatt in 1990. It is a sister-company of Safari Air (see page 179), though is not directly connected to any of the lodges. Thus it can independently recommend options for you, and is another good choice for helping you to organise a last-minute mokoro trip or safari.

Ensign Services Mophane Rd, PO Box 66, Maun; tel: 6860351 or 6860978; fax: 6860571; email: ensign@info.bw. Almost opposite the Power Station, Ensign isn't a travel agent, but I've included it here as it's a really useful place to know about. The office here, run by Alison, offers office services including typing, photocopying, email and acts as a Maun base and representative for various companies, including Moremi Safaris, Mack Air and Guma Lagoon.

Merlin Air Services P Bag 13, Maun; tel: 6860351; fax: 6860571. No guide to Maun would be quite complete without a mention of Merlin Services. Situated on the corner of Mathiba I Road and Airport Road, immediately outside the airport's gates, Merlin acted as a communications hub and booking centre for a few of the area's older, independent camps – when communications meant telex and radios rather than cellphones and satellite phones.

Okavango Tours & Safaris The Power Station Building, PO Box 39, Maun; tel: 6860220; fax: 6860589; email: okavango@info.bw; web: www.okavangotours@okavango.bw. Found inside the Power Station, on the left side as you enter, OTS is very closely associated with Lodges of Botswana (see page 173) who own Delta Camp and Oddballs (both in NG27B). Both companies are owned by Peter Sandenbergh. That said, OTS also arrange trips to other lodges and on a variety of other safaris, if requested. It's an efficient, professional company that knows its business. Note that it's totally different from the tour operator of the same name in the UK.

Travel Wild PO Box 236, Mathiba I Road, Maun; tel: 6860822; fax: 6860493; email: t.wild@info.bw. Opposite the airport, a few doors down from Merlin Air Services, Travel Wild is another good, independent travel agent. Talk to them if you want a fairly unbiased view, though be aware that they also act as a communications hub and representatives for the Panhandle's Shakawe Fishing Lodge (see page 355) and the new Motsentsela Tree Lodge, near Maun.

Flight companies

With the exception of Air Botswana, all the companies mentioned here are small charter companies operating light aircraft out of Maun Airport and around the camps and lodges of northern Botswana.

I include these not because you need to ever book your own flights between the camps; you don't. That's always done for you by the camps concerned, or your tour operator back home; it's better that way.

I include a list of the main airlines and their contact details here so that, in case of emergency, you can contact them. More likely, you may want to charter a plane somewhere fairly unusual – like the Tsodilo Hills for the day, for a pleasure flight over the Delta, or even to take you to Windhoek! These details should give you some idea of who to contact to arrange this.

Note that booking inter-camp flights through the camps is invariably cheaper than chartering them directly with the airlines. For rough guidance, a nine-seater plane (ten if you include the pilot!) and an hour's flying time costs around P1,350 plus P10 per person airport departure tax. Similarly a Cessna 206 which would accommodate five passengers would cost around P700 per hour, plus P10 per person airport tax. These basic prices will usually vary very little between the various companies.

Air Botswana PO Box 191, Maun; tel: 6860391; fax: 6860598. Their main reservations office is a dramatic thatched building on Airport Road, near the corner with Sir Seretse Khama Road, almost beneath the large radio mast in the centre of town. It's generally easier to reconfirm flights and make further arrangements here, than it is at the airport.

Delta Air PO Box 39, Maun; tel: 6860044/6861682; fax: 6861791; synergy@info.bw. With an office opposite the airport, just east of the old Duck Inn, Delta Air has a close association with Lodges of Botswana – and hence usually operates the transfers for Delta Camp and Oddballs. In addition, it offers all the usual charter services including pleasure flights over the Delta.

Northern Air PO Box 159, Maun; tel: 6860436; fax: 6861248; email: nair@kerdowney.bw. Face the airport building, Northern Air's offices are on the corner on the right – again very close to the old Duck Inn. Northern Air is part-owned by Ker & Downey, and hence is frequently used by them for inter-camp transfers. They can also arrange pleasure flights over the Delta.

Mack Air Mathiba I Rd, P.Bag 329, Maun; tel/fax: 6860675; email: mack.air@info.bw. Situated just opposite the airport, between the offices of Merlin Air Services and Okavango Wilderness Safaris, Mack Air is run by Stuart McKisock and maintains a good reputation as an reliable, high-quality air charter company which doesn't have ties to any of the camps.

Moremi Air Just next to Merlin Air Services. Run by Mark Smith.

Safari Air Linked with Desert & Delta.

Sefofane Mathiba I Rd, P.Bag 159, Maun; tel: 6860778; fax: 6861649; email: sefofane@info.bw. Based out of the Okavango Wilderness Safaris' block of offices, just outside the airport's gates, Sefofane is part-owned by Wilderness Safaris. Hence they organise virtually all the flying in Botswana for clients to Wilderness's camps, making them the biggest 'small' airline here. In an emergency, if they're not available on the numbers given above, then try getting hold of them via Okavango Wilderness Safaris in Maun, or even by ringing Wilderness's Jo'burg office (see pages 96–7).

Swamp Air P Bag 33, Maun; tel: 686 0569; fax: 686 0040; email: gunnscamp@info.bw. This is really just the private charter arm of Gunn's Camp, used for ferrying clients into and out of Gunn's Camp.

Wildlife Helicopters Mathiba I Rd, P Bag 161, Maun; tel/fax: 6860664; email: wildheli@info.bw. Situated with the rest of the flight companies, opposite the airport on Mathiba I Road near Moremi Air, this is Maun's only helicopter company.

THE ROAD NORTH OF MAUN
Shorobe
Shorobe is a sizeable village about 26km north of Maun, and 53km south of South Gate, Moremi. Drive slowly through here as you can usually expect plenty of goats and people wandering on the road. On the south side of the village you'll see Shorobe Primary School, and dotted throughout are a few small, local shops which sell soft drinks and very basic supplies.

The one place that is worth seeking out here is the Babomoso Basketry Co-op, which was set up as an income-generating project for the local people by Conservation International. It sells a wide range of baskets at generally lower prices than you'll find in Maun. What's more, you know that the money you pay is going straight back to the local community.

From Maun to Moremi or Chobe
Leave Maun heading northeast – passing the radio mast and airport turn-off on your left. After about 10km you'll reach a large and newish roundabout with a right turn to Francistown and a left to Shorobe. Taking the left, you'll shortly pass Island Safari Lodge and Crocodile Camp.

Just under 40km after Maun you'll pass straight through the village of Shorobe. This is a good gravel road, but beware of travelling too fast as you'll find domestic animals and some quite large rocks on the road – quite apart from a steep camber to the road that encourages careless drivers to slide their cars off to the side.

Around 19km from Shorobe you'll reach the Veterinary Control Fence, or the 'Buffalo Fence' as most people know it. Just 2km after the fence you'll meet a fork, signposted with a green concrete bollard. Turning left will bring you to Moremi Reserve's South Gate after about 32km. See the section on South Gate, page 272, for comments on this road.

There are three places beside the road that you may want to stay, one community campsite and two relatively new lodges.

Sankuyo Village

Sankuyo Tshwaragano Management Trust have recently developed a campsite and traditional village about 25km south of Sankuyo, south of the split between the roads to Moremi and Chobe. This is signposted from the road, about 70km north of Maun, 7km from the Mowana Gate on the buffalo fence.

This is on the eastern side of NG34 – see pages 340–5 for more on that area – but has been included here for continuity, as it's most applicable to people who are driving themselves through this area.

Kaziikini Campsite

Kaziikini Campsite has a bar and a restaurant offering a range of traditional and European meals. There is a supervised playground, guided walks and (at a push!) you can use it as a base for driving into Moremi or Chobe.

Unfortunately the main bar/restaurant here was burnt down in early 2002 and, as I write, the plan for four simple rondavels had not yet materialised. They have five large, private pitches.

For more details contact: People and Nature Trust; tel: 6865126; email: pantrust@info.bw; web: www.duke.edu/~sas21/sankuyo.html. A daily shuttle service between this and Maun was also planned – though it seems very unlikely that this will ever happen.

Shandereka Traditional Village

Beside Kaziikini, Shandereka Cultural Village offers village tours and activities with the local people, the revenue from which goes directly to them. If you've the time to stop it's a project that's worth your support.

NG34 Reserve – Starling's

The Chobe road until a little north of Sankuyo and all of the road from the Veterinary fence to South Gate are in NG34 concession – Starling's Reserve. See pages 340–5 for more details of the camp, and note that with a prior reservation you can drive yourself there.

NG43 Reserve – Mankwe

To the east of Sankuyo is the drier NG43 concession, where you'll find Mankwe Bush Lodge. See pages 345–6 for more details of that private reserve area.

Continuing to Chobe

If you're heading straight to Chobe, follow the directions above for South Gate, but just after the Buffalo Fence take the right turn.

This right turn leads, after about 24km, to Sankuyo Village. Shortly after Sankuyo the road forks again. Take the right fork to reach Mababe Village after about 30km. Leave Mababe Village with a left turn to head west of northwest. From there keep right as the track forks after a kilometre or so. After crossing the cut-line that marks Chobe's boundary, you'll soon be heading north towards Chobe's Mababe Gate (⊕ MABGAT 19°06.182'S; 23°59.119'E), which is about 22km from Mababe Village.

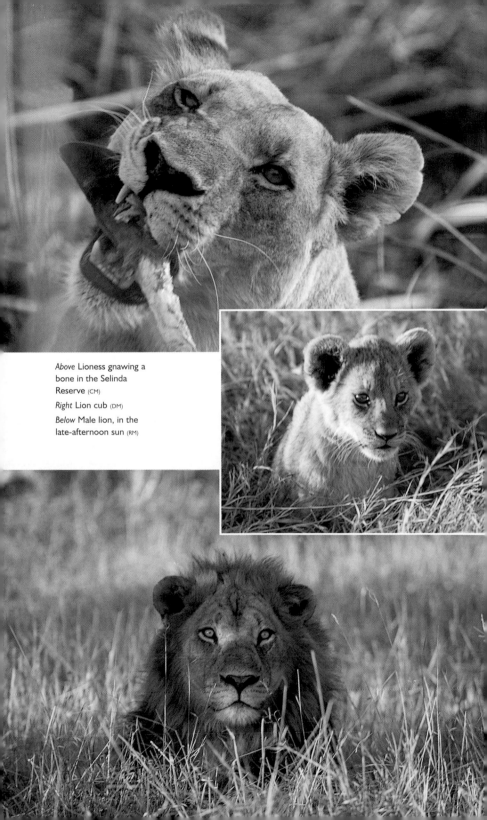

Above Lioness gnawing a bone in the Selinda Reserve (CM)

Right Lion cub (DM)

Below Male lion, in the late-afternoon sun (RM)

Above Elephants drinking at the edge of the Chobe River (CM)

Right Hippopotamus in the Khwai River, Moremi (CM)

Below Lions crossing the Chobe River into Namibia's Caprivi Strip (CM)

Had you taken the left fork after Sankuyo, you would travel about 33km due north along the Moremi cut-line before joining the road which links the Mababe Gate with Moremi's North Gate, and crosses the Magwikhwe Sand Ridge. From this junction, a left would take you to North Gate (about 22km away), and a right would lead you across the sand ridge and, eventually (29km), back to the road mentioned above – from Mababe Village to Mababe Gate.

Kasane and the Northeast

KASANE

Kasane itself is just a small town standing on the southern bank of the Chobe River, in the northwest corner of Botswana, a few kilometres from its confluence with the Zambezi – where the borders of Zambia, Zimbabwe, Namibia and Botswana meet at a point.

Although it is of little interest to the visitor in itself, Kasane is an important gateway: to the Chobe National Park, Victoria Falls in Zimbabwe, to the road across the Caprivi Strip, and to the small charter flights which ferry visitors between the various lodges in northern Botswana.

So if you're passing through this area it's quite likely that you'll come through Kasane, even if only on a transfer bus. And if you've organised your own travelling then you're likely to want to stop here, to refuel and refresh before continuing.

Getting there and away
To/from Francistown

Kasane is about 316km of good tarred road from Nata, and 506km from Francistown. It's a straight and easy drive, though not very interesting scenically; most people stop at Nata to fill up with fuel and relieve the boredom. If you are hitching or travelling by bus, then this road is easy by Botswana's standards – make an early start from Francistown and you can expect to reach Kasane by nightfall.

Note that there are often plenty of elephants on this road, so despite it being tar you should drive with caution. As with most roads in rural Africa, driving at night is asking for trouble – especially as grey elephants are well camouflaged against the grey tarmac.

To/from Zimbabwe
At Kazungula

There is an excellent tarred road from Zimbabwe to the Kazungula border and across into Botswana (open 06.00–18.00). This means that one of Africa's biggest centres for travellers is a day-trip away from Kasane – and, more noticeably, that Chobe can be visited as a day-trip from the Falls.

About 2km after entering Botswana at the substantial immigration office, there's a T-junction. The right turn is for the ferry to Zambia only; left leads you immediately past a disease control post. Here your vehicle will be driven through a puddle of insecticide and you'll be asked to stamp your shoes on an impregnated mat. You'll also be checked to make sure that you're not importing banned animal products – like fresh meat, milk, bones or skins. (All part of Botswana's zealous efforts to protect their national herd from diseases.) Under 2km later and there's a right turn to Kasane, while straight on leads to Nata and Francistown. This is about 12km east of Kasane town.

KASANE & THE NORTHEAST

Katima Mulilo (Namibia)

Ngoma Bridge

Chobe

Game Scout Camp

Savuti via Kavimba

Ihaha campsite

CAPRIVI STRIP (Namibia)

Zambezi

ZAMBIA

Serondella campsite (disused)

Puka Flats

Sedudu Island

Rapids

Nantanga Game Scouts Camp

Chobe Game Lodge

Kasane

Chobe

Sidudu Scout Camp & entrance gate

Kazungula

Kasane Forest Reserve

Chobe National Park

Kasane Forest Extension

Savuti

Ngwezumba Pans Area

Nogatsaa Pan

Tchinga Pan

N

Bradt

0 ———— 10km
0 ———— 10 miles

Maikaelelo Forest Reserve

Kazuma Forest Reserve

Kazuma Pan

KEY

Tar road
Track
International boundary
Nature reserve

Pandamatenga Farms

Nata

Padamatenga

If you're on an organised trip then it's very easy to have a road transfer arranged for you between Kasane and Victoria Falls. It'll take about two hours, and cost in the region of US$45/£30 per person, one-way.

At Mpandamatenga

About 93km south from Kasane, and 223km from Nata, this is one of the country's few arable farming areas. It's easily distinguished by the prominent grain silos, which tower over the surrounding sorghum and maize fields. There's a small border post here for crossing into or out of Zimbabwe. It opens 08.00–16.00. This is under 50km from Robins Camp, deep in the heart of Hwange National Park, so it can be a convenient way to drive between Chobe and Hwange.

To/from Zambia

About 2km from the disease-control post mentioned above, is the ferry over the Zambezi to Zambia (open 06.00–18.00). This often takes quite large trucks and is a substantial size. The ferry journey costs about US$25 per vehicle, the precise amount depending on the vehicle's size. Once on the north bank, it's about 60km of pot-holed tar heading east to reach Livingstone, though if you want to get to Livingstone then it's usually faster to go via Zimbabwe – even taking into account the extra time at border crossings.

Alternatively, heading west on the Zambian side, it's about 130km to the small town of Sesheke. This is the gateway to Zambia's Western Province, although given that Sesheke can be reached painlessly on good tar roads, through Namibia via Ngoma, this would usually be my first choice of route.

Thus you may find that the ferry is mainly used either by very local traffic, or by haulage companies who wish to minimise the number of customs officials that their trucks come into contact with.

If you want to hitch across to Zambia, then try standing where the Zimbabwean and Zambian roads fork, hitching on both of them. To get into Kasane or to head for Nata, the disease control post makes a perfect hitchhiking spot as vehicles have to stop here anyway.

There is a plan to span the Zambezi with a bridge here, at an estimated cost of about P402 million (mid-2001). If built, it would be one of only five bridges to span the width of the Zambezi anywhere along its length. (The others are at Chirundu, Tete, Livingstone, and a footbridge at Chinyingi mission.)

To/from Namibia

Ngoma (see page 217) is the location for a bridge across the Chobe, and a border with Namibia (open 06.00–18.00). It's about 51km from the centre of Kasane by good tar road, or rather more if you take the scenic riverside road (4WD advisable) through Chobe National Park. From Ngoma, it's a further 69km of good tar to the main town of Namibia's Caprivi Strip, Katima Mulilo.

By air

Kasane (airline code: BBK) is a busy gateway for the light aircraft that taxi visitors around the camps of northern Botswana, but it's otherwise fairly quiet. Most travellers coming through Kasane will also pass through Victoria Falls or Livingstone, and find it best to use the frequent flights to/from that airport to reach either Harare or Johannesburg.

That said, August 2001 saw Air Botswana launch direct flights between Kasane and Johannesburg. This was the result of travellers wanting to avoid the unrest in Zimbabwe, and access Kasane directly from the main regional hub of

Johannesburg. However, at time of press the continued success of this route was looking in doubt.

Kasane Airport

Turn away from the river up a good tar road on the west side of Kasane town, just east of the Chobe Safari Lodge. After 1.4km you meet the main road to Ngoma at a T-junction. Turn right and after less than a kilometre you'll see a left turning clearly signposted to Kasane Airport.

Here there is a small, neat and very organised little airport, though being a short distance from town it's very quiet and lifeless between planes.

By bus

There are buses and regular small combies plying between Kasane and Nata, and linking on to both Francistown and Maun – but relatively little else. As with most long bus journeys, get there early in the morning to be sure of getting away. Expect Francistown to cost about P45 and take seven hours, Maun to be about P50 and take a little longer.

Orientation

It's fairly easy to get your bearings in Kasane. The Chobe River meanders roughly from east to west. This is the border with Namibia. A road shadows its course near its southern bank, the Botswana side. Kasane is a fairly linear town, spread out along that road. Most of the visitor's lodges stand on the river bank, accessed by short side-roads.

One tar road loops around away from town and the river to reach Ngoma, the border with Namibia. This actually cuts inland through the Chobe National Park, though isn't usually of interest for game viewing. A spur from this leads north, down the sandy game-viewing roads beside the Chobe riverfront. Another tar road heads south and slightly west before bending more east and heading towards Nata and the rest of the Eastern Corridor area. The latter offers the only 2WD access to the rest of Botswana.

Maps

There are few good maps of Kasane or its environs, perhaps because it's such an easy town to find your way about. For Chobe National Park, you need the excellent Shell map, by Veronica Roodt. See the section on maps on page 86 and *Chapter 6* for details. This is usually available from African Easel bookshop, in the Audi Centre near Barclays.

Where to stay and eat

When planning where to stay here, you should also consider the lodges which are just inside the national park, see pages 208–10, and even those on the east side of the Chobe Forest Reserve, near Ngoma (see pages 215–17).

If you're just passing through Kasane, then it might make sense to choose to stay in one of the lodges listed here, as they tend to be a little cheaper than those in the park, and you may also save a few days' park fees. However, if you're visiting the Kasane area specifically to see northern Chobe, and can afford to use one of the lodges in the park or near Ngoma, then you might be better there.

Here I'll note lodges and camps that are outside the national park, in and around Kasane.

Chobe Chilwero Lodge (8 chalets) contact via Sanctuary Lodges, page 97.
For many years, Chobe Chilwero was a delightful small bush lodge run by Linyanti

Explorations, who still run the Selinda concession in the Kwando-Linyanti area (see page 243). However, in the late 1990s they sold it to A&K, the multinational luxury travel company. To avoid the label of 'an A&K lodge', it's since been re-branded as one of three Sanctuary Lodges in Southern Africa (see page 176) – which remain controlled by the shareholders of A&K.

In the last few years, Chobe Chilwero has been rebuilt to exclusive and luxurious standards. All 15 of its large timber-and-thatch bungalows have air conditioning, imported terracotta floor tiles, sunken handmade baths, indoor and outdoor showers, and private terraces that overlook landscaped gardens. The South African architect, Jonathan Ridler, is responsible for this and has created the atmosphere of an ethnological museum with tasteful décor including many beautiful African artifacts. It includes a comfortable lounge area, a small library with an excellent selection of books and magazines, a beautifully landscaped pool (with showers, toilets and sunbeds) and a business centre for those who can't live without email. Much effort goes into the food here, with treats like bread-sticks and truffles made at the lodge. The service is impeccable – but friendly, and the wine cellar extensive.

Chobe Chilwero looks out over the Chobe's floodplains from behind a relatively discreet electric fence. Game drives are conducted by knowledgeable, enthusiastic guides although the lodge's location effectively limits these to the eastern part of Chobe's riverfront. They use high-quality 4WDs taking a maximum of six guests. Evening sunset cruises are also offered in small single-deckers boats – a pleasant change from some of the larger boats on the river.

Chobe Chilwero is a luxurious lodge in an accessible spot on the edge of Chobe, which offers great comfort and excellent game viewing. It makes an ideal excursion for 2–3 days if you're staying in Victoria Falls or Livingstone but is not isolated enough to offer a real wilderness experience.

Rates (2005): US$485/630 per person sharing/single from July to October; US$335 per person sharing or single from November to June. Includes all meals, activities, park fees, laundry, and most drinks. Excludes transfers. Open: all year.

Chobe Safari Lodge PO Box 10, Kasane; tel: 6250336; fax: 6250437; email: chobelodge@info.bw
Overlooking the river, on the western fringes of town, Chobe Safari Lodge was started around 1960 making it the oldest of Kasane's camps. (Just to confuse everyone, it was initially called the 'Chobe Game Lodge', and later changed its name.) It is immediately adjacent to the park, on the riverside road that used to lead to the entrance – though now this is blocked off and visitors must drive past the airport on the Ngoma road to get into the park. So whilst this is the closest lodge to the park for boat trips, it makes little difference if you're driving.

There's a wide choice of different rooms, at slightly different prices. At the top end there are 20 'river rooms' (plus two family rooms) which each have en-suite showers and toilets, air conditioning, a television and a telephone. Then there are nine simple rondavels (plus three bigger ones for families) with fans rather than air conditioning. If you are a party of four, then the family rooms are particularly good value.

The lodge has plans to build a whole new wing of about 32 'safari rooms', which it promises will be its most luxurious yet. If all goes to plan, these are due to open sometime in 2002. Meanwhile, the old established campsite by the river changes little, though has acquired a few pre-erected tents in recent years. The lodge's facilities include two bars, a swimming pool, a squash court and a volleyball court. The restaurant runs on a set-menu system, with a full breakfast for around P45, braai lunch P55 and dinner for P65.

Game drives (P85/60 for adults/children, excluding park fees) depart four times per day at 06.00, 09.30, 13.00 and 15.30 – running with a minimum of two people. River cruises

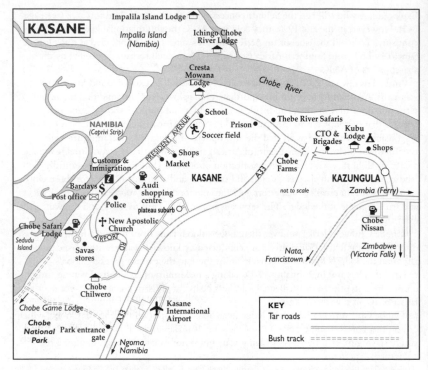

(P65/50) leave at 09.00 and 15.00. For something a little more intimate you can also hire a small motor boat for P90 per hour (minimum of 2 hours) anytime from 07.00 to 18.00, with a driver to explore the river.

Costs: P450 per night for a twin river room (P485 for the family room), P385 for a twin rondavel (P400 for a family room). Camping is P35/25 for adults/children.

Chobe Valley Lodge (8 tents) Landela Safaris, Landela House, 29 Mazowe Street, PO Box 66293 Kopje, Harare, Zimbabwe; tel: (263) 4 734043-6; fax: (263) 4 708119; email: bookings@landela.co.zw

Chobe Valley Lodge (⊕ CHOBEV 17°51.193'S; 25°14.585'E) was built in 1999 in the Lehsoma Valley adjacent to the Chobe Forest Reserve, about 8km from Kazungula and 10km from Kasane. It's easily reached from the Kazungula–Nata road – and used to be known as Elephant Valley Lodge.

The lodge has eight walk-in tents at ground level, each with its own veranda and en-suite shower (heated by a gas boiler) and toilet. The decor is fairly simple, using wrought iron and wood, and there are electric lights, stand-alone fans and safety deposit boxes in all the tents.

Facilities include a swimming pool, a bar, lounge area, curio shop and small bookshelf with reference books. Beside the lodge is a small waterhole modestly named Alan's Pan, allegedly after the lodge's builder – Alan Elliot, the Zimbabwean founder of the 'Touch the Wild' chain of safari camps.

Activities here include boat trips, drives and walks. For cruises you drive into Kasane and then take out the lodge's own large boat on the Chobe. If water levels are low, then mokoro excursions may be possible. Game drives from the lodge into Chobe usually transit through the Chobe Forest Reserve, where the guides can use spotlights on the way back in the evening. Given its distance from the park, a feature here are the all-day drives into the park with a picnic lunch. If you stay here, then request at least one of these longer drives before you arrive. Walking trips with a guide are also offered, though see my comments on walking safaris in Botswana (pages 127–8) before you go.

Rates: US$275/375 per person sharing/single from July to October; US$220 per person sharing or single for the rest of the year. This includes all meals, laundry and two activities per day – it excludes drinks and transfers. Open: all year

Kubu Lodge (11 chalets) PO Box 43, Kasane; tel: 6250312; fax: 6250412/651092; email: kubu@botsnet.bw

About 9km from the centre of Kasane town and 3km from the control point at Kazungula, Kubu stands beside the river. It has two signposts pointing to it from the main road – but best approach following the westerly one, as the lodge is only about 500m from there.

Kubu's chalets are all substantial wooden buildings raised off the ground with stairs up to the veranda at the front, set in lush green lawns under shady trees beside the river. Solid wooden tree trunks have been used to construct the beds, and each chalet is well furnished with rugs on the wooden floors, wickerwork chairs and a laundry basket. (Laundry is usually included in room rates here.) Kubu has mains electricity, and under the high, thatched roof you'll find some unexpected modern conveniences like a coffee machine, a fan, and a system of emergency fire sprinklers. The small bathroom has a flush toilet, shower, and a vanity unit where you can plug in a shaver. Most rooms have a double bed, and also a three-quarters bed.

Kubu's restaurant is a solid building, in the style of a Swiss chalet, overlooking the river. It includes a small bar, and has tables indoors as well as some under umbrellas outside. Expect lots of ethnic prints on the tables and good food. Lunch/dinner costs around US$10/20 per person. By the river there's a swimming pool surrounded by lawns, with a braai area and boma next to it. Kubu's office doubles as a large curio shop, selling a variety of statues, masks, a few books and plenty of postcards.

Kubu organises boat cruises and game drives. The jetty at the lodge itself is used for boat cruises eastwards, up the confluence of the Chobe and Zambezi, whilst game-viewing cruises heading west into Chobe National Park actually depart from Wenela harbour, in Kasane. (The drive there and back is included.)

Boat cruises and game drives from Kubu last about three hours each. Boat cruises go 10.00–13.00 or 15.00–18.30. Game drives three times a day: 06.00–09.30, 10.00–13.00 and 15.00–18.00. All cost about US$20 per person plus park fees.

Rates: US$130/185/225 for single/double/triple rooms.
Open: March 1–January 5.

Kubu Camping PO Box 43, Kasane; tel: 6250312; fax: 6250412/6251092; email: kubu@botsnet.bw

A few minutes' walk from the lodge, Kubu's campsite is a popular site for individual private campers. Its toilets and hot showers are clean and functional, if a little institutional, but the funky egg-shaped swimming pool shows more originality. Each of the pitches has a braai stand, some also have power points and standpipes for water. They're dusty and dry, but there's ample room to pitch your tent in the shade under trees, which can be very welcome.

Nearby is a very simple open-air laundry, and four basic A-frame shelters for those who don't want to pitch a tent. Each has simply two beds with linen provided; the window is gauze.

Part of the campsite slopes steeply down to the river and it's not well lit at night, so if you eat at the restaurant make sure that you take a torch for the walk back.

Rates: P38.50 per person camping, P66 per person to sleep in an A-frame.
Open: March 1–January 5.

Mowana Safari Lodge (110 rooms) PO Box 266, Kasane; tel: 6250300/6250478; fax: 6250301; email: mowana@info.bw or resmowana@cresta.co.bw

Opened in April 1993 by the president, Mowana Lodge is the Botswana flagship of the Cresta group of luxury hotels. This typically Botswanan hotel, conceived on a grand scale and built around a baobab tree with over a hundred rooms, including 10 suites, 16 family rooms and two rooms suitable for paraplegics. All are spacious, indeed luxurious, with river views, remote-control air conditioning, fans, telephones and well-appointed bathrooms. In terms of facilities, they're typical of a hotel appealing to international business-people.

You'll find an outdoor landscaped swimming pool, a restaurant and a bar, both overlooking the river and named 'Serondella' and 'Savuti Bar' respectively. The restaurant serves breakfast for P70, lunch for P70 and dinner (with a game bias) for around P75. Then there's also a terrace for lighter snacks, various smart jewellery and curio shops, and even a hairdressing salon – for essential last-minute styling between safaris.

For the true business visitor there are conference facilities available for groups of up to 800 people, whilst most others will content themselves with the game drive and boat cruises that venture into Chobe National Park.

Rates: US$346 per person sharing, US$376 single, including three meals and two activities per day. Discount of US$10 per person per night for the 'low season' (Jan–Jun). B&B rates also available at around US$210 per person sharing, US$440 single. Each activity costs around US$38 per person. Open: all year.

Thebe River Camping PO Box 5, Kasane; tel/fax: 6250314; email: thebesafaris@botsnet.bw

Used mostly by overland companies and small groups with local safari operators, it's on the north side of the road, northwest of Kubu Lodge and about 5km from the centre of town. This is the base for Thebe River Safaris (see page 193) which is usually occupied by overlanders or travellers taking a trip with Thebe. The campsite's very pleasant and beside the river, though if you want to camp here you must make arrangements in advance.

For campers there is a small bar, a swimming pool, a kitchen that will prepare meals, basic flush toilets and open showers. There are also five permanent tents under thatched shades. Twin beds and bedding are provided, facilities are shared with the campers.

Rates: P30.80 per person per night camping, P143 per tent per night
Open: all year.

Kasane Marina Lodge

The newest lodge in the area – partially still under construction – and an innovative timeshare-type development. Investors 'buy' a 25-year lease on a fully furnished chalet. This confers on them the right to use it for a specified number of weeks per year, plus some income from its use, and also a sales commission on any visitors that they send to the lodge.

Obviously they must rely on tourists making up the bulk of their visitors, in order to bring a good return on the investment. Watch this space for more news.

Liya Guest Lodge PO Box 212 Kasane; tel/fax: (09) 267 651450; cellphone 71756903; email: Liyaglo@botsnet.bw

If you're passing through and just want to spend a night or two in Kasane itself, this is a convenient budget place very near the airport. They will meet flights, arrange transport and, like most lodges in the area, arrange game drives.

Rates: Singles are US$38.50 en-suite or US$36.50 with shared toilet; doubles US$58.50 en-suite or $54.50 with shared toilet.

What to see and do

Kasane's only real attraction is probably its **Reptile Park**, which is virtually next to Kubu Lodge. This holds guided tours around its collection of fauna at 09.00, 11.00, 14.00, and 16.00. Admission is good value at P10 for adults and P5 children, giving visitors a chance to see animals that they would rarely spot in the wild.

On a quirky note, historians observe that in the early 1900s the police in the area used a large hollow Baobab tree, with a locking door, as a prison. This still stands today, behind the present police station.

Kasane is mainly used as a stopping-off point in the middle of a trip, and as a base for excursions into Chobe National Park – which can be organised either through your lodge, directly with one of a handful of small local safari operators, or you can drive yourself.

Game drives

These generally head west straight into the national park, and then cover the game drive roads and loops around the riverfront area. See *Chapter 10* for more details of these areas. If you're organising a trip with a local company, when comparing the various options available, remember to ask how long the drive is, and how much of that time it takes to get to the park gates and back. Typically they'll last about three hours, though generally the lodges further east will spend more of this getting to and from the park than those further west.

Either way you're going to find yourself mostly around the eastern side of the riverfront area, where traffic densities are relatively high.

The national park only allows driving in daylight hours, but several of the lodges now advertise 'night drives.' Note that these are conducted outside the park, in areas where quantities of big game are much more limited.

Boat cruises

These can vary from ten-seater motorboats to double-storey boats taking 40 people on a champagne breakfast. The game viewing from the river can be surprisingly good, especially in the later afternoon during the latter half of the dry season. Large numbers of elephants are virtually guaranteed, and often whole herds will cross the river from one side to the other.

Motor boat trips

Many of the lodges/operators will send you out on a private little boat with a driver and a coolbox. It's certainly my favourite way to see the Chobe Riverfront area, and probably remains one of my favourite safari experiences in Africa. It can be magical.

The small boat gives you a lot more flexibility in what you concentrate on, and how long you stop somewhere, as it's just a question of requesting what you want to do from your driver/guide.

Because of the number of lodges in the area, the river can become quite full of boats at times. So if you want a quieter experience, try and arrange for a boat at the crack of dawn. Most of the cruises don't leave until 9am, so you'll have the river almost to yourself for a few hours – apart from the occasional Namibian fisherman in a mokoro (there's no fishing allowed in the national park from Botswana.)

Getting around

Most visitors to the Kasane area will either have their own transport, or they'll be visiting as part of an organised trip with an all-inclusive package – so the general lack of transport won't be a problem. If you're backpacking then there are a few small minibuses that ply up and down the main road... but the town is so small that you can walk around it with ease.

Getting organised
Banks and money

Remember that you'll need to pay all your park fees in cash (Pula) if you are entering Chobe National Park in your own vehicle. Kasane is an obvious spot for changing money and has only one main bank – so the bank's 'foreign exchange' teller is usually quite busy.

Barclays Bank (PO Box 27, Kasane; tel: 6250221; fax: 6250269), occupies a central spot in town on the north side of the road. (For reference: ✪ KASANE 17°47.97'S; 25°9.015'E.) It's now in a modern, architect-designed building – though I still have memories of changing money here in 1988 when it occupied a small, picturesque thatched rondavel. Both the Barclays branch and Kasane have grown a lot since then, and the service has become a lot swifter!

Failing that, there's a small bureau de change outside the Audi Centre which may be quicker and usually offers a similar rate.

Shopping

Kasane isn't one of the world's shopping capitals, but you'll be able to get most of what you need here.

Just east of the turn-off to Thebe River Safaris is the Metro Cash & Carry for large-scale shopping expeditions, whilst Savas Stores (P Bag K4, Kasane; tel: 6250341; fax: 6250647) is run by Geoff and Patricia Williams – a friendly couple who have lived here for years. They're a good source of general information, as well as having an eclectic and interesting stock, from groceries and fresh produce to maps, guides and travel books. It is just opposite the Engen garage and Chobe Safari Lodge, and they can get hold of just about anything for you if you order it and can wait a few days.

In the heart of town, almost opposite Barclays, is the small Audi Shopping Centre and here you'll find the excellent bookshop: Africa Easel (tel/fax: 6250828). If you're looking for wildlife books, local guidebooks, or the more common maps, then this is the place to get them. In the same complex, the Stationery Box (tel: 6251415) has gifts and curios as well as stationery, and there's an office for Impalila Island Lodge (see pages 194–5).

Adjacent to this, heading westwards, is the grandly titled Chobe Commercial Centre which encompasses Pharma Africa (tel: 6251492), a convenient pharmacy, and also Simple Simon Pieman selling what they claim are the best pies in town.

Almost opposite this complex is the customs and immigration office, then Barclays and then the post office, outside which you'll find a small row of public telephones.

Local safari companies

Because overland truck companies that are not officially registered in Botswana can't use their own vehicles in the park, there's a strong market in Kasane for day-trips into Chobe.

African Odyssey PO Box 350, Kasane; tel/fax: 6250601; email: odyssey@info.bw. A small safari company offering local game drives, boat trips and transfers.

Chobe Travel Shop PO Box 55, Kasane; tel/fax: 6250828; email: travel@info.bw

Go Wild Safaris PO Box 56, Kasane; tel/fax: 6250468; email: go.wild@info.bw. This is the in-house travel and tours agency based at Chobe Safari Lodge, offering various safaris from short game drives (P75 plus park fees for 3 hours) to full mobile trips across the country (typically P230-320 per person per night). They have had a temporary bushcamp, called Peteke, at Buffalo Ridge (Ngoma).

Into Africa Mowana Safaris PO Box 266, Kasane; tel: 6250478; fax: 6250469; email: intoafrica@info.bw. This is the in-house travel and tours agency based at the Mowana.

Linyanti Explorations PO Box 22, Kasane; tel: 6250505; 6250352; email: info@linyanti.com; web: www.linyanti.com. Based at Kazungula, near Kasane, this long-established Botswana company runs the good-value, upmarket camps in the Selinda Reserve (NG16), northwest of Chobe. See pages 239–45 for more details.

Mantis Safaris/Nkwazi Fishing P Bag K48, Kasane; tel/fax: 6250051; cell: 7130 4159. Small operator specialising in boat trips on the Chobe and Zambezi rivers.

Safari Excellence P Bag K33, Kasane; tel/fax: 625099. Run by Stefan du Plessis and Stephanie Molloy, this small operator offers local drives and transfers, as well as longer overland safaris.

Thebe River Safaris PO Box 5, Kasane; tel/fax: 6250314; email: thebesafaris@botsnet.bw. As well as a campsite (see page 190), this is the base for a mobile safari operation which sends trips around northern Botswana and up to Zambia. It's run by Jan, Annatjie, Jannie and Louis van Wyk, who pitch trips as 'budget, middle or luxury' – depending on how much effort/cash you are willing to expend. Prices vary from about US$110 per person per day for budget trips, where you do the chores and supply some of the kit; to US$185 for the luxury trips where they do more work and supply the kit. (Both assume a minimum 4 people for a 7-night trip.) Thebe also arranges boats, vehicles and guides for game drives/boat trips in the park, costing around P75 per person per drive/cruise. These require a minimum of 4/6 people, and don't include park fees (about P70 each).

Car hire

For self-drive car hire just about the only choice is Avis, which operates out of the Mowana Lodge (see page 189); tel: 6250144; fax: 6250145; emergency tel: 6251136. Note that it'll usually be cheaper to make a reservation and pay outside Botswana (indeed, outside of Africa), rather than turn up here and take the rate at the counter.

Vehicle repairs

If you must break down, then Kasane's not a bad place to do so, as it's used as a supply base by several of the safari operators and has several garages. Certainly if you're heading across Chobe and Moremi you should make sure your vehicle's in tip-top shape before you head off. The best is probably:

Chobe Nissan PO Box 287, Kasana; tel: 6250673; fax: 6250674. Situated near Kazungula, just past the disease control post on the way to Nata, about 14km from the centre of town. They're agents for Dunlop tyres and Nissan, although will service and repair most makes. They will also sell spare parts, and undertake wheel-balancing.

Useful addresses

If you need any tent repairs, then contact The Wearhouse (tel: 6251140 or 6250289), at Kazungula – just next to the Chobe Nissan garage.

AROUND KASANE

Although technically on Namibian soil, there are several lodges on the northern side of the Chobe River which use Kasane as a base. Most of their visitors and supplies come through Kasane, and their activities feature trips on the river beside the park.

Two of these – King's Den and Chobe Savannah Lodge – stand on land directly opposite the national park, hence I'll cover them in the chapter on *Chobe National Park*, page 197.

Two others stand northeast of Kasane, on Impalila Island, and I'll discuss these here. For more details of the Impalila area, and the rest of Namibia's Caprivi Strip, see one of my other guidebooks – *Namibia: The Bradt Travel Guide*. Because Namibian accommodation is generally much less expensive than that in Botswana, both are very good value for money.

Impalila Island area

Around Kazungula is the confluence of the Chobe and the Zambezi, and trapped between the two is Impalila Island, at the far eastern tip of Namibia. The Zambezi flows relentlessly to the sea but, depending on their relative heights, the Chobe either contributes to that, or may even reverse its flow and draw water from the Zambezi. Between the two rivers is a triangle of land, of about 700km², which is a mixture of floodplains, islands and channels that link the two rivers.

This swampy, riverine area is home to several thousand people of Namibian nationality, mostly members of Zambia's Lozi tribe. (The main local languages here are Lozi and Subia.) Most have a seasonal lifestyle, living next to the river channels, fishing and farming maize, sorghum, pumpkins and keeping cattle. They move with the water levels, transferring on to higher, drier ground as the waters rise.

Flora and fauna

The area's ecosystems are similar to those in the upper reaches of the Okavango Delta: deep-water channels lined by wide reedbeds and rafts of papyrus. Some of the larger islands are still forested with baobabs, water figs, knobthorne, umbrella thorn, mopane, pod mahogany, star chestnut and sickle-leafed albizia, while jackalberry and Chobe waterberry overhang the rivers, festooned with creepers and vines.

Large mammals are scarce here, and most that do occur swim over from Chobe. Elephants and buffalo sometimes swim over, and even lions have been known to swim across into Namibia in search of the tasty-but-dim domestic cattle kept there.

Even when there are no large mammals here, the birdlife is spectacular. Large flocks of white-faced ducks congregate on islands in the rivers, African skimmers nest on exposed sandbanks, and both reed cormorants and darters are seen fishing or perching while they dry their feathers. Kingfishers are numerous, from the giant to the tiny pygmy, as are herons and egrets. However, the area's most unusual bird is the unassuming rock pratincole with its black, white and grey body, which perches on rocks within the rapids and hawks for insects in the spray.

Where to stay

The largest island in this area, Impalila Island, is at the very tip of Namibia. It gained notoriety during the 1980s as a military base for the SADF (South African Defence Forces), as it was strategically positioned within sight of Botswana, Zambia and Zimbabwe. It still boasts a 1,300m-long runway of compressed gravel, but now its barracks are a secondary school, serving most of the older children in the area.

Charter flights into this landing strip are possible, though most visitors usually reach Impalila with a short boat transfer from Kasane.

There is a **customs and immigration post** on Impalila, which opens from 07.00 to 17.00. It's fairly laid back and informal as borders go, but remember that you'll have to clear customs and immigration for Botswana and Namibia when you arrive/leave at the start/end of your stay. Also note that neither of these can organise game drives in Chobe; they're limited to boat trips.

Impalila Island Lodge (8 double chalets) PO Box 70378, Bryanston 2021, South Africa; tel: (27) 11 706 7207; fax: (27) 11 463 8251; email: info@impalila.co.za
Situated on the northwest side of Impalila Island, overlooking the Zambezi's Mambova Rapids, Impalila Island Lodge has in many ways brought the island to people's attention.

BATTLE FOR AN ISLAND

The precise boundary between Namibia and Botswana in this area has been defined to follow the deepest channel of the Chobe River – a definition which works well for most river boundaries. However, the Chobe splits into many streams, whose strengths and depths seem to gradually alter over the years.

Sedudu Island (or Kasikili Island, as it's called in Namibia) is a very low, flat island which covers about 3.5km^2 when the waters are low, but shrinks to a much smaller size when it is flooded. It's used mainly for grazing cattle.

Both Botswana and Namibia have claimed that the island belonged to them. In the 1990s it was occupied by the BDF (Botswana Defence Force) who built several watch-towers on it – chunky structures towering over the island's grassy plains, and cunningly disguised with variegated military-pattern netting. In early 1995, both Botswana and Namibia agreed to put the issue before the International Court of Justice (ICJ) in The Hague, and in February 1996 they both agreed to abide by its eventual judgement.

Botswana argued that the northern channel was the main river channel, while Namibia maintained that southern channel was the larger one. Finally, in December 1999, the ICJ pronounced that the border should 'follow the line of the deepest soundings in the northern channel of the Chobe River around Kasikili-Sedudu Island'.

That said, the court also diplomatically ruled that 'in the two channels around Kasikili-Sedudu Island, the nationals of, and vessels flying the flags of, the Republic of Botswana and the Republic of Namibia shall enjoy equal national treatment'.

For visitors, this means that game-viewing boats from both countries are allowed on both sides of this tiny, troublesome patch of floodplain!

Accommodation is in one of eight wooden chalets, each with twin beds or a king-size double. It is fairly luxurious, and was built by Karen and Dusty Rodgers and opened in December 1994. Much is made of polished local mukwa wood, with its natural variegated yellow and brown colours. The raised-up chalets have a square design, enclosing a bathroom in one corner, giving blissfully warm showers from instant water heaters. Below the high thatch ceilings are fans for warmer days, and mosquito nets for most nights. Large adjacent double doors open one corner of the room on to a wide wooden veranda, overlooking the rapids. These doors have an optional mosquito-net screen for when it's hot, though are more usually glass. Being next to the river can be quite cold on winter mornings.

Activities at Impalila include guided motor boat trips on the Zambezi and Chobe: the Zambezi mainly for bird watching and fishing, while longer boat trips to Chobe offer remarkable game viewing on the edge of the national park there. Mokoro trips explore the shallower channels, and even run the gentle rapids, whilst guided and independent walks are possible on the island. Superb fishing (especially for tiger-fish, best caught on a fly-rod) is all around, and the guides are experienced enough to take beginners or experts out to try their luck.

Since the lodge was merely a project on the drawing board, the team at Impalila has worked in a very low-key, but positive way to involve the local community. Currently the lodge pays into a 'community development fund' that is utilised by the community for various projects – the clinic, the school, measures to encourage preservation of wildlife and to conserve the local environment – and administered by Dusty and the local chief. Now there are long-term plans to start a wildlife conservancy including Impalila Island, but these could take years to realise. However, because of their excellent approach, don't miss the visits that the lodge organises to local villages, as they can be very rewarding.

Note that Impalila has a super sister-lodge in Namibia's Caprivi Strip (on an island in the Kwando River, just northeast from the Kwando concession in Botswana). It's also a first-rate spot with an even more progressive programme of community involvement.

The main part of the lodge is a large thatched bar/dining area and comfortable lounge built around a huge baobab. This is open to the breeze, though can be sheltered when cold. The wooden pool deck has reclining loungers, umbrellas, and a great view of the river. Impalila's food is excellent and candle-lit three- or four-course meals around the baobab make a memorable scene. It is a stylish, well-run lodge ideal for fishing, birding, or just relaxing, with the added bonus of game viewing from the river in Chobe.

Rates (2005): US$265/395 per person sharing, including all meals and activities.
Open: All year.

Ichingo Chobe River Lodge (7 twin-bed tents) PO Box 55, Kasane, Botswana; tel/fax: (267) 6250143 (on island); fax: (267) 6250223 (in Kasane town); email: ichingo@iafrica.com
First set up in 1993, Ichingo was the idea of Dawn and Ralph Oxenham. Ralph was originally working in Livingstone, when they both embarked upon their own canoe trip from Katima Mulilo to Livingstone for one holiday. Dawn overturned her canoe in the Muwomba rapids and, exhausted and frustrated, ended up staying on the island where she had scrambled ashore. That was Impalila Island, and the inspiration for starting a lodge here.

Initially managers ran Ichingo, but in 1996 Dawn and Ralph decided to refurbish and run it themselves. It stands on the south side of Impalila, just east of the Cresta Mowana and a few kilometres from Kasane. It overlooks the quiet backwaters of some of the Chobe River's rapids, and there is no noise from the mainland.

Ichingo's accommodation is walk-in Meru tents, which are more rustic than Impalila's chalets. The shower/basin/toilet are en suite, at the back under thatch, and there's a balcony at the front, overlooking the river through thick vegetation.

Activities include game viewing, birdwatching and fishing from motor-boat trips, mokoro excursions, fly-fishing in rapids, and walks around the island and along nearby floodplains. Unusually for a bush lodge, the camp actively welcomes children, even when not accompanied by adults, as craft activities can usually be organised for them.

Ichingo's large thatched bar and dining areas overlook rapids on Chobe River, and this relaxed, rustic camp makes a super base for river trips and game viewing from boats along the Chobe River.

Rates: N$833 single, N$722 per person sharing (plus N$360 per extra child sharing), including all meals and activities.
Open: All year.

Chobe National Park and Forest Reserve

Chobe National Park takes its name from the Chobe River, which forms its northern boundary, and protects about 10,700km² of the northern Kalahari. Its vegetation varies from the lush floodplains beside the Chobe River to the scorched Savuti Marsh, dense forests of cathedral mopane to endless kilometres of mixed, broadleaf woodlands. This is classic big game country, where herds of buffalo and elephant attain legendary proportions, matched only by some exceptionally large prides of lion.

Much of the park is devoid of water in the dry season, and the vast majority of it is inaccessible, so this chapter concentrates on the four main areas of Chobe that are accessible: the Chobe Riverfront, Ngwezumba Pans, Savuti, and the Linyanti. It also covers the Chobe Forest Reserve, a populated enclave almost surrounded by the park.

BACKGROUND INFORMATION
History

The Chobe's original inhabitants were the Bushmen, followed by the Hambukushu, Bayei and Basubiya. The 1850s saw David Livingstone pass through the area, on his way to seeing the Victoria Falls, and a succession of big game hunters seeking trophies and ivory. It was first protected as a game reserve in 1961, and then proclaimed a National Park in 1968, which was none too late.

Despite its distant trophy-hunting past, the game density in some areas of the park remains remarkable, ensuring the park's continued popularity. Simply driving a few kilometres along the Chobe Riverfront in the dry season is demonstration enough, as you'll be forced to halt frequently to allow game to wander slowly across the road, or to watch herds coming down to drink from the river

However, perhaps more than any of Botswana's parks, Chobe has felt the impact of tourism. In the 1980s, park fees were low and the few basic campsites were full. Rubbish became a problem, solitary game viewing was almost impossible and the animals became habituated to people. While Chobe has never been busy by East African standards, its three or four basic public campsites and simple network of game-viewing roads couldn't cope with so many visitors.

Fortunately, around 1987, the government started to implement a policy of 'high cost, low density' tourism. Park fees went up and the numbers of visitors dropped. The situation has now changed. With regular increases in these park fees the flood of visitors through the park has turned into more of a moderate flow. Once again, most of the park feels like a wilderness area. Even the 'honey pot' of the northern Chobe Riverfront area isn't quite as busy, though the proximity of Kasane's lodges and campsites ensure that it's never going to be that quiet either.

see page 204

KEY

Tar road	———————
4WD track	======
National park/ forest reserve	– – – – – –

GPS co-ordinates ⊕

CNP1	18° 30.243'S;	24° 34.497'E
CNP2	18° 34.679'S;	24° 23.381'E
CNP3	18° 38.152'S;	24° 24.928'E
GCHOHA	18° 23.25'S;	24° 14.732'E
MABABE	19° 06.182'S;	23° 59.119'E
MARSAN	18° 36.078'S;	24° 03.678'E
SAVUTE	18° 34.005'S;	24° 03.902'E

0 ——————— 20km
0 ——————— 10 miles

N

Bract

CHOBE NATIONAL PARK & FOREST RESERVE

Geography

The geography of Chobe National Park and adjacent Forest Reserve, and indeed most of northern Botswana, is one based on an undulating plain of Kalahari sand that slopes very slightly from the northwest down to the southeast. Its altitude varies from about 950m at Linyanti, to around 930m at Ihaha and 942m at Savuti. In many ways its most defining feature is its northwest boundary: the Chobe-Linyanti river system.

On the ground, Chobe's geographical features are subtle rather than striking. Various vegetated sand dunes and sand ridges occur, including the large Magwikhwe Sand Ridge. Natural pans are dotted throughout the park, reaching their highest densities around the Nogatsaa and Tchinga areas, and also the Zweizwe area east of Savuti. Only occasional rounded hills break the Kalahari's flatness.

Whilst the region is bounded by great rivers, within this area there are only dry, or at least very seasonal, watercourses. The Savuti Channel is the most famous of these – and that did flow, on and off, until 1982.

Geology

See *Chapter 3*'s section on *Geological history*, on pages 45–54, for a comprehensive overview of Botswana's geological past. Here it's enough to note that by around three million years ago the Kalahari's longitudinal dunes had formed, channelling rivers south and east into the Limpopo. Then, around two million years ago, a tectonic shift blocked this drainage, leaving the rivers feeding a super-lake in the heart of Botswana – Lake Makgadikgadi. Geologists think that the level of this fluctuated in time, but that it reached as far as the Savuti area. Compelling evidence for this are the great sand-ridges in the area, and the presence of smooth, wave-washed pebbles and boulders – for example those found on the southern side of the Gcoha Hills.

Flora and fauna

Trying to describe Chobe as a whole without any comment or sub-divisions would be very misleading. Unlike some of Africa's national parks, Chobe is best considered as a handful of totally different areas. Each with a different feel, slightly different vegetation and distinct populations of animals.

Later in this chapter I'll treat separately: the wildlife highlights of the **Chobe Riverfront**; the variation to be found around the **Ngwezumba Pans**; the unique situation around **Savuti**; and the isolated corner of the park that reaches northwest to the **Linyanti**. In passing, I'll also mention the circumstances of the populated Chobe Forest Reserve enclave.

Meanwhile, here I'll try to give a brief overview, and cover some of the species which are found throughout the park.

Flora

In general, across the whole park you'll find many similarities. Near any of the permanent rivers the vegetation is varied, with a large number of tree and bush species. It's classic riparian forest – as occurs throughout southern Africa.

Away from water, Chobe has fairly thick and sometimes thorny bush with relatively few open areas. Much of this is Kalahari sandveld, often with a high proportion of acacias and species that love deep sand, like the silver terminalia (*Terminalia sericea*). Some of Chobe, especially in the south, is covered with mopane woodland, containing almost exclusively *Colophospermum mopane*.

The main exceptions to this are a few areas of (geologically) recent alluvial deposits, like Savuti Marsh, which look totally different. Here you'll find the skeletons of various acacias and leadwoods (*Combretum imberbe*) on open plains covered in couch grass (*Cynodon dactylon*) – the latter being the principal attraction for zebra to the area.

Animals

Most of Chobe's wildlife is found across the whole park. Occasional elephants and buffalo are seen everywhere, but the large herds generally follow a highly seasonal pattern of migrations. These are principally dictated by the availability of water.

As the dry season progresses, all the small clay pans in the bush (and particularly the mopane woodlands) dry up. Then the elephants and buffalo start to form larger herds and migrate to the permanent waters of the Chobe and Linyanti rivers. These gather in their thousands by the rivers, having come from as far away as Zimbabwe's Hwange National Park. Then, as soon as it rains and the small pans in the bush start to fill with rainwater, the animals move away again and disperse.

Many of the parks animals will follow a smaller-scale, less noticeable version of this type of seasonal migration to the water, and this is what makes the game viewing in Chobe so remarkable towards the middle and end of the dry season.

At any time of year, Chobe's big game includes blue wildebeest, Burchell's zebra, impala, kudu, tssesebe, giraffe, impala, common duiker, steenbok, warthog, baboon and vervet monkey throughout the park. Eland, sable and roan antelope also range across the park – but are relatively scarce, just as they are elsewhere in southern Africa.

Lion and spotted hyena are very common, and are generally the dominant predators, whilst leopard, cheetah and wild dog all occur, though are seen much less frequently. Both side-striped and black-backed jackal are present – though the former are found more in the north of the park, and the latter in the south. Brown hyena probably occur, though rarely, in the drier parts of the south – though they don't seem to co-exist happily with a high density of lion or spotted hyena.

Cape and bat-eared fox are found here, though again the Cape fox prefers the drier south. I once had a particularly good sighting of a whole family of bat-eared foxes in the middle of the open plains on Savuti Marsh, early in the morning on a cold September day. There are a variety of mongooses found here; the most often seen of these are probably the banded and dwarf species – both of which are social, and very entertaining to watch.

Serval, caracal, aardwolf and aardvark are found all over the park, though are only occasionally seen due to their largely nocturnal habits. Pangolin are found here too, though they're very rarely seen.

If you have the chance to take any night drives in areas adjoining the park (no night drives are allowed inside the park) then you've a good chance to spot scrub hares, spring hares, lesser bushbabies, porcupines, genets (small-spotted and large-spotted), civets, African wild cats and honey badgers.

Though white and black rhino would occur here naturally, as they should throughout northern Botswana, they have all been wiped out through poaching. There have been occasional reports of individual animals living in the most inaccessible corners of the region... but we are sure that that a viable breeding population doesn't exist here.

In October 2001, white rhino were finally re-introduced into Mombo area, on Chief's Island in the Moremi Game Reserve. It's hoped that a number of black rhino will shortly follow. If these thrive and breed, then perhaps, eventually, we'll see rhino in Chobe once again – given continued CITES protection and the continuation of a very effective anti-poaching regime.

Birdlife

Over 450 species of birds have been seen in Chobe – too many to even try to list here. Thus I'll cover the birding highlights in the separate sections concerning the specific areas within the park. Note that the summer migrants generally arrive around October and leave again in March.

When to visit

Noting the general comments made in *Planning and preparations*, page 77, you'll generally find a wider variety of bird species here in the wet season, many of which will be in their breeding plumage.

The movement of the animals is rather more complex. Most of Chobe's larger herbivores migrate with the seasons, to find water to drink and pastures new. These movements are, to a large extent, predictable, so bear them in mind as you plan your trip to maximise your chances of good game viewing.

Like most of Africa's game migrations, the principle behind this one is simple. The animals stay close to the permanent sources of water during the driest months, then they disperse into the forests and (especially) the open grasslands at the start of the rains to take advantage of the fresh grazing and browsing.

In northern Botswana, this means that game becomes more and more prolific near the permanent watercourses – the Chobe, the Linyanti, and the edges of the Okavango – as the dry season wears on. Then as soon as the rains come, many animals head south and east into the interior's forests and plains (especially the Makgadikgadi area and Nxai Pan). This gives the vegetation beside the rivers a little time to recover, so that when the dry season returns the animals will again find some grazing near the water.

The finer details of this are more complex, and slightly different for each species. Zebra, for example, have been the focus of a research project which tracked them using radio transmitters and a micro-light aircraft, based in Savuti. This study suggested that they spend the rainy summer, from November to about February, in the Mababe depression – venturing south to Nxai Pan, and then following the Boteti River down to around Tsoe, before heading across to the Gweta area and back north to Nxai Pan.

In March and April they pass through Savuti for a few months, where they foal. This makes a particularly good foaling ground as the rich alluvial deposits from the old Savuti Channel have left the area with mineral-rich soil supporting particularly nutritious grasses. A few months later, as dryness begins to bite around July, they move again towards the Linyanti for the dry season. Finally in late October and November, they return to the Mababe area as the rains begin and the grasses start to sprout.

Similarly, Sommerlatte (see *Further Reading*) studied elephant movements in the park in the mid-1970s. He found that the highest wet-season concentrations were around the Gcoha Hills, the eastern side of the Mababe Depression, and the mouth the Ngwezumba River (the Nogatsaa/Tchinga pans area). Though clearly movements have changed since then, if only because the Savuti Channel has dried up.

For the visitor, this means that the game in the dry season is best in the river areas. In the wet season, and just afterwards, the interior pans are definitely worth a visit. Savuti is unusual in that, remarkably, it has good game all year, but is especially interesting around April/May and November.

GETTING ORGANISED

As with most of Botswana's wilder areas, there are basically three ways to visit Chobe: on a fly-in trip staying at the lodges and camps; on a mobile safari trip, organised by a local safari operator; and on a self-drive trip with all your own equipment and food.

Only the self-drive visitors really need to do much of their own planning, and they should take everything they'll need to live on (including supplies of water) between Maun and Kasane. Chobe is often combined with Moremi on such a trip – which, taken at a relaxed pace, typically takes about ten days. You should stock up on food, fuel and supplies before you leave. There are a few small local shops in the villages of the Chobe Forest Reserve, but otherwise there's nothing available on the whole route.

Orientation

Though the maps make Chobe look complex, it's really very simple. In the northeast corner is Kasane, and in the southwest corner the road leaves for Maun and Moremi. Most visitors drive in on one side, and exit the other – and in the middle all roads lead to Savuti. There are concessions and camps planning to open up around Chobe, which may change this, but for now work on this basis!

North of Savuti there's a 'direct' road that links it to Kasane via the Chobe Forest Reserve and the Chobe Riverfront area. Then there's an indirect route that travels to Kasane via the Nogatsaa Pans area in the forested heart of the park. Most visitors choose one of these routes; see *Driving from Kasane to Savuti* on page 210 for a discussion of their relative merits in various seasons. In all the above I use the word 'road' loosely – to mean two adjacent tyre tracks in the sand. You need a high-clearance 4WD for a trip to Chobe, and lots of time.

Maps

There is really only one map of Chobe that is worthwhile for normal navigation and that's the Shell Map of Chobe National Park, by Veronica Roodt. The main map itself is fairly small, but it has a good inset of the game-viewing tracks of the Chobe Riverfront area, and also aerial photograph backdrops for first-rate insets of the area around Savuti and Nogatsaa. Veronica's map of Savuti is especially good for navigation! See *Further Reading* for more details of where to find the Shell series.

Booking and parks fees

If you're flying into organised camps, then your park fees will probably already be included in the price of your safari. If you're driving into Chobe then you'll need to have booked all your campsites in advance – see pages 142–3 for details of the National Park's offices in Maun and Gaborone, and a scale of the fees.

You'll need to have a copy (or preferably an original) of this confirmation with you, then you'll need to pay your parks fees on the gate when you arrive. Note that this is best done in Pula, and that credit cards are never accepted (though for the first time US$ or UK£ cash became acceptable in 2001 – albeit at fixed and fairly unattractive exchange rates).

CHOBE RIVERFRONT

Perhaps the park's greatest attraction is its northern boundary, the Chobe River. In the dry season animals converge on this stretch of water from the whole of northern Botswana. Elephant and buffalo, especially, form into huge herds for which the park is famous. In November 1853 David Livingstone passed through the area and described the river:

> … though the river is from thirteen to fifteen feet in depth at its lowest
> ebb, and broad enough to allow a steamer to ply upon it, the suddenness
> of the bending would prevent navigation; but should the country ever
> become civilised, the Chobe would be a convenient natural canal.

CHOBE RIVERFRONT AREA

Fortunately that kind of civilisation hasn't reached the Chobe yet – there are no canal boats to be seen – and today's traveller must make do with 4WDs or the small motor-boats which weave along the river, amongst channels still ruled by hippos.

Orientation

The southern bank of the Chobe River is slightly raised above the river, perhaps 3–4m high. Below this is a fairly level floodplain of short green grass and reeds, through which the river follows a very meandering course, roughly west to east – with many switchbacks, loops and adjacent old lagoons.

High on the bank is the main riverfront track, which is wide but sandy. This leads from the Kasane to the Ngoma gate fairly directly. Looping off from this are game-viewing tracks. Most of those on the north side drop down to the floodplains, and then loop around by the river. Those few heading off south usually follow straight firebreaks into the dry woodlands that make up the bulk of Chobe behind the thin band of riparian forest.

You can't get lost, provided that you don't cross to the south of the main road. Head east and you'll reach Kasane, west and you'll find Ngoma.

The game densities are generally at their best between Kasane and Ihaha, although the density of vehicles is also high here. When you head west past Ihaha, towards Ngoma, you'll find an increasing number of Namibians herding cattle on the floodplain areas beside the Chobe River. Game densities in the Forest Reserve are significantly lower than those in the park, but you do have better chances of spotting some less common species like sable and roan antelope.

Flora and fauna highlights

The Chobe River meanders through occasional low, flat islands and floating mats of papyrus and reeds. These islands, and beside the river, is always lush and green – and hence attracts high densities of game. Beside this the bleached-white riverbank rises up just a few metres, and instantly becomes dry and dusty. Standing on top of this are skeletons of dead trees, sometimes draped by a covering of woolly caper-bushes.

In several areas this bank has been eroded away, perhaps originally where small seasonal streams have joined the main river or hippo tracks out of the water have become widened by general animal use to access the floodplains. Here there are often mineral licks, and you'll see herds of animals in the dry season coming down to eat the soil as well as drink from the river.

Flora

On the bank beside the river the vegetation contains many of the usual plants found in riparian forest in the subcontinent. Yet despite this it has a very distinctive appearance, different from that any other African river – and perhaps largely this difference is due to the sheer volumes of game, and especially elephants, that visit it during the dry season.

The main tree species found in this riverine forest include Natal mahogany (*Trichilia emetica*) – which isn't found in the rest of Botswana, plus Rhodesian teak (*Baikiaea plurijuga*), large fever-berry (*Croton megalobotryus*), umbrella thorn (*Acacia tortilis*), knobthorn (*Acacia negrescens*), raintree (*Lonchocarpus capassa*), African mangosteen (*Gardenia livingstonei*), bird plum (*Berchemia discolor*), jackalberry (*Diospyros mespiliformis*) and the odd sausage tree (*Kigelia africana*).

Because of the intense pressure from elephants, you'll often see the remains of dead trees still standing which have been ring-barked by elephants; with the termite-resistant skeletons, probably leadwoods (*Combretum imberbe*), being particularly noticeable.

These riverside forests can seem quite denuded towards the end of the dry season, which many naturally blame on heavy grazing by the game. Clearly this has an impact here, but commercial logging took place along this riverside before and during World War II and also took its toll of some of the larger trees.

Despite this, several different types of bushes thrive here. Buffalo thorn (*Ziziphus mucronata*) and knobbly combretum (*Combretum mossambicense*) are common, though Chobe's most distinctive bush must be the remarkably successful woolly caper-bush (*Capparis tomentosa*). This sometimes grows into a dense, tangled shrub, but equally often you'll find it as a creeper which forms an untidy mantle covering an old termite mound. Sometimes you'll even find it covering the crown of dead trees, or draped continuously over a series of bushes.

If you're out game viewing with a Botswana guide, then ask him or her if they know of any local medicinal uses for woolly caper-bush. The plant has very strong antiseptic qualities, and both Palgrave and Roodt (see *Further Reading*) report that this is one of the trees most widely used in Africa for its magico-medicinal properties.

Fauna

The game densities in the Chobe Riverfront vary greatly with the seasons, but towards the end of the dry season it is certainly one of Africa's most prolific areas for game. It is an ideal destination for visitors seeking big game. Elsewhere in the dry season you'll find fascination in termites or ground-squirrels; but here you can find huge herds of buffalo, relaxed prides of lion, and perhaps Africa's highest concentration of elephant – huge herds which are the hallmark of the area.

One of the main attractions of the boat trips on the Chobe is that large family groups of elephants will troop down to the river to drink and bathe, affording spectacular viewing and photography. You'll find these here at any time of day, but they're especially common in the late afternoons, just before sunset.

When it's very dry you'll also find elephants swimming across the river at night to raid the relatively verdant crops and farms on the Namibian side – often coming back to Botswana during the day when the villagers feel more confident to emerge and scare them.

If you are not floating but driving, then be cautious. Read my specific comments on driving near elephants, pages 211–12, and err on the side of caution. Most of Chobe's elephants are in family groups containing mothers with calves. They can be sensitive to any perceived threat – so keep a respectful distance from them. This can be especially difficult when you see licensed guides driving closer, but you should still keep your distance. Their experience, and general coolness in case of elephant aggression, will allow them to do relatively safely what would be dangerous for you to attempt.

If you find your car surrounded by elephants, then try to relax. Virtually all of Chobe's elephants have seen lots of vehicles before, and so are unlikely to get too upset. Don't panic or rev your engine, just sit quiet and still until the animals have passed. Ideally switch off your engine – but this is not for the faint hearted.

See pages 201–2 for a general comment on the game species found throughout Chobe. However, the riverfront is the best chance to see hippos, crocodiles and the odd sunbathing leguvaan (water monitor). Whilst there also look out for the delightful Cape clawless and spotted-necked otters, which make their homes in the riverbank.

Perhaps the Riverfront's most talked-about antelope is the Chobe bushbuck. This is a localised race, or perhaps a subspecies, of the bushbuck (*Tragelaphus scriptus* and if a subspecies then *ornata*) which has wide distribution within sub-

Saharan Africa, from the edge of rainforests to the edges of the Kalahari and throughout the eastern side of southern Africa. Their colouration exhibits a lot of regional variation, and there is certainly a distinctive race which occurs only in this Chobe Riverfront areas – with brighter colouration and clearer markings than are found in the rest of southern Africa.

Bushbuck are small, attractive antelope which usually occur singly or in pairs. Only the males have horns, which are short and spiralled. They are well camouflaged, with a red-brown coloration, like the soil, and a covering of white spots that blend into the shadows of the riverside's thick vegetation. They will freeze if disturbed, and there are reliable reports of lions and hyena passing within 10m of a plainly visible bushbuck and not noticing it. Only eventually, if disturbed, will they bolt for cover as a last resort.

Another antelope often noted here is the puku (*Kobus vardonii*) – which some sources claim is rarely seen. This is true, but only if you've never been to Zambia, where puku are probably the most common antelope. South of the Chobe they probably only occur in this Chobe Riverfront area, and especially around the aptly named 'Puku Flats' peninsula of the floodplain.

The red lechwe (*Kobus leche*) is another water-loving antelope which is resident here, and easy to confuse with the puku at first glance. Look closely and you'll see that the lechwe's underparts are much lighter, their coats seem less shaggy, and the males' horns larger. Also notice that when they run, Lechwe usually seem to hold their heads close to the ground, while Puku usually run with their heads held much higher. This makes identifying them from a distance much easier – and soon you'll realise that red lechwe are usually the most common antelope on the Chobe's floodplains.

Waterbuck and reedbuck are also usually found in wetter areas, and so are found around Chobe Riverfront and Linyanti but not elsewhere in Chobe. Roan are also found here, but are fairly scarce, as befits an antelope that is sought-after by private game areas and expensive to buy. Finally, the beautiful sable antelope are common nowhere, but I've seen large and relaxed herds here on several occasions. Being specialist grazers, they are more commonly found in the wooded south of the Riverfront, though as sable and roan usually drink during the middle of the day, you will quite often see a small herd near the riverfront road, between Ngoma and Kasane.

Birdlife

From a boat on the main river in the park you're likely to spot numerous beautiful kingfishers (pied, giant, some malachite and the occasional half-collared) – with the pied seeming to be particularly numerous, perching on reeds by the river, or hovering to hold their eyes static above the river's surface. You'll also see plenty of reed cormorants and darters, various bee-eaters; hammerkops, wire-tailed swallows, a high density of fish eagles and even African skimmers (November–March only; the best place to see them is probably near Hippo Pools, beside Watercart Drive).

The fringes of the islands and floodplain are particularly good for birding, being home to many storks, herons, geese, egrets and a wide variety of plovers (blacksmiths, long-toed, crowned, wattled and, of special interest, white-crowned). Particularly unusual and worth seeking are rufous-bellied and white-backed night herons, slaty egrets, brown firefinches and wattled cranes.

For a totally different environment attracting several different species, head downstream and out of the park, to the shallow rapids dotted with rocks, which are adjacent to Impalila Island on the Chobe and Zambezi rivers. (The Chobe's are the

Kasane Rapids, whilst those on the Zambezi are known as the Mambova Rapids.) In the dense waterside vegetation before the rapids look out for the shy finfoot, whilst around the rapids themselves there's a thriving population of rock pratincoles.

If you have the chance to explore the Kasane Channel (which connects the Zambezi and Chobe Rivers), then do so. Technically you'll need to cross into Namibia, so this trip is probably easiest to undertake from one of the lodges on Impalila Island. Here you'll find small lagoons beside the main channel covered in water lilies, and bird species that include the uncommon lesser and purple gallinules, lesser jacanas and moorhens, pygmy geese and African rails. On the edge of these, in the adjacent reeds and papyrus beds you'll probably hear (if not see) chirping cisticolas, greater swamp warblers and swamp boubous.

Back inside the park, in the band of forest beside the river, you'll find many drier-country species, including coucals (Senegal and coppery-tailed), oxpeckers, sunbirds (you can find coppery sunbirds here), rollers (look out for the racket-tailed), hornbills, flycatchers, weavers, shrikes and francolins. Large flocks of helmeted guineafowl seem particularly visible here, and are especially fond of loitering along the tracks in front of vehicles. Or so it seems!

There's a tremendously wide range of raptors here, from the ubiquitous fish eagles perching on dead trees overlooking the river, through to the huge martial eagles patrolling the drier woodlands. Other resident eagles include the uncommon western banded snake eagle, black-breasted and brown snake eagles, bateleur, tawny, long-crested, Ayres' and African hawk eagle. These are joined in the summer by migrant eagles, including Steppe and Wahlberg's eagles, and all year by many species of falcons, goshawks, harriers, kites and even the rarely-seen bat-hawk.

Where to stay

Many people visit the Chobe Riverfront whilst staying in Kasane (for which, see the previous chapter and page 186–90), or possibly from a base at Ngoma (see page 217). Generally the choices inside the park are more expensive, but they have better locations. Within northern Chobe, there are only two choices: the basic public campsite at Ihaha or the stylish Chobe Game Lodge. There are also two lodges on the opposite side of the river. Although they are technically in Namibia, I've included them here for completeness as they are lodges used primarily to visit Chobe.

Serondela Public Campsite (now closed, but mentioned for completeness)
For years the only site in northern Chobe was Serondela, which is about 17km west of Kasane town. It was quite a famous campsite, having sprawled along the riverside, vaguely around a set of very basic toilets and cold showers. The local animals had all lost their fear of man. Hence all the dangerous big game seemed to make a point of regularly sauntering through camp. Ignorant tourists had, over the years, fed some animals and the baboons, particularly, became a menace – aggressive, adept at stealing food if you turned your back for a second, and even able to open zips on unguarded tents.

On one occasion a lone male bounded on to the tailgate of my 4WD, snatching a packet of biscuits from a food box in its jaws, and sprinted off – all in a matter of seconds whilst myself and a companion were a few steps away at the front of the vehicle. Before leaping up into the back it knew that we'd seen it and were coming back to chase it, but also knew that it was faster and so continued. It was obviously very well practised at this sort of smash-and-grab raid.

Further, Serondela was relatively close to the eastern side of the park, so it added considerably to the density of traffic in the peak dawn and dusk time for game viewing. So for several reasons this site was wisely closed in the late 1990s and superseded by the new Ihaha site.

Ihaha Public Campsite (see page 142 for National Parks' bookings)
About 15km west of the old site at Serondela, Ihaha (⊕ IHAHA 17°50.484'S; 24°52.748'E) is the new and only camping site for private visitors within northern Chobe. If you're taking the riverfront road you can't miss this, as there are two sharp turns in the road and a small National Parks' office past which you must drive. Earthwork ramparts effectively surround the site, so one has to turn away from the river road and pass through the main camp office to get to the site.

The ablutions here are a great improvement on Serondela's, consisting of two tall, whitewashed, thatched buildings, each with two showers, two toilets and several sinks for men and women.

Chobe Game Lodge (46 rooms) Desert and Delta, see page 171.
Situated about 9km from the park's Sidudu Entrance Gate, Chobe Game Lodge is the largest lodge in any of Botswana's national parks, and at first sight seems like just another luxury hotel. Its design is unusual though, with tribal antiques in almost Moorish surroundings, which blend together very well. Having opened in 1972, it's become something of an institution. Despite its size, it has maintained a first class reputation for personal service since I've known it; perhaps because of an experienced staff who understand how to give attention to detail.

Chobe Game Lodge's rooms are mostly spread out along the riverbank, about 60m from the water's edge, and were all upgraded and refurbished in 1999 and 2000. Each is set slightly into the bank with a barrel-vaulted ceiling and one full wall of glass overlooking the river. Their design, together with punkah-punkah ceiling fans and air conditioning, keep them cool through the day. Inside the red-tiled floors are dotted with rugs, the furniture is very solid and the decor well thought out. Each has its own mini-bar and tea/coffee making facilities. The comfy beds have little canopies, and the en-suite bathrooms have a bath with an efficient shower attachment, a toilet, a washbasin, and an electric point for hair-dryers and shavers.

The Game Lodge also has four large suites, furnished equally well but with a 'lounge' as well as a bedroom. Each has its own small, secluded swimming pool. The lodge's PR was greatly enhanced when Elizabeth Taylor and Richard Burton chose it as a romantic place in which to be re-married, and spent their honeymoon in a suite.

As you'd expect, there's a large pool, a pleasant bar and also a 'cigar bar' with a full-sized billiard table. The lodge's food is good, and usually eaten outside on a covered veranda, or in the boma by the river. Breakfast and lunch are buffet-style, while dinner is even more leisurely, à la carte by candlelight.

The activities offered here are amongst the most varied of any of the region's lodges. Game drives typically go out three times a day – early or late morning and late afternoon. All last about three hours and use open-sided 4WDs. It's possible to take out a small boat with a driver/guide, usually either in the late morning or the early afternoon. Short walks on the riverbank and around the forest reserve are usually best done when it's cool, and it may be possible to take a long excursion to explore the Botswana side of Kazuma Pan on foot with an armed guide. Generally you're not limited to two activities a day – they're quite flexible about organising all-day trips or midday boat rides if you ask them. You can take as many activities as you have the time and energy for, and if the lodge isn't full then they're quite flexible about the timing of, say, the outings in small boats. There are usually nightly shows of wildlife videos in the conference room, which seats up to 100. (If you need access to a business centre, then the Game Lodge is your only choice in Chobe or the Okavango!)

Rates (2005): US$323/446 per person sharing/single from July to October; US$252/265 per person sharing or single for the rest of the year. Open: all year

Chobe Savannah Lodge (12 rooms) contact Desert and Delta, see page 171.
This is the smaller sister-lodge of Chobe Game Lodge and it stands on a private concession of land on the Namibian side of the river, facing west out over the Puku Flats area. Its main centre is a double-storey thatch-and-timber building, which has superb views across the flat landscape of the river and its floodplains. Inside this is a lounge, library and a dining room, whilst outside is an open boma for evening fires, a plunge pool and a wooden sun deck.

The 12 brick-and-thatch suites all have en-suite facilities with separate showers and oval baths, air conditioning, overhead fans, mini-bars and tea/coffee making facilities. It's a stylish spot, designed carefully with lots of rich dark earthy browns.

Activities here major on game viewing by motor boat, as well as sunset cruises and guided canoeing. Nature walks along the river and trips to one of the local villages are also offered.
Rates (2005): US$323 per person sharing/single from July to October; US$252/265 per person sharing or single for the rest of the year. Open: all year

King's Den (20 chalets, plus a boat) PO Box 98, Katima Mulilo, Namibia; tel: Botswana 650 814
Owned by the Zambezi Lodge, a hotel in the Caprivi Strip's main town, Katima Mulilo, King's Den overlooks the Chobe National Park from Kasikili Island. It can be reached by taking a boat west from Kasane.

It has ten wooden chalets constructed on stilts on the edge of the island, all with en-suite facilities. In addition to these, there is a 13-cabin riverboat, the Zambezi Queen. Some say it's moored here, others allege that it's stuck.

While the site has potential, King's Den seems to be currently used mainly for fishing trips and doesn't offer the quality that you'll discover in many of Botswana's lodges.
Rates: around N$1,000 single, N$800 per person sharing, including all meals and activities.

What to see and do
Game viewing and birdwatching are the main activities here; walking and night drives are not allowed in Chobe. Most visitors explore along the floodplains beside the river; this is relatively easy game viewing even without a guide.

If you're driving yourself though and have a little time to spare, don't ignore the roads away from the river on the western side of this riverfront section, particularly the Kaswabenga and Simwanza Valley roads, as well as the fire-breaks marked on Veronica Roodt's maps of Chobe. The landscape here is very different from anything else you're likely to see in Chobe. It's broken country with rocky hillsides and gullies; classic leopard country. Driving around here in October, you'll often find surprisingly good concentrations of game, despite its apparent distance from the river. This is because the game will often rest in the shade of the forest on its way to and from the river.

Driving from Kasane to Savuti
There are two routes through the park between Kasane (✪ KASANE 17°47.97'S; 25°9.015'E) and Savuti. Certainly the shorter, and probably the more beautiful, is the western route, which takes about 172km to reach Savuti from Kasane and can take in the Chobe Riverfront drive if you have time. The alternative is the eastern route, which is about 207km long. This stays within the park and passes through the Nogatsaa Pans area.

Note that in the wet season, you're recommended to use the western route. Firstly, because it's probably slightly more frequented by vehicles. Secondly, you'll find it particularly easy to get stuck in the clay soils found around the pans (both Zweizwe and Nogatsaa/Tchinga). That said, if you do brave the pans route, the birding can be particularly good at that time of year.

DRIVING NEAR ELEPHANTS: AVOIDING PROBLEMS

Elephants are the only animals that pose a real danger to vehicles. Everything else will get out of your way, or at least not actively go after you, but if you treat elephants wrongly there's a chance that you might have problems.

To put this in perspective, most drivers who are new to Africa will naturally (and wisely) treat elephants with enormous respect, keeping their distance – simply out of fear. Also in the more popular areas of Chobe or Moremi, where the elephants are habituated to vehicles, you'd have to really annoy an already grumpy elephant for it to give you trouble.

To give specific advice is difficult, as every elephant is different. Each is an individual, with real moods and feelings – and there's no substitute for years of experience to tell you what mood they're in. However, a few basics are worth noting.

Firstly, keep your eyes open and don't drive too fast. Surprising an elephant on the road is utterly terrifying, and dangerous for both you and the elephant. Always drive slowly in the bush.

Secondly, think of each animal as having an invisible 'comfort zone' around it. (Some experts talk of three concentric zones: the fright, flight, and fight zone – each with a smaller radius, and each more dangerous.) If you actively approach then you breach that zone, and will upset it. So don't approach too closely: keep your distance. How close depends entirely on the elephants and the area. More relaxed elephants having a good day will allow you to get within 25m of them, bad-tempered ones that aren't used to cars may charge at 250m! You can often approach more closely in open areas than in thick bush. That said, if your vehicle is stationary and a relaxed, peaceful elephant approaches you, then you should not have problems if you simply stay still.

Thirdly, *never* beep your horn or flash your lights at an elephant (you shouldn't be driving yourself at night anyhow!). Either is guaranteed to annoy it. If there's an elephant in your way, just sit back, relax and wait; elephants always have right of way in Africa! The more sound and fury – like wheel spins and engine revving – the more likely that the elephant will assume that you are attacking it, and this is especially the case with a breeding herd.

Finally, look carefully at the elephant(s):

Are there any **small calves** around in the herd? If so expect the older females to be easily annoyed and very protective – keep your distance.

Are there any **males in 'musth'** around? These are fairly easy to spot because of a heavy secretion from penis and temporal glands and a very musty smell. Generally these will be on their own, unless they are with a cow on heat. Such males will be excitable; you must spot them and give them a wide berth.

Are there any elephants with a lot of seepage from their **temporal glands**, on the sides of their heads? If so, expect them to be stressed and easily irritable – beware. This is likely to have a long-term cause – perhaps lack of good water, predator pressure or something as random as toothache – but whatever the cause that animal is under stress, and so should be given an extra-wide berth.

DRIVING NEAR ELEPHANTS: FACING A CHARGE

If you get into a hair-raising situation with elephants, then you've probably not kept your distance. The key was prevention, and you failed. Now you must keep cool, with your logic ruling your fear. A few words here are inadequate – you need experience – but I'll outline some basics.

Firstly, if your vehicle is stationary and switched off, and you become unexpectedly surrounded by peaceful elephants, don't panic. Don't even start the engine, as that would startle them. Just sit there and enjoy it; there's no real cause for concern. Only when they've passed and are a distance away should you start up. When you do start – never start and move off simultaneously, which will be interpreted as the vehicle being very aggressive. Instead start up quietly, wait a little, and then move.

More often a situation occurs when one from the herd will be upset with you. In that case you've approached too closely. (The key was to keep your distance – remember?) Then an annoyed elephant will usually first **mock charge**. This usually first involves a lot of ear flapping, head shaking and loud trumpeting – mock charges are often preceded by 'displacement activities', and the animals often show uncertainty about charging. The individual then runs towards you with ears spread out, head held high, and trumpeting loudly. This is terrifying, especially if you're not used to it. But be impressed, not surprised; elephants weigh up to 6,000kg and have had several million years to refine this into a really frightening spectacle.

However terrifying, if you stand your ground then almost all such encounters will end with the elephant stopping in its tracks. It will then move away at an angle, with its head held high and turned, its back arched, its tail raised, and the occasional head-shake. Often you'll find the 'teenagers' of the herd doing this – testing you and showing off a bit.

However, if you flee or back off rapidly during such a mock charge, the elephant will probably chase your vehicle, perhaps turning a mock charge into a full charge (see below). So, before you move, make very certain that you have a swift escape route, and that you can drive faster than the elephant can run. (In deep sand, you can forget this.)

As a fairly desperate measure, not normally needed, if the elephant is really getting too close, then increasing the revs of your engine – commensurate with the threat – will encourage the animal to stop and back down. Don't beep your horn, don't rev up and down, but do steadily press your accelerator further down as the elephant gets closer. (I've never needed to do this; it's overkill for most mock charges.)

However, if you're really unfortunate then you'll come across an upset or traumatised animal, or one that really perceives you as a threat and that makes a **full charge**. This is rare – expected only from injured elephants, cows protecting calves, males in musth and the like. Then the individual will fold its ears back, put its head down, and run full speed at your vehicle. I'm pleased that I've never faced one of these, but if you do then your only option is to drive as fast as you can. If you can't get away then I'd try revving, as above, matching it's threat with your engine's noise. But I'd also start praying – this is a *seriously* dangerous place to be.

Don't imagine that the western route is always easy at that time. Most of this is fairly thick sand and you'll often be crossing fossil dunes with woodland on the crests and scrub or grasslands in the valleys. Veronica Roodt (see *Further Reading*) reports that there's a patch where water sometimes gathers just south of the Gcoha Hills. So beware of problems there too after heavy rains.

Eastern route – via the pans

For the eastern route, you need to take the fast road from Kasane to Ngoma, away from the river. About 16km after the Sedudu Entrance Gate, near Kasane, you'll reach a crossroads. A right turn, north, would take you to the riverfront road in the Serondela area. Left leads you through the Nantanga Gate, onto the only road through Chobe, and within a kilometre to the Nantanga Pans.

About 35km later there is a left turn to the complex of roads around Nogatsaa airstrip, Ngwezumba Dam and the old Nogatsaa and Tchinga campsites. Continue straight and after about 22km you'll pass another left, leading back to the same area. Shortly after this the road begins to follow the dry bed of the Ngwezumba River.

Around 22km from this (at ⊕ CNP1: 18°30.243'S; 24°34.497'E) you pass a small track on the right, which leads after almost 4km to Nxunxutsha Pan (⊕ NXUNXU: 18°29.312'S; 24°32.537'E), which is the southernmost point of the Chobe Forest Reserve.

About 60km later after the second Nogatsaa turn-off, this road takes a more southerly direction and leaves the riverbed behind (⊕ CNP2: 18°34.679'S; 24°23.381'E). About 7km later the road splits it (⊕ CNP3: 18°38.152'S; 24°24.928'E), with the right turn leading southwest through the pans. About 11km later the road turns west and finally northwest towards Savuti. This track enters Savuti by the south side of Qumxhwaa Hill (Quarry Hill) and joins the western route from Kasane just north of the channel.

At this final split in the pans route, there is an alternative left fork (which is not recommended as a route) which leads south for a few kilometres before passing Chosoroga Pan. One spur from this used to swing west around the pan and join into the roads on the south side of Savuti Marsh (from where you bear north and slightly west to reach the centre of Savuti). Another track apparently heads down directly from this pan to Mababe Village. I'm unsure of the current state of either of these tracks, so I would welcome news on either (preferably accompanied by details and GPS co-ordinates if they're navigable).

The total distance from Kasane to Savuti along the eastern route is about 195km, and takes five or six hours to drive in the dry season. An advantage is the possibility of a midway stop at the Ngwezumba Pans, although scenically this route lacks the beauty of the Chobe River.

Western route – via the riverfront

Taking the western route you have a choice of ways to start. If you're in a hurry, or starting late in the day, then drive to Ngoma from Kasane on the tar. Alternatively, and much more enjoyable, is to meander along the riverfront road, which passes Serondela and Ihaha. Both are a little over 50km. The fast route will take under an hour, whereas the river route will take several, depending on how much you stop to watch animals or take photographs.

Either way you'll reach the scout hut at Ngoma, where you will probably be required to sign the register. Then you should take a left turn heading roughly southeast, signposted to Mabele (12km), Kachikau (36km), Parakarungu (70km) and Savuti. This is sometimes referred to as the B334 and it appears to be good tar – but don't let that deceive you, for after a little over a kilometre it reverts to gravel.

AVOIDING THE SAND NORTH OF GCHOHA

The final 50km or so north of the Gchoha Entrance into Chobe can be very thick, heavy sand and the road has been badly churned up by trucks in the past. To avoid this, watch carefully and about 3.5km after you pass through Kachikau, there's the start of a track (⊕ DETOR1 18°10.147'S; 24°28.545'E) which bears off slightly to the right of the main track. This more-or-less shadows the main road, crossing it again at least twice, most clearly at (⊕ DETOR2 18°15.25'S; 24°19.087'E), which is about 22.5km from Kachikau and 16.6km from the Gchoha Gate.

If you follow this you'll often find it much easier, although rather than leading directly to the gate it leads to a point on the cut line (⊕CUTTUR 18°21.82'S; 24°10.633'E) which is about 7.7km northwest of the gate. Thus you just need to turn left along the cut line to return to the main track, and turn right to the gate.

For anyone heading in the opposite direction, from Savuti to Maun, you would simply turn left up the cut line immediately after exiting the gate, and then take a right turn (CUTTUR) just after the end of a band of mopane trees.

This brings you into the **Chobe Forest Reserve**, mentioned in more detail after this route description.

About 11.5km past the turning you'll pass a big baobab near a few simple buildings and a large sign proclaiming Mabele. You'll still be able to see the Chobe floodplain off to the right, but with little game on it. Mabele has a 'Hi-life' bar and a soccer pitch. Mabele General Dealer (⊕ MABELE 17°59.182'S; 24°38.858'E), on the right, is the best shop in town though it's very limited.

Whilst the road through Mabele is a slow sand surface, after Mabele it becomes a faster grey gravel again. The vegetation is mostly acacia species here, with lots of umbrella thorn, *Acacia tortilis*. The scenery becomes less inspiring, and almost 22km after Ngoma you pass a police camp on the right-hand side (various prefabricated houses) which overlooks the floodplain again.

Shortly afterwards, almost 25km from Ngoma, you reach the small town of Kavimba, which has a landmark in the form of two baobabs which stand in the road (⊕ KAVIMB 18°4.192'S; 24°35.02'E). Entering town there's a new Apostolic church on the right.

A little over 10km later you'll reach Kachikau, which is marked on some maps as Kachekabwe. You'll be able to buy a limited range of drinks and foodstuffs at the shops here if you need them. There's a forestry camp here, and the smart, well-built Lizwasani Community Secondary School. In the centre of town (⊕ KACHIK 18°9.143'S; 24°30.172'E) there's a right turning signposted to Setau, a small settlement in the communal area to the north of the Forest Reserve, near Lake Liambezi. Ignore that turning and just afterwards you'll pass the Chobe Craft Shop on the left, which sells a very good range of baskets.

After Kachikau the sand starts to get deeper and the track worse. (See box for a possible detour to avoid this.) The country around here is rolling vegetated dunes, which mean lots of corrugations and deep, deep sand. Plenty of leadwood trees are around, so beware of punctures (especially if you've reduced the pressures in your tyres for the sand). The long, strong leadwood spines will cause punctures in even the sturdiest of 4WD tyres.

About 80km after Ngoma you'll meet what looks like a crossroads, although in reality you are crossing the cut-line that marks the end of the forest reserve, and the start of Chobe National Park. If you were to turn right here, then this (very rough and bumpy) cut line would lead you to a spot on the Linyanti River just east of the Linyanti Campsite. If you were heading directly from Kasane to the Linyanti or Selinda concessions, you would probably use this track (the right side is better when it's wet, the left better in the dry season).

Continuing straight across the cut-line, however, and less than a kilometre later you'll reach the impressive Ghoha entrance gate (✪ GCHOHA 18°23.25'S; 24°14.732'E), which was completed as recently as May 1999. This is about 80km from Ngoma, and 28km from Savuti. Here you'll need to produce your camp reservations, sign in and pay any required park fees.

As you enter Chobe you'll see the Gchoha Hills on your left in the distance – the first set of hills. A few kilometres later you'll pass the first of the hills, which is dotted with baobab trees. The road inside the park is generally less sandy and better than that which is outside – although it does cross the northern edge of the Magwikhwe Sand Ridge just south of the hills.

About 25km after the entrance gate you'll pass a (sharp-angle) right turn which leads to Savuti airstrip, and a couple of kilometres further on you'll reach the main Savuti waterhole on your right, where you'll often find vehicles game viewing. The road eventually approaches Savuti from a northeasterly direction. Although this route is shorter (about 166km in total) and arguably more spectacular, it is probably more difficult and time-consuming to drive than the eastern route described above.

CHOBE FOREST RESERVE

Chobe Forest Reserve is an enclave largely surrounded by the Chobe National Park. To the northwest of it are seasonal marshes, Lake Liambezi and eventually Namibia.

The Chobe Forest Reserve and the area to the north of it, concessions known as CH/1 and CH/2, are areas designated for community-managed livestock and hunting. The carefully managed hunting of this is currently administered by a company, Rann Safaris, which has a few small hunting camps here. Amongst a number of high-profile guests, it's alleged they were recently visited by Norman Swartzkop – the US general better known as 'Stormin' Norman'.

The 'hunting' aspect of this should not deter photographic guests from visiting, as the reserve contains good populations of wildlife that are managed sustainably by the community and Rann Safaris.

Many visitors simply pass through this reserve en route between Kasane and Savuti. See the route described above *Driving from Kasane to Savuti: Western Route – via the Riverfront* for more details of the drive through the area.

Where to stay

There is a campsite and a few lodges here. These are generally more moderately priced than staying on the eastern side of the park. You'll also find Chobe's game-drive loops become quieter as you move from east to west – from the Kasane area to Ngoma. So think of this as an alternative to the Kasane area, as well as a potentially convenient stopover.

Muchenje Safari Lodge (10 chalets) P Bag K31, Kasane; tel: 636001; fax: 36000/1 or 650223; email: much@info.bw
Matt and Lorna Smith built Muchenje (✪ MUCHEN 17°57.115'S; 24°42.361'E) in 1996, and have owned and run it ever since. To get there follow the signs from Ngoma towards Mabele and Savuti; Muchenje is about 3km along on your right.

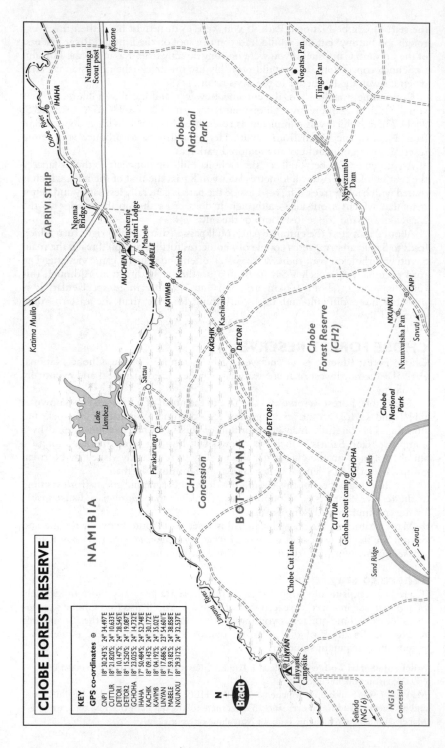

CHOBE FOREST RESERVE

KEY

GPS co-ordinates ⊕

CNPI	8° 30.243S; 24° 34.497E
CUTTUR	8° 21.820S; 24° 10.633E
DETOR1	8° 10.147S; 24° 28.545E
DETOR2	8° 15.250S; 24° 19.087E
GCHOHA	8° 23.025S; 24° 14.732E
IHAHA	7° 50.484S; 24° 52.748E
KACHIK	8° 09.143S; 24° 30.172E
KAVIMB	8° 04.192S; 24° 35.02E
LINYAN	8° 17.686S; 23° 54.601E
MABELE	7° 59.182S; 24° 38.858E
NXUNXU	18° 29.312S; 24° 32.537E

N

Brădt

The wooden chalets were refurbished in 2001 and all ten are comfortably furnished with twin beds surrounded by a walk-in mosquito net. Each has an en-suite shower and toilet, electric lights, and its own balcony overlooking Chobe's floodplain.

The lodge is perched on the escarpment overlooking the floodplain. It has a dining area, a bar, a small curio shop and a modest library, all under a high thatched roof. Above the dining room, on a second floor, is a game-viewing platform with a great view. Outside there's a swimming pool with loungers around it and an impressive view.

Activities include game drives into the national park – using an area which tends to be more private and less busy with vehicles than those from lodges around Kasane, as less traffic reaches this far west. Bush walks with armed guides are also offered in the Forest Reserve, as are birdwatching and fishing trips on the river. Alternatively, especially if you're staying for three nights or more, you can arrange an all-day activity. One good combination is a boat cruise along the Chobe in the morning, followed by a picnic lunch in the bush and then an afternoon game drive through the park back to the lodge.

Rates (2005): US$275/375 per person sharing/single from November to March; US$325/475 from April to June; US$375/550 from July to October. These include activities, meals, local drinks, laundry, and transfers to/from Kasane. Open: all year

Buffalo Ridge Campsite & Baobab Safari Lodge Tel/fax: 6250430; cell: 082 659 1232; email: rosi@botsnet.bw

From the scout post at the Chobe's Ngoma Gate, it's a few kilometres north to the border post. Driving this way, down into the Chobe floodplain and the bridge, Buffalo Ridge Campsite is shortly on your left – almost opposite the Botswana border post itself.

The lodge here doesn't seem to be accepting any visits from private individuals, and they're not good at all at responding to communications. Both this and the campsite are run by the very busy Rosi Slogrove.

Rates: P30 per person camping. Open: all year

Kavimba Community Campsite

If you need to camp whilst passing through the forest reserve then I've heard that recently the community at the Kavimba Village have established a simple campsite on the edge of the Chobe Forest Reserve. I haven't seen this yet, but would welcome news of it.

Ngoma border post

The conversion of the gravel road into tar from Namibia's Katima Mulilo to the Botswana border at Ngoma has taken years, but now it's finished. Thus you can drive from Kasane into Namibia and right across the Caprivi Strip on a good tar road.

At Ngoma, there's little there apart from the border post. Botswana's smart border post is a fairly new (mid-1990s) building, perched high above the river, almost opposite the Buffalo Ridge Campsite. Namibia has a less imposing office next to the bridge on the other side of the Chobe River, about 2km further on. Both are efficient, pleasant, and generally quiet. This crossing is fine for 2WD vehicles, and opens 06.00–18.00. As with many borders, don't be alarmed if you see the odd soldier wandering around with a gun, and don't even think about taking any pictures near the bridge without permission.

Lake Liambezi area

This large, shallow lake is located between the Linyanti and Chobe rivers. When full, it covers some 10,000ha, although it has been dry (something of a dustbowl) since 1985. People and cattle now populate its bed.

Lake Liambezi's main source of water used to be the Linyanti River. However, even in recent years of good rain it has been unable to fill the lake after filtering through the Linyanti Swamps (which themselves are very dry). Despite good water levels in the Kwando-Linyanti system in the 2001/2 rainy season, it didn't break through as far as Liambezi.

Although over recent decades there has been a trend towards less and less water, and more villages, in the lake and the marshes around it, in early 2002 there was sign of a possible change. For the first time in many years Lake Liambezi has a few inches of water on it, due to good rains and possibly some flow-back from the Chobe River.

NGWEZUMBA PANS

About 70km south of the Chobe River lies a large complex of clay pans surrounded by grassland plains, mopane woodlands and combretum thickets. There are well over a dozen individual pans: Noghatsau, Gxlaigxlarara, Tutlha, Tambiko, Kabunga, Cwikamba and Poha, to name but a few, and all hold water after the rains. This makes them a natural focus during the first few months of the year, when the animals tend to stay away from the permanent waters of the Linyanti and Chobe rivers.

If any of the water pumps here are working consistently then it also ensures that they are excellent during the dry season too. However, if visiting in the heart of the dry season then check with the scouts at Savuti or Nantanga; ask if the pumps are working before you head this way.

Flora and fauna highlights

With water there, the pans are excellent in the dry season. Early in the dry season they're quite likely to hold water anyway – so taking the eastern route certainly makes sense around May–August. Once the natural water dries up, the pumps are vital. With water in the late dry season you can expect herds of Chobe's game interacting; it's a place to just sit and watch for hours.

Curiously, perhaps the area's most notable game doesn't need permanent water and so is found here all year. This area is perhaps the only place in Botswana where oribi antelope occur naturally. These small, elegant grazers are orange-red above, white underneath, have a dark circular scent gland under their ears and a short bush tail with a black tip. Only the males, which are very territorial, have short, straight horns. They are usually seen in pairs, or small groups, feeding in the open grasslands during the morning or late afternoon. If startled they will often emit a shrill whistle before bounding off at a rapid rate with a very jerky motion.

AN UNEASY ALLIANCE

Co-operative relationships between mammals and birds are unusual, but the honey badger enjoys two. Its association with the greater honeyguide is well known. This small bird uses a distinctive song to lure the honey badger to a bee's nest, whereupon it feasts on the grubs after the badger has ransacked the nest and had its fill of honey.

Less well known is the honey badger's association with the pale chanting goshawk. This relationship is of no benefit to the badger, since the goshawk – or sometimes a pair of them – simply follows the bigger predator around as it digs and forages for prey, and pounces on any rodent or reptile that slips past. The badger may have the last laugh though, since goshawk eggs and nestlings are among its 59 different prey species that have been recorded in the Kalahari.

This is also the only area of Chobe where you've any real chance of spotting gemsbok (or oryx). This is the dominant large antelope species in the parks south of here, but it's relatively unusual to see them in Chobe. These pans, together with the complex around Zweizwe, are probably the park's best place to spot roan antelope – which never thrive in areas of dense game but seem to do well around here.

For birdwatchers the pans, and especially the larger ones like Kwikamba Pan, can be superb during the rains. Expect a whole variety of aquatic birds passing through including Egyptian and spurwinged geese, lesser moorhen, redknobbed coot, redbilled and Hottentot teal, African pochard, dabchick and even the occasional dwarf bittern. The large grassland plains here also attract grassland species such as yellow-throated sandgrouse, harlequin quail, croaking cisticola and, occasionally, Stanley's bustard.

Where to stay

Nogatsaa/Tchinga Public Campsite (see page 142 *Bookings*)
There used to be two campsites here, at Tchinga (alias 'Tshinga' and 'Tjinga') and Nogatsaa. However, both have been strictly closed to private visitors over recent years. There are certainly HATAB camping facilities in the area, so you ought to have no problems visiting here with a mobile safari run by a licensed Botswana tour operator (see page 94 for explanation).

Nogatsaa, the more northerly site, is situated overlooking Nogatsaa Dam and used to have toilets, cold showers and a game-viewing hide. It used to be a great place for just sitting and watching the game coming to bathe and drink.

Tchinga is about 21km south of Nogatsaa, and even years ago had no facilities other than a water tank with a very temperamental mechanical pump.

SAVUTI

Unlike most game-viewing areas, Savuti isn't just about animals. Its game can be great, but that's only half the story. To understand the rest, and discover some of its spirit, you must dig into its history – from the geological past, to the first humans and then the European hunters, 'explorers' and conservationists – and learn of the reputation of some of its famous characters. Savuti seems to have more 'stories' linked with it than all the other game areas in Botswana combined. So seek these out before you come, as only then will you really appreciate why Savuti has a legendary quality about it.

History

The key to its attraction is the mysterious Savuti Channel, which is often dry (as it is now) but sometimes, inexplicably, flows. Its journey starts in the Zibadianja Lagoon, at the southern tip of the Linyanti Swamps. In past years when it flowed, it meandered a little south and then eastwards until it entered the national park about 35km away.

Continuing east, it flowed through a wide gap in the Magwikhwe Sand Ridge, around which are a number of low, rounded hills – the Gubatsaa Hills. (In former times, its flow probably formed this gap.) This is about 54km due east of the lagoon, and this is the place usually referred to as 'Savuti.' It's also the place where the modern National Park's campsite stands.

From here the channel turned abruptly south, and spilled out into the Mababe Depression, a huge flat area which was once the bed of an ancient lake (see page 48 for more details), and formed the flat expanse of the Savuti Marsh covering about 110km².

SAVUTI AREA

Ngoma, Kasane

Linyanti Campsite

Savuti
Airstrip

KEY

4WD track ═══════════

GPS co-ordinates ⊕

SAVUTE	18° 34.005'S; 24° 3.902'E
SAVSAF	18° 33.927'S; 24° 3.441'E
SAVELE	18° 34.207'S; 24° 3.269'E
MARSAN	18° 36.078'S; 24° 3.678'E

Khlaxhlane
Pan

Quaïxhwaa
Hill ▲

Savute
Safari
Lodge
SAVSAF ⊕ ▲ SAVUTE

SAVELE ⊕
Savuti
campsite

Small
Qumxhwaa Hill ▲

Savute
Elephant
Camp

Damagosera
Hills ▲

Savuti Channel

Nogatsaa,
Tchinga

Tanxhwaa Hill ▲

▲ Tsonxhwaa Hill

Sexaxamba
Pan

N

Bradt

MARSAN ▲
Leopard Rock ▲ ⊕   ▲ Twin Hills
Kwando
Pan

0 ────────── 3km
0 ────────── 2 miles

Old
Airstrip

Motsibi
Island

Savuti Marsh

Magwikhwe Sand Ridge

SAND RIDGE ROAD

MARSH ROAD

Mababe Gate

Mokgweba
Island

At its peak, with the channel and marsh full, it must have been like a huge drinking trough over 100km long, penetrating the heart of the dust-dry northern Kalahari. It's no surprise that it attracted huge quantities of game and, in turn, whatever people were around at the time.

San/Bushmen

The early hunter-gatherers certainly had settlements here, evidenced by at least five sites in the hills around Savuti containing rock art. Archaeologists link these paintings with those in the Tsodilo Hills, and with the traditions of people of the Okavango.

A few of these sites are known to some of the guides at the lodges here, and if you are staying at one then request for your guide to take you to see them. Don't try to find them on your own. Not only is exploring on foot against the park's rules, but the density of lion and elephant here is sufficiently large that it's dangerous for the inexperienced.

The Rock Art Research Institute at the University of the Witwatersrand provides information about Bushman paintings in general on its website www.wits.ac.za/raru; email: enquiries@rockart.wits.ac.za

Early explorers

There are many reports of this area from the early European explorers – fascinating if only to look back and see what they recorded of Savuti. In June 1851 when Livingstone passed through here the marsh was a 'dismal swamp' some 16km long, fed by both the Mababe (now called Khwai) River, which spilled over from the Okavango system, and also by the 'strongly flowing' Savuti Channel.

Chapman also crossed the channel around 1853, when he recorded it as dry. Then when the great white hunter, Frederick Courtney Selous came, in 1874, the channel was full and flowing into the marsh. However, when Selous came back in 1879 he noted that the channel had partially dried out, and no longer fed the marsh. Mike Main, in his excellent book on the Kalahari (see *Further Reading*) concludes that sometime in the 1880s the channel dried up.

Modern history

It seems to have remained dry until a heavy rainy season, 1957–58, when the channel began to flow strongly once again. This continued until 1966, when it dried up again. It then flowed from 1967–81, when it seemed permanent and enhanced the area's reputation as a top game destination.

In the 1970s Lloyd Wilmot started a camp here, Lloyd's Camp, which was to put both Lloyd and Savuti on the map. Lloyd is, in fact, the son of one of the Okavango's famous crocodile hunters, Bobby Wilmot – and has many sisters, most with strong connections in the area.

A safari here was always off-beat. Lloyd built up a reputation for empathy with the game, and a total lack of fear for his own safety when dealing with it. Everyone who visited here came away with stories of remarkable animal encounters, and Savuti's reputation grew.

However, the channel's flow was gradually reducing and, in 1982, it ceased to flow completely. Gradually the water shrank into a few remaining pools, and then they dried up too. With them went the fish, hippos, crocodiles and all the other creatures that had lived there. During this time Lloyd was frequently photographed kneeling or lying in front of a thirsty elephant, excavating sand from a hole in the bottom of the channel until he reached water. This sad time was well chronicled in a video, *The Stolen River*, by Derek and Beverley Joubert. It's also one of the main subjects of Clive Walker's book, *Savuti – the Vanishing River* (see *Further Reading*).

Nobody really knows why it stopped, as nobody understood why it started again after almost 80 years of dryness. Explanations range from changes in the paths used by the Linyanti's hippos to tectonic shifts – see Mike Main's book, *Kalahari*, for a more detailed discussion.

However, even with the channel now dry, Savuti remains a classic area for game. Experts observe that the soil here is especially good, and the grazing particularly rich. Furthermore, there are now several permanent waterholes in the area. The oldest is pumped by the National Park, near the centre of Savuti, while two others are in front of the two lodges in the area. A further two are towards the bottom of the marsh, on opposite sides of it – and these try to attract the game, and especially the elephants, away from the centre of Savuti which has been so heavily impacted by game over the years.

Orientation

The Savuti Channel is a (currently dry) riverbed, which starts from the Zibadianja Lagoon, at the southern tip of the Linyanti Swamps. It flows through the Linyanti Reserve, before entering the national park about 35km away. Heading east, it first cuts through a wide gap in the Magwikhwe Sand Ridge, around which are a number of low, rounded hills – the Gubatsaa Hills. There it spreads out into the Mababe Depression, forming a large marshy area known as Savuti Marsh.

This area is now dry and known as 'Savuti.' It's about 54km due east of the lagoon, and here within the Chobe National Park you'll find a campsite, two up-market lodges and several waterholes.

Maps

There are numerous small, winding roads around Savuti, relatively few landmarks and very few signs on the tracks. It's easy to become disoriented. If you want to explore the area in detail, you should have with you Veronica Roodt's excellent Chobe map (see *Further Reading*), and preferably also a GPS.

Flora and fauna highlights

Flora

Savuti's habitat is a mostly undistinguished thick thorny scrub, with camelthorn (*Acacia erioloba*) and silver terminalia (*Terminalia sericea*) making up much of it, though there are also large areas of mopane (*Colophospermum mopane*). You'll also find substantial stands of shaving-brush combretum (*Combretum mossambicense*) and Kalahari appleleaf (*Lonchocarpus nelsii*), and it's perhaps the most westerly area where you can find the lovely paper-bark albezia (*Albezia tanganyicensis*). Dotted all over the drier parts of the area are landmark baobab trees (*Adansonia digitata*); their ability to survive being ring-barked is essential to survival here.

The main contrast to these wooded areas is the Savuti Marsh. Here open plains covered with a variety of perennial grasses stand above the (geologically) recent alluvial deposits of the channel. These grasses are tolerant of the slightly higher salinity levels present, and some are particularly nutritious and a great attraction for the game when there's moisture about.

Here you'll also see the skeletons of dead trees, still standing in the flat grasslands. These were mostly camelthorns, umbrella thorns (*Acacia tortilis*) and leadwoods (*Combretum imberbe*) which are thought to have seeded and grown up between the 1880s and the 1950s, when the marsh was dry. Then when it flooded in the late 1950s they were drowned – though the hard, termite-resistant wood still stands.

On the southern side of the marsh you can see the bush gradually starting to invade the grasslands again, with the distinctive, low 'round mounds' of candle-pod acacia (*Acacia hebeclada*) leading the aggressors.

Fauna

At the heart of the park, Savuti sees most of the park's species (see page 201), with the exception of the Chobe bushbuck and the water-loving species. Reedbuck and waterbuck used to occur here, but even they have deserted with the demise of the channel's flow.

Now much of the interest is concentrated around the three remaining waterholes, and especially the old one pumped by the National Parks department. Here there's invariably a lot of game. Lion are frequently found lying around, and big herds will pause as they approach, or wait until their thirst overcomes their fear.

Savuti's elephants are notable for a number of old bulls which live in the area permanently, and are often individuals known to guides who have spent a lot of time in the area. These are augmented by large breeding herds which pass through. Whenever it's dry you can be sure that with such limited water resources, there's action and jostling for drinking positions at the waterhole.

Visiting in recent years, at least one of the local lion prides has grown so large that they will kill elephants to satisfy their hunger – traumatising the local elephants in the process. (The Khwai River area in Moremi has a similar phenomenon.)

Spotted hyena have always been numerous and very noticeable at Savuti. In the late 1980s and early '90s they would appear at the campsite, skulking around the bins, as soon as the sun set. After dark, and when people had gone to sleep, they'd pick up anything that they could carry, and eat anything small enough to crunch up – including, I was once assured, a glass lens from a 35mm camera! My aluminium camping cooker was stolen by a hyena once at Savuti, and still bears the scars of its strong jaw.

S M Cooper (see *Further Reading*) studied the clan sizes here in 1986–88, and found that there were five territorial clans in the area, and a number of transient animals passing through. The clans averaged about 18 adult females each, six males, five of unknown sex and ten cubs under two years of age – so around 39

BABY HUEY

One of Savuti's more famous residents was an elephant named Baby Huey, who had become very relaxed around people. He'd also picked up a liking for oranges, after foolish visitors fed him. Gradually he came to associate people with food. When I first visited Savuti in 1998, this was a problem.

Nobody drives around at night, but on that trip we were woken at 05.00 one morning by a vehicle driving up to our tent. The couple inside it had seen our fire burning, and come to seek sanctuary. It seems that they, and their small son, had been sleeping in the back (the pick-up section) of their 4WD when Baby Huey had passed by. Smelling oranges, he'd used his tusk on the front cab like a can-opener on a tin, and then delved inside for a snack.

The couple were completely traumatised, and left Chobe at first light. Two days later Baby Huey was shot – and camping visitors are still banned from bringing citrus fruit into the park. And all because people were naive enough to feed the animals.

members of each clan. They tend to prey on reliable, low-density resident game species like impala and warthog throughout the year, and augment this by feasting on the herds as they pass through the area, especially the new-born zebra foals.

Despite the presence of so many lion and hyena, leopards also do well here, perhaps helped by the presence of the rocky kopjes which make a perfect habitat for them. Daryl and Sharna Balfour have some lovely shots of leopard at Savuti in their book on Chobe (see *Further Reading*).

Once driving with one of Lloyd's guides (who shall remain nameless) we realised that there was an early-morning commotion in the air, and followed this to a young female leopard that had *just* killed an impala. Nearby the guide knew that she had a cub to feed. However, our vehicle's approach had, unwittingly, frightened the leopard off its kill, and soon after we arrived so did a hyena – which proceeded to claim the prize.

Such was the maverick nature of Lloyd's Camp that this guide simply jumped out of the cab, grabbed the hind quarters of the impala, and started upon a tug-of-war with the hyena for the carcass. Spurred on by this, and the realisation that the cub would otherwise miss a meal, I joined in. Eventually we won the carcass and hauled it up onto a low branch hoping that the leopard would reclaim it.

But nature, once upset, isn't so easily put right. As we pulled back from the scene the hyena returned, stretched up on its hind legs, and plucked the impala from the branch with ease. Others swiftly joined it, devouring it within minutes. The leopard had already given up and disappeared, perhaps in disgust.

In the wet season there are still movements of buffalo, zebra and wildebeest which come onto the marsh to graze, though the huge herds of buffalo that came when the channel flowed have now stopped coming. In his book on Botswana (see *Further Reading*) in 1968, Alec Campbell describes the scene on the marsh when the channel was flowing:

> Here the Savuti Channel carries water from the Linyanti... forming a
> marsh about a meter deep. From June to December huge herds of buffalo
> visit the marsh to feed in the surrounding scrub mophane and one can see
> as many as 6,000 daily. Out on the flats which surround it on the
> southern and western sides are herds of bull elephants, wildebeest, impala,
> giraffe, tsessebe and sometimes large numbers of zebra. Lion are also quite
> common.
>
> Cow elephants with their young spend much time in the taller mophane
> to the east of the marsh but come down to drink in the afternoon.
>
> Hippopotami and waterbuck are to be seen in the Channel especially near
> the mouth where it enters the marsh.'

Numbers now probably don't match what was seen then, though April–May is still the prime time for the zebra and wildebeest herds to pass through, usually foaling here as they go. The precise timing of this is heavily dependent upon the local rainfall patterns.

The dry season can witness large numbers of tsessebe move onto the marsh area to graze. Occasionally, at the end of the dry season, oryx have been known to appear at the south end of the marsh, but they are very uncommon this far north. Always you'll find groups of giraffe in the acacia woodlands on the edge of the marsh and all over the area.

Finally, if you're anywhere around the hills in the area, then P C Viljoen (see *Further Reading*) notes that several klipspringer were spotted here on the Qumxhwaa Hill (Quarry Hill) in 1978 and 1979. If there are still individuals here then they are very isolated, as the nearest significant klipspringer population is probably in Zimbabwe's Hwange National Park, about 130km to the east.

Birdlife

The list of bird species found in Savuti runs to over three hundred species, but a couple of the more unusual include the Marico flycatcher, crimson boubou, capped wheatears, pennant-winged nightjars (only during the summer, October–January; look especially on the roads at dusk) and Bradfield's hornbill.

In addition, when you're in areas of acacia woodland then keep a look out for racket-tailed rollers and the spectacular displays of the male broad-tailed paradise whydahs in breeding plumage (February–April).

On Savuti's open areas you'll find the occasional secretary birds, Stanley's bustard, and plenty of the larger kori bustards. The Balfours' coffee-table book on Chobe (see *Further Reading*) has a wonderful picture of a carmine bee-eater using the back of a kori bustard as a perch from which to hawk around for insects. Kori bustards are Africa's heaviest flying birds, but heavier still are the flightless ostrich, which can sometimes be seen here. During the summer, Abdim's and white storks congregate in numbers on the marsh.

Where to stay

Savuti's two luxury camps and its campsite are all close to each other. All face onto the Savuti Channel, and all are near the old bridge over the channel, just to the north of the marsh. Being a day's drive from either Kasane or Maun, most guests of the lodges fly in to Savuti's airstrip (which can take planes as large as a DC3), but visitors to the campsite usually arrive driving their own fully-equipped 4WDs, complete with all their supplies.

Stay in the area for long and you'll hear of the legendary Lloyd Wilmot and his famous camp – Lloyd's Camp. This became something of an institution here, but has sadly now closed. (Lloyd still visits occasionally, but has left the safari business.) Despite this, you'll still find books and websites that haven't caught on to this. Similarly, Allan's Camp and Savuti South were opened here (by Gametrackers) and subsequently closed – only to be combined and re-built as the Savute Elephant Camp (see below).

The current options for visitors are:

Savuti Campsite see page 142 for National Parks' booking offices
Savuti's campsite (⊕ SAVUTE 18°34.005'S; 24°3.902'E) has moved over the years, and now is more central and has better infrastructure than ever. Previously it had just a few taps that had been ingeniously encased in concrete to prevent elephants from pulling the pipes to access the clean water (they would often make such an effort for clean water, rather than drinking from the dirty waterhole!) whilst showers and toilets were almost non-existent. An electric fence was even erected at one stage – but was swiftly broken and trampled by the elephants.

Now, moved to a place nearby, the new public campsite has a relatively new ablution block, surrounded by an ingenious circular wall. This has been designed to be elephant-proof, and also so that smaller animals like cats can easily get out over the wall, but not easily get in. The toilets and showers (with hot water) are relatively clean and in good order. The idea of a fence around the whole site has been abandoned, though the site now has an impressive office and entrance gate.

Savuti remains a wonderful place to camp. It's speciality has always been spotted hyenas and, of course, elephants. Like the area's private camps, it has nightly visits from spotted hyenas which, I once discovered, can carry away a full rucksack at high speed, despite being pursued. They will steal and eat anything from a camera lens to a bar of soap, so leave nothing outside.

The camping pitches (eight at last count) are separated and marked, albeit not always clearly. Many sit under old camelthorn trees, with site number one being particularly good. The size of the site, and the distance between the pitches, is such that some campers even drive to the ablution block after dark. Visibility is good, with not too much undergrowth around, though there's often the low whine of a water pump or a generator in the background.

Sit back after dinner. Turn off your lights, and shield your eyes from the fire. Now, when your vision has adjusted to the dark, shine around a powerful torch. With a little patience you should be able to pick out the ghostly green eyes of hyena, just beyond your firelight. (Torches are useful for this, but beware of shining one accidentally at a passing elephant. They don't like this at all!) If you do have any hyena problems, remember that they will push their luck, but are essentially cowardly animals. Chase them and they will always run, sometimes dropping their spoils. Just be very careful of what else you might run into during the chase!

Savute Elephant Camp (12 tents) Contact Orient-Express Safaris, see page 174 Situated (✪ SAVELE 18°34.207'S; 24°3.269'E) close to the Safari Lodge, this was the first of Gametracker's camps that I visited following their reconstruction, and I was amazed at its scale. 'Tents' is really far too flimsy a word for the guest accommodation here. Each is built on a large, raised platform of wooden decking about 18m long and 6m across. At the front of this are a few safari chairs overlooking the bottom of the channel from quite a height, and behind them is a huge shaded canvas tent.

Inside this, on the polished wooden floor, are two adjacent three-quarter size beds under a walk-in mosquito net, with plenty of walking space around, several comfy chairs plus a writing-desk and a chair, and some solid and fairly stylish furnishings/fabrics.

Walking around the reverse of the wooden headboard reveals a place for suitcases, a wardrobe with a clothes rail, and the middle area of the tent, which is a dressing room. This has twin basins, several large mirrors and acres of hardwood surrounds. Through polished hardwood doors you'll find separate rooms for the large shower (easily big enough for shared showers) and the flush toilet.

Above the head of the bed, facing over it, are two air-conditioning units. These augment the large ceiling fan in the centre of the room, which can be used all day and night – as can the room's lights (which run on a 12V system). Savuti will often drop below freezing on winter nights, so if you get cold then there's a gas/oil/electric radiator to help take the chill off the enormous room.

However, what really makes the camp feel so substantial are a number of huge wooden 'walls' near to the main footpath through the camp. These have been designed to 'dissuade' the local elephants from idly wandering through – but they do nothing at all to help the camp blend in.

The camp's bar, lounge and dining room stand under a huge canvas roof with open sides. Around this is a veranda overlooking the large swimming pool, which itself overlooks a pumped waterhole in the Savuti Channel. That said, visiting at the height of the dry season you may be uncomfortable wallowing in the pool whilst stressed elephants argue over precious gulps of muddy water below you.

The lodge emphasises the quality of the food and accommodation, which are both high, and it's very similar indeed to its sister-camp, the Khwai River Lodge (see page 258). Activities here concentrate on 4WD game drives during the day (night drives, and driving off-road, are not allowed in Chobe). It also has a small hide nearby, and will arrange visits to local bushman paintings on request.

Rates (2005): Jan–Mar US$503 per person sharing, Apr–Jun US$574, Jul–Oct US$571, Nov–Dec US$503; single supplement US$145 per night. Open: all year.

Savute Safari Lodge (12 rooms) Desert and Delta Safaris, see page 171
Savute Safari Lodge (⊕ SAVSAF 18°33.927'S; 24°3.441'E) opened in March 1999 and most
of its visitors reach here by plane, like those of the Elephant Camp. It's been built right
next to the site of the old Lloyd's Camp, and so the local wildlife is exceptionally relaxed
with people – to the point that lions are occasionally found sleeping on the paths between
rooms. (As with most wildlife camps in Botswana, guests here are always escorted by the
staff if walking around the camp after dark.)

The Safari Lodge's rooms are unique in Botswana. In size and quality they're not
dissimilar to the Elephant Camp's rooms – at least 16m long and 6m wide, with double or
twin beds, a huge, high thatched ceiling, wooden structure, simple baths, roman blinds, and
all based on a slightly raised, smooth wooden floor. Most of the walls are wooden, but one
side of each chalet is glass sliding doors. (Those down by the river, with one long side of
glass, are certainly the most spectacular.) Inside the glass doors are mesh mosquito screens.

However, the décor is the shock – as it's modern Scandinavian in appearance: bright,
mostly light colours, clean lines and functional designs. If you're used to shades of green
and khaki, this will surprise you. 'Ikea meets Habitat' was the description of one guest,
referring to its similarity with some European furniture stores.

Each chalet has lots of space. There's a comfortable two-seater couch and an armchair,
and around are thoughtful touches including chic lamps with arresting blue shades and a
tea/coffee maker. Expect lots of white with flashes of bright colours and especially a strong,
royal blue. On the veranda are safari chairs and roll-down blinds designed to cover the
windows. The white-tiled bathroom is modern with a sink, a glass-screened shower, a flush
toilet and a large mirror. Some have large floor-to-ceiling picture windows which can be
unnerving until you realise that you're not overlooked.

The bedroom has twin or double beds with quality linen surrounded by a (cleverly
designed) walk-in mosquito net, below a ceiling fan. There is no air conditioning in the
chalets, though their design does help to moderate the excesses of the climate. During the
day there is electricity from a generator, while at night the chalet's main lights work from a
back-up battery system.

Hilary Bradt and Janice Booth visited here recently, only to be woken by the yelps of
wild dog which had made a kill directly under their chalet. They watched as the dogs were
joined by a cohort of Savuti's numerous hyena, who then challenged the dogs for their
booty – dim shapes wheeling and criss-crossing in the moonlight.

The lodge's dining room has a high, thatched ceiling, tiled floors and light-coloured
wooden tables with solid chairs, pretty tablecloths and a few plants around. However, meals
are often served outside, on a new covered terrace which has a direct view of a waterhole in
the channel. (Much to the delight of a local genet who often drops in for the buffet.)

There's a small library and various board games to pass the heat of the day, and a hi-tech
Jetmaster fireplace in the centre of the room for cold winter mornings. The lodge's curio shop
has a reasonable range of handicrafts, clothing and local jewellery. A small pool, surrounded by
decking has been built overlooking the channel, where the lodge pumps its own waterhole.

If you're staying in several camps, and/or come to Africa on safari often, then the lodge's
design works and will probably seem like a refreshing change. Activities are limited to 4WD
game drives, and the occasional wander to see a Bushman painting. The young guides here
when I last visited were keen on their nature, and enthusiastic about finding it.

*Rates (2005): US$323 per person sharing/single from July to October; US$252/265 per person
sharing or single for the rest of the year. Open: all year*

Savuti Camp – see the section on the *Linyanti Concession*, pages 238–9
This is a small camp situated further up the Savuti Channel, in the private Linyanti
Concession west of Savuti. It is nowhere near the marsh, or in the area that has,
historically, been known as 'Savuti'.

What to see and do

Game viewing and bird-watching are the main activities here, and there's always something going on if you can find it! Start at the main waterhole, which is often the centre for action – though sadly often also quite busy with vehicles.

Driving at night is not allowed, though often the wildlife will come quite close enough if you just stay in your campsite/lodge and keep looking around you.

Driving south from Savuti

About 5km south of the campsite, just before the hill known as Leopard Rock, the track splits two ways. This point (⊕ MARSAN 18°36.078'S; 24°3.678'E) is shown very clearly on Veronica Roodt's Chobe map. In October 1999 there was still one of Chobe's rare old signposts standing here, but since then it appears to have vanished.

The left-hand track is the **marsh road**, signposted Savuti Marsh; it's more scenic but becomes very rutted and bumpy in parts following the western side of the marsh itself. This is fine during the dry season, and you'll see great views of the marsh. It's often a particularly good area for giraffe due to the high number of acacia trees around. However, it's a bad route to choose during the rainy season, as you will almost certainly get stuck.

The right fork is the **sand ridge road** and heads more directly towards Maun, west of the marsh. Taking this you will cut across the Magwikwe Sand Ridge about 26km south of Savuti. Don't expect this to be too obvious, as the ridge is little more than a wide, vegetated sand dune. You will climb slightly to get on to it, and drop slightly to come off – and in between the driving is more difficult than normal as your vehicle's tyres will sink deeper into the sand.

Both meet up again about 20km north of the park's Mababe Gate. The sand ridge road takes 37km to reach this, and the marsh road takes about 44km. The sign here reads: Khwai 45km, North Gate 54km and Maun 133km.

Before you reach that you'll reach the old Mababe Gate, at around (⊕ OLDGAT 19°00.770'S; 23°59.360'E), which is marked on some maps as the gate. Around here the road becomes more difficult during the rains. In contrast to Savuti's relatively lush vegetation, there is little ground cover here, and only low stunted mopane trees to protect the soil from the extremes of the elements. The road's fine earth is hard-baked when dry, and very slippery when wet.

Around 10km further on is the new Mababe Gate (⊕ MABABE 19°06.182'S; 23°59.119'E), where you sign out of (or into) Chobe, and pay your park fees. Just south of this the road forks, without a signpost in sight, and you have a choice... right for Moremi, or left for Maun directly.

Continue into Moremi

Turn right and head west at this junction and a few kilometres later you climb slightly onto Magwikwe Sand Ridge. This takes about 3km of very slow driving to plough through (from about 16km to 19km after Chobe's exit gate), and shortly after you reach the other side you enter the stunningly beautiful river valley of the Khwai River. In the dry season the contrast could not be sharper. After the unrelenting dryness of southern Chobe, the Khwai's lily-covered waterways and shady glades under huge spreading umbrella thorns (*Acacia tortilis*) are completely magical.

About 6–7km after joining the river, you'll reach the boundary of the Chobe and Moremi parks, and then 22km later you'll reach the bridge over the River Khwai at North Gate (see also page 256).

Along this road, at OKAV24 (⊕ 19°05.500'S; 23°49.971'E), you'll find a turning north signposted to Seronga marked by one of the park's old signs, in the form of

Above Overview of Maun, gateway to the Okavango Delta (CM)

Below left Buffalo on one of the Chobe's floodplains (CM)

Below right Large male kudu in the mopane woodlands near South Gate (CM)

Above left Malachite kingfisher (CM)

Above right Pied kingfishers (CM)

Right Carmine bee eaters are commonly resident in sandy banks during the summer (RT)

Below left Spoonbill (CM)

Below right Darter, or snake-bird (CM)

HITCHING A RIDE

The Kori bustard (*Ardeotis kori*) is one of the world's heaviest flying birds, weighing up to 17kg, and – despite a wingspan of 2.8m – it is a reluctant flyer, needing a good run-up to get airborne. On the ground, these stately birds strike conspicuous figures, and are often seen around the pans, either picking their way hesitantly across the grassland in pairs, one at least 100 metres from its partner, or resting in the midday shade of an acacia.

Kori bustards often associate with game herds, whose trampling hooves disturb the locusts, beetles, reptiles and other small creatures on which they feed. In turn, they sometimes provide a similar service for the carmine bee-eater (*Merops nubicoides*). This dazzling bird arrives from Central Africa in October, and spreads out across the grassland in large flocks. Its usual hunting technique is to hawk for insects – particularly bees – in acrobatic sorties from a fixed perch, such as an anthill or bush, and return to the perch to dispatch and swallow the catch. In open grassland, where fixed perches are in short supply, a kori bustard provides an ideal mobile alternative.

In fact the bustard goes one better than a bush by actively stirring up food for the bee-eater, which snaps up whatever it can catch around the bigger bird's feet before settling again on its back. Bee-eaters are not known to try this trick from the backs of mammals, yet the bustard remains surprisingly tolerant of its passengers, and sometimes two or more of them will hitch a ride.

a green concrete pillar. Beware of this, especially if you're heading in the opposite direction towards Chobe, as it will lead you astray through private concessions towards Selinda (see page 239).

Continue to Maun

Turning left, southeast at the fork here will lead you much more directly and quickly to Maun, effectively reaching the village of Kudumane (also known as Mababe Village) first, about 22km from the Mababe Gate. Here you'll take a right turn, passing through Sankuyo, the veterinary fence, and then Shorobe before Maun. (See pages 179–81 for this route – and if you have a GPS then set it for ⊕ MAUN at 19°58.508'S; 23°25.647'E to keep you in roughly the right direction!)

If your destination is Maun, then don't imagine that travelling through the edge of Moremi (on the direct road from North Gate to South Gate) is a quick option. It'll take a good six or seven hours to reach Maun this way. You'll have some slow, heavy driving across the sand ridge, and have to pay an extra set of park fees for Moremi (even if you have just paid some for the same day in Chobe).

However, if you have pre-arranged a few nights in Moremi, then do take this road and don't miss the chance to stop off. It offers a completely different experience.

On the road to Maun, just north of Sankuyo, you'll spot a right turn to Mankwe Bush Lodge (see page 346). About 25km south of Sankuyo, the Sankuyo Tshwaragano Management Trust is reported to have recently developed a campsite and traditional village. This is signposted from the road, about 70km north of Maun.

LINYANTI

The Linyanti River acts as a magnet for game during the dry season, just as its continuation, the Chobe, does further north. However, reaching this area does require the visitor to 'side-track' from the established Moremi-Savuti-Ihaha route across Chobe. This means that it gets few visitors. Further, with only a few kilometres of riverfront accessible to private visitors, and some very, very thick riverside reedbeds and vegetation, it can be a disappointing area.

To the east is the CH/1 concession – which has a mixture of local villages and hunting camps within it. To the west of this is the NG15 photographic concession, the Linyanti Concession (see pages 234–9), which has several good camps, the nearest of which is Linyanti Tented Camp. Visitors driving themselves are restricted in both, so to see this area at its best you are probably well advised to visit one of the Linyanti's camps on a fly-in safari.

Note that despite there being a track marked on the maps from Seronga towards the Linyanti, this is not a practical one to use to get here from the west. Firstly, neither private self-drive vehicles nor mobile operators are allowed to drive through the private concessions between the Linyanti and Okavango. Secondly, as a private visitor you're not allowed to enter Chobe National Park at the Linyanti – you can only enter it from the south or the north. And thirdly, even with a GPS, navigation would be a complete nightmare, and the hunters in the centre of the concessions wouldn't be at all welcoming.

Flora and fauna highlights

This area has a very similar ecosystem to that of the Chobe Riverfront area (pages 205–8), although the vegetation here beside the water seems to have many more large trees and be in a more natural state. Here I didn't feel that the vegetation had been hammered in quite the same way as it has been along the riverfront at Chobe. That said, with a hunting area a few kilometres to the east, and an area that used to allow hunting to the west, the game was much more scarce than the relatively 'tame' herds beside the Chobe.

See more extensive comments on the waterfront area of the Linyanti Reserve, which is part of this very same area on pages 235–7.

Getting there and away

You'd normally approach the Linyanti Campsite from Savuti. To get on to the right track, drive over the old bridge over the Savuti Channel (or what's left of it) and onto its north bank, and then turn left. Thus you pass the campsite on the other side of the channel on your left, whilst heading northwest. Ignoring various right turns, you'll approach a T-junction within a few kilometres, and take a left heading westwards. This crosses the sand ridge (though you may not notice this!) and about 5km later there are two left turnings. Ignore these. Follow the road around to the right, heading in a more northerly direction.

The first 10km of this drive is easy. It's mostly a hard, fast track that's marked clearly on Veronica Roodt's Chobe map. However, after this there's about 30km of trickier driving – very deep sand and tougher going. The scenery is gently rolling dunes, with many flatter areas of low mopane. Visiting last in October, I found large numbers of elephants on the road north. Towards the river there was also a pall of dust-and-wood-smoke hanging over the woods near the river, and a tremendous amount of fine, grey dust in the air. Some of this was clearly coming from fires raging across the river in Namibia.

Where to stay

Linyanti Campsite (see page 142 for National Parks' bookings)
Linyanti Campsite (✦ LINYAN 18°17.686'S; 23°54.601'E) is about 40km from Savuti. When last visited, it had about half a dozen green, metal rondavels with thatch over tin

roofs, all in an advanced state of dilapidation. If you're camping here, then you should certainly come with all your water as well as supplies – although filtering and treating river water to drink would be possible in an emergency.

What to see and do

With only 7km of riverfront accessible, and basically only one track to access it, the driving opportunities are limited here. However, there are plenty of reed beds next to the bank, which can be a delight for birdwatchers, and I've come across the occasional person who absolutely adores this area.

KWANDO, SELINDA, LINYANTI AREA

KEY
4WD track
National park
Private park
GPS co-ordinates ⊕

LINYAN	18° 17.686'S; 23° 54.601'E
MARSAN	18° 36.078'S; 24° 03.678E
OKAV16	18° 40.219'S; 23° 29.856E
OKAV22	18° 43.931'S; 23° 46.320E
SAVBRI	18° 34.979'S; 23° 33.018E

Chobe Forest Reserve

Gchoha scout post

N

Chobe National Park

Chobe National Park

Mabbe Depression

Savuti Campsite, Savute Elephant Camp & Savute Safari Lodge

Savuti Marsh

Δ MARSAN ⊕

Magwikhwe Sand Ridge

CHI

Linyanti Campsite
Δ
⊕ LINYAN

Linyanti Tented

Mamili NP

NAMIBIA

Kings Pool

LINYANTI (NG15)

North gate

OKAV22 ⊕

KHWAI COMMUNITY (NG18)

Savuti

Savuti Channel

Duma Tau

Zibadianja Lagoon

⊕ SAVBRI

Old pole bridge

Selinda

Zibalianja

OKAV16 ⊕

Lebala

Kwando River

Lagoon

0 ___ 20km
0 ___ 10 miles

KWANDO (NG14)

SELINDA (NG16)

Tsetse Fly control cut line

Magwegqana or Selinda Spillway

KWARA (NG20)

Kwara area

Veterinary fence

gate

NG11

Seronga

NG12

NG22

Linyanti, Selinda and Kwando Reserves

Almost parallel to the Okavango, the Kwando River flows south from Angola across the Caprivi Strip and into Botswana. Like the Okavango, it starts spreading out over the Kalahari's sands, forming the Linyanti Swamps. In wetter years this is also a Delta, complete with a myriad of waterways linking lagoons; a refuge for much wildlife. It's a wild area, much of which is on the Namibian side of the border, in the Mamili National Park, where it's difficult to access. A fault line channels the outflow from these swamps into the Linyanti River, which flows northeast into Lake Liambezi, and thence into Chobe.

Both the Kwando and the Linyanti rivers are permanent, so for the animals in Chobe and Northern Botswana they are valuable sources of water. Like the Chobe and Okavango, they have become the ultimate destination for migrations from the drier areas across northern Botswana – and also sought-after safari destinations, especially in the dry season.

In recent years this area, between the Chobe National Park and the Okavango Delta, has been split into three large concessions – Kwando in the north, Linyanti in the east, and Selinda in the middle.

In some ways these are similar, as each encompasses a large area of mopane woodlands and smaller, more prized sections of riparian forest and open floodplains on old river channels. Look at the locations of the camps and you'll realise that much of the interest lies in these floodplains and riparian forests – diverse habitats rich in species.

Away from the actual water, two fossil channels are also worthy of attention: the Savuti Channel and the Magwegqana Spillway. Both offer contrasting and interesting wildlife spectacles.

BACKGROUND INFORMATION
History
The Kwando River has its headwaters in Angola, from where it flows south across Namibia's Caprivi Strip, forming one boundary between Namibia and Botswana. Progressing over the Kalahari's sands, it is thought that once it continued southeast, probably through the course of the present-day Savuti Channel, into the Mababe Depression to swell the vast Lake Makgadikgadi – around one or two million years ago. (See *Chapter 3* for more on the geological history of the region.)

Then, at some point in the last million years, tectonic shifts raised up a fault line running northwest which effectively 'captured' this river, and diverted it along the fault to flow into the Chobe and Zambezi Rivers, thus creating what we now call the Linyanti River.

Around the same time, a parallel fault – the Thamalakane Fault – is also thought to have halted the Okavango's course, trapping it and ultimately silting it up to form an inland delta. As the gradients in this part of the northern Kalahari are very small indeed (1:4000 is typical of the gradient in the Okavango Delta) the routes taken by these watercourses are very susceptible to the tiniest tilts in the earth's surface. As an aside, these faults probably mark the most southerly extent of Africa's Great Rift Valley.

Like the trapped Okavango, silting gradually allowed the Kwando/Linyanti river to spread out into a small inland delta, forming what we call the Linyanti Marshes today.

There is one further geographical feature of note in this area: an ancient river course known as the Magwegqana (spelled in various different ways), or the Selinda Spillway. This splits off from around the Okavango's Panhandle area, and heads northeast entering the Linyanti River system just north of the Zibadianja Lagoon. This doesn't seem to be the obvious product of any local fault lines – although it does roughly follow the line of the Linyanti-Gumare Fault. It's either some form of overflow from the Okavango Delta, or perhaps an ancient river course, or both. Either way it's highly visible from the air, and on the ground offers a rich and open environment for game.

Geography

The geography of the various parts of this area follows on directly from its geological history, and can easily be divided into four types of environment.

Firstly, there are the Linyanti Swamps, comprising of river channels, lagoons, reedbeds and banks of papyrus. Secondly, adjacent to these is a narrow belt of riparian forest that lines these waterways – on the northern edge of the Linyanti Reserve, and the eastern edge of Kwando.

Thirdly there are two dry riverbeds, the Selinda Spillway and the Savuti Channel. Both flood periodically, but both have been dry for a number of years. There are similarities as well as differences between them, most notably the sheer width of the Spillway as it approaches the Linyanti Swamp compared with the relatively narrow Savuti Channel.

Finally, and common to all the concessions, are large areas of dry woodland dominated by large stands of mopane trees, which cover most of the three areas but are usually of least interest to the visitor on safari.

LINYANTI CONCESSION (NG15)

The Linyanti Concession covers 1,250km² of the northern Kalahari, dominated by large areas of mopane woodlands. However, its northern edge is bounded by the waters of the Linyanti River, complete with a string of lagoons and marshes. Adjacent to this is a narrow band of highly varied riparian forests which is the focus of most safari activities.

Cutting from west to east, through the centre of the concession, is the bed of the Savuti Channel. This is usually a dry sand river, where a number of waterholes attract game during the dry season.

Getting organised
Getting there and away

Getting to any of the camps in the Linyanti Concession is simple: you fly. Wilderness Safaris (who run all four camps) include light aircraft flights with their trips into these camps, and it's very easy to fly here from Maun, Kasane, or another camp in northern Botswana.

There are two main airstrips in the concession; one on the river's floodplain near to King's Pool (see page 238; ⊕ KINAIR 18°26.734'S; 23°41.095'E), and another cleared from the bush between Duma Tau and Savuti Camp (see page 238; ⊕ DUMAIR 18°31.948'S; 23°39.264'E).

All these camps work on the basis that the logistics are worked out well in advance. Everybody who arrives has a prior reservation (most made months ago) and everyone arrives and leaves by light aircraft.

No self-driving visitors are allowed into these camps, even by prior arrangement. So if you just drive in, you can expect to be escorted off the property and pointed in the direction of a public road!

When to visit

Note the general comments made in *Planning and preparations*, pages 76–7, and then also the specific comments made for *Chobe Riverfront* area, on page 202 – because the Linyanti's riverfront has broadly the same kind of game movements as that area. In short: game concentrates around here when it needs the water, and spreads out when it can easily drink elsewhere.

This means that the game will be better here when it's drier, although you'll find a wider variety of bird species here in the wet season, many of which will be in their breeding plumage.

Flora and fauna

Technically the Linyanti Reserve is a 'multi-purpose concession' which means that both photographic safaris and hunting are allowed. However, currently Sable Safaris and Wilderness, the companies running the reserve, have a no-hunting policy in order to concentrate on photographic tourism, and reduce the negative impacts that hunting has on the animal populations.

Flora

As with the animals, in many ways the vegetation here is very similar to that of the Chobe riverfront area, though it generally seems in much better condition. It's thicker, older and more lush – though perhaps that is simply the result of much less logging by humans and slightly less pressure from the animals.

In the dry season there is usually at least a kilometre of open ground between the slightly raised riverbank, dotted with mature riparian forest, and the actual waters of the Linyanti. Most of this is open grassland (making a conveniently smooth runway for King's Pool), and this will flood occasionally at times of very high water in the river system.

In this area you'll find some smaller bushes, like russet bush-willows (*Combretum hereoense*) and Kalahari star-apples (*Diospyros lycoides*) – the latter also known as toothbrush bushes after a surprisingly effective use for their thinner branches. (You may also hear this called the blue bush.)

Beyond the floodplain, and up the riverbank, you'll find classic riparian forest with plenty of tall species like knobthorn (*Acacia negrescens*), raintree (*Lonchocarpus capassa*), leadwood (*Combretum imberbe*), jackalberry (*Diospyros mespiliformis*), African mangosteen (*Gardenia livingstonei*) and some marvellous spreading sycamore figs (*Ficus sycomorus*). There are some woolly caper-bushes (*Capparis tomentosa*) in the lower vegetation, but fewer of them than you'll notice beside the Chobe.

Inland, far from the river, is dominated by mopane (*Colophospermum mopane*), though there are also mixed areas, notable for their Kalahari appleleaf (*Lonchocarpus nelsii*), wild seringa (*Burkea africana*), and others in the areas of deeper sand, like old watercourses. Baobabs (*Adansonia digitata*) are dotted around infrequently.

The area around Savuti Camp is very much like this dry woodland, interlaced with sandy fossil riverbeds, whilst along the narrow Savuti Channel itself you'll find more open grassland.

Fauna

All year round here you're likely to see impala, kudu, giraffe, reedbuck, steenbok, warthog, baboon and vervet monkeys throughout the area. Lion and spotted hyena are common, and generally the dominant predators, whilst leopard are often seen in the riparian forest and can be the highlight of night drives.

Cheetah occur here, but not very frequently – though the Savuti Channel is perhaps an exception to this as they are seen here periodically. Wild dog usually stay near their dens from around June to September (with July and August being the most reliable time for them), and then range widely over most of northern Botswana. A den hasn't been located here recently, though pups were being seen here (in September 2001), so there must have been one in the region somewhere. (This is no surprise, as most dens are never found in wild areas like this.)

Blue wildebeest and Burchell's zebra are around all year, although around May they will arrive in larger numbers, remaining within reach of the water until just before the rains begin in around November–December when they head off southeast towards Savuti Marsh.

Elephants and buffalo follow a similar pattern with small groups around all year, often only bulls, but with much larger breeding herds arriving in June–July and staying until December. During this time you'll regularly find very large herds of both buffalo and elephant, hundreds strong.

Tsessebe occur, but are uncommon. In very dry years sable and roan start appearing around September–October. Eland are very rare here, and gemsbok don't occur this far north.

Waterbuck are permanent residents, especially towards the northeast of the concession. This is one of relatively few areas of Botswana where they're found. Keep a look out around King's Pool and Linyanti Tented Camp, particularly at the interface between the mopane woodlands of the interior and the riparian forest by the river. Sitatunga are occasionally sighted from boat trips on the river.

Side-striped and black-backed jackal are around, the latter reaching the extreme northern edge of its distribution here (and so isn't common). Bat-eared fox are regularly seen; the area around King's Pool airstrip seems to be a particularly favourite. Mongooses are always around, especially the banded and dwarf.

Serval, caracal, African wildcat and aardwolf occur, and Savuti Camp has a notably excellent record of sightings in the channel for these, especially serval. Aardvark are occasionally seen, and one local expert reports they used to be spotted frequently in the riverine forest near the Zibadianja Lagoon. I've no reports of pangolin here.

When you're out on night drives, you've also got a chance to see scrub hares, spring hares, lesser bushbabies, porcupines, genets (small-spotted and large-spotted), civets and honey badgers.

Birdlife

In the riparian woodlands, birds of particular interest include wood owls, swamp boubous, brown firefinches, white-rumped babblers and collared sunbirds. Of particular note is the beautiful Schalow's lourie, a local race of the Knysna lourie found in this region.

There are numerous summer migrants, including carmine bee-eaters that nest here. There are several colonies in the area, including one almost opposite the

Livingstone hide. Carmines tend to arrive around September and leave March–April. Some appear to have learnt to follow vehicles down the Savuti Channel, catching the crickets that jump away from the moving wheels. Others use the kori bustards, which frequent the channel as moving perches.

Other summer visitors include the thick-billed cuckoo and the narina trogon, although one expert on the area's birdlife, Mark Tennant, comments that the latter may be resident.

The raptors are well represented. Bateleur and fish eagles are probably the most numerous, but you're also likely to spot African hawk, and tawny, martial and black-breasted snake eagles. Gymnogenes are relatively common. When the first rains come in December, migrants like Wahlberg's and steppe eagles seem notably attracted to the first flush of green in the Savuti Channel – hence December to February can be a particularly good time here.

Throughout the year, western banded snake eagles are also sometimes seen, though they're not common, along with giant eagle owls, bat hawks (look out on the edge of the forest, by the river, in the evening) and the occasional Pel's fishing owl.

On the water there's a host of different species, though some of the marshes and lagoons here can be difficult to access, even from the camps. (The canoeing possible at Linyanti Tented Camp goes some way to remedy this.) Some of the more unusual residents include slaty and black egret, rufous-bellied heron, painted snipe, long-toed plover, African rail and wattled crane. African skimmers usually nest here in September, with Zibadianja Lagoon, amongst others, being a favourite spot for them.

Where to stay

All four camps in the Linyanti Reserve are owned by Sable Safaris, but exclusively marketed by Wilderness Safaris (see page 174). They range from the substantial comfort of King's Pool to the much more simple bush-camp style of Linyanti Tented Camp. All cater exclusively for fly-in visitors and none will accept visitors who want to drive in.

Here I'll describe them from north to south:

Linyanti Tented Camp (5 tents)
Linyanti Tented Camp has long been one of the smallest, simplest camps run by Wilderness Safaris, and it's now marketed as one of their 'Vintage' camps (along with Kaparota, Jacana, Tubu and Pom Pom). These have slightly lower prices than the rest of their camps in Botswana, and promise modest comforts in place of plush luxuries.

Linyanti Tented Camp is about 10km southwest of Chobe's Linyanti Campsite (see pages 230–1) and despite having five simple Meru-style tents, it will normally only accept a maximum of eight guests at a time. All these tents have en-suite hot shower, washbasin and toilet. Together with the dining and bar area, which are also under simple canvas, they all overlook the Linyanti River. Linyanti is very much an old-style safari camp, with traditional tents, far from the interior-designer chic found elsewhere.

Activities here include 4WD game drives by day and night, most of which are taken in the riverine forest beside the water. Short walks and boat trips are possible, as well as self-paddle canoeing excursions in large, Canadian-style canoes on the nearby lagoons – an activity which, despite the amount of water around, is almost unique here and not generally possible at other camps in Botswana.

Rates: US$400/490 per person sharing/single from July to October; US$240/330 for April, May, June and November. Includes all meals, activities, park fees, laundry, and most drinks. Excludes transfers. Open: April to November.

King's Pool (10 raised chalets)

This is the Linyanti's flagship camp, the largest and most luxurious. It overlooks the Linyanti River and the swamps beyond from a position (✪ KINGSP 18°26.276'S; 23°42.415'E) in the very centre of the reserve, almost 19km northeast of Duma Tau and a similar distance from Linyanti Tented Camp.

Accommodation is in ten substantial chalets with canvas walls, all supported by raised decks and perched on the edge of a high river bank. These rooms all have private, tiled bathrooms with a hot shower, toilet and handbasin, as well as a separate outdoor shower. All have balconies overlooking Kings Pool Lagoon (a broad bend in the Linyanti River) and when I was last there a herd of elephants wandered through camp in the middle of the day for a drink below the chalets.

In the centre of the camp is a large lounge, bar and dining-room, all under thatch, whilst outside there's an open-air boma for meals under the stars. On the edge of camp there's a swimming pool and, separately, a hide for game viewing (though it's questionable if this offers better game viewing or birdwatching than is already possible from the balconies of the chalets).

Activities here are mainly on 4WD game drives and night drives. These concentrate on the riverine forest areas beside the water and, when dry, the wide grassy floodplains between the river's water and the high bank. Short walks are also possible, and when the water levels are high enough (eg: around April to August) there's a double-decker boat for gentle river cruises.

There are two small game hides in the vicinity of the camp: Inkwe Hide, which is near the river on the east side of camp, and Livingstone's Hide, which is halfway between King's Pool and Duma Tau. (Almost opposite the latter, on the other side of the river, is a colony of carmine bee-eaters.) Visitors can be dropped and collected later from these, and if you book early and request it then it's theoretically possible to sleep over in one. (Though marketed as an option, this rarely happens in practice and is not for faint-hearted visitors!)

Rates (2005): US$870 per person sharing/single from July to October; US$545/600 from December to March; US$595 for April, May, June and November. Includes all meals, activities, park fees, laundry, and most drinks. Excludes transfers. Open: all year.

Duma Tau (9 raised tents)

At the western end of the Linyanti, overlooking the Zibadianja Lagoon from its southeastern shore, Duma Tau is found just east of the source of the Savuti Channel (✪ DUMATA 18°32.217'S; 23°33.917'E) under a canopy of mangosteen trees.

The camp has nine luxurious tents raised on wooden platforms, all with en-suite facilities: hot showers (one indoors and one outside) washbasins and flush toilets. There is a central dining-room, bar and lounge, and a small plunge pool for afternoon dips.

Activities centre around 4WD game drives, and night drives which visit the riverine forest beside the Linyanti, as well as the drier areas along the upper reaches of the Savuti Channel and the mopane forest between. Short walks are sometimes possible, and there's a boat which can be used on the lagoon and in nearby waterways when water levels are high.

Duma Tau also shares the use of Livingstone's game hide with King's Pool – and visitors can be dropped and later collected here, and even sleep over if requested early enough. (I last saw the hide in passing, as a large pride of lion had brought down a buffalo within about 30m of it!)

Rates (2005): US$595 per person sharing/sharing from July to October; US$390/430 from December to March; US$430 for April, May, June and November. Includes all meals, activities, park fees, laundry, and most drinks. Excludes transfers. Open: all year.

Savuti Camp (6 raised tents)

Savuti Camp (✪ SAVUTI 18°35.834'S; 23°40.412'E) stands beside the Savuti Channel,

DRIVING THROUGH THE PRIVATE CONCESSIONS

If you thought that Botswana's national parks were badly signposted, the tracks through private concessions are even worse. Basically, they've not been set up for private vehicles to drive through them. A few specified 'transit routes', set up for use by occasional supply vehicles, are the only tracks on which you can legally drive. Venturing off these is illegal, as is camping anywhere at all here. It's effectively private land.

Many visitors here are lost – accidentally finding themselves off the main tracks in the national parks. One story, told by the team at Selinda, is of a party of apparently 'experienced' travellers in a 4WD from South Africa who arrived in the dead of night one year. They'd got lost driving from North Gate to Savuti, and been slowed down by an expensive new trailer which got stuck in every patch of sand on the way. Eventually they abandoned their expensive trailer at Selinda – swearing that they'd never return to Botswana's bush again.

So the only way to use these routes is with the permission from the reserves. You'll then need your GPS, all the maps you can find, bags of common sense ... and then you can still expect to get lost!

about 42km due west of the Savuti Marsh – the area that's always been commonly known as 'Savuti' within the Chobe National Park. (See pages 219–29). It's about 13km as the eagle flies, from Zibadianja Lagoon and the rickety wooden bridge which spans the start of the Savuti Channel (✪ SAVBRI 18°34.979'S; 23°33.018'E).

The camp has five Meru-style tents raised up on individual wooden decks. All have en-suite showers, toilets and wash basins with hot and cold water. Three of the rooms have inside bathrooms, whilst the other two are open to the skies with views beyond.

Each has a small veranda, with everything under the cool shade of a large canvas roof. The camp has a separate dining room and bar/lounge area under a thatched roof, and a small plunge pool.

Activities here concentrate on 4WD game drives, by day and night, although walks are also possible. There are several elevated hides to visit, and the waterhole in front of the camp is the only source of water in the dry season for miles around. Hence the camp has a justified reputation for lion and elephant. What's less well known is the channel's apparently high concentration of serval, which appear with surprising regularity on the night drives here.

Note that the camp is highly seasonal, with the channel flushing a verdant green with the first rains, but subsequently becoming quite arid and harsh towards the end of the dry season in October/November.

Rates (2005): US$595 per person sharing from July to October; US$390/430 from December to March; US$430 for April, May, June and November. Includes all meals, activities, park fees, laundry, and most drinks. Excludes transfers. Open: all year.

SELINDA CONCESSION (NG16)

Selinda covers a long swathe of 1,350km², including a large section of the Magwegqana Spillway, the often-dry waterway that links the Okavango to the Linyanti Swamps.

Most of its camps are in the far east of the concession, in a very open area where small tree-islands stand amidst large dry plains. The eastern side of the concession is largely thick mopane forest; Motswiri Camp is a seasonal camp used for hunting here.

Getting there and away

The vast majority of visitors fly into the Selinda Reserve. It's certainly the easiest and quickest way, taking only about an hour from Maun or Kasane, and very easily organised by the camp or your tour operator. There's an airstrip situated halfway between the Selinda and Zibalianja camps, less than 5km from either of them. However, it is possible to drive here. So for the sake of completeness, I'll include directions. Note that these tracks are generally used much less than even the sand tracks through Chobe or Moremi, so unless you are highly self-sufficient and bush-wise you would be much, much wiser to fly. With little or zero passing traffic, you would face a major problem in the event of a breakdown, or an argument with an aggressive elephant.

Driving from Chobe's Linyanti Campsite

From northern Chobe, the Selinda Reserve is easiest to approach coming from the Linyanti Campsite, driving through the south side of the Linyanti Reserve on what's known as the 'transit route'. However you intend to arrive, you must book in advance, and make sure that the Selinda team know exactly when you're arriving, and by which route you intend to approach.

Firstly, to get to the Linyanti Campsite in Chobe you must either come about 40km from Savuti (see page 230), or a similar distance along the cut-line of the Chobe Forest Reserve (see page 215), from near the Ghoha Entrance Gate. The latter is rarely used, and most people would want to stop for a few days at Savuti anyhow.

From the Linyanti Campsite in Chobe, take the only track westwards and after 4km you'll reach the edge of the Chobe National Park, with a clear signpost from 'Linyanti Investments' directing you left, away from the river, to Maun, Kwara, Kwando – and Selinda. You are now driving along the cut-line that marks the edge of the Chobe National Park. This will lead you south for about 7km, before a right turn branches off, which you should follow. This is now the transit route – sometimes signposted as 'Transit Route A' – and it continues roughly west, parallel to the river, for a further 22km. The scenery here is almost exclusively mopane woodlands.

About 10km after leaving Chobe's cut-line, you'll pass a crossroads. Then for the next 12km there are various small right turns which you must ignore – they all lead up to the Linyanti's camps (Linyanti Tented Camp and King's Pool) and most are marked clearly with 'No through road' signs.

This transit route is designed to allow vehicles to cross this private concession whilst causing the minimum of disturbance to the guests. Note that if you drive off the transit route, you'll be an unwelcome intruder on a private concession!

About 22km after you leave Chobe's cut-line, the road forks and you keep right, heading between north and east. (A left turn would take you to Linyanti's Savuti Camp.) About 11km later you'll reach a crossroads where you take a left onto a deep sand road. Here again there are various right turns from the road (to Duma Tau Camp) that you should ignore.

Continue for about 10km until you reach the old, rickety bridge (✪ SAVBRI 18°34.979'S; 23°33.018'E) made of poles. This spans the start of the Savuti Channel, just south of Zibadianja Lagoon, and is the concession boundary. If it's dry then you might prefer to just drive across the channel on land to the left of the bridge, rather than across the poles themselves.

On the far side of the channel, turn right. (The alternative track, heading left, would lead along the channel to Linyanti's Savuti Camp.) You'll find a sign saying Selinda Concession, and the road bends to the left. It's quite striking how different the landscape is; on the left is mixed forest, and soon on the right are open plains with the odd palm island and lots of game around. To reach Selinda's HQ keep heading left, and you'll find it on the left in a forest island within a few kilometres. From there they'll direct you to your pre-arranged camp.

Driving to the Khwai River area

It's about 100km to North Gate from Zibalianja Camp, taking perhaps four hours in the dry season. If you drive south through Selinda, then all the tracks will converge into one, and then cross the TFC (Tsetse Fly Control) cut-line about 9km due south of Zibalianja Camp.

This point is noted as OKAV16 (⊕ 18°40.219'S; 23°29.856'E). You'll see a wide variety of signs at this intersection, including one denoting 'military zone 1999 – no hunting beyond this point'. Another, referring to the road northwest, indicates the village of Beetsha, confirming that (believe it or not) this is the main road up to the east side of the Okavango's Panhandle area. If you were heading north from here then, rather more cheerfully, you'd read one saying 'Welcome to Selinda,' as well as others indicating Kwando and Linyanti.

From here turn left along the cut line, heading about 10° south of east. Generally you'll find this is a good and very straight track, though there are a few patches of deep sand. As you might expect, it's all mopane woodlands here with less and less variation in the vegetation as you travel. Typical of such an environment, the area is dotted with small pans, and where the track crosses them it can become very muddy in the wet season.

After 30km of very straight road, you'll reach OKAV22 (⊕ 18°43.931'S; 23°46.320'E), where you'll take a right turn heading south and slightly east. If you had continued straight here, you would cross the Magwikwe Sand Ridge and then meet the sand ridge road (see page 228) at a T-junction, west of Savuti Marsh. This track into Chobe is not used frequently; I'm unsure of its condition.

Heading south and east from OKAV22, the road isn't as straight as the cut-line, but makes its way through large areas of mostly stunted mopane. This is NG18, a concession designated for 'community utilisation of the wildlife by the Khwai Community'. See pages 286–7 for more details on this, but note with interest that in 1999 the Khwai community had an income of US$240,000 from the sale of its hunting quotas in this wildlife area.

Passing through NG18 fairly swiftly, in the middle of a hot day in late September we spotted a few kudu, impala and steenbok, and hyena spoor on the track – so there is a fair amount of game around here.

Towards the south side of NG18 the land opens up a little and you'll pass more open areas of grassland and low bushes. A little over 35km after OKAV22 you'll reach an old airfield at OKAV23 (⊕ 19°02.415'S; 23°50.194'E), which is a large, flat grassy area that seems disused now.

After this the road continues south, though the mopane changes from rather low, stunted trees to some of the most impressive continuous stands of cathedral mopane that you'll see anywhere. Only as you approach the main game area around Khwai itself do you start to find this broken down more by elephant damage, and interspersed with open areas.

Finally, about 6km south of the airstrip you'll reach a junction (⊕ OKAV24 19°05.500'S; 23°49.971'E) with the main road from Moremi to Chobe. It's still marked by one of the park's old green concrete pillars that function as signs: left (northeast) 27km to Chobe and right 14km (southwest) to Moremi. Seronga, on the east of the Panhandle, is signposted back north.

Approaching this sign from Moremi can be quite confusing. The Selinda road, described above, is apparently marked as 'Chobe'. It's not unknown for careless self-drivers to make the mistake of taking this road, thinking it leads to Savuti. One party, who were lost for several days having done this, eventually turned up at Zibalianja Camp, desperately seeking help. They'd been lost for several days, frequently stuck in the sand, and didn't want to continue. They just wanted the nightmare to end and to leave as fast as they could. So with the right directions in hand, they abandoned their brand new trailer and quit Botswana.

Flora and fauna
Flora
The area around Selinda and Zibalianja camps is the wide mouth of the Magwegqana Spillway – which is largely composed of open floodplains dotted with small palm islands. The spillway floods only very rarely, but when it's done so in the past it has cleared, or killed off, many small trees and bushes on the plains, leaving only flat marshes and grasslands behind.

Because it hasn't flooded fully for a long time, these areas are now dry and are gradually being colonised by 'pioneer species' of invading bushes – species which can quickly take a hold and will thrive in areas which have been disturbed like this.

Chief amongst these is the wild sage (*Pechuel-loeschea leubnitziae*), which covers large areas of the spillway with its aromatic grey-green foliage. (In *Trees and Shrubs of the Okavango*, Veronica Roodt comments that 'All over Africa wild sage is used [to treat] a variety of venereal diseases.')

Another pioneer is the candle-pod acacia (*Acacia hebeclada*) which form lovely, round bushes. If you've come here after Savuti Marsh, you may have seen them on the south side of the marsh there.

Dotted amidst this are small, slightly raised 'islands' of trees. These have been here for decades, and can survive the periodic flooding – though see the comments on pages 52–3 regarding island formation if you're curious as to how such 'islands' are formed.

The trees found on these are typical in many ways of those in the riparian forests, though with the addition of lots of the real fan palms (*Hyphaene petersianna*). Some are tall trees, many are only bush-sized, but all help to make Selinda's environment a particularly attractive one. Amongst the other tree species here, African mangosteens (*Gardenia livingstonei*) seem particularly common and lush – their branches all apparently flung outwards, as if a green bomb had exploded inside.

Fauna
Like the Linyanti and Kwando, there's a population of resident game, which is swelled from about June onwards by the arrival of large numbers of game which move into the reserve for its proximity to the permanent waters of Zibadianja Lagoon and the Kwando–Linyanti river system.

Permanent game includes impala, red lechwe (on the east side near the lagoon), kudu, tsessebe, giraffe, reedbuck, steenbok, warthog, baboon and vervet monkeys. Lion and spotted hyena are common, whilst leopard are seen more rarely, usually around the larger tree islands. The very open country is certainly good for cheetah, and though I've never seen them myself, I do get regular reports of them here.

Selinda certainly is one of the best reserves for wild dog; the pack known locally as the 'Selinda pack' denned here in 2001 and 2002. Although wild dog do range over the whole of northern Botswana, if you want any chance of seeing them then you'll need a place where your guide can drive off-road, to stick with them as they hunt, and where there's lots of dry, open grassland with not too many trees, so that the driving is relatively free of obstacles.

This narrows your choice down to a few of the private reserves, but would certainly include Selinda, Mombo, Vumbura and the southern side of Kwando. I don't wish to imply here that you won't see dogs elsewhere; you will. However, if I were going out specifically to look for dogs, then I'd start in these areas.

On my last visit I followed them hunting on one occasion for over an hour. Following them at speed across the open ground, they would frequently run through the small palm islands to try and flush out any game hiding there. At the same time we'd drive around the islands, and wait for them to come out on the other side again.

Herds of wildebeest and zebra arrive around May, staying here until just around November–December. Elephants and buffalo follow a similar pattern with individuals around all year, and larger breeding herds arriving around June-July and staying until December. Eland, sable and roan occur here, but none are common.

Side-striped jackal, bat-eared fox and various mongooses are resident, as are the more nocturnal serval, caracal, African wildcat and aardwolf. Night drives will usually locate scrub hares, spring hares, lesser bushbabies, genets (small-spotted and large-spotted), civets, sometimes honey badgers or porcupines, and rarely aardvark.

Birdlife
Virtually all of the birds typical of riparian woodlands in the neighbouring Linyanti and Kwando reserves (see pages 236–7 and 247) also occur in the tree islands of Selinda.

In addition to this, the reserve is noted for good sightings of collared palm thrush, plus species of open grasslands like ostriches, secretary birds, kori bustards, red-crested korhaans, various sandgrouse and both common and (from November to March) harlequin quails. The family of coursers is well-represented here – with the uncommon bronze-winged and three-banded varieties occurring as well as the more widespread Temminck's and double-banded coursers.

During the summer months flocks of Abdim's and white storks can be seen, whilst raptor concentrations are always good.

Where to stay
All of the camps in the Selinda Reserve are run by Linyanti Explorations (Pty) Ltd., PO Box 22, Kasane; tel: 6250505; fax: 6250352; email: info@linyanti.com; web: www.linyanti.com

Run by Brian and Jan Graham, Linyanti Explorations are one of Botswana's last remaining small, owner-run operations. They've been operating in this area since 1976, based entirely in Kasane where they founded Chobe Chilwero (selling it only relatively recently, in 1999).

In January 1995 they took on Selinda Reserve, and hence built Selinda, Zibalianja and two small fly-camps used for walking trails (Mokoba and Tshwene). Photographic visitors from these camps have exclusive use of the eastern side of the reserve.

In the far west of the concession near the buffalo fence and NG22, about 60km from Zibalianja, there is also a small hunting camp called Motswiri – though in the long term, it is planned to phase this out.

Like most of Botswana's high-quality camps, bookings must be made in advance and virtually everyone flies in. Linyanti Explorations encourages travellers to book through good overseas tour operators that specialise in Africa; they include a list of suggested operators on their website.

Selinda (6 tents)
Standing on the edge of the Selinda Spillway, Selinda Camp (✪ SELIND 18°31.897'S; 23°31.354'E) is the reserve's main camp though it still feels small.

Its tents are all traditional Meru-style walk-in tents with comfortable twin or double beds, wooden furniture and a relaxed, comfortable feel. Each has an en-suite bathroom, partially open to the skies, at the back with shower, washbasin and flush toilet. This is shaded by a thatched roof to keep it cool. When the generator's running there is 220V electricity available, at night there's a 12V system of battery lights.

The camp's main building is thatched and two storeys high, containing a bar (often self-service), a small curio shop, a comfy lounge and an upstairs dining room – where the candlelit dinners are marvellously atmospheric. Outside is a small plunge pool for when it's hot, and a boma area with central campfire for cool mornings and evenings.

The team is very enthusiastic about their activities, which concentrate on 4WD game drives in the morning and afternoon/evening. The former can start very early in the morning (a good sign of commitment to their game spotting!), the latter eventually becoming spotlit night drives.

Short walks can also be organised, often as part of a drive. Depending on the Zibadianja Lagoon's levels, boating and fishing trips are sometimes possible. As part of its continued monitoring of the reserve, the team assists with monthly game counts that take place every full moon. Enthusiastic visitors with stamina are invited to take part. (They also undertake aerial counts three times a year, as part of their overall monitoring programme of the reserve, though logistics mean that these aren't open for visitor's participation.)

Rates (2005): US$490/765 per person sharing/single from July to October; US$425/575 from March to June or during November. If you stay for four or more nights in the reserve, then these drop to US$440/620 and US$385/535 respectively. Includes all meals, activities, park fees, laundry, and most drinks. Excludes transfers. Open: March to November.

Zibalianja (4 tents – but usually takes a maximum of 6 visitors)
This (✪ ZIBALI 18°35.577'S; 23°30.670'E) is probably Botswana's smallest permanent camp, built on a small tree-island amidst the plains just a few kilometres west of the Zibadianja Lagoon. (The slightly different spelling of the camp's name and the lagoon's name is intentional.)

Zibalianja has just four twin-bedded Meru-style tents standing on raised wooden platforms, shaded by canvas fly-sheets. Each has an en-suite bathroom, with a shower, washbasin and flushing toilet. These are of traditional design but very comfortable, with a system of 12V lighting from solar power.

There's also a small, informal dining area, though meals are often eaten outside. The camp's focal point is a supremely photogenic little bar perched on a wooden platform under its own tree just off the edge of the tree-island. This has superb views all around.

Activities here, and the team's enthusiasm for them, mirror those at Selinda, and the guiding when I last visited was both intelligent and excellent. Zibalianja is a super little camp for those who are serious about their game viewing and birdwatching.

Rates (2005): US$490/765 per person sharing/single from July to October; US$425/575 from March to June or during November. If you stay for four or more nights in the reserve, then these drop to US$440/620 and US$385/535 respectively. Includes all meals, activities, park fees, laundry, and most drinks. Excludes transfers. Open: March to November.

Walking trails camps (3 tents each)
Usually referred to as simply Selinda's walking trails camps, you won't find their names, Mokoba and Tshwene, used very often. Both stand along the Selinda Spillway (the Magwegqana, towards the northeast of the reserve).

Tshwene is further west, where the spillway is still relatively narrow, standing under some lovely old leadwood (*Combretum imberbe*) and knobthorn (*Acacia nigrescens*) trees. It is one of the smallest and simplest camps that you'll find in Botswana. Mokoba is in the far northeast corner of the reserve, close to the Kwando River. Neither is more than about 6km from Selinda Camp, and typically visitors spend a few days at one of the permanent camps (Selinda or Zibalianja), then a few days walking to one of these camps, and then continue to the other camp for their last nights.

Accommodation in either of the walking camps consists of mini-Meru tents. These have large panels of airy (but insect-proof) mesh, and solar lighing inside. Inside is enough space in which to stand, two proper single beds, a small bedside table and a couple of chairs.

A separate fly-sheet extends to create a tiny veranda, next to which you'll find a washbasin in a stand with a screen around it. Bucket showers (hot water provided on request) and flushing toilets are separate; the showers are shared between the guests.

Meals are very relaxed and al fresco; the table is usually set up under the stars, and the food is good despite having only the simplest of bush kitchens.

These camps focus on walking safaris, although short night drives are also possible. Each camp takes just four walkers at a time (six if all in one group!) and the reserve has earned an excellent reputation as one of the very best reserves in Botswana for walking. The guides here are always armed, and accompanied by a tracker. Guiding standards are high because they are specialist walking guides.

A typical day here would be perhaps 6–8km between camps in a morning, and a shorter walk of perhaps 4–5km in the afternoon.

Rates (2005): US$490/765 per person sharing/single from July to October; US$425/575 from March to June or during November. If you stay for four or more nights in the reserve, then these drop to US$440/620 and US$385/535 respectively. Includes all meals, activities, park fees, laundry, and most drinks. Excludes transfers. Open: March to November.

KWANDO CONCESSION (NG14)

On the northern edge of Botswana, bordering Namibia across the Kwando River, the Kwando Concession covers an enormous area of 2,320km^2 of very wild bush. It's one of Botswana's larger wildlife concessions. Beside its eastern boundary, the river, is a narrow belt of riverine forest. In the south this opens out into some large tree islands and open floodplains. There are two photographic camps on this productive eastern side.

The vast western part of the concession includes huge tracts of thick mopane woodland. Here, far from the river, there is a seasonal hunting camp.

Getting organised
Getting there and away
Like most of Botswana's private concessions, Kwando is reached by a short flight from Maun, Kasane, or one of Botswana's other camps. Both these camps work their logistics out well in advance. Trips here are always pre-arranged, and they don't welcome 'drop-in' visitors, or ever really get any. There are two main airstrips in the concession; one near Lagoon, and the other near Lebala.

Thus virtually nobody would consider self-driving into these camps, even by prior arrangement. However, if you did then you'd pre-arrange your visit with the camps and take the transit route north through Selinda. It's about 14km in a straight line from Selinda to Lebala, and a further 30km by road from there to Lagoon.

When to visit
Game viewing revolves around the reserve's riverfront on the Kwando River and its adjacent riverine forest. Thus note the comments made in *Planning and preparations*, pages 76–7, and also the specific comments made for Chobe

Riverfront area, on page 202. The Kwando's riverfront has broadly similar game movements to the Chobe or Linyanti riverfronts. In short: game concentrates around here when it needs the water, and spreads away again when it can easily drink elsewhere.

This means that the game viewing improves as the land dries out. Then buffalo and elephants move into this area from the west and south and zebra and wildebeest move in from the great plains of the Chobe. Later, when it rains, so the animals will move away – although birdwatchers will find more of interest in the wet season when there's greater variety of bird species, many of which are in breeding plumage.

Flora & fauna
Flora
Kwando's environment and ecosystems are similar to those of the Linyanti and Selinda reserves. The north of the reserve is most like the Linyanti Reserve, in that it's dominated by the presence of the river, which runs on its eastern border in a roughly straight line. Adjacent to this is a band of riverine forest, characteristically rich in its variety of trees. These include African mangosteen, *Garcinia livingstonei* (which remind me of a bomb exploding, as all the stems grow out straight from the top), jackalberry, *Diospyros mespiliformis*, sausage tree, *Kigelia africana*, leadwood, *Combretum imberbe*, and knobthorn, *Acacia nigrescens*.

As you move further south in the reserve, around Lebala Camp, you're getting into the northern side of the Magwegqana Spillway, and here the riverine forest opens out, becoming a mosaic of open areas covered in low bushes and grasses. These open areas are often dominated by wild sage, *Pechuel-loeschea leubnitziae*, and interspersed with patches of forest, which become smaller and more island-like as you move further south.

These forest patches and islands contain many of the same riverine trees species, and you'll also find marula trees, *Sclerocarya birrea*, occasional baobabs, *Adansonia digitata*, and increasing numbers of real fan palms, *Hyphaene petersiana*. Plus many camelthorns, *Acacia erioloba*, and the invasive candle-pod acacia, *Acacia hebeclada*.

Further south still, the land becomes even more open as you approach the reserve's southern boundary and the Selinda Reserve.

Fauna
Like the Linyanti and Selinda, Kwando's resident game is augmented in about June by migrant game which arrives here from the drier areas south and west, attracted by the permanent waters of the Kwando River.

Common species found here include include impala, red lechwe, kudu, tsessebe, giraffe, steenbok, warthog, baboon and vervet monkeys. Roan, sable and common duiker also occur, but are not common. Lion, leopard and spotted hyena are common, whilst cheetah are rarely seen. Hippo and crocodiles frequent the river, along with the playful spotted-necked otters.

Herds of wildebeest and zebra are resident here from around May to December. Elephants and buffalo follow a similar pattern with individuals around all year, and larger breeding herds arriving around June–July and staying until December. These large herds are particularly common near the river during the dry season, and the elephants seem to have a penchant for aggression if approached too closely. When driving around with one of the camp's guides, he would refer to them nonchalantly as 'cheeky' animals; but driving myself through the area once I found it much more nerve-racking. They reacted completely differently to the relatively passive elephants found in the busier parts of Chobe and Moremi.

Kwando is also a good reserve for seeing wild dog, especially in the south of the reserve around Lebala, helped by Kwando Safari's policy of actively 'tracking' animals across the bush – and having both a tracker and a driver/guide on all of its vehicles.

Highlights of the night drives here include Selous' mongoose, genets and aardwolf – along with more usual sightings of scrub hares, spring hares, bushbabies, genets, civets, honey badgers and porcupines.

Birdlife

The birdlife here is almost identical to that of the Linyanti Reserve (see pages 236–7), with plenty of variety. I particularly remember a huge colony of carmine bee-eaters that we seemed to have discovered by accident when stopping on a drive for a 'sundowner' drink.

Sacred and hadeda ibis are particularly common in the waterways here, whilst rarer residents include slaty and black egrets, and rufous-bellied herons.

Where to stay

Both the camps here, Lagoon and Lebala, are owned and run by Kwando Safaris, based in Maun. See page 172 for details.

Lagoon Camp (6 tents)

Overlooking the Kwando River, Lagoon Camp (✆ LAGOON 18°12.980'S; 24°24.790'E) is the smaller and more northerly of Kwando's two camps here in the riparian forest belt. It stands amidst tall, mature forest that includes some fine marula (*Sclerocarya birrea caffra*) and jackalberry (*Diospyros mespiliformis*) trees.

The large tents here are of a custom design, with two three-quarter size beds, or a double, overlooking the river. The large front door can be opened into an entirely gauzed area; wonderful to wake up to! These have a solid wooden bed-head, matching the tent's wardrobe and furniture – though no fan. Outside each the veranda has two khaki chairs overlooking the river. All is covered by a canvas shade, shielded from the sun by a thatched roof. At the back of each is a private, en-suite, reed-walled enclosure with an open-air shower, a washbasin (in front of a large mirror) and a flush toilet. Hot water comes from individual gas-fired boilers.

The food at the camp is good, and served in a thatched dining room which overlooks the river. The bar's largely self-service, and a small curio shop has local handicrafts and some useful books. The lounge area has comfortable armchairs, a small library and various boardgames.

Game frequently wanders into camp and on my last visit here one old bull elephant came to within touching-distance of the dining room as we ate brunch, in search of some tasty morsels in the tree above. It was very relaxed; apparently oblivious to the camera flashes and general fuss that it was causing.

Lagoon Camp has a plunge pool for the hotter months, but its main activities are 4WD game drives, usually one early in the morning (after coffee and biscuits), and the second in the late afternoon, which usually turns into a night drive as the light fades. With a tracker accompanying every drive, and a maximum of six people per vehicle, there's a willingness here to drive cross-country and actively track coveted game – like the big cats and wild dogs. The guides are enthusiastic about their big game here, and sometimes positively zealous in their tracking of it.

There is also a two-storey floating pontoon-type boat on the river, which can be used for gentle sundowner cruises. If you're keen on fishing then spinning for tiger fish and bream is also an option.

Lagoon's atmosphere is laid-back, friendly and not at all regimented – mealtimes are usually adjusted around game-viewing times, rather than vice versa. A slight minus is that the tents are quite close together (although all have canvas blinds that can be closed.

Rates (2005): US$615 per person sharing/single from July to October including all meals, most drinks, activities & park fees; US$250/385 per person sharing or single for the rest of the year. Open: all year.

Lebala Camp (8 tents)
Lebala (✷ LEBALA 18°24.760'S; 23°32.540'E) is a slightly larger and more substantial camp than Lagoon, in a very different location. Lebala means 'open space', which is appropriate as there are lots of plains around it. It's just 14km from Selinda, and yet 26km (measured in a straight line) from Lagoon – and hence it's no surprise that its environment is close in character to that of Selinda, but quite different to the area around Lagoon.

Lebala's substantial and custom-designed tents are built on raised decking. This is mostly made of polished mukwa wood – a very colourful and durable local wood from the *Pterocarpus angolensis* tree. Each chalet encompasses a very large bedroom, with two three-quarter-size beds and a sprinkling of mukwa furniture. Outside the bedroom is a large private veranda for sitting out, with a few chairs and a table.

Canvas room-divisions separate the bedroom from the 'entrance hall' where there is a spot to put suitcases, a hat-and-coat stand, a large wardrobe and a writing desk – as well as a zipped tent door to the outside world. The large bathroom has a stand-alone claw-footed bath, with taps on the side, and also his & hers washbasins and a toilet. Outside is a large semi-circular shower. (Hot water comes very efficiently from each room's individual gas geyser.)

Good meals are served in the separate thatched dining area, adjacent to which is a comfy lounge and bar area. This has a modest library of books, and one side open to the plains around. There's a campfire for the cooler months, and a small plunge-pool for the warmer ones.

Activities here concentrate on 4WD game drives, and as with Lagoon the guides always drive with a tracker and will actively seek the game. Last time I visited here I arose late one morning, only to learn that wild dog had sprinted through camp just before sunrise.
Rates (2005): US$615 per person sharing/single from July to October including all meals, most drinks, activities & park fees; US$250/385 per person sharing or single for the rest of the year. Open: all year.

The Okavango Delta –
Moremi Game Reserve

Much of what is covered in this section, and especially concerning *Flora and fauna* and *When to visit*, is applicable to the Okavango as a whole – hence I've covered this information here in detail, and made reference to it elsewhere where appropriate.

Remember that Moremi and its surrounding reserves are only separated by lines on a map; their ecosystems blend together seamlessly. Birds and animals move without hindrance across almost the whole of the Okavango, Linyanti and Chobe regions. Thus all the country covered in *Chapters 12–16* is really one continuous area dedicated to wildlife. The enormous size of this, together with the diversity of ecosystems that it contains, are two of the main reasons why the wildlife of northern Botswana is so spectacular.

BACKGROUND INFORMATION
History

In his *Travels and Researches in South Africa* (see *Further Reading*) David Livingstone recounts what he was told by the local people near Lake Ngami in 1849 about the origin of a river there:

> While ascending in this way the beautifully-wooded river, we came to a large stream flowing into it. This was the Tamunak'le. I enquired whence it came. 'Oh, from a country full of rivers – so many no one can tell their number – and full of large trees.'

However, within a hundred years of Europeans finding this 'country full of rivers', its environment and wildlife were under threat. In an exceedingly far-sighted move, the BaTawana people proclaimed Moremi as a game reserve in 1962, in order to combat the rapid depletion of the area's game and the problems of cattle encroachment.

Initially Moremi consisted mainly of the Mopane Tongue area, then in the 1970s the royal hunting grounds of Chief Moremi, known as Chief's Island, was added. Since then, in 1992, the reserve has been augmented by the addition of a strip of land to the northwest corner of the reserve, between the Jao and Nqoga rivers. This was done to make sure that it represented all the major Okavango habitats, including the northern Delta's papyrus swamps and permanent wetlands which had not previously been covered by it.

As an aside, it's often cited that this was the first reserve in Africa that was created by native Africans. This is true and recognises that the native inhabitants were the prime movers here, rather than the colonial authorities. However, beware of ignoring the fact that Africa's original inhabitants seemed to coexist with the wildlife all over the continent without needing any 'reserves' until Europeans started arriving.

MOREMI OVERVIEW

NG22

NG23
Vumbura
Duba Plains

Moanachira Lagoon
Xugana
Xugana Lagoon
NG21
Shindi
Kwara

Camp Okavango

GCODIK

Nqoga River

Jao River

Gcodikwe Lagoon

Mombo & Little Mombo

Kwetsani

NG25 Jacana

Jao Camp

Zepa

Chief's

Chief's Island

Xigera

MOREMI

Xo Flats

Abu Camp

Nxabega

Macatoo

Xudum River

Kanana
Eagle Island
Oddballs
Gunn's Camp

Gubanare
Delta Camp
Semetsi Camp

NG26
NG27a
NG27b

Pom Pom

Ranns Camp

Sandveld Tongue

Mantis
Eden

Moklowane
Xudum

NG30

Kujwana

NG29

Qwaapu

Boro River

KEY		GPS co-ordinates ⊕	
4WD track		1BRIDG	19° 17.099'S; 23° 23.531'E
Vet cordon fence		3BRIDG	19° 14.368'S; 23° 21.430'E
Wildlife reserve		4BRIDG	19° 15.128'S; 23° 24.173'E
Region		CAMPMO	19° 11.322'S; 23° 24.489'E
Safari camp or lodge		GCDDIK	19° 09.731'S; 23° 14.507'E
		NOGATE	19° 10.261'S; 23° 45.055'E
		OKAV24	19° 05.500'S; 23° 49.971'E
		SOGATE	19° 25.548'S; 23° 38.733'E

Geography

Moremi Game Reserve protects the central and eastern areas of the Okavango Delta. It forms a protected nucleus for the many wildlife reserves/concessions in the region. Physically Moremi is very flat, encompassing extensive floodplains, some seasonal, others permanent, numerous waterways and two main landmasses: the Mopane Tongue and Chief's Island.

Its area is defined in some places by rivers, although their names and actual courses are anything but easy to follow on the ground. Its northern boundary roughly follows the Nqoga-Khwai river system, whilst its southern boundary is defined in sequence by the Jao, Boro and Gomoti Rivers.

It's worth noting that since the middle of the last century it seems that the western side of the Delta (specifically the Thaoge River system) has gradually been drying up. As this has happened, an increasing amount of water is entering the Moanachira/Khwai River system, on the eastern side of Chief's Island – helping to raise water levels around the Khwai River area, and increase the incidence of flooding on the roads there.

Flora and fauna

The ecosystems of Moremi Reserve are amongst the richest and most diverse in Africa. Thanks to generally effective protection over the years, they have also been relatively undisturbed by man. Now with wildlife tourism thriving around the park as well as in the private concessions, we can be really optimistic about its future. The regime of conservation supported by money from benign tourism is gaining ground. As I write this, rhino have been reintroduced into Moremi; the first to be sent back into the wild areas of northern Botswana since poaching wiped them out.

Flora

There are over 1,000 species of plants recognised in Moremi, yet large tracts of the reserve are dominated by just one: mopane, *Colophospermum mopane*. This covers the aptly named Mopane Tongue and parts of Chief's Island. Because the park has had effective protection for years, and the soils are relatively rich but badly drained, much of this forest is beautiful, tall 'cathedral' mopane – so-called for the gracefully arching branches which resemble the high arches of a Gothic cathedral. You'll often find large areas here where there are virtually no other species of trees represented.

Beside the many waterways you'll find extensive floodplains, and some lovely stretches of classic riparian forest with its characteristically wide range of tree and bush species.

Laced through the areas of mopane you'll also find open areas dotted with camelthorn trees (*Acacia erioloba*) and sandveld communities following the sandy beds of ancient watercourses, dominated by silver terminalia, *Terminalia sericea*, wild seringa, *Burkea africana* and Kalahari apple-leaf, *Lonchocarpus nelsii*. You'll find much, much more detail on this vegetation in Veronica Roodt's essential *Trees and Shrubs of the Okavango Delta* (see *Further Reading* for details).

Fauna

Moremi protects as dense and diverse a population of animals and birds as you'd expect to find in one of the Africa best wildlife reserves. With the reintroduction of rhino, you can see all the big five here, and a lot more besides.

Elephant and buffalo occur here year-round in large numbers, and you're likely to see blue wildebeest, Burchell's zebra, impala, kudu, tsessebe, red lechwe, waterbuck, reedbuck, giraffe, common duiker, bushbuck, steenbok, warthog, baboon and vervet monkey throughout the park. Eland, sable and roan antelope also range across the park but are less common, as they are elsewhere in Africa. Sitatunga live deep in the swamps.

Lion, leopard, cheetah and spotted hyena all have thriving populations here. Moremi is central to wild dog, which range widely across most of northern Botswana.

Both side-striped and black-backed jackal occur – though the latter are more common. Brown hyena probably occur, but relatively rarely and only in the drier areas with lower densities of the other large predators. Similarly, bat-eared fox are found here, though not so commonly as in Botswana's drier areas. There is a wide variety of mongooses found here, including the banded, dwarf, slender, large grey, water and Selous' mongoose. Meanwhile in the water, Cape, clawless and spotted-necked otters are often glimpsed though seldom seen clearly.

Serval, caracal, aardwolf and aardvark are found all over the park, though are only occasionally seen due to their largely nocturnal habits. Pangolin are also found here, and seem to be slightly less rare than in other areas of their range.

Although night drives aren't allowed within the reserve itself, some of the camps near North Gate will finish their afternoon drives outside the park, and hence do short night drives back to camp. Then you have a chance to see scrub hares, spring hares, lesser bushbabies, porcupines, genets (small-spotted and large-spotted), civets, African wildcats and honey badgers. Black and white striped polecats are also nocturnal, though very seldom seen.

Up until 2001 rhino had been absent due to poaching, though in November of that year the first white rhino were reintroduced into the Mombo concession, in northeast Moremi. They're now free to roam, but they are effectively constrained to Chief's Island.

Birdlife

Moremi boasts over 400 bird species, a great variety, which are often patchily distributed in association with particular habitats; though visiting any area, the sheer number of different species represented here will strike you as amazing.

Although there are no birds that are truly endemic to Botswana, the Okavango is a hugely important wetland for many species, amongst which are a number of rarities worth noting here. Top of the Okavango's list of 'specialities' is the slaty egret. Expect to find this in shallow, reedy back-waters and pans. Besides the Okavango, this rare egret is only resident in the quieter corners of the Chobe and Linyanti rivers, and the Bangweulu Wetlands in Zambia. To identify it look for its overall slate-grey colouring, except for its lower legs and feet which are yellow, as are its eyes and some of its face, while the front of its neck is a rufous red. (The less uncommon black egret lacks the yellow on the legs and face, or the rufous neck.)

Much easier to spot are magnificent wattled cranes which can be seen in the delta fairly readily, usually in pairs or small groups wandering about wet grasslands or shallow floodplains in search of fish and small amphibians and reptiles.

For keen birdwatchers, other specials here include brown firefinch, lesser jacana, coppery-tailed coucal, Bradfield's hornbill, pink-throated longclaw and the inconspicuous chirping cisticola.

When to visit

See *When to go* in *Chapter 4* for more general comments on the whole of northern Botswana, and note that the best times to visit are dependent upon how you intend to visit, exactly which camps you are visiting, and why.

Flying in

If you're flying into a camp in Moremi or the Delta then the season won't make much difference to the access; virtually all the camps open all year. The Okavango's camps used to close down during January and February, but now most keep open throughout the year, despite being much quieter during the green season (December to March). The exception to this has been the January to March period in 2002, when many camps closed down due to reduced bookings from America after the tragedy of September 11.

In terms of vehicle access to the various game-viewing areas from your camp, the rains are often less of a concern than the flood, the peak of which usually lags behind the rains by several months (depending on how far up the Delta you are). However, generally there will be the most dry land from about August to January.

Driving in

If you're driving yourself into Moremi, then understand that only a restricted area of the reserve will be accessible to you, and the wet season will make this access more difficult. As the rains continue, their cumulative effect is to make many of the roads on the Mopane Tongue much more difficult to pass, and it simply submerges others.

The direct track between North Gate and Xakanaxa has been particularly problematic recently. It was waterlogged for traffic for virtually all of 2001, due to a combination of rain and floods. Thus only the experienced and well-equipped need even think about driving anywhere through Moremi between about January and April.

Most visitors who drive themselves come to Moremi in the dry season, between around May and October. Then the tracks become increasingly less difficult to navigate, although even then there are always watercourses to cross.

Flora and fauna

The flora and the birdlife are definitely more spectacular during the rains. Then the vegetation goes wild, migrant birds arrive, and many of the residents appear in their full breeding plumage. So this is a great time for birders and those interested in the plants and flowers.

The story with the animals is more complex. In most of Moremi there is water throughout the year. Higher water levels here simply means less land area available for animals that aren't amphibious. However, around the edges of the Delta, animal densities are hugely affected by the migration towards the water from the dry central areas of the country.

Thus game viewing generally gets better the later in the dry season that you go … although this trend is probably less pronounced in the centre of the Delta than it is at the edges.

Activities

The water levels will affect the activities that you can do whilst here. In some areas mokoro trips are possible only for a few months every year, when water levels are high enough. Similarly, the game drives from a few of the camps are generally possible only when water levels are low enough.

Costs

The cost of some camps in the Okavango varies with the season. This depends very much on the company owning/marketing the camps, but in general you can expect July to October to be the highest cost level; December to March to be the time of lowest cost; and November, April, May and June to be pitched somewhere in the middle.

Getting organised
Orientation
Moremi Game Reserve covers a large tract of the centre of the Okavango Delta, and a wide corridor stretching east to link that with Chobe National Park.

At the heart of Moremi is a long, permanent island, Chief's Island, oriented from southeast to northwest. At about 60km long and around 10km wide this is the largest island in the Delta, and it's usually cut off from the mainland by waterways and floodplains. Within the eastern side of Moremi is a triangular peninsula of dry land covered (mostly) in mopane trees, known as the 'Mopane Tongue'.

Between and around Chief's Island and the Mopane Tongue, Moremi is a mosaic of rivers, lagoons, floodplains and small islands which slowly and gradually change with the passage of time.

Maps
Once again, Veronica Roodt's definitive map of Moremi Game Reserve (see *Further Reading*) can't be recommended too highly for visitors to Moremi, and is essential for anyone planning a self-drive trip there.

Booking and parks fees
If you're flying into an organised camp, then parks fees will probably already be included in the price that you've paid. If you're driving in you'll need to have booked all your campsites in advance – see page 142 for details of the National Park offices in Maun and Gaborone, and a scale of the fees.

You'll need to have a copy (or preferably an original) of this confirmation with you, then you'll need to pay your parks fees on the gate when you arrive. Note that this is best done in pula, and that credit cards are never accepted.

Opening hours
The park's opening hours vary with the season, roughly corresponding to 'dusk 'til dawn'. This is when the park's gates and offices open, and you're not allowed to drive around the park before morning opening time, or after evening closing time.

Currently these are: December, January and February: 05.30–19.30; March, April and May: 06.00-19.00; June, July and August: 06.30–18.30; September, October and November: 06.00–19.00.

Moremi Reserve's regulations
With your entry permit and booking you'll usually be given a photocopied set of the park's regulations, which are worth familiarising yourself with before you get here.

Amongst the more notable ones is a strict ban on camping away from the campsites or without a valid permit; driving off-road; driving faster than 40km/h; walking away from your vehicle (except for designated campsites); or swimming anywhere.

You aren't allowed to bring any firewood into the reserve, or take any out. However you *are* allowed to collect it from within Moremi for your own use. Remember that, and collect it as you drive around during the day. If you forget to do so until you're setting up camp, you'll usually find the campsites devoid of even the smallest combustible dead twigs! (Needless to say, never take branches from living trees or bushes, however dead they may seem.)

THE MOPANE TONGUE

Within eastern Moremi, the dry triangle of the Mopane Tongue juts into the Delta from the east, between the Khwai and Mogogelo rivers. Each side of this is about 40km long, and roughly marking the corners are the campsites of South Gate, North Gate and Xakanaxa – a reminder that this is the only area of Moremi that's accessible for visitors driving themselves.

Aside from the riverine forest which lines its edges, the vast majority of the interior of this peninsula is covered in forests of mopane – including many stretches of very mature and beautiful forests.

Khwai River and North Gate

Near the northeastern edge of Moremi, the northernmost waterways of the Okavango gradually narrow and are spanned by a wooden pole-bridge. The tracks that run beside the river and around the floodplains here are often stunning in their beauty, and prolific in their wildlife. It's a spectacular area, and especially beautiful if approached from the dusty heartlands of Chobe during the dry season.

Orientation

It's easy to orient yourself here. The Okavango's waters approach from the west down the Khwai River. To the west they're flanked by floodplains, loops, meanders and lagoons, but gradually travelling east this valley narrows and concentrates the river water into a small channel.

Central to the whole area is the bridge at North Gate, which spans the channel. South of this is Moremi, and north is the small settlement of Khwai Village, the community-controlled concessions beyond NG18 and NG19 (see pages 286–7), and the area's airstrip.

Although the lodges in this area are technically inside these concessions, I've included them in this chapter as their focus is essentially on this corner of Moremi.

Flora and fauna highlights
Flora

All along the edge of the Khwai's floodplain you'll find some of the region's most beautiful, mature riverine forest. Stunning trees, tall and old abound, including a large number of camelthorn, *Acacia erioloba*, and some almost pure stands of leadwood, *Combretum imberbe*. There are also patches of acacia woodlands, usually standing on sandy patches of ground between the river valley and the mopane woodlands of the Tongue's interior.

Mammals

The Khwai area seldom fails to deliver some very impressive wildlife spectacles when visited in the dry season. This is perhaps to be expected, as it marks the boundary of the Okavango's waters that flow east and north – and so is the closest drinking water for large numbers of thirsty animals in southern Chobe during the late dry season.

Of particular note here are the lion prides. In 1999 one was so large that it had started taking down small elephants – a practice which visibly worried the area's large elephant herds.

I've had some particularly good leopard sightings here, seeing the cats lounging around in shady trees during the day, usually on the edge of the riverine forest. Mixed areas of broken woodlands and open areas is classic leopard territory, and because it's been protected for so long, many of the residents are very relaxed in the presence of game-viewing vehicles.

NORTH GATE AREA

KEY

Main 4WD track
Other track
Seasonal track

GPS co-ordinates ⊕

KHWAIL	19° 08.860'S; 23° 48.019'E
KHWAIR	19° 09.052'S; 23° 47.543'E
MACHAB	19° 07.448'S; 23° 48.758'E
NOGATE	19° 10.261'S; 23° 45.055'E
OKAV24	19° 05.500'S; 23° 49.971'E
TSARO	19° 09.976'S; 23° 44.049'E

Khwai Community Concession (NGI8)

0 _____ 3km
0 _____ 2 miles

Chobe, Maun
Selinda
OKAV24

ZAMBWAYA RD
XWAZARA RD
Xwara Pan
Xhloromotsaa Pan
Lepapaha Pans
MAKGAPHA ROAD

XHLEBA ROAD
LEPAPANA ROAD

Makgapha Pan
Jeremotsaa Pan
Big Qonimotshaa Pan
Xiflu-oro Pan
Small Qonimotshaa Pan
Xhleba Pan
Motswiri Pan

MACHAB
Machaba Camp ⊕

KHWAIL
Khwai River Lodge
Khwai Airstrip

KHWAIR ✦
Saguni Hippo Pool

Moqwara Pan

Kaunga Pan

SEPANYANE ROAD

North Gate campsite
NOGATE

Khwai Village
North Gate (pole bridge)

Tsaro Elephant Lodge
TSARO ⊕

South Gate

Segagana Pans

Seolo Pan

Xugana

Xgaba Pan

Samahundu Pool

Domba Hippo Pool
Baobab
Xokanoxa

Qoa Lediba

Mopane Tongue

N

Bradt

At Khwai you probably have a better chance than in most places of seeing the normally elusive roan antelope, which come down to the river to drink regularly.

Birdlife

Khwai's birdlife is varied, like the habitats found here, though with only a narrow channel of water in the dry season, you'll usually have to search elsewhere for large numbers of the more aquatic species. That said, even in the dry season you will find storks (saddle-billed and marabou) and wattled cranes pacing around the open areas in search of fish, frogs and reptiles to eat.

Khwai does have a reputation, especially towards the end of the dry season, for having a very high density of raptors – with which I can concur. I've been closer to a martial eagle here than anywhere else, had a lovely sighing of a marsh harrier hunting, and both bateleur eagles and giant eagle owls seem particularly common. So as you drive along, keep glancing into the sky and checking the tops of trees for the distinctive outline of a perched raptor.

Where to stay

There are three lodges and one campsite here. All stand overlooking Moremi from the north side of the Khwai River, and so are technically in the NG19 concession. However, as they all concentrate on safaris into the reserve, I've described them here for completeness. Note that all, even the campsite, must be pre-booked before you arrive. You are likely to be turned away if you simply turn up.

Khwai River Lodge (15 canvas rooms) Contact Gametrackers, see page 174
I've very fond memories of the original Khwai River Lodge (✪ KHWAIL 19°08.860'S; 23°48.019'E) which once stood here, with understated little bungalows dotted around amongst the leadwood trees on the edge of the river's floodplain. It was one of the Okavango's oldest lodges, and full of character. Now this has sadly been demolished, apart from the basic structure of its old office that has been preserved as a small museum and curio shop. Around this is now an opulent Gametrackers lodge, built between about December 1998 and May 1999 and modelled on the same design as that used for Savute Elephant Camp.

At its heart is a central area, which is slightly raised on a timber platform and topped by an enormous thatched roof. This encloses a lounge, a bar and a dining room. The lounge has a fireplace with leather surround, chess sets, a TV with a library of wildlife videos, comfy couches and a small library. Next to this is a dining area where candles light long, wooden tables for stylish dinners – adjacent to a wide area of decking overlooking the narrow, shallow river valley. There's a central fireplace, for drinks outside, and a huge swimming pool built into the decking. Next to the main complex, an adjoining raised observation deck with thatched roof shelters a small telescope; it's a good spot for game viewing or perhaps the occasional intimate private dinner.

The lodge's 15 canvas rooms are really far too opulent to be called tents. All are built on high timber platforms, facing the river valley. Because these are spread out in a line, each a distance from the next, the camp stretches for over a kilometre in length and the furthest tents are a significant walk from the central lounge. Each large platform has a wide veranda at the front, with safari chairs overlooking the river, and a huge canvas structure measuring about 18m x 6m.

Inside, each 'tent' is fully furnished with polished wooden floors, rugs and plenty of proper, comfy furniture – not just the usual safari chair or two. Twin three-quarter-sized beds, which are usually pushed together, have high-quality cotton bedding, bedside tables and twin (battery-powered) lamps. The beds are surrounded by mosquito netting, and surmounted by two air-conditioning units which, when I last visited in October, fought a valiant but losing battle to keep the room cool. At the back of the tent is a toilet and a large (two-person) shower, each behind a wooden door. The lodge's build-quality is very high, and clearly no expense has been spared – though there seems to have been little attempt to blend the lodge into the surrounding area.

Activities here focus on two game drives per day. The morning drive usually commences after a light breakfast, and returns in the late morning for a substantial brunch. The afternoon drive commences after afternoon tea, and aims to leave the park as it closes, at sunset. Driving at night in the park is not allowed, though a spotlight will sometimes be put on when the vehicles have passed over the bridge and are heading for home.

Rates (2005): Jan–Mar US$503 per person sharing, Apr–Jun US$574, Jul–Oct US$751, Nov–Dec US$503; single supplement US$145 per night. Open: all year.

Tsaro Elephant Lodge (8 rooms) Desert and Delta Safaris, see page 171
Barely 2km west of North Gate, Tsaro Elephant Lodge (⊕TSARO 19°09.976'S; 23°44.049'E) is another of Moremi's old, established camps. For many years it was the sister-camp of Xugana until sold by Hartley's Safaris, though now it's run by Desert & Delta. It's still one of the very few remaining lodges with a solid construction of stone or brick (Sandibe, pages 334–5, also springs to mind here), and has an atmosphere and a slight quirkiness which befits its age.

Each of Tsaro's eight rooms are unique, having been developed and augmented over time. (Room number one usually counts as the honeymoon suite, and is regarded as the best!) All have a high, thatched roof covering a concrete veranda, on which there are usually a couple of easy chairs. These all look south over the Khwai River into Moremi. The river's about 80m away from the lodge, and before that there's an expanse of floodplain dotted with tall, grey termitaria and usually a sprinkling of lechwe and impala.

Inside each chalet you'll find polished concrete floors scattered with mats, a few dark, wooden armchairs, a simple wardrobe, a luggage rack and two single beds. In the en-suite bathroom there's a large shower (hot water heated by gas geyser), washbasin, mirror and flush toilet.

Up in the high thatched ceiling there's a strong fan which works on the lodge's own electric generator during the day. At night this is switched off and the camp is lit with a system of battery-powered lights. Tsaro's simple and pleasant but not luxurious.

Note Late in 2001 Tsaro unexpectedly closed. It had recently been substantially refurbished, and its closure was certainly a surprise to Desert & Delta. Apparently, the lease on the lodge's land had come up for renewal and renegotiation. Sadly, Desert & Delta were unable to reach an agreement with the local community over the terms and conditions of the new lease. We have left the information in here as we wait to see if Tsaro will reopen, or if it will simply fall into disrepair, and also if there will be similar difficulties in the future between the community and Khwai or Machaba.

Machaba Camp (8 tents) Contact Ker and Downey Safaris, see page 172
The contrast between Machaba (⊕ MACHAB 19°07.448'S; 23°48.758'E) and its neighbour is striking – despite Machaba being only about 3km northeast of Khwai River Lodge.

Machaba feels like one of the Okavango's last old-style camps, with traditional tents on the ground amidst a rather lovely glade of riverine forest, with old knobthorne, red bushwillow, raintree and leadwoods above and around it.

Each green canvas Meru-style tent stands on a solid concrete deck, with a shaded veranda and deck chairs at the front. Inside there's coir matting on the floors, a little cloth-shaded wardrobe and twin beds separated by a little table – on which there's usually a cool container of drinking water and a battery-powered lantern. Each has a flush toilet, shower, a washbasin and a shower at the back (hot water from efficient individual gas geysers.) These tents have no electricity, but the camp's generator can individual gas geysers.) These tents have no electricity, but the camp's generator can charge video batteries.

Similarly the canvas-roofed lounge at the camp's centre is equally simple, with a small dining and bar area, a cozy lounge, and a very good, well-maintained 'sightings board'. This shows how frequently the big game species (lion, leopard, cheetah, wild dog, buffalo) have been seen, and when, plus bird charts and maps. The lack of data for elephants simply demonstrates that they're almost always around.

Slightly east, about 1km downstream, Machaba has a game-viewing hide overlooking the river at which guests can be dropped off, and then collected again at a pre-arranged time. Other activities at Machaba centre around two game drives per day. The first usually starts after a light breakfast, returning in time for a late-morning brunch. The second begins after afternoon tea, and then leaves the park around sunset. Last time I visited, Machaba was being run temporarily by Bruce Cantle, whose experience of, and enthusiasm for, the area made it a lovely place to stay. The tents were looking old, but these are due to be replaced for 2002.

Rates: US$440/640 per person sharing/single from July to October; US$370/420 per person sharing/single for the rest of the year. Open: March to the end of November.

North Gate Campsite Contact National Park's booking office, see page 142
This campsite is another lovely National Park's site with only the most basic of facilities. It's situated on the south side of the Khwai River, immediately on your left as you cross into Moremi. There's a simple toilet block, a supply of fresh water, and about a dozen campsites dotted amidst wonderful, tall woodlands.

Look out in this campsite area for especially impressive specimens of sickle-leaved albezia, *Albizia harveyi*. Their fine leaves and flattened seed-pods might look like acacias, but trees of the Albezia family don't have thorns. You'll also find a few huge sycamore figs, *Ficus sycomorus* – easily spotted because of their yellow-orange bark, and a tendency for parts of their wide trunks to form buttresses. Old Africa hands will avoid camping directly under a fig tree if possible, though, as their fruits are sought after by everything from baboons and bats to elephants – any of which can make for a messy tent in the morning, and a very disturbed night's sleep.

What to see and do
Wherever you stay here, however you travel, your activities during the day will be almost exclusively game drives – as walking and night drives are forbidden by park rules, and the Khwai is too shallow and narrow for safe boating.

Game-viewing roads and loops spread out on both sides of North Gate, to the west and east. Most stick close to the Khwai River, either exploring the river's floodplain or the adjacent band of riverine forest. You'll need Veronica Roodt's map of Moremi (see *Further Reading*) to get the best from these, as they're not shown on the main map of Botswana.

If you're visiting in the wet season, then consider taking one of the long drives that loop away from the river east of North Gate – like Sepanyana Road. These give you access to some of the pans in the mopane area, which might prove more productive for game at that time.

Getting there and away
By air
Virtually all of the visitors to the three lodges here arrive at the airstrip (⊕ KHWAIR 19°09.052'S; 23°47.543'E), which is just outside Khwai River Lodge. This is a short hop from Kasane, Maun, or any of the other airstrips in the region. There are no facilities at the airstrip; it's just a flatish section of low grass with a windsock next to it.

Driving from North Gate to Savuti, Chobe

Note that the reverse of this route is described in slightly greater detail in *Chapter 10*, pages 228–9. Here I've repeated the basics, as this is often a route that is taken by self-drive visitors on their first trip to Botswana, and it's one that can be confusing.

Cross North Gate's wooden bridge (⊕ NOGATE 19°10.261'S; 23°45.055'E) to the north side of the river, and follow the main track through Khwai Village. This bends to the right, and heads roughly northeast, passing the Khwai Airstrip, at KHWAIR (⊕ 19°09.052'S; 23°47.543'E) on the right. Near the airstrip, a right turn leads to Khwai River Lodge, while a few kilometres later a second right heads to Machaba.

About 8km after the airstrip, the road forks at OKAV24 (⊕ 19°05.500'S; 23°49.971'E). The branch to the north, signposted to Seronga by one of the park's old green concrete pillar signs, heads off to Selinda Reserve and the northeast side of the Delta. To reach Chobe take the right turn which initially bends east, following the stunningly beautiful Khwai River Valley.

Around 9km after this you technically cross into Chobe National Park and there's a right turn onto a cut-line road which heads due south, marking Moremi's border. This takes about 33km to join the road to Maun near the village of Zankuyo.

Ignoring that right turn, about 16km after OKAV24 the road leaves the river and splits again. Both forks join the Savuti–Maun track: head right for Maun, but left for Savuti. Shortly after you'll cross the Magwikwe Sand Ridge – a relic from the period when central Botswana was covered by the giant super-lake, Lake Makgadikgadi. (See page 48 for more on the origins of this ridge.) You may not see the ridge itself, but after 3km stuck in low gears ploughing through thick sand, you'll realise that you've crossed it.

It's about 6km from the base of the sand ridge to Chobe's Mababe Gate (⊕ MABABE 19°06.182'S; 23°59.119'E), and the earth on some of this road is very fine with a high clay content: hard-baked when dry; sticky and difficult when wet. At the gate, stop and sign in before continuing roughly north towards Savuti.

About 20km north of the Mababe Gate, the road splits. Both forks lead to Savuti. The right fork is the **marsh road**, which is more scenic, but can be very rutted and bumpy during the dry season, with great views of the marsh. It is certainly going to be the worse of the two during the rainy season, when you'd be wise to take the left fork, the more direct sand ridge road. This stays closer to the Magwikwe Sand Ridge, climbing onto it at one point. It's less interesting, but certainly the better route in the wet.

After about 37km on the sand ridge road, or 44km on the marsh road, these routes converge (⊕ MARSAN 18°36.078'S; 24°3.678'E) beside Leopard Hill Rock, which is about 5km south of the heart of Savuti.

Driving from North Gate to Xakanaxa

Important note on the road between North Gate and Xakanaxa Note that between 2000 and (as I write) 2002, the main North Gate–Xakanaxa road has been largely closed because of high water levels. Before setting off along it you should always ask the warden at the camp you are leaving if it's passable. If not then you have no choice but to route via South Gate and the 'central' road through the Mopane Tongue (a total distance of about 72km).

That said, even when blocked by high water levels, the main problems are often in the middle of the route – allowing you to access some of the more northerly game-drive loops from North Gate on a drive from the east. But having seen these, you've then got to re-trace your steps.

This route is really very straightforward. Start from North Gate's wooden bridge and follow the road southwest towards South Gate for less than a kilometre. Here you'll find a substantial right turn signposted to Xakanaxa, heading in a more westerly direction. Follow this and after about 44km it'll lead you straight there, mainly through old, established mopane woodlands.

However, the real joy of this route is the numerous side-loops which detour to the right of the road. There are endless small loops and side-roads, but if you feel lost remember that heading west and south will generally keep you going in the right direction. Heading north will go deeper into the detours and usually bring you back to the Khwai River.

The main problem arises when the tracks are waterlogged. When I drove this route in 1999, most of the loops were fine. A few – often those marked as 'seasonal roads' on Veronica Roodt's map of Moremi (see *Further Reading*) – were tricky and required one to cross quite deep water in the vehicle. The scenery on the road around Qua Ledibe (Lediba is the local word for lagoon), particularly looking out west towards the Xuku floodplain, was very beautiful as we meandered between the dappled light of the forest and open lagoons.

However, west of Qua Lediba, the road became progressively more difficult, with deeper and deeper stretches of water to cross. Several times we forded water across the road, until one large pool stopped us. Forest to the left and lagoon to the right. There was no easy way around. The track was flat sand; solid not slippery. Vehicle tracks had been this way recently – a good sign.

As we considered our next move, two large trucks, run by a mobile safari operator, approached and drove across, showing us the depth; we crossed safely. We avoided the next pool, but in a third the vehicle lurched alarmingly to the right – my passenger falling across me as I drove. The Land Rover didn't blink though and pulled us through. Nerve-racking when alone, such puddles are more fun with a party of two vehicles, as then one can pull the other out of difficulty if necessary.

Back on the main road, heading west we found a drift, where the road had been washed away. Various alternatives circled off left, finding shallower, but slippier, places to cross. The water at the main road was deeper – but the substrate was more solid. On the whole, a safer bet.

Driving from North Gate to South Gate
Again, this is a very straightforward route, on a very straight road – only without the game drive loops of the previous route. From North Gate's wooden bridge you simply follow a substantial track for about 30km, which heads southwest, directly towards South Gate (⊕ SOGATE 19°25.548'S; 23°38.733'E)

Driving from North Gate to Maun
This isn't a route that people often want to take, but the quickest way is probably to follow the first part of the *North Gate to Savuti* instructions, above. Then around 9km after OKAV24 (⊕ 19°05.500'S; 23°49.971'E), turn right onto the cut-line which heads due south. This takes about 33km to join the road to Maun near the village of Zankuyo.

Note that crossing the Khwai River here can be tricky, and this road is especially sticky and difficult during the rainy season.

Tip of the tongue: Xakanaxa and beyond
One corner of the Mopane Tongue's triangular peninsula juts towards the centre of Moremi, and at the end of the tip is Xakanaxa Lagoon. Beyond it, on three sides,

is the Delta's maze of channels, floodplains, lagoons and islands. A few of the larger, closer islands are accessible via simple pole bridges – like Goaxhlo and the large Mboma Island. Beyond this, Moremi becomes inaccessible without a boat: that's the realm of the small, fly-in safari camps.

The patchwork of environments found here is typical of the inner reaches of the Delta. It's also phenomenally beautiful, and one of the most reliably good areas for wildlife on the subcontinent. Expect phenomenal densities of game and birdlife here and, as it's been protected for years, the animals are generally very relaxed.

For the self-driving visitor, the game and scenery here is as good as it gets in Botswana – don't miss this area.

Orientation

The main route from North Gate to Xakanaka roughly follows the northern edge of the Mopane Tongue. Similarly, the main road from South Gate to Third Bridge roughly follows the southern edge of the Tongue. This sections covers the area around and between Xakanaka and Third Bridge.

In Veronica Roodt's map of Moremi (see *Further Reading*) there are some detailed insets of the road layouts around this area, so make sure that you buy a copy of this before you get here. You'll also find plenty of useful references and background information on the reverse of the map.

Flora and fauna highlights

Picking out the 'wildlife highlights' for an area like this, and trying to point out what's special here, is virtually impossible. There's usually something special around every corner. It's not that you'll see different things here than you will elsewhere in Moremi, or even Botswana, it's just that you'll see them all in a very small area here.

Where to stay

There are three camps, catering mostly to pre-arranged fly-in visitors, and one campsite all clustered around the Xakanaxa Lagoon, a huge open lagoon which is fed by the Moanachira River. This can be traced upstream, passing close to Camp Okavango, Shinde and Xugana – allowing these isolated water-based camps to be used as 'satellites' for sojourns of a few days into the Delta, linked by a boat journey of a few hours.

Note that because of the particularly high game densities here, and the relaxed, fearless nature of the animals, even walking around within camp can be an experience at times. Lion, hyena, leopard, buffalo, wild dogs and elephants all wander though the camps and campsites very frequently – so be careful when you are walking around your camp or campsite here, especially after dark.

Camp Moremi (11 tents) Desert and Delta Safaris, see page 171
Approaching Xakanaxa Lagoon from either of Moremi's entrance gates, Camp Moremi (⊕ CAMPMO 19°11.322'S; 23°24.489'E) is the furthest left (southwest) of the adjacent camps at the tip of the Mopane Tongue.

Camp Moremi is a very well-kept, established camp, with a central lounge area for breakfast and lunch, as well as a separate elevated (and very comprehensively stocked) bar, lounge and dining room. Most of this has walls that are partially open to the breeze, and is cooled by overhead punkah-punkah fans. Underneath this is a well-stocked curio shop (open for guests only) selling clothes, T-shirts, videos and books.

All of this is shaded by huge old trees, apart from an open area of lawn which is kept short by the hippos that regularly graze here at night. A lot of other animals venture into

XAKANAXA

Channel to Xugana, Shindi
Kwara, Camp Okavango

Salvinia Lagoon

Moanachira River

Xhobega Lagoon

Gcodikwe Lagoon

GCODIK

Xhamu Lagoon

Xakanaxa Lagoon

Camp Okuti
Xakanaxa

Camp Moremi
CAMPMO

Nchunga
Island
Goashio
Lagoon

Goashio
Island

Xakanaxa public campsite

Xakanaxa Airstrip   XAKAIR

Old
Xakanaxa
Airstrip

Kio-oro Pool
Gomo-oro Pool

Nyandambesi Lagoon

Khwai

South Gate

M o p a n e   T o n g u e

Botelele Pool

4BRIDG
Fourth
Bridge
Dobetsaa Pans

Maya Pool

Bodumatau
Bridge

South Gate

Bodumatau
Lagoon

B o d u m a t a u

First Bridge
1BRIDG

Second
Bridge
2BRIDG

Magwexhlana Pools

I s l a n d

Monxa Bridge
(small poles)

Third Bridge
campsite

Third Bridge
3BRIDG

Lebala Pan

Tsau Pan

Lechwe Pans

M b o m a

Mboma Lagoon

MBOMA SANDVELD RD

MBOMAT

0   5km
0   3 miles

KEY		
4WD roads		
Seasonal track		
Pan		
Swamp/marsh		

GPS co-ordinates ⊕		
1BRIDG	19° 17.099'S,	23° 23.531'E
2BRIDG	19° 17.003'S,	23° 22.553'E
3BRIDG	19° 14.368'S,	23° 21.430'E
4BRIDG	19° 15.128'S,	23° 24.173'E
CAMPMO	19° 11.322'S,	23° 24.489'E
GCODIK	19° 09.731'S,	23° 14.507'E
MBOMAT	19° 1.574'S,	23° 17.126'E
XAKAIR	19° 11.778'S,	23° 26.342'E

the perimeter. Amidst the lawn, there is a swimming pool raised up on a wooden deck and also a high observation platform with a super view over the Xakanaxa Lagoon.

Like all the camps in this area (and indeed most in Botswana), you'll find a lot of wildlife inside the bounds of the camp. As well as animals which pass through, a resident attraction here is Pavarotti, an elderly hippo who apparently feel safer with humans around – having switched his lifestyle (to avoid other hippos) so that he's on land by day and in the water at night. But be wary – he is still a wild animal and should not be approached.

Guests stay in one of 11 Meru-style tents, with proper doors (which must be kept locked because of kleptomaniac baboons) each positioned on raised teak platforms. These are well-furnished with sisal matting covering the floor, bright rugs and fabrics, wooden wardrobes, luggage racks, dressing tables, a table-top electric fan and director's chairs. Each room has facilities for making tea and coffee, and a private bathroom – with flush toilet, a large shower with glass screen, mirror and washbasin – next to the tent and the raised platform.

At the end of camp, the honeymoon suite (number 11) is raised up quite high and has been built with flair and imagination around a rather marvellous old jackalberry tree (*Diospyros mespiliformis*), which has five separate trunks growing up right through the middle of the room.

Activities concentrate on 4WD game drives in the area, though it's also possible to take motorboat trips around the lagoons and waterways. Note that Camp Okavango and Xugana (see pages 292–3) are also owned by the same company, and it's a good combination to also stay for several nights at one of these as well as Camp Moremi, transferring between them using motorboats.

Rates (2005): US$323 per person sharing/single from July to October; US$252/265 per person sharing or single for the rest of the year. Open: all year.

Xakanaxa (13 tents) Moremi Safaris, PO Box 2757, Cramerview 2060, South Africa; tel: (2711) 465 3842/3; fax: (2711) 465 3779; email: moremi@yebo.co.za
Less than a kilometre northeast of Camp Moremi, Xakanaxa has long been run by Bob and Flo Flaxman. It's a classic old camp, and one of the few independents in northern Botswana, (ie: camps that aren't run by a large company as part of a group). In the last few years their lounge/dining room area and reception had a major fire, but the camp's been rebuilt with energy and has bounced back.

Twelve of the tents here are traditional Meru-style tents which all stand on wooden decks, with verandas which overlook the lagoon. Inside these you'll find solid wooden twin beds and, at the back of the tent, a hot shower, handbasin and flush toilet. The whole of the tent, and the toilet and shower behind, is covered by a large canvas roof on to which, when I last visited, they were experimenting with innovative ways of spraying water, to cool the air inside. An unusual thirteenth chalet has eight beds (complete with its own lounge, dining room and pool) which is sometimes used by families or small groups.

Xakanaka's raised, thatched dining area overlooks the lagoon. It's memorable for a long table, made from reclaimed old railway sleepers, on which dinners are served, lit by candlelight.

There's a swimming pool here, and the whole camp is surrounded by a high, 3-strand electric fence. This is designed purely to keep elephants out of the camp, which can be destructive to the trees as well as dangerous. Xakanaxa is better than most camps in Botswana at catering for families and children.

Activities from here are 4WD game drives and boat trips onto the lagoon – though if you're combining this with a trip to Camp Okavango, then you'll stick mainly to game drives here.

Rates: US$420/595 per person sharing/single from July to October including all meals, activities & park fees; US$300 per person sharing or single for the rest of the year. Open: all year.

Camp Okuti (10 chalets) Ker & Downey Safaris (see page 172)

Sandwiched between Xakanaxa and the campsite, Okuti has quite a tight spot in many ways. It was taken over by Ker & Downey in July 1999, which puzzled many as it didn't seem to fit in with the rest of the their more upmarket camps – Shinde, Kanana, Pom Pom (which was then run by them) or Machaba.

Okuti has nine small, thatched A-frame chalets all in a relatively small area by the side of the lagoon. The close spacing between these was typical of safari camps in the 1980s, but it's very unusual in more modern camps.

Each of these chalets has low brick side-walls and steeply angled thatched roofs, which comes down to within a foot or two of the ground. Inside all have twin beds (though one 'family unit' has four beds) and at the back a tiled area with a shower, toilet and washbasin. Hot water comes from wood-fuelled 'Rhodesian' boilers behind the chalets, whilst the lights run from a generator during the day, and a battery at night.

These are set amongst shady trees, and there are a few sun-loungers around and a small bar, but no swimming pool. There's a small rondavel selling curios. Okuti's dining area has brick walls and a tented roof. Activities here concentrate on 4WD game drives and trips by motor boat.

Okuti was a top camp a few decades ago, though when I last visited it looked very sad and outdated. Because it's effectively surrounded on all sides, it seems to have no way to create a more spacious atmosphere – and so even rebuilding it couldn't bring it up the spacious standards of its neighbours.

Rates (2005): US$350 per person sharing, low season (March to June and November), US$520 per person sharing high season (July to October), including all meals, drinks and activities. Open: March 1 to November 30.

Xakanaxa Campsite see page 142 for National Parks' booking offices
On arrival in this area, campers should stop and sign in at the smart new wooden office of the camp's warden, which you'll find immediately next to Xakanaxa airstrip (✪ XAKAIR 19°11.778'S; 23°26.342'E). This is about 3.5km southeast of the camps. If you arrive from North Gate, then you'll pass this on your right; if you're coming from Third Bridge or South Gate then follow the signs to North Gate and watch for it on your left as you start to drive east. (Don't confuse this with a disused strip that's about 1km west of the new one.)

On the east side of Camp Okuti, the Xakanaxa Campsite is a marvellous place to stay. Here about eight vaguely marked sites blend into one long camping area, which stretches along this tip of the Mopane Tongue. Facilities are very limited, with very basic toilets and showers, plus water taps dotted around the sites, their knobs encased in huge slabs of concrete to protect them from the elephants who love such clean water.

I've always loved these sites, and on my last visit in September the purple hanging flowers of the Kalahari appleleaf (*Lonchocarpus nelsii*) were in full force, reminding me of small jacaranda trees. However, as with Third Bridge, this is an area of particularly dense game, so always remain vigilant as you move about the campsite, making sure that you keep your eyes out for animals at all times.

Third Bridge Campsite see page 142 for National Parks' booking offices
Third Bridge (✪ 3BRIDG 19°14.368'S; 23°21.430'E) is about 8km in a straight line from Xakanaxa, although driving takes about 18km, depending on the route used. Despite being relatively close, if you're camping in the area for four or five nights then, ideally, try to split this between the two sites.

Approaching from Xakanaxa you'll first see a fairly new wooden office, raised off the ground and surmounted by a radio mast. Stop here to sign in before proceeding slowly over the pole bridge. You'll see that the water's crystal clear as it passes over the sandy bottom of the narrow waterway, but despite the apparently impenetrable stands of papyrus all around, it's a dangerous place to swim. People used to often bathe here, but there were regular attacks by crocodiles, and hence the plethora of notices warning you against

regular attacks by crocodiles, and hence the plethora of notices warning you against swimming.

This site is quite large, and the pitches spread out. It's notable for some attractive large fever-berry trees (*Croton megalobotrys*), and at its eastern end you'll find an ablution block, with two flush toilets and two showers for each sex. Outside these are the two wood-fired 'Rhodesian' boilers and a water tower. So if you do need hot water, then you may have to collect firewood, build a fire and heat it for yourself.

Specialities of this site included, the last time I visited, a troop of very cheeky baboons, who had developed stealing food into a form for sport – and they usually won. So what's good practice anywhere is absolutely vital here: lock everything away when you're not using it, or it'll be stolen. That said, staying here tends to be more private than Xakanaxa simply as there are less vehicles around, so it's certainly my favourite site in Moremi.

What to see and do

Until very recently all self-drive visitors ever did here was drive on their own game drives, or perhaps take a boat trip for a few hours from one of the lodges. Recently more organised water activities have started to become available, which seem likely to become very popular in time.

By vehicle

There's a lot of exploring to do in this area which is veined by game-viewing loops and tracks. So take your time. Drive around slowly, and stop frequently. There are a number of specific areas that you might aim for, or just end up at:

Floodplain Roads The network of tracks to the west of the main track between Xakanaxa and Third Bridge are probably the most rewarding in Moremi for game. Many are also very beautiful.

Goaxhlo Island and Pan Also known as Dead Tree Island, you'll recognise it by the number of skeletal trees that surround the pan of open water. Like those at Savuti, these were killed by drowning – when the channels changed and inundated the area. Most are mopane trees, and because of their resistance to termites, and semi-submerged state, they're decomposing very, very slowly indeed.

This is quite an eerie sight, and photographers will find plenty to inspire them, especially if there are any animals present. Keep a particular lookout for the graceful pink spoonbills which breed here.

Gcodikwe Lagoon Gcodikwe Lagoon (⊕ GCODIK 19°09.731'S; 23°14.507'E) is one of the Okavango's largest and most famous lagoons. This is a huge, ox-bow lagoon that's now almost circular and has several large tree-islands in it. It is only reachable by boat. Xakanaxa is 18km away, or about 90 minutes by boat. It is perhaps best visited from one of the lodges just outside of the park, the best being Kwara which is 6km northeast, Shinde, 11km northwest or Camp Okavango, 15km west – though you can double all these 'straight-line' distances to allow for meandering through the waterways.

These 'islands' are made up mainly of water fig trees and a little papyrus growing in shallow water. Over the millennia these have accumulated a mass of bird guano and detritus under them to raise their levels and grow. Now they're large, but still isolated from any predators that are not aquatic. Hence they've become a vital breeding ground for the Okavango's waterbirds. Thousands of pairs of birds come to this heronry to breed, including herons, egrets, storks, ibises, cormorants and many others.

Most of the nest-building activity starts around August, and breeding seems to be timed so that the chicks hatch around October and November, when water levels are low and thus the birds find fish easiest to catch. Certainly when I last visited in late February, there were only a few birds around.

Watch carefully and you'll see that the larger, more robust species like marabou and yellow-billed-storks tend to nest in the canopy of the trees, while the smaller, more vulnerable species can be found within the trees. Also keep an eye out for water snakes and Leguvaans, which both come here in search of chicks.

Dobetsaa Pans Take a left in a southerly direction, perhaps a kilometre after crossing Fourth Bridge on the way to Third Bridge, and you'll find a short loop leading down past a few very scenic pans. Veronica Roodt comments that this is 'one of the few places in Moremi where the African skimmer can be seen'. But even without the skimmers it's a good birdwatching spot with some very open pans.

Mboma Island West of Third Bridge is a large, long island, circled by a loop road which stretches for about 50km around it. There's a spur to this at the north end, and a short cut back to Third Bridge halfway round. It's worth spending a day here, as Mboma's environments are varied and beautiful, though different from the floodplain loops nearer to Xakanaxa. I've had great sightings of cheetah on the northern side of the island, and the south is said to be a popular haunt of buffalo herds.

By boat

If you're staying at the campsite then I'd strongly recommend that you take at least one trip onto the lagoons and waterways by boat or mokoro. It's certainly worth the cost, unless you're due to be going to a camp with water activities later in your trip.

Until recently, you had to rely on the boats of the lodges around Xakanaxa – which was often not possible in the high season, when they were full. It required you to approach them politely, whilst there, and ask to hire a boat and driver for a few hours to explore the lagoons and channels, or to take a half-day trip out to Gadikwe Lagoon. Usually you had to enquire, and then set a time for the trip. Xakanaxa and Camp Okuti were the best chances for this; Camp Moremi, though friendly, is least likely to be able to help. Mokoro trips were not possible; the water of Xakanaxa Lagoon is far too deep.

However, the good news is that a new 'boat station' has been set up in Moremi, at the far northwest tip of Mboma Island. This is about an hour's drive (15km) from Third Bridge, or three hours (63km) from South Gate. The turn-off to this from the main loop road is at ⊕ MBOMAT 19°1.574'S; 23°17.126'E, and the station is about 1.5km drive west of there. Remember that boat fuel is costly to buy and transport, and you're in a very remote location, so these trips aren't cheap.

For **short trips** a motorboat and driver can be hired in advance for about P250 per hour, which takes up to nine people. If you just turn up in hope, and there's a boat available, this reduces to P180. Alternatively mekoro trips are P90 per mokoro (seating two) per hour when reserved in advance, or P60 if you take your chances and turn up.

Longer trips are possible if pre-booked, and there are three islands nearby on which camping is now allowed: Gcodikwe 1, Gcodikwe 2, and Xhobega. These islands are in the area of the Gcodikwe and Xhobega lagoons, just northwest of Mboma Island. See above for a description of the Gcodikwe Lagoon with its heronries. To stay overnight here you will need your own camping equipment and food; only a boat and driver are supplied.

Costs for these longer trips are P1,000 per boat per day, and P350 per mokoro per day – plus, of course, your park fees for the game reserve and any camping fees. However, note that you cannot, yet, stay overnight on islands as part of a mokoro trip. The water is too deep to reach any of the the designated islands for camping. Instead your mokoro will explore the floodplains just off Mboma Island, on the southeastern side of the boat station, and return to the boat station each afternoon.

Note that vehicles can be left safely at the boat station. Contact Kgori Safaris in Maun, (see page 172) who run this boat station, for bookings and further details.

Getting there and away
By air
Virtually all of the visitors to the three lodges arrive and leave via Xakanaxa airstrip, which is easily linked with any of the other airstrips in the region.

Driving from Xakanaxa to North Gate
It's about 44km to drive directly from Xakanaxa to North Gate; just head east from Xakanaxa airstrip (⊕ XAKAIR 19°11.778'S; 23°26.342'E). See pages 261–2 for more comments on this route, and ask advice from the camp's office before you set off as sometimes this road is blocked by high water levels. If that's the case, then you have no choice but to go the long way around – via South Gate (see the routes given below).

Driving from Xakanaxa to South Gate
Many would travel from Xakanaxa to South Gate via Third Bridge, using the route described in the next section, as the scenery's more varied and, in the dry season, I'd expect the game to be better – especially around the Mboma Island area.

However, if you do need the most direct route, then a track heads southeast from near the western end of Xakanaxa's airstrip, and takes about 42km to reach South Gate. The route is generally good, even when it's wet, apart from a number of clay pans which can be sticky.

Driving from Third Bridge to South Gate
I always find the tracks around Mboma Island confusing, but to reach South Gate you set off west onto Mboma Island from Third Bridge. Keep bearing left when the road forks and after 3–4km you'll be travelling south. The road then bends east, south and even west until you reach another pole bridge which is known, rather unimaginatively, as Second Bridge (⊕ 2BRIDG 19°17.003'S; 23°22.553'E).

Crossing this, you'll then head southeast towards another pole bridge referred to as (surprise!) First Bridge (⊕ 1BRIDG 19°17.099'S; 23°23.531'E). From here it's an uncomplicated drive southeast to South Gate, with the vast majority of the trip through mopane woodlands.

South Gate
Also known as Maqwee Gate, South Gate (⊕ SOGATE 19°25.548'S; 23°38.733'E) is usually treated as a transit stop for most visitors as it's in the midst of fairly unexciting mopane forest. Camp amongst the trees; there are toilets, showers and water here.

Having described it as unexciting, this may just be my failure to really get to know the area well. I've only stayed here for three individual nights, one during each of three different trips (always at the start or the end of a trip across Chobe and

Moremi). However on one of those occasions, just as I was getting up, about half a dozen wild dogs gently jogged through the camp and into the forest. I don't think our roof tent has ever been packed away so rapidly – but try as we might, tracking them was a waste of time with park rules forbidding off-road driving in Moremi!

On another trip entirely I found a whole pack of wild dogs lounging in the road a few kilometres south of South Gate, in the NG33/34 concession area. They posed for photographs just a few metres from my vehicle for twenty minutes or so – totally unconcerned with our presence. So perhaps, especially in the earlier months of the year, South Gate warrants a closer look and more than just an overnight stop.

Orientation

The geography of South Gate is very straightforward. There are no game-viewing loops as such, just four clear roads: one to Maun via the veterinary checkpoint, another to North Gate, one to Third Bridge which stays close to the southern side of the Mopane Tongue, and another to Xakanaxa which cuts through the heart of the Tongue.

Flora and fauna highlights

Flora

Around Third Bridge the trees are almost all mopane (*Colophospermum mopane*), with their distinctive butterfly-shaped leaves. Tall, undamaged specimens can reach 18m in height, when they're known as 'cathedral mopane' for their gracefully arching branches. In neighbouring areas, where the nutrients are not as plentiful or the trees have been damaged by elephants, this same species grows much lower – and is known as 'stunted mopane.' In both you'll find their leaves hanging down and tending to fold together during the heat of the day, leaving little shade underneath.

This tremendously successful tree is one of the commonest species in the hot, dry areas of the subcontinent. It's notable for its tolerance of poorly drained, alkaline soils – and often occurs in areas where there's a lot of clay. Driving in mopane country during the rainy season usually involves negotiating lots of sticky, clay-filled mud-holes.

For the camper, the mopane wood is a dark-reddish colour, hard, heavy and termite-resistant. Thus even long-dead pieces won't have been completely eaten by termites. It burns exceedingly well, smelling sweetly and producing lots of heat, so think of collecting some firewood if you're passing through here on the way to Xakanaxa or Third Bridge. (Turn each piece over, looking under it carefully for snakes and scorpions, before picking it up.)

Animals

With relatively dense forests this area can seem devoid of wildlife. But don't be mistaken; it isn't. Because the soil in mopane forest areas is often very poorly-drained, it's dotted with small pans, temporary shallow ponds, during and shortly after the rains. This allows most of the big game species to leave the over-populated areas beside the watercourses and disappear into these huge areas of forests.

Elephant, zebra, impala, kudu, tsessebe, common duiker, bushbuck, steenbok, eland, roan warthog, baboon and vervet monkey can all be found here, as will lion, leopard, spotted hyena, wild dog and many of the smaller mammals. But you will have to look much harder here for them than on the open floodplains and beside the watercourses where they congregate during the dry season.

What you are guaranteed to see here at any time of year are lots of bush squirrels (*Paraxerus cepapi*), which are so common in mopane woodlands that they're often known as 'mopane squirrels'. See the *Wildlife Guide*, page 516, for more details.

Birdlife

The high density of small rodents in mopane woodlands, especially tree squirrels, means that it's a good place for small raptors which hunt from perches (rather than the air). These include barn owls, smaller hawks and kestrels, and even martial eagles.

Meanwhile two very common species here are the small, black and white Arnot's chat, which appear in pairs or small groups, often hopping about the ground or lower branches in search of small insects – memorably described by a friend on first sight as 'little flying zebras.'

Also the red-billed hornbill, which seems to be everywhere with it's heavy flap-flap-flap...glide... flap-flap-flap...glide... style of flight. Remember Rowan Atkinson's performance as the hornbill in Walt Disney's *The Lion King* and you'll never be able to watch one again without smiling.

Where to stay

There's only one place to stay:

South Gate Campsite Contact National Park's booking office, see page 142
This campsite is immediately next to the National Park's gate, and has basic facilities which are a hallmark of Botswana's parks: two very simple ablution blocks, each with one shower and one toilet each for ladies and gents. You can fill up with fresh water, and there are about a dozen places to camp.

Getting there and away
From South Gate to Third Bridge

Take the most westerly exit from the campsite and the route is very easy. After about 24km you'll pass a right turn, marked by an old green cement block. One side of this notes that Mboma and Third Bridge are off to the left. There are no indications where the right turn goes, though it actually leads around the east side of the Bodumatau Lagoon.

Keeping on the main road (left), you'll then pass in order First Bridge (⊕ 1BRIDG 19°17.099'S; 23°23.531'E) and Second Bridge (⊕ 2BRIDG 19°17.003'S; 23°22.553'E), before finally reaching the campsite and Third Bridge (⊕ 3BRIDG 19°14.368'S; 23°21.430'E).

From South Gate to Xakanaxa

Usually the best route is to follow the directions to Third Bridge, above, then continue southwest to Fourth Bridge (⊕ 4BRIDG 19°15.128'S; 23°24.173'E). From there proceed north, keeping slightly east until Xakanaxa airstrip (⊕ XAKAIR 19°11.778'S; 23°26.342'E), where you turn west. You can navigate through this labyrinth of game-viewing loops using Veronica Roodt's map, or by sticking to the main track, setting your GPS for Xakanaxa, and then keeping slightly east of the direct-line direction.

However, if it's late in the dry season and you've plenty of time, then you may want to take a detour around the Bodumatau Lagoon, which avoids Third Bridge completely. (This track is marked as 'seasonal' on most maps, and is much less reliable than the main track, especially when wet.) In that case, take the right turn at the green concrete block which is about 24km from South Gate. In that case you'll take around 16km to reach the Bodumatau Bridge, and then a further 13km will lead you to Fourth Bridge.

One local operator refers to the first part of this road after the green concrete block as 'Elephant Alley' – for its winding road though dense mopane is often frequented by elephants. Drive carefully.

From South Gate to North Gate

A very direct, straight road leads about 30km north-northeast from South Gate to North Gate (✪ NOGATE 19°10.261'S; 23°45.055'E). There are no game-viewing loops off this road.

From South Gate to Maun

Leaving the park from South Gate, after a few hundred yards there's a well-signposted fork: right to San-Ta-Wani Lodge (and then south to Maun); left directly to Maun. See page 340 for brief comments on San-Ta-Wani.

Keeping left on the main road, you should still keep looking out for wildlife. I drove this way some years ago, in May 1993, and about 14km from the gate the road was virtually blocked by a large pack of lazy wild dogs wandering about the road, showing little interest in our vehicle. There are several areas of sandy thornveld shortly after the gate, with some stunning, tall old camelthorn trees, *Acacia erioloba*, which are a particular favourite of the local giraffe. Within these sandier areas, the road is so wide that during the rains it can seem like a series of small lakes. Although the centre of these tend to be deeper than the edges, they are generally firm, whereas the shallower edges can be much more muddy.

To the right of this road is a non-hunting area, NG33, whilst to the left is an area managed by the community, NG34. Both are good wildlife areas, but note that technically the road you are on is a 'transit route,' and as such the land and the wildlife here are managed – so you are not allowed to stop and camp here.

About 32km from South Gate you join the main road from Chobe to Maun. Bear right for Maun or double-back left for Sankuyo Village and Chobe National Park. (This road north to Chobe is referred to as 'the Mababe Road' by the signpost.) Your nearest camping site would probably at Mankwe Bush Lodge (see page 346) in NG45, just north of Sankuyo Village.

Shortly after that junction, about 34km from South Gate, you may need to stop to pass through the Veterinary Cordon Fence. After a further 17km you'll reach the sizeable village of Shorobe (see page 179), from where the road to Maun is tarred. The total journey from South Gate to the Okavango River Lodge and Crocodile Camp, on the outskirts of Maun, is about 80km.

Shorobe Village

About 54km south of Moremi's South Gate is the village of Shorobe – which marks the furthest extent of the tar road from Maun. You'll be able to buy a cold drink from one of the roadside vendors, and the Babomoso Basketry Co-operative on the east side of the road is worth a look. However, there's little else to tempt the passing traveller.

THE PRIVATE AREAS OF MOREMI – NG28

Aside from the Mopane Tongue, the only way to access any of the rest of Moremi is from one of the small private safari camps to which you must fly in. There are three main camps within Moremi: Mombo and Chief's camp at the north end of Chief's Island, and Xigera right on the western edge. These are described below.

However, there are a number, like those in NG19 near North Gate, which stand just outside the edge of the park, but conduct many of their activities within the park. These include the camps in NG21 (Camp Okavango, Shindi and Xugana –

see pages 290–4), and also the old camps along the south end of the Boro River in NG27B (Oddball's Camp, Delta Camp, Gunn's Camp, Semetsi and Eagle Island – see pages 317–23).

Because these two areas are very different I'll subdivide this concession into two sections – one covering Xigera's area, and the other concentrating on the camps on Chief's Island: Mombo and Chief's Camp.

Xigera

If you had to place a pin on the map in the centre of the Delta, you'd probably put it near to here. The Xigera (pronounced Keejera) area is within the boundaries of Moremi Reserve, near its western border. Technically it's within Moremi's only private concession area, NG28. (Although the concession is also split between Mombo and Chief's Camp, their dry-land areas are so different in character from Xigera's that I'll discuss them in a separate section, after this one.)

Concession history

Look at an old map of the Delta and you'll realise that the western boundary of Moremi used to be further east than it is now. Then the Xigera and Mombo areas were part of the NG28 concession and outside the park. Xigera was originally built as long ago as 1986 by Hennie and Angela Rawlinson, two well-known Maun residents, at a place that Hennie called Paradise Island.

Then in 1992 Moremi was expanded westwards and northwards. This was done in order to bring under its protection all the major Okavango habitats, as until then none of the northern Delta's papyrus swamps or permanent wetlands had been included. This expansion swallowed up NG28, including the Xigera and Mombo areas. Thus these camps occupy prime sites within Moremi Game Reserve.

The lease for Xigera expired in 1998, but the Rawlinsons got it back again for another 15 years. Between December 1999 and April 2000 the camp was completely demolished and rebuilt from scratch a short distance away. It opened in May 2000.

Getting there and getting away

Only pre-booked guests who fly in visit this area, and all the marketing, management and reservations for Xigera are done by Wilderness Safaris (see page 174 for details).

The airstrip serving the camps (XIGAIR) is located at ✛ 19°23.155'S; 22°44.618'E. Note that there's no practical dry-land access to Mombo, Chief's Camp or the nearby Nxabega from here. Driving here isn't an option.

When to visit

Because the focus here is more on the environment and birdlife than game per se, this area can be visited any time of the year – although the tiny Zepa bushcamp is really not designed for rainy conditions, and so closes during the rains.

What to see and do

Motorboat trips and mokoro excursions have always been the main activities from Xigera; from Zepa only mekoro are usually possible. That said, Xigera's team has worked hard and in 2001 they located a good area for game drives, and have come up with a way of stationing vehicles on the larger islands there. So usually, water levels permitting, it's now possible to drive there too.

Thus from about May until October, whilst the water is high, you boat to the game-drive vehicles, and then drive from there. Then it's possible to do motorboat trips as well as mokoro trips directly from the camp.

PAPYRUS

The graceful, feathery papyrus is a giant sedge which dominates large areas of the Okavango. It grows in areas of permanent swamp in thick floating mats, unmistakable for its feather-duster heads that sway in the breeze. At first it's perhaps surprising that such vigorous, lush, emerald-green vegetation thrives here with apparently few nutrients available from the clear water or the poor Kalahari sands beneath.

The secret lies in a number of remarkable adaptations. Firstly, papyri have nitrogenous bacteria between their scale-leaves which 'fix' nitrogen from the air into a form that the plants can use. Secondly they photosynthesise using a special 'carbon-4' pathway, thus making more efficient use of the sun's energy than most plants.

With these adaptations, water and sunshine, papyri are amongst the fastest-growing plants in the world. You'll quickly see another factor that helps them here if you cut a stem of papyrus (preferably a dying one!). Observe that although thick and strong, it's very light. So the plant is committing relatively little energy or materials to raise such a tall, strong stem.

In fact papyri store most of their energy in long, thick rhizomes which form part of the tangled floating mat. From this base, their shoots can rise up to about 2.5m high, and yet typically have a life cycle of only three months. Within this they grow swiftly to maturity, flower and die – leaving a tangle of brown, dead stems near water level. The nutrients from these old stems are withdrawn back into the rhizome, ready to power the birth of another shoot. This rapid recycling of nutrients is another of the keys to the plant's lush, vigorous growth.

However, between about November and May, the water level is lower and it's then possible to keep the vehicles near camp and drive directly from there, though, the motor boats have to be stationed in deeper water a short distance north of camp, and are reached by mokoro.

Because the camp is within Moremi Reserve, night drives, fishing and off-road driving is not allowed. Short walks are conducted, but the guides are not allowed to carry rifles.

Flora and fauna

The area around Xigera is one of the Delta's few truly deep-water experiences. (Jedibe, when it was open, used to deserve this accolade. It really was surrounded by apparently endless papyrus swamps, with only the odd island. Camp Okavango, Kwara, Xugana and Shinde could also lay claim to have deep-water experiences to some extent.)

Here at Xigera itself you're very close to the Jao River, which feeds the Boro and is one of the Okavango's major waterways.

Flora

Spending most of your time on the water, you're probably going to be most aware of the aquatic grasses and sedges. Of these the graceful, feathery papyri (*Cyperus papyrus*) are perhaps the most striking, and certainly one of the most interesting (see box).

In shallower sections you'll also find large areas of common reeds here, *Phragmites australis*, and the tall miscanthus grass, *Miscanthus junceus*. There are also a few lovely stands of pure water fern, *Thelypterus interrupta*, on the edges of some of the channels and lagoons.

On the islands you'll find the normal trees of the Delta, including a good number of confetti trees, *Gynmosporia senegalensis*. The English name for these comes from the small, scented white flowers which come out around May-June, and then fall underneath the tree in large enough quantities to be scooped up.

Mammals

This area isn't a bad one for big game, though that's not why I'd go to Xigera. If you're staying at Xigera then remember that the bridge across the channel, linking the camp on one island with the main vehicle track to the airstrip on the other, isn't only used by people. Many other animals find it convenient, especially at night. Spotted hyenas cross it almost religiously every night, lion regularly and leopard occasionally too. Monkeys and baboons play on it during the day. Look underneath at the fish in the clear water and you may even see the odd spotted-necked otter fishing for bream.

On the larger island elephants are often in evidence, and when I was last here the floodplain beyond my tent's veranda was dotted with lechwe. Elephant are often around, sometimes in substantial herds of 50 or so, and on game drives you've a good chance of spotting impala and tsessebe.

As you'd expect for the environment, the Xigera area has one of the highest densities of sitatunga antelope in the Delta. These lovely creatures are notoriously difficult to spot, but gliding around silently in a mokoro probably offers you the best chance possible – just keep yours eyes wide open and your mouth tightly shut!

LIFE IN PAPYRUS SWAMPS

Papyrus swamps are in many ways a difficult habitat. Below the waterline, little light penetrates the floating mat of dead, tangled stems and rhizomes. The constant decomposition of dead papyrus stems mean much organic debris, and water which is acidic and low in oxygen. With no light, there's no chance for algae or any other higher plantlife.

Above the waterline the stems form a dense, tangled mass. The stems themselves are fibrous, difficult to digest and very nutrient poor. Combined with a floating base that can't support any weight, this makes life here almost impossible for most larger animals. Only the specially-adapted sitatunga antelope is at home here.

For animals as small as rats and mice, the situation isn't so bad. They don't generally stay in the papyrus beds, but they are light enough to make forays there, supported by the floating mat and individual stems. Greater cane rats are the largest of these, growing up to about 80cm on a diet of papyrus shoots, reeds and other vegetation. Although they swim well, they normally live in small family groups in burrows on permanent dry land, leaving these at night to forage in the reedbeds and papyrus.

A few birds also use the papyrus for shelter and nesting, including several species of weavers, the red-shouldered widow and red bishop bird – which will tear the feathery umbels of the papyrus as material to weave their intricate nests. Many more will come into papyrus areas to hunt for fish or insects, and there will be very few trips here when you won't see at least a few malachite and pied kingfishers.

On one occasion here recently, an eminent guide was leading a number of mekoro, trying to get as close as possible to a sitatunga. When the antelope made a break to get away, it jumped directly over one of the mekoro.

Birdlife

Given the environment of large areas of permanent papyrus and swamp vegetation, plus some islands, this is a good camp for seeking the more water-dependent birds in the Delta.

Notable amongst these are the African skimmers, which usually arrive at Xigera Lagoon around September or October. About twenty pairs of these amazing birds were noted here in 2001, and if they're new to you then take a few moments to watch one of them through binoculars. You'll see it using the most amazing flying skills to place its lower mandible in the lagoon at a fixed depth, and steadily scythe through the water. Then periodically you see the bill snap shut with its catch of an unfortunate small fish. This is compulsive viewing, even if you never normally look at anything smaller than a lion; an amazing fishing technique.

Whilst floating around you can expect to see assorted kingfishers, herons, egrets and other water birds. Included in this list, if you're lucky, will be purple (but not lesser) gallinules, lesser jacanas, moorhens, lesser moorhens and green-backed herons. It should be a good area for bitterns (including the dwarf and little), though I've never seen one here.

Other unusual birds that enthusiastic ornithologists should look out for include chirping cisticolas, tawny-flanked prinias and palm swifts, all of which are regularly sighted here.

Where to stay

Although there are two camps here, Zepa is a tiny, almost temporary camp that is usually visited only as part of a set itinerary. For most visitors, Xigera is the only option here. Both camps are run by Wilderness Safaris (see page 174).

Xigera (8 tents)
Sited on a new location (✪ XIGERA 19°23.647'S; 23°45.535'E) on Paradise Island, the 'new' Xigera Camp opened in April 2000. If you've never been to the Delta, then simply conjure up an image of a luxurious safari camp in the heart of the swamps, enveloped by a green, tropical lushness. You've probably come close to visualising Xigera.

All of Xigera's tents are raised a few metres above the island floor on wooden decks. These are widely spread out along one fringe of the island, each looking eastwards, past the easy chairs and table on the veranda and onto a small lagoon that seems to attract good game. These tents are all linked together, and to the central hub of a lounge and dining room area, by a total of about 800m of raised boardwalks.

The tented rooms themselves are part wood, part canvas. The front is made of wood, with two large sliding doors and huge gauze windows. It's easy to really open up for good views and airflow, the latter assisted by an efficient, free-standing, antique-style electric fan.

Inside, the double or twin beds are enclosed in a walk-in mosquito net, with a large trunk and easy chairs. Behind the bed is a bamboo screen and towel rack, a dressing table, twin basins, an inside flush toilet and separate shower. Through the tent's rear door is a blissful outdoor shower.

The camp's generator charges batteries, which supply 220V electricity to the chalets constantly and even power the (very efficient) electric showers.

Overlooking a perennial channel, and the footbridge across it, is the camp's comfortable thatched dining room, bar and exceedingly cozy lounge. Close by, the camp has a small curio shop selling materials, jewellery, postcards, film T-shirts and a few hats. There's also

Above Leopard are often caught napping in old riverine trees by day (CM)
Right Caracal are seen occasionally on night drives (CM)
Below right Spotted hyena cubs emerging from their den (DM)
Below Wild dogs in the Selinda Reserve (CM)

OKAVANGO DELTA

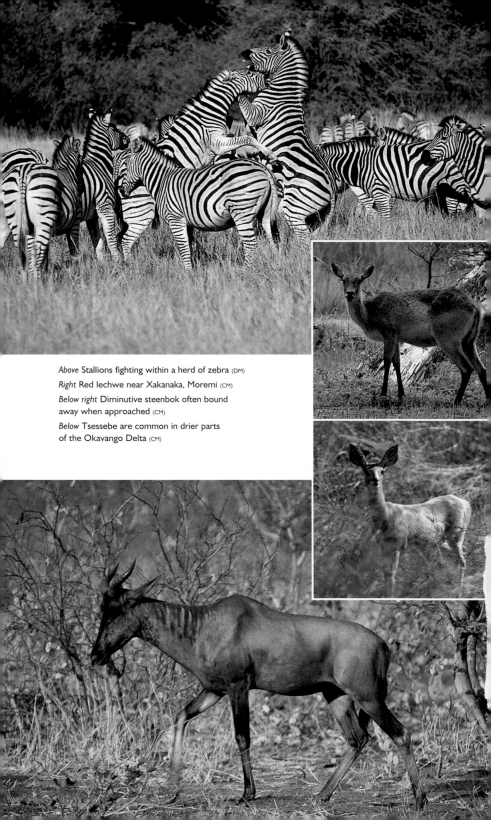

Above Stallions fighting within a herd of zebra (DM)

Right Red lechwe near Xakanaka, Moremi (CM)

Below right Diminutive steenbok often bound away when approached (CM)

Below Tsessebe are common in drier parts of the Okavango Delta (CM) in such an environment, though clearly litigious-minded visitors aren't encouraged to find 'safe' places to swim in the Delta itself!

Like Jao, Xigera feels like one of the Delta's most tropical, slow and romantic camps. It offers a great water experience, though I'd suggest that most visitors spend only two nights here, rather than three or four that might be the norm at a camp with more emphasis on game activities.

Rates (2005): US$595 per person sharing/single from July to October; US$390/430 from December to March; US$430 for April, May, June and November. Includes all meals, activities, park fees, laundry, and most drinks. Excludes transfers. Open: all year.

Zepa (5 tents)

Zepa is seldom mentioned in any literature as it's a tiny, simple 'trails camp' used on the guided safari marketed by Wilderness as the *Mopane Itinerary*. It's never usually sold as a stand-alone camp; I include it here only for the sake of completeness. Zepa has been erected (✪ ZEPA 19°22.221'S; 23°44.894'E) on a small island about 3km northwest of Xigera. It's hidden within a dense stand of wild date palm, overlooking the open, salty clearing at the heart of the island.

At Zepa you'll find a basic canvas roof, supported by iron struts, used as a mess tent – though the tables will often be laid out under the open skies instead. Zepa's five small tents are 3m x 3m dome tents, which are roomy enough for a few mattresses, though you can't stand up comfortably.

Each has a flap to shade the door, and a large window on each of its four sides that can be opened to reveal mosquito-netting and allow a good flow-through of air whilst you sleep. Outside each is a canvas basin on a stand, while long-drop toilets are shared between the visitors.

Zepa's really only designed as a base for mokoro trips, with the possibility of short walks on the islands. (See my comments on walking, on pages 127–8.) Look around this small island and you'll see reeds and papyrus all around.

Mombo and Chief's Camp

Mombo and Chief's share a concession within Moremi, but they are about 25km apart – which is a long way in the Okavango. Hence, unless they *want* to cross paths, you'll never normally see one of the vehicles from the other camp.

Concession history

Since the mid-1980s the rights to run Mombo were owned by Jao Safaris (now defunct). They sub-leased this to many safari companies including Ker & Downey, Bonadventure (who were one of the main tour agencies when I first visited Maun in 1987) and, lastly, Wilderness Safaris. During this time, and especially the last few years, it gained a first-class reputation for game, helped by an exceedingly large and successful pack of wild dogs.

When Jao Safaris' lease expired in 1998, there was clearly going to be very stiff competition for this area. Because it was recognised as such a prime area, the Land Board (ie: the government body responsible) allowed for two sites to be put up for tender, at opposite ends of the concession. About 29 companies entered. There was tremendous competition: the best proposal and overall management plan would win.

Eventually two bids were accepted; one from Wilderness Safaris and another from A&K (whose Botswana operations have recently become 'Sanctuary Lodges'). Each needed to promise the government the highest possible revenue, as well as the best (that is, most sustainable and productive) management plan.

To achieve this, they both arrived at the obvious solution: each built one of the

To achieve this, they both arrived at the obvious solution: each built one of the country's most upmarket camps, and attached an appropriately high price tag to it. It was the only way to make financial sense with such high concession fees.

Thus the new, much more luxurious Mombo came into being, near the old Mombo site, and Chief's Camp was built south of that, on the northwestern side of Chief's Island. The tender process had maximised the government's revenues, and pushed part of the area's tourism a step further upmarket.

Getting there and getting away
Only pre-booked guests flying in visit this area, as there is no practical dry-land access to Chief's Island. Driving here isn't an option. Each camp has its own airstrip on Chief's Island; Mombo's airstrip is found at ⊕ MOMBOA 19°12.680'S; 22°47.510'E.

When to visit
Because the focus here is firmly on game viewing, the dry season is the obvious time to visit. That's when the game is at its most visible and most dense. That said, from July to October the camps (especially Mombo) have substantial 'high season supplements', which can make the costs at other times of the year seem very attractive.

If you decide to come at a less popular, and cheaper, time then remember that Chief's Island is a large, permanent island with its own large, permanent population of game. Thus you'll still see some first-rate game even if the game viewing isn't quite as good as it would have been during October.

What to see and do
Game drives are the main activity here, though both camps are constricted to some extent by the park's rules. Night drives, fishing and off-road driving are not allowed – though the camps have been campaigning to have these rules softened. Short 'nature walks' are conducted, although these are restricted as the guides are not allowed to carry rifles under the park's current rules.

In addition to drives, Chief's also offers mokoro trips. When the floods arrive, up to 70% of Chief's Camp's network of roads become covered in water, and mokoro trips can start off right there at the lodge.

Flora and fauna highlights
Flora
The environments found here aren't unique in the Delta, but they are old, established, and have long been protected – and so are basically pristine and undisturbed.

Perhaps the most interesting, and certainly the most photogenic, habitats here are the shallow floodplains which surround the northern end of Chief's Island. (It's such a distinctive landscape that an image of it has remained deeply engrained on my mind since my first visit here, in the mid-1990s.)

Looking at the whole Delta, you'll realise that this area is very close to the permanent swamps at the base of the Panhandle. Because of this, the floods here are more regular and predictable than they are lower down the Delta. This regular seasonal flooding has created a very photogenic environment of short-grass plains, amongst which are a number of tiny islands fringed by dense, feathery stands of wild date palms (*Phoenix reclinata*). For me, this is the quintessential Delta landscape – and it's sufficiently open to be excellent for game viewing.

(Away from the Okavango Delta, the only place that I've seen which is similar to this in southern Africa is the Busanga Plains of northern Kafue, in Zambia. These are again consistently flooded every year, and have very little disturbance.)

Go back on to the dry land of Chief's Island and you'll find a range of more familiar landscapes and floral communities. Mopane woodlands are dominant across much of the island, with some areas of impressive, tall 'cathedral' mopane (*Colophospermum mopane*); often a popular retreat for the game during wetter months.

Running through this you'll find lines of Kalahari sandveld, reflecting the locations of old, long-dry watercourses. Here you'll find sand-loving species like the silver cluster-leaf (*Terminalia sericea*), the Kalahari appleleaf (*Lonchocarpus nelsii*), perhaps some camelthorn (*Acacia erioloba*) and umbrella thorns (*Acacias tortilis*) and the odd leadwood tree (*Combretum imberbe*).

Where the land meets the water, there are bands of classic riverine forest including fine specimens of raintree (*Lonchocarpus capassa*), sausage tree (*Kigelia africana*), jackalberry (*Diospyros mespiliformis*), African mangosteen (*Garcinia livingstonei*), figs (mostly *Ficus sycomorus*) and some wild date palms (*Phoenix reclinata*). Throughout the area's forests you'll occasionally find huge old baobab trees (*Adansonia digitata*) – which probably have lived long enough to see the environment change around them!

Fauna

The game in this area is at least as dense as anywhere else in the Okavango (or indeed the subcontinent), and because the area's a private one, the game viewing is just about the best you'll find in southern Africa. It's dense, varied, and good sightings of predators are virtually guaranteed.

See the *Flora and fauna* section at the start of this chapter for more extensive comments on Moremi as a whole; in this particular area impala, tsessebe, zebra and giraffe are usually the most numerous of the larger herbivores – although warthogs are remarkably common. (So numerous that they have become a major prey species for both lion and leopard.) Elephant and buffalo are resident here in good numbers, with more individual animals seen during the rains, and generally larger herds recorded as the dry season progresses.

Herds of red lechwe are common in the flooded areas when the water's high, but rarely venture into the drier parts of the reserve. Kudu and wildebeest also occur, as do the occasional reedbuck and steenbok; sable and roan are usually never seen here.

Though most of the Delta's usual line-up of nocturnal animals do occur, without taking night drives most are difficult to spot. The exception seems to be honey badgers, porcupines and spring hares which are sometimes seen around the camps at night.

The area has a justified, first-class reputation for excellent sightings of all the major predators. Spotted hyena are probably the most successful large carnivore in the area, though lion are also very common – as they are in many areas of the Delta.

What's less usual is the thriving permanent cheetah population here. The sprinkling of slightly raised date palm islands and termite hills make ideal look-out posts – suiting the cheetah's hunting style perfectly. The area's open environment makes sightings of cheetah relatively frequent. I've a recent report of one sizeable pair of brothers taking sub-adult zebra and wildebeest – bigger prey than might normally be expected.

As an aside, long-standing guides comment that there were a lot more cheetahs in the Mombo area until a recent demise in the dominance of the lion and a rise in the fortunes of the hyaena. This is really just a small-scale example of the constant ebb and flow of power struggles in the animal kingdom – and cheetah sightings here are still much better than in most other areas of the Delta, or indeed southern Africa!

There are good numbers of leopard around – although their appearances during the day are relatively limited. Originally Mombo, and this area, built its reputation on some of Africa's best sightings of wild dog – largely because of a very successful pack of about 40 dogs (which is a very large size for a pack) that denned here for several years in the mid-1990s. With this pack in residence, visitors were virtually guaranteed amazing sightings, and the area's dry open floodplains proved marvellous for following the animals as they hunted.

Now that pack has broken up, as is the usual process when the alpha female dies. Thus while the wild dog sightings are as good as most of the areas in the eastern Delta, they're not better as there's no sizeable pack in regular residence. That said, the fact remains that if you do see dogs here, the floodplain areas are the perfect place to be able to follow them.

Finally, a real good news story for this area, and the Delta as a whole. Black and white rhino used to occur here naturally, but by the 1980s they had been exterminated by poaching. Finally, on November 9 2001, the first white rhino were brought back into this area. Five of them were set free to roam, and have since settled down well on to Chief's Island. This has been so successful that there are plans to bring in more, and in time it's likely that black rhino will also be reintroduced to the area.

Birdlife

At the heart of the Delta, and with a large and diverse area of dry land and floodplains, this area of Moremi gets periodic visits from virtually all of the birds in the Delta – so singling out a few to mention here is inevitably a flawed process.

However, top of the list for a special mention are the vultures, attracted by the game densities and predator activity. Most numerous are the white-backed, hooded and lappet-faced vultures – though you'll also find a surprising number of white-headed vultures. Palm-nut vultures occur here (usually frequenting the real fan palms) though they're not common.

Also attracted by the game, both kinds of oxpecker are present here – though yellow-billed (which feed on the backs of hippos) seem more common than the red-billed variety.

As happens everywhere in the Delta, when the waters recede, isolated pools of fish are left behind. As these gradually dry up the fish become more and more concentrated, attracting the most amazing numbers of predatory birds. Pick the right day (usually one between about May and October) and the right pool, and you'll be entertained for hours by large concentrations of pelicans, saddle-billed storks, marabou storks, black egrets, grey and Goliath herons to name but a few. It's an amazing sight. In other receding pools you'll find congregations of pelicans or, in those which aren't so frantic, painted snipes can be seen if you look hard (or have a good guide!).

The short-grass floodplains here suit wattled cranes, which are often found in numbers, and on the drier plains watch for secretary birds and kori bustards. The latter occasionally have carmine bee-eaters using their backs as perches. In plains with longer grass you may be able to spot an African crake, while ostriches are very rarely seen (perhaps because there are too many large predators).

On the water look for pygmy geese and dwarf jacanas in the quieter areas – along with many species of more common water-birds. There's often a good number of the relatively rare slaty egrets about too.

Both Mombo and Chief's are top-of-the-range camps in one of southern Africa's very best game areas. Both come at a high cost – though Chief's hasn't been around long enough to build up quite the same reputation that Mombo has. However, note that some safari purists contend that elements of the clientele who visit this camp are attracted more by the image of the camp rather than the reality of the game viewing, which can be to the detriment of the atmosphere at times.

Mombo is run by Wilderness Safaris (page 174), and Chief's is run by Sanctuary Lodges (see page 176).

Mombo (9 tents)

This is the flagship Wilderness Safaris' camp in Botswana – one of their two 'Platinum' camps (the other of which is Jao, page 304) and probably the most expensive photographic camp in Botswana.

It all stands on wooden decking raised high off the ground. The main dining area has, under a high thatched roof, a long polished wooden table for candlelit dinners. One side of this structure opens on to the decking outside, via roll-down grass blinds (used for rare bouts of inclement weather).

The adjacent lounge/bar overlooks wide floodplains and is furnished comfortably with hand-woven 'sea-grass' coffee-tables and colonial leather sofas. Next to this are the glass-fronted cases of a well-stocked small library, amidst easy chairs around a wooden Pygmy bed, imported from the Congo, which doubles for a coffee table.

Behind the lounge is a large boma where braais are sometimes served, while in front on the decking is a campfire, surrounded by deck-chairs, for after-dinner drinks. Near to the small plunge pool some loungers and hammocks cluster in a patch of shade.

Mombo's 'tents' are very large. They're made of canvas, supported by wooden poles, and connected by raised wooden walkways. There are five to the east of the main area, and four to the west, plus Little Mombo (for details, see below). The furthest, number nine, is the 'honeymoon tent' – close to a small 'honeymoon lounge' that is used for private dinners.

Each tent's large wooden door opens to reveal twin beds, or a double, surrounded by walk-in mosquito nets, a sofa, a writing desk, two bedside tables with lamps and a free-standing electric fan. To one side the bathroom has a double indoor shower (two shower heads and lots of space), free-standing twin sinks (the plumbing disguised by a crisscross wooden lattice) and a rather magnificent mirror – 7ft tall with a wide polished wooden frame. Underfoot is polished parquet, held together using dowels.

The zipped gauze panels at the front of each tent open on to a decked balcony, where a table, chairs and a lounger are shaded from the sun by the canvas roof. On one side is a thatched 'sala,' or small gazebo, with a mattress and cushions, which makes a nice shady spot from which to watch game. That said, the area underneath the decking of the chalets themselves seems to be a popular evening spot for buffalo.

Rates (2005): US$1,200 per person sharing/single from July to October; US$1,200/1,335 from December to March; US$1,200 for April, May, June and November. Includes all meals, activities, park fees, laundry, and most drinks. Excludes transfers. Open: all year.

Little Mombo (3 tents)

Continuing along the decking, past Mombo's tent number nine, you find it's smaller sister camp, Little Mombo. This camp has only three tents and, although adjacent to the main camp, it operates as a separate entity. Its tents have the same design as those of its neighbour, and its main lounge/dining/bar area is similarly furnished, though smaller. Little Mombo has its own outdoor boma, small pool and communal *sala* – as well as individual ones for the rooms.

Rates (2005): US$1,200 per person sharing/single from July to October; US$1,200/1,335 from December to March; US$1,200 for April, May, June and November. Includes all meals, activities, park fees, laundry, and most drinks. Excludes transfers. Open: all year.

Chief's Camp (12 tents)

Chief's Camp is about 25km from Mombo, just off the western side of Chief's Island. It is the pride of Sanctuary Lodge's operations in Botswana, and used extensively by A&K companies worldwide.

Chief's main area is raised on decking where its high thatch roof covers a large, open plan area. This is dotted with expensive ethnic curios and the odd bookshelf, where there is a varied mix of interesting reading. Adjacent to this you'll find the lounge and a well-stocked bar, with wooden coffee table and weaved 'sea-grass' sofa, and a dining room with a number of tables. Here guests tend to dine with their own guide, who is generally allotted to you when you arrive. (You tend to stick with the same guide and take all your drives with him/her). When last visited, Chief's food was good and imaginative, and accompanied with an impressive selection of wine.

Outside this dining/lounge area, an expanse of wooden decking acts as a veranda, where you can sit in the shade of large jackalberry (*Diospyros mespiliformis*) and marula (*Sclerocarya birrea*) trees. Slightly below this, a large (8m long) swimming pool is surrounded by loungers and a small 'sala'. Those with a passion for shopping might also seek out the efficient shop that sells T-shirts, film, books and some stylish curios.

Chief's has 12 tents, all secluded and slightly raised off the ground on decking. They are reached from a simple bush path, lit at night by electric hurricane lamps. Tent numbers one to seven are on the eastern side of the main area, the others on the west. All have private verandas overlooking the plains (which usually flood from around June to the end of August, when the water may come all the way up to the lodge).

Each tent has a wooden door and polished wood floor. Bedside the twin or double beds, adjustable aluminum lamps stand on the bedside tables. The decor is stylish and partly modern, partly ethnic – including masks made by the Teke people of Cameroon. But it's not at all rustic. In the tents you'll find a solid wardrobe, with roll-down canvas door, a couple of chairs and tables, a free-standing lamp and a ceiling fan, powered by 24-hour (110/220V) electricity.

The bathroom is within the main body of the tent, but feels different. It has proper partition walls and a brick shower cubicle with glass door, opposite which is a large glass mirror. The toilet is adjacent, behind a wooden door, and there are twin washbasins, both with individual mirrors – completing the impression that this is the bathroom of a plush hotel rather than a safari camp.

Rates (2005): US$735/955 per person sharing/single from July to October; US$440 per person sharing or single from November to June. Includes all meals, activities, park fees, laundry, and most drinks. Excludes transfers. Open: all year.

The Okavango Delta – Private Reserves around Moremi

In his book *The River Okavango*, the Victorian-era explorer and trader Charles John Andersson wrote:

> On every side as far as the eye could see, lay stretched a sea of fresh water, in many places concealed from sight by a covering of reeds and rushes of every shade and hue; whilst numerous islands, spread over its whole surface, and adorned with rich vegetation, gave to the whole an indescribably beautiful appearance.

For modern visitors the Okavango Delta has lost none of its beauty. However, finding reliable information on the various areas from brochures can be as challenging as Andersson's expedition. This chapter aims to demystify these areas, and to identify some of the strengths and weaknesses of the areas and their camps.

It aims to cover all of the private reserves around the Okavango and the main camps within these. But before you read any of my comments, here are a few general observations on the chapter:

- I've covered the reserves in the order of their concession numbers, from NG12 to NG34.
- There are virtually no fences between these areas, so the game flows freely between them. It's won't always be where I suggest it is.
- Remember that differences in environment and game can be as great *within a reserve* as they are between one reserve and its neighbour. Despite this some trends are evident, which I've tried to draw out.
- The marketing leaflets of the reserves usually claim that every animal/bird is found in their particular areas – particularly the 'sexy' ones like wild dogs and Pel's fishing owls! There is some truth in this, in that virtually all the animals/birds do occur in all the reserves. However, I've tried to get behind the spin with a realistic assessment of what you're most likely to see, and where you're most likely to see it. I've tried to make my comments reflect realistic probabilities; but they can't be definitive.
- I've made comments largely from my own first-hand experience, informed when in these areas by guides and experts. Occasionally, I have used reliable local sources. That said, I have not spent a year in each reserve, so my observations have been snap-shots from the times that I've visited, augmented by comments from travellers sent by my travel company. They don't pretend to be comprehensive, systematic surveys – but I do believe that they're broadly representative.
- Under each reserve I've tried to cover the basics of the wildlife and the practicalities. This has necessitated some repetition, but it's a reflection of the fact that there are more similarities between the various reserves in the Delta than there are differences.

OKAVANGO'S PRIVATE RESERVES CAMPS & LODGES

THE LILIES

The two main species of waterlilies in the Okavango are the day-lilies, *Nymphaea nouchali caerulea*, and the night-lilies, *Nymphaea lotus*, which are sometimes called lotus lilies. The day-lilies are more common, and the species are fairly easy to tell apart.

As you might expect, day-lilies open in mid/early morning, and close in the afternoon. Their large floating leaves have smooth edges; their flowers start off as a delicate shade of violet-purple (earning them the name of 'blue lily') with only the centre having a yellowish tinge. These last for about five days, gradually turning whiter as they age, before the stem twists and drags the pollinated seed-head under water. There it matures until the seeds are eventually released, complete with air-filled bladders to help them float and disperse better.

Night-lilies are similar but have much darker green leaves, sharply serrated at the edge. The flowers have creamy white petals, edged with yellow, and a strongly yellow centre; these flowers often lie very flat on the surface, facing directly upwards. They open in the late afternoon and close in the early morning, relying for their pollination on night-flying insects.

GUDIGWA (NG12)

Outside the buffalo fence, north of Vumbura and Duba Plains, the Magwegqana Spillway starts here in an environment similar to southeast Vumbura – though generally NG12's islands are bigger and its vegetation more established. In the south there is good game viewing and extensive mopane woodlands; last time I was in the area, two cheetah left Vumbura heading north to hunt in NG12.

Several villages stand on this concession's northern boundary including Betsha (Betsaa), Eretsha (Eretsa), Kangara, Ganitsuga, Kombo and Gabamukuni. In 2003 this area received its first visitors thanks to an exciting project to create the Delta's first upmarket, community-run 'cultural camp', Gudigwa (US$355–400 per person, per night). This comfortable camp is owned and run by the local San communities, who showcase their culture and skills to visitors. This ground-breaking project, catalysed by a timely grant from the UK's Department for International Development (DFID), is supported by Conservation International and Wilderness Safaris (see page 174), who are marketing this camp. It promises to be very successful, allowing visitors a fascinating experience of San culture in the middle of their trip, whilst providing poor communities with a sustainable, direct income. Don't miss it!

KHWAI COMMUNITY CONCESSIONS (NG18 AND 19)

On the southern edge of the small NG19 concession, where hunting is illegal, are Tsaro Lodge, Khwai River Lodge and Machaba Camp. For the sake of continuity, I've described these in the North Gate section, on pages 258–60 of the chapter covering Moremi Wildlife Reserve.

The larger NG18 area, which stretches north to the Linyanti concession, east of Kwara and west of Chobe, is owned and managed by the small, local community of Khwai Village. Here the people have formed themselves into the Khwai Development Trust, and in 1999 they earned about P1.2million (US$240,000) by auctioning off their hunting quota to different hunting organisations.

The only time that I've been here is when driving on the 'transit route' between Moremi and the Linyanti and Selinda reserves, which I describe briefly in *Chapter*

11, page 241. The interior of this concession appeared to be fairly monotonous mopane, but there were signs of game around.

Future developments
There are also plans to develop two campsites here, Xamotese and Zou, presumably to compete with the main National Parks' campsite at North Gate. However, neither of these is yet operating.

Some details of these two campsites are given on their website (www.khwai.org) although this doesn't appear to have been updated for several years. Failing that, they can be contacted on: Khwai Development Trust, PO Box 657, Maun; tel: 660791; fax: 662671.

You may be able to email them at: merafekhwai@yahoo.com or AfricanFishEagle@yahoo.com or browner_bw@yahoo.com.

KWARA RESERVE (NG20)
Kwara covers a huge area of 1750km², in the middle of the Delta's northern edge. It's bounded to the north by Selinda, to the west by Vumbura and to the east by the Khwai Community's concession, NG18.

On the south side, near to Kwara Camp itself, the reserve is adjacent to Moremi Game Reserve and the small enclave of NG21 (which includes Camp Okavango, Xugana and Shinde). This location gives Kwara access to the shallow floodplains and deep-water areas on the north side of the Delta, as well as a huge, dry, game-viewing area to the north of that.

Concession history
Kwara's been an established safari camp for many years, since it was originally built in 1996. For several years in the mid-1990s it was privately owned and marketed by Wilderness, and was also the base for Sarah-Jane's early horse safaris – which are now run from Macatoo Camp in NG26 (see pages 310–11).

It was taken over by the Kwando Safaris team in 1999, to add a real Delta experience to their Lagoon and Lebala camps. They have subsequently brought Songwe Village to their portfolio, giving them a successful 'circuit' of four camps encompassing Victoria Falls, the Kwando/Linyanti region and the Okavango.

Getting there and getting away
Kwara could be reached by boat from Camp Okavango, Camp Moremi, Xugana, or Shindi, but in practice virtually all visitors arrive by air into the small airstrip a short distance from camp. Like most camps in the Okavango, you can't just drop in here, and even if you could the camp wouldn't welcome you. It's essential to pre-book your visit.

Flora and fauna highlights
Kwara Reserve is very large, and covers a wide spectrum of environments from deep-water lagoons and thick papyrus to dry-country scrub and mopane. Thus trying to describe here any dominant species of plants or animals is at best inconclusive, and at worst completely misleading.

These are a few general notes on what you're likely to find here, plus observations of what I found most interesting on my last visit.

Flora
South of the camp lie the permanent swamps; a true deep-water environment. You'll find large stands of both papyrus and phragmites reeds, often with

waterberry and water fig trees dotted amongst them. Look down in some of the deeper main channels here and you'll find the water opaque; heavy with sediment.

However, in most of the lagoons and the slower channels you'll be able to see right to the Kalahari sand at the bottom, and any water creatures or plants there. Amongst the tangle of weeds, ask your guide to point out the delicate tangle of stems belonging to one of the Okavango's many species of bladderwort (*Utricularia* species). These usually form a submerged tangle of green, hair-like stems with tiny, thin leaves. Dotted amongst these are numerous small 'bladders' which, when touched by a small invertebrate like a mosquito larva, can suck the animal in and capture it. The bladder then digests the animal, and in the process gets valuable nitrogen, which is in very short supply in the mineral-impoverished waters of the Okavango.

Much easier to locate, floating on the surface of the lagoons, you'll find the fan-shaped, serrated leaves of the water chestnut, *Trapa natans*. This is often found on the edges of the lagoons, and is interesting not so much for its white flowers, but for the horned seedpod which it forms. The barbs on this will latch on to the fur or skin of animals, as an aid to dispersing its seed. Their large size suggests that the area's numerous hippo are involved.

Move away from the water, north of camp, and you'll start entering the drier parts of the Kwara Reserve. You'll see that between the dry and wet, there's a transition zone where the bush is a mixture of ancient tree-islands surrounded by plains that were once flooded. The tree-islands here were once more distinct, and surrounded by true floodplains, but as this area has dried out, the vegetation on the plains has grown and blurred the distinction between plains and tree-islands. Similarly, the salt deposits that are often found at the heart of the tree-islands have dissipated.

Like many areas on the edges of the Delta, this is in the very slow process of change. This zone was once wet, and now its landscapes and vegetation are very, very gradually reverting to landforms and vegetation of the drier areas – a process that will take millennia to complete.

Here you'll find most of the Delta's usual species of trees, from African mangosteens to jackalberries and both real fan and wild date palms. Plus a few species more often seen in the drier areas of Chobe like Kalahari appleleaf, *Lonchocarpus nelsii*, and silver cluster-leaf, *Terminalia sericea*.

Mammals

In the drier areas, Kwara's dominant antelopes appear to be tsessebe and impala, with very healthy populations of reedbuck, kudu and giraffe. You'll also find wildebeest, zebra, bushbuck, warthog and steenbok, plus a liberal sprinkling of elephant and the odd herd of buffalo. On the floodplains around camp, lechwe are also common, whilst deep in the papyrus there are sitatunga, though these are not often seen here.

All the big cats are around – lion, leopard and cheetah – and given the open nature of some of the environment, and Kwando Safaris' policy of tracking game as actively as possible, it is a good area for wild dog. I last made a very short visit here in February, which is usually a very difficult time for spotting predators. But despite the thick, green vegetation the guide and spotter managed to locate a pack of wild dogs as they killed an impala – having tracked them for several miles across the bush.

Birdlife

As with the range of animals, the birdlife is inevitably very varied. About 6.5km southwest of Kwara is Gcodikwe Lagoon. This is within Moremi Reserve, but Kwara is the nearest camp to it and so makes a good base for visits here. See the more comprehensive notes on pages 267–8 of *Chapter 12* about Gcodikwe, but note that within a boat ride you'll find one of the region's most important breeding colonies of storks, egrets, herons and spoonbills. It is at its busiest between September and November, but there are always a few birds there.

Elsewhere in Kwara you'll find a good range of the usual species found in and around the Delta. The more common residents here include reed cormorants; darters; African and lesser jacanas; malachite, pied and giant kingfishers; pygmy geese; fish eagles and marsh harriers. Meanwhile the coucals are particularly well represented with Senegal, coppery-tailed and, (in summer) even black coucals all seen here. More unusual sightings include fulvous duck, swamp boubous, black and slaty egrets, black-crowned and white-backed night herons, and the occasional migrant osprey.

In the drier areas north of the permanent waterways, some of the commoner residents include blacksmith plover, red-billed francolins, double-banded sandgrouse, lilac-breasted rollers, yellow-billed hornbills, Meyer's parrots, fiery-necked nightjars, palm swifts, white-rumped babblers, red-eyed and Cape turtle doves, black-crowned Tchagras, Heuglin's robins and black-breasted snake eagles.

More unusual sightings might include western banded snake eagles, Dickinson's kestrels (often perching on palm trees), red-necked falcons, bat hawks, swallow-tailed bee-eaters, red-billed helmet shrikes, brown-throated weavers and wattled cranes.

When to visit
As with much of the Delta, the big game here is generally more prolific during the dry season; and although many of the birds breed between December and March, Gcodikwe is generally at its most spectacular before then. That said, visiting in February still allowed me some first-class game viewing, including wild dog, as commented above. So don't write off the green season as a universally lousy time for game: it just takes a bit more tracking down then.

What to see and do
Kwara is big on activities, and has a wider range available through the year than many camps in the Delta. Game drives and night drives are the norm, and the camp boasts that there are never more than six guests on a vehicle with a guide and tracker. Together with very knowledgeable guides, this makes the game-viewing experience here amongst the best in the Delta, and certainly better in the green season than most dry-land camps. Much of this is due to their willingness to actively track the game, heading off-road and into the bush at the slightest sign of something interesting.

On the water, the varied terrain means that motor boats and mekoro trips are possible all year, and the camp also has a double-decker 'pontoon'-type boat. Climbing on top of this in the papyrus-lined channels is magical, and will give you a completely different view of the waterscape.

Where to stay
Kwara Camp is owned by Kwando Safaris (see page 172) and often linked with its sister camps in NG14, Lebala and Lagoon (see pages 245–8). At time of press, another camp is being planned here, Tsum Tsum, for late 2003. This is likely to be in the locale of 'Four Rivers', an area that's long been known for its good game.

Kwara Camp (8 tents)
Kwara (⊕ KWARAC 19°06.473'S; 23°15.867'E) stands on a small tree island amidst floodplains and has eight tents, most of which are raised on teak decks with good views over the surrounding plains and lagoons.

These were all enlarged and virtually re-built at the start of 2002. The tents now measure about 3.5m by 7m by about 2m high – and are lined in a light green canvas that makes them much brighter than a normal tent. The large windows are a traditional insect-proof mesh, and they're furnished with solid teak furniture including a wardrobe, luggage rack, bedside tables, chairs and beds, all standing on a polished floor which is dotted with rugs.

The bathroom is within the tent, though in a separate part, and includes twin washbasins, a flush toilet, and an inventively designed large shower that's enclosed but surrounded by a screen that's partially open to the outside. The honeymoon suite (number 8) also has a free-standing bath as well as a shower.

Beneath a large jackalberry tree (*Diospyros mespiliformis*), Kwara's thatched bar-lounge and dining area is cosy, comfortable and slightly raised up on decking. It overlooks a shallow lagoon that often attracts good numbers of game. The camp's food is good and the bar well-stocked, as you'd expect from a high-quality camp. Nearby there's a small splash pool and a gift shop. Kwara shares a fairly informal approach with its sister camps, Lagoon and Lebala, which have all been deliberately designed slightly differently as part of a real effort by Kwando Safaris to ensure that the camps have their own individuality.

Rates (2005): US$615 per person, sharing or single, from July to October, including all meals, activities and park fees; US$250/385 per person sharing or single for the rest of the year. Open: all year.

XUGANA, CAMP OKAVANGO AND SHINDE (NG21)

This concession is relatively small by Botswana's standards, but shares a long southern boundary with Moremi Reserve, and is entirely devoted to photographic safaris. To the north NG21 adjoins the Kwara and Vumbura concessions.

Within the reserve, the activities are primarily water-based, although Shinde also offers game drives and a programme of walking safaris from fly-camps.

Getting there and getting away

All the camps have their own nearby airstrips. Camp Okavango's airstrip (✪ CAMPOA 19°07.720'S; 23°05.930'E) is a short walk behind the camp, and from the air you'll realise that this takes up most of the very small island on which the camp is situated!

Shinde's airstrip (✪ SHINDA 19°07.070'S; 23°09.180'E) is a short drive, less than 3km, northeast of the camp. Xugana's airstrip (✪ XUGAIR 19°02.200'S; 23°05.710'E) is slightly closer and northwest of the camp.

All guests pre-arrange their trips here, and most fly into the camps. However, because Camp Okavango and Xugana have a sister-camp, Camp Moremi, on the tip of the Moremi Tongue there are a number of boat transfers between these camps. It's quite common, for example, to fly into Camp Moremi for a few days of game activities, then transfer by boat to Camp Okavango for water activities, before flying out.

When to visit

Whilst game viewing under the clouds of the green season can be quite rewarding, the attraction of sitting on a boat or a mokoro is more elusive. To appreciate the magic of boating through the Okavango, most people need at least dryness and preferably a blue sky and tropical sun.

Last time I visited Camp Moremi during the green season, the weather one morning was glorious. This prompted the enthusiastic manager to ask me why

Sunvil Africa sends relatively few visitors to the Okavango between January and March. 'It's almost empty of visitors and often the weather's superb,' he beamed. Later that day the clouds drew in and it rained on and off for 36 hours, foiling any ideas I had about photography for the rest of my stay. Hence I'd advise that water-based camps like Xugana and Camp Okavango are best visited during the dry season.

Flora and fauna highlights

NG21 is adjacent, and in many ways very similar, to the southern parts of the neighbouring reserve NG20 (Kwara Reserve). Thus read my comments on the *Flora and fauna* there (pages 287–9) for a complete picture. That said, a greater proportion of NG21 reserve is permanent swamp, as it has several large, permanent rivers flowing through it. The Moanachira passes through heading east to feed the Gcodikwe Lagoon, before flowing into the Xakanaxa Lagoon which forms the source of the Khwai River that eventually reaches to the far eastern corner of the Delta.

A less clear channel, the Mborogha, flows southeast almost to Chief's Island where it ultimately feeds into the Gomoti and Santandibe Rivers – both important watercourses of the lower Delta (though in the last few decades there seems to have been a change of flow between these two major rivers, from the Mborogha to the Moanachira).

In *Okavango: Jewel of the Kalahari* (see *Further Reading* for details), Karen Ross notes that the eastern rivers, the Moanachira and Mborogha, carry far more water today than they did a hundred years ago. So with all these waters concentrated into NG21 it's perhaps not surprising that it's an area where you'll find plenty of deep-water lagoons and channels.

The majority of the NG21 reserve has too much water to be one of the Delta's prime game-viewing areas, but in the dry area around Shinde you'll still find good numbers of game, including impala, lechwe, tsessebe and giraffe. Lone bull elephants are around for most of the year, whilst the breeding herds migrate here from the dry interior towards the end of the dry season.

Reedbuck, kudu, sable and buffalo are infrequently seen, while sitatunga are common in the areas of thick papyrus but rarely sighted. Zebra and wildebeest are relatively rare in this area. It's a good place to look for water-based mammals like the very common hippo and the more elusive spotted-necked otters.

The dominant predators are lion and hyena, with leopard and wild dog also found here. From around September to November 2001 a pack of dogs, known locally as the Four Rivers Pack, denned and raised pups in the area used by the Footsteps Walking Camp.

What to see and do

Xugana and Camp Okavango both operate motorboat excursions to explore the lagoons, plus mokoro trips to visit the areas of shallower water nearby. Often the mokoro trips are combined with walking on the islands, though these are usually led by an unarmed poler, so read my comments on walking (pages 127–8) before you depart. Note that if you're keen to visit Gcodikwe Lagoon then Camp Okavango or Shinde are much nearer to it than Xugana.

Both water activities are primarily for birdwatching and to learn about the general environment rather than for game viewing, though it's also possible to go fishing (for bream and tiger fish normally) from the motor boats.

In addition to these water activities, Shinde also has permanent access to dry land and so can offer 4WD game drives and night drives (a maximum of seven guests per vehicle) and walks accompanied by an armed ranger. However, those serious about walking would be better to spend a few nights on Shinde's Footsteps fly-camps.

Where to stay

Of the three camps in this area, the two water-camps, Camp Okavango and Xugana, are both owned and marketed by Desert & Delta Safaris (see page 171). The third camp, Shinde, is run by Ker & Downey – see page 172 for details.

Xugana Island Lodge (8 chalets)

Though its been periodically reinvented, Xugana is one of the Delta's older camps; it is said that it may have been started as a hunting camp as early as the 1960s, probably by Henry Selby (of the hunting company Ker, Downey & Selby). Subsequently, in the early 1980s, it was bought by a local businessman, David Harvey, as a private family retreat in the Delta. This eventually became more commercial and in 1986 Tsaro Elephant Lodge (see page 259) became a sister-camp for Xugana. Both were marketed under the banner of Hartley's Safaris. Finally both were bought by Desert & Delta Safaris in 2000.

One of the few things that hasn't changed about Xugana over the years is its location (⊕ XUGANA 19°04.097'S; 23°06.014'E) on the banks of a forested island beside a large, deep lagoon. It's a spectacular site, fitting for a camp that concentrates entirely on water-based activities. It's about 7.5km north of Camp Okavango (and yet the most direct route by boat covers about 16.8km of waterways).

The camp's lounge, bar and dining areas are set back slightly under fig and leadwood trees; all have thatched roofs and open sides which face the water. That said, the camp often makes a point of arranging their dinners al fresco, either around camp or at locations nearby.

For many years Xugana used the lagoon itself as a swimming pool, suspending a crocodile-proof wire cage in the lagoon for bathers to cool off in. Whilst environmentally admirable, some of the camp's less enlightened guests clearly found this pool's occasional murkiness off-putting, and so in 2001 a new swimming pool was built amongst the landscaped lawns at the centre of camp. These are dotted with natural vegetation, with everything protected from hungry elephants by an electric fence. (What remains of the old swimming pool is now a floating deck, used for the odd al fresco dinner on the lagoon.)

Along with the new pool, Xugana's eight chalets were completely refurbished in 2001, basically to bring their standards up to compete with more modern camps. Each is built of reed and thatch, raised up on wooden decking, with twin beds or a double under a large, walk-in mosquito net. Each has a ceiling fan under its high ceiling, which operates from the camp's generator during the day. There's a 12V lighting system in the rooms for use at night. Their bathrooms are en suite with a walk-in hot shower, flush toilet and washbasin, and outside, facing the lagoon, is a private wooden deck with a pair of canvas safari chairs.

The camp has a good small curio shop, the 'Xugana Gallery', with a fair selection of local books and wildlife guides, plus a few T-shirts, handicrafts and postcards.

Rates (2005): US$323/446 per person sharing/single from July to October; US$252/368 per person sharing or single for the rest of the year. Open: all year.

Camp Okavango (12 tents plus a suite)

On the south side of this concession, Camp Okavango (⊕ CAMPOK 19°08.118'S; 23°06.035'E) stands on the west side of Nxaragha Island amidst floodplains, lagoons and waterways. Because of its location, Camp Okavango is one of the Delta's easiest camps in the permanent swamps to arrange to visit by boat (see *Getting there and getting away*, above). However, it's a measure of the meandering geography of the Delta's waterways that although its sister-camp, Camp Moremi, is only about 33km away as the egret flies, the most direct route by boat (coincidentally, via the Gcodikwe Lagoon) takes slightly over 60km.

'Camp O' as it's usually known was started by an American woman, Jessie Niel, in the early 1980s, and was swiftly followed by Camp Moremi in around 1985. She ran and marketed them as a pair under the banner of Desert & Delta Safaris until, around 1993 or 1994, the whole operation was taken over by a group called Chobe Holdings, associated with Chobe Game Lodge and AfroVentures – though the name was kept.

Camp Okavango is quite a large camp by Okavango standards, and its spacious thatched dining, lounge and bar area reflect this. All open out onto a large area of lawn, which is often the venue for meals outside – usually accompanied by lots of candles and flaming torches!

For seclusion during the day, there's a raised viewing hide that's been built into a sausage tree (*Kigelia africana*) and three knobthorn trees (*Acacia nigrescens*) near the end of the jetty. It's a good spot to relax with comfy chairs, and the view over the papyrus and reeds might interest patient birdwatchers. The plunge pool, sundeck or the sprinkling of hammocks around camp, however, are probably better venues for relaxation.

Sand paths link the tents and main areas – which is a pleasant change from the usual acres of hardwood walkways. Camp Okavango has twelve large Meru-style tents, each raised up on individual wooden platforms. These are very comfortably furnished, with twin or double beds, crisp linen, a teak wardrobe, luggage rack, dressing table, bedside pedestals and canvas safari chairs. You'll also find rugs on the floor and co-ordinated linens and blinds to cover the mesh windows. Each has an en-suite bathroom with a hot shower, washbasin and flush toilet.

As well as the tents, the camp also has one suite available, which they call the 'Okavango Suite'. This is the old house of the camp's former owner, Jessie Neil. It's a unique, open-plan bungalow that's clearly been built to a personal specification. At its centre is a lounge with old-style settees and, nestling in a wooden room-divider, a TV and video. On one side of this is the large bedroom, dominated by a bed shrouded in mosquito netting. On the other is a dining room built for entertaining (though if staying in the suite then even just two guests can arrange to have dinner served here). It's all floored, panelled and furnished in wood.

However, the suite's pièce de résistance is its bathroom. Down a few steps from the bedroom you'll find a black bathroom suite lit by recessed lighting in a room lined with black tiles and mirrors. Urban gothic, circa 1970, in the heart of the Okavango. It's wonderful: don't miss it!

In addition to boat and mokoro trips, bush walks on the islands are possible, though see my comments on walking trips in Botswana (pages 127–8) before you set off. Camps like this which concentrate on water activities tend to have a slower pace than those which also offer game drives; you'll have more time to just relax. As befits this, the tents also have their own tea- and coffee-making facilities and even towelling robes. The team here are also adept at varying the routine, and including the odd torch-lit barbecue on islands away from camp, and other bush surprises.

The camp's curio shop is notable for a fine collection of baskets, all made by the staff, with the proceeds going to them. There are also a few books, T-shirts and film.

Rates (2005): US$323/446 per person sharing/single from July to October; US$252/368 per person sharing or single for the rest of the year. Open: all year.

Shinde (8 tents)
Shinde stands in the heart of the NG21 Reserve, about 6km east of Camp Okavango, 12km west of Kwara and 8km southeast of Xugana. It's also been here a long time, and since the early 1980s has been under the ownership of Ker & Downey.

The central bar/dining area is built on raised, wooden decking on various levels, rising towards a canvas roof that's bowed, a little like an old ox-wagon. The camp also has a swimming pool and a well-stocked curio shop.

Shinde has eight tents, of several different designs, though all in a relatively traditional safari style. Three of these have wooden poles for frames and canvas walls, built on individual, raised wooden decks and shaded by thatched roofs. These form an 'enclave' with its own small area of decking, which can be used together for a small group of six who seek privacy. The rest are more traditional, walk-in, Meru-style tents protected by large shade cloths. These have mesh windows and either wooden or tiled floors dotted with rugs. Inside each you'll find a bright colour scheme dominated by lively African fabrics, wonderfully firm mattresses, bedside tables, an open armoire for clothes and a luggage rack.

Two of these tents, including the 'honeymoon suite' with its queen-size bed, have been built on raised wooden platforms. All have en-suite bathrooms with hot and cold running water, a washbasin, shower, flush toilet, a large mirror and the usual array of tiny bottles of lotions and potions that most camps supply these days. Outside each tent is a shaded porch with a couple of comfy chairs.

Rates (2005): US$550/800 per person sharing/single from July to October; US$450/525 from March to June and November. Includes all meals, drinks, activities and laundry, but not air transfers. Open: beginning of March until the end of November.

Footsteps across the Delta (3 tents)
In 1998 Shinde started to run walking trails in NG21, which they now market as 'Footsteps across the Delta'. Along with Selinda's walking trails (see pages 244–5), this is one of the few operations in the Delta that take walking safaris really seriously.

As with any good walking safari, numbers here are small and these camps take a maximum of six people at a time. Accommodation is in small, twin-bedded tents that are moved each day to a different location. Each is lit by gaslight, and set up with an adjacent private bucket shower and long-drop toilet.

It's all very rustic with dinner usually eaten under the stars, although standards of food are good with lots of effort made to use fresh fruit and vegetables, bake fresh bread each day despite the camp's remote locations, and (of course) to provide a well-stocked bar.

The days here revolve around walking, though occasional trips by mokoro are also possible; you can normally expect two walks of 3–4 hours in duration, one in the morning and one in the evening.

Rates (2005): US$395/520 per person sharing/single from July to October; US$350/400 from March to June and November. Includes all meals, drinks, activities and laundry, but not air transfers. Open: beginning of March until the end of November.

VUMBURA AND DUBA PLAINS (NG22 AND 23)

Immediately north of Moremi's Mombo concession, the Vumbura and Duba Plains reserves (NG 22 & 23) share many similarities of game and landscape with Mombo. This northern area of the Delta is one of my favourites, but because of the similarity between Vumbura or Duba, if you are planning a trip to this area then it's best to include only one of them in your itinerary.

Vumbura is a very varied reserve, and the areas through which you drive are often very pretty. Much of its landscape consists of wide-open plains with tiny islands – almost a cliché of one's preconceived view of the Okavango. Vumbura's game is notably diverse, so most visitors will see a wide range of antelope and have a good chance to spot the less common predators.

Duba Plains, to the west of Vumbura, is visually similar but with larger open plains. It doesn't quite have Vumbura's diversity of game, but instead is the long-standing venue for battles between large herds of buffalo and sizeable prides of lion. Thus, it will often provide a very impressive spectacle of big game.

Both can access water activities, Vumbura for the whole year, although the areas aren't quite so picturesque as, say, the Jao Flats.

Background information
Concession history
Until around 1997 this was a hunting area, but then Wilderness Safaris started Vumbura, Little Vumbura and Duba Plains camps.

For several years there were two small, seasonal hunting camps running in the northeast of the Vumbura concession (one of which was on the site of Kaporota). These had closed by 2001 and while the reserve is designated by the government for 'mixed wildlife utilisation', hunting is no longer practised in either area; both are now used solely for photographic safaris. (As an aside, Dereck and Beverly Joubert, the wildlife photographers, are closely involved with the Vumbura concession.)

As is increasingly the case with reserves in Botswana, both Duba and Vumbura have an element of local community involvement. Five local villages – Seronga, Eretsa, Betsaa, Gudigwa and Gunitsugwa – have some control over the concession, and derive considerable benefit from its success. Most of the staff for the camps come from these villages too, thus there's a flow of revenue from these camps going back to the communities by way of wages. (See *The anatomy of a community partnership* on page 296, and comments on NG12 on page 286.)

Getting there and away
All the camps here only accept pre-booked guests who fly in. Driving isn't possible without permission – and permission is never given. (Though it would be only a few hours drive from Seronga, if you knew the way!). Note that both camps have their own separate airstrips. Vumbura's airstrip (VUMAIR) is located at ⊕ 18°57.504'S; 22°49.063'E.

When to visit
In common with the rest of the Okavango, you'll find the big game more diverse and prolific during the dry season, although the birdlife is generally better between December and March. Driving around the reserve can be more difficult then, as there's a lot of water around and many roads are submerged.

Flora and fauna highlights
Both these reserves are broadly similar in character, although Duba Plains (as you might expect) has more extensive open plains, whereas the plains at Vumbura are often partially flooded, and they're broken up by more islands, including many small palm islands.

Flora
Much of these concessions consist of very beautiful, open floodplains dotted with islands, many of which are tiny. The vegetation of the larger islands is dominated by many of the Okavango's usual tree species, including raintrees, *Lonchocarpus capassa*, leadwoods, *Combretum imberbe*, African mangosteens, *Garcenia livingstonei*, jackalberries, *Diospyros mespiliformis*, sausage trees, *Kigelia africana*, and sycamore figs, *Ficus sycomorus*.

You'll also find knobthorn trees, *Acacia nigrascens*, although relatively few of them, and some particularly large, wonderful specimens of fever-berry trees, *Croton megalobotrys* – named after the anti-malarial properties of the seeds and the bark. (These properties had been known to local African residents for centuries, but were brought to the attention of a wider audience by an article in the medical journal, *The Lancet*, in 1899. Apparently there has still not been any detailed research on these medicinal properties.)

THE ANATOMY OF A COMMUNITY PARTNERSHIP

Though 'community-based natural resource management' is recognised as one of the main strategies for achieving sustainable development in the rural areas of Botswana, really good examples of it are few and far between. Wilderness Safaris have a strong track record with successful community projects in other countries, like Damaraland Camp in Namibia, and here in Botswana their flagship community project is the Vumbura and Duba concessions. The camps in these private reserves or concessions started in 1997 when the safari company and their partners made an agreement with the community to which the government had given management of concession areas NG22 and 23.

The community, in this case, consists of five villages to the north of the Okavango Delta: Seronga, Eretsha, Betsha, Gudigwa and Ganitsuga. The villagers had to set up a trust, with a fully constituted board to represent all the villages and people of the area (NG22 and 23) in their dealings with the government, the Land Board and with the safari companies. The ten-person board is made up of two elected people from each of the five villages. Wilderness pays a six-figure US-dollar lease fee each year to the board (this is a lot of money in rural Botswana). The board decides how to use that money for the benefit of the community. Further, as part of the deal Wilderness has to employ at least 118 people from the villages (though they actually ended up giving jobs to around 150), and to deliver on a number of community projects. These projects have resulted in the setting up and supporting of a number of secondary cottage industries in the villages, like basket-weaving and vegetable gardens; in addition they have sponsored an inter-village soccer tournament; helped with transport problems; and set up village shops, mortuaries etc.

Perhaps the most difficult issue about this kind of agreement for any safari company is the short duration of the leases; the community can swap their safari company after the first year if it wishes to, then again after the second year, the fifth year and the tenth year. Given the huge investment in infrastructure and the long-term nature of the marketing, this is difficult for most safari companies to contemplate. However, Vumbura and Duba are now six years into the project, and Wilderness Safaris are slowly starting to reap the benefits of a stable, long-term relationship with the community as their partner. Equally, guests to these camps know that their safari is actively benefiting the communities in the area – and so know that they're helping the villagers and the wildlife by coming to these camps.

Amongst the main bushes that you'll find here are the Kalahari star apple, *Diospyros lycioides lycioides*, which is often also called the blue bush, for its overall bluish tinge, or the toothbrush bush – as the roots of this bush can be peeled and used as a toothbrush. (Veronica Roodt reports that on using it 'at first my mouth burnt and I became extremely worried when my whole mouth turned yellow. The result, however, was remarkable – white teeth and fresh breath'.) Another very common bush in this area is the evergreen magic gwarri bush, *Euclea divinorum*. Also sometimes known as the 'toothbrush bush' for the use of its branches, both these bushes can produce dyes that are used to colour palm leaves used in weaving baskets in Botswana.

In the northeast of Vumbura there are some fine acacia woodlands, whilst as you travel west from Vumbura into Duba you'll find more and larger open floodplains, slightly less thick wooded islands, and more clusters of the wild date palm, *Phoenix reclinata*.

As well as the drier areas, there are many small channels near the Vumbura camps, and some open, lightly reeded lagoons. The channels are lined intermittently with a mixture of papyrus and common reeds, and periodically open out onto floodplain areas. Scenically the areas near these camps don't quite match up to the sheer beauty of the Jao Flats – as there are very few feathery real fan palms or lily-covered lagoons.

Mammals

When last visited, I was very impressed by the varied line up of antelope that I saw in the Vumbura Reserve in a few days. Unlike many of the areas further from the heart of the Delta, there wasn't just a high density of one or two species, to the virtual exclusion of the rest.

Species that you can expect to see here include tsessebe, impala, lechwe, kudu, zebra, wildebeest, giraffe, warthog and steenbok. Sable are seen fairly often, especially near the airstrip. Waterbuck are common here; Vumbura is one of the few places within northern Botswana where you'll find good numbers of them. Duiker, reedbuck and bushbuck are seen infrequently, whilst roan antelope are rare here, though have been seen occasionally in the late dry season. I know of one sighting of sitatunga in Vumbura (which was one February).

Wild dogs had denned here for several years running prior to my visit, and I was lucky enough to be able to watch a beautiful pack with pups at its den, situated in the mopane woodlands on the east side of the Vumbura. However, in a thick band of mopane woodlands it wasn't possible to follow them when they moved off.

Cheetah are also resident, though, like the rest of the smaller game, they will move through the buffalo fence and out into the huge NG12, to the north. In the dry season, when many of the open floodplains are dry, it's a classic open environment that is perfect for cheetah, rather like Mombo and parts of Selinda, so it's a particularly good area in which to seek them.

Leopard are occasionally seen on night drives. Lion and spotted hyena are both relatively common. Both black-backed and side-striped jackals occur here, though the black-backed are seen much more regularly.

Moving westwards, Duba Plains is noted not only for its huge open plains, but also for having some of the best concentrations of buffalo in Botswana. Particularly large herds are found here during the dry season. These can easily number over a thousand animals, and inevitably they attract a very high concentration of lion – which in the Duba Plains area, is very much the dominant predator. The converse of this is that Duba doesn't have the same balance of species, or the diversity, that you'll usually find in Vumbura, giraffe, zebra and impala being the notable absentees, though Duba is curiously popular with warthogs!

Spotted hyena are flourishing here, despite the sizeable prides of lions, and side-striped jackals are seen fairly frequently whilst black-backed are largely absent.

Birdlife

The birdlife here is as varied as you'll find in any area of the Delta with a good mix of dry and wet environments. Certainly in one afternoon of very casual bird spotting on the river from Vumbura you can expect to find a range of kingfishers (malachite, pied, and giant), jacanas, several species of egrets (including slaty), black-winged stilts, open-bill storks and reed cormorants. In addition, the open floodplains with short grass seemed to attract very good numbers of various waders plus saddle-billed storks, glossy and sacred ibises, spoonbills and – relatively unusually – pelicans.

Similarly, the birds enjoying the waterlogged plains of Duba Plains last October included wattled cranes and, an unusual treat in the Delta, flamingos.

What to see and do

The Vumbura camps, and to a lesser extent Duba Plains, have year-round access to deep permanent water, and so boat trips are possible all year, with opportunities to fish if you wish. There are also mokoro excursions, 4WD game drives and night drives. (Though night drives when flood levels are very high, from May to August, may sometimes be restricted.) Short walks are also offered by these camps, though I would generally go to a specialist walking camp if I wanted to do much walking.

Where to stay

All the camps in Vumbura and Duba are marketed by Wilderness Safaris (see page 174). Vumbura, Little Vumbura and Duba Plains are currently all the same cost, whilst Kaparota is marketed as one of Wilderness's rustic series of 'vintage camps' and hence costs slightly less.

There is also a little-known fourth camp in this area, called Vundimtiki. This is used exclusively by one overseas tour operator from the USA. Visitors from elsewhere are unlikely to even hear about it, and I haven't visited it and so include no further comments on it here.

Little Vumbura (5 tents)

Although less than 2km from its larger sister-camp, Little Vumbura feels quite separate, perhaps because it's on a small island and always approached by boat (⊕ LVUMBU 19°00.070'S; 22°51.710'E).

Little Vumbura has a small dining area and a comfy lounge/bar section. All is under canvas on decking about a metre off the ground, and attached, via a 50m jetty, to the launch area for the boats.

Over the dining-room/bar stands a large waterberry tree, *Syzygium cordatum*, and the open sides of the canvas structure (which can be rolled down) are shaded by dense surrounding stands of wild date palms, a couple of fig trees (*Ficus sycomorus*) and an assortment of jackalberry trees (*Diospyros mespiliformis*). This all leaves you with the very comfortable feeling that the camp's been built from within the vegetation, and you're cocooned in a small, tropical hideaway.

The walk-in tents are comfortable, with wickerwork shelves, wardrobe and furniture. They stand on the ground and have an en-suite shower cubicle, washbasin and toilet inside. A few paces away outside is a much more natural open-air shower, with a view of the surrounding floodplains.

Aside from the main area, there's also a small curio shop (with a few books, materials and local baskets for sale), a plunge pool and a wonderful open hexagonal section of decking (with a fire pit in the middle) which extends into the reeds and is used for dinner, drinks and stargazing.

Up to 2001, this little camp accepted just eight people and was certainly one of Wilderness's hottest properties in Botswana. Now to capitalise on this, Little Vumbura has been made slightly larger to take up to ten people, while the main Vumbura Camp been slimmed down in size.

Rates (2005): US$595 per person sharing/single from July to October; US$390/430 from December to March; US$430 for April, May, June and November. Includes all meals, activities, park fees, laundry, and most drinks. Excludes transfers. Open: all year.

Vumbura (6 tents)
Although the concession's main camp, Vumbura seems to have been in the shadow of its smaller, sexier sister-camp; for 2002, however, it has slimmed down to just 12 guests, rather than 16 – and has thus become a lot more attractive.

That said, Vumbura (⊕ VUMBUR 18°59.801'S; 22°50.782'E) has always been a good, well-built camp. The main dining/bar area is built on wooden decking, whilst the tents are situated at ground level and stand in deep shade under a canopy of mostly jackalberry and mangosteen trees. The tents are widely spread out, most with good views over an open *vlei* area. (See page 57 for an explanation of 'vlei'.)

Each has a double or twin beds, with the back of the headboard extending into a small wardrobe and laundry basket. There are twin washbasins, a separate toilet and hot shower, chairs and a table and a 24-hour fan that works from a battery backup system when the generator's off at night. The tent's large gauze windows can be closed with canvas flaps. Outside there's a small veranda and a large open-air shower.

The camp has a small curio shop sellings books, shirts, locally made baskets and toy mekoro, and a comfortable central dining/bar/lounge area dominated by an impressive oval table – all under canvas supported by gum poles. *Rates (2005): US$870 per person sharing/single from July to October; US$390/430 from December to March; US$595 for April, May, June and November. Includes all meals, activities, park fees, laundry, and most drinks. Excludes transfers. Open: all year.*

Kaparota (5 tents)
Kaparota is a small camp on the northeast side of the Vumbura concession, about 50 minutes drive from the Vumbura airstrip. It stands on an island dominated by sausage trees, *Kigelia africana* – a location that (like many of the sites in the Delta now used for camps) was first used as a hunting camp. Then in 2001 hunting stopped in the reserve, and this rustic camp converted to cater to photographic safaris. It's designated by Wilderness as a 'vintage' camp which means that it's not as luxurious as many of their camps – but instead is a little more rustic and a little less costly.

The five simple Meru-style tents are all raised up on individual platforms, complete with a small veranda furnished with a couple of canvas deckchairs. Each tent has a private 'bathroom' at the back, which is roofless and separate from the sleeping area. Here you'll find a washbasin, a flush toilet and a (hot and cold) shower. Inside are twin beds, a basic wardrobe and a few chairs.

Kaparota is, in some ways, simply a cut-down version of the concession's plusher camps. It offers the same range of activities and guiding standards as the other camps here. However, its game drives do often head back southwest, towards the area of the other camps, which is generally a more productive area of better game. *Rates: US$400/490 per person sharing/single from July to October; US$240/330 for April, May, June and November. Includes all meals, activities, park fees, laundry, and most drinks. Excludes transfers. Open: April to November.*

Duba Plains (6 tents)
Of all the 'usual' fly-in camps in the Delta, Duba Plains is one of the most northern. It is north of Moremi Reserve, about five minutes' flight west of Vumbura.

Duba is a fairly small camp with the main dining area built on raised decking under a high thatched roof, around a large jackalberry tree. The cozy lounge/bar area is adjacent, on a slightly lower level, with armchairs and a couple of sofas around a wicker coffee table. Judicious use of sapling screens lends it a pleasant rustic feel.

The thatched guest toilet is nearby, and beyond is another area of raised decking. On one side of this is a swimming pool; opposite is an observation deck with chairs, tables and loungers. This commands a good view over the plains, and is often used for brunch. To the side of this is a quiet 'sala' (a small gazebo), with a couple of wicker chairs and a bench. It's perfect for relaxing in the afternoon. About 150m from the main lounge is a small hide for birdwatchers, with a copy of Newman for those 'hard to identify' species.

Duba's six tents are linked by bush paths, and raised on decks to give good views of the plains. Outside each there's a small veranda with a table and two chairs, in front of the tent's wooden door. Inside, wood has been used extensively for simple, tasteful decor. The headboard at the back of double or twin beds extends into twin washbasins, and there's a small wardrobe and laundry basket. The tent has mosquito-proof gauze, so mosquito nets are not usually provided. Inside at the back is a flush toilet and a shower, beyond which a door opens onto raised decking where an outdoor shower has a great view of the plains.

Because of its location near the Panhandle, Duba is one the first camps in the main Delta to be flooded. From about May to the end of August the shallow-water plains around it usually have enough water for mekoro trips.

Rates (2005): US$720 per person sharing/single from July to October; US$500/550 from December to March; US$550 for April, May, June and November. Includes all meals, activities, park fees, laundry, and most drinks. Excludes transfers. Open: all year.

COMMUNITY AREA (NG24)

Currently this is the only one of the Delta's photography-specific areas (ie: hunting is not allowed) which has no proper safari operation in it. Until about 1999 this was the location for Jedibe Camp, which had long been run by Wilderness Safaris (see page 174) and was one of their earliest camps in the Delta.

I visited Jedibe in about 1996. It was located deep within a maze of deep-water channels and papyrus, and the main activity there was exploring on motorboats. This was superb fun (although motorboats are probably the most expensive activity to run for any camp, given their thirst for fuel!) as the boats could reach some stunning areas of the most beautiful floodplains, as well as exploring the papyrus-lined channels of the main rivers. Mokoro trips, incorporating walks on the islands, were also possible but usually of secondary interest.

However, in 1999 Jedibe's lease came up for 'tender' – which means a re-opening of negotiations between the government, the community (the Okavango Jakotsha Community Trust), and anyone who is interested in taking responsibility for the area's lease.

Since Jedibe was built, many new mixed land-and-water camps have come into existence in the Delta, and proved very successful. Furthermore their range of game drives and water activities are wider than Jedibe's options. This left Jedibe looking less commercially attractive, with a very specific, limited niche as a deep-water camp in permanent papyrus running mainly (inherently costly) motorboats. Jedibe's northerly location, far from Maun, meant expensive transport links and running costs too.

These factors all made Jedibe less commercially attractive, at a time when the local community was expecting to get more for the concession. Eventually no agreement could be made.

This process has now been re-started and as I write (June 30 2002) the deadline for companies to finally deliver their bids is closing. They are asking companies to run a photographic operation in part of the concession for five years. I don't know if they'll be able to find a company and make an agreement, or if they'll hit a stalemate again.

If they succeed, and you do visit this area, then don't go for the animals. Although there are animals on the islands, this is a deep-water area and you should treat any game sightings as a bonus. Instead come for the bird and water-life. Expect lots of deep, fast-flowing channels and endless banks of papyrus, which periodically open out onto spectacular floodplains.

Where to stay

There is now one, small backpacker's camp on the edge of the reserve, accessed from Etsha 6, on the Panhandle road:

Makwena Camp (camping only) Tel: 674299; email: makwena@dynabyte.bw
This small, budget camp is reached about 14km from Etsha 6 on the Panhandle – usually 12km of 4WD track from the road, followed by a 2km boat ride. These 4WD transfers to/from Etsha 6, if you can organise them, are P100 per person return.

Makwena is currently being run as a campsite for budget travellers, and charges P33 per person per day for camping. From there a boat transfer to a fly-camp on an island is P100 per person (return), from where you can hire mekoro for P100 per day. Each mokoro seats one or two people.

If you want to go for longer than a day then there's a P300 per mokoro per night 'sleep-out' fee, which enables you to stay out on one of the islands; note, too, that there's an entry fee into this community area of about P25 per person.

If you're interested then apparently Mr Malcolm Thomas who works in the Co-op supermarket at Etsha 6 can get in touch with the camp from there. However, this didn't work when I last tried, as he wasn't around. It's certainly best to contact the camp at least two or three days in advance, and you will need to arrive with all your food and camping equipment; Makwena cannot supply either.

JAO, KWETSANI, JACANA AND TUBU CAMPS (NG25)

Close to the Panhandle, west of Moremi, NG25 is a particularly beautiful concession covering about 600km^2 of the upper Okavango Delta. Most of this is a fairly wet environment, with extensive floodplains especially around the Jao Flats, though there is a substantial, drier section to the west of the reserve, where the new Tubu Camp is situated. The annual flood generally reaches this reserve around April or May, instantly expanding the area of the floodplains.

Getting there and away

As with most camps, flying in here is the only option, and almost always booked in advance. Driving here is totally impractical.

When to visit

For the water activities anytime is fine as long as it doesn't rain. Hence from April to November would be my choice of time to visit. However, if you're on a serious game-viewing trip then better to come towards the end of the dry season where this area's diversity of species does pick up, with dry-country species like cheetah being seen here periodically.

Flora and fauna highlights

The area around Jao, Kwetsani and Jacana feel very much like most people's image of the Okavango: watery and terribly picturesque. It's a lovely environment. Whilst the game diversity in the area might not quite match some of the areas further east yet, lechwe and lion are exceedingly prolific here and those alone will keep most people entertained.

The birding is also good, with enough diversity of habitat to mean that you'll find most Delta species here if you look hard enough. I've had great luck in the past here with gallinules and pink-throated longclaws.

The area around Tubu Tree Camp, on the eastern side of the concession, is much drier and totally different from the eastern part of the reserve where the three older camps are situated.

Flora

The reserve's most memorable area must be the beautiful Jao Flats, a series of huge open floodplains, dotted with tiny islands that are often only a few metres across. These vast floodplains are covered in a mix of very sparse vegetation, much of which is the aptly-named hippo grass, *Vossia cuspidata*, which has round, slender leaves, pointing periodically out of the water by up to a metre. Often these have a tiny flower spike on top, reminiscent of a minute papyrus head.

Much taller and denser are the stands of tall common reeds, *Miscanthus junceus*, and even areas of the attractive bulrush, *Typha capensis*. The latter have distinctive velvety seedheads and edible roots (which taste a little like chewing gum or sugar cane!). As you'd expect in such a watery area, the deeper parts have thick stands of papyrus.

There's usually plenty of open, shallow water around, and in the slow-flowing channels look out for water lettuce plants, *Ottelia ulvifolia*, underwater, with its wavy leaves, long trailing stems and delicate, trumpet-shaped flower held above the surface by a single airbladder.

The many small islands in the area are often little more than bases for the emergence of a ring of bushy wild date palms, *Phoenix reclinata*, and perhaps the odd real fan palm, *Hyphaene petersiana*, springing up through the centre of the low canopy, perhaps around a termite mound.

Also look out for the wild dagga plant, *Leonotis nepetifolia*, with its bright red flowers, like baubles from a Christmas tree. These will remain standing long after they turn brown and die. There are also thickets of the uncommon magic gwarri bush, *Euclea divinorum* – which is believed by some local people to have wood with supernatural powers. Above these you'll find rain trees, *Lonchocarpus capassa*, woodland waterberry trees, *Syzygium guineense*, and the occasional birdplum, *Berchemia discolor*.

Some of the bushes on the larger islands here are more typical of drier areas, including the Kalahari appleleaf, *Lonchocarpus nelsii*, the Kalahari star apple, *Diospyros lycioides lycioides* – with its bluish-tinge which gives it the name of 'blue bush' sometimes. Ask your guide and s/he may show you how its twigs can be used as a toothbrush!

Similarly these larger islands have bands of acacias here, including the umbrella thorn, *Acacia tortilis*. These become more prevalent as you move further east in the reserve, where you find larger islands, with thicker belts of acacia bush and areas of mopane also. This is the area in which you'll find Tubu Camp.

Animals

The majority of the reserve around the Jao Flats is a superb area for lion and lechwe, which are both exceedingly common. The lechwe occur in large herds and will frequently startle; listen to them splash as they run across the flooded grasslands. The lion are certainly the dominant predator, with a number of large prides in the area.

Other game is usually present in lower densities, but in this eastern section you can expect to spot blue wildebeest, zebra, small groups of tsessebe and elephants in the area. Kwetsani, in particular, is noted for the increasingly relaxed bushbuck which seem to frequent its island. Sable and roan are virtually never seen here, but the large areas of papyrus are home to sitatunga, though as ever these take a lot of effort to see.

Lone male buffalo will pass through, especially from June onwards, and later in the dry season larger breeding herds move across the reserve. Elephants have a broadly similar pattern, and their herds get larger as the dry season progresses.

Cheetah aren't usually seen on the eastern side of the reserve until the waters have receded a long way, which means around October. Then they'll move west again as the waters rise in February. Leopard and hyena are seen occasionally but infrequently throughout the reserve and the year. Sightings of wild dog are very unusual (for example, there was one sighting during the whole of 1999 – but things are improving).

The western area of the reserve, accessed from Tubu, have a much drier habitat around them and you can expect giraffe, kudu, and impala here in the mixed acacia woodlands.

Like most of the reserves around the Okavango, Jao Reserve had previously been used for hunting. However, questions have been raised if the hunting in this area was ethical or not. It is alleged that leopard were baited and snared in numbers, and hyena shot. This would have enabled the lion prides to grow with little competition, thus satisfying the demand for lion trophies – and explain the present very high numbers of lion and relative scarcity of other predators.

Fortunately all hunting has been stopped in the Jao Reserve for several years, and the animal populations should be slowly returning to a more natural balance.

Birds

This is a good reserve for birdwatching, particularly for some of the less common water-based species. During a few gentle boat rides on the eastern side of the reserve, I had good sightings of many of the commoner waterbirds, plus lesser jacanas, lesser moorhens, purple and green-backed herons, slaty egrets, white-faced whistling ducks, lesser moorhens, and both purple and lesser gallinules. (Both of the gallinules were seen in small lagoons close to Kwetsani.)

Meanwhile driving in the drier areas we came across a similarly good range, and noted several flocks of Meyer's parrots, Dickenson's kestrels nesting at the top of an old palm tree, wattled starlings, and a tree full of open-bill storks. Then, again near Kwetsani, we found some very uncommon pink-throated longclaws (a big tick!) in a wide marshy plain where they seem to be resident.

Though not too unusual, African snipes can be found here. Listen carefully around dusk, as the sun sets and darkness falls. Then, during the breeding season, the birds fly high and zoom back to the ground. Their fanned-out tail feathers make a noise like a percussion instrument – called 'drumming'.

The western side of this reserve, around Tubu, should have a wider range of raptors than the east (Jao, Kwetsani and Jacana), simply because it's drier.

What to see and do

I would visit Jao and Kwetsani primarily for their water activities, trips by boat and mokoro, which they can generally offer all year (though motor boats at Kwetsani may be restricted by water levels around October-January). That said, day and night game drives (and sometimes short walks on the islands) are also possible here, and will make a bonus for your stay.

Jacana is also best regarded as a water-based camp, with motor boats and mokoro trips all year, as well as game drives when the water levels are not in high flood. Tubu is quite the opposite: a dry-land camp for game drives which can also arrange mokoro trips when the flood levels are high. A couple of nights at Jacana, and a few at Tubu, make a relatively inexpensive combination, at least by the standards of the Delta.

The comfortable game-drive vehicles in this reserve tend to use vehicles with three rows of three seats, of which a few are often left empty. When I last went walking, the guide was a capable, experienced walking guide who gave an appropriate pre-departure safety briefing and clearly knew how to use the rifle that he carried. He also escorted the mokoro trip, which I was pleased to see eschewed the easier hippo trails in favour of a more difficult, but much safer, route through a shallow floodplain. Though he's now left this reserve, I hope that the standards of safe practice, which he set, will remain.

Where to stay

All four camps in the Jao Reserve are marketed and run by Wilderness Safaris (see page 174). They range from the opulence of Jao, to the relative simplicity of Jacana. All cater exclusively for fly-in visitors:

Jao Camp (9 rooms)
Imagine what Tarzan would have built if he'd had a few million dollars and some chic Italian designers, and you're close to imagining Jao Camp. Standing on the southeast side of the Jao Reserve (✪ JOACAM 19°18.431'S, 22°36.071'E), Jao is one of Wilderness Safaris' flagship 'platinum' camps (the other being Mombo, which was designed by the same architect).

Arriving at Jao, you walk through a profusion of lush wild date palms before eventually finding the large, two-storey main building. It's about 30m long and 8-10m wide, with designer-inspired scraggy thatch and hints of an Indonesian longhouse. Upstairs here is the dining room, where everybody usually eats around a long elegant table (handcrafted on site, apparently, using Zimbabwean rosewood!); a spacious lounge with comfy leather sofas, a chess table, and stylish lamps; there's a long outside balcony where breakfast is sometimes served.

Down a magnificent set of stairs there's a small library, a snug and a curio shop. A few paces away from this you'll find a round swimming pool and a few sun-loungers amidst the palms.

The rooms at Jao are probably the most luxurious and spacious in the Okavango region. All are on stilts, accessed by raised wooden walkways. They have one long side, facing the nearby channel, and equally scraggy thatch to match the central longhouse. Their position gives lots of privacy, though also makes the walk from the farthest rooms as much as 600m from the centre. (Less fit visitors can request chalets closer to the centre!)

Entering at the side of the chalet, through a large, swivelling door, you find a lounge with huge coffee table, big comfy settee and a lockable safe for valuables. This is only half of the open-plan room, which also has twin (or double) bed(s) under a walk-in mosquito net, complete with a fan underneath. The chalets are effectively insect-proofed, though one long side of the room is made of gauzed or glass doors which can all be opened and folded back, concertina-style. This opens up the front of the chalet onto the wide balcony outside. All of the floors are held together with wooden dowels and studs rather than nails or screws and beautifully finished with 'adzed' edges to the light, wooden floorboards.

A slight partition divides the main bedroom and lounge from a dressing area with a wardrobe, an old-style claw-footed bath, and two conical sinks placed centrally; a stylish use of space. Another partition separates this from a toilet, then outside is an open-air shower, surrounded by circular clay walls (with a view over the channel).

Set a few metres away from each room is a 'sala', a small outside gazebo, with a mattress and cushions, under a shady thatched roof. This makes a lovely perch for relaxing in the afternoon, raised far off the ground in the heart of the date-palm forest, overlooking the channel.

In short, Jao is visually stunning and exceedingly comfortable; if you want private luxury in the Delta then it's superb. It's an obvious choice for honeymoon couples. However, it's a large camp where guests will stay in their rooms rather than mix socially, so doesn't have quite such an intimate atmosphere or sociable feel that you may find at some of the smaller camps.

Rates (2005): US$870 per person sharing/single from July to October; US$545/600 from December to March; US$595 for April, May, June and November. Includes all meals, activities, park fees, laundry, and most drinks. Excludes transfers. Open: all year.

Kwetsani (5 tents)

Kwetsani (⊕ KWETSA 19°14.594'S, 22°32.200'E), faces east, towards the rising sun, from a long, narrow island about 10km northwest of Jao, its larger, more opulent neighbour. (This can take 40 minutes if the roads are dry, or an hour by boat.)

The main lounge/dining room area at Kwetsani is slightly raised and stands under a high thatched roof, with one side open, overlooking an open plain. There's a dining table under part of this, a trendy metal fireplace in the centre (handy when it's cool in the morning), and an open lounge area with comfy chairs, a leather sofa and a small bookshelf. Nearby is a well-stocked bar, complete with a jackalberry, *Diospyros mespiliformis*, growing up through it.

The wooden decking floor extends from under the thatch on to a wide veranda, which has been built around a huge sycamore fig, *Ficus sycomorus*, a marula, *Sclerocarya birrea caffra*, and a sausage tree, *Kigelia africana*. There's usually a spotting scope standing on the deck here. Nearby is a guest washroom/toilet, which has not only a tree growing up through it, but also has half of its wall cut away to give a view. Down a sloping walkway, almost on the level of the surrounding plains, a few sun-loungers, umbrellas and chairs surround a small splash-pool (about 5m by 3m). On the other side of the lounge is a viewing platform about 3m up from the main deck – though the view from the rooms is usually as good.

The five chalets are all raised off the ground, and linked by wooden walkways. Two are south of the main area, three are on the north side. Each has twin beds, or a double, under a large mosquito net, with a fan above it. Behind the substantial wooden bed-head is a large mirror, twin wash basins and a small wardrobe with shelves. On either side of this, two separate doors lead into small rooms, one containing an indoor shower, the other a toilet.

There is also a reed-walled outdoor shower on the balcony, along with several easy chairs and a table. Kwetsani is a lovely small camp which, perhaps helped by its small size, had a very relaxed and positive atmosphere when I last visited.

Rates (2005): US595 per person sharing/single from July to October; US$390/430 from December to March; US$430 for April, May, June and November. Includes all meals, activities, park fees, laundry, and most drinks. Excludes transfers. Open: all year.

Jacana Camp (5 tents)

Although less than 4km north of Jao, Jacana (⊕ JACANA 19°16.766'S, 22°36.619'E) is a 35-minute boat ride from it. Jacana was originally a basic 'trails camp.' It started life being used as a base for mokoro excursions for small escorted-group itineraries that run across Chobe and Moremi. However, for 2001 Wilderness changed its emphasis and was marketing it directly for individual visitors as part of the small group of 'vintage' camps (see page 174).

It's a much smaller, simpler camp than most in the Delta, and stands on a small island in the very beautiful Jao Flats area. Like Jao, the density of date palms lends Jacana the feeling of a 'tropical island'. The dining/bar area is a simple two-storey structure with a canvas roof and roll-down screens around its side. Downstairs this has a neat, well stocked bar and a small lounge/reading area with easy chairs and a sofa. Upstairs is the dining area, with a polished wooden floor and a large dining table.

Behind this is a thatched hut, which they call a 'hustshi', and a few hammocks. Meals are sometimes eaten outside, in the open area behind at the centre of camp – which reminds me of eating in a traditional African *kraal*.

Each of the tents here are raised slightly on decking, and fairly small by the standards of the Delta (about 3m x 3m).

These have simple low-voltage electric lights, twin or double beds, and a basic wardrobe. There's a small veranda at the front with two canvas directors' chairs and a table. Behind each is a private toilet, shower and washbasin, which are all open to the skies. (It's lovely to have a hot shower under blue skies and palm trees, but this isn't an ideal design for use during the rains, between January and April!)

One of the camps most entertaining features is the 'guest toilet', which is down a rough walkway from the main upper deck. There's an impressive cement-moulded bowl, a great view, and a pulley made in 'Heath-Robinson' style to flush the toilet. In a similar vein, the camp has several painted concrete features, a hippo, a crocodile, and a purple sofa that pay tribute to the builder's imagination. They may not sound fun, but they are.

From around April to September, flood levels are high and the area around the camp is flooded. Then Jacana is best visited as a base for mokoro excursions, as game drives would entail a 20-minute boat ride to reach the jetty, the nearest point where Jacana's vehicles can be parked.

During the rest of the year game drives are possible from the island. Though simpler than some of the Delta's camps, Jacana is a beautiful and a very good-value choice for a couple of nights, especially towards the end of the dry season.

Rates (2005): US$595 per person sharing/single from July to October; US$430 for April, May, June and November. Includes all meals, activities, park fees, laundry, and most drinks. Excludes transfers. Open: April to November.

Tubu Tree Camp (5 tents)
Newly opened in June 2002, Tubu is one of Wilderness Safaris' vintage camps. This means that it's one of their simpler, less expensive camps (see page 174). It has five small tents on decks with en-suite shower, toilet and washbasin inside, plus a separate shower outside. The separate dining and lounge areas are also raised up and tented.

Tubu is west of the other three camps in the concession, with access to large areas of dry mopane and acacia woodlands. From around April to September, and perhaps later, mokoro trips and fishing ought to be possible – but for the rest of the year activities are limited to game drives and walks.

Rates (2005): US$595 per person sharing/single from July to October; US$430 for April, May, June and November. Includes all meals, activities, park fees, laundry, and most drinks. Excludes transfers. Open: 15 June to 15 November.

ABU CAMP AND MACATOO (NG26)

Visiting this large concession west of Moremi, the focus is more about the activities that you do here, rather than the environment. Abu Camp is the main place in the Delta for riding elephants, and Macatoo Camp is one of the Delta's two centres for horse-riding. The third camp, which I won't cover here, is the relatively famous hunting camp, Selby's.

Getting there and away
The only option for these camps is to make advanced bookings and fly in; there's an airstrip near Abu Camp which is used by both operations. Driving here is totally impractical.

When to visit
Because the focus of a trip here is the experience of horse-riding or the interactions with elephants, it's fine as long as you avoid the rains. So visit anytime from late-April/May to around mid–end December.

Flora and fauna highlights
The finer details of the wildlife in this concession tend to be eclipsed by the experience of the horses that you ride, or the elephants that you're with – hence I will make only relatively sketchy comments here on the wild fauna in this area.

However, you will find here most of the Delta's usual big game, including elephant, buffalo, giraffe, blue wildebeest, kudu, tsessebe, red lechwe, impala, zebra, reedbuck, steenbok, warthog, baboons and vervet monkeys. Lion and spotted hyena are the dominant predators, with occasional appearances by leopards and wild dogs.

That said, like NG25 to the north, and NG29 and 30 to the south, I don't think that the variation and density of game is quite up to the levels of, say, central Moremi or some of the areas on the north side of the Delta. However, rest assured that you'll still see plenty of game when visiting here.

Elephant-back safaris

This is the original elephant-back safari operation, which has since been emulated by several camps in various parts of southern Africa. (Grey Matters, in NG26, is the Okavango's only other place which offers interactions with non-wild elephants.) It's the Delta's most expensive place to visit and is run by Randall Jay Moore, one of its more colourful characters.

Some claim it's simply the ultimate in amazing safari experiences; others detest the whole idea of riding on trained elephants. If you can afford it, you can make up your own mind.

Basic trip information

For further information, contact Elephant Back Safaris: P Bag 332, Maun; tel: 661260; fax: 661005; email: ebs@info.bw; web: www.elephantbacksafaris.com.

The elephants

The camp is named after the lead elephant, Abu, which has starred in various films, including *White Hunter Black Heart* and *The Power of One*. Abu was brought over to Africa from the USA by its trainer, Randall Moore, and gradually a small herd of 12 elephants has been assembled – most of which are orphans. They range from youngsters of six months to Abu, who is 40 years old.

The experience

The activities here are flexible, depending on both the guests and the elephants, but will usually include either a morning elephant ride, or a whole-day excursion, travelling with the elephants to a shady spot for a long picnic lunch, and then back with them in the late afternoon. Alternatively 4WDs and, depending on water levels, mekoro or boats are always available.

Riding on the elephants involves using large custom-made saddles. Although comfortable, in many ways this feels more detached than walking beside them. When you're riding, the other game is largely unaware of your human presence, but the real fascination of these trips is not the other game that you see, or even the 'riding' itself. It is the experience of being so close to the elephants; being able to walk beside them as they plod along and being comfortable with them at close quarters, rather than viewing them from afar.

Abu Camp (5 tents)

When Ker & Downey was involved with this operation, Abu Camp stood on the site that today is occupied by Nxabega. The new Abu Camp also overlooks a lagoon and consists of five very luxurious tents raised up on teak decking. They've been carefully designed using an interior skeleton of wooden poles with walls of canvas stretched between them. Despite being far from most people's image of a tent, they retain the zipped doors and roll-down windows of more traditional safari tents.

ABU CAMP'S ELEPHANTS

There are about a dozen trained elephants at Abu Camp at the moment. The older ones have mostly come from zoos in the USA, whilst many of the younger ones are orphans from the Kruger National Park, in South Africa. They include:

Abu – a large bull with matching tusks, born around 1960. Probably from East Africa or the Kruger Park, he was taken when small to the United States, where he was used for rides at a wildlife park in Grand Prairie, Texas. He was returned to Africa in 1988, to feature in the movie, Circles in a Forest, and moved to Botswana in 1990. He's appeared in many films since, and Randall Moore describes him as an exceptionally calm, intelligent and gentle bull.

Cathy – the matriarch of the herd, distinguished by her shorter left tusk, is the herd's largest adult cow and was also born around 1960. She was captured in Murchison Falls National Park, Uganda, when young, and taken to a zoo outside Toronto. She returned to Africa with Abu in 1988, and came to Botswana in 1990.

Benny – a large, mature bull, Benny has a floppy right ear and no tusks. Born around 1959, he was captured in the Kruger, moved to Brookfield Zoo in Chicago and later to the Fort Worth Zoo, in Texas. He returned to Africa with Cathy and Abu, though took a long time to adapt to his new surroundings and is described as 'shy and nervous'.

Mthondo mbomvo – a strong and stocky bull with a broad head and even, splayed tusks, Mthondo was born around 1975. He was originally from Zimbabwe, but translocated when young to South Africa's Pilanesburg Reserve. There he caused trouble, knocking down tents in a hunting camp and harassing visitors, and so in 1993 he was moved to this herd. Now he is regarded by the trainers as quiet and dependable.

Nandipa – is one of the herd's young female elephants, distinguished by the hole in her right ear. Her tusks are even and straight, close to the trunk. She was born around 1988, orphaned in Kruger, and moved here in 1990.

Inside they're all slightly different, but very stylish; they're amongst the most luxurious rooms in the Delta. Some beds are mahogany antique 'sleigh-style', whilst others are four-posters. The floors are beautifully polished teak, dotted with matching rugs. Bathrooms are all spacious and en suite, with a stand-alone shower, flush toilet, washbasins and either a copper or a porcelain bath. Pictures, ornaments and carvings of elephants (and especially of Abu) are all over the camp. Outside each is a shaded deck with comfy canvas chairs.

The dining area is set on an expanse of tiered teak decking punctuated by jackalberry trees, *Diospyros mespiliformis*, and sycamore figs, *Ficus sycomorus*. This stands in front of the main lounge, which has comfy chairs and a small library. The food is good and the service attentive, as you'd expect of a camp which regularly hosts the world's glitterati as guests.

The costs

This is Botswana's most expensive camp. Trips here take a maximum of 10 visitors, and last a fixed duration of 5 nights – always starting on a Wednesday and ending on a Monday. (Thus leaving two days of the week when the elephants do not have any guests to deal with!)

Shirheni – Shirheni, another young female, was born around 1986 and was also orphaned in Kruger. She is similar to Nandipa but slightly larger in size. She moved here in 1989 and gave birth to a young bull in November 2000, named Pula, after she was mated by a wild bull on February 20 1999.

Pula – born to Shirheni on November 27 2000 at 6.30 am, after a night of heavy rain. Pula is the Setswana word for rain or success, as well as the name of Botswana's currency. At birth he was 91cm high and it took an hour before he made his first hesitant steps. He is described as very playful and confident.

Jika – has very short tusks that are close to her trunk. Another Kruger Park orphan, she was born around 1988. She also joined Elephant Back Safaris in 1990, and is described as the herd's 'dizzy blonde'!

Seba – Seba was born around 1995, and is also an orphan from Kruger. Seba is said to be often surrounded by the young females in the herd, and is the star of the Walt Disney film, Whispers, which was released in 2000.

Thando – with some distinctive 'red' hair on his head, Thando was born around 1986 and brought to Botswana as an orphan from Kruger in 1990.

Kitimetse II – a name which means 'I'm Lost', was found at the end of 1999 after she had been injured by a crocodile and abandoned by her own wild herd. She was brought to the boma at Abu Camp, where her wounds were treated and she was slowly introduced to the rest of the herd. She seems to have been completely accepted by the other elephants, and formed close bonds with Jika, Nandipa and Shirheni. She is thought to have been born around 1996.

Mufunyani – which means 'The Irritable One', is another orphan from Kruger who joined this herd in 1990. In February 2002, the 14-year-old bull was released back in to the wild with a satellite tracking collar, as part of a research project. So far, he is becoming accustomed to a new life as a wild elephant, but usually stays fairly close to Abu Camp.

Costs for this trip are US$7,500 per person sharing, or US$10,500 if you're travelling alone, and this includes flights to/from Maun, accommodation, meals, drinks, laundry and all activities.

The terms and conditions of the company's fine print are, unusually, worth noting as they insist on a high (30%) deposit. Read them very carefully if you're thinking of booking, and be sure to book at least a year in advance.

Safety issues

In common with many safari camps throughout Africa, all visitors here are required to sign an indemnity form which, basically, absolves the camp from any responsibility for your safety whilst participating in a trip. And as when visiting any camp in the bush, you accept that you're taking on certain risks to do with Africa's animals and their unpredictability that you wouldn't face sitting on the couch at home.

The only difference here is that being in such close proximity to such huge, strong animals does present a greater risk than most normal photographic safaris.

As an example of this, in early May 2000 a 27-year-old bull named Nyaka Nyaka killed one of the camp's professional guides, Andre Klocke. He had approached the elephant from behind to take its saddle off and accidentally startled the animal. The incident had equally grave consequences for Nyaka Nyaka, who was subsequently shot.

That said, no client has ever been injured by one of the elephants in its eleven years of operation. Despite this sad incident, the camp prides itself on a very high safety record.

Riding safaris

For African Horseback Safaris (PO Box 20538, Maun; tel/fax: 663154; email: sjhorses@info.bw; web: www.africanhorseback.com) see page 167.

These riding safaris are run by Sarah-Jane Gullick, who is English by birth and clearly has horses in her blood, having been involved in hunting, eventing and even worked on a Dude ranch in Wyoming before getting hooked on Africa. She set this operation up in 1994, originally with Ker & Downey Safaris (based out of a camp called Macateer Camp).

Basic trip information

Below is some basic information for these trips. Contact African Horseback Safaris if you need more precise details as they've a lot of information about their trips that they can send.

Riding ability required.

These safaris are for experienced riders aged 12 years and over. Riders over 60 need to be 'riding fit' and strong. These trips usually involve about 4–6 hours in the saddle each day. Thus riders need to feel competent about keeping up with the group, capable of riding at all paces; rising to the trot and controlling your horse at the canter. They may also be required to gallop out of trouble, so these trips do not take beginners. For safety reasons, if they think that your riding is not up to standard, you won't be allowed to ride here.

The horses

The horses are a variety of thoroughbreds, Namibian Hanovarians, Arabs and Kalahari-Arab crossbreeds ranging from 14 to 16.2 hands (140–165cm) high.

Weight limits

There's a weight limit of 15 stone per person (210lbs or 95kg), over which they can sometimes make special arrangements for advanced riders.

Tack and clothes

Good quality English- and Western-style trail saddles are supplied, each with its own water bottle. They can lend riders half chaps; long leather boots are impractical.

African Horseback Safaris does not supply hard hats or safety helmets; you must bring your own. They suggest that riders wear their riding clothes and boots on the plane, and bring their hat and wash bag as hand luggage, in case your luggage gets delayed.

The experience

See the section on Okavango Horse Safaris, pages 327–30, for more general comments about the fascinating experience of riding through the Okavango. These apply equally well to both operations. Suffice to say that once you step into the saddle, most of the Okavango's resident game will treat you and your horse as a single, composite four-legged herbivore. So antelope will relax around you, and predators will give you pause for thought!

African Horseback Safaris request visitors come for a minimum of seven nights. This will always start on arrival in camp with an introductory talk on the safari, and a safety briefing. Two guides will accompany each riding safari; they carry a first-aid kit, rifle and radio.

Such trips normally incorporate not only riding, but also the occasional game drive, walk and night drive. Boating, canoeing and fishing are also possible sometimes, depending on water levels. Their riding groups have a maximum of 6–8 guests, and a typical 7-day trip would include a few nights spent out at a fly-camp away from the main camp. Note that these trips usually start and end on Tuesdays and Fridays, and seven- or ten-day safaris are the norm.

The camps
These aim to be comfortable and simple, and all are staffed. As with most camps, the service is a good standard with high-quality food prepared freshly. Dinner is usually a stylish three-course affair, served by candlelight. The main camp used as a base is:

Macatoo Camp (4 tents)
Like Okavango Horse Safaris' camps in neighbouring NG29 (see pages 327–30), this is a specialist camp used purely for riders. Each of this small camp's four large tents has twin beds, and each tent has its own en-suite shower and loo. There is a furnished mess tent, a small splash pool and a daily laundry service here.

Fly-camps (set up as/where required)
The longer safaris here usually include a couple of nights sleeping at a mobile fly camp, where the ablutions are a traditional bucket shower and loo.

The costs
A stay here costs US$330 per person per night, including all meals, drinks and activities from March to May, and November to January. This rises to US$445 in the 'high season' between June and October, though if you stay 7 nights or more then the cost is US$395 per person per night. There's a minimum stay allowed of three or four nights, and safaris are generally timed to start and end on Tuesdays and Fridays.

Transfers to/from Maun are US$137 per person, one way. Macatoo use Abu's airstrip, which is between one and two hours' drive from camp.

POM POM, KANANA AND NXABEGA (NG27A)
This large, strictly photographic concession is now effectively split between three safari companies: Ker & Downey who run Kanana, CCAfrica who run Nxabega, and Wilderness Safaris who recently took over Pom Pom.

Concession history
By the early 1970s there were a number of camps throughout the Delta, most of which accepted either hunting or photographic guests. One of the bigger companies involved here was Safari South, who ran many camps including Khwai River Lodge, Four Rivers Camp (near the present Kwara), Queenie, Splash, Jedibe, Machaba, Mombo, Pom Pom, Shindi and others.

Around 1985 Ker & Downey was split from Safari South, as a wholly-owned subsidiary, to differentiate the photographic camps from those used for hunting.

Then Ker & Downey had four photographic camps in the Delta: Shinde, Mombo, Jedibe & Machaba.

A company called Jao Safaris owned Mombo at that time. Various contracts changed, which resulted in Ker & Downey leaving Mombo and Jedibe. (These were eventually taken up by Wilderness Safaris, in 1989.) Meanwhile, the government had designated NG27 for photographic use only, and Ker & Downey took over the running of Pom Pom, which had been another old hunting camp run by Safari South.

From 1985 Pom Pom was the only major camp here, but in 1990 they started a 'partnership' with Randall J Moore. He brought trained African elephants over from the USA to start 'Elephant Back Safaris' and Ker & Downey built Abu Camp – which from 1991 stood on the site that Nxabega now occupies, in the north of the reserve.

In 1993 I was very excited to visit Pom Pom – and to get here I took my first flight over the Delta! It was then one of Botswana's most upmarket camps, and all of the rest of the clientele during my stay were from America. The combination of staying at Pom Pom for a few days, and then Abu Camp was a winning one; business was good for them. (Note that throughout this time there were also a few simple bushcamps in the area, used by various operators.)

However, the following year Randall Moore tendered for, and obtained, his own concession next door: NG26. This upset the apple cart, as he then built the camp that is today known as Abu Camp – thus taking away a highly profitable chunk of business from Ker & Downey.

NG27 concession has always been subdivided. First AfroVentures (who subsequently merged with CCAfrica) built Nxabega Camp on the site of the old Abu Camp, in the north. Then in 2000 Ker & Downey opened their own new camp, Kanana – which they now own.

Most recently, in 2001, Wilderness Safaris have taken over the marketing and management of Pom Pom, building a completely new small camp here, but keeping the name and location of the 'old' Pom Pom.

Getting there and away

All of these camps work only with guests flying in, usually having made their bookings months before they travel. Driving here is not possible without permission and totally impractical.

When to visit

Slightly less seasonal than the areas further south and west, there's still a big difference between the game densities through the seasons; they're a lot better when it's drier. As usual, the birding is as good as it gets during the wetter time of the year (December to around March).

Flora and fauna highlights

Travelling from south to north, the landscapes, flora and fauna change very slowly, but there are slight differences between the different parts of the reserve. Bear in mind whilst reading this that the similarities between the different areas are much greater than their differences.

Flora

The NG27 concession is in the heart of the Delta and contains most of the environments that are to be found in the Delta. Everywhere you'll find thickets and stands of riverine forest, more open areas of invasive bushes, and occasional floodplains.

The area around Pom Pom is very open and pretty, notable for many tiny islands amidst wide open floodplains, which are often submerged between May and September. These distinct islands are often covered, or at least fringed, by real fan (*Hyphaene petersiana*) and wild date palms (*Phoenix reclinata*), and between them are large marshy floodplains. There are quite a few baobabs in the area, and the forest patches here are fairly sparse.

Moving northeast to the area of Kanana, there are less of the flat, open plains and more areas colonised by expanses of wild sage. Around these are larger islands and woodland patches with plenty of the Delta's usual riverine tree species – sausage trees, *Kigelia africana*, jackalberries, *Diospyros mespiliformis*, knobthorns, *Acacia nigrescens*, the occasional marula, *Sclerocarya birrea caffra*, and the odd raintree, *Lonchocarpus capassa*. (Also sometimes called the appleleaf, the raintree gets it name from the droplets which are secreted by froghopper insects as they suck the sap from the leaves. This keeps the soil beneath the tree moist, and in exceptional cases can even form pools.)

Further northwest, around Nxabega, the forests become more in evidence with large, dense lines of broadleaf forests and patches of acacia. Mixed with these are a few open plains, fringed by real fan palms (*Hyphaene petersiana*) and stands of riverine trees. In the midst of the larger floodplains you'll see occasional islands crowned with an African mangosteen, *Garcinia livingstonei*, or perhaps a large sycamore fig, *Ficus sycomorus*, growing out of an old termite mound perhaps surrounded by a few russet bush-willow bushes, *Combretum hereroense*. Some of the Nxabega's floodplains have thick coverings of hippo grass (*Vossia cuspidata*) that turn a lovely shade of orange-red around September.

Fauna

The variety of game in NG27 certainly seems wider to me than that found in areas further south and west – though I feel that it's not as wide as some of the reserves on the northeast side of the Delta. Tsessebe, impala, wildebeest, lechwe, steenbok, baboon and zebra are all common and seen here very regularly. Giraffe do particularly well here, they're very relaxed amongst the many acacia thickets, and there is a good number of resident elephants.

THE LIZARD

There's a tale of a slightly fussy, older woman coming to stay on her own in a tented safari camp. Over lunch she complained about a lizard in her room, but was told this was nothing to worry about – and it'd probably vanish of its own accord soon.

That afternoon after lunch, whilst most of the camp was having a siesta, she wandered out in search of one of the staff. 'That lizard is still in my room,' she proclaimed, with agitation, to one of the managers that she found in the dining room. He then explained that this was really nothing to worry about, as lizards often came in and out of the rooms. In fact, he elaborated, 'it's very good as they're natural way of keeping the mosquito population down.' So, she could go back and sleep, relaxed in the knowledge that it wouldn't do her any harm at all.

Off she went, but 20 minutes later she was back again. She couldn't sleep, claiming that the lizard was making too much noise. Unimpressed, but determined to satisfy the guest, the manager took her back to the room – only to be completely embarrassed by finding a huge monitor lizard thrashing about, trying to find a way out of the tent.

Lion and spotted hyena are the commonest large predators, though the mixed woodland is a perfect habitat for leopard that are numerous, though only seen occasionally. Cheetah are seen here only rarely, when the reserve is at its driest (October to March); they're not at all common. Wild dog pass through periodically (as they do through most areas of northern Botswana) though not frequently. Both black-backed and side-striped jackal are common here.

As with most of the Delta there's always plenty of smaller animals, too widespread to be worthy of particular comment ... though I recall a great sighting of an entertaining troop of dwarf mongooses here once!

Birdlife

The birding is good and very varied in this concession. Kanana has immediate access to the deep channel of the Xudum channel that is lined with a mixture of water figs, huge floating mats of graceful papryus and anchored sections of miscanthus grass (*Miscanthus junceus*). Amongst the birdlife here, there's a notable profusion of squacco herons. However, what is really interesting in the Kanana area is the recent discovery (October 2001) of two heronries. One is small, whilst another is described as being as big as the heronry at Gcodikwe Lagoon. When found this had many birds breeding there, including yellow-billed, marabou and open-billed storks, darters, cormorants and egrets. (I haven't yet seen this, but how such a large heronry went 'unnoticed' for so long is a complete puzzle.) However fascinating, visitors must remember the problems that disturbances can cause to the birds; don't encourage your guide to approach too close to the birds.

Nxabega doesn't have the heronry, though one recent September over 500 open-billed storks and about 1,000 squacco herons were seen gathering to roost just a little west of Nxabega. It does, however, have a couple of very old pole bridges across small waterways in its reserve. These prove particularly attractive perching places for waterbirds that can then be seen while driving. (This is an advantage if, like me, it's a help to have a stationary base from which to use a camera and tripod, rather than a rocking boat.) Lots of hamerkops, small herons, egrets (including a good number of slaty), black crakes and bee-eaters. Kingfishers are well-represented; here I've got closer to photograph a diminutive malachite kingfisher than I ever have whilst on a boat.

Read the marketing literature for almost any camp in the Delta and you'll realise that claims for sightings of 'the elusive Pel's fishing owl' are a tedious marketing cliché. Every camp simultaneously trumpets their rarity, and yet claims you'll see one whilst staying there. That said, when I last visited Nxabega, one such owl was making predictable, regular appearances on one of the old bridges, and the guides advised that three pairs were regularly seen in different locations in the area. Meanwhile, I'm reliably informed that in 2002 a pair of Pel's fishing owls were seen in, and said to be nesting in, trees about 100m from camp.

Having said all that about the resident birds that associate with water, you'll find an equally good variety of drier-country birds in this reserve. On my last visit just amongst the eagles, I spotted tawny, bateleur, Wahlberg's and, most remarkable, near Pom Pom a martial eagle battled with a large monitor lizard on the ground beside our vehicle. (We found both locked in combat, but at a stalemate. Eventually they disentangled themselves and the great lizard made a hasty retreat under a bush.)

Finally, on a more domestic note, the staff at Nxabega seems to have 'tamed' a pair of wild yellow-billed hornbills sufficiently for them to come along to afternoon tea on most afternoons.

Where to stay

All the camps are totally different, perhaps because they're run in different ways by different companies.

Kanana (8 tents) contact Ker & Downey, see page 172
Opened in May 2000, Kanana is built a few kilometres from the site of an old basic bushcamp known as Khurunxaragha Camp (which was formerly used by Wilderness for their mobile safaris, and was located near the present airfield). Kanana stands at roughly the centre of NG27 (✪ KANANA 19°32.577'S; 22°51.731'E), and overlooks the reedbeds of the Xudum River. This gives the camp access to a permanent, deep-water channel for boating all year.

Accommodation is in one of eight very comfortable tents that spread out on the left side of the main area. These are separated by about 20m, and so even the furthest room isn't miles from the centre of camp. These have sewn-in insect-proof groundsheets and six large mesh windows – even the front of the tent can be opened up into a large mesh area, giving a wonderful airy feel when it's warm.

Inside, the floor's teak, covered with sisal matting. These tents are comfortable and well furnished with a wooden wardrobe and a luggage rack, dressing table and chairs, and plenty of thoughtful touches. The raffia bedside tables have electric lights powered by solar-powered batteries – the camp's generator is usually only switched on during the day. Twin or double beds have good-quality cotton sheets and down pillows with blankets. A canvas divider separates the en-suite flush toilet, washbasin and shower (very efficient too – hot water from individual gas geysers).

Outside on the shaded veranda, to the front and side of the tents, there's a table and comfy chairs, and all the tents face the river from under a cover of riverine trees – jackalberries, knobthorns and sausage trees. These are linked by sandy paths, illuminated at night by electric lanterns, one of which passes the small, circular waist-deep plunge pool.

Kanana's main area is a U-shaped wooden building with a large tree in the centre and a long dining room, several small lounge areas (one with a small library), a bar and down nearer the water, a 'sandpit' for fires.

Activities possible here include boat trips (including fishing for bream or catfish), mokoro excursions (often including short island walks) and game drives. Though their comfortable vehicles have been carefully thought out, with canvas pockets for binoculars and lots of space, the camp's strongest suit is its mokoro trips. It's particularly convenient that when water levels are good, these can be launched directly from the side of the lodge's main area, and into the reedbeds which surround the Xudum River.

As with most camps, Kanana works on the basis of one long safari activity after breakfast, then siesta time after lunch, and another afternoon/evening activity after afternoon tea, before dinner. Sometimes a late night drive is possible after dinner.
Rates (2005): US$495/695 per person sharing/single from July to October including all meals, activities and park fees; US$410/460 per person sharing/single for the rest of the year. Open: March to the end of November.

Nxabega (10 tents – but maximum 18 guests) contact CC Africa, see page 170
Built on the site of the original Abu Camp, Nxabega (✪ NXABEG 19°29.080'S; 22°47.670'E) is the most northerly of the camps in NG27. It's about an hour's drive north of Kanana (though only around 12km as the birds fly!) and 11km south-southeast of Xigera, which is in Moremi. However, for most of the year Xigera is inaccessible by land from Nxabega because of the Boro River.

Nxabega first opened in 1997, designed simply but with style, like its sister-lodge, Sandibe. However, in September 1999 the whole of the central lounge/dining area burnt to the ground, along with the closest tent (number seven). These were rebuilt and re-opened six months later. This seems to have combined in Nxabega the benefits of a new camp, like design lessons learned from the previous one, with an experienced team of staff.

Nxabega's new lounge/dining area is constructed on a grand scale from wood, stone and a high shaggy thatched roof – around a huge jackalberry tree. Inside, it is swish but understated; with clean lines and teak-panelled walls. The large dining table area stands under two electric candelabras. Nearby in the lounge are two separate groups of luxurious settees. Heavy glass-topped coffee tables rest on game-skin patchworks, supporting the odd picture book, cigar boxes and a backgammon set. It's comfortably done with style and the odd striking African artefact (sadly of West rather than southern African origin!). The bar is almost hidden, but stocked exceedingly comprehensively with obscure liqueurs, imported spirits and good wines. (Unlimited house wine, beers and soft drinks are normally included in the rate, but if you want to drink their cellar of vintage wines dry, they'll charge extra!)

The ten rooms are high quality, large tents raised up on platforms about a metre above the ground, overlooking the floodplain. All are well spread out, with a discreet 30–40m between them. Number one is on the far right of the lodge (as you look over the water); numbers six and seven are on either side of the main area; and number ten (the honeymoon suite) is past the large swimming pool on the left side. Each has a shaded veranda with table and chairs outside. Inside, twin or double beds stand on a smooth wooden floor, draped with quality cotton sheets, down duvets and assorted pillows.

These tents are furnished well – with chairs, a dressing table, wardrobe and bedside lamps (powered by a solar-powered battery system). At the back of each tent is a small en-suite bathroom with a flush toilet, hot shower (heated by a gas geyser), and a washbasin.

Activities include day and night 4WD game drives, mokoro excursions and boat trips (good fishing is possible on the Boro River). Nxabega's been constructed with care and generally seems to be run with a higher complement of staff than most lodges (average two staff per guest). This gives it an air of quality. The food is particularly good, but what I appreciated more was the flexibility that visitors have over everything, from the timings of breakfast and lunch, to the scheduling of activities. These are seldom regimented, and the staff make real efforts to organise activities to suit you. If you've ever wanted to do a late-night drive after dinner to look for aardvarks, or a mid-day boating trip … Nxabega is a good choice!

Rates: US$430/645 per person sharing/single from July to October including all meals, activities and park fees; US$355/530 per person sharing/single for the rest of the year. Open: all year

Nxabega Trails Camp (4 tents) contact CCAfrica, see page 170
In the same area as Nxabega is a small, simple bushcamp used by some of the mobile safaris run by AfroVentures. This is one of the places that the brochure blurbs refer to when they say that a trip will stay 'in the Delta in a small bushcamp'.

The camp itself is essentially temporary, and when I visited it had just a few simple 3m by 3m dome tents on a small palm island. Each has twin beds with mattresses, pillows and blankets. All four sides of these particular tents opened up to reveal sides of gauze netting. Outside each was a canvas wash-stand, and the whole area was lit by oil lamps. Toilets were shared and there were bucket showers (suspended from convenient trees and screened off behind reed walls).

Activities were mainly mokoro trips with short walks on the islands, plus perhaps the occasional drive. They were arranged so that the visitors to the trails camp never saw anything to do with Nxabega, and vice versa – how a wilderness experience ought to be.

Rates: A stay here is never sold on its own, it's always part of a larger mobile trip visiting a number of bushcamps with a private guide. Open: all year.

Pom Pom (6 tents) contact Okavango Wilderness Safaris, see page 174
One of the original upmarket camps in the Delta, Pom Pom (⊕ POMPOM 19°35.072'S; 22°50.560'E) is barely 5km southwest of Kanana, though this is about 45 minutes' drive. Pom Pom was originally opened here by Ker & Downey in 1985, but was later re-built by Wilderness when they took it over in 2001.

Pom Pom's six tents are all on the ground on the edge of a small island overlooking a lagoon. Two are west of the central area; four are on the east side. These are standard Meru-style tents furnished with twin or double beds, a wicker chair, and a wooden dresser and wardrobe. The toilet and washbasin are en suite, whilst the private (hot) shower is reached through a zipped entrance at the back of the tent and covered by a canvas roof.

Activities here include day and night drives, mokoro trips and short walks. These walks were expertly led by one of the camp's managers, Brian, on our last visit. Excursions by boat are only occasionally possible when water levels are very high. (The main flood hits here around May, often filling the dry lagoon in a day. The area's highest water levels usually occur around June to August.)

This rustic camp looks out on to a small permanent lagoon, fringed by lilies. The bar is a simple wooden counter with a few stools built around a large strangler fig and there are two dining areas, one under canvas and the other open. The wooden coffee tables and wicker chairs of the lounge stand under a canvas roof, together with a small but informative selection of books and a backgammon set. This proved a very friendly and compact little camp when last visited; it had a great atmosphere.

Rates (2005): US$595 per person sharing/single from July to October; US$430 for April, May, June and November. Includes all meals, activities, park fees, laundry, and most drinks. Excludes transfers. Open: April to November.

DELTA, ODDBALLS, GUNN'S AND EAGLE ISLAND (NG27B)

Between NG30, NG32 and Moremi stands a fairly small photographic reserve, just off the southwest side of Chief's Island. This was the first area of the Okavango where tourism really took off in volume, and it's now very interesting to see it making the transition to smaller numbers of visitors, and more upmarket camps.

Concession history

A short history of the Delta and Oddballs camps is an interesting illustration of the transition between different types of tourism mentioned above. It started shortly after *Lodges of Botswana* bought Delta Camp in 1983. During their first year they not only catered to upmarket visitors, but also used the camp as a base for the mokoro trips of more budget-conscious travellers.

This mix didn't work in one camp, and so in 1984 they built a separate lower-budget camp at the other end of their island. The nickname of their first manager was 'Oddball', and so this became Oddball's Camp. Oddball's marketing was astute and well targeted, portraying a relaxed, hippie hangout where spaced-out campers could find paradise on their own island in the Delta. This became a buzzing base for budget mokoro trips in the heart of the Delta – *the* backpacker's place in the Delta, known in hostels from Nairobi to Cape Town, and beyond.

It was very successful. At first they just had showers, toilets and a (fridge-less) bar; campers brought all their own food and kit. It grew fast, eventually encompassing a shop for campers and food, as well as chilled drinks from a fully-fledged bar.

When business peaked during the late 80s and early 90s, they had up to 120 visitors *per day* flying in, some camping for a night in the camp and others heading out on mokoro trips. Then there were no limits on how many visitors the camp could accept. The camp had a rule that every visitor had to stay at Oddball's for at least one night.

Then two things happened which changed this business. Firstly, in July 1989 the government raised its national park fees from P10 per person per week to P30 per person per day. Mokoro trips from Oddball's had always been to Moremi, and this increased their prices dramatically.

Secondly, there had long been a process of 'tendering' for camps – whereby safari operators bid for the lease to operate safari camps. In 1996 the government introduced new leases to camps in many of the Delta's reserves, insisting that safari companies not only produce large cheques for rental and royalties (per visitor), but also a 'management plan' for the reserves. These became effective in January 1997.

In drawing up these detailed management plans, the safari companies were forced to look not only at their game and environmental policies, and the sustainability of them, but also how they trained their staff, and what they were doing to help the wider community in the area. This process raised the issues of sustainability, responsible tourism and community development – and placed them in the centre of the government's decision-making process. Thus, it made them important to the safari operators.

Oddball's had started a programme of training their polers as early as 1988. Like all camps, it now insists that all of its polers have a qualification as a professional mokoro guide. The government insists that standards like these are now applied across the board for all the camps in the region.

By 1997 Oddballs alone had about 35 mokoro guides working for them. They were able to renew their leases on Oddball's and its smaller, upmarket sister-camp, Delta Camp. However, the government had made a hard bargain: they had to reduce the number of visitors down to a maximum combined total of 60 people at any one time. That was 40 guests at Oddball's and 20 at Delta Camp, a fraction of past numbers.

Immediately prices had to be increased in order to cover their costs from a much smaller base of visitors. In December 1999 both camps were extensively renovated; the economics dictated that they had to move more upmarket, charging more, to stay in business. The camp on the Oddball's site was rebuilt in much greater style, as a fully fledged upmarket camp that could command high prices. Then the names of the two camps were switched. This newly built camp on the site of Oddball's old site is now known as Delta Camp. Whilst the older camp which was once known as Delta Camp became Oddballs (without an apostrophe this time).

Thus the budget 1980s camp has became an upmarket camp for the next century; whilst the original budget camp has been totally rebuilt and refurbished as a new luxurious camp, to standards which are now so much higher than they were.

This is a text-book example of what has happened right across Botswana. Pressure from the government, using park fees and the concessions as tools of implementation, has led to lower numbers of visitors right across Botswana's wild areas, and hence to more costly safaris and more upmarket lodges. For their money visitors now get a much more exclusive experience, guided by polers who have more training and better skills than before – and are paid better as the result.

In summary: the environment benefits, the local people benefit, Botswana's finances benefit, and even the visitors get a better experience – that is, those who can still afford to visit!

Geography note

As with the whole Delta, the floods in this area are variable and unpredictable, in both duration and timing. The flood usually arrives between March and August, and remains for an average of four months. However, hydrologists note that there has been a measured decrease in the amount of water flowing down the Boro River since the late 1980s. In the 1994/5 period of water inflow, it was estimated that the lower Boro River received little over half of its long-term average. That water flow has since gradually decreased.

This could be explained by postulating that the western side of the Delta is gradually rising relative to the eastern side. Hence the Thaoge is gradually flooding less, and the Khwai is flooding more. The Boro is fairly central to the Delta, and derives its flow from the Nqoga River (the source of the Khwai River). However, it breaks from this at a very sharp, acute angle, and hence some experts suggest that it should be considered as being influenced the same way as the rivers on the western side of the Delta.

Having said all this, some say that changes in water flows could be caused simply by a hippo changing its regular path in the higher reaches of the Delta! Whatever the cause, this reduced flow isn't necessarily good or bad for the visitor; but it is a help in understanding some of the gradual changes which are happening (over decades) to the area's vegetation.

Getting there and away

Although years ago safari operators used to offer boat transfers up the Boro River from Maun to here, now flying in is really the only way. There are several airstrips, including Delta airstrip (✪ DELAIR 19°31.840'S; 23°05.430'E), which is closest to both Oddballs and Delta Camp, and about 4km southwest from there is Xaxaba airstip (✪ XAXAIR 19°33.220'S; 23°03.510'E).

When to visit

Though open all year, these camps rely primarily on mokoro trips and so are certainly at their best when the sun is shining and the sky blue. That is between April and November. If you're camping out then it makes for a better trip if it's not too cold at night, thus my favourite months for visiting here would be around May–early June and September–October time.

Flora and fauna highlights

The Boro River and its associated floodplains dominate this reserve. In a recent land survey (1996) they estimated that only about 4% of the whole reserve was permanent swampland, but 75% was classed as seasonally inundated swamp and grasslands. The remaining 22% is dry land: riverine forests and grasslands on the islands. So this is a very seasonal environment, which changes annually with the floods.

Flora

As noted above, there is relatively little permanent swamp here. Small patches of papyrus are found though, usually in photogenic little clumps beside the main Boro River. Look carefully and you'll also find areas of common reeds (*Phragmites australis*), Miscanthus grass (*Miscanthus junceus*), bulrushes (*Typha capensis*) and a number of floating leafed, emergent and submerged species.

Perhaps the major feature of the area is some splendid, mature patches of riverine forests that line sections of the Boro River. Here you'll find lots of real fan palms (*Hyphaene petersiana*), often in beautiful dense stands. There's also a scattering of all the 'usual suspects' that you'd expect in riverine forest in the region, including leadwoods (*Combretum imberbe*), jackalberries (*Diospyros mespiliformis*), knobthorns (*Acacia negrescens*), sausage trees (*Kigelia africana*), large fever-berries (*Croton megalobotrys*), woodland waterberries (*Syzygium guineense*) and occasional baobab trees (*Adansonia digitata*). However, perhaps the area's most unusual flora are the huge strangler figs (*Ficus* species, probably *thonningii*, *natalensis* or *fischeri*). There are several specimens here enveloping large leadwood trees – an amazing sight.

On the larger island, and particularly on Chief's Island (in Moremi, but visited from these camps), you'll find permanently dry forest areas. These vary from mopane woodlands in areas of clay soil, to areas of acacias where there's more sand.

In the deepest areas of sand you'll find *Terminalia sericea* – the source of the best wood from which to craft traditional mokoro poles.

Adjacent to the river are large areas of very shallow floodplains. A wide variety of grasses, sedges and herbs are found in these areas with various species of *Eragrostis, Imperata, Panicum, Aristida* and *Cymbo*pogen being common. Over 200 plant species have been recorded here, though the floodplains are very often dotted with a sparse covering of *Imperata cylindrica* – a plant sometimes known as 'silver spike', which has long, rigid leaf spikes growing from a rhizome, some with a small 'spikelet' at the end.

Mammals
None of the camps in this reserve conduct game drives, so a visit here is usually much more about the ambience of the Delta rather than spotting game. Come for the experience, let any game sightings be a bonus, and you'll have a good trip.

That said, there are good game densities in the area, and especially on the adjacent Chief's Island. Even from a mokoro you're likely to see hippopotami and crocodiles in the water. Elephants are frequently seen in the drier months, from May to October, wandering through the floodplains; from December to April they are around in smaller numbers.

When out walking on the islands there is a chance of much more game. The area's dominant antelope is the red lechwe, but you will also find tsessebe, impala, zebra, kudu, reedbuck, giraffe, warthog and buffalo. As the area becomes drier with time, blue wildebeest are being seen more often. Roan, sable and waterbuck remain absent from this area. When the flood is at its height, sitatunga are occasionally seen. With the recent reintroduction of rhino to Chief's Island, there's a very slim chance that you could bump into one of these.

The most common predators here are lion, spotted hyena and jackals. Leopard are rarely seen, but they will be relatively common as the riverine forest suits them perfectly. Wild dogs and cheetah also occur here, but are rare sightings. There was even a report from this area of a brown hyena sighting, though this is certainly a rarity here.

Birdlife
Birding is an important feature of all the trips here; you'll probably spend much of your time exploring the area from a mokoro. As mentioned above, the water levels can vary hugely – in October 2002 they dropped by 15cm in just three weeks. So expect the channels and the birdlife to vary greatly through the seasons.

When water levels are lowest, around November to February, you may find skimmers on some exposed sandbanks. Meanwhile knob-billed ducks, long-toed and blacksmith's plovers, and saddle-billed storks are amongst a whole host of permanent residents. As levels rise, red-winged pratincoles gather in large flocks, and there is always a good variety of kingfishers, from giant and pied to the tiny pygmy and malachite. Woodland kingfishers appear for the summer around the end of October – insectivorous birds which are usually seen hunting for insects in the riverine forest. They arrive with a variety of migrants, including the carmine bee-eaters, aerobatics yellow-billed kites, and paradise flycatchers, the males of which have the most spectacular tails. I've a reliable report of black coucals in front of Delta Camp, but haven't seen them there myself.

Much of the Boro's channel usually sees the annual catfish run (see box on page 359), and this area is no exception. If you're lucky enough to catch this then you can spot 30 species or more in a 100m stretch of waterway. Pelicans, skimmers and a wide variety of herons, egrets, storks, stilts, snipes and cormorants all appear in quantity then, to take advantage of the abundant food.

What to see and do

Though these camps differ slightly in their activities, they are essentially water-camps from which you take guided mokoro trips along the Boro River, and out onto its associated floodplains.

Most also offer walking trips on the islands – just as camps here have for decades. These generally use the bush-wise local polers as guides, whose local knowledge can be excellent (even if their communication skills in English are more variable). They will almost never be carrying any firearms for protection, so see my general comments about *Walking trips and safaris* in *Chapter 6*, for a further discussion of the safety issues raised by this approach.

Where to stay

Of the four camps in this reserve, Delta and Oddballs are run by Lodges of Botswana (see page 173); Semetsi Camps, and Gunn's Camp and Bushcamp are run by Crocodile Camps Safaris (see page 170).

Delta Camp (10 chalets)
Bought by Lodges of Botswana in 1983, Delta Camp has been run by them ever since – although at the start of 2001 the new camp built on the site of the old Oddball's Camp was renamed as Delta Camp.

The camp still overlooks the Boro River and its ten reed-and-thatch chalets all have open verandas looking northeast into Moremi. All have an en-suite bathroom, including a shower, toilet and wash basin.

Activities centre around mokoro trips, with walks on the islands guided by your poler. With a little advanced notice, it's possible to go on day-trips with picnic lunches.
Rates: US$360/450 per person sharing/single for November to March, May and June; US$420/490 for April and July to October. These prices include meals, all drinks, activities and park fees. US$65 per seat (each way) for flights between Maun and Delta's airstrip – with a strict 10kg luggage allowance. Open: all year.

Oddballs Palm Island Luxury Lodge (20 dome tents)
Southeast of Delta Camp, but still beside the same Boro River, Oddballs is still thought of as a destination in the Okavango for budget travellers, even though it's *much more* expensive than it was.

For your money, you now have your own 2.4m by 2.4m (three-person) dome tent which stands on a raised wooden deck, surmounted by a roll of reeds for shade. Outside is a view over the Delta, inside are two camp beds, with a mattress and pillow included, and on its veranda is a small table and two stools.

Unlike the backpacker's camp of old, a stay here now includes all your meals and activities. It usually includes a first and last night at Oddballs itself, with the intervening nights camping out on the islands. Then all your camping kit and food is provided (drinks are not – you buy these separately), but you do your own cooking whilst you're on the mokoro trail.
Rates: US$180/240 per person sharing/single, including meals, activities, and park fees for both the camp and the mokoro trails. Meals are cooked for you at camp; or by yourself whilst on the trails (ingredients provided). US$65 per seat (each way) for flights between Maun and Oddballs' airstrip – with a strict 10kg luggage allowance. Open: all year.

Gunn's Camp (7 tents and 1 chalet)

Gunn's is situated on the Boro River, overlooking Moremi Game Reserve, and was founded and run for years by the brusque Mike Gunn. It used to be accessed as often by motorboat as by plane from Maun, and in the 1980s it ran week-long 'fitness in the wilderness' courses which, amongst other things, taught you how to punt your own mokoro.

Since then it has been upgraded to a more upmarket camp, and in June 2002 Crocodile Camp Safaris took over the its management. Now it has seven Meru tents, each with twin beds, colourful fabrics and teak furniture. All have en-suite bathrooms with flush toilets and showers at the back, and a small sitting area outside with comfy chairs. The eighth room is their honeymoon chalet, which is thatched and raised up on wooden decking with a large veranda. This has a four-poster bed with mosquito net drapes. All have electric lighting run from a generator, with battery back-up.

The camp's central dining/bar area is wood and thatch, with an excellent sitting area on the first floor, overlooking the adjacent river and its floodplains. Nearby is the camp's small swimming pool.

Activities are organised in the morning and evening, usually involving mokoro trips and perhaps including a walk on one of the islands. If the channels are deep enough, then motor boat trips along the Boro are also possible. With prior notice, it's also possible to take a mokoro and poler out for a whole-day trip, with a picnic lunch for a long stop on one of the islands.

Rates: US$325/425 per person sharing/single, including meals, most local drinks, activities and park fees. US$88 each way per seat for flights between Maun and Gunn's – with a strict 10kg luggage allowance. Open: all year.

Gunn's Bushcamp

Gunn's Bushcamp is a campsite near to Gunn's Camp that is used as a base for mokoro excursions around the Delta. It has a restaurant, a bar, a swimming pool, and a shop where food can be bought and limited amounts of equipment are available for rental.

The options are flexible. You can bring your own camping equipment and food, or you can hire tents and kit (best booked in advance) and eat in their restaurant. That said, the equipment hire is relatively expensive: P40 per day for a two-person tent, or P10 per day for a towel! Meals cost around P25 for a full breakfast, P20 for a lunch special, and P38 for a two-course dinner.

Activities are mokoro trips with walks on the islands. These cost about US$70 per mokoro per day, and can be as short or as long as you wish – camping on the islands as you go. Packs consisting of a day's food and equipment hire cost US$50/60 per person sharing/single per day; camping fees are US$10 per person per day, and park fees are US$15 per person per day.

Thus a four-day/three-night mokoro trip would cost around US$356 per person sharing (including flights). Add on another US$150 each, making a total of US$506 each, if you need food and equipment – which you probably will given the strict weight limits for the flights.

Transfers between Maun and Gunn's Bushcamp cost US$88 per person one-way, and note that the 10kg luggage allowance on the flight out here is fairly keenly enforced. *Open: all year.*

Semetsi Camp (8 tents)

Overlooking the Boro River, and Moremi Game Reserve beyond that, Semetsi has eight walk-in 'mini-Meru' tents, each raised on a wooden platform. Inside these are twin beds with mattresses, duvets, towels and linen. It's clean and comfortable, but fairly spartan by the standards of most camps in the Delta. Flush toilets and showers are shared, and set back from the tents.

Semetsi has a reed-walled bar and dining area, topped by a thatched roof, and a campfire outside for drinks at the end of the day. Lighting throughout the camp is by paraffin lantern, which I still think is the most beautiful way to light a camp in the bush! There is a laundry service included in the costs.

Activities here take place normally mornings and evenings, generally mokoro trips including a walk on a nearby island.

Rates: US$170/242 per person sharing/single, including meals, drinks, activities and park fees. US$80 per seat (each way) for flights between Maun and Semetsi – with a strict 10kg luggage allowance. Open: all year.

Eagle Island Camp (12 tents)
One of the Delta's first photographic camps was built here at Xaxaba Island (Unless you're fluent in one of the local Khoisan languages and used to the various clicks, this is usually pronounced as 'Kakaaba' – with a 'Ka' as in the word 'cat.'). It was known as Xaxaba Camp and, at one point, was bought by Lloyd Wilmott (of 'Lloyd's Camp, Savuti' fame) before it was run for many years by Gametrackers (see page 174 for details). There's still a bushcamp used by wildlife researchers on the same spot today, known as Baboon Camp. Now the main camp nearby is this reserve's plushest: Eagle Island.

As you might expect, it's built to basically the same design and specification as its sister-camps: Khwai River Lodge (pages 258–9) and Savute Elephant Camp (page 226).

This means large, opulent canvas rooms built to high-quality standards on timber platforms, each with a wide veranda at the front and safari chairs. They're well spread out and linked by illuminated pathways. Inside, each tent is fully furnished with polished wooden floors, rugs and luxurious furniture. The twin three-quarter-sized beds, which are usually pushed together, have high-quality cotton bedding, bedside tables and twin (battery-powered) lamps. The beds are surrounded by mosquito netting and surmounted by two air-conditioning units. Yes, really – as well as the ceiling fan! And there's 110/220V power augmented by and 24-hour battery electricity. At the back, each of these tents has a separate toilet room, a large shower room, and acres of polished wood.

Activities are mainly mokoro trips and guided walks on the islands, though during high-water periods (usually June to September) motor boat trips are also practical. There's also a large 14-seater 'sundowner cruiser' which can slowly coast along the main channels for most of the year.

On very rare occasions, it's been known to be so dry here that there's not enough water for good mokoro trips, and then the camp has organised game drives. Otherwise, Eagle Island is a camp for water-based activities.

Rates: (2005): Jan–Mar US$503 per person sharing, Apr–Jun US$574, Jul–Oct US$751, Nov–Dec US$503; single supplement US$145 per night. Open: all year.

XIGERA, MOMBO AND CHIEF'S CAMP (NG28)

Although technically in the NG28 concession, on the north and west side of Chief's Island, this concession was effectively swallowed up by Moremi Game Reserve in 1992 – hence I'll cover these three private camps, and their satellites, within a separate section of *Chapter 12* which deals with Moremi Game Reserve. See pages 272–82.

GUBANARE AND XUDUM (NG29 AND 30)

Together these equally large concessions cover a total of about 2,000km² on the southern edge of the Delta, sandwiched between southern Moremi and the Sandvelt Tongue. They're designated as 'multi-use' concessions, and so part of them is used for hunting and a different, separate part is used for photographic trips – all pay a 'lease fee' to the local community for their use of the land.

I've only described the non-hunting camps here, which are split between two operations: photographic safari camps run by Landela, and a specialist horse-riding operation run by Okavango Horse Safari.

Background information
Getting there and away
Getting here is always organised by Landela or Okavango Horse Safaris, and it's usual to fly. There's one airstrip, called Kiri (✪ KIRI – 19°36.726'S, 23°02.367'E), in the northeast of NG30 that's used by Gubanare, and Xudum airstrip (✪ XUDUMA – roughly 19°41'S, 22°52'E), in the centre of NG29 that's used by the other camps. (Though this second was out of action on my last visit.) In case of emergency, it's sometimes possible to be driven into some of these camps – though it's a dusty, bumpy six-hours from Maun!

These camps work on the basis that guests have prior reservations and are getting in and out by light aircraft. No self-driving visitors are allowed into these concession areas.

When to visit
On the edge of the Delta, these areas have more seasonal variation than areas further north – so the game really is significantly better later in the dry season than earlier. Though as with anywhere in the Delta, the wetter times of the year are better for birdwatching.

Geography note
Be aware that the western side of the Delta (from the Thaoge into Lake Ngami) has been drying up since the middle of the last century. As a result of this (or vice versa) an increasing amount of Okavango's water is finding its way into the Muanachira/Khwai system, on the eastern side of Chief's Island.

Thus the floodplains of the west are gradually drying out and being invaded by flora used to drier conditions, whilst the drier areas of the Khwai River, and areas like Sandibe, are gradually becoming wetter.

Flora and fauna highlights
Visiting one September, I concentrated my time in the area around Gubanare, which is in the far northern corner of the concession – and probably its most productive area for wildlife.

There the land was relatively dry, with only a few areas of floodplain; which is probably fairly typical of these areas towards the southwest edge of the Delta. Because of this location, the annual flood hits these areas relatively late – typically around the end of May or June. Then good water levels last until around the end of October or November.

Vegetation
Around Gubanare there are lots of large, open plains covered in tall grass and interspersed with dry established thorny thickets. Among these are dense stands of leadwood trees, *Combretum imberbe*, and knobthorns, *Acacia nigrescens*. The latter are so numerous that their beautiful, creamy flowers combine to form a powerful perfume.

Perhaps as the result of fires in the past, there are large areas of chest-high wild sage, amidst occasional 'islands', typical of the Delta, where termite mounds are dotted with African mangosteens, raintrees, marulas, sausage trees and jackalberrys. Amongst the larger stands of trees are umbrella thorns, *Acacia tortilis*,

Left The Laurens van der Post panel of the Tsodilo Hills (CM)

Below right Detail of eland and giraffe on the same panel (CM)

Below left The main paintings of the Rhino Shelter, Tsodilo Hills (CM)

Above left Lilac-breasted roller (AZ)

Above right Banded mongoose (DM)

Right Elephant shrew (RT)

Below Warthog digging for roots and tubers (CM)

and real fan palms, *Hyphaene petersiana*. But these islands of forest are relatively infrequent and quite poorly defined.

In the far north, the concession has a short boundary with Moremi, the Boro River, which is one of the Delta's best known channels and is lined in parts by mature riverine forest.

Overall the mixed environment contains a wide variation of tree and plant species, though it doesn't have the beauty of some of the more mature, established forests or floodplain areas.

Animals

There's a good range of species here, typical of the Delta, though game densities didn't appear to me to be very high. They are certainly highly seasonal with animals proving scarce during the rains, and then numbers improving as the land dries out in the dry season.

The dominant antelope here is probably tsessebe (in one study of the Delta these made up 70% of all lion kills), though wildebeest and impala are also fairly common, occurring frequently in small groups. Family groups of giraffe and small numbers of zebra are also seen in the drier areas, along with kudu and steenbok. Red lechwe are dominant in the wetter areas, and there's no shortage of hippos or crocodiles in the deeper waters around the Boro River.

Roan, eland and gemsbok are seen but very rarely, and generally only in the drier areas on the south side of the NG29 concession nearest to Xudum, in an area not usually visited from these camps.

Between about December and June elephants occur here in small family groups (this is typical of their behaviour in the whole region when food is plentiful). Then they tend to be most frequently found in the mopane scrub areas in the south of the concession. Later in the year, as the land dries up, they gradually coalesce into larger herds, hundreds strong, which move north and east, nearer to the heart of the Delta. Buffalo tend to occur in large herds that move through the concession in the dry season; smaller groups are seldom seen.

Of the predators, lion are by far the most common in these concessions; there is a big population here (it's probably slightly *over* populated). Leopard are also permanent residents, although they are shy and rarely seen, despite the night drives. I didn't see any spotted hyena on my visit, though they're almost certainly around – but perhaps restricted by the density of lion.

Cheetah are very scarce, and generally only seen in the driest of months, around October to December. Then the grass is shorter, and there's more dry land, and so less pressure from lion. At other times of the year the cheetah move away from the water, south and west out of the concession.

Recently there's been a family group of caracal which are seen fairly regularly (about once per month) near Xudum airstrip. Given how rarely these cats are seen, this represents a really good chance – so keep a sharp lookout.

Birds

The varied habitat leads to good birdwatching, and my explorations of the Boro River area from here were excellent. Old favourites spotted included saddle-billed storks, knob-billed ducks, night herons, long-toed plovers and spurwing geese. Very large flocks of red-winged pratincoles were congregating on the exposed sandbanks, where the grass had been cropped short thanks to the grazing lechwe. May witnesses the biggest pratincole colonies here, which first appear as the Boro River begins to rise. Before that, while the sandbanks are exposed, you'll sometimes find African skimmers around.

In the area's drier grasslands black-bellied khorans were highly visible, with their eye-catching courtship displays. The wild sage areas here are often burnt and, immediately after this, wattled cranes arrive in numbers to dig up snails and other creatures that are exposed by fires.

Raptors which are frequently seen here include various vultures; bateleur, fish and tawny eagles, and the occasional martial eagle. The opportunist yellow-billed kites and steppe eagles usually start arriving for the summer in late August, and whilst the smaller raptors are more scarce, black-shouldered kites are often spotted (and easily recognised because they hover in mid-flight).

The safari camps
There are really two totally different operations in this area although, as a visitor, reserves are so large that you'll never come across Landela's camps if you're riding, or vice versa. Here I'll treat them separately.

The following five safari camps are run by Landela Safaris, based originally in Zimbabwe – see page 96 for contact details. They're fairly simple camps by Botswana's standards, in areas that don't have the best game densities – which are reflected by their relatively moderate prices. The camps here may be perfectly suited to keen birdwatchers on modest budgets who aren't that motivated by game sightings.

Gubanare Camp (8 tents)
In the very northern corner of NG30 (⊕ GUBANA – 19°32.733'S, 22°57.832'E), Gubanare is about 11km due east of Kanana and almost exactly the same distance from its own airstrip, which is 45 minutes' drive southeast of camp. It's a relatively new camp, having opened in August 1999, and is just a few kilometres' drive from the Boro River, slightly upstream of the old riverside camps in NG27B.

Its design is a fairly standard, classic safari camp. The main lounge, bar and dining area is raised up on a hardwood deck with two comfy sitting areas and a long dining table. The bar is made from an old mokoro and over the whole open-plan area is a canvas roof. A relaxed ambience is helped by atmospheric candles and paraffin lanterns (although the camp does have a generator for essentials like fridges and charging video batteries).

Gubanare's rooms are all large Meru-style tents based on solid plinths to raise them slightly off the ground. The tiled veranda at the front has a couple of canvas director's chairs, kept cool by a large shade that extends right over the tent. Inside are two single beds with bedside tables, a wardrobe, a safety deposit box, a fan and a suitcase stand. At the back there's a large toilet area with flush toilet, washbasin and hot shower.

Activities revolve around 4WD game drives and night drives in Toyotas (with three rows of three seats in the back). Short walks are often possible, though with Landela's walking camps nearby, the emphasis is on driving. The Boro River is a 45-minute drive from camp, and it's also usually possible to go on a boat trip. (The river is about 10–15m wide here, and usually 2–3m deep.) While water levels are high, around June to Oct, there are sometimes enough shallow-water areas for mokoro trips. If you fancy a swim ... use the pool back at the lodge!

Rates: US$325/425 per person sharing/single from July to October; US$220 per person sharing or single for the rest of the year. This includes all meals, laundry and two activities per day – it excludes drinks and transfers. Open: all year.

Rann's Camp (8 chalets)
Built in 1997, Rann's Camp (⊕ RANNS – 19°38.032'S, 22°53.980'E) is southwest of Gubanare in NG29, about 8km southeast of Pom Pom. Its main bar, dining room and lounge are protected under a thatched, wooden area furnished comfortably with teak furniture, and a jetmaster fireplace that's great for cooler mornings. A raised wooden deck extends around the lounge and has a small swimming pool set into it.

The wooden chalets are also thatched, with simple decor inside and en-suite shower, flush toilet and washbasin (hot water from gas geysers). The windows are protected by mosquito gauze. Note that although chalets 1–4 are close to the main areas, the others are more spread out. Number eight is wonderfully secluded, but about 550m from the centre of camp!

Activities include 4WD game drives by day and night, walking trips, and mokoro excursions. When the flood is high, between about May to September, Rann's can be cut off from the airstrip – and then the only way to get here is by plane to Xudum airstrip, then 4WD trip to Mantis Camp, followed by a short mokoro ride from there to the camp.

Rates: US$325/425 per person sharing/single from July to October; US$220 per person sharing or single for the rest of the year. This includes all meals, laundry and two activities per day – it excludes drinks and transfers. Open: all year

Xudum Camp (8 tents)
Built around 1995, Xudum (⊕ XUDUM – 19°42.665'S, 22°52.987'E) is the oldest and the furthest south of Landela's camps in Botswana. It's situated to the south of both of its satellite walking camps, Eden and Mantis, towards the middle of the NG29 concession.

The tented dining room and lounge areas are comfortable, and overlook a wide floodplain on the fringes of the Xudum River. Nearby, the bar is built in a fork in the branches of an impressive jackalberry tree (*Diospyros mespiliformis* – which is also known as the 'African ebony' tree, although it's only a cousin of the true ebony from North Africa which produces the sought-after, heavy black wood used for piano keys). In front of these, closer to the water, is an open-air fireplace for the cooler evenings.

Xudum has eight Meru-style tents with verandas and chairs. Seven are twin rooms, the eighth is a 'honeymoon' tent with a double bed. All have en-suite showers, flush toilets and washbasin (water heated by good gas geysers).

Activities are similar to Rann's Camp – with the emphasis on the driving.

Rates: US$325/425 per person sharing/single from July to October; US$220 per person sharing or single for the rest of the year. This includes all meals, laundry and two activities per day – it excludes drinks and transfers. Open: all year

Eden and Mantis – the Walking Trails camps – (4 tents each)
Xudum has two satellite trails camps, Eden and Mantis, both of which were built around 1995 when Xudum was built. Recently a third walking-trail camp was added – Baobab – but that's since been taken down.

Both are small, simple tented camps designed for small numbers of walkers. Dining and relaxing is in the open air under the trees, and the tents are raised up on a platform, basically furnished with simple camp beds (linen provided). On the ground next to the tent, screened off with a reed wall, is a private flush toilet and bucket shower. There's gas for cooking and paraffin lanterns, but no electricity here. Activities at both concentrate almost entirely on walking, led by a guide accompanied by a tracker, though there's usually a vehicle at each camp for emergencies.

Rates: US$275/375 per person sharing/single from July to October; US$200 per person sharing or single for the rest of the year. This includes all meals, laundry and two activities per day – it excludes drinks and transfers. Open: all year.

Riding safaris
All these riding safaris are run by Okavango Horse Safaris, based in Maun. Contact: Private Bag 23, Maun; tel: 661671; fax: 661672; email: ohsnx@info.bw; web: www.okavangohorse.com

Basic trip information
Perhaps unlike most of the other camps in this book (except African Horseback Safaris, page 167), the precise details of OHS's camps are really much less

important than the arrangements made for the riding activities. Thus here I'll cover briefly the basics of these safaris, before mentioning the camps and itineraries.

Riding ability required

You must be able to ride well. This isn't a place to learn to ride, or to come if you feel at all nervous on a horse. This means the ability to 'post to the trot' for stretches of ten minutes at one time, to be comfortable at all paces, and to be able to gallop out of trouble. It is a great advantage if you are fit and a proficient rider.

The horses

OHS advises that they use Pure Arab, Anglo Arab, American saddle bred, part- and full-thoroughbred, Kalahari and Kalahari cross horses. All are between 14 and 17 hands high, well schooled, responsive and have fairly even temperaments.

Weight limits

The maximum weight for any rider is 95kg (15 stones or 210lbs), and they even insist that potential riders may be required to step on a pair of scales! That said, for heavier riders there is an alternative programme of shorter rides, game drives and walks that is possible, but this must be discussed with them when you arrange your trip.

Tack and clothes

The tack used is English style, and each saddle has a seat-saver for comfort. Australian Wintec and an assortment of leather saddles are used, including Barnsby and Kieffer. The tack is generally of a high quality and kept in good condition. Only a limited assortment of half chaps and riding gloves are kept in the camp for guests' use.

OHS produces specific 'clothes lists' for their trips, but they can do laundry in their camp. Like all operations, the air transfers dictate that you stick to a strict weight limit (excess can be left in Maun). Note that proper riding clothes, and clothes of bush colours, are important here.

Information about you

To book on to one of their trips, OHS will ask you for you age, weight, height, and riding experience – as well as the more usual questions of your preference in drinks and any specialised diet that you require, or allergy that you have. They'll also require you to fill out an indemnity form in camp before beginning your trip – a practice which is becoming increasingly common in camps throughout southern Africa.

Having established that you can cope with the rigours of a riding safari here, you have a choice between a five-day and a ten-day safari, and these are normally scheduled in advance on set dates throughout the year. This does lack flexibility, but it means you are with a group of people and get to know each other, and as a group you can cover the ground.

On all trips there's a demonstration and talk at the beginning of the safari on how to handle big game situations, as well as a familiarisation session with the tack. After that, expect to spend between about four and six hours in the saddle each day, broken by refreshment stops. Typically this means that you'll have some picnic breakfasts and lunches, and also ten-minute walks every couple of hours spent in the saddle. (This acts to rest the rider by giving him/her the chance to use different muscles, and it also helps to relieve the horse from the constant pressure of a rider's weight).

Although the focus here is firmly on horse riding, alternative activities are often possible during afternoons which are not 'day rides'. These can include game drives, bird-watching walks, mokoro rides and night drives.

Riding in big game country can be difficult, especially when a horse looks very much like an antelope to a hungry lion. Thus safety is a big issue; it's at the root of why this isn't a place for inexperienced riders. An extremely experienced guide, usually P J or Barney, accompanies every ride, and they do carry a 375 rifle in case of emergency.

These riding itineraries take a maximum of eight riders at once (again, for safety reasons). They will accept children to visit, though these must be strong, competent riders (a pony club test pass is insisted upon) and the cost for a child is the same as an adult.

The experience

Provided that you are a competent rider, seeing the Okavango from horseback can be totally magical. From the point of view of most of the rest the Delta's animals, once you step into the saddle you become part of a four-legged herbivore (albeit, a strange-shaped one).

Thus generally they relax around you, allowing you to ride with herds of antelope without disturbing them, and see the place from a kudu's eye view. The palm islands, grassy floodplains, mopane forests and clear streams all ensure that the ground under you is always changing. Your horse will wade from island to island, where the going is normally quite good and firm along the edges – allowing the ride to move on at a trot and canter.

Having said all this, just as the herbivores perceive you as an antelope, so will the predators. Hence the emphasis on safety that a horse-riding operation must have in this environment. It's not unusual to have to gallop to safety from a pride of lion – usually with the guide at the rear, gun in hand.

The riding camps

These aim to be comfortable and simple, and all are staffed. Three meals a day are prepared, with saddlebag picnic breakfasts. As with most camps, they emphasise fairly healthy food with fresh vegetables and salads, and bake fresh bread each day. Dinner is often a three-course affair, usually served by candle light at a dining table beside the campfire.

Kujwana Camp (5 tents)
Kujwana is situated on the Xudum River (⊕ KUJWAN – 19°44.370'S, 22°57.115'E) about 8.5km southeast of Xudum Camp. It's about 11.5km northwest of Qwaapu Fly-camp, and almost 20km southeast of Moklowana.

Accommodation here is in Meru-style tents with a shaded veranda and a en-suite bathroom. This includes a long-drop toilet and a bucket shower (that's the type where the bucket is filled with hot water and raised on a pulley for you by the camp staff!) The beds are separate stretcher-type beds, with bedrolls, cotton sheets, duvets and towels provided.

Moklowane Camp (4 tents)
Moklowane is the most northern of the horse-riding camps (⊕ MOKLOW – 19°37.137'S, 22°49.277'E), and is situated in open flood plains only about 8km east of Rann's camp, and barely 5km southwest of Pom Pom camp (in the adjoining NG27 Reserve). That said, it's about 19km northwest of Kujwana, and 30km northwest of Qwaapu Fly-camp – which just goes to emphasise what a large amount of ground these horse-riding safaris can cover.

Accommodation here is very similar to Kujwana, with Meru-style tents with verandas and en-suite bathrooms – complete with long-drop toilets and bucket showers.

Qwaapu and Kiri fly-camps (8 tents)
Qwaapu and Kiri fly-camps are different from Kujwana and Moklowane. Firstly because they are less fixed, and can be moved. Secondly because they're a little more simple.

Qwaapu Fly-camp is on the southeast side of the reserve (GPS: QWAAPU 19°47.553'S, 23°02.666'E) and Kiri is often moved, depending on the water levels, but is usually somewhere on the northeast side, towards the Boro River and Kiri airstrip (⊕ KIRI 19°36.726'S, 23°02.367'E).

These camps have walk-in dome tents with separate, but private, long-drop toilets and bucket showers. There's also a central tent for dinner, though meals will often be eaten under the sky.

The costs
The trips are all five- or ten-night safaris, which are usually arranged around set dates in the year. There are no trips during the rains, between December and February.

From March to May, and November, trips cost around US$365/345 per person sharing per night for a five-/ten-night trip. This includes all accommodation, meals, drinks, guiding, riding, game drives, walks and mokoro trips. From June to October the cost is US$400 per person sharing per night, for either the shorter or the longer trip. (These prices include a fee paid to the concession of US$14 per person per night.)

Visitors who want single accommodation should add 50% to these costs, though this is usually waived if you're prepared to share a tent with another visitor. The flight between Maun and the camps costs US$90 per person, one-way (US$180 return).

CHITABE AND SANDIBE (NG31)
Background information
NG31 Reserve covers a relatively small 360km² of the eastern Okavango Delta. However, it's a superb location which looks on a map like a bite out of the southern side of Moremi Wildlife Reserve – between Chief's Island and the Mopane Tongue. Sandibe and Chitabe share this reserve, though generally keep to their own sides of it. Sandibe have about 160km² on its northern side, and Chitabe (and the adjacent Chitabe Trails Camp), occupies the southern 200km². These two camps are relatively close, about 12km apart, and they share one airstrip.

The reserve is particularly interesting as it's experiencing a period of change. The Gomoti River, which forms the northern and eastern border of the reserve, had been dry from about 1984. Then it began to flow again in 1999, spilling onto the seasonal floodplains here. This has dramatically increased the amount of water in this area. Previously only about 5% of Sandibe's area had water on it; now it's closer to 50% permanent water.

Getting there and away
All visitors to these camps pre-book their time and fly to the camps. NG31's main airstrip (⊕ CHITAA 19°27.952'S, 23°22.443'E) is about 7km north of Chitabe and 8km east of Sandibe.

This is barely 60km from Maun, making it one of the closest of the Delta's airstrips for camps. However, this doesn't usually affect the price of a trip here. Wilderness Safaris, for example, usually charges a set rate for a package including time at its camps and flights to/from them. This price doesn't vary with the position of the camp within the Delta.

When to visit

As with the rest of the Okavango, the big game here is more diverse and prolific during the dry season, although the birdlife is generally better between December and March. That said, NG31 really is in the heart of the Okavango where the water is basically permanent, and so these differences aren't as great here as you'll find in some of the more outlying, western areas of the Delta.

Flora and fauna highlights

NG31 is a varied reserve; there are quite marked differences between the northern sides (east and west) and also between these two and Chitabe's area further south, even if the list of species which occur in both are broadly the same. There is a complex mix of environments in this reserve; what follows here is very much a simplification.

The most striking difference is that the northwest of the reserve is a wetter environment than the rest. Just north of this reserve, in Moremi, the Mboroga River flows south between the dry-land areas of Chief's Island and the Mopane Tongue. Forming a number of large lagoons, it splits into two channels. One branch, the Gomoti River, then forms part of this reserve's northern boundary, and all of its eastern side. The other branch, the Santantadibe River, is a deep, wide channel that leads to lots of lagoons and runs down this reserve's southwestern side.

Flora

Sandibe overlooks the permanent Santantadibe River from within this watery side, on the reserve's northwestern corner. Around it there are plenty of open-water areas and floodplains, fringed by belts of riverine vegetation with a high proportion of real fan palms, *Hyphaene petersiana*. The islands here can be large and continuous, and on the larger of these you will find occasional baobab trees growing – an indication that they've been dry islands for a long time.

The northeastern side of the reserve, around the location of the airstrip, is a spit of dry land where the habitats seem to occur in belts. There are belts of thick mopane forest interspersed with belts of dry 'acacia thornveld', where you'll find mixed stands of camelthorn trees, *Acacia erioloba*, umbrella thorns, *Acacia tortillis*, and the very similar, but thorn-less, sickle bush, *Dichrostachys cinerea africana*. Also buffalo thorn, *Ziziphus mucronata*, with its two types of thorn, which snag on any passing animal (especially on clothing), and have earned it the name 'wag-'n-bietjie' in Afrikaans, meaning 'wait-a-bit.'

There are also bands of lower, more 'scrubby' vegetation, including classic species of deep Kalahari sand like the silver cluster-leaf, *Terminalia sericea*, and some very striking areas forested with large numbers of dead leadwood trees, *Combretum imberbe*. These trees, with their hard, termite-resistant, wood were killed by flooding when the water levels in the area changed – but will probably stand for many years, like a river of dead trees from the air.

Moving to the south side of the reserve, nearer to where Chitabe stands, you will find a lot of mixed forest areas with classic riverine species of trees lie the large fever-berry, *Croton megalobotrys*, sausage tree, *Kigelia africana*, and jackalberry, *Diospyros mespiliformis*.

Around here there are some smaller islands surrounded by shallow floodplains covered with hippo grass, *Vossia cuspida*. The deeper channels are mostly lined by phragmites reeds, *Phragmites australis*, and miscanthus grass, *Miscanthus junceus*. These are permanent channels which don't dry up, and seem to have relatively little seasonal variation; they simply spread out onto wider floodplains when the flood finally arrives here (around May or June usually).

At the southern end of the reserve is a belt of soil with a high clay content, providing the perfect substrate for large stands of mopane trees, *Colophospermum mopane* – which sometimes seem so uniform that it almost appears to be a monoculture.

Fauna

This reserve has a wide range of game species, dominated by impala, tsessebe, kudu and, on the floodplains, red lechwe. Zebra are fairly numerous, blue wildebeest less so, and giraffe are very common in the bands of acacia thornveld. (Thirty-five were observed together at one point on the airstrip.) Reedbuck, duiker and steenbok are often seen; whilst eland and roan are found only rarely (usually towards the south of the reserve), and sable seem to be totally absent.

The sightings here of buffalo and elephants seem to follow the same broad patterns. Throughout the year there are small resident herds of both around, plus odd old bulls and small bachelor groups. However, from around June to October large breeding herds pass through. Then buffalo herds can number well over 1,000, and herds of 100 elephants are not unknown.

The key to understanding this is to realise that when there has been rainfall, usually starting around November–December, the big herds move into the large swathes of mopane forest between the Okavango and the Kwando–Linyanti River system. That is, into the interior forests of Kwando (NG14), Linyanti (NG15), Selinda (NG16), Khwai Community (NG18) and Kwara (NG20). Whilst there, their water needs are sustained by the seasonal clay pans which hold water. However, when these pans start to dry up, around May or June, they move back to the areas of permanent water, including this reserve.

The reserve has plenty of lion including, when I last visited, a resident pride 17-strong. Recently they seem to have mainly concentrated on hunting buffalo, though that may have been just the natural response to having a lot of mouths to feed.

Leopard are common here, with the mixed woodlands and floodplains being an ideal habitat for them. I've had one of my best leopard sightings in Botswana near Chitabe, and hence tend to regard it as one of the country's best camps for leopard.

Cheetah stay here throughout the year, and are most frequently seen in the drier, more open eastern side of the reserve. Their populations are perhaps helped here by relatively low numbers of spotted hyena.

The reserve seems to have made a name for itself for wild dog. This may partially be due to the involvement in the reserve's management of Dave Hamman, who took many of the photographs for the book *Running Wild* (see *Further Reading*) – about the 'Mombo' pack of wild dogs in Moremi.

There certainly is a healthy population of dogs here. They seem to like the marginal floodplains, and will flush the antelopes through plains and islands to catch them. In 1999 there were three dens in the concession, though as these are usually moved from one year to the next... the situation is relatively unpredictable between the years. Having said this, I'd probably choose a more open and less wooded area than Chitabe if I were specifically hoping to track down some wild dogs.

Finally, on a more unusual note, this reserve seems to have had a very high incidence of pangolin sightings: they have recorded about six sightings in the last two years. (Most camps would count themselves lucky with one such sighting, as these are very rare animals.) Many of these sightings have been on full-moon night-drives, when the pangolin has been seen foraging around in the open. Aardvarks and aardwolves are also frequently seen here at night. Perhaps this, and the pangolin sightings, are really a reflection of the camps' enthusiasm for (or at least willingness to organise) serious late-night game drives, rather than a higher density of these animals in this area *per se*.

Birdlife
A recent survey counted about 386 species in this immediate area. In general, Sandibe is a better location for waterbirds. Along with many more common species, Okavango 'specials' like the Pel's fishing owl, slaty egret (thought to be the world's rarest heron), black coucal and black egret have been recorded here.

Chitabe has a wider variation of dry-country birds, with its most common raptor being the bateleur eagle, though there are also good numbers of many other eagles including martial, brown snake, black snake, tawny and western banded snake eagles. Marsh harriers are found in the wetter areas, along with the inevitable fish eagles and even the uncommon migrant European marsh harriers. Look out for bat-hawks in the late evening. Less spectacular, though almost equally uncommon, brown firefinches can certainly be found here.

What to see and do
The camps differ in their activities. Chitabe and Chitabe Trails are essentially dry-land camps, which concentrate on game drives and night drives, plus occasional guided walks.

Sandibe offers more of a mix of activities with game drives, boating and mokoro trips. They have recently had the huge advantage of a battery-powered boat here – called Lily – which gives up to 12 people (more usually six or so) trips along the Santantadibe River. Its slow speed and minimal wake, combined with very quiet operation, help it to have minimal impact and thus approach the shyer game and birds more closely with less disturbance.

When on mokoro trips at Sandibe, it's usual practice for an armed guide to accompany each group in a separate canoe with his/her own poler, as well as the mekoro which the guests are in.

Unusually for the Delta, both Sandibe and Chitabe Trails welcome children. At Sandibe they're even given a 'planet manager's workbook' to keep them busy whilst teaching them about the area, and the camp staff are adept at ensuring that they don't disrupt the activities or ambience for the other guests. At Chitabe Trails there is one 'family room' – where two halves of the room each have two beds, and share an interconnecting bathroom area.

Where to stay
There are just three choices here. Chitabe and Chitabe Trails are run by Wilderness Safaris (see page 174), whilst Sandibe is run by CCAfrica (see page 170). These are all very good, but very different, camps.

Chitabe Camp (8 tents)
Chitabe is set on an old, established tree island and first opened in July 1997. The whole camp is raised up on wooden decking, and walkways lead between the eight tents and the lounge and dining area which form the centre of the camp.

Here you'll find a large central area with a bar on one side, under thatch, and a separate dining area. Scattered around the open areas of decking are tables and chairs. One walkway leads from here down to a largish plunge-pool (about 8m by 3m), and all of this is under typical tall, shard trees of riverine forests – including jackalberries, *Diospyros mespiliformis*, knobthorns, *Acacia nigrescens*, and sausage trees, *Kigelia africana*.

There are four tents on each side of camp, and all have a solid door which leads into a large Meru-style tent. Here you'll find twin beds, or a double, surrounded by mosquito netting under a fan, plus a few wicker chairs, a table and a simple wardrobe. The en-suite bathroom is part of the tent, with a shower cubicle, a washbasin and a flush toilet. There's also a (much nicer) outdoor shower, enabling you to watch the stars as you refresh.

Rates: US$495/625 per person sharing/single from July to October; US$215/305 from December to March; US$335/485 for April, May, June and November. Includes all meals, activities, park fees, laundry, and most drinks. Excludes transfers. Open: all year.

Chitabe Trails (5 tents)
This is a smaller version of the main Chitabe Camp, built a few hundred metres from the main camp, on the other side of the same island. It uses exactly the same style of tents and furniture as the main camp. However, here the tents are built on the ground, not on platforms, and they're linked by natural paths through the bush rather than polished wooden walkways. (Note one of these rooms is a new 'family unit' where two tents, with two beds each, are linked by a shared en-suite bathroom.)

Although very unprepossessing, Chitabe Trails remains one of my favourite camps in the Delta. I often prefer the Delta's smaller, more intimate camps and the experience that I had here on my last visit was magical.

Rates: US$495/625 per person sharing/single from July to October; US$215/305 from December to March; US$335/485 for April, May, June and November. Includes all meals, activities, park fees, laundry, and most drinks. Excludes transfers. Open: all year.

Sandibe (8 chalets)
Sandibe opened in August 1998, about a year after Chitabe, and takes its name from the Santantadibe River that it faces. It stands in a band of thick riverine vegetation, and the pathways through the camp weave between the natural bush, which has been disturbed as little as possible. There are no wooden walkways here!

The main lounge and dining area has a unique design, influenced (I'm told) by styles from Mali and even Santa Fe. The roof is two storeys high, supported on long tree-trunk timbers and trendily decked in shaggy thatch. Under one side of this is a small lounge, on the other are tables set for meals. Up a few steps here is a small sitting area and a boardwalk with a hammock and more easy chairs. The whole structure is very open with rough wooden banisters and adobe walls.

A favourite feature of the lodge is the boma area, outside, where at night they have a central fire under tall trees, surrounded by lots of magical candlelight.

As with its sister-camp (Nxabega), Sandibe has a well-stocked wine cellar. Here it is kept cool in fine traditional style by an eco-friendly cool room with porous charcoal walls. (Ask to see this – it's how safari camps survived before refrigerators!) Though unlimited good house wine is included as part of your stay, if you want access to the vintage wines and more esoteric, imported spirits then these will cost extra.

Sandibe's relatively simple rooms are of a solid, terracotta-coloured construction with mesh windows (no glass) and big double-doors. Inside the twin or double beds have high-quality cotton sheets and linen, covered during the day by an unusual woven leather bedspread, and one walk-in mosquito net.

In these cool rooms is a writing desk, wooden bedside tables with lamps, tall mirrors, a wall-safe for valuables and a fan high in the ceiling. There's a small toilet and wash basin inside, plus a wonderful en-suite outdoor shower. Outside each chalet is a polished concrete veranda with chairs and a table, and a raised viewing platform for watching the wildlife.

The camp has a small circular plunge-pool, perhaps 5m in diameter, surrounded by sun-loungers, and a semi-circle of natural leadwood poles jutting up from the ground. There's also a curio shop, with the usual T-shirts, postcards, film, books, hats, maps, pictures, baskets and cuddly toys. Sadly they also sell imported West African and East African crafts, rather than concentrating on locally produced ones.

Like Nxabega, Sandibe has a large enough staff complement to be better than most camps at tailoring its activities around what guests want, and when they want it.

Rates: US$430/645 per person sharing/single from July to October including all meals, activities and park fees; US$355/530 per person sharing/single for the rest of the year. Open: all year.

STANLEY'S AND BUDGET MOKORO TRIPS (NG32)

This is a 'multi-purpose area', which is controlled by the local communities. Operations here have changed over the last few years, and a number of camps that have been planned (and even marketed) have not come into being. Specifically, note that despite being described in some travel guides, **Baines' Camp** has *never* actually existed. It was merely marketed as an idea at one stage in the early 1990s. (Gorokgwe Camp and Ivory Camp are also in this concession, but take a lower profile as they are hunting camps, in the separate, designated hunting area of NG32.)

Currently the concession is subdivided into areas for different uses. Two of these are of interest to visitors. Stanley's Camp and Grey Matters elephant project occupy one area, whilst a second is used for budget mokoro trips by many operators from Maun. Because these are such separate operations, I've described them separately below – after the natural highlights.

Flora and fauna highlights
Flora
NG32 is the concession on the other side of the buffalo fence from the relatively populated areas around Maun. It's at the southern end of the Delta, relying on the Boro and Santantadibe rivers for flooding – and last in line to receive the water. In a dry year, the floods can be very low and patchy here.

This means that there are relatively few short-grass plains which are regularly flooded, but significant patches of floodplains which are only intermittently wet. These provide an idea base for a profusion of the invasive wild sage (*Pechuel-loeschea leubnitziae*), which covers large open areas with its aromatic grey-green foliage. Where they've had slightly longer to become established, you'll find the distinctive rounded outlines of candle pod acacias bushes (*Acacia hebeclada*) starting to appear in these areas – as one of the first shrubs to move in it usually indicates that an area has been dry for many years. In some of these open areas where the recent floods haven't reached you'll find a profusion of termite mounds.

Aside from this, driving around NG32 near Stanley's the vegetation seems to occur in strips, including linear expanses of riverine forrest where the major tree species are leadwoods (*Combretum imberbe*), jackalberries (*Diospyros mespiliformis*), marula (*Sclerocarya birrea*) and sausage trees (*Kigelia africana*). There are relatively few areas of deep, deep sand here and not that many acacia glades, but there are some quite dense – and very attractive – concentrations of real fan palms (*Hyphaene petersiana*).

When visiting with a mokoro poler, you'll see a very different side to the area. Unless the flood has been very high, you'll probably be poling within the vicinity of the Boro or the Santantadibe. This is at the very shallowest end of the Delta, so expect large areas of miscanthus grass (*Miscantusus junceus*) and common reeds (*Phragmites australis*), plus the occasional floodplains of hippo grass (*Vossia cuspidata*).

If you do actually pole up the Boro, then you'll find the environment generally gets more interesting as you continue. After a few days, you'll leave behind some of the more boring stretches of reeds, and start finding wider floodplains around you, and more lagoons. Wherever you pole, the islands on which you stop will often be classic little palm islands fringed with palms and the riverine forest.

Fauna

The game densities generally get better as you head further north in the area. Impala are probably the commonest antelope here, with tsessebe a close second and red lechwe certainly dominating any areas which are flooded. Kudu, giraffe zebra, reedbuck, warthog and occasionally wildebeest are all found here; sable, roan and waterbuck are not. Elephant and buffalo occur singly during the wetter parts of the year, and pass through in larger herds as the dry season reaches its end.

When the flood is at its height, there may be the occasional sitatunga around, but apart from a few places on the rivers, there isn't enough papyrus reedbeds to support them.

Lion are around in good numbers, and while leopard occur, they're not frequently spotted. Wild dog pass though, and sightings of them seem to increase between about October and December. However, the open wide plains where you could follow them are limited in the concession.

Cheetah are certainly around here and often seen in the drier areas – on one drive here during a fairly brief visit one of the book's contributors spent a magical 25 minutes with a male cheetah as he strolled from termite mound to mound searching for the perfect vantage point.

Birdlife

NG32 is a classic edge-of-the-Delta reserve that has a good mix of dry-country and shallow-water bird species. The most common species include red-eyed, mourning and Cape turtle doves, which all greet the morning with a variety of gentle coos. Identify the latter by their lyrical exhortations to 'word harder, work harder'.

Other birds frequently seen here include long-tailed shrikes, red-billed quelia, buffalo weavers, lilac-breasted rollers, blacksmith plovers and long-tailed and glossy starlings. Crimson-breasted shrikes provide startling flashes of red; Meyer's parrots can often be seen as a flash of colour flying at speed.

In more open areas you'll find red-billed and Swainson's francolins, flocks of helmeted guinea fowl, kori bustards and occasional ostriches. Sandgrouse are common in acacia groves, as are yellow-billed hornbills, whilst their red-billed cousins prefer the reserve's mopane woodlands.

The floodplains support a varied cast of waders and waterbirds, including the occasional wattled cranes. This is a good reserve for raptors; bateleur eagles, black-breasted and brown snake eagles are especially common, and Gabar goshawks are frequently seen.

Stanley's camp

Getting there and getting away

If you're staying at Stanley's Camp, then access is by air to the strip near camp; you're not allowed to drive yourself here.

When to visit

Like most of the areas on the edge of the Delta, the game densities are better during the dry season than during the rains. So whilst from June to October is the best time to visit for game, the birdwatching is usually more interesting during the rains – from around December to March.

Accommodation

Stanley's was originally built by the maverick local character Alistair Rankin (the subject of a number of local bush myths – some involving mokoro trips, buffalo and uncomfortable nights spent in trees). It's owned and was run for several years by Sarah Collins, of Planet Okavango. These origins explain why it may appear surprising rustic – and quite a contrast – if you arrive here from either of Sanctuary's other lodges (Chief's or Chobe Chilwero); it wasn't (re-)built or designed specifically for Sanctuary.

The open-plan dining/lounge area is simply a large canvas tent (think of a 'big top' circus), on a slightly raised wooden decking – with a large jackalberry tree (*Diospyros mespiliformis*) that's growing right through the centre and out the top. Under here are a couple of comfy sofas and a few leather chairs. The 'library' is slightly separate, and here you'll find a leather sofa with a couple of old wooden suitcases into which is packed a slightly eccentric collection of novels, magazines and reference books. Beside this is a chessboard, with table and chairs – a thinking option to while away hot afternoons.

Stanley's has a small curio shop with a couple of glass-fronted cabinets in which there's a selection of various souvenirs, T-shirts and a basic selection of film. It also sells baskets made by the staff, which are hanging around – all very low key and in keeping with the generally relaxed, unpretentious feel of the camp.

Most meals are social affairs, taken with everybody eating together at a long table. That said, if you're staying for a few days then you can take the opportunity to request a picnic lunch to be made up, so that you can stay out in the bush all day. After dinner in the evening, everybody usually retires for drinks and a chat to a small fire pit, outside in front of the big top.

The camp has eight tents on solid red-painted concrete bases, all of which are to one side of the main area, connected by bush tracks. These are fairly simple, and inside you'll find a couple of beds, a desk with drawers and a chair, a couple of bedside tables and an old-style wooden wardrobe in one corner. Lighting is by electric 'hurricane'-style lamps, and there are rugs on the floor – but no fans in the rooms.

Each tent has its own en-suite toilet and shower – complete with original and wood-and-canvas shower cubicles, a wooden dresser with sink and mirror (and the usual range of complimentary toiletries), and another electric lamp. Even the cracks in the floor seemed to somehow blend well with the 'bush' air of the lodge – helping to make this a very lovely, traditional old-style camp.

Rates: US$440/580 per person sharing/single from July to October; US$230 per person sharing or single between December and March; US$230/335 per person sharing/single for the rest of the year. This includes accommodation, meals, most drinks and normal activities. It excludes transfers, a few imported drinks, laundry and elephants trips with Grey Matters – which cost an extra US$210 per person per activity.

What to see and do

Activities at Stanley's Camp usually revolve around 4WD game drives and night drives, though it's usually possible to take mokoro trips for at least a few months a year – typically around June to September. The water's not consistently deep enough to run motor boat trips. Aside from these normal activities, many people here will pay the extra US$210 per activity to spend time with Doug and Sandi Groves and their elephants…

LIVING WITH ELEPHANTS

Doug and Sandi Groves started this not-for-profit organisation in 1999, aiming to secure the future of their trio of elephants, and to work through various projects towards a more harmonious relationship between Botswana's elephant and human populations.

Projects undertaken include their 'Outreach programme' whereby children from Maun and nearby villages spend two days at Grey Matters with the three elephants – interacting with the elephants and learning about them through hands-on experience and discussions. See www.livingwithelephants.org for more details.

Grey Matters

Doug Groves started out working with elephants in American zoos, including Washington Park Zoo and San Diego Wild Animal Park. Subsequently, in 1987, he came to Africa as the trainer of four elephants who were being returned from the US to South Africa for a film, *Circles in a Forest* – the first of many filming projects for him. As an aside, the main elephant involved in this was Abu – who now leads the herd at the Okavango's only other operation that offers visitors time in the company of elephants which are not wild (Abu Camp, in NG26).

In 1994, Randall Moore and Ker & Downey went their separate ways – and almost simultaneously Ker & Downey invited Doug to Botswana, to set up and run an elephant-based tourism project. Now Grey Matters isn't linked to Ker & Downey, and instead works closely with Stanley's Camp – and is the base for the 'Living With Elephants Foundation' (see box).

What to see and do

Elephant activities are arranged through Stanley's Camp, where all the guests stay, and hence guests rarely need to contact Grey Matters directly (PO Box 66, Maun; tel: 6863198; email: groves@livingwithelephants.org).

THE ELEPHANTS AT GREY MATTERS

There are three trained elephants with Doug and Sandi at the moment; all are orphans from culling programmes:

Jabu is short for Jabulani, which means happiness; he was born in about 1986 and orphaned when two by a cull in the Kruger National Park, South Africa. He is described as a proud bull who enjoys leading this small herd – playful, dependable, and the most independent and confident member of the herd. He now stands about 2.9m tall at the shoulder.

Thembi, a smaller female, is about the same age as Jabu, and was also orphaned by a cull in the Kruger. She's said to be smart and very social, and loves being the centre of attention. Originally a very insecure calf, she's gradually becoming much more confident.

Morula came to Doug in 1994 as a maladjusted 17-year-old, lacking confidence and with a troubled background. Doug comments that she started off being exceedingly submissive to him and the other elephants, but then vented frustrations on trees. He adds that she's gradually become more secure and relaxed here.

These activities cost US$210 each, and normally consist of about four hours in the morning – a leisurely foraging walk with the camp's three elephants, which allows you to get used to observe and interacting with them at close quarters. You'll be encouraged to touch and walk with the elephants as they forage – and to view them as individuals. Riding the elephants is not usually part of these trips. At the end of this there's usually a picnic lunch in the bush.

The maximum number of guests at any one time is eight – if there are more people then they'll organise an afternoon walk for a second group.

Budget mokoro trips
Background information
NG32 is the end destination for virtually all of the one- to four-day mokoro trips offered from Maun which begin with a road transfer into the Delta. These may be marketed differently by the different companies, but they're all basically the same. It's worth explaining these in detail, so that you will understand these budget trips if you're shopping around Maun.

A Maun-based company called Planet Okavango has made an agreement with the communities in the NG32 concession to co-ordinate mokoro trips on the Boro and Santantadibe rivers. There are a number of communities in the area, where work as polers and guides provides a valuable income.

Government rules limit the numbers of visitors (and hence the impact of tourism). A maximum of 30 mekoro are allowed on each river system at any one time. These start off, and return to, one of three 'launch sites' on the Santantadibe, and one site on the Boro River.

Planet Okavango runs a booking system which co-ordinates all the mekoro in the area. They take bookings from a variety of different Maun tour operators (in particular Audi Camp, Delta Rain, Drifters, Bushways, Crocodile Camp Safaris, Quadrum Safaris, Island Safari Lodge and Okavango River Lodge – though these aren't the only ones). They make sure that the limits on the numbers of visitors are strictly followed, and they give permissions to the various Maun operators to take visitors to the various launch stations for trips. Planet Okavango also employ launch site organisers, who co-ordinate the various trips – and are in radio contact with the Maun office, and so understand exactly how many mekoro are required.

Meanwhile the tour operators from Maun book slots for trips on a first-come, first-served basis with Planet Okavango; they also pay the freelance polers and guides from the community directly. It's a strict rule that there should be one professional poling guide from the villages for every party of up to eight visitors. The rest of the mekoro are usually poled by locals from the different villages who don't have this qualification.

Trips here are basically mokoro trips, with short walks on the islands, and visitors usually bring all their own food and camping kit. All the polers bring is their own food – and when I last took a trip here, the poler appeared to have arranged our route to stop at friends on various islands.

The bottom line of all of this is that the actual polers, mekoros and areas being offered by the various competing companies in Maun are all exactly the same. And because they all pay the polers about the same ... the costs of the trips are virtually identical. So by all means shop around for these trips – but be aware that what's on offer is basically the same everywhere, and will cost about the same.

Getting there and getting away
For all of the budget mokoro trips, the operator organising it will drive you here. It takes about 90 minutes to most of the launch sites. You're not allowed to drive

yourself here, and these trips must be booked through one of the participating companies in Maun. See the list of Maun operators and try Planet Okavango – then perhaps one of two from: Audi Camp, Delta Rain, Drifters, Bushways, Crocodile Camp Safaris, Quadrum Safaris, Island Safari Lodge and Okavango River Lodge. There's usually no point contacting them all!

If you want to combine a mokoro trip with a dry-land safari, then Planet Okavango and Starling's Camp (in neighbouring NG34) have combined to offer a five-night/six-day 'Sitatunga Trail'. This is two nights at a mokoro fly-camp, three at Starlings, and includes all transfers and activities for US$750/850 per person sharing/single, excluding drinks and laundry. It's a good deal to a good area and makes efficient use of your transfers.

When to visit

These trips aren't really about game, although you may see some. They're more about enjoying the experience of being poled along the waterways, and seeing some of the birdlife, and water-life, close up. From my experience, mokoro trips are much more fun when the sun's shining and the sky is blue; grey skies and (even worse) rain do take the edge off it. Thus best avoid January and February if you have a choice – and ideally come between about April and November.

What to see and do

Relax, take a bird book and a pair of binoculars, and enjoy the experience. My first trip into the Delta was like this – and it was magical. Subsequently I've seen more interesting areas of the Delta, and infinitely better game, but it's still hard to beat the sheer joy that you'll get from floating around on a mokoro in such an amazing environment for the first time.

See my comments on walking on pages 127–8 before you go walking in search of big game with your poler – as none of these trips are likely to be led by someone that I'd describe as a professional walking guide, and none of the polers carry any guns.

SANKUYO TSWARAGANO COMMUNITY TRUST (NG33)

The small NG33 reserve is really an enclave that has been cut out of NG34. It borders Moremi, and this is where the old San-Ta-Wani Safari Lodge used to be, which was one of the Delta's older, dry, photographic camps. Gametrackers ran it, before Orient Express Hotels bought their whole operation and changed it. They stopped using this camp as part of their 'circuit', and after that San-Ta-Wani fell into a downward spiral. It was used as a self-catering stop for mobile safaris for a while, but is currently disused.

In character it's very similar to the area around South Gate and parts of NG34. However, with no major watercourse or other focal point, it's not an easy area in which to run a stand-alone operation.

Currently I'm told that the community is trying to develop something here by itself – though it seems unlikely that anything will materialise in the near future.

SANKUYO COMMUNITY TRUST AND STARLING'S (NG34)

NG34 covers an area of about 900km², and you drive through the eastern side of this when you leave the Moremi Reserve's South Gate and head towards Maun. It's an area with good game, and is easily accessibly (by 4WD) from Maun. Thus, and very unusually for the region, it's a private concession to which you can drive yourself.

Background information

NG34 is run for the benefit of the local community, through the Sankuyo Tshwaragano Management Trust – and it's a reserve which sees more frequent changes than most. Until about 2001 it was the location for Gomoti Camp, run by Crocodile Camp Safaris – but they then lost the rights to run a camp here.

Meanwhile in mid-2002 the rights for photographic safaris here were taken over by a first-rate company from Maun, Capricorn Safaris. They built and are currently running Starling's Camp. This promises to be a real success, although as I write there's still one issue outstanding with the Land Board – which needs to be resolved before we can be sure that the camp will remain here.

Meanwhile there's long been an intermittent presence here of animal researchers, many of whom seem to have subsequently written books! Naturalist and lion researcher Peter Katz has been here conducting lion research for about five years. He had a book, *Prides*, published in 2000 – and more recently the three children staying with him and his partner have written *Lion Children* which was published in 2001. They are all still in residence, at the inevitably-named 'Lion Camp', which is about 2km from Starling's Camp.

Before that, John 'Tiko' McNutt began a wild dog research unit based here in 1989. The project broadened and developed since then, and in 1996 a book that he co-authored was published: *Running Wild: Dispelling the Myths of the African Wild Dog.*

Getting there and away

Years ago, it used to be possible to fly here; the old San-Ta-Wani airstrip is found at ⊕ STWAIR 19°30.820'S, 23°37.700'E. That's about 10km due south of South Gate, in NG33. However, this strip is currently out of action, and needs upgrading – so for now the only access to NG34 and Starling's Camp is by vehicle.

It takes about two hours to drive from Maun. First follow the directions for Moremi (see pages 179–80) through Shorobe, and head right up to South Gate. Within sight of the gate, about 500m from it, there's a concrete plinth just where you turn left, to drive roughly southwest down Moremi's cut-line. (That is the straight line of cleared vegetation that separates the park from the private reserve.)

From there it's a straight 10.5km until the cut line turns right. Follow this for a further 7.9km until you reach a junction (⊕ STARTU 19°31.599'S, 23°31.987'E). Here you've effectively reached the edge of the riverine forest beside the Gomoti River, and you turn to head roughly southeast and to shadow the river. About 2.5km along here is the old site of Gomoti Camp (⊕ GOMOTI 19°32.424'S, 23°33.174'E), around which are various confusing tracks.

Ignoring all of those, about 6.1km past STARTU junction you'll reach Starling's Camp (⊕ STARLI 19°33.330'S, 23°34.134'E). Expect to have a number of game-viewing tracks branching off to confuse you when you're on the last section of this trip, beside the river, but follow your nose (and your GPS); it's not difficult to find.

This route requires a 4WD, but isn't difficult and should be accessible all year round. However, if you haven't got your own vehicle then Capricorn's road transfers are very reasonable indeed at US$50 per person return from Maun (for a minimum of two people).

When to visit

Big game animals are more prolific here during the dry season, as with the rest of the Okavango – although the birdlife is generally better between December and March. Because NG34 is on the southwest side of the Delta, the flood reaches it last. Also note that NG34 contains some of the closest dry-season watering points for the game that spreads out towards Nxai and Makgadikgadi during the rains. Around this, there is a much higher density of game in the dry season than the wet.

That said, quite a lot of the reserve is mopane woodlands, a favourite location for animals during the rains and early dry season – so expect it to have some game around all year.

Flora and fauna highlights

Look on a map of the reserve's vegetation and you might be struck by the amount of mopane woodlands here – which generally isn't a huge attraction for safari-goers. However, drive on the ground and you'll realise that most of the area around the Gomoti River, where Starling's Camp and its safaris are concentrated, is a much prettier combination of big open flood plains with occasional islands.

Like much of the Delta around eastern Moremi, the flood patterns here do seem to have changed recently. When Tico McNutt first came in 1989, the Mogogelo River, near San-Ta-Wani, still had water in it; since then this has dried up. The flood has been generally poor elsewhere in the area, but these indications are mixed – observe the Gomoti River, which flows seasonally, and seems to have been flooding further and better during the last few years.

With something as complex as the changes in water flows and levels in the Delta, everyone has a slightly different opinion. Perhaps one of the most pertinent comments on this was, allegedly, from local wit, Willy Philips, who commented that 'the only reliable water in the Okavango is the water in the toilets.'

Flora

As mentioned above, much of NG34 is quite thick, and relatively unproductive, mopane woodlands. However, the western side of the reserve, adjoining the Gomoti River and some of its floodplains, is much more interesting.

Even driving on the main road south from South Gate to Maun you'll get a flavour for this, as you pass through some superb stretches of open acacia savannah – where you'll find very good populations of giraffe, if you're not speeding through too fast. The dominant species here is camelthorn (*Acacia erioloba*), though you'll also find a few umbrella thorns (*Acacia tortilis*) and the odd old leadwood (*Combretum imberbe*) mixed amongst them. It's classic mature Kalahari sandveld – and matches many people's image of Africa. These areas run like veins through the reserve, marking out the areas of deepest sand.

Around the Gomoti River, things are different. Here you'll find plenty of lovely areas of old riverine forest, containing all the usual species including sausage trees (*Kigelia africana*), marula trees (*Sclerocarya birrea*), jackalberries (*Diospyros mespiliformis*), African mangosteens (*Gardenia livingstonei*) and sycamore figs (*Ficus sycomorus*). You'll also find knobthorns (*Acacia negrescens*), which are immediately obvious around September and October for their creamy-white flowers and almost sickly-sweet perfume. Occasionally you'll find small islands, or patches, of these standing together.

The floodplains here come in two broadly different varieties. Those plains that still regularly flood are usually covered with short grass – a photogenic environment that's easy for game viewing. The others, which have been dry for a number of years, have often been largely covered with wild sage (*Pechuel-loeschea leubnitziae*). This classic 'pioneer species' can quickly take a hold when a floodplain dries out; it thrives in areas that have recently been disturbed. Other, slower growing species of shrubs and trees will eventually germinate and take over these areas, though not for some years yet.

Amidst all of these plains, you'll find islands, large and small. These have riverine trees and shrubs on them, including a scattering of real fan palms (*Hyphaene petersiana*) and a notably high density of knobthorn trees (*Acacia negrescens*).

Mammals

I haven't spent a lot of time in this area though my first memory of it was a good one. In May 1993, I'd been driving myself through Chobe and Moremi with a friend. It had been a good trip, though we were disappointed not to have seen any wild dogs. By the time we left South Gate, in the heat of midday, we had given up trying to spot animals. We were in NG34, but didn't think of this as a wildlife reserve.

After about 14km along the main track, we slowed down to find our way blocked by a large pack of very lazy wild dogs wandering about the road, and lounging by the side of it, yet showing little interest in our vehicle. They posed for photographs, as harmless lapdogs, for about 30 minutes until they finally wandered off – thus providing us with one of the best game sightings of our whole trip. Only now, knowing how long researchers spend following the dogs in this area, do I understand why these dogs were so totally relaxed with our vehicle.

The commonest antelope here is probably the impala – a favourite prey of wild dogs, although you'll also find good numbers of tsessebe, kudu, giraffe and warthogs. Elephant are fairly common and, like buffalo, often move through here in the dry season in large herds. Roan are seen occasionally, while a real treat is the small herds of sable which appear fairly regularly in front of camp and near the Gomoti River.

Of the predators, lion are dominant although the area certainly has a permanent presence of wild dogs also. Leopard and cheetah both occur, but aren't seen often. The landscape should suit leopard; I guess that after a few more years leopard will become less shy here, showing themselves a bit more.

Birdlife

The birdlife here reflects the variety that you'll find anywhere in the Delta, and obviously depends heavily on the water levels. One recent checklist for NG33 and 34 lists 208 species, but doesn't even pretend to be exhaustive.

However, the more common birds which are most frequently seen on the Gomoti floodplain and around the camp area include the long tailed and glossy starlings, from which the lodge takes its name; plus red-eyed, Cape turtle and mourning doves; blacksmiths and crowned plovers; long-tailed and crimson-breasted shrikes; red-billed quelias; buffalo weavers; lilac-breasted rollers, and white-backed and hooded vultures. Wattled cranes and paradise whydahs are also spotted periodically.

Meanwhile in the acacia woodlands, along with the ever-present doves, you're likely to find kori bustards; large flocks of helmeted guinea fowl; red-billed and Swainson' francolins; red- and yellow-billed hornbills; Meyer's parrots; double-banded, Burchell's, Namaqua and yellow-throated sandgrouse; plus the occasional Gabar goshawk, bateleur and ostrich.

What to see and do

The main activities here are game drives and night drives, which are usually conducted using open-topped Toyota Land Cruisers which take a maximum of seven guests. That said, when the river's dry the camp is pumping water up into a small pan in front of camp – so your veranda can also be a good venue for game sightings.

Serious walking trips are also a feature here, and Capricorn advise that they will only use top professional walking guides who are armed. ('The standard of a Zimbabwe professional guide, with experience' – which is pretty much the gold standard of guiding in southern Africa, see pages 127–8 for comments.) Thus if you are keen on walking, then I'd let them know this when you book into the camp. If they consistently live up to this promise, then Starling's will be one of the few places in the region that really offers high-quality walking trips.

Depending on the season, mokoro trips are also possible from here. Water levels for this are generally feasible from around late-May to September, though obviously this varies from year to year. Similarly, the camp offers boating trips when possible. The Gomoti is rarely navigable and so they usually use one of the boat stations up at Mboma Island or Xakanaxa, in Moremi. This requires a game drive of about 90 minutes each way, and the pay-off is that you're then boating in a very interesting area at the heart of Moremi.

If you've a yearning for more culture, then a visit to the Shandereka Cultural Village (see page 180), on the eastern side of NG34 near Sankuyo, can be organised. These trips usually take most of a day and include a picnic lunch. They give you a chance to meet and interact with the local Bayei people – perhaps taking part in some of their domestic and ceremonial life, as well as go for walks in the bush to learn about tracking animals and gathering wild plants.

Finally, if you want to combine a mokoro trip with a safari here, then Starling's Camp has combined with Planet Okavango (in neighbouring NG32) to offer a combined five-night/six-day 'Sitatunga Trail'. This includes two nights at mokoro fly-camp, three at Starlings, and includes all transfers and activities for US$750/850 per person sharing/single. It excludes drinks and laundry, but even so looks like a very good deal – and makes efficient use of your road transfers.

Where to stay

Starling's Camp must be pre-booked through Capricorn Safaris in Maun (see page 169), and it has no campsite attached to it. Note that the number of visitors allowed to use this part of the reserve at any one time is very strictly limited – and so you cannot just turn up and hope for a space.

If you find yourself travelling between South Gate and Maun and need a space for the night, then better to camp at the Kaziikini Community Campsite, on the eastern side of this concession, near Sankuyo Village (see *From Maun to Moremi or Chobe* at the end of *Chapter 8*).

Starling's Camp (8 tents)

Built beside the Gomoti River, about 3km downstream from the old site of Gomoti Camp (which has now been dismantled), Starling's Camp is a rare thing – a species of the Delta that's become more endangered over the past few years: it's a camp that isn't aiming for the latest in luxuries.

Instead Capricorn have built an old-style safari camp without ever referring to a design consultant, an interior decorator or a chic stylist. Here you'll find walk-in Meru-style tents built on solid plinths with en-suite flush toilets and (gas-heated) hot showers. These tents have simple wooden furniture in them and a full set of linen and towels. They're clean, comfortable and functional. Lighting around the camp at night is by paraffin lamps, whilst inside the tents small lights are powered by a 12V battery system.

The camp's main social area, simple and tented, is built on a huge wooden deck with a great view over the Gomoti River and its floodplain into NG32. This stands under a huge murula tree (*Sclerocarya birrea*), around which a few smaller knobthorns (*Acacia nigrescens*) are clustered. This is the focal point of camp, where tasty meals are served. It's adjacent to a comprehensively stocked bar and a comfy lounge area.

Although I haven't yet visited this new camp myself, Capricorn are a first-rate company. If Starling's Camp can continue to deliver what it is achieving at the moment, then it's excellent value for visitors who can drive here. It makes an ideal final stop on a self-drive safari from Kasane through Chobe and Moremi to Maun.

Rates: US$150/200 per adult sharing/single. Children (5-12) are welcome and cost US$75 if sharing with adults; under-5s are free. This includes accommodation, meals, teas and coffees and activities in the reserve. It excludes transfers, drinks, laundry and any trips into Moremi.

MANKWE (NG43)
To the east of NG33 and 34, NG43 is really a huge (3,460km²) patch of the Kalahari, east of Moremi's South Gate and south of Chobe's Mababe Gate. It's not an area where there's easy or prolific game viewing. I include it here because it is the base for a new bush lodge, and this may prove a very convenient stop between Maun and either Moremi or Chobe. In time, as the areas under wildlife protection effectively expand, it may even become more of a game-viewing destination in its own right.

Getting there and away
Virtually all visitors travelling directly between Maun and Chobe will pass through a section of NG43, even if you haven't noticed it. The lodge is situated in the northwest corner of the reserve, just north of Sankuyo Village, and between the roads that lead to Chobe and Moremi (⊕ MANKWE: 19°22.030'S, 23°53.510'E).

To reach it from Maun, head towards Chobe's Mababe Gate. (That is, follow the directions to Sankuyo covered at the end of *Chapter 8* under the heading *From Maun to Chobe*.) Shortly after Sankuto Village the track splits. The right turn goes to Chobe, the left northwest to the cut line which runs north-south and divides Chobe from Moremi. You'll find turn-offs to 'Mankwe' signposted on both roads.

Return transfers between the lodge and Maun can also be organised by the lodge for P100 per person (for a minimum of four people).

What to see and do
Mankwe really works in two different ways, with different sets of activities. Firstly, if you're just passing through on the way to Chobe, and decide to stop for a day or two, they will organise bush walks in their area led by a guide, or game drives. These can be shorter drives on NG43 itself, including afternoon/night drives with a sundowner, or whole day-drives which usually head into the Khwai River area. Night drives after dinner are also an option.

These guided activities are offered for a minimum of four people – at least, you must pay for four. Bush walks (2–3 hours) are P40 per person, short gamedrives (3–4 hours) are P60pp, full-day drives are P100pp, and short (2-hour) night drives are P40pp.

Secondly, you can use Mankwe's position close to South Gate as a base for mobile safaris into the Moremi Game Reserve, often combined with overnight trips into the Delta from Mboma Boat Station, which they run. (See pages 368–9 for full details.)

A full day drive in Moremi or Chobe is P500 per person, and an overnight boat trip in Moremi is P880 per person per night, including food and equipment. Again, these assume a minimum of four passengers.

They're also starting to offer wilderness 4WD trails across the NG43 concession, though these require two vehicles for safety reasons. A local guide accompanies each trip (in your 4WD), and s/he costs P100 per day.

Where to stay

There is only one place to stay, **Mankwe Bush Lodge**, and it is run by Kgori Safaris, P Bag 146, Maun; tel: 665788 or 661073; fax: 665787; email: kgorisaf@info.bw; web: www.mankwe.com. Reservations for this are currently being administered from South Africa at tel: (27) 12 3617464; fax: (27) 12 3617464; email: tourism@mankwe.com.

Mankwe Bush Lodge (8 tents)

Far from any other lodge, constructon of Mankwe started in November 2000, and it opened for business in April 2001.

The main lodge is raised up on a wooden deck, with a thatched lounge, an outside boma area to sit around the campfire and a small swimming pool. Accommodation is in one of eight Meru-style tents. All are fairly large, about 4m x 8m, and stand on wooden decks overlooking the plains around. Inside are twin beds, simple furniture and an en-suite bathroom including a flush toilet, washbasin and a hot (gas-fired) shower.

Rates: P750/1100 per person sharing/single, including all meals, activities in NG45 and laundry. If you're staying for only one night then 'bed and breakfast' costs P500/750 per person sharing/single. Open: all year.

Mankwe Campsites (6 pitches)

About 1.5km from the main lodge there are six private campsites, half under camelthorn trees and the other half under mopane trees. (Thus they're known as the 'camelthorn' and 'mopane' sites respectively!) Each campsite has its own small ablutions, with a flush toilet, a bucket shower and a washbasin. By prior arrangement, meals can be eaten in the lodge.

Limited firewood is available (you're asked to collect your own after the first night), and you'll need all your own drinking water as well as food and fuel.

Rates: P70/50 per adult/child per night. Open: all year.

The Okavango Panhandle and Northwest Kalahari

If much of the Okavango Delta is the preserve of the privileged few who can afford to fly-in to exclusive safari camps, then the Panhandle presents more egalitarian options. Here you'll find the raw edge of Botswana's safari industry, camps on the edge of the Delta run by idiosyncratic owners or local communities – without marketing aids or slick glossy brochures. This is the Okavango's safari scene as it was 20 years ago!

Go west, into the Kalahari, and it's wilder still. Here there's almost nothing organised, yet the amazing Tsodilo Hills have been declared as Botswana's first world heritage site. Adventurers will want to dig deeper here, reaching the caverns of the Gcwihaba Hills and the remote Aha range.

THE PANHANDLE

Look at a map of the Okavango Delta and you'll see that it's shaped like a frying pan, with the main river flowing down the handle, from the northwest. Thus this area gets its name.

Orientation

The Panhandle's western side is very easy to access with a 2WD, as the road between Sehithwa and Shakawe is tar. Once you leave the main road and the larger settlements, a high-clearance 4WD is essential to cope with the sand in the area.

The track that follows the river on the eastern side is used much less, though it's not intrinsically difficult. Visitors very rarely travel along this as the only practical access to it is via the ferry that crosses the Okavango at Mohembo, north of Shakawe.

Geology and geography

All of this area is in the Kalahari, though here it's dominated by the influence of the Okavango River. This comes south into Botswana from the Angolan Highlands, having crossed Namibia's Caprivi Strip.

Entering Botswana, the river's gradient is very low. However, it is constrained from spreading out by steep riverbanks on either side. Underneath the sand lies a more fundamental constraint; parallel fault lines in the earth's crust which run southeast, about 10–15km apart. Thus the river meanders gradually southeast, between them, forming a series of wide, sweeping curves and the odd ox-bow lagoon – but always remaining within the constraints of the banks.

Where the river's meanders kiss the banks at the edge of the floodplain, villages have sprung up: Shakawe, Sepupa and Seronga. The southern extent of the fault-lines lies around Seronga, so south of here the river begins to spread wider to form the main body of the Delta.

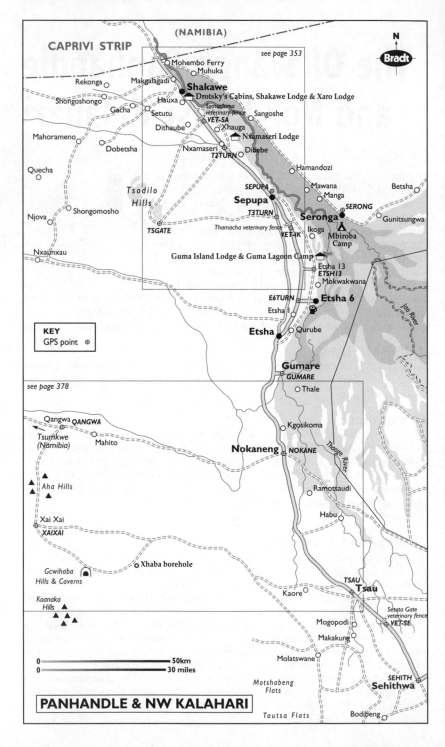

(NAMIBIA)

CAPRIVI STRIP

see page 353

N

Bradt

Mohembo Ferry
Muhuka
Rekonga
Makgalagadi
Shakawe
Drotsky's Cabins, Shakawe Lodge & Xaro Lodge
Shongoshongo
Gacha
Hauxa
Setutu
Somachima
veterinary fence
VET-SA
Sangoshe
Mahorameno
Dithaube
Xhauga
Nxamaseri Lodge
Dobetsha
Nxamaseri
Dibebe
T2TURN
Quecha
Hamandozi
Mawana
Manga
Betsha
SEPUPA
Tsodilo Hills
Sepupa
SERONG
Njova
Shongomosho
T3TURN
Seronga
Gunitsungwa
Thamacha veterinary fence
Ikoga
Nxaunxau
TSGATE
VET-IK
Mbiroba Camp
Guma Island Lodge & Guma Lagoon Camp
Etsha 13
ETSH13
Mokwakwana
KEY
GPS point ⊕
E6TURN
Etsha 6
Etsha I
Etsha
Qurube
Etsha
Gumare
GUMARE
see page 378
Thale
Qangwa **QANGWA**
Kgosikoma
Tsumkwe (Namibia)
Mahito
Nokaneng
NOKANE
Thaoge River
▲ *Aha Hills*
Ramotsaudi
Xai Xai
XAIXAI
Habu
Xhaba borehole
Gcwihaba Hills & Caverns
Koanaka Hills
TSAU
Tsau
Kaore
Setata Gate
veterinary fence
VET-SE
Mogopodi
0 ————— 50km
0 ————— 30 miles
Makakung
Molatswane
SEHITH
Sehithwa
PANHANDLE & NW KALAHARI
Motshabeng Flats
Tautsa Flats
Bodibeng
Jao River

Iao River

GPS REFERENCES FOR PANHANDLE AND NW KALAHARI MAP (opposite)

E6TURN	19°06.706'S, 22°16.152'E
ETSH13	19°00.975'S, 22°19.125'E
GUMARE	19°22.242'S, 22°09.242'E
NOKANE	19°39.694'S, 22°11.184'E
QANGWA	19°31.868'S, 21°10.281'E
SEHITH	20°28.259'S, 22°42.372'E
SEPUPA	18°44.150'S, 22°10.625'E
SERONG	18°48.771'S, 22°24.988'E
T2TURN	18°35.834'S, 21°59.986'E
T3TURN	18°50.292'S, 22°10.011'E
TSAU	20°10.294'S, 22°27.265'E
TSGATE	18°47.275'S, 21°44.856'E
VET-IK	18°50.327'S, 22°13.756'E
VET-SA	18°29.256'S, 21°55.142'E
VET-SE	20°15.775'S; 22°33.926'E
XAIXAI	19°52.867'S, 21°04.934'E

Flora and fauna

The Panhandle isn't a prime area for game viewing, so don't come here expecting masses of big game or you'll be disappointed. That said, you may catch glimpses of the occasional sitatunga or small herds of lechwe, and you're almost bound to see numerous hippo and crocodile.

However, there are some first-class areas for birding, and plenty of areas with deep-water channels and lagoons.

Flora

Looking from the Panhandle's banks, often all you can see is a gently swaying mass of feathery *papyrus* heads. Here, more than anywhere else in the Delta, the environment is polarised: there's deep-water channels, and there's the *papyrus* beds that surround them.

Occasionally you'll find sections of *phragmites* reeds and, when the waters are low, open stretches of sandbanks. Sometimes the odd day lily, *Nymphaea nouchali caerulea*, will take hold in a quiet inlet on the edge of the channel, but mainly the vegetation here is huge expenses of floating *papyrus*.

Birdlife

The birdlife here is as varied as anywhere in the Delta, though getting to actually see the birds that inhabit the papyrus can be tricky. Some of the more sought-after sightings here would be painted snipes, rufous-bellied herons, lesser jacanas, chirping cisticolas, brown-throated weavers and coppery-tailed and white-browed coucals. Greater swamp warblers and swamp boubous can often be heard calling from the papyrus, but are less easy to spot.

The Panhandle is a particularly good area for the white-backed night heron, whilst perching on the sandbanks look out for white-backed ducks (sometimes in large numbers), long-toed plovers, red-winged pratincoles and, of course, the Panhandle's most acrobatic birding attractions: African skimmers.

These distinctive, black-and-white birds fly south to the Delta between about September and December. They mainly come to breed on the sandbanks of the

Panhandle which are then exposed while the water is low. Here they'll gather in small flocks, each pair excavating a shallow depression in the sand where they'll lay their eggs and raise their young.

One of the Delta's most amazing sights is to watch these birds feed. With long, graceful wings they fly fast and low, holding their elongated lower mandible just low enough to cut the water's surface. This is hollow and has sharp edges, shaped to minimise its drag in the water. When this touches a small fish near the surface, it is quickly raised against the upper mandible, trapping the fish firmly. I always marvel at their flying skill, moving their body in all directions whilst their bill traces a constant, steady path through the water.

Note that because they nest very near the waterline, on low sandbanks, their nests and young are very vulnerable to both predators and to damage from the wash caused by fast-moving motorboats. So boats operating in these areas should never be driven too fast.

Another spectacular migrant, better seen in the Panhandle than anywhere else in the Delta, is the carmine bee-eater. These come to southern Africa to breed, and stay from about October to March. They nest in large colonies, building their nests underground at the end of tunnels which they excavate into the side of sandy riverbanks. You won't forget the sight of hundreds of these bright carmine-pink birds twittering around a river bank that's holed with nests like a piece of Swiss cheese.

Above the water you'll always see fish eagles around. Marsh harriers and even the occasional migrant osprey are also sometimes seen. Beside the waters and papyrus there's the narrow band of thick riverine forest on the banks before the bush becomes that of the dry Kalahari. Here there's a wide variety of different birdlife – typical of any of the riverine areas in this region. Notable sightings here would include the tiny brown firefinch, Bradfield's hornbills, western banded snake eagles and Pel's fishing owls.

Getting around
By vehicle
The main road on the west side of the Panhandle is very easy to get along in a 2WD; it's all tar and maintained to a high standard. For anywhere else in this area, you really need your own fully-equipped 4WD.

By bus
There are several buses per day which ply between Maun and Shakawe, stopping at the main villages on the way. The whole trip takes about 7 hours and costs a total of P40. These will turn off to the larger centres, like Gumare and Etsha 6, but just pick-up/drop passengers on the main road near the smaller villages. Most go from Maun to Shakawe in the morning, and back in the afternoon – but ask locally for more precise timings.

By air
There are small airstrips dotted around, so if you charter a plane you can get to most places here: Shakawe, Nxamaseri, Nokaneng, Tsau and Guma Lagoon. The Tsodilo Hills has an airstrip, but you really need a vehicle whilst you're there to get the most out of it. There are no airstrips anywhere near the Gcwihaba or Aha Hills.

The Eastern Panhandle
Visitors relatively rarely see this side of the Okavango's Panhandle, largely because there is little to attract visitors here. However, there is a good gravel road that runs

down the eastern side of the river from Mohembo to Seronga. This is how these villages get the bulk of their supplies.

Between Mohembo and Seronga you'll find a large number of small villages which survive mainly on fishing and, away from the river, a number of tiny 'cattle-post' settlements used by the people when tending their cattle in the interior of NG11 – which is fairly continuously cattle-ranching country.

The main reason for visitors to come here is for mokoro trips based out of Mbiroba Camp, run by the Polers' Trust, at Seronga. This is one of the few options left to see any of the Okavango for travellers who are constrained by a relatively tight budget.

Getting there and getting away
By air
Seronga has an airstrip (⊕ SERAIR 18°49.180'S, 22°25.020'E) that is now in regular use from Maun bringing visitors to the Okavango Polers Trust, and this is now by far the easiest and most convenient way for most travellers to access this village. Check in Maun with Island Safari Lodge or Audi Camp for details of the options.

By vehicle
The only practical way to access the eastern side of the Panhandle with a vehicle is to cross the Okavango River on the ferry at Mohembo, in the far north.

There appears to be another route, which every year is tried by a clueless few, following what looks like a good road on the Shell map of Botswana. This appears to go around the eastern side of the Delta and link into Seronga from the Linyanti area, via the village of Betsha.

However, the tracks on this side have very few users and no signposts. They cross a number of different private concessions and hunting areas, none of which will welcome your visit. Straying off designated 'transit routes' will get you into trouble. Meanwhile, when the tracks meet villages they split and vanish. But perhaps the greatest danger here is of water levels blocking the route. It's easy to get dangerously lost in this region and to then run out of fuel, water or supplies. There's no help here, so I'd strongly advise against trying to use any of these tracks.

By bus/hitching
If you're travelling without a vehicle, then both Shakawe and Sepupa are fairly easy to access with one of the local busses that run up and down the road between Shakawe and Sehithwa. There are then two ways across to the eastern side.

The easiest way (and if you're aiming for Seronga, then the most convenient way) is to take the bus to Sepupa and then catch the small motor-boat ferry which shuttles between Sepupa and Seronga.

The alternative is to use the vehicle ferry at Mohembo, and then hitch south down the road on the eastern bank.

By boat
There's a regular motorboat ferry between Seronga Boat Station (⊕ SERBOA 18°49.316'S, 22°24.855'E) and Sepupa (see page 358). This takes a couple of hours to reach Sepupa (it's faster in the opposite direction, downstream), via a variety of winding channels. In the highly unlikely event that you ever need to navigate yourself to Seronga by boat, the turn-off from the main channel towards the boat station is at ⊕ SERTUR 18°49.776'S, 22°24.350'E, which is about 1.2km away.

On the motorboat ferry, a one-way trip costs only about P20 per person, but you'll have to wait for the boat to fill up. Alternatively, it may be possible to arrange boat transfers here from Guma Island Lodge (see pages 362–3) on the west of the Panhandle, if you're staying there for a period of time. Sepupa Swamp Stop charges a minimum of P600 for a private motorboat to do the return journey between Sepupa and Seronga.

Seronga
Seronga (✪ SERONG 18°48.771'S, 22°24.988'E) is a sizable village at the base of the Panhandle. It's the regional centre for a number of small settlements to the east of it, along the northern edge of the Delta, as well as a focus for the people who still live in the northern areas of the Delta.

Where to stay
There's only one option here – but it's one of the best budget options in the Delta; the base for a local co-operative of polers in the area:

Mbiroba Camp (5 chalets plus rondavels and camping) The Okavango Polers Trust, PO Box 24, Seronga; tel: 676861; fax: 676939; email: mbiroba@okavango.co.bw; web: www.mokoro.org (this may change to www.okavango.co.bw – and neither was working when I last tried!)
This is one of the region's more established community ventures which is succeeding by offering a simple, good-value product to travellers who are not expecting five-star luxury. Despite this, there's still a bar and a curio shop!
The camp's five chalets are simple, double-storey constructions with solar-powered lighting, and solar-heated water for the outdoor shower. All are of traditional Meru-style design, set on wooden decks, with up to four beds and an en-suite bathroom.
Alternatively, there's a campsite and a few simple rondavels, which share ablutions and can sleep up to three people. Limited numbers of tents and other camping equipment can be hired here; expect to pay about P25 for a two-person tent, and P10 for a folding mattress and sleeping bag.
Rates: P220/275/363/440 for a chalet to sleep 1/2/3/4 people; P55 per person per night for a rondavel. Camping costs P30 per night.

What to see and do
Mbiroba Camp is used as a base from which to take mokoro trips into the Delta with a poler. You need to bring all your food and equipment; you'll be camping 'rough' without any facilities. That said, if you're prepared this is a lovely way to see the Delta. Just make sure you read *Chapter 6* before you go.
Current costs for this are P165 per mokoro (seats two) per day, plus a one-off charge of P55 for transfers, and P25 for 'service' – but I'd expect these to change more rapidly than most camp's costs.

The Western Panhandle
Mohembo border and ferry
Heading north about 13km after Shakawe, you reach the area of the border with Namibia. A left fork takes you to the neat, newly built customs and immigration area for those crossing into Namibia by road.
A right fork leads swiftly to the (free) Mohembo Ferry, which usually takes a few vehicles at a time across the river, including the occasional small truck. Expect to find a lot of people waiting around here – some to cross, others to meet those who have crossed, or to buy and sell things here.

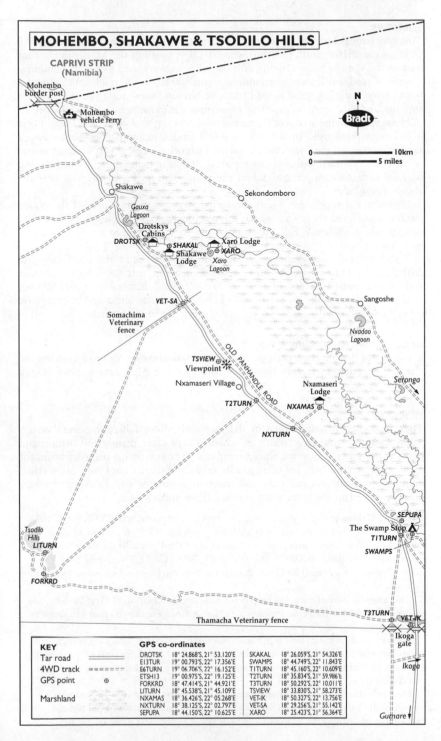

MOHEMBO, SHAKAWE & TSODILO HILLS

CAPRIVI STRIP
(Namibia)

Mohembo
border post

Mohembo
vehicle ferry

N

Bradt

| 0 | 10km |
| 0 | 5 miles |

Shakawe

Sekondomboro

Gauxa
Lagoon

Drotskys
Cabins

DROTSK

SHAKAL
Shakawe
Lodge

Xaro Lodge

XARO

Xaro
Lagoon

VET-SA

Somachima
Veterinary
fence

Sangoshe

Nxadao
Lagoon

OLD PANHANDLE ROAD

TSVIEW
Viewpoint

Nxamaseri Village

T2TURN

Nxamaseri
Lodge

NXAMAS

Seronga

NXTURN

SEPUPA
The Swamp Stop
TITURN

SWAMPS

Tsodilo
Hills
LITURN

FORKRD

T3TURN
VET-IK

Thamacha Veterinary fence

Ikoga
gate

Ikoga

Gumare

KEY		GPS co-ordinates			
Tar road		DROTSK	18° 24.868'S, 21° 53.120'E	SKAKAL	18° 26.059'S, 21° 54.326'E
4WD track		E13TUR	19° 00.793'S, 22° 17.356'E	SWAMPS	18° 44.749'S, 22° 11.843'E
GPS point	⊕	E6TURN	19° 06.706'S, 22° 16.152'E	TITURN	18° 45.160'S, 22° 10.609'E
		ETSH13	19° 00.975'S, 22° 19.125'E	T2TURN	18° 35.834'S, 21° 59.986'E
		FORKRD	18° 47.414'S, 21° 44.921'E	T3TURN	18° 50.292'S, 22° 10.011'E
Marshland		LITURN	18° 45.538'S, 21° 45.109'E	TSVIEW	18° 33.830'S, 21° 58.273'E
		NXAMAS	18° 36.426'S, 22° 05.268'E	VET-IK	18° 50.327'S, 22° 13.756'E
		NXTURN	18° 38.125'S, 22° 02.797'E	VET-SA	18° 29.256'S, 21° 55.142'E
		SEPUPA	18° 44.150'S, 22° 10.625'E	XARO	18° 25.423'S, 21° 56.364'E

Shakawe

This very large fishing village stands on the northern banks of the Panhandle of the Delta, some 281km north of Sehithwa and 13km south of the Mohembo border post on the Caprivi Strip. Driving into the village always used to feel like entering a maze of reed walls, each surrounding a small kraal, as the track split countless ways between the houses. The odd trap of deep sand was enough to stop you for an hour, and thus serve up excellent entertainment to numerous amused locals.

However, with the arrival of the tarred road, visiting Shakawe is less fraught that it has been previously. In the village you'll find a major police station, and a significant base for the army (the Botswana Defence Force), as you'd expect in one of the country's more sensitive border areas. If you're going to be doing anything unusual here, then stopping to ask at the police station if it is OK to proceed is always a good idea.

If you've the time, take a walk along the river that is just behind the police station. Sometimes there's a mokoro ferry shuttling local people to and from the eastern side of the river, full with their wares to sell or recent purchases to take back home.

There are also a few shops here, many concentrated within the small shopping centre around the bus stop. On the west side of town, just 400m off the tarmac, you'll find a good paved airstrip, with a very neat, round thatched terminal building.

If you can't leave the modern world behind you then Shakawe has cellphone coverage which usually extends to Drotsky's, but not much further.

Getting there and getting away

If you're not driving here, then there are good daily bus services to Maun via the rest of the western Panhandle from the centre of town. Alternatively, hitch-hiking is relatively easy.

Where to stay

There's nowhere practical to stay in Shakawe itself, though there are several water-based camps on the river south of town. These cater mainly for fishing and birdwatching. In recent years, since Namibia's Caprivi Strip has been off-limits for many visitors, trade here has dramatically fallen and these camps have often relied on business from visiting road construction engineers and local government officials. Listed are the three main options, from north to south:

Drotsky's Cabins (6 chalets & camping) PO Box 115, Shakawe; tel: 675035; fax: 675043
Almost 8km south of the radio mast in Shakawe you'll find a left turn off the tar road. This sandy track will lead you east, crossing the old road up the Panhandle for about 3km to reach Drotsky's Cabins (⊕ DROTSK 18°24.868'S, 21°53.120'E). You should be able to drive across this in a normal 2WD car, though the sand can be very thick, so some driving skill is needed.

This long-established camp has been run by the delightful Jan and Eileen Drotsky, and their family, who have seen the Shakawe area change from a remote outpost to a thriving little town.

Drotsky's Cabins stands on a high bank, overlooking the river, which is already several kilometres wide. Below is a network of deepwater channels and large beds of papyrus. It's excellent for birdwatching or fishing, though there's little game around except for hippos and crocodiles.

Drotsky's six chalets are set amongst well-watered lawns in a shaded haven under a canopy of thick riverside trees. Colourful shrubs and banana trees have been planted between them, creating the welcoming impression of a green and tropical haven.

Two of the chalets sleep two people, whilst the other three are bigger and built on two levels, and so can sleep four. All are A-frame design with low brick sidewalls supporting a tall, steeply angled thatched roof. These are insect-proofed with mesh on the window and lit by mains electricity. They all have simple furnishings, rugs on the floor, and a tabletop electric fan. Central to the lodge is a bar (which often seems to play host to an eclectic selection of local characters) and a very large dining area, built over the river. Look out for the rather beautiful wooden top to the bar here!

Drotsky's is a very genuine old camp, where hospitality hasn't been learned from a manual. If you are willing to take it on its own terms, then it can be a super lodge, and offer you fascinating insights into the area, its history and its ecosystems.

Rates: P236/P385/P495 for a single/twin/4-person chalet, or P33 per person camping. Breakfast P35, lunch P50, dinner P60. Boat hire varies in cost depending on the size of the boat, and transfers to or from Shakawe airport are P25 per person.

Shakawe Lodge (10 bungalows) contact via Travel Wild in Maun (see page 178); tel: 660822; fax: 660493; email: t.wild@info.bw

Shakawe Lodge (⊕ SKAKAL 18°26.059'S, 21°54.326'E) has been known as the Shakawe Fishing Camp for decades. You'll find the turning to it on the main road about 5.5km north of the Somachima Veterinary Fence (⊕ VET-SA 18°29.256'S, 21°55.142'E), and 12km south of the radio-mast in Shakawe Village.

The lodge stands on the bank of the Okavango River, a little less than 3km east of the main road. It was started as long ago as 1959; subsequently its present owners, Barry and Elaine Price, now very well-known local characters, took over the fishing camp in 1975. Now this offers ten large, thatched, brick bungalows. Each has a fan and mains power throughout, and an en-suite bathroom. All are carpeted, though very basic. There's a circular thatched boma, used as a bar/dining room, adjacent to a small lily-covered lagoon that's behind the splash pool.

Under shady trees on the river bank, a few metres south of the main lodge, is the campsite. This is a lovely, grassy site with simple ablutions and a few metal drums that act as braai stands for cooking.

Most visitors here come to fish, though bird watching – through the riverside forest or from boats – is also popular. When Namibia's Caprivi is safe, the Mahango Game Reserve is within reach of a day-trip, though most visitors would opt to stay there as a separate destination.

Beside the bank at the lodge, look for the Okavango's only armoured boat. This is a relic of the Angolan war from the late 1970s. Apparently it was used by 32 Battalion of the South African forces, who were stationed in the Caprivi Strip, near the site where Ngepi Campsite is now. However, it broke loose and drifted south, and has been gentle rusting in Botswana ever since! Barry has some stories to tell you about this if you ask him.

Rates: chalet P275/P418/P637 for single/double/triple, camping P35 per person incl. tax. Breakfast P35, lunch P45, dinner P65. Boat hire is P85 per hour, plus fuel. Transfer to/from Shakawe airport is P75 per vehicle. Or US$250 per person per night, including everything except drinks, for overseas groups.

Xaro Lodge (8 chalets) Book via Drotsky's Cabins, above.

Xaro (⊕ XARO 18°25.423'S, 21°56.364'E) is about 8.5km downstream from Drotsky's Cabins, its parent camp, and is usually reached from there by boat – a 15-minute trip. The lodge is built on an outcrop from the mainland, amidst an old, established grove of knobthorn (*Acacia nigrescens*), mangosteen (*Garcenia livingstonei*) and jackalberry (*Diospyros mespiliformis*) trees.

Once there, it's hard to escape the feeling that this was once an absolutely beautiful, old-style Okavango camp. It was originally built in about 1984 by Hartleys Safaris, before passing through several hands until it was acquired by Jan Drotsky, whose son now runs the camp. Here you'll still find a thatched, stone dining area with a large table in the centre and various old books on the bookshelves in the walls.

Accommodation is currently in Meru-style tents built on permanent concrete bases, each with a shaded veranda and a separate toilet and shower. These are adequate, though there are plans to build eight more modern, octagonal thatched rondavels with en-suite facilities to replace them in the future.

Look around and you'll also find a garden of succulents and cacti here, banana trees and even a small baobab tree (*Adansonia digitata*) on the left of the camp as you look out onto the river.

Talking to Royal, one of the marvellous staff who have been here for years, he recalled that the lodge has always been used for fishing and birdwatching from motor-boats, never from mekoro, and that's still the situation.

Rates: P247/P385 for a single/twin tent. Breakfast P35, lunch P50, dinner P60. Boat hire varies in cost depending on the size of the boat, and transfers to or from Shakawe airport are P50 per person.

Nxamaseri

Though the small village of Nxamaseri is not a stop for most visitors, I've included a section here because the area around Nxamaseri Camp is a very interesting one, and capable of providing a deep-water Delta experience which is as interesting as most of the reserves further east.

Specifically, the Nxamaseri Channel here is a side-channel of the main Okavango River. Like Guma Lagoon, further south, it's fairly easily accessible due to the presence of a lodge. If you want a real Delta experience in the Panhandle, then this should be high on your list of places to visit – though getting here either requires your own vehicle or a flight.

Flora and fauna highlights

The Nxamaseri Channel is north of the point where the main Okavango River divides at the base of the Panhandle, and is a stretch of open, clear water up to about 30m wide in places. Beside the edges you'll find stands of papyrus and common reeds, whilst its quieter edges are lined by patches of waterlilies, including many night lilies, *Nymphaea lotus* (aka lotus lilies) as well as the more common day lilies, *Nymphaea nouchali caerulea*. Look out also for the heart-shaped floating leaves, and star-shaped white or yellow flowers of the water gentian, *Nymphoides indica*.

As with the rest of the Panhandle, this isn't a prime area for game viewing. You may catch glimpses of sitatunga or the odd lechwe, and you're almost bound to see hippo and crocodile, but big game is scarce.

However, the channel is a super waterway for birdwatching; home to a tremendous variety of waterbirds. Without trying too hard, my sightings including many pygmy geese, greater and lesser jacanas, lesser galinules, colonies of reed cormorants, darters, numerous species of bee-eaters and king-fishers, green-backed herons, a relaxed black crake, numerous red-shouldered widows and even (on a cloudy morning in February) a pair of Pel's fishing owls. Beside the channel are pockets of tall riverine trees and various real fan and wild date palms, whose overhanging branches house several colonies of weavers (masked, spotted-backed and brown-throated).

Upstream of the lodge, on the main Okavango River, there's a colony of carmine bee-eaters at a location known locally as 'the red cliffs'. This is occupied from around early September to the end of December, but is probably at its best in late-September/early-October (the best time for most migrant species here).

Getting there and getting away

About 19km north of Sepupa (over 37km south of Shakawe) there's an unmarked turning (⊕ NXTURN 18°38.125'S, 22°2.797'E) onto a vague track through the bush which leads northeast, about 5.5km from the main road, to Nxamaseri Lodge (⊕ NXAMAS 18°36.426'S, 22°5.268'E). This is little more than a number of confusing tracks in the deep sand which initially head slightly left of the straight-line direction to the lodge, before finally bending right.

If you're approaching from the north this is about 21.5km south of the Somachima Veterinary Fence (⊕ VET-SA 18°29.256'S, 21°55.142'E). After 10km you'll pass a slight rise marked by a sign as 'Tsodilo View' (⊕ TSVIEW 18°33.830'S, 21°58.273'E). From here, on a clear day, you can see the hills to the southwest. Less than 3km south of this viewpoint you'll pass a sign to Nxamaseri, which leads to the village of the same name. The camp's unmarked turning is almost 9km south of this.

Nxamaseri will only accept advanced bookings, and it is surrounded by water for most of the year. So you *always* need to make advance arrangements to stay here. You'll usually be met if you're arriving by vehicle, and a boat and mokoro are often needed to ferry you the final few kilometres – so this is not a lodge to try and drop into unannounced.

What to see and do

As mentioned, this isn't a lodge for big-game safaris, but the boat trips for bird-watching are first class, and whilst there tends to be less emphasis on mokoro excursions, these are also possible when the water levels are high and there are suitable areas of shallow water nearby.

Fishing is another major activity here, and is possible throughout the year. For enthusiastic anglers, the very best tiger-fishing months are from August to November, and the best times for bream are between March to June. During the first three months of the year the rain and new floodwaters are said to disturb the fish, which move out to the floodplains – and so fishing in the channels can be more difficult.

The record tiger-fish catch here is about 6.7kg, though in a normal season they'd expect to have 10–15 catches over the 6kg mark. Fly-fishing and lure/spinning fishing are done here, and Nxamaseri pride themselves in keeping their equipment in good condition. Like most Okavango Lodges, Nxamaseri operates a 'catch-and-release' system with fishing, except for the occasional bream taken for the table. They have two large, flat, barge-like boats which provide a very stable platform for several people fishing, and is also ideal for photography.

Where to stay

Nxamaseri Lodge (6 chalets) PO Box 159, Maun; tel: 678016 or 660778; fax: 678015; email: suzyl@sefofane.bw or nxa.lodge@info.bw

Nxamaseri Lodge stands beside the Nxamaseri Channel, in an area where, when water levels are high, there are plenty of open marshy floodplains covered with an apparently unblemished carpet of grass, and dotted with tiny palm islands. It's very like the Jao Flats, and is one of the Okavango's most beautiful corners.

Nxamaseri is a long-established camp that has sometime in the past been written off as 'just a fishing camp'. That is how it started: built in about 1980 by PJ and Barney Bestelink, who now run Okavango Horse Safaris. It is claimed that fly-fishing in the Delta was pioneered here, and certainly it remains an attraction for people who fish seriously. However, given that much of the magic of the Delta, and especially its wetter parts, are the birdlife and the scenery, then Nxamaseri's environment and attractions are at least comparable to most of the other water camps in the Delta.

Accommodation is in one of six chalets. Looking from the river, there's a double (most camps would call this a 'honeymoon') chalet on the right of the main lounge/dining area, and five twin-bedded chalets on the left. All are brick with thatch and, above a waist-high wall, one side is largely open to the river. (A rain-proof screen can be rolled down, but is seldom needed.) All have high thatched roofs and very simple, wooden furniture.

With a free flow of air from outside, a walk-in mosquito net protects the beds from insects. Each has an en-suite bathroom with flush toilet, hot shower and a washbasin. The camp has a generator running during the day, and that feeds batteries which supply power at night for two bedside lights in each chalet. They're very comfortable, but not luxurious.

The camp's central lounge/dining area is under a large thatched roof, with one side open to the river. Again, this is simple and comfortable though not ornate. What does strike one about the camp is the way that it's been built within a wonderfully thick and tropical patch of riverine vegetation. All around there are knobthorn (*Acacia nigrescens*), waterberry (*Syzygium cordatum*), sycamore fig (*Ficus sycomorus*) mangosteen (*Garcinia livingstonei*), jackalberries (*Diospyros mespiliformis*), sausage trees (*Kigelia africana*) and some of the most wonderfully contorting python vines (*Cocculus hirsutus*) that you'll see anywhere.
Rates: US$220/330 per person sharing/single per night from December to June; US$295/440 from July to November. Includes all meals, activities and local drinks – but excludes other drinks and transfers. Open: all year.

Sepupa
Sometime spelt 'Sepopa', 223km north of Sehithwa and perhaps 58km south of Shakawa, Sepupa can be reached via a turning from the main road (⊕ SEPUPA 18°44.150'S, 22°10.625'E), which is about 1.7km away.

There you'll find a few shops including a bottle stall, a general dealer, a radio mast and a bakery advertising 'fresh palatable skilled-made bread'. Irresistible!

However, if you're not tempted then there's a turning off this linking road to the south, about halfway between the village and the main road. This is signposted to the Swamp Stop, and also leads to the motorboat ferry to Seronga.

The ferry to Seronga
On the right of the Swamp Stop, a few hundred metres downstream, is the very informal mooring for the ferry. This is really just a motorboat with a shade cover that's driven across the river when full. It normally leaves around 12.00–14.00pm, provided there are enough people, and takes 90 minutes to cross the river (diagonally downstream, via a variety of winding channels) to Seronga. A one-way trip costs P20 per person.

Where to stay
There's really only one option here:

Sepupa Swamp Stop (camping plus fixed tents) contact via Island Safari Lodge in Maun; tel: 6860330; fax: 6862932; email: island@info.bw
The Swamp Stop itself (⊕ SWAMPS 18°44.749'S, 22°11.843'E) is just a simple campsite under trees, with a few Meru tents erected on concrete bases for those who haven't brought their own tents; all share ablutions. Firewood is available for P10 per barrow.

However, the owners have marketed it well and positioned it as one of the very few remaining bases for budget safaris into the Delta, and a possible springboard for getting to Seronga, which is one of the other possible bases!

Activities here include self-catering mokoro trails. Costs depend on group size and duration, but expect a typical three-night trip to cost around US$255/145/135/110/110 per

THE CATFISH RUN

The amazing phenomenon of the catfish run is unique to the Okavango Delta. It happens every year, between early August and the end of November, though its timing is difficult to predict precisely.

As the water level starts to drop in the northern part of the Panhandle, it is still rising in the southern part of the delta. The catfish runs start in the north of the Panhandle, where the lowering water levels concentrate the Delta's smaller fish in the channels and papyrus banks – especially the relatively small churchill, *Petrocephalus catostoma*, and bulldog, *Marcusenius macrolepidotus*.

The main predatory species involved include the sharp-toothed catfish, *Clarias gariepinus*, a hardy, omnivorous species which grows up to 1.4m in length, and 59kg in weight, and the much smaller blunt-toothed catfish, *Clarias ngaensis*. These catfish hunt in packs and a 'run' starts with the catfish swimming upstream inside the papyrus banks. Here they slap their powerful tails on the surface of the water, making a noise like a gunshot, and against the papyrus to stun the smaller fish, their prey.

Hundreds and sometimes thousands of catfish will work their way upstream like this, making the water 'boil' with their frenzy of activity. All this noise and commotion attracts an eager audience of herons, storks, egrets, fish eagles, and other fish-eating birds on the banks, while crocodiles, snakes and tiger fish lurk beyond the papyrus in the deeper channels waiting to snap up anything that escapes from the papyrus.

Although in each run the catfish swim upstream, when it's finished they pause and drift back down, subsequently re-joining other catfish and starting new runs. So as the water levels drop further down in the Delta, so the location of the runs move south also.

These runs occur in many different sizes. There will be several per day in different areas of the Delta, each covering a distance of a few kilometres before fizzling out. A couple may be longer than this, perhaps continuing for as long as two weeks and covering a lot of distance – but these are the exception rather than the rule.

Eventually, signalled by the onset of the rising waters, the catfish will themselves move out onto the floodplains and spawn.

---

person for 1/2/3/4/5 people. Alternatively you can take the river-taxi to Seronga, and organise trips directly with the Okavango Polers' Trust (see page 174).

Motor boat trips cost P80 per hour, or P550 per day, plus fuel (P3.75 per litre). There's a houseboat here that takes a maximum of 12 people at a time for P150 per hour or P800 per day, plus fuel. (This comes with a small tender boat attached.) Either of these boats can be used for overnight camping trips on the islands for P15 per person, plus the appropriate boat charges.

Transfers to Seronga cost P100 per person one-way – but require a minimum group size of six people, making the ferry next door a much more economic option for most people. *Rates: P25 per person camping, erected (and services) tent is P200 per night (max of 2 nights). Open: all year.*

THE DELTA'S WESTERN FRINGES

Ordered from north to south, here's a brief listing of the main landmarks and villages on the road between Sepupa and Sehithwa. If it gets a little repetitive, then take that as a fair reflection of the road which is long and well surfaced with tarmac.

Most of this has a low, wide verge of groundcover which is often cut – helping to ensure that big game can be seen before it is standing in front of you. But for all this visibility, the scenery is uninteresting.

Although you're travelling at times very close to the western edge of the Okavango Delta, the road passes through apparently undistinguished areas of bush. You may see the occasional animal, but with man and cattle as the dominant species in this area, only bird-watchers are likely to find much of interest on the drive.

Sepupa to Etsha 13

Tsodilo turning

About 0.5km south of the Sepupa junction on the main road is a smaller turning (✪ T1TURN 18°45.160'S, 22°10.609'E) onto a track which is very clearly signposted to the Tsodilo Hills. This is the most southern approach to the hills (see page 373 for more details).

Ikoga Gate

At about 211km north of Sehithwa, 12km south of the Sepupa turn-off, you will have to stop at the Ikoga Gate (✪ VET-IK 18°50.327'S, 22°13.756'E), which is a checkpoint on the Thamacha Veterinary Fence.

Ikoga turning

About 206km north of Sehithwa, there's another turning east, this time to Ikoga.

Etsha-13

About 32km south of the Sepupa turn-off, or 191km north of Sehithwa, is a turning (✪ E13TUR 19°0.793'S, 22°17.356'E) which leads slightly over 3km east to Etsha 13. This small town has a few basic shops, but little more.

Guma Lagoon

On the western side of the Delta, at the very base of the Panhandle, Guma is a large, papyrus-lined lagoon. It is linked to the Thaoge River, the main eastern finger of the Okavango's river system, by a short channel (40 minutes by boat from the camp or the lodge).

Guma Lagoon and the main Thoage River are excellent spots for fishing and bird-watching. This combination, with relatively easy access from Etsha 13, has encouraged two different camps to set up here.

Flora and fauna highlights

Guma isn't a place for big game; it's a deep-water environment that offers good bird watching and fishing.

The vegetation around the lagoon itself is mainly papyrus, though you'll also find large stands of phragmites reeds. You'll also find the odd waterberry, Syzygium cordatum, and water fig, Ficus verruculosa, especially in the smaller channels and backwaters.

On the banks, the riverine vegetation is thick and lush. It includes plenty of wild date palms, Phoenix reclinata, river beans, Sesbania sesban, and potato bushes, Phyllanthus reticulatus, which are members of the euphorbia family, and are not related to potatoes at all – but smell the air on a warm evening and you'll realise where their name comes from.

Also keep an eye out for large sour plum, Ximenia caffra, water pear, Syzygium guineense, jackalberry trees, Diospyros mespiliformis, and the occasional sausage tree,

Kigelia africana – one of which greets you as you enter Guma Lagoon Camp. Further from the water, you'll often find acacias: camelthorn, *Acacia erioloba*, knobthorn trees, *Acacia nigrescens*, and umbrella thorn, *Acacia tortilis*, are the main species here. There are a few baobabs, *Adansonia digitata*, in the area, but they're not common here.

The more common birds include fish eagles, many species of herons, egrets, warblers, bee-eaters and kingfishers, pygmy geese and greater and lesser jacanas. Look for red-shouldered widows in the papyrus, and reed cormorants and darters sunning themselves on perches over the water.

In the riverine forest areas you can find Heuglin's robins, crested and black-collard barbets, green pigeons, various sunbirds and, in the summer, the spectacular paradise flycatchers in breeding plumage.

Getting there and away

Starting at the small town of Etsha 13 (⊕ ETSH13 19°00.975'S, 22°19.125'E), the route to either of the lodges at Guma Lagoon is only about 13km of very sandy 4WD track. If you're driving a 2WD then with prior notice the lodges can arrange to collect you from Etsha 13, leaving your car somewhere safe whilst you're at Guma.

There are some small signposts on this route, but they're not always consistent and the route is far from straight. Start off by heading through the village on a track going east southeast. Gradually this turns east, then northeast, and finally north – as the scenery gets prettier with less domestic animals and settlements, and more small date palm islands and open floodplains.

A GPS is sensible for this route. Waypoints for one possible route, from Etsha13 to the Guma Lagoon lodges, are as follows. In order:

ETSH13   19°00.975'S, 22°19.125'E (the village of Etsha 13)
GUMA00   19°00.900'S, 22°19.171'E   GUMA01 19°00.933'S, 22°19.362'E;
GUMA02   19°01.317'S, 22°20.135'E;   GUMA03 19°01.236'S, 22°20.318'E;
GUMA04   19°01.017'S, 22°20.533'E;   GUMA05 19°01.210'S, 22°21.354'E;
GUMA06   19°00.734'S, 22°22.192'E;   GUMA07 19°00.204'S, 22°22.831'E;
GUMA08   19°00.042'S, 22°22.912'E;   GUMA09 18°59.252'S, 22°22.825'E;
GUMA10   18°59.060'S, 22°22.912'E;   GUMA11 18°58.537'S, 22°22.609'E
GUMAIL   18°58.245'S, 22°22.101'E (Guma Island Lodge)
GUMA13   18°58.098'S, 22°22.228'E;   GUMA14 18°57.749'S, 22°22.370'E
GUMALC   18°57.73'S, 22°22.404'E (Guma Lagoon Camp)

There are certainly more direct routes than this, as the whole area is criss-crossed with a variety of confusing bush tracks. However, many will be seasonal and depend on the water levels, so beware of getting stuck!

Alternatively, the Island Lodge has a relatively new airstrip, or you can fly into the small airstrip at Gumare and be collected from there by the lodge. It may also be possible to fly into Seronga, and be transferred to the Island Lodge by boat from there.

What to see and do

Precise activities depend on where you're staying, though boat trips are really the main draw here. On the whole, the water's deep enough to limit the scope of mekoros for most of the year, and so motor boats are the vehicle of choice. If you're not a devout angler, or birdwatcher, then just take a few rods and a pair of binoculars out and do a little of both – it's very relaxing.

Where to stay

There are only two choices at this lagoon. These are both quite different and don't generally work closely together.

Guma Island Lodge (8 tents & camping) P Bag 13, Maun; tel/fax: 674022; email: gumacamp@info.bw; web: www.gumalodge.com
Built on the northwestern edge of the lagoon, this lodge was opened in June 2000 by its owners, Geoff and Nookie Randall, who have lived in the area for years. (Geoff played an important part in starting the building of fiberglass mekoro in the area – and thus is partially responsible for saving an enormous number of the Delta's old trees!)

There are eight tents here, all raised up on high wooden decking. Inside you'll find comfortable twin beds made with colourful fabrics, chairs, a small table and a wooden wardrobe behind. At the back of each tent is an en-suite shower, toilet and washbasin. The power at the lodge, and the lighting in the tents, comes from the lodge's own generator and a system of back-up batteries for the lights at night.

The main lounge and dining area is a large log cabin, again raised up on decking, which houses a comfortable lounge, a dining room and a well-stocked bar. There's a better collection of local baskets and craftwork here than in most curio shops, and some are for sale in the lodge's own small shop.

THE ETSHA VILLAGES

In 1969, the war in Angola (which, in many ways, was an extension of the Cold War of the superpowers though using African proxies) displaced a large number of mostly Hambukushu people from the Caprivi area into Botswana. There they were accepted as refugees. Initially they were received at Shakawe, but eventually the plan was to move them to a new village called Etsha, south of there.

However, whilst at Shakawe it's said that they naturally split into thirteen separate groups. So when they were moved, they naturally split into thirteen villages which spread out along the western edge of the Delta. These were each a kilometres apart, and so were called, somewhat unimaginatively, Etsha 1, Etsha 2, Etsha 3, and so on up to the most northerly, Etsha 13.

Now the old track which links them and runs close to the Delta has been largely superseded by the new tar highway, which takes a more direct route on the east of the old road. However, you'll still find tracks linking the two, one of which is close to Etsha 13, and another close to Etsha 6.

The tents and main area are all widely spread out and linked by fairly high wooden walkways. This keeps everything above water if levels rise to a high flood. Normally the ground beneath is dry, with cool lawns dotted with date palms. There are plans to install a swimming pool here.

There's also a campsite here, slightly separate from the lodge, but under the same cool canopy of trees as the main lodge. Toilets and showers are simple, with wooden-clad showers and toilets, and there are also braai stands and facilities for washing up, though if you arrange it in advance, you can have your meals in the main lodge. Campers here are often serious about their fishing!

In the last year or so Guma has become a favourite stop for overland group trips and activities major on mokoro trips, which cost around P130 per mokoro per day. That said, various boat trips, booze cruises and fishing excursions are also possible.

Finally, after visiting the lodge and writing this, I've since seen the lodge referred to as 'Nguma Luxury Lodge' and also as 'Nguma Island Tented Lodge' – the latter by Audi Camp (see page 168) who promote it as a base for fly-in mokoro trips.

Rates: P720 per person sharing, including all meals and activities. Camping is P20 per person per night. Open: all year.

Guma Lagoon Camp (3 tents and camping) P Bag 23, Maun; tel: 674626/7; fax: 674626; email: guma.property@info.bw

Barely a kilometre northeast of the lodge is Guma Lagoon Camp, which is very different. It's run by an enthusiastic couple, Guy and Beverley Lobjoit, who ran Nxamaseri Lodge for many years before moving here to start their own place in 1999. Guy's an angler of some repute (one of the Okavango's fly-fishing experts) as well as an accomplished birder.

Here their operation caters mainly for self-catering visitors who drive themselves here – although meals can sometimes be arranged if you book far enough in advance. They have a campsite with toilets and hot showers, and also three very comfortable 4m x 4m dome tents, set on shaded stands overlooking the lagoon and furnished with beds and linen. Each of these tents has its own toilet, shower and washbasin built beside the tent.

The camp has a fully equipped kitchen, with pots, pans, cutlery, cooking equipment and freezing facilities. This is next to a shaded dining/bar area with a deck extending over the lagoon.

It's a relaxed and friendly spot. Guy and Beverley also run a fish farm here (which is fascinating to look around) and Guy can be hired as a specialist fishing guide for around US$100 per day. Note that the camp also hosts the bush offices and main supply base for Okavango Horse Safaris (see page 327), so don't be surprised if you see horses galloping around as you approach.

Rates: P33 per person camping, P82 using the dome tents; P90 per hour for boat hire or night boat drives. P40/80/90 for a one-way boat or vehicle transfers to or from Etsha 13/Gumare/Seronga. Open: all year.

Etsha 6 to Toteng
Etsha 6
About 45km south of the Sepupa turn-off (178km north of Sehithwa) there's a signposted turning (⊕ E6TURN 19°6.706'S, 22°16.152'E). This leads, in slightly less than 3km, due east of here to the village of Etsha 6.

When I last drove along the main road here, there was a concentration of pot-holes in the road between the two turnings for Etsha 6 and 13. So drive carefully here. (That said, I only noted these because the overall standard of the tar road up the eastern side of the Delta is excellent, and pot-holes are rare on most of it.)

The town itself has the most reliable fuel in the area, from a Shell Station in the centre. Thus most people passing through and travelling any distance should stop here. It's also a place where buses turn off the road to stop. Etsha 6 has a bakery and take-away, behind the bus stop, that sells good fresh bread (and some less impressive pies, chips and other fast food).

Across the road from the fuel station is a Co-op which stocks cutlery, crockery, non-perishables like tinned food, and basic staples like rice and maize in quantity. There's very little fresh produce here, but they do usually have chilled soft drinks and bottled water.

There is one camp to the east of here that can be accessed from Etsha 6 – Makwena Camp, in NG24 Reserve. See page 301 for brief comments.

Gumare
About 146km north of Sehithwa, 37km from Nokaneng, and 77km south of Sepupa, there's a turn-off east to Gumare (⊕ GUMARE 19°22.242'S, 22°09.242'E). This is one of the main towns of the Panhandle area. Signboards (only some of which are current!) crowd beside the turn-off, virtually all pointing the 700m or so west to town.

There you'll find a hospital, a school, a small community of overseas aid workers and a thriving small business centre. Again, there's also a highly-visible radio mast in town (with good cellphone coverage even for my UK phone!).

It's worth seeking out the small curio shop in town that has good local baskets at very reasonable prices, and there's a good little supermarket here and also a fuel station (where, sadly, supplies can be erratic). Being about halfway between Sehithwa and Shakawe, buses travelling along this route usually detour to Gumare, and will often stop here briefly.

About 4km north of the turn-off is another turning, west from the main road, signposted to Gumare's small airstrip.

Nokaneng
About 109km north of Sehithwa, 114km south of Sepupa, there's another radio-mast (⊕ NOKANE – 19°39.694'S, 22°11.184'E) amidst a group of houses, some of traditional design and others modern, complete with satellite dishes. Just south of the village there's a small turning to the northeast signposted to Nokaneng airstrip.

There's also a track heading east from here that leads to the Namibian border, near Tsumkwe, which opened recently, but check it before you go. Near the border, it's also possible to turn south and access the Aha Hills area and Gcwihaba Hills and Caverns. See pages 377–87 for more comments on these areas.

Habu turn-off
About 79km north of Sehithwa you'll find another radio mast and a signpost eastwards to the village of Habu, which is about 18km away. There you'll also find a small settlement with a few small shops.

Tsau
About 43km north of Sehithwa, or 180km south of Sepupa, you'll come across a turning to the village of Tsau. (This is also often referred to as 'Tsao'.) The settlement itself is just to the east of the main road, and its prominent radio mast is quite a landmark (✛ TSAU 20°10.294'S, 22°27.265'E). Here you'll find lots of small huts, though relatively little tree or vegetation cover, and a few small, general shops.

Setata Veterinary Fence Gate
At about 27.5km north of Sehithwa you'll have to stop and pass through the Setata Gate (✛ VET-SE 20°15.775'S; 22°33.926'E) in the Veterinary Fence.

Sehithwa
Also spelt as 'Sehithwa' on road signs, Sehithwa (✛ SEHITH 20°28.259'S; 22°42.372'E) is about 29km from Toteng, and a more substantial settlement. When I last passed through here there was a lot of road works here, apparently for a new tar road that was being built to link to the main road to Ghanzi due south of town. Locals commented that there is some cellphone coverage for about 10km north of town, though I didn't pick this up at all.

Toteng
Though a significant dot on the map, Toteng (✛ TOTENG 20°21.407'S; 22°57.204'E) is little more than a road junction. It's about 64km from Maun on the good, tar (A35) road to Sehithwa, and is notable for the left turn onto the A3 road to Ghanzi, about 222km away. Today you'll find a bottle store and a general dealer at this junction, and a sprinkling of small cattle-farming homesteads in the local area.

Despite its apparent insignificance, Toteng has historical importance as a centre for the Batawana – Campbell (see *Further Reading*) comments that: 'When they arrived in Ngamiland in 1795 they settled at Kgwebe and later moved to Toteng.' This was also one of the areas that received an influx of Herero people after their defeat at the battle of Waterberg.

Lake Ngami
The existence of a great lake within the Kalahari was known to Europeans from early reports of Bekwena and Batawana people, though it wasn't reached by them until the mid-19th century. Livingstone arrived on August 1 1849, with Cotton, Oswell and Murray, narrowly beating Charles Andersson, who set out specifically to reach it from present-day Namibia.

In his book, entitled Lake Ngami (see *Further Reading*), Andersson was hugely disappointed with what he first took to be Lake Ngami. He wrote:

> At last a blue line of great extent appeared in the distance, and I made sure
> it was the long-sought object; but I was still doomed in my
> disappointment. It turned out to be merely a large hollow in the rainy
> season filled with water, but now dry and covered with saline
> encrustations.

However, he hadn't reached the lake at this stage, and after getting beyond some pans and reed beds, and over a series of sand ridges, he finally glimpsed the water, and described the moment:

> There, indeed, at no very great distance, lay spread before me an immense
> sheet of water bounded only by the horizon – the object of my ambition
> for years, and for which I have abandoned home and friends, and risked
> my life.

Visiting the lake is certainly easier than it was for those first explorers, though it's by no means well signposted, and at times it can still be very disappointing. Note that although very large when full, a high rate of evaporation and a very shallow profile means that the area covered by water can vary enormously.

Getting there and away

The lake's bed is surrounded by a triangle of good roads, so approaching it is a matter of turning off one of these and following your nose (or, perhaps better, your compass or GPS). If you're feeling cautious then start by checking out the road which leaves Sehithwa heading south-southeast. This was a rough gravel track across the dry bed of the lake when I last travelled on it, but it may be tar now. If there's any water in the lake then it's likely to be on the eastern side of this road.

If so, then the road between Sehithwa and Toteng passes close to the northern shore. To maximise your chances of getting close to the water even when it's receded a little, strike off this about a third to half way from Sehithwa to Toteng, and try to find tracks heading south and slightly east. You should reach the shore within about 5km of the road.

When to visit

The pithy answer to this question is: 'whenever it's full of water!' And there lies the rub; it's only worth going if there's water in the lake, and few people will have been there and be able to tell you. Your best chance of getting up-to-date information is probably from operators in Maun, and especially the pilots, because if the lake's empty it's better to save yourself a trip. If it's just a wide expanse of clay, then you won't find it that exciting.

The state of this mystical lake varies greatly, depending upon whether the Delta's flood, which has historically been Lake Ngami's main source of water, has been high enough to overflow into the Nhabe River which feeds the lake. The lake was an empty dustbowl for the late 1980s and 90s, but then filled to a shallow depth during 2000 and 2001. So ask around to find out what's happening.

If and when it really floods, Lake Ngami comes alive with birdlife. From October, the ducks, geese, waders and other northern migrants arrive, lining the muddy shores until the weather cools towards the end of April. The flamingos, both greater and lesser, don't choose their times so carefully – being found here in their thousands whenever the conditions are right for the algae on which they feed. They appear from the shore as a pink haze settled on the water's surface.

Where to stay
There's nowhere official to stay here, but the land is open enough to camp rough – provided that you ask permission from the nearest local villagers. On my last visit the local villagers suggested that we go a few kilometres away from the lake itself to avoid the mosquitoes. This was a very wise move. You'll need to be self-sufficient, of course, and don't rely upon any drinkable water here.

What to see and do
This is purely a birding destination, though because visitors here are really very rare there are no tracks or pathways (for 4WDs or walkers) designed for bird-watchers. All the tracks here have been made to serve the villagers and their many, many cattle. All this makes getting around time-consuming and at times difficult – but if there's water here then it might be worth it.

THE NORTHWEST KALAHARI
This area is Botswana at its most enigmatic. Here you'll find huge tracts of the Kalahari, punctuated only by isolated Bushman settlements. It's an area where you need to have a good 4WD (or two), and you must be totally self-sufficient – travelling with all your own food, water, fuel and equipment.

It's not somewhere which will attract visitors for its game viewing or bird-watching, though you will find both game and birds here. In fact, it's not an area that attracts many visitors at all. But old Africa hands are drawn here for its isolated ranges of hills. One displays a breathtaking cultural heritage of paintings, another hides a labyrinthine cave system, and a third – well... the Aha Hills are just there. On the map. In the middle of the Kalahari. Waiting to be visited.

For more information on the science and explorations of this area, interested readers are directed to numerous articles in *Botswana Notes and Records*, some of which have been noted as reference in *Further Reading*.

Tsodilo Hills
Rising to 400m above the monotony of the Kalahari's thick bush, archaeologists say that the hills have been sporadically inhabited for about 30,000 years – making this one of the world's oldest historical sites. For only about the last millennia has this included Bantu people: previously, for thousands of years, the San lived here, hunting, using springs in the hills for water and painting animals (over 2,000 of them) on the rocks.

For both San and Bantu, the Tsodilo Hills were a mystical place, 'home of very old and very great spirits' who demanded respect from visitors. As told in *The Lost World of the Kalahari* (which is essential reading before any visit here, see *Further Reading*), they created much trouble for some of the first Europeans to visit – as recently as the 1950s. Long ago it must have been, in van der Post's words,

> ... a great fortress of living bushman culture, a Louvre of the desert filled with treasure'

The Tsodilo Hills remain a remarkable place, an important national monument and, in December 2001, was declared Botswana's only World Heritage Site. Whilst this should help to safeguard the hills for future generations, I can't visit without wondering what it was like when the San were here. What we regard now as the high art of an ancient people is remarkable, but it's very sad that our understanding of it is now devoid of the meaning and spirituality with which it was once imbued.

It's really worth spending several days here to search out the paintings of the Tsodilo Hills. It's a long drive across deep Kalahari sand to get here, and once

TSODILO HILLS

KEY

4WD track	
Cliff trail	
Rhino trail	
Lion trail	
Male hill trail	
GPS point	⊕

Key to numbers

1 Pictures 2/8 up ravine and on top
2 Pictures 9/10 including the 2 rhino
3 Picture 11 whales and a penguin
4 Picture 13 Laurens van der Post panel (high up)
5 Pictures 14/16

Child Hill

NORTHERN APPROACH

MALATS
Malatso campsite

Start of Cliff trail

MLTURN

Female Hill

SQCAMP 1
Squirrel Valley campsite

Remains of old settlement

5
4 2
3

LITURN

Lion panel & start of Lion trail

Headquarters & main campsite

Cave 12 with a signboard next to it

Pipeline

MAKOBA
Makoba Woods campsite

Male Hill

Borehole

White Paintings Shelter

N

Bradt

OLDVIL
Old San Village

Airstrip
TSOAIR

420m

CENTRAL APPROACH

0   2km
0   1 mile

Borehole

TSGATE

Tshukumutshu

Hambukushu Village

FORKRD

SOUTHERN APPROACH

San Village SANVIL

GPS REFERENCES FOR TSODILO HILLS MAP (opposite)	
FORKRD	18°47.414'S, 21°44.921'E
LITURN	18°45.538'S, 21°45.109'E
MAKOBA	18°45.688'S, 21°44.586'E
MALATS	18°43.608'S, 21°43.910'E
MLTURN	18°44.243'S, 21°43.575'E
OLDVIL	18°46.386'S, 21°44.782'E
SANVIL	18°48.147'S, 21°43.903'E
SQCAMP	18°45.385'S, 21°44.248'E
TSGATE	18°47.275'S, 21°44.856'E
TSOAIR	18°46.870'S, 21°44.645'E

you're here then even just exploring the marked trails can easily take three or four days, though a longer stay would be better.

However, after several visits over the years, I am left remembering the captivating feeling of spirituality in the hills far more than simply the images of the paintings, however remarkable. I've known this to disturb some visitors profoundly; they were uneasy to the point of wanting to flee the hills, and couldn't wait to get away – whilst others find the hills entrancing and completely magical.

So if you come here, then do so with respect and take some time to stay here – don't just come to tick it off your itinerary and leave.

A word of warning

In *The Lost World of the Kalahari*, you can read Laurens van der Post's story of his first visit to the hills. Of how his party had ignored the advice of their guide, and thus disturbed the spirits of the hills, by hunting warthog and steenbok on their way. Once at the hills, his companion's camera magazines inexplicably kept jamming, his tape recorders stopped working, and bees repeatedly attacked his group – and the problems only ceased when they made a written apology to the spirits.

So perhaps the spirits here are one more reason why you ought to treat the Tsodilo Hills with the very greatest of respect when you visit them.

Folklore and archaeology

The Tsodilo Hills hold a special spiritual significance for the people of the region, and are of immense archaeological value to the wider world for what can be learned about some of our earliest ancestors.

Folklore

The San believe the hills contain the spirits of the dead, and that their powerful gods live in caves within the Female Hill, from where they rule the world. They believe that these gods will cause misfortune to anyone who hunts or causes death near the hills.

They have many beliefs, all specific to places within the hills. For example, there's a cave on the western side of the Female hill which contains a permanent source of water and, the San believe, a giant serpent with spiralling horns, like a kudu. If a San guide takes you around the hills, then ask them about legends and stories associated with the places that you visit on the hills.

Meanwhile the Hambukushu people, who live in the area, believe that God lowered man to earth at the site of the hills, and he landed on the Female Hill. For proof they point to footprints which are engraved into the rock, high up on the hill. However, modern sceptics claim these are simply natural marks in the rock, or even suggest that they might be the prints of dinosaurs!

Archaeology

Archaeologists think that people (*Homo sapiens* as opposed to *Homo erectus*) have occupied the area for at least about 60,000 years. Estimating the age of rock paintings is very difficult, and usually done by linking a style of painting with nearby artefacts which can be scientifically dated with precision (eg: by carbon 14 dating techniques).

However, the Tsodilo Hills have had more archaeological research than most of southern Africa's sites – so we do have an idea about the people who lived here. So far, most of the evidence unearthed here dates from the Middle Stone Age period. There have been several major excavations including ones at the Depression Shelter, the Rhino Cave and White Paintings. (See *Further Reading* for various articles in *Botswana Notes & Records* for more details. There's also a more personal view of a visit to one of these excavations in Mike Main's *Kalahari: Life's variety in dune and delta*.)

Excavations at White Paintings, a site at the base of the Male Hill, indicate habitation going back to at least 40–50,000 years ago. For this the archaeological team excavated as deep as 7m below ground level, finding a variety of stone blades and scrapers. Of these, it's estimated that over 55% of the raw materials don't occur in the hills, and must have been brought in from outside. This indicates at least a movement of people, and perhaps early bartering or trading networks.

Excavations at the Depression Shelter certainly indicate that people were using coloured pigments here, probably for painting, more than 19,000 years ago. However, despite what you'll often read, nobody really knows exactly how the painters used to make their paints. Many things have been suggested, but animal fats and derivatives of plants seem the likely binding agents, probably mixed with pigments obtained largely from ash, various minerals and plant dyes. Iron oxide, in the form of ochre, seems a particularly likely mineral to have been used.

Meanwhile much more recently, about AD800–1,000, specularite was being mined here intensively. This mineral was historically used for cosmetic purposes by groups within South Africa, further emphasising the likelihood of a long-standing trade network that included the people of the Tsodilo.

The paintings

The paintings at the Tsodilo Hills chart thousands of years of human habitation, and include some of the world's most important and impressive rock art. It is 'a Louvre of the desert filled with treasure.'

Its special nature is augmented by the realisation that these hills are 250km from the nearest other known rock art. They are totally removed from all of southern Africa's other rock paintings. Even within the hills, some of the paintings are located on high, inaccessible cliffs, with commanding views over the landscape. This was surely a deliberate part of the painting for the people who created them.

Campbell and Coulson, in their excellent book African Rock Art (see *Further Reading*), assert that the Tsodilo Hills 'contain some 4,000 red finger paintings composed of about 50% animals, 37% geometrics, and 13% highly stylised human figures.'

The paintings here belong to several different styles and if you take the time to look closely at them will often amaze you with their detail. Although most of the animals painted are wild, Campbell and Coulson noted that there is a much higher incidence of paintings of domestic stock than any other similar sites in southern Africa.

The human figures painted include many with schematic men painted with erect penises. It's thought that these could be associated with the trance dance – a traditional dance of the San in which rhythmic breathing often produces an altered state of consciousness.

Geology

The Tsodilo Hills are formed from what's technically known as 'micaceous quartzite schists'. These metamorphic rocks started out as shales, probably deposited as mud on the surface of an ancient sea. Great heat and pressure in the earth changed them, and you can see the small crystals of minerals formed during this process if you look carefully.

Tsodilo's schists have particularly high mica and quartz contents, and a coarse-grained surface. Conveniently, this texture means that rocks give a good grip to rubber-soled shoes, so they're relatively easy to clamber around. In many places there are piles of boulders, and you'll often need to hop between these if you want to explore the hills.

There are a few permanent springs of water in the hills, but these are very difficult to find without a local guide. They were certainly important to the early inhabitants of the area though, as they would have been the only water sources for miles around.

Flora and fauna

Unlike most destinations for visitors in Botswana, a visit to the Tsodilo Hills really isn't about looking for animals, birds or plants. The focus is much more cultural and historical. That said, don't forget that you are in a very sparsely populated area of the northern Kalahari and there is wildlife around.

On the roads that approach the hills I've been very aware of fresh elephant dung, and fleeting glimpses of occasional fleeing small buck. There are certainly kudu, steenbok and duiker here permanently, as well as leopard and probably spotted hyena.

In his 1934 book *The Mammals of South West Africa* (see *Further Reading*), Shortridge records that klipspringer were found here at the hills, although I've not come across any reports of them here more recently, so it seems unlikely that there is any population of them left now.

Everywhere around the hills you'll find quite a wide variety of birdlife, including the ubiquitous grey hornbills – easily heard as well as seen with their descending call of 'phe, phephee, pheephee, pheeoo, phew, pheeoo-pheeoo' (with thanks to Newman, see *Further Reading*, for expressing this song so well on paper!)

Look out also for the Tsodilo gecko (*Pachydactylus tsodiloensis*) a small, nocturnal gecko with yellow and brown stripes which is endemic to these hills.

Looking at the vegetation, keep your eyes open for stands of mongongo trees, *Ricinodendron rautanenii*, which occur on the hills and sometimes in pure stands on the Kalahari's sand. These can reach between 15-20m tall, characterised by smooth, often peeling bark on grey to light-brown stems and compound leaflets a little like the chestnut trees of Europe. After sprays of yellow flowers around October to November, they produce egg-shaped grey-green fruits from February onwards. These can be up to 3.5 x 2.5cm in size, covered with smooth hairs. Inside these are mongongo nuts, which can be cracked open to reveal an edible kernel – one of the most important, and celebrated, foods for the San across the Kalahari. Palgrave (see *Further Reading*) comments that this is a protected tree in South

Africa, and that its light, strong wood is sometimes used as a substitute for imported balsa wood.

Getting there

There are now three routes into the Tsodilo Hills from the main Shakawe-Sehithwa road. All the tracks described here are difficult, sandy 4WD-only routes that will take you about two and a half to three hours to complete, despite the relatively short distances involved. Expect to use your low-range gears a lot in the sand, and travel as early in the day as you can (driving is easier when the sand is cooler).

All of these approaches boast an unusual type of corrugation. Rather than the usual high-frequency vehicle rattle, there are corrugations here which make the whole vehicle bounce up and down. If you attempt to drive over this faster than about 10km/h, you find your heads hitting the ceiling. It's painful, but ensures that getting to the hills is always a long and tedious drive.

Whilst complaining about the road – look on the bright side. Firstly, if you have to make an effort to get there, you should appreciate it more. Secondly, these corrugations ensure that visitors will never over-run the hills, as only those who are really keen to be here will stomach the journey!

Although animals aren't prolific in this area, there is big game here, including elephants. So drive carefully because trying to beat a hasty retreat from a surprised elephant whilst your vehicle is in thick sand simply isn't very practical!

That said, the main danger here is fire from grass seeds and stems blocking up your vehicle's radiator and collecting near its hot exhaust system. So if you're driving here, your must take steps to prevent this. (See page 122 of *Chapter 6*.)

Considering the three possible driving routes, from north to south:

Northern approach

The turning from the main road is immediately next to the south side of the Somachima Veterinary Fence (✪ VET-SA 18°29.256'S, 21°55.142'E). This is about 17.4km south of Shakawe. This route follows the fence for a little while, before forking off left. It takes about 36km to reach the hills.

This used to be the best of the routes to the hills. However, on my last visit in February 2001, I tried this route in reverse, from the hills to the road. To find it take the track between the Male and Female Hills, head for ✪ LITURN 18°45.538'S, 21°45.109'E, and then ignore the turning right to the start of the Lion Trail. However, when I tried the track was very overgrown as it left the hills. It didn't appear to have been used for some time, and wasn't easily navigable. So unless this has improved, this northern track will probably swiftly become impassable and vanish back into the bush.

Central approach

This is a relatively new road to the hills, that has been built fairly recently. A lot of vegetation has been cleared for this along the way, and there's one track going in either direction. However, both are still very slow, bumpy sand tracks, and this route has the limited, formal character of a cut line through the bush. So though perhaps a slightly faster route than either of the two older approaches, I prefer the older approaches. Note that in mid-2002 there were rumours that this track was about to be surfaced with gravel, though old hands aren't holding their breath in anticipation.

The central route starts on the main road at (✪ T2TURN 18°35.834'S, 21°59.986'E). This is 4.8km southeast of the 'Tsodilo View' (✪ TSVIEW

Above Springbok 'pronking' across the open, flat plains of the Central Kalahari (CM)

Below left Pale-chanting goshawk, the most common raptor in the Kalahari, often seen on telegraph poles (CM)

Below right A straight sand track runs beside this veterinary fence, typical of roads in the Kalahari (CM)

Above The gemsbok, or oryx, is perfectly adapted for the Kalahari's high temperatures and lack of water (CM)

Below left Salt, or *trona*, deposits form the barren white hearts of many of the smaller islands in the Okavango Delta (CM)

Below right Stone-Age arrowheads can still be found on Makgadikgadi's salt pans (CM)

18°33.830'S, 21°58.273'E), which is signposted on the road, and almost 15km south of the Somachima Veterinary Fence (⊕ VET-SA 18°29.256'S, 21°55.142'E).

From there the tracks head southwest beside each other, averaging a bearing of about 230°, and to the left of the hills. It passes around the southern side of the Male Hill and joins the southern approach at (⊕ FORKRD 18°47.414'S, 21°44.921'E), about 34km from the tarred road. You then bear right to reach the main gate.

To leave the hills this way, find the main gate (⊕ TSGATE 18°47.275'S, 21°44.856'E) and head south of the Male Hill, following the track slightly south of east. Shortly the road forks, (⊕ FORKRD 18°47.414'S, 21°44.921'E), and you take the left hand track which bends around the Male Hill towards T2TURN heading northeast at a bearing of about 50°.

Southern approach

This begins about 10km south of Sepupa, but first you get yourself onto the untarred track that is marked on the Shell map as joining Etsha with Sepupa. To do this it'll be easiest to head to Sepupa and then, about 500m south of the turning to the village itself, take the turnoff (⊕ T1TURN 18°45.160'S, 22°10.609'E) that leads south-southwest of the main road. This is, in fact, part of the old road up the Panhandle.

About 9.5km later there's a clearly signposted turning (⊕ T3TURN 18°50.292'S, 22°10.011'E) on to a track that leads west to the hills. Follow this and after a further 22km this passes through a small cattle post. Finally you'll approach the hills from the south side, with the Male Hill the first to come into view. Within sight of the hills you pass a fork in the road (⊕ FORKRD 18°47.414'S, 21°44.921'E), and soon reach the main thatched 'gate' turning (⊕ TSGATE 18°47.275'S, 21°44.856'E) about 55.5km after leaving the road at T3TURN.

If you're leaving the hills by this route then simply find the main gate (TSGATE) and then head out south of the Male Hill and follow the track slightly south of east from there (a bearing averaging about 95°). Keep straight (right) where the road forks (⊕ FORKRD 18°47.414'S, 21°44.921'E), and head fairly directly for ⊕ T3TURN 18°50.292'S, 22°10.011'E.

Hitchhiking

I wouldn't even entertain trying to walk or hitchhike here. With more animals around than vehicles, and no water, it would be unpleasant at best, and life-threatening at worst.

By air

There's a good bush airstrip at the hills, so it's quite possible (albeit at significant cost) to charter a plane to get you here from Maun, or anywhere else in the region. However, once on the ground you'll usually want a 4WD to get around the base of the hills, and to the start of the various walking trails.

You may be able to persuade one of the Panhandle's lodges to send a 4WD with a driver for your use. However, the drive is so tough on their vehicles that they are reluctant to do this if you're not also spending time staying at their lodges. So however you look at this, it won't be a cheap option.

Approaching from the air you'll appreciate the hills' uniqueness within the desert, though you'll miss the excitement as they're first sighted over the treetops – and the sheer sense of achievement of having completed the long drive here.

Orientation

The Tsodilo Hills rise up from the bush-covered undulations of the western Kalahari, about 45km west of the village of Sepupa. They consist of four hills, roughly in a line, with names from San folklore.

The most southerly is known as the Male Hill. This is the highest hill, rising 410m above the surrounding bush, and the San believed that the most sacred place is near the top of this. Their tradition is that the first spirit knelt on this hill to pray after creating the world, and they believe that you can still see the impression of his knees in the rock there.

Close to the Male, on its northern side, is the Female Hill, which covers almost three times the area of the Male, but only reaches about 300m in height. This seems to have most of the main rock art sites on it.

About 2km north of the Female is the Child Hill, which is smaller still at only about 40m high. Then beyond this, about 2.2km northwest of the Child, is a smaller kopjie that is said by the San to be the first wife of the Male Hill who was then left when he met the Female Hill.

Most visitors spend their time on the Female Hill, and may visit the Male. Few visit the Child or the kopjie beyond, to which there are no vehicle tracks.

There are several man-made landmarks that might help you to orientate yourself when in the area of the hills:

The gate

As you'll see when you arrive, there's a large and sturdy gate been built, complete with a small office and an impressive thatched top, which makes a clear landmark (⊕ TSGATE 18°47.275'S, 21°44.856'E). This was originally intended as a gate within a cattle fence, but when I last visited there was no fence here and the gate stood on its own in splendid isolation.

Hambukushu village

Just south of the gate is a small settlement with some corrals for animals. This is the Hambukushu village, and it's one possible place where you may be able to find a guide to take you around the hills.

San village

The San village at the hills has, rather sadly, been moved from its old location, between the hills (⊕ OLDVIL 18°46.386'S, 21°44.782'E) to a new location about 3.8km south-southwest of there, well away from the hills. It's now found at ⊕ SANVIL 18°48.147'S, 21°43.903'E.

It has been alleged that this has been done with the intention of 'tidying up' the area for visitors. If so, it's deeply misguided, as most visitors will want to drive out here to try and hire San guides to the hills anyway.

Tshukumutshu track

On the way from the main gate to the San Village a track heads off right, on a northwest bearing of about 305°. I've followed this for 7–8km, and it remains a good track, and believe that it heads for a place called Tshukumutshu. I'd welcome more information on it if readers have gone further.

What to see and do

Apart from soaking up the atmosphere, exploring the hills and their rock art is the main reason to come here. For both you'd be wise, if possible, to take a local guide with you – which also helps to give the small local community some income in an area where there must be very few other opportunities for paid work.

Hiring a guide

On my last visit, I drove to the San village and, with sign gestures and improvisation, tried to ask for a guide. The man of the family that I was speaking to eventually sent me off with two of the children, a boy called Xashee, aged 10, and a girl called Tsetsana, aged 16.

At first I thought that I'd been fobbed off with the children, who were silent in the presence of their family. However, as soon as we got into our car to drive back to the hills, it transpired that Tsetsana was on holiday from school, and spoke excellent English. Her brother spoke much less to us, but seemed to know more of the sites with rock art.

They bounded up the hills with bare feet faster than we could in walking boots. They knew their way about very well and although we only followed on the 'standard' trails, we would have missed many of the paintings without their help.

The trails

There are four trails that I know of on the hills: the Rhino Trail, the Cliff Trail, the Lion Trail and the Male Hill Trail. That said, one source refers to there being six trails, and several sources refer to the 'Divuyu Trail,' which I don't think exists! The best source for information will be the office at the hills, which was closed when I last visited. I'd welcome detailed descriptions of the routes, preferably with GPS positions of all the paintings, from any readers who have time to explore these trails and write to me about them.

The Rhino Trail is marked with sturdy numbered posts, indexed for a series of annotated route plans that are, apparently, being produced. I believe that Alec Campbell, a world-renowned authority on both African rock art and Botswana, has written them – and the national museum is meant to be producing them. However, these have been 'in production' for so long that some doubt if they will ever be seen. If you can get hold of one, I'd expect them to be the best guide to the hills.

The best sites for rock art are on the Female Hill, and especially towards its north end. The hills are a place to explore for yourself, preferably with a local guide. Here are a few notes from my own observations. I'm aware they may contain errors as well as omissions, but I hope that they'll spur readers to explore – and perhaps send me any corrections or additional comments.

Rhino Trail This is the only one of the trails that the author has walked, and it starts from the close to the Squirrel Valley Campsite (⊕ SQCAMP 18°45.385'S, 21°44.248'E). Each of the pictures is marked with sequentially numbered posts, though in the lush vegetation of February there were some of these that neither us, nor our young guides, could locate. The GPS references here should be a help to make sure you're in roughly the right place, but you'll probably still have to search a bit to find the paintings. It's certainly best to take a local guide with you anyhow.

This trail starts with **Picture #1** (⊕ PICT1 18°45.336'S, 21°44.195'E), which is high, about 10–15m above the ground, facing a baobab on the right hand side of a broad ravine near the campsite.

Picture #2 (⊕ PICT2 18°45.331'S, 21°44.225'E) is deeper into the ravine and higher up, at an altitude of 1,063m. There's quite a lot of steep rock-hopping to climb up this ravine at the beginning of the trail. It won't be suitable for anyone who is uncomfortable clambering around rocky slopes.

A spot that I've located nearby, and called **Picture #2A** (⊕ PICT2A 18°45.291'S, 21°44.239'E), is less than 100m north-northwest of #2, and higher up again. Here there's a beautiful picture of a rhino that's perhaps 100cm across, with gemsbok below.

But the time you reach **Picture #5**, which includes an impressive giraffe, you're at the centre of the Female Hill, and **Picture #7** is found on rocks beside a flat track here.

Picture #8 (⊕ PICT8 18°45.150'S, 21°44.576'E) is at an altitude of 1,102m (you can see the Male Hill from here); it's a picture found under an overhang of several men – known as 'the dancing penises'.

Pictures #9 (⊕ PICT9 18°45.437'S, 21°44.723'E) and #10 are almost adjacent to each other, on vertical walls of rock slightly off the trail. **Picture #10** has a plaque next to it reading 'Rhino Trail', and its main figures consist of two rather beautifully painted rhino. These are the most famous of Tsodilo's paintings, as they now form the logo of The Botswana Society (see page 149).

Shortly this trail joins the main track which leads west between the Female and Male hills. Detour to the right of this, and **Picture #11** (GPS: PICT11 18°45.635'S, 21°44.862'E) is on the Female Hhill and appears to be of several whales and a penguin.

This trail then leads around to what I'll refer to as **Cave #12** (GPS: CAVE12 18°45.673'S, 21°44.842'E) – which is a large cave at the base of the Female Hill, facing the Male Hill. This has little in the way of paintings, but it does have a 'Museums of Botswana' board outside it urging visitors to treat the hills with respect.

Continue from here by following the main vehicle track that leads north along the west side of the Female Hill. The plaque for **Picture #13** (⊕ PICT13 18°45.627'S, 21°44.436'E) stands next to a notice proclaiming 'Rhino Trail' – and marks where you should turn right from the vehicle track onto a footpath which runs closer to the hill than the larger track.

When at #13, look up and slightly back at the hills and there, high up, you'll see what is now known as the 'van der Post panel.' In his inimitable style, Laurens described first seeing this:

> Over the scorched leaves of the tops of the bush conforming to a contour nearby, and about a hundred feet up, was a ledge of honey-coloured stone grafted into the blue iron rock. Above the ledge rose a smooth surface of the same warm, soft stone curved like a sea shell as if rising into the blue to form a perfect dome. I had no doubt that I was looking at the wall and part of the ceiling of what had once been a great cave...
>
> But what held my attention still with the shock of discovery was the painting that looked down at us from the centre of what was left of the wall and dome of the cave. Heavy as were the shadows, and seeing it only darkly against the sharp morning light, it was yet so distinct and filled with fire of its own colour that every detail stood out with a burning clarity. In the focus of the painting, scarlet against the gold of the stone, was an enormous eland bull standing sideways, his massive body charged with masculine power and his noble head looking as if he had only that moment been disturbed in his grazing. He was painted, as only a bushman, who had a deep identification with an eland, could have painted him.'

Take this footpath which follows the west side of the Female Hill, heading roughly north. Very close to the path, **Picture #14** depicts rhino, warthog and several antelope. Next, less than 400m from the Squirrel Valley Campsite, **Picture #15** (⊕ PICT15 18°45.556'S, 21°44.361'E), includes lots of very clearly painted giraffe, rhino, gemsbok and other antelope on a wonderfully colourful outcrop of rock.

Finally, just before arriving back at the Squirrel Valley Campsite, **Picture #16** has a curious circular design – almost geometrical – on the right. It is reminiscent of a shield, the shell of a tortoise, or even a wheel.

Cliff Trail This is at the north end of Female Hill, and to find the start try heading north on the track to Malatso Campsite, and then turn right at (✪ MLTURN 18°44.243'S, 21°43.575'E). You'll reach the steep base of the cliffs, about 50m away, where there's a turning circle for vehicles.

The trail appears to circle clockwise around the northern part of the Female Hill, before taking a shortcut back to near its start over a col. I'd welcome a detailed description of this route and its paintings from anyone who has completed it (with GPS locations if possible).

Lion Trail This is a trail that stays at ground level, and doesn't include any climbing. It overlaps with some of the Rhino Trail's paintings at the base of the south end of the Female Hill, as well as visiting sites on the north side of the Male Hill. To find its start point, take the vehicle track which heads east between the Male and Female Hills, and then turn right at ✪ LITURN 18°45.538'S, 21°45.109'E, to find a turning-circle for vehicles at the base of the Male Hill.

Male Hill Trail This starts from the same place as the Lion Trail, though eventually goes up and over the top of the Male Hill, including some strenuous scrambles.

Where to stay

There's a relatively large, new park's office on the west side of the Female Hill which, if it's operating, should be your first point of call when you arrive at the hills. Here you'll have to sign in, pay a small entry charge, and then they will direct you to a campsite.

This will either be to one of the camp pitches next to the office, which is in excellent condition with pristine facilities, or one of a couple of other sites dotted around. These are wilder, as they have nothing but a fireplace, and they can be a little indistinct.

When I last visited there were no staff on duty, or any other visitors at the hills. We stayed for three days and saw nobody apart from the local villagers. The official campsites include:

Makoba Woods Campsite (✪ MAKOBA 18°45.688'S, 21°44.586'E). Just beside the southern tip of the Female Hill, you'll pass this as you head north to the Main Camp and office from the entrance gate.

Squirrel Valley Camp (✪ SQCAMP 18°45.385'S, 21°44.248'E). Nothing more than a turning circle for vehicles really under trees at the base of the Female Hill where the Rhino Trail starts, this is also known as the Baobab Campsite.

Malatso Campsite (✪ MALATS 18°43.608'S, 21°43.910'E). Near the far northern end of the Female Hill, close to the Cliff Trail, there's an enclave here between some of the low rock outcrops from the northern end of the Female Hill. (For comparison with other altitudes mentioned above, this camp at the base of the hill stands at 1,011m.) This is a lovely, remote spot – though the track to reach it was overgrown in places, and a little tricky to reach in the fast-fading light of dusk.

Aha and Gcwihaba

Over 150km southwest of the Tsodilo Hills lies an even more remote area, populated by scattered San villages and dotted with a number of hills. This is one of the most remote areas of the Kalahari, and it attracts the most experienced bush travellers simply 'because it's there'. This is expedition territory, best reserved for those who are well equipped and bush-wise.

AHA & GCWIHABA HILLS, NOKANENG & TSAO

GPS REFERENCES FOR AHA AND GCWIHABA HILLS MAP (opposite)

DOBEVI	19°34.830'S, 21°04.428'E
GCWIHA	20°01.250'S, 21°21.230'E
GTURN1	20°07.047'S, 22°22.291'E
GTURN2	19°39.577'S, 22°11.010'E
GTURN3	19°54.286'S, 21°09.418'E
GTURN4	19°57.556'S, 21°44.541'E
QANGWA	19°31.868'S, 21°10.281'E
TSAU	20°10.294'S, 22°27.265'E
WAXHUN	19°43.532'S, 21°03.489'E
WAXHUS	19°46.643'S, 21°02.518'E
XAIXAI	19°52.867'S, 21°04.934'E

Most go to visit the Aha Hills, which straddle the border with Namibia, and nearby Gcwihaba Hills, which contain the well-known Gcwihaba (or Drotsky's) Caverns. These are easily located, not commercialised and fascinating to visit.

In reality, though the Gcwihaba Caverns are the only cave system here that's practical for most visitors to see, there are a number of others in the area which have been unearthed by local scientists in the last few decades. The locations of these are usually kept secret to avoid visitors damaging them, or having a serious accident (which would be all too easy).

Geology and geography

Turning east from Tsau, you'll soon start notice the road's gentle decline. It's entering the Gcwihaba Valley, a fossil river valley which may have been an ancient extension of the Okavango Delta. Within this, a group of six low hills protrude above the sand and rise to a maximum of 30m above the surrounding valley. (Compare this to the Male Hill at the Tsodilo, which reaches 410m.) About 40–50km northwest of these, the Aha Hills share a very similar geology and appearance.

All of these low hills are made almost exclusively of dolomite marble which, early in its formation, is thought to have been steeply folded causing many of its strata to stand vertically. It's estimated to be about 800–1,000 million years old.

This rock has been weathered into a very jagged, sharp surface and many loose blocks which aren't always easy underfoot. Underneath numerous faults and fractures split it. When weathered it appears a grey colour, but if you break it you'll find a pearly-white colour beneath. There are occasional bands of muscovite in the marble, and beds of more recent limestone and calcrete.

About 15–20km southwest of the Gcwihaba are the Koanaka Hills. These are also similar in geological origin, but essentially inaccessible to visitors. There has been some recent exploration of these (see *Discovery and Exploration of Two New Caves in the Northwest District*, in *Further Reading*), one of which – called the 'blue cave' – is Botswana's largest cave complex found to date.

Formation of the caves

Like many cave systems in the world, the Gcwihaba Caverns have been formed by the action of acidic groundwater flowing down through the faults in the rock. This gradually dissolves the alkaline limestone over the centuries. Some of this limestone has been redeposited as stalagmites and stalactites.

That said, this simple and quite standard explanation for the cave formation doesn't

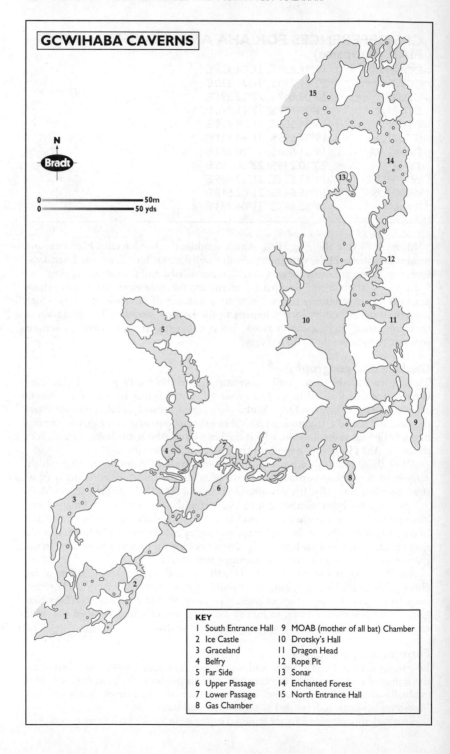

GCWIHABA CAVERNS

N

Bradt

0 ——————— 50m
0 ——————— 50 yds

KEY

1	South Entrance Hall	9	MOAB (mother of all bat) Chamber
2	Ice Castle	10	Drotsky's Hall
3	Graceland	11	Dragon Head
4	Belfry	12	Rope Pit
5	Far Side	13	Sonar
6	Upper Passage	14	Enchanted Forest
7	Lower Passage	15	North Entrance Hall
8	Gas Chamber		

entirely explain why the cave system is more-or-less horizontal throughout. (It has northeast and southeast entrances, and appears to have had two levels at different times.) Because of this, Cooke (see *Further Reading*) notes that from the size of the caves and passages, it seems likely that very large volumes of groundwater must have moved within the rock here – perhaps a course of the old Gcwihaba River flowed through, underground. This would explain the sheer size of some of the caves here.

For that to have been the case, the area's water table must have been much higher for at least one period historically, and probably two. After these levels had subsided, and the caves emptied of water, then stalagmites and stalactites would have been formed gradually by a trickle-through of more moderate volumes of water (eg: rainfall) through fault-lines.

History

Though people have occupied the area for at least 12,500 years, it doesn't seems as if the caves were used extensively. Excavations in Gcwihaba Caverns (in 1969 by Yellen, et al, see *Further Reading*) did find evidence of charcoal, ostrich eggshell and bone fragments, thought to be the remnants of human occupation, but the finds were limited and there is no rock art here at all.

These caves were first brought to the attention of the outside world in June 1932 when the local !Kung people showed the cave to a farmer from Ghanzi, Martinus Drotsky. Hence for many years this was known as 'Drotsky's Cave.' (As an aside, Martinus was the grandfather of Jan Drotsky who currently runs Drotsky's Cabins, near Shakawe.)

The local !Kung refer to these hills as '/twihaba' – and hence now the hills and main cave and this cave system are now usually referred to as the Gcwihaba Hills and Caverns, respectively. (Although you'll see this spelt in a variety of ways in various publications.)

Since then, they were declared a national monument in 1934 and the Director of the Bechwanaland Geological Survey visited the caverns with Drotsky in 1943. The first cave survey was undertaken in 1970 by a school group from Falcon College in Zimbabwe (then Rhodesia). Various scientific explorations and surveys have been done since then, including an expedition in October 1991 by the British School's Exploring Society (including Heather Tyrrell, one of the contributors to this book).

Nowhere else in this area has had as much time or attention given to it as the Gcwihaba Caverns have had, though the two sinkholes in the Aha Hills have been surveyed on at least two occasions, most recently by the BSES in 1991.

The people

The people of the area are mostly Ju/'hoansi Bushmen, together with a few Herero (Mbanderu). Because of the lung disease that swept through this area of the country and the subsequent eradication of cattle here in the late 1990s, work patterns changed here in the 1990s. Thus many people are employed by branches of the government; working to clear roads and similar public works.

A particularly detailed and interesting article on the community in the Xai Xai area, with a lot of detailed facts from a study there, can be found at www.kalaharipeoples.org/documents/Ju-pap.htm

Flora and fauna

Though visits to this part of the Kalahari are usually for caves and culture, there is some wildlife around. As with most places in the Kalahari, this area is at its most beautiful and the flora and fauna is at its most vibrant during and shortly after the summer rains (January to about April).

Flora

This classic Kalahari environment is dominated by the silver terminalia, *Terminalia sericea*, identified by the silvery sheen on its blue-grey leaves. and the Kalahari appleleaf, *Lonchocarpus nelsii*. You'll also find some bushwillows, *Combretum callinum*, and wild seringa bushes, *Burkea africana*.

Raisin bushes, *Gwewia flava*, are here accompanied by sandpaper raisin bushes, *Grewia flavescens*, and the false sandpaper raisin bushes, *Grewia retinervis*. Rub a leaf of either of the latter between your fingers and you'll soon realise how they got their common names.

One tree worth noting here is the Namaqua fig, *Ficus cordata*. This is well known throughout the central highlands of Namibia and down to the Cape – but otherwise unrecorded in Botswana. Here you'll find it growing all over these hills, its roots often flattened against the rocks. Several strong specimens grow around the entrances to the Gcwihaba Caverns, green and thriving even during the dry season, perhaps due to the cooler, moister microclimate in the air of the caves.

Similarly, the mopane aloe, *Aloe littoralis,* is found here and throughout Namibia, but nowhere else in northern or central Botswana. It's a striking plant with a single, vertical stem, succulent leaves with serrated edges and a flower head that branches into pointed spikes of red flowers.

All around the region you'll certainly find the Devil's claw creeper, *Harpogophytum procumbens procumbens*. Recognise it for its pinky-mauve flowers with a hint of yellow in the centre in January to March, and after that its small but wicked oval fruit that has hooks on all sides – like some tiny medieval jousting ball with grappling hooks. (This could be confused with the large Devil's thorn, *Dicerocaryum eriocarpum*, which has a brighter pink flower but a much less elaborate fruit.)

The Devil's claw is found all over the Kalahari, but has recently been in demand from overseas for its medicinal properties. Extracts of this are variously claimed to aid in the treatment of intestinal complaints, arthritis, and many other ailments. Hence anywhere near a centre of population is likely to be largely devoid of these plants, but in the more remote areas of the Kalahari you'll often find it beside the sandy track.

Birdlife

As with anywhere in the Kalahari, the birds here can either survive without drinking water, or will routinely fly long distances to find it every day. Guineafowl and red-billed francolin are very common, though coqui and crested francolin do also occur here. Sandgrouse are common, particularly the namaqua and double-banded species, though you'll also find Burchell's and, occasionally, the yellow-throated varieties. Doves are here too, with cape turtle, laughing and namaqua species always around.

The area's LBJs ('Little Brown Jobbies' as keen bird-watchers refer to the plethora of smaller, brown birds whose similarities tax their identification skills) include chestnut-backed finchlarks, sabota larks and penduline tits.

Larger and more visible birds, which are easier to spot and identify, include double-banded coursers, black-bellied and red-crested khorans. Both of these khorans show interesting displays during the mating season. You may also come across of the world's heaviest flying bird here, the kori bustard, and ostriches are not unknown, though they are very uncommon.

Of the raptors, by far the commonest is the pale chanting goshawk, which is usually seen perching atop a bush, small tree or post, surveying the area. When disturbed it'll usually swoop off, flying low, to a similar perch not far away. The very similar, but slightly larger, dark chanting goshawk may also be found here, on the edge of its range. (These are distinguishable in flight, from above, as the pale variety has a white rump, whereas the dark chanting goshawk has a darker colouring and a darker, barred rump.)

Animals

Big game is present throughout this area, but it's relatively scarce especially near to settlements where you're more likely to come into contact with dogs and domestic stock. That said, gemsbok, springbok, eland, steenbok, duiker and kudu all occur in the area. Veronica Roodt reports seeing six very relaxed wild dog near the entrance to Gcwihaba Caverns, and there are also occasional lion, leopard, cheetah and spotted hyena around here. Hence there must be a reasonable population of their antelope prey – even if these seem elusive due to the relatively thick vegetation, and lack of waterholes at which they might gather and be more easily spotted.

Given the huge distances that elephant can cover, and the spoor that I've seen near the Tsodilo Hills, I wouldn't be surprised to find lone bulls wandering around in this area during the wet season. Drivers, be warned.

If approaching this area then, whilst looking for big game, don't forget the smaller stuff. Small seasonal pans here will fill with a noisy mélange of bullfrogs which have spent the dry season underground, attracted by the water and the number of grasshoppers and crickets around.

There's no better time to see plenty of small reptiles, from the Kalahari serrated tortoise, with its bold, geometric patterns, to the flapnecked chameleon. Around sunset, and for the first few hours after that, listen out for the click-click of the barking gecko, sometimes described as like rattling a box of matches. The onomatopoeic name 'Aha' is said to come from the sound made by these often-unseen residents.

Inside the Gcwihaba Caverns is a different story. Some of the earlier scientists to visit the cave noted that leopard inhabit it, and found fresh spoor here. Meanwhile, its name derives from the !Kung word for 'hyena's hole'. Whilst I don't know of any more recent visitors who have come across large predators in here, you can't help but notice the bats! These can be noisy and smelly, but are otherwise harmless.

The most common species here is probably the insectivorous Commerson's leaf-nosed bat, *Hipposideros commersoni*. These are the largest insectivorous bat in southern Africa which, although they only grow to a weight of about 120g, can have a wingspan as large as 60cm. These have short, pale fawn coloured hair all over and black feet. Males have distinctive tufts of white fur on their shoulders. These are the bats that leave the caves in large numbers at dusk.

Also found here in numbers are the tiny Dent's horseshoe bat, *Rhinolophus denti*, which weigh a mere 6g and measure about 7cm long, with a wingspan of 20cm, when fully grown. Horseshoe bats like this are identified because of complex 'nose-leaf' structures on their face between their mouths and their foreheads (used to locate their insect prey using the animal equivalent of radar).

A third common bat here is the Egyptian (also called 'common') slit-faced bat, *Nycteris thebaica*, which is easily identified by its long, rounded ears and the 'split' running down the centre of its face. They fly efficiently but relatively slowly, eat insects, and grow to about 10cm long with a wingspan of about 24cm.

Given the presence of these bats, it's quite likely that these support a small ecosystem of invertebrates in the caves. In similar caves in Namibia, several hundred kilometres to the west of here, scientists have recently also discovered small but highly poisonous spiders. So tread carefully…

Getting there

I'm not aware of any landing strips in this area, so to get here you need at least one fully equipped 4WD, with all your food and water. There is water usually available at Xai Xai village, and a small very basic shop at Qangwa, but it's better to bring with you everything that you might need.

As with any tracks in the Kalahari, and especially those that are rarely used, a major danger is fire caused by grass seeds and stems blocking up your vehicle's radiator, or collecting near its exhaust system. If you're driving here, especially during the first few months of the year, you must take steps to prevent this. (See page 122 of *Chapter 6*.)

There are two roads which head west from the main Shakawe-Sehithwa road, and then loop around and join up with each other around the Aha Hills. Both are very long, very sandy and hard going, though navigation is not difficult. Here I'll briefly describe both:

The northern route

About 300m north of the centre of Nokaneng there's a track heading west (✪ GTURN2 19°39.577'S, 22°11.010'E). This is the longer and the sandier of the two routes, but there's relatively little mud this way so if rains have been heavy it may be the easiest route.

From Nokaneng, it twists and turns quite a lot but after a little over 120km you'll reach the tiny village of (✪ QANGWA 19°31.868'S, 21°10.281'E). This name is sometimes seen spelt Xangwa, or even Gcangwa.

From there one track heads west towards Namibia, ultimately to Tsumkwe (✪ TSUMKW 19°35.507'S, 20°30.184'E). You take the one which leads southwest for over 10km to another small village, Dobe (✪ DOBEVI 19°34.830'S, 21°4.428'E). From there the track heads due south, and actually picks its way through the Aha Hills. It passes west of the small group of hills which contain Waxhu North Cave (✪ WAXHUN 19°43.532'S, 21°3.489'E), and east of the main range of hills, within which is found the Waxhu South Cave (✪ WAXHUS 19°46.643'S, 21°2.518'E). Finally it reaches the village of Xai Xia (✪ XAIXAI 19°52.867'S, 21°04.934'E) after about 37km.

In some literature you'll find this designated as 'Nxainxai' or 'CaeCae' or, more recently, /Xai/Xai. However you want to spell it, this is one of the largest villages in the area with a population of about 300–400 Ju/'hoansi San people, and perhaps 50 Herero (Mbanderu) people. Here there is a borehole, a small school, a basic health post, and small administrative centre for the people.

From there the route turns east, becoming the route described below which ultimately ends on the main road near Tsau. About 10km east of Xai Xai you pass a clear right turn (✪ GTURN3 19°54.286'S, 21°9.418'E) which takes almost 30km to reach the Gcwihaba Hills and Cave (✪ GCWIHA 20°01.250'S, 21°21.230'E).

The southern route

Although it can be confusing to locate the start of this route in the east, once you're on it, this is the best route out to the hills and caves unless there has been very heavy rain in the area.

Around Tsau (✪ TSAU 20°10.294'S, 22°27.265'E) there are a number of tracks heading roughly west to northwest. Some of these will fizzle out at smallholdings, bush homesteads, and villages whilst some join into one road which heads out towards the hills. The turning onto one of the easiest tracks (✪ GTURN1 20°07.047'S, 22°22.291'E) is found about 10.5km north of the centre of Tsau, whilst another cuts off the main road about 1.5km from Tsau.

During the dry season, the first few hours from Tsau are generally fairly easy driving, as the hard, compacted track gently descends into the fossil river valley.

However, during the rains a number of wide, shallow pans hold water here, turning it into a series of connected mud-holes and a challenging route even for experienced drivers. (Hence in the rains you might consider taking the longer northern route instead.) After that, the country becomes rolling dune-land with thick sand, which is slow-going but not as treacherous as the mud.

About 90km from Tsau there's a left turning (⊕ GTURN4 19°57.556'S, 21°44.541'E) to Xhaba borehole. This passes the Xhaba borehole, a satellite cattle post of /Xai/Xai village, after about 26km, and then reaches the hills another 26km later. It's the quickest way to the hills. If you miss this turn-off then continue on to the main turning (⊕ GTURN3 19°54.286'S, 21°9.418'E), used by the Northern route, above, and take a left there. This is over 150km from Tsau.

Where to stay

Most people camp near the main entrance to the caves, though there are sufficiently few visitors that you're unlikely to see anyone else here. Note that there is no water here (the nearest is at Xai Xai), or any other facilities, so it's vital that you bring everything that you need with you, and take away all of your rubbish. (Or at least everything that cannot be burned and reduced to ash.)

When using the toilet, take a spade, a box of matches and your tissue paper. Bury your waste deeply and always burn your toilet paper.

The alternative would be to visit the community at Xai Xai which is starting to get involved with tourism. You'll find more information on this at www.xaixai.org, or try to email: xaixaibw@yahoo.com (though this didn't work for me).

To get the best out of such an experience, you're probably wisest to come here with an experienced mobile safari operator who (and this is vital) knows the village and villagers well. They'll also know what's possible, and enable you to get the most out of your trip, whilst the community benefits in just the same way. Operations who may be able to help include Uncharted Africa Safaris (page 455), Phakawe Safaris (page 175), or New Moon Safaris (page 174). This will be more costly than trying to do something yourself, but probably much more satisfactory.

Gcwihaba Hills and Caverns

The low, rounded hills here are not the attraction, but beneath them is a labyrinth of passages and caves, some with enchanting rock formations of stalagmites, stalactites and spectacular 'flowstones' which seem like waterfalls of rock.

Some of these chambers reach up to 10m in height, whilst other passages are so narrow that you'll need to clamber and squeeze through. All were formed by the dissolving and depositing action of acidic water on the limestone of the rocks around, though now the caves are totally dry.

What to see and do

To explore the caves you'll need *several* good torches, plus extra batteries and bulbs (a fail-safe emergency backup is essential, as there's no one here to help you), and perhaps a lighter or matches. If you bring a huge ball of string (you'll need about a kilometre for it to be much use!) then remember to collect it up again and take it away with you.

There are lots of dead ends, closed off passages and caverns to penetrate. If your curiosity flags, then remind yourself of the legend of Hendrik Matthys van Zyl, the wealthy founder of Ghanzi, who is said to have stashed a portion of his fortune here in the late 1800s.

Orientation

There are two main entrances to the caves that are about 250m apart. There is a route between them, but it's not straightforward or obvious, so getting through may tax your map-reading skills. (You won't be able to rely on your beloved GPS either, as they're useless under the rock ceilings of the caves!)

Most of the caves are on one level, though there is a section, slightly nearer to the south entrance than the north, where several of the corridors split into two different levels, one raised several metres above the other.

Start exploring the caves from the main (north) entrance. Here, on one of the large boulders towards the right of the main entrance hall, you'll find the inscription 'Discovered 1 June 1932, M Drotsky.'

You'll also realise that a string marks a route through the caves. Given how easy it is to get lost in here, this can be very comforting. It starts at the lower entrance, and proceeds down an increasingly steep and narrow passageway. There's a short vertical climb down into what's been christened the 'rope pit', before you emerge up the other side onto a shelf. Then it's a bit of a squeeze before you find yourself in a large chamber.

From here the route basically climbs, though there are lots of side-passages to distract you, and part way is where there are two different levels to the passages. You'll also come across the chambers with the bats in them, deep within the cave complex, before finally emerging from the southern entrance (where there's a ledge that is now used as a roost by a resident barn owl).

Aha Hills

About 40–50km northwest of the Gcwihabe Hills, and visible from them, is a range of low, rounded hills: the Aha Hills. These straddle the Botswana-Namibia border, and are one of the most remote and little-visited destinations in Botswana.

Like the Gcwihaba Hills, this range is made of dolomite marble that has been split by weathering into numerous faults and fractures. This presents a very jagged surface, with many loose blocks underfoot, and isn't easy to walk on.

The range covers about 245km², most of which is in Botswana, and very little of which has been properly mapped or documented. That said, it's interesting to note that on the Namibian side the range is much easier to reach than the hills in Botswana, being only about 20km from the good, gravel road which links Tsumkwe to Gam.

What to see and do

In some ways the hills are attractive simply because they're so remote, and because you can camp wherever you like. Though it's important, as always, that if you find yourself near a village then you ask permission to stay from the head villager.

Clambering around isn't as much fun here as in the Tsodilo Hills, simply because the rock surface is totally different. Instead of large boulders with an even surface and an easy grip, the Aha Hills are made of endless jagged little blocks. So if you do come here, then stout walking shoes with strong soles make clambering around a lot easier.

Two sites on the Botswana side have attracted some interest, and both are 'sink holes' – large holes in the ground. The local people apparently know both as simply 'Waxhu', which means 'house of god'.

Both can only be visited using specialist climbing/caving equipment, so don't be tempted to try and climb down. There are no mountain rescue teams in Botswana!

Waxhu Cave (north) Found at ✪ WAXHUN 19°43.532'S, 21°03.498'E, this was first described in 1974 and is about 70m deep.

Waxhu Cave (south) Also known by some of its recent visitors as 'Independence Cave', because they first visited it on the fifth anniversary of Botswana's independence. This cave is about 50m deep and can be found at ✪ WAXHUS 19°46.632'S, 21°02.518'E.

Botswana Notes and Records (see *Further Reading*) records many more details on these sink-holes, including rough maps of them and the various expeditions which have explored them recently.

Bradt Travel Guides

Africa by Road Charlie Shackell/Illya Bracht
Albania Gillian Gloyer
Amazon, The Roger Harris/Peter Hutchison
Antarctica: A Guide to the Wildlife
  Tony Soper/Dafila Scott
Arctic: A Guide to Coastal Wildlife
  Tony Soper/Dan Powell
Armenia with Nagorno Karabagh Nicholas
  Holding
Azores David Sayers
Baghdad Catherine Arnold
Baltic Capitals: Tallinn, Riga, Vilnius, Kaliningrad
  Neil Taylor et al
Bosnia & Herzegovina Tim Clancy
Botswana: Okavango, Chobe, Northern Kalahari
  Chris McIntyre
British Isles: Wildlife of Coastal Waters
  Tony Soper/Dan Powell
Budapest Adrian Phillips/Jo Scotchmer
Cameroon Ben West
Canada: North – Yukon, Northwest Territories,
  Nunavut Geoffrey Roy
Cape Verde Islands Aisling Irwin/
  Colum Wilson
Cayman Islands Tricia Hayne
Chile Tim Burford
Chile & Argentina: Trekking Guide
  Tim Burford
Cork Linda Fallon
Croatia Piers Letcher
Dubrovnik Piers Letcher
East & Southern Africa: The Backpacker's Manual
  Philip Briggs
Eccentric America Jan Friedman
Eccentric Britain Benedict le Vay
Eccentric California Jan Friedman
Eccentric Edinburgh Benedict le Vay
Eccentric France Piers Letcher
Eccentric London Benedict le Vay
Eccentric Oxford Benedict le Vay
Ecuador: Climbing & Hiking in
  Rob Rachowiecki/Mark Thurber
Eritrea Edward Denison/Edward Paice
Estonia Neil Taylor
Ethiopia Philip Briggs
Falkland Islands Will Wagstaff
Faroe Islands James Proctor
Gabon, São Tome & Príncipe Sophie Warne
Galápagos Wildlife David Horwell/Pete Oxford
Gambia, The Craig Emms/Linda Barnett
Georgia with Armenia Tim Burford
Ghana Philip Briggs
Hungary Adrian Phillips/Jo Scotchmer
Iran Patricia L Baker
Iraq Karen Dabrowska
Kabul Dominic Medley/Jude Barrand

Kenya Claire Foottit
Kiev Andrew Evans
Latvia Stephen Baister/Chris Patrick
Lille Laurence Phillips
Lithuania Gordon McLachlan
Ljubljana Robin & Jenny McKelvie
Macedonia Thammy Evans
Madagascar Hilary Bradt
Madagascar Wildlife Nick Garbutt/
  Hilary Bradt/Derek Schuurman
Malawi Philip Briggs
Maldives Royston Ellis
Mali Ross Velton
Mauritius, Rodrigues & Réunion Royston Ellis/
  Alex Richards/Derek Schuurman
Mongolia Jane Blunden
Montenegro Annalisa Rellie
Mozambique Philip Briggs/Ross Velton
Namibia Chris McIntyre
Nigeria Lizzie Williams
North Cyprus Diana Darke
North Korea Robert Willoughby
Palestine, with Jerusalem Henry Stedman
Panama Sarah Woods
Paris, Lille & Brussels: Eurostar Cities
  Laurence Phillips
Peru & Bolivia: Backpacking and Trekking
  Hilary Bradt/Kathy Jarvis
Riga Stephen Baister/Chris Patrick
River Thames, In the Footsteps of the Famous
  Paul Goldsack
Rwanda Janice Booth/Philip Briggs
St Helena, Ascension, Tristan da Cunha
  Sue Steiner
Serbia Laurence Mitchell
Seychelles Lyn Mair/Lynnath Beckley
Slovenia Robin & Jenny McKelvie
South Africa: Budget Travel Guide Paul Ash
Southern African Wildlife Mike Unwin
Sri Lanka Royston Ellis
Sudan Paul Clammer
Svalbard Andreas Umbreit
Switzerland: Rail, Road, Lake
  Anthony Lambert
Tallinn Neil Taylor
Tanzania Philip Briggs
Tasmania Matthew Brace
Tibet Michael Buckley
Uganda Philip Briggs
Ukraine Andrew Evans
USA by Rail John Pitt
Venezuela Hilary Dunsterville Branch
Your Child Abroad Dr Jane Wilson-Howarth/
  Dr Matthew Ellis
Zambia Chris McIntyre
Zanzibar David Else

Bradt guides are available from all good bookshops, or by post, fax, phone or internet direct from:
Bradt Travel Guides, 19 High Street, Chalfont St Peter, Bucks SL9 9QE, UK
Tel: +44 (0)1753 893444   Fax: +44 (0)1753 892333
Email: info@bradtguides.com   Web: www.bradtguides.com

The Kalahari's Great Salt Pans

The great salt pans lie in the heart of the northern Kalahari, forming an area of empty horizons into which the blinding white expanse of the pans disappears in shimmering heat-haze. In winter, dust devils whirl across the open plains; in summer many become undulating seas of grasses beneath the turbulence of the stormy skies. It is a harsh, spare landscape, not to everybody's taste, but it offers an isolation as complete as anywhere in southern Africa, and a wealth of hidden treasures for those prepared to make the effort – including Stone-Age ruins and prehistoric beaches.

The wildlife is rich, but highly seasonal and nomadic. At times you'll find great concentrations of plains game, with all their attendant predators, and, in good years, spectacular breeding colonies of flamingos crowd the shallow waters of Sua Pan. At other times the stage seems empty. But even then, there is always a cast of smaller Kalahari residents behind the scenes – from coursers and korhaans to mongooses and molerats.

BACKGROUND INFORMATION
Orientation
The tarred Nata–Maun road bisects this barren region. To the south of this lie the vast, dry depressions of Sua and Ntwetwe, with their scattered 'islands' of granite and fossilised dunes, fringed by grassland and acacia savannah. To its north is the Nxai Pan complex, including Nxai and Kgama-Kgama pans, now grassed over, and Kudiakam Pan which is overlooked by the famous Baines' Baobabs.

Much of the region is unfenced ranching country, where wildlife has largely been supplanted by cattle. However, the fauna and flora are protected in a number of reserves. Makgadikgadi Pans National Park extends south of the Nata-Maun road, between the western shore of Ntwetwe Pan and the Boteti River. Nxai Pans National Park adjoins this to the north of the Nata-Maun road, and includes the Nxai Pans complex and Baines Baobabs. Meanwhile the much smaller Nata Sanctuary is situated in the northeast corner of Sua Pan, and was proclaimed to protect the seasonal breeding waterbirds of the Nata River Delta. Each of these areas has its own distinct attractions and seasonal peculiarities.

Geography
The Magkadikgadi Pans consists of an immense expanse of largely flat and featureless terrain in the north of the Kalahari. The pans themselves are located roughly between the diamond town of Orapa in the south, the village of Nata in the northeast and the Boteti rivercourse in the west. This falls away northwards towards the Mababe Depression and the Chobe-Zambezi river catchment system.

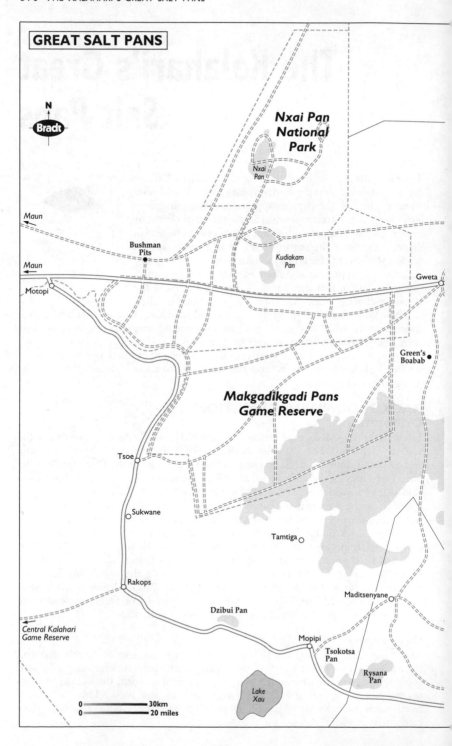

GREAT SALT PANS

N

Bradt

Nxai Pan
National
Park

Nxai
Pan

Maun

Bushman
Pits

Kudiakam
Pan

Maun

Gweta

Motopi

Green's
Boabab

*Makgadikgadi Pans
Game Reserve*

Tsoe

Sukwane

Tamtiga

Rakops

Maditsenyane

Dzibui Pan

Central Kalahari
Game Reserve

Mopipi

Tsokotsa
Pan

Rysana
Pan

Lake
Xau

0 — 30km
0 — 20 miles

KEY

Tar road	
4WD track	
National park	
Veterinary fence	
Salt pan	

Kasane

Nata

Tsigara

Nata Sanctuary

Sowa Spit

Chapman's Boababs

Sowa

Francistown

Sua Pan

Thabatshukudu

Ntwetwe Pan

Tshwagong

Kubu Island

Kukome Island

Guquago Pan

Nkokwane Pan

Ntsokotsa Pan

Mmatshumo

Mosu

Mea

Francistown

Orapa (closed town)

At its centre lie two huge adjacent salt pans – Sua (to the east) and Ntwetwe (to the west) – which cover an estimated combined area of roughly 12,000km². Around them are a number of smaller pans, including Nxai Pan to the north and Lake Xau to the south.

Geology

To grasp the complex geology of this area, you really require a broader understanding of the way in which the whole Kalahari was formed (see pages 47–52). In brief, the pans are the desiccated vestiges of the huge 'superlake' which, several million years ago, covered most of central Botswana and moulded the landscape of the entire region. Subsequent climate change, seismic upheavals and the diversion of rivers (the details of which divide geologists) starved this lake of its water supply, shrinking it to today's flat, caustic depressions of grey clay, and withering its surrounding wetlands into arid savannah.

Today the pans receive no more than 400–500mm of rain annually, and have no permanent standing water. After good rains, however, they briefly become shallow lakes again, fed by the seasonal Boteti river from the west – bringing the overspill from the Okavango – and the Nata River from the northeast.

Flora and fauna

The plant and animal life of the region reflects its harsh climate. The plants are hardy and resilient species; the animals comprise either nomadic species that follow the rains in large seasonal movements, or specialised sedentary species adapted to arid Kalahari conditions. Populations fluctuate wildly according to rainfall. Consequently wildlife viewing is a 'hit and miss' affair, depending entirely on the time of year and local conditions. However, in the right place at the right time, it can be spectacular, and the wide, open spaces make for excellent visibility.

Flora

The flora of the Makgadikgadi Pans region can be graded into a loose series of zones, each determined by the soil in which it grows. At the centre lie the pans themselves: barren, windswept and devoid of any plant life. These sterile, salty dustbowls are surrounded by extensive grasslands which flourish on Kalahari sands, comprising a mixture of salt-tolerant species around the pans, coarse 'finger' grasses across the sandy plains, and nutritious 'sweet grasses' on the margins. The grasslands are punctuated with scattered trees and thickets, consisting primarily of acacia species.

Further from the pans, where the soil has a richer sand and clay mix, this acacia savannah becomes a denser bush, interspersed with other woodland trees, including various combretum and terminalia species. To the north and east, the acacias are replaced by a belt of mopane trees (*Colophospermum mopane*), which flourish on the more heavily clay soils.

To the west, the alluvial soils and hidden water-table of the Boteti riverfront support a strip of dense riverine woodland. Here typical Kalahari species, such as camelthorn (*Acacia erioloba*) and blackthorn (*Acacia mellifera*), grow alongside riverine giants such as sycamore figs (*Ficus sycomorus*), sausage trees (*Kigelia africana*) and many of the other riverine species that are usually associated with wetter areas.

Across the region, towering real fan palms (*Hyphaene petersiana*) cluster in elegant, waving stands above the grasslands, forming extensive groves of palm woodland to the west of Ntwetwe Pan. Equally conspicuous are the scattered baobabs, which sprout incongruously around the pans and on isolated rock outcrops, each with centuries of history recorded in its swollen limbs.

Mammals

Fossil evidence unearthed on the pans shows that in wetter, prehistoric times, the region supported the whole spectrum of African big game – including abundant elephant, buffalo and rhino. Today, the selection of large mammals is more limited than the game-rich areas of Moremi and Chobe to the north and west. Rhino have disappeared altogether, while elephant and buffalo only occur occasionally, in small numbers on the fringes.

However, the grasslands draw huge herds of grazers, which can, despite recent declines, still rival anything outside Tanzania's Serengeti for sheer numbers. Zebra and wildebeest gather in tens of thousands, supported by smaller numbers of gemsbok, eland and red hartebeest. Movements are unpredictable, but in general the highest concentrations occur in the western Boteti region during the late dry season (August–November) and further north in the Nxai Pan area during the rainy season (December–April).

Hardy springbok are impervious to drought and remain scattered across the grasslands throughout the year. In the Nxai Pans area, the mopane woodland shelters browsers, including impala (which supplant springbok where the bush thickens), kudu, sable and tsessebe. Here, giraffe are common and a few breeding elephant frequent the fringes of the northern pans.

Another pocket of diversity occurs along the Boteti River, where the thicker bush provides cover for grey duiker, bushbuck and waterbuck. Giraffe and elephant also visit this area, while the permanent pools even support a few hippos and crocodiles – emigrants from the Okavango.

A variety of predators prowls the region. Lions generally follow the game, particularly the zebra herds in the Boteti area and the winter springbok in Nxai, but seldom occur on the pans themselves. Cheetah are most often seen around Nxai Pan, while leopard frequent the denser bush of the Boteti waterfront. Spotted hyena keep to the woodland fringes, while the brown hyena – a Kalahari specialist – is found around the pans themselves.

Wild dog are highly nomadic and though unusual, can turn up anywhere. Here they are most often seen in the vicinity of Nxai Pan. Smaller predators include bat-eared fox, black-backed jackal, aardwolf, honey badger, African wildcat, small-spotted genet and striped polecat. Yellow mongooses are common on the grasslands, while the slender mongoose prefers acacia thickets.

Without much in the way of fruiting trees, the Makgadikgadi is not a good region for primates – except along the Boteti, where both vervet monkeys and baboons do find food and cover. However, throughout the region the lesser bushbaby, which feeds mostly on insects and acacia gum, thrives in the acacia savannah.

Other mammals of the grasslands include the ubiquitous aardvark and porcupine, and the bizarre spring hare is particularly abundant. Most smaller mammals are nocturnal, allowing them to avoid the high daytime temperatures, when a larger surface area to body ratio quickly causes overheating. On this principle a variety of rodents make their home in burrows and emerge at night, including the desert pygmy mouse, hairy-footed gerbil, and Damara mole rat (see box on page 437).

The black-tailed tree rat avoids the burning sun by hiding in tree holes, and protects the entrance to its lair with a scruffy 'nest' of twigs. At night this species can be seen scampering through the branches of a camelthorn, using its prehensile tail for added agility.

One exception to the nocturnal rule is the ground squirrel, an animal of the deep Kalahari that occurs in the sandy south of the region. This highly sociable rodent can forage in the full glare of the sun by using its tail as a parasol to cast protective shade.

Birds

The Great Salt Pans region offers several distinct habitats for birds. The open grasslands support typical ground-nesting, arid country species such as coursers, korhaans, sandgrouse, chats, larks and pipits. Both the world's largest bird – the ostrich – and the world's largest flying bird, the kori bustard, strike conspicuous figures in this featureless terrain, while greater kestrels, pale-chanting goshawks, marsh owls and the statuesque secretary bird are among the more common resident predators.

Any isolated stands of trees are beacons for birds: red-necked falcons breed in fan palms, while baobabs provide roosts for owls and breeding sites for hornbills and rollers. Elsewhere, typical arid woodland residents dominate the thicker scrub, including red-billed francolin, grey lourie, fork-tailed drongo, pied babbler, glossy starling, white-browed sparrow weaver and a wide variety of shrikes, barbets, flycatchers, robins, sunbirds, warblers, waxbills and whydahs.

Eagles, including martial and bateleur, roam the skies. Smaller predators such as gabar goshawk and pearl-spotted owl hunt the thorn scrub, and vultures follow the herds across the region, hoping for casualties.

In summer the resident bird population is swelled by a huge influx of migrants drawn to the seasonal bonanza of seeds and insects. Some are non-breeding visitors that come from as far afield as Europe and central Africa. White storks (from Europe) and Abdim's storks (from East Africa) arrive wheeling on thermals to stalk the savannah; carmine and European bee-eaters hawk their insect prey just above the grass; shrikes, including red-backed and lesser grey, claim prominent territories on thorn bushes from where they ambush hapless lizards and grasshoppers.

Other more local breeding visitors include seed-eaters such as wattled starlings, doves, finchlarks, canaries – and the prolific red-billed quelea, whose flocks reach swarm proportions. Migrant raptors are lured by the brief abundance of prey, with many different species – including western red-footed falcons, steppe buzzards, yellow-billed kites and tawny eagles – congregating at mass termite emergences (see page 396).

After good rains, when Ntwetwe and Sua Pans turn briefly into glassy lakes, waterbirds arrive in their thousands. The shallow, saline conditions are ideal for both greater and lesser flamingos, which construct their clay nests under the blazing Kalahari sun and filter-feed on algae and brine shrimps. Meanwhile pelicans, darters, cormorants and ducks flock to the brackish waters of the Nata River delta, in the northeast of Sua Pan. Here, waders such as stilts, sandpipers and avocets forage along the shoreline, while jacanas, pied kingfishers, weavers and bishops frequent the reed beds.

Smaller fauna

Further down the evolutionary scale, a variety of reptiles and amphibians thrive in Makgadikgadi's arid expanses, though most pass unseen by the visitor. Acacias, with their deeply fissured bark and abundance of insect prey, provide havens for skinks and geckos above the open grassland. At ground level, the ground agama ambushes termites from a hollow at the foot of a shady bush, while the legless Kalahari burrowing skink swims just below the surface of the sand in search of beetle larvae, and is often found drowned when pans fill up overnight. In sandier areas, barking geckos emerge from their burrows on summer evenings and fill the Kalahari night with their bizarre territorial clicking calls.

Perhaps *the* highlight of Makgadikgadi's smaller animals is one that few have either heard of or seen: the Makgadikgadi Spiny Agama (*Agama makarikarica*). This is a small species of the agama family – a lizard – that's endemic to Makgadikgadi. It feeds on termites and beetles, and lives in tunnels at the base of bushes.

The acacia woodland is home to a broad cross-section of typical bushveld reptiles, including monitor lizards (both water and rock), flapneck chameleons and leopard tortoises. Snakes encountered at ground level include black mamba, snouted cobra, African egg-eater, mole snake and the ubiquitous puff adder, while arboreal species such as boomslang and spotted bush snake hunt chameleons and birds' eggs among the thorny tangle.

To survive this harsh habitat, many frogs aestivate below ground during the dry season. Giant bullfrogs emerge from their mud cocoons after seasonal rains to take over temporary pans in a frenzy of breeding. These frogs are so aggressive that they have even been observed snapping at lions. The much smaller rain-frogs of the *Breviceps* genus, like the bushveld rain frog, *Breviceps adspersus*, have toughened feet, evolved for digging their burrows. They also appear with the rains, and gather at the surface during termite emergences, cramming in as many of the hapless insects as time will allow.

The Kalahari teems with invertebrate life. Good years bring swarms of locusts and mass migrations of butterflies to the grasslands, while countless termites demolish and carry away the dead vegetable matter that carpets the ground. Termites are fundamental to the ecology of the region. Not only do they recycle and enrich the soil, but they are also a vital prey species for everything from eagles and aardvarks to skinks and spiders.

There are 14 genera of termites, each of which has a different mode of foraging: harvester termites (*Hototermitidae*) nest in underground burrows, while *Odontoterme* termites construct the enormous raised mounds that can be seen for miles across the grasslands – each one a miracle of air conditioning.

Among a multitude of other insects are the wingless tenebrionid beetles, which scuttle rapidly across open ground on long legs and squirt a noxious fluid at attackers. More visible are the chunkier dung beetles, which swarm on strong wings to fresh animal dung, then roll it away and bury it as 'brood balls' in which their eggs are laid and their larvae mature.

On hot summer days, thickets throb with the stridulating calls of cicadas, the adults having only two weeks of life in which to mate and deposit their eggs, after up to 17 years underground larval development.

Termites and other insects feed a host of invertebrate predators. Sand divers (*Ammoxennidae*) are small, fast-moving spiders that paralyse termites with their venom and bury themselves if disturbed. Golden orbweb spiders (*Nephiladae*) string their super-strong webs between thorn bushes to ensnare flying insects.

Contrary to popular belief, sun-spiders, or solifuges (*Solifugae*), are not venomous, but pursue insects at high speed across the ground and despatch them audibly with powerful mandibles. You'll often see these large arachnids running across the ground at night near campfires. Though frightening at first, they're totally harmless and don't bite people!

Not so harmless are the resident scorpions, which detect the vibrations of prey through their body hairs. As a rough rule of thumb for the nervous, species with larger pincers and slimmer tails have less powerful venom than those with smaller pincers and larger tails.

Red velvet mites are parasites on larger invertebrates and often gather in sandy areas in the early morning after rain showers, looking like tiny scarlet cushions. Another tiny parasite, the voracious tampan tick, lurks in the sand beneath camelthorn trees

HIGH-RISE LIVING

The towers of mud built by termites, known as termitaria, are often the only points of elevation for miles across the Makgadikgadi grasslands. Not all termites build mounds – harvester termites (*Hodotermitidae*), which are common on Kalahari sands, leave little evidence of their underground tunnels above the surface – but those that do, the *Macrotermitidae* species, are responsible for one of the true wonders of nature.

Communicating entirely through pheromones, millions of blind worker termites can raise several tons of soil – particle by particle – into an enormous structure over three metres high. Below the mound lies the nest, where separate chambers house brood galleries, food stores, fungus combs (where termites cultivate a fungus that can break down plant cellulose for them) and the queen's royal cell. The queen produces up to 30,000 eggs a day, which means – since she lives for many years – that the millions of inhabitants of the colony are all brothers and sisters.

The whole structure is prevented from overheating by a miraculous air-conditioning system. Warm air rises from the nest chambers, up a central chimney, into thin-walled ventilation flues near the surface (you can feel the warmth by placing your hand just inside one of the upper vents). Here it is cooled and replenished with oxygen, before circulating back down through separate passages into cavities below the nest chambers. Finally, before returning to the nest, it passes through specially constructed cooling veins, kept damp by the termites. In this way, termites maintain the 100% humidity and constant temperature of 29–31°C required for successful production of eggs and young. (These conditions are exploited by monitor lizards, who seal their eggs inside termitaria for safe incubation.)

After the rains, when conditions are right, the queen produces a reproductive caste of winged males and females – known as imagoes – who leave the colonies in huge swarms to mate, disperse and establish new nests. *Mass termite 'emergences'* are one of the bonanzas of the bush, offering a seasonal feast to everything from frogs and spiders to kites, falcons and tawny eagles.

and, chemically alerted by an exhalation of its victim's CO_2, emerges to drain the blood from any unsuspecting mammal that fancies a nap in the shade.

GETTING ORGANISED

Once you leave one of the few main roads in this area, you generally need to be in a self-sufficient 4WD vehicle. Bringing along all your food and water with you is always a good idea, as whilst you will find water in some places, there is very little in the way of shops!

If you're venturing off across Makgadikgadi, then you really should take at least two vehicles and have a GPS and a compass; an environment of flat salt without any landmarks at all can be very disorienting, especially during a windstorm. In such a situation, breaking through the pan's crust and getting stuck can create a life-threatening situation.

Maps

The 'usual suspects' both cover this area well – the *Shell tourist map of Botswana* map and the *Contimap*. Both have a variety of useful GPS points. Although I find the

Shell map a little easier to use, with its more detailed maps on the reverse side, the *Contimap* is much newer (2001). Take both if you can.

If you plan on exploring a lot of the pans, then you should also get hold of a copy of the excellent *Visitor's Guide to Botswana* by Mike Main (see *Further Reading*). This has a number of carefully described routes through the area – as well as much interesting general information. However, note that the most recent edition that I'm aware of was 1996, and some of the tracks will have changed since then.

Booking and park fees

If you want to stay in either of the national parks then you must book ahead for a campsite. See *Chapter 7*, pages 142–3, for details of the park fees for these national parks.

Similarly Nata Sanctuary, Jack's Camp and Makgadikgadi Camp are certainly best booked in advance – though most of Sua and Ntwetwe Pans are not controlled, and so you can sleep anywhere.

NXAI PAN NATIONAL PARK

Nxai Pan National Park lies to the north of the Nata-Maun road at the northern fringe of the ancient lake Makgadikgadi basin. It is contiguous with Makgadikgadi Pans National Park, to the south of this same road. Nxai is probably the easiest area of the pans to drive yourself into and from December to around July will also have the best game. Add in the spectacular sight of Baines' Baobabs to make a super destination for a three- to four-day self-drive trip.

Note that Nxai is usually pronounced to rhyme with 'high', unless you're familiar with the clicks of the Khoisan languages, in which case the correct pronunciation of the 'x' is actually a palatal click (i.e. press tongue against the roof of your mouth, and then move down).

Background information
Geography

The park covers an area of 2,658km², comprising Nxai Pan itself, Kgama-Kgama Pan complex to the northeast, and the Kudiakam Pan complex (including Baines' Baobabs) to the south. The latter were added to the original park in 1992.

The pans themselves are ancient salt lakes, ringed to the south and west with thick fossil dunes of wind-blown Kalahari sand. Today they are completely grassed over, but scattered across their surfaces are smaller pans or waterholes that fill up during the rainy season. Some of these are artificially maintained by the park authorities to provide surface water throughout the year, but the watercourses that once fed the area from the northeast have long since dried up.

The park's general topography is flat and featureless, with the famous baobabs being the most striking landmarks, and one of the higher points of elevation. To the north and east the soils become increasingly clayey, supporting the encroachment of mopane woodland and integrating with the dense mopane woodlands of the Chobe/Zambezi river catchment system.

Flora and fauna highlights
Flora

The open grassland that covers the pans consists of many palatable 'sweet' grasses (eg: *Themeda* species), which sustain the large herd of grazers that invade the area in summer. These grasslands are studded with 'islands' of acacias, consisting mostly of candle-pod acacia (*Acacia hebeclada*). This is easily recognised from around October to March, as its seedpods stand upright, like candles. Other very

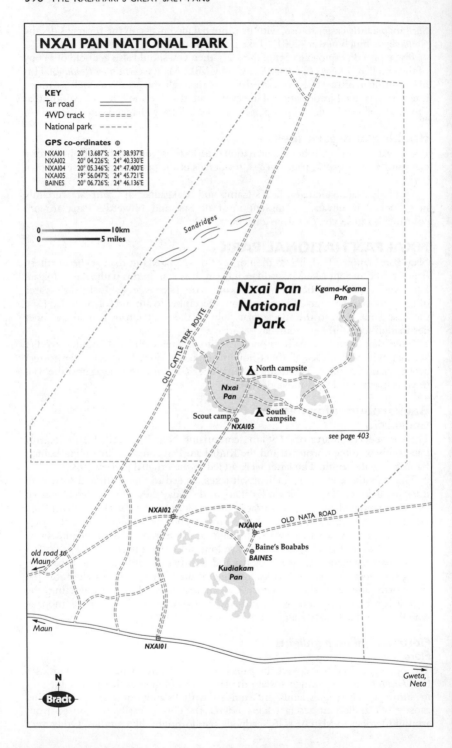

NXAI PAN NATIONAL PARK

KEY
Tar road
4WD track
National park

GPS co-ordinates ⊕
NXAI01   20° 13.687'S;   24° 38.937'E
NXAI02   20° 04.226'S;   24° 40.330'E
NXAI04   20° 05.346'S;   24° 47.400'E
NXAI05   19° 56.047'S;   24° 45.721'E
BAINES   20° 06.726'S;   24° 46.136'E

0 ━━━━━ 10km
0 ━━━━━ 5 miles

Sandridges

Nxai Pan
National
Park

Kgama-Kgama Pan

OLD CATTLE TREK ROUTE

North campsite

Nxai Pan

Scout camp
⊕
NXAI05

South campsite

see page 403

NXAI02 ⊕

NXAI04 ⊕

OLD NATA ROAD

old road to Maun

Baine's Boababs
⊕
BAINES

Kudiakam Pan

Maun

NXAI01 ⊕

N

Gweta, Neta

Bradt

common species here are the umbrella thorn (*Acacia tortilis*) and bastard umbrella thorn (*Acacia leuderitzii*).

During the rains, the pans sprout a profusion of wildflowers, including the spectacular brunsvigia lily (*Brunsvigia radulosa*), which brings a splash of red to the summer landscape.

Around and between the pans the vegetation differs according to soil type. Acacias are the dominant trees on sandy soils, with stands of silver clusterleaf (*Terminalia sericea*), and – particularly in disturbed areas – dense thickets of sickle bush, *Dichrostachys cineria*. Mopane (*Colophospermum mopane*) dominates the richer clayey soils to the north and east, carpeting the dusty ground with its golden butterfly leaves and bursting into a flush of green with the rains. Elsewhere, mixed sand and clay support various combretum species, with their wind-borne winged pods, while a richer selection of shrubs thrive on the lime-rich calcrete ridges, including the trumpet thorn (*Catophractes alexandrii*), Western rhigozum (*Rhigozum brevispinosum*) and purple-pod terminalia (*Terminalia prunoides*). Visit South Camp to see some fine examples of these.

Of all the area's trees, the best-known must be the great baobabs (*Adansonia digitata*). In particular the famous Baines' Baobabs that overlook Kudiakam Pan, which were painted by the renowned Victorian explorer and artist Thomas Baines on May 22 1862, and have changed little in 140 years since. They are not the only baobabs around, but they're certainly the most celebrated.

Mammals

From December to April, Nxai Pan is a breeding ground for large herbivores. Game viewing can be spectacular at the start of this season, when thousands of animals are dropping their young and predators are drawn to the easy pickings. After good rains the lush green grasslands teem with huge concentrations of Burchell's zebra, blue wildebeest and springbok (here at the northeastern limit of their range), while healthy numbers of other grazers include gemsbok, eland and red hartebeest.

Large giraffe herds, sometimes over 40 strong, move across the pans between the acacia 'islands', which they prune into characteristic hourglass shapes. The mopane woodland, mainly to the north of Nxai Pan, shelters browsers such as impala and kudu, which often venture out onto the pans for the permanent waterholes and rich mineral salts. The impala is a versatile species, being able to adapt its diet to graze or browse, according to what is on offer, and Nxai Pan is one of the few areas where impala and springbok occur side by side – their habitats elsewhere generally being mutually exclusive.

In summer, small herds of breeding elephant can sometimes be seen around Kgama-Kgama Pan in the northeast of the park, while lone bulls disperse across the area at other times – generally on the fringes of the mopane. Other visitors from the north include the occasional tsessebe, at about the southern limit of their appearance in the Kalahari. In winter the great herds disperse from the pans, leaving few grazers except the hardy springbok, and a few timid steenbok that find shelter in the thickets.

Predators are well represented on Nxai Pan. Lion can be heard throughout the year: in summer they follow the zebra and wildebeest herds; during the dry season they remain to hunt springbok around the few permanent waterholes. The springbok herds also draw cheetah – Nxai Pan offers perfect open terrain for this coursing predator, and has a good reputation for sightings. Meanwhile wandering packs of wild dog occasionally turn up in pursuit of the same quarry.

Spotted hyena can sometimes be heard at night, especially when there are large concentrations of game around, while the more elusive brown hyena hunts and scavenges for smaller prey items around the pans. Black-backed jackal and honey badger are both versatile smaller predators that occur throughout the area – the latter sometimes foraging in association with the pale-chanting goshawk.

Aardwolf and bat-eared fox snap up harvester termites on the open grasslands: the former is strictly nocturnal and seldom seen; the latter may still be about at sunrise, foraging in loose family groups with ears cocked to the ground for termite rustlings.

African wildcat and small-spotted genet hunt the acacia bush after dark for small rodents and roosting birds, while by day yellow mongoose comb open sandy areas for scorpions, slender mongoose hunt the acacia scrub, alone or in pairs, and banded mongoose rummage through the woodland in large, sociable colonies.

Other smaller mammals found here include lesser bushbaby, aardvark and porcupine, with spring hare on the grassland and scrub hare in the woodland. By day, tree squirrels are common and noisy inhabitants of the mopane.

Birds

Nxai Pan's rich avifauna comprises a mixture of grassland, acacia scrub and mopane woodland birds, with a total of 217 species recorded in Hugh Chittenden's *Top Birding Spots in Southern Africa* (see *Further Reading*). Each habitat has its own typical residents.

Grassland birds include ant-eating chat, white-browed sparrow weaver, capped wheatear and pale-chanting goshawk. White-browed robin, pied babbler and chinspot batis are found in the acacia scrub. Red-billed hornbill, red-billed francolin and barred owl prefer the mopane.

The distinction between adjacent habitats is reflected in the parallel distributions of similar species. For example, double-banded coursers and white-quilled korhaans – both Kalahari specialists – occur only on the open grasslands, while bronze-winged coursers and red-crested korhaans, their close relatives, stick to the surrounding woodlands.

Resident raptors, such as bateleur, martial eagle, tawny eagle and brown snake eagle, are joined in summer by an influx of migrants, including steppe buzzard, western red-footed kestrel and yellow-billed kite. Raptor watching can be superb at this time, with more unusual species such as lesser-spotted eagle and hobby sometimes joining the throng at termite emergences.

Kori bustards, secretary birds and (in summer) white storks hunt the grasslands, and after good rains wattled cranes sometimes appear on the flashes. In spring the air resounds to the breeding displays of larks, including sabota, rufous-naped, red-capped, fawn-coloured, dusky and clapper. During summer the game herds are a focus of bird activity, with carmine and blue-cheeked bee-eaters hawking insects around the feet of springbok and zebra, red-billed and yellow-billed oxpeckers hitching rides on giraffes, and white-backed and lappet-faced vultures dropping from the sky onto carcasses.

Away from the pans, the campsites are a good place to search out the smaller passerines: violet-eared, black-cheeked and blue waxbills occur in the sandy acacia scrub together with melba and scaly-feathered finches, while shaft-tailed and paradise whydahs – brood parasites on waxbills (see box on page 401) – dash about in extravagant breeding finery. Baobabs are always worth checking, since they often provide roosting or nesting sites for rollers, hornbills and various owls.

Getting there and getting away

To visit Nxai Pan National Park you really need a vehicle, either your own or one driven by one of the mobile safari operators from Maun. Either way, you

BROOD PARASITES

Cuckoos are not the only cheats of the bird world. Whydahs (*Viduidae*) are also brood parasites that lay their eggs in other birds' nests. Like cuckoos, each species of whydah exploits a specific host, and all of them choose waxbills (*Estrildidae*). However, unlike cuckoos, whydahs do not evict the eggs or nestlings of their host, so young whydahs grow up alongside their step-siblings, not instead of them.

To enhance the deception, a whydah's eggs – and there are usually two of them – perfectly mimic the colour of its host's clutch, and, once hatched, the whydah nestlings have exactly the right arrangements of gape spots inside their bills to dupe their step-parents into feeding them. A male whydah can even mimic the song of its host to distract it from the nest while the female goes about her devious business undisturbed. Breeding male whydahs are lively, conspicuous birds, who flaunt extravagant tail plumes in dancing display flights – though outside the breeding season they are indistinguishable from the drab females.

Three species of whydah occur in the pans region, of which the most typical is the shaft-tailed whydah (*Vidua regia*), easily recognised by the long thin tail-plumes of a breeding male, each tipped with a pennant. This species frequents sandy clearings in acacia thickets, often in association with its host, the violet-eared waxbill, and apparently without any animosity between them. The other two species are the pin-tailed whydah (*Vidua macroura*), which parasitises the common waxbill and prefers well-watered areas, and the paradise whydah (*Vidua paradisaea*), which parasitizes the melba finch and is a common bird of acacia savannah.

should come with all your fuel, water and food – there are no shops or petrol pumps here.

The route here is very easy to find, and starts with a northerly turn-off from the main Maun–Nata road at (⊕ NXAI01 – 20°13.687'S, 24°38.937'E). This is about 134km from Maun and 158km from Nata, and is very well signposted so you're unlikely to miss it.

There's one track north here, and after 18km of fairly thick, corrugated and fairly unpleasant sand driving, you'll reach a right turn at (⊕ NXAI02 – 20°04.226'S, 24°40.330'E). This leads to Kudiakam Pan and Baines Baobabs – see page 404 for directions.

Continue straight, bearing north-northeast for a further 18km and you'll reach the entrance gate (⊕ NXAI05 – 19°56.047'S, 24°45.721'E), which is at the south end of the main pan.

When to visit

The game at Nxai is fairly erratic – it can be excellent, though sometimes it will disappoint. If there has been good rains, then between December and April you have a very good chance of witnessing large herds of springbok, gemsbok, giraffe and migrating zebra, plus a scattering of other species. However, note that this is also the time when the pans are at their most treacherous, and the driving is at its most muddy.

I last visited in late May, after a year of good rains, and we had excellent general game, with very large numbers of springbok, although in three days we didn't see a single large carnivore. Reliable reports suggest that this continues until around August, when game densities start to decrease. Then as the dry season progresses and the waterholes dry up, the game becomes sparser and less dependable. Nxai can be a hot and unrewarding park at the height of October's heat.

Where to stay

There are just two campsites here, both a short distance off the main Nxai Pan. One to the south, called South Camp, and one to the north, unsurprisingly called North Camp. Both usually have standpipes for water and, if you're lucky, you'll find working flush toilets and showers here.

There's also an old, disused campsite on a short (0.8km long) loop road on the eastern side of Nxai Pan at ⊕ NXAIOL 19°55.571'S, 24°49.282'E.

South Camp

South Camp (⊕ NXAISO 19°56.159'S, 24°46.598'E) is the closest to the entrance and probably the busier site – but also the nicer one. It's situated in a grove of purple-pod terminalia trees (*Terminalia prunioides*) which cast a good shade, making it relatively cool.

North Camp

North Camp (⊕ NXAINO 19°52.707'S, 24°47.358'E) stands in a less inspiring grove of stunted mopane trees, which don't offer nearly the same shade as the terminalias. However, if South Camp is busier then you may find more solitude here.

What to see and do

Nxai's a great park for watching the herds of plains game, and is certainly somewhere that you need to be patient. Don't rush around in search of predators; instead take your time and you'll see much more. The waterholes are very open and exposed here, so park a good distance away and you won't disturb the animals drinking.

Finally, note that the night sky here is often phenomenally clear – as it is across the centre of the Kalahari. So if you can bring a star chart as well as your route maps, you'll enjoy it all the more. First on your list should be to identify the Southern Cross, and use it to find due south.

When gazing up, try using your binoculars and you'll be amazed how many more stars you can see.

Nxai and Kgama-Kgama pans

This is the main pan of the complex. It's covered with grasses and dotted with clumps of acacias – and has always provided me with the best game viewing in this park.

Getting around

In the dry season you'll find most of the roads in the area of the pan are good and hard – a pleasant contrast to the thick sand that you ploughed through to reach here.

When the rains come you'll have to be much more careful as many roads on the pan itself turn very muddy. Then the sand road in will be the easiest section, and the park itself will provide the problems. Make sure your self-sufficient vehicle includes a spade, and always carry some wood with you – both for campfires and for sticking under the wheels when you get stuck.

From Nxai Pan to Kgama-Kgama Pan

Visiting most recently in May, the roads which leads off east towards Kgama-Kgama Pan had clearly been used very little during the previous rains, and was very overgrown.

To reach this, head east from the scout post for about 10km, passing South Camp on your right. This should bring you to a junction of the tracks (⊕NXAI16 19°55.803'S, 24°50.986'E). From here one track leads off (and is clearly marked on most maps) to loop around to the southeast and then turn north. This is in a very poor state, totally overgrown, and is fast becoming impassable.

However, another track leads off heading north of east, before turning northeast, and after almost 5km reaches another junction (⊕ NXAI14 19°53.902'S, 24°52.744'E). The road northeast to Kgama-Kgama Pan was not in good shape, though later in the dry season it should be fine.

The alternative, which leads roughly west, across the north end of the small pan to the east of Nxai, heads through an interesting area of mostly mopane woodland, mixed with some denser groves of terminalias, and even in May, some of the pans here retained water. This eventually leads west to North Camp (⊕ NXAINO 19°52.707'S, 24°47.358'E).

Kudiakam Pan and Baines' Baobabs

Sandwiched between Nxai Pan and the main road, Kudiakam is the largest of an interesting complex of pans lying in sparse bush east of the track to Nxai. The game here doesn't usually match Nxai's, but the main attraction is an extraordinary beautiful group of trees known as Baines' Baobabs, which stand at a spectacular site on the eastern edge of the pan. They were immortalised in a painting by Thomas Baines who came here in May 1862 with James Chapman and wrote:

> A lone circuit brought me, with empty pouch, to the clump of baobabs we had seen yesterday from the wagon; five full-sized trees, and two or three younger ones were standing, so that when in leaf their foliage must form one magnificent shade. One gigantic trunk had fallen and lay prostrate but still, losing none of its vitality, bent forth branches and young leaves like the rest... The general colour or the immense stems was grey and rough: but where the old bark had peeled and curled off, the new (of that peculiar metallic coppery-looking red and yellow which Dr Livingstone was wont so strenuously to object to in my pictures) shone through over large portions, giving them, according to light or shade, a red or yellow, grey or a deep purple tone.

The baobabs themselves have changed very little since Baines painted them: the one lying prostrate is still thriving, having lost none of its vitality.

Having thought of the baobabs with reference to a fairly recent Victorian painter, it's perhaps worth reminding ourselves that Baines was far from the first person here. Lawrence Robbins (see *Further Reading*) and others have conducted archaeological surveys of this area and discovered extensive remains dating from the Middle Stone Age period 'especially on the eastern side within a 4km radius of the Baines baobab grove'. Many stone tools were found, plus ostrich eggshell remains, a zebra's tooth and the bone of a fossil hippopotamus.

This site has been dated to between about 105,000 and 128,000 years old, around which time this was probably a beach location on the edge of the great superlake. This Middle Stone Age period has a special resonance, as this is the period during which we think the first homo sapiens appeared.

Getting there

The easiest way is to follow the directions to Nxai by turning off the main Maun-Nata road at ⊕ NXAI01 20°13.687'S, 24°38.937'E, which is well signposted to Nxai. After heading north for 18km, you'll find a track off to the east at ⊕NXAI02 20°04.226'S, 24°40.330'E.

When I last drove this way there was the rusting shell of a burnt-out VW combi a short way along this track. Either grass seeds had clogged the radiator to overheating, or the sheer effort of the deep sand here had simply been too much for it. This track splits very soon, after about 0.9km, and both roads lead to the baobabs.

Dry season route

The right fork heads almost directly for Baines' Baobabs (⊕ BAINES 20°06.726'S, 24°46.136'E). It is the more direct route, but it crosses the surface of the pans, so do not try this unless you know what you're doing and are sure they will be dry. (It should be fine after about August, though don't take this as a guarantee!)

Wet season route

Taking the left fork is more reliable if you're travelling earlier in the year, as it bends around slightly to the north, taking about 14.4km to reach a crossroads at ⊕

NXAI04 – 20°05.346'S, 24°47.400'E. Here you meet the old road between Maun and Nata; this is about 3.6km from the trees themselves. There's a network of small tracks around here, so head straight and then look for tracks off to the right, or turn right and find a track to your left – you can't miss them (⊕ BAINES 20°06.726'S, 24°46.136'E).

Where to stay
In the last few years, there has been an increasing numbers of visitors to Baines' Baobabs, and in the last decade this pan and its trees have been included in the National Park to protect them. Campers were becoming a problem here, and their fires a real danger to the trees, so camping is no longer allowed here.

MAKGADIKGADI PANS
The Sua and Ntwetwe Pans that comprise Makgadikgadi cover 12,000km² to the south of the Nata–Maun road. The western side is protected within a National Park, while the east is either wilderness or cattle ranching land.

These are amongst the largest saltpans in the world and have few landmarks. So you're left to use the flat, distant horizon as your only line of reference – and even that dissolves into a haze of shimmering mirages in the heat of the afternoon sun. During the rains this desolate area comes to life, with huge migrating herds of zebra, wildebeest, and occasionally (if the pans fill with water) pelicans and millions of flamingos. A couple of odd outcrops of isolated rock in and around the pans add to their sense of mystery, as well as providing excellent vantage points from which to view the endless expanse of silver, grey and blue.

Makgadikgadi Pans National Park lies on the west of the pans, incorporating the western end of Ntwetwe Pan and a larger adjacent area of grassland and acacia woodland. The flora and fauna here is sufficiently different, especially around the Boteti River, to warrant a separate section. This is towards the end of this chapter, entitled *Makgadikgadi Pans National Park* (pages 422–7).

Background information
This section concentrates on the main saltpans, Sua and Ntwetwe, and the areas of grassland immediately around them which encompass many scattered smaller pans.

Geography and geology
As discussed on page 51, Sua and Ntwetwe lie at the centre of the great prehistoric lake basin that circumscribes the whole region. On top of this is an ancient mantle of windblown Kalahari sands – deposited during the tertiary period, as the subcontinent was levelled by erosion. Exposed rock is a rarity on the surface of this scrubbed and scoured landscape. However, beneath the sand lie ancient Karoo deposits 300 million years old, comprising basalt larva, sandstone and shales and containing such valuable minerals as gold, silver, copper and nickel.

During the Cretaceous Period, 80 million years ago, rifts and buckles in the Earth's crust allowed 'pipes' of molten material – known as kimberlite – to punch their way up from below. Diamonds formed under conditions of massive heat and pressure in these kimberlite pipes. Today they are mined at Orapa, just south of Ntwetwe Pan.

A few isolated outcrops of igneous rock extrude from the surface of the pans, notably Kubu Island and Kukome Island on Sua Pan. Apart from these, and some fossilised barchan (crescent-shaped) dunes to the west, the pans themselves are flat and featureless expanses of dry, sterile salt. However, after good summer rains they are transformed into shimmering lakes, giving a glimpse of what the great superlake must once have been like. The rainwater that pours down on them is augmented in really wet years by seasonal flows from the east: the Nata, Tutume, Semowane and Mosetse rivers. Also, again only in exceptional years, an overspill from the Okavango makes its way to the west side of Ntwetwe, via the Boteti River.

Flora and fauna highlights

The saline conditions of the pans themselves have a strong local influence on their surrounding vegetation. Broadly speaking this becomes richer and more diverse the further you travel from the pan edges, creating a loose concentric series of 'succession' zones, each of which supports a distinctive fauna. These zones effectively chart the gradual demise of the ancient super-lake.

Flora

There is no plant life on the surface of the pans, since nothing can tolerate the excessively high concentration of mineral salts, and wind erosion scours the exposed dusty surface, quickly denuding it of any vegetation that tries to take hold. The immediate fringes are carpeted with more-or-less uninterrupted grassland, consisting primarily of *Digitarias* species, which can survive despite the irregular herd movements. Between the pans can also be found patches of prickly salt grass (*Odyssea paucinervis*), a yellowish, spiky species that tolerates high salinity (salt crystals can sometimes be seen on the leaves).

Summer rains bring lush growth to the grasses, which flower in a wind-rippled sea of green. Then you'll also see a scattering of short-lived wild flowers bloom

KALAHARI MELONS

There are at least eight species of the pumpkin family in Botswana, of which the tsama melon, *Citrullus lanatus*, is the most distinctive and frequently seen. It is found throughout the region, and is particularly common after a good rainy season. Then, even after most of the rest of the vegetation is brown and shrivelled, you'll find tempting round melons beside the sandiest of roads – often apparently on their own.

During the dry season these become important sources of moisture for many animals, especially the gemsbok, and are also used by the local people. To get drinking water from one of these, you first cut off the top, like a boiled egg. The centre can then be cut out and eaten. Then take a stick and mash the rest of the pulp whilst it's in the melon, and this can be eaten. Take care not to eat the pips. These are best roasted and pounded, when they make an edible meal that can be cooked with water. Sometimes you'll come across a bitter fruit, which you should not eat as it may cause poisoning.

Another fairly common species is the gemsbok melon, *Citrullus naudianus*, which has similar sprawling tendrils and an oval fruit, covered in blunt fleshy spines. Unlike the tsama melon, this is a perennial plant with a long underground tuber. Inside the fruit is a jelly-like, translucent green which can be eaten raw (again, discarding the pips usually), though it doesn't taste very good. It's slightly more palatable when roasted beside the fire overnight – but I wouldn't recommend that you throw away your muesli or yoghurt before tasting it!

among the grasses, including crimson lilies, acanthus and wild hibiscus (*Hibiscus calyphyllus*). In areas of thicker sand ridges, the runners of the tsama melon (*Citrullus lanatus*) sprawls across the sand, its swollen fruit providing life-sustaining moisture for a myriad of animals, from gerbils to gemsbok. In winter, cropped and shrivelled, the grasses are reduced to a sparse golden mantle over the dusty plains, scattering their seeds to the wind.

Here and there, small hollows in the rolling grassland trap windblown detritus, creating pockets of richer soil that support scattered trees and shrubs. The commonest trees are various acacia species, such as the umbrella thorn (*Acacica tortillis*) which, with their fine leaves for minimizing water loss and wicked thorns to deter browsers, are ideally suited to survive this arid environment. The hardy camelthorn (*Acacia erioloba*) thrives in areas of deeper sand, often in an almost lifeless state of disintegration, by tapping deep reserves of ground water with its long roots.

The shepherd's tree (*Boscia albitrunca*) with its distinct white trunk and dense, invaluable shade, is another versatile pioneer of sandy Kalahari soils. The grasslands are studded with stands of fan palms (*Hyphaenea petersiana*), with their hard, cricket-ball sized fruit known as vegetable ivory. Thick groves of this elegant tree occur beyond the northwest shores of Ntwetwe Pan and along the Maun-Nata road.

In the far northeast of Sua Pan, the seasonal Nata River spreads out into a small delta formation which is quite different to the rest of the region. Here there's a band of tall dry riverine forest along the banks of the Nata, and a thickening of the ground cover lining the braided channels. Phragmites reeds thrive in the brackish conditions here, and when this delta is in flood the area can seem quite lush.

Further from the pans, the grassland gives way to a denser bush. To the east, a mixed sand and clay soil supports a greater variety of woodland trees, including tamboti (*Spirostachys africana*), marula (*Scleoroclarya birrea*) and monkey thorn (*Acacia galpinii*), while a belt of mopane woodland (*Colophospermum mopane*) also grows in the more heavily clayey soil around Nata and along the eastern boundary of Sua Pan.

The mighty baobabs (*Adansonia digitata*) are perhaps the region's best known and most easily identified trees. These grotesque, drought-resistant giants occur scattered around the pans and on isolated rock outcrops such as Kubu Island, where they have stood as landmarks for millennia. The swollen trunks of many are engraved with the signatures of generations of thirsty travellers. Among the baobabs on Kubu some other more unusual species take advantage of this rocky, island niche, including the African star-chestnut (*Sterculia africana*) and common corkwood (*Commiphora pyracanthoides*).

Mammals

Large mammals are scarce around the pans. This is partly because of the hostile nature of the terrain, partly because this is cattle ranching country, where wild animals have been marginalised by the activities of people. and partly because of the destructive effect that veterinary control fences have had on animal migration patterns.

There is no doubt that cattle fences to the south (see page 61) have had a significant impact on the populations of herbivores, and especially the blue wildebeest. Now blue wildebeest are seldom seen around Sua Pan and certainly not in the vast herds that built up during the 1950s, when populations were estimated to peak at about 250,000.

Today a permanent scattering of springbok inhabit the surrounding grasslands. These hardy and versatile antelope manage without water for long periods, and withstand the harshest daytime temperatures by orientating their white rumps towards the sun to deflect the worst of its ultraviolet rays.

Other large mammals are thin on the ground, being more abundant towards the west of Ntwetwe and the adjacent grazing grounds of Makgadikgadi Pans National Park (see pages 423–5). However, a scrutiny of the pan surface can reveals the tracks of a surprising range of visitors, including rare (perhaps lost?) wandering elephants or giraffe. Zebra and gemsbok are sometimes seen trekking wearily through the heat haze as they cross the pans between grazing areas, while red hartebeest are frequent visitors to the grasslands, where they can subsist on poorer grasses than many species.

The encrusted tracks of lion or cheetah sometimes appear on the pan surface, particularly towards the west, but the comparative lack of large herbivores means that larger predators are scarce, and a wandering lion is apt to be shot by cattle ranchers. More common are the smaller nocturnal carnivores that can survive the harsh conditions and thrive on smaller pickings.

Brown hyena inhabit the area, and a habituated clan of these elusive predators may be observed at close quarters from Jack's Camp, on the western shores of Ntwetwe, where they have been studied by zoologists. Their catholic diet includes tsama melons and ostrich eggs, as well as spring hares, young springbok, smaller mammals and carrion.

Black-backed jackal, bat-eared fox and African wildcat are widespread, while yellow mongoose is common in sandy areas, where it is an accomplished killer of scorpions. At night, a legion of smaller mammals moves out across the grasslands. Spring hares thrive on damaged grassland and are common around villages, where up to 60 may occur per hectare. Their eyes shine brightly in torchlight, and casting a beam around your campsite will usually reveal at least one foraging nearby.

Aardvarks are found (though seldom seen) in open areas with plenty of termites, scrub hares hide up in acacia thickets, and porcupines occur anywhere. Acacias provide shelter for lesser bushbabies, which feed on their gum during winter when insects are less abundant. This diminutive, nocturnal primate performs astonishing leaps from tree to tree and seldom comes to the ground, progressing on its hind legs in huge hops when it does. Common rodents include typical Kalahari species such as ground squirrel, Damara mole rat, hairy-footed gerbil and black-tailed tree rat.

Birds

The Makgadikgadi Pans are perhaps best known for their birdlife; specifically the great concentration of waterbirds in the Nata River delta after good rains (December–April). In good years, tens of thousands of flamingos, both lesser and greater, arrive to breed, visible from the air as a pink shimmer across the surface of the lake. They are sustained by a rich soup of algae – and brine shrimps, whose eggs had lain dormant in the baked clay of the pan surface throughout the dry season.

This gathering represents the largest breeding flamingo population in southern Africa, and can peak at over 100,000 birds. However it is a very unpredictable phenomenon. Even after good rains the flamingos have a life-and-death race against time to breed before the waters dry up, and they may not return again for years. In 1976, over 5,000 young flamingos, still unable to fly, were observed from the air trekking en masse across the barren pans in search of new water when their breeding shallows evaporated. What became of them is not recorded.

The flamingos can best be seen in the Nata Bird Sanctuary (see page 412–13). Here, when the flood is full, you will also find pelicans (both white and pink-backed), herons and egrets, cormorants and darters, waders (including avocet,

SPRING HARES

The spring hare is actually a true rodent, and not a hare at all. Weighing about 3kg, this bizarre animal looks like a cross between a rabbit and a kangaroo, with its long ears and thick black-tipped tail. It progresses in ambling hops on long hind legs, with forelegs clasped in front and tail balanced behind.

Spring hares live in burrows by day, in which they doze off upright, having plugged the hole with dirt. By night they graze on grass and crops, and dig for roots, corms and tubers. This animal is a prized delicacy for many nocturnal predators, including owls, honey badgers and caracals. It also figures prominently on the local human menu. It has been estimated that over 2.5 million spring hares are hunted annually in Botswana – hooked out of their holes during the day – providing the protein equivalent of 20,000 cows.

blackwinged stilt, blacksmith plover, wood sandpiper and ruff), black-necked grebe, red-knobbed coot, and ducks (including red-billed teal and white-faced duck). Other species more typical of the Okavango floodplains also occur at this time, including fish eagles, saddle-billed storks and, occasionally, wattled cranes. The reedbeds themselves provide a breeding habitat for weavers, bishops and reed warblers.

The open grasslands surrounding the pans are home to many typical Kalahari ground-nesting birds, including ostriches, which are sometimes seen far out on the pans themselves, kori bustards and secretary birds. Some smaller species, including capped wheatear and ant-eating chat, take this a stage further by nesting, like rodents, in underground burrows. All four of southern Africa's sandgrouse (Namaqua, Burchell's, double-banded and yellow-throated) occur around the pans. These delicately plumaged birds are most often seen in the evening, flying rapidly towards a waterhole with rippling calls. Males will waddle in to immerse their absorbent belly feathers and carry water back many kilometres to their young on the nest.

More conspicuous by day is the boldly-marked male white-quilled korhaan, who calls with a noisy 'karak karak karak' as he takes off and circles slowly in territorial display, before fluttering to the ground with yellow legs dangling. Like all korhaans, the brooding female relies on her cryptic camouflage to remain hidden. Another common species, the double-banded courser, is superbly adapted to withstand the harsh conditions of the pans. It does not need any drinking water, and can survive extreme overheating while protecting its single egg from the fierce Makgadikgadi sun.

In this largely featureless habitat, any point of elevation can prove a good spot for birds. The baobabs on Kubu island provide roosting and nesting sites for barn owls and rollers (both lilac-breasted and purple). Many tall stands of date palms harbour breeding palm swifts, and the occasional pair of red-necked falcons. Isolated thorn trees support the massive untidy nests of secretary birds or vultures (both white-backed and lappet-faced).

The acacia woodland holds a wide selection of birds typical of this habitat across the region (see *Nxai Pan* page 400). Red-billed francolin, white-browed robin and violet-eared waxbill forage low down in the thickets, while lilac-breasted roller and long-tailed shrike perch more conspicuously in the taller acacias. Bateleurs and martial eagles patrol the skies, and a host of bulbuls, babblers, hornbills, barbets, sunbirds, flycatchers and others occupy the niches in between.

The area around Nata Lodge is particularly rich in woodland species. In summer, migrant raptors such as steppe buzzard, western red-footed kestrel and yellow-billed kite join resident predators such as greater kestrel, pale chanting goshawk and marsh owl, and after good rains, Montagu's and pallid harriers may be seen quartering the grasslands in drifting, elegant flight.

Other common summer migrants include white stork, red-backed and lesser grey shrikes and European and carmine bee-eaters, while seed eaters such as red-billed quelea and black-eared finchlark arrive to breed in large numbers, taking advantage of the seasonally abundant grass seeds.

Getting around
With a large number of tracks in the area, I have not even tried to describe them all in detail here. However, if you're driving around by yourself, rather than with a local guide who knows the area well, then navigation issues should preoccupy you! Outside the national park, visiting the pans is all about exploring for yourself. If you want set routes to follow, perhaps it's not for you.

If you're ready for a small expedition, then take note of the highlights and landmarks mentioned here, with GPS co-ordinates, and use the maps (mentioned on pages 396–7) to keep some realistic idea of where you are. That said, because of the size of the pans and its very remote situation, you must follow some basic safety rules:

- Take at least one reliable GPS with you – and many more batteries than you think you'll need.
- Carry much more fuel that you expect to use.
- Carry enough water and food for your whole time in the pans area, plus a few days safety margin.
- Travel with a minimum of two fully equipped 4WDs, and preferably also a satellite phone.
- Arrange a rendezvous for when you leave the pans, and someone to raise the alarm if you don't arrive. Leave a rough route plan with them.

It's difficult for me to emphasise enough just how dangerous the pans can be. There are periodic deaths of people who visit the area without the proper back-up and preparation, and then get into difficulties. It's different from many areas in Botswana because:

- The sun is merciless on the pan's surface; there's absolutely no shade.
- If you break through the crust of the pans to the wet silt beneath, then getting out is very difficult, even with a second vehicle. Remember: there will be no wood around, or branches to put under the wheels.
- There are so many different tracks on the pans (each diverging vehicle makes a new one), that often there simply isn't a 'right' track which most vehicles take. Thus, it may be weeks or months before someone takes the same route that you do, and passes you.

Nata
Nata itself is a very small place at the junction of the tar road to Maun, Kasane and Francistown. For many years it was little more than a filling stop for most people, where the vital garage relied on hand-cranked petrol pumps, and the well-stocked 'Sua Pan Bottle Store' was always busy.

Little has changed over time, although the place feels a lot more modern than it used to – and the nearby Nata Sanctuary has made this pan a bigger attraction than it was. It is still usually sensible to refuel when you pass through Nata.

Where to stay

Most visitors who are deliberately visiting this area stop at Nata Lodge, though if you're on the road and need a cheap place to lay your head – the Sua Pan Lodge might be all that you need.

Sua Pan Lodge Tel/fax: 6211263
Behind the back of the Shell petrol station, this has a few simple and clean rondavels, with basic en-suite showers and flush toilets, for P150/200 per person sharing/single. Or you can camp here for P25 per person.

Nata Lodge (12 three-bed chalets, 10 twin-bed tents and camping) PO Box 10, Nata, Botswana, Tel: 611210/611260; fax: 611265; email: natalodge@info.bw
Nata Lodge lies about 10km south of Nata, and is well signposted just off the road. It stands in a patch of sparse woodland with real fan palms and marula trees.

The thatched family chalets here have one bedroom and sleep two or three; alternatively two can share a twin-bedded Meru-style tent, tucked into the bush and raised up on a low platform. All have en-suite bathrooms with a shower, toilet and washbasin. Nearby there is a very large camping area. Meals can be arranged in the restaurant; a full breakfast costs P38, a braai dinner is P66, and light lunches are possible from the snack menu. The lodge's pool is right in front of the main lounge/dining area, and nearby the lodge has a curio shop. Mike Unwin reports that on his last visit here there was a family of bushbabies leaping from tree to tree, across the swimming pool.

On an ad hoc basis, the lodge organises early-morning and sunset trips into the Nata Sanctuary and on to the pans, costing about P77 per person for a 3-hour trip (minimum four people).
Rates: Two/three-bed chalets are P375/420, whilst the tents are P310. Camping is P30/22 per adult/child per night. Open: all year.

Sua Pan

Sua Pan is the eastern of the two twin pans, and extends roughly southwards from the town of Nata in its northeast corner. On its southern shore is the village of Mosu; to its north lies the Maun-Nata road; to its west it is divided from Ntwetwe Pan by a thin strip of grassland. Sua (sometimes spelt 'Sowa') is the Tswana word for salt, and this mineral residue from the vanished super-lake dominates the geology and ecology of the pan.

Once salt was laboriously collected from the pan surface by the San and carried away on donkeys. Today it is mined by the Sua Pan Soda Ash Company – a joint South African and Botswana government enterprise – who supply sodium carbonate on an industrial scale for use in the manufacture of paper, glass and steel. Their mine is situated along the Sua Spit; a tongue of grassland that extends halfway across the pan from its eastern shore.

The Nata River feeds Sua Pan from the northeast (bringing the rains from Zimbabwe) and, in good years, it floods from December to April with shallow, warm water. Where the fresh water of the river meets the saline pan, a brackish delta of silted reedbeds has formed. In summer, this corner of the pan attracts great concentrations of breeding waterbirds, notably flamingos (see *Fauna* below). This delta is now protected within the Nata Sanctuary – an area of 230km². The flamingos can usually be viewed from the bird hide on the eastern shore.

Evidence of the former lake exists in the form of fossil pebble beaches along the shores of Kubu Island and other granite outcrops around the pan, and fossil diatoms and molluscs on the pan surfaces. These reveal that there was a prolonged wet period about 14,000–17,000 years ago and, more recently, a flood only 1,500 years ago. Near the village of Mosu in the south, an escarpment rises some 40

FLAMINGOS

Of the world's half-dozen or so species of flamingo, two are found within southern Africa: the greater, *Phoenicopterus ruber*, and the lesser, *Phoenicopterus minor*. Both species have wide distributions, from southern Africa north into East Africa and the Red Sea, and are highly nomadic in their habits.

Flamingos are usually found wading in large areas of shallow saline water where they filter feed by holding their specially adapted beaks upside down in the water. The lesser flamingo will walk or swim whilst swinging its head from side to side, mainly taking blue-green algae from the surface of the water. The larger greater flamingo will hold its head submerged while filtering out small organisms (detritus and algae), even stirring the mud with its feet to help the process. Both species are very gregarious and flocks can have millions of birds, though a few hundred is more common.

Only occasionally do flamingos breed in southern Africa, choosing the Makgadikgadi Pans, Namibia's Etosha Pan, or even Lake Ngami. When the conditions are right (usually March to June, following the rains) both species build low mud cones in the water and lay one (or rarely two) eggs in a small hollow on the top. These are then incubated by both parents for about a month, until they hatch. After a further week the young birds flock together and start to forage with their parents. Some ten weeks later the young can fly and fend for themselves.

During this time the young are very susceptible to the shallow water in the pans drying out. In 1969, a rescue operation was mounted in Namibia when the main Etosha Pan dried out, necessitating the moving of thousands of chicks to nearby Fisher's Pan – which was still covered in water.

The best way to tell the two species apart is by their beaks: that of the greater flamingo is almost white with a black tip, while the lesser flamingo has a uniformly dark beak. If you are further away then the body of the greater will appear white, while that of the lesser looks smaller and more pink. The best place to see them in Botswana is certainly Sua Pan – although even there they will only appear if the rains have filled some of the pan.

metres above the edge of the pan, showing the erosive force of the great lake that once washed against these cliffs. Here there is also one of several subterranean springs that emerge around the fringes of the pans.

What to see and do

Nata Sanctuary makes a very easy place to visit for a day or two, either based at Nata Lodge or camping in the sanctuary itself. Aside from this, the pan is a remarkable area to explore, with the occasional spot like Kubu Island that has a magic all of its own. That said, there's a lot more than just Nata Sanctuary and Kubu here – but it does need time to explore it. Read my warning under *Getting around*, on page 410; then get a copy of Mike Main's book (see *Further Reading*), a few good maps, and enjoy it!

There's not much traffic around, and the pans are huge and desolate – so it's best to travel in a two-vehicle party and tell someone reliable where you plan to go, and when you'll be back. This is especially important during the first part of the year when the pan is wet, and there's a significant risk of getting a vehicle badly stuck in the mud.

Nata Sanctuary

A conservation area was originally established in the northeast corner of Sua Pan with the help of the Kalahari Conservation Society in the 1980s, to protect the important seasonal wetland areas around the Nata Delta. However, although the villagers at Nata were consulted about the plans, the wider community in the area didn't benefit from it.

This area encompassed cattle-grazing land owned by four communities: Nata, Sepako, Maposa and Mmaxotae. However, in the early 1990s it was realised that without the support of these local communities, conservation in the area couldn't be effective. Eventually, as part of the ground-breaking community project, the communities moved about 3,000 head of cattle out of the area, and fencing began. In 1993 Nata Sanctuary was opened to the public, and in the same year it won the prestigious 'Tourism for Tomorrow' award for the southern hemisphere

Now Nata Sanctuary conserves an ecologically sensitive and important natural environment, and also effectively returns money to the communities for doing so.

Getting there

The entrance to Nata Sanctuary is about 17km south of Nata next to the main road to Francistown. There's a small reception here where you must pay entry fees to the sanctuary of P20 per person per day, plus P10 per vehicle.
Open: daily 07.00–19.00, all year.

Where to stay

If you're not staying at the nearby Nata Lodge then there are some simple bush campsites in the sanctuary, complete with basic long-drop toilets and cold showers. Camping here costs P25 per person per night, payable at reception.

Flora and fauna

See above for notes on the general flora and fauna of the pan, but note that a number of mammals have been enclosed (or reintroduced) within the fenced boundaries of this reserve, including gemsbok, springbok, hartebeest, kudu, eland, zebra, reedbuck, jackal, fox, monkey, steenbok, squirrel and spring hare.

Kubu Island

In the southwest of Sua Pan lies an isolated granite outcrop, some 10m high and a kilometre long, known as Kubu Island. It forms the shape of a crescent, and its slopes are terraced with fossil beaches of wave-rounded pebbles, providing startling evidence of the prehistoric lake's former water levels. Crowned with an array of ancient, gnarled baobabs and surrounded on three sides by a vast grey emptiness, Kubu has a unique atmospheric beauty.

At night, with the wind moaning through the baobabs, it is easy to imagine the waves of a great inland sea lapping at its pebble beaches. Many of the island's rocks are white, covered in ancient, fossilised guano from the water-birds that used to perch here when it was surrounded by the lake. The moonlight reflecting off the pan's white surface gives the place an almost supernatural atmosphere, which is heightened by the mystery of Kubu's former inhabitants. The shoreline is littered with Stone-Age tools and arrowheads, while concentric dry stone walls on the islands survive from a much more recent village, perhaps around AD1400–1600, and outside this are a number of stone cairns.

GPS REFERENCES FOR SUA PAN MAP (opposite)

KUBU-I	20°53.737'S, 25°49.421'E
KUKOME	20°55.001'S, 26°12.203'E
KWADIB	20°54.907'S, 26°16.571'E
MMATSH	21°08.590'S, 25°39.214'E
THABAT	20°42.606'S, 25°47.476'E
TSHWAG	20°48.094'S, 25°45.608'E
TSIVET	20°58.620'S, 25°37.178'E
TURNMI	21°19.468'S, 25°33.742'E
TURNM2	20°55.990'S, 25°40.015'E

Archaeologists have linked these with the dynasty of Great Zimbabwe, and think that these were probably the most southwestern tip of that state. In *Riddle of the Stone Walls* (see *Further Reading*) Alec Campbell explains the theory that they could have been remote 'circumcision camps' to which the boys of the tribe were taken for circumcision and ceremonies leading to adulthood. It is suggested that perhaps ceremonies took place within the walls, and every class that 'graduated' then built a separate cairn.

Campbell also noted that the people of the nearest village, Tshwagong, hold Kubu and the nearby Thithaba Islands as sacred, and men over 16 years of age visit the islands to make contact with God, singing a particular song for rain and leaving offerings on the ground.

Note that Kubu is a national monument, and there are plans to station a warden here to ensure that visitors don't damage anything.

Getting there

From the north there are endless possible routes to Kubu Island (✪ KUBU-I 20°53.737'S, 25°49.421'E), and you can expect it to take about 3–4 hours from the main Maun–Nata road. Easiest is probably to take one of the many tracks that leave the main road between about 30km and 15km west of Nata. Follow your nose (or, more practically, your GPS) towards Thabatshukudu Village (✪ THABAT 20°42.606'S, 25°47.476'E), which is about 70–75km south, depending on the track that you take.

From there it's about 10km southwest to the Tswagong Veterinary Gate, through which any north–south traffic between Sua and Ntwetwe pans passes – so tracks will lead you there. This is about 3km north of the small village of Tshwagong (✪ TSHWAG 20°48.094'S, 25°45.608'E), from where it's about 14km in a straight line southeast to Kubu Island. (There are several tracks here, so just head southeast and follow your GPS.)

Note that the track that leaves Gweta in a south then southeasterly direction, ending at the Tswagong Veterinary Gate, passes over several long stretches of Ntwetwe Pan, and so is dangerously muddy during the earlier months of the year.

From the south, it's best to start by heading for the village of Mmatshumo (✪ MMATSH 21°08.590'S, 25°39.214'E. Again you'll find a number of tracks from the Orapa-Francistown road which will lead you here; the shortest leaves the main road around ✪ TURNM1 21°19.468'S, 25°33.742'E. From there it's about 23km to Mmatshumo. Heading north from there, there's a good view of the pan to your right after about 5km, before the track bends west and back north to cross the small Tsitane Pan, crossing the veterinary fence at ✪ TSIVET 20°58.620'S, 25°37.178'E.

Then a straight track heading north by northeast brings you to Tshwagong (⊕ TSHWAG 20°48.094'S, 25°45.608'E) after about 20km.

Note that during the dry season you can take a short cut about 7km north of the vet fence, at around ⊕ TURNM2 20°55.990'S, 25°40.015'E, which heads east-northeast across the pan to Kubu; but don't try this when the pans are wet!

Sua's landmarks
Note that you should never attempt to drive across the pan from the east side to the west, or vice versa – even during the dry season.

Sowa Pan Mine (Soda-ash factory)
This modern industrial complex seems strangely out of place here, especially as it is easily reached, 40km along a tarred road. The turn-off is about 48km south of Nata on the road to Francistown.

South Islands
About 7km south of Kubu, far out on the pan, are two other small islands. They too have Baobab trees and the larger one, on the east, has a series of rocks cairns along its spine.

Kukome Island (also spelt 'Kukonje' Island)
On the eastern shore of Sua Pan, roughly opposite Kubu, Kukome Island (⊕ KUKOME 20°55.001'S, 26°12.203'E) has similar fossil beaches and ancient remains. To reach here, first head for the Kwadiba Veterinary Gate (⊕ KWADIB 20°54.907'S, 26°16.571'E) on the east side of Sua Pan, from where a track leads west for about 7km to Kukome Island. (Beware: the GPS point given for the Kwadiba Gate on older editions of the Shell map doesn't seem correct to me.)

Mmatshumo Village
Mmatshumo (⊕ MMATSH 21°08.590'S, 25°39.214'E) is a small village on the south side of the pans, between Sua and Ntwetwe pans – as well as an important waypoint when you're navigating yourselves around.

Thabatshukudu Village
Thabatshukudu (⊕ THABAT 20°42.606'S, 25°47.476'E) is another village, notable for the landmark of its colourfully painted general dealer's store – and another useful waypoint when navigating yourselves around.

Ntwetwe Pan
Ntwetwe Pan is the western twin of Sua, and is of a similar size and general topography, though aligned more east–west. It lies due south of the Nata–Maun road, between Gweta in the north and Orapa and Mopipi in the south. One finger extends to the north of the road, while to the southwest the pan breaks up into several smaller pans, including Lake Xau, just south of Mopipi. The old north–south trading route between Gweta and Mopipi crosses the centre of the pan, and the two famous isolated baobabs (Green's Baobab and Chapman's Baobab) that marked this route for early European explorers, including Livingstone who left his initials here, still serve as landmarks for today's travellers.

Ntwetwe lacks the famous granite outcrops of Sua; its main points of elevation are fossilised barchan dunes that once crept across the surface of the lake during a dry period and were left stranded when waters rose again. Gabasadi Island is the largest of these. The profiles of the dune islands show steps and lines of vegetation which, like Sua Pan's pebble beaches, are evidence of former higher lake levels.

Stone-Age sites are scattered among the smaller pans that form the western shore of Ntwetwe. At Gutsha Pan, near Chapman's Baobab, there is a perennial spring. Here the San once dug pit traps lined with poisoned stakes to trap the plentiful game that came to drink. The remains of these traps, and the calcrete blinds behind which the hunters hid, are still visible today.

What to see and do

Like Sua Pan, Ntwetwe is an area for experienced old Africa hands to explore in their own vehicles – though bear in mind my comments on safety under *Getting around* on page 410.

Alternatively, and much safer, there are three camps situated on the northwest side of the pan. All are expensive, even by Botswana's standards. But if you can afford their high prices, then fly in here from Maun for three or four days and explore the pans and surrounding area with expert guides; on foot, by 4WD and on quad bikes.

Where to stay

Though Jack's Camp (and its sister-camp, San Camp) and Makgadikgadi Camp are the only camps on the pans themselves, you could also visit this area on an excursion from Planet Baobab (see pages 428–9) near Gweta. This is a cheaper option, aimed at backpackers and people driving on the Nata–Maun road.

Makgadikgadi Camp is marketed by, and easiest to book through, Okavango Tours and Safaris in Maun (see page 178). Jack's Camp, its smaller satellite, San Camp, and also Planet Baobab can be contacted at Uncharted Africa Safari Co, PO Box 173, Francistown; tel: 241 2277; fax: 241 3458; email: unchart@info.bw; web: www.unchartedafrica.com

Note that Jack's and San camps are usually reached by light aircraft from Maun; a private airstrip (GPS: SANAIR 20°29.504'S, 25°11.054'E) is ten minutes' drive from camp.

Jack's Camp (8 tents)

Jack's Camp was the original camp on the pans. When all the other safari operators in Botswana focused on game and the Delta, Jack's dared to offer something totally different – and succeeded in style.

A bushcamp was originally started in this area as early as the 1960s, by the late Jack Bousfield. After his tragic death in an aircraft accident, his son, Ralph Bousfield, started to build a camp for visitors here which first opened in 1993. It's set in sparse forest of real fan palms, in grasslands on the edge of Ntwetwe Pan, overlooking Makgadikgadi Pans National Park.

Jack's has eight tents, and it prides itself on 'traditional East African 40s safari style'. This means it's very comfortable, with first-class attention to detail, but doesn't have indoor plumbing or electricity. It is not a 'super-luxurious lodge' by any means. Jack's green tents are classic Meru-style and furnished in keeping with the theme. Inside six of the tents have twin beds with individual canopies, while the other two have four-poster double beds, all with down pillows and duvets, and high-quality linens. Outside at the front is a shiny copper washing bowl, to which hot water is delivered in the morning or on request. Each tent has a private toilet and shower, set back a little from the tent (but en-suite facilities are planned for 2003). The showers are bucket showers, to which water is delivered on request, and the toilets (in a concession to pampered modern guests) flush. At night, lighting is by paraffin lamp – much more magical than electricity!

THE CLANS OF MAKGADIKGADI

The brown hyena (*Hyaena brunnea*) is one of the three hyena species in southern Africa, the other two being a successful scavenger and hunter, the spotted hyena, and the insectivorous aardwolf. Brown hyena are classed as 'near threatened', with a total population of under 10,000 – of which the Makgadikgadi National Park has about 50 adults.

The brown hyena has evolved to life in desert systems throughout southern Africa, where it occurs at low densities. This shy, nocturnal animal is a solitary forager that can survive independently of permanent surface water. Brown hyenas will eat virtually anything, apart from grass or herbage – and here their diet ranges from melons and scorpions to ostrich eggs or old carcasses.

As part of his PhD from Pretoria University, Glyn Maude has been running a project researching these animals for three years, based near Jack's Camp. He has habituated a clan to the presence of his vehicle, and observed that individuals will often cover over 65km in a night when foraging in the Makgadikgadi. Here lion kills are an important source of food. Over the wet season, these are often zebra and wildebeest, whilst over the dry season, when food is more scarce, they can frequently be cattle and other livestock.

Brown hyenas are not truly solitary animals; they live in clans of between two and ten members. In the Makgadikgadi, Glyn has measured clans' territories as covering 300–750km². However, clan members are rarely seen together as they forage alone, only interacting with other clan members either by a chance meeting while foraging, or at a communal den site. Some brown hyenas are not part of a clan but are nomadic, the males in particular. Clan members will often be tolerant of an intruder of the opposite sex, but will chase away same sex intruders.

Brown hyenas are usually almost silent: their vocalisations are minimal. Long-distance communication is by a unique double scent mark deposited on grass stalks. These marks can be made as often as every 150m of foraging, and as well as communicating with other clan members, the scent mark is also a marker for the clan's territory. Defecations are also used as territorial markers and can be found in concentrations in 'latrine sites' which are often located along territorial boundaries. The presence of brown hyenas is more often indicated by their spoor or scent marks, as sightings of the animal in the wild are very uncommon.

Jacks has a central 'mess tent' – which is really a series of grand canvas pavilions. The interior is lined with amber printed cotton, whilst the green of the outside blends with the surrounding bush. This is really a canvas field museum, sheltering an eclectic selection of items (mostly local) including various stone tools, fossils of extinct mega-fauna (like giant zebra), prints, maps, historical etchings, and a fair size collection of beadwork made by Bushman.

There's also a drinks tent, a library tent, a centralised dining tent and a separate tea tent, its floor scattered with a mass of Persian rugs and cushions, where tea and delicious cakes are usually served before the afternoon activities.

The activities here vary with the season. When it's dry, from around May to December, there's likely to be very little game around. That's fine, as it's not the focus of a trip here. Instead you'll explore the pans in 4WDs, on individual quad bikes and on foot, often with a

San tracker. These trips will concentrate on the area's smaller wildlife, and also its history and archaeology – often including a visit to the baobabs in the area, and a part of the pan where old Stone-Age flint axe- and arrow-heads can be just picked up off the surface. (Quite rightly, my guide insisted that they were also to be left there by us!)

When it's wet, from around January to April, the pans can become quagmires. It's often not possible to use the quad bikes, and the 4WD drives tend to stick to the grasslands on the edges of the pans. However, then there is a much greater density of wildlife around, with many migrant birds and, if you're lucky, large herds of plains game.

Amongst all the camps that I know in Africa, Jack's Camp stands out for its unique style of guiding. Anyone can find you a herd of elephants in Moremi, but to find fascination in a barren salt pan requires a lot more skill. Jack's usually use a mixture of very capable resident guides from Botswana, plus a handful of zoology and biology graduates who come here to combine a few years guiding with a PhD specialising on some of the local wildlife. Wits comment that these are often British, Oxbridge and good-looking – but this can often mean an informed and very intelligent level of discussion.

As the camp is outside the national park, night drives are possible – when there's often more wildlife around than during the day. Recently, thanks to the lion research that's been done from here, sightings of lion have increased hugely. Also in the last few years they've had a zoologist based here, Glyn Maud, who has been researching brown hyenas. He has habituated one clan to vehicles, which has enabled Jack's to virtually guarantee sightings of these very shy creatures to interested visitors. Though they occur widely, you'd be very, very lucky to see brown hyena elsewhere!

Rates: US$465/625 per person sharing/single, including all meals, drinks, activities, laundry and park fees. Flights transfers to/from Maun are US$140 per person each way; road transfers from Gweta are US$110 per person each way. Jack's Camp does not take credit cards. Open: start of February to end of December.

San Camp (6 tents)

Ten minutes' drive from Jack's Camp, San is run by the same team in very similar style, though uses white canvas rather than green Meru-style tents. Again, it's rustic but stylish and comfortable. It works in the same way with similar activities and approach, although is only open during the dry season. It has just six tents, of which two have four-poster double beds and the rest have twins. Note that the toilets here are long-drop, rather than flush, and are also private but set back from the back of the tents.

Both Jack's and San Camp are first-rate camps offering something totally different to virtually all of the rest of Botswana's camps. Either makes a great three- or four-night stop, best at the very end of a fly-in trip to Botswana, though both are expensive.

Rates (2005): US$420/500 per person sharing/single, including all meals, drinks, activities, laundry and park fees. Flights transfers to/from Maun are US$140 per person each way; road transfers from Gweta are US$110 per person each way. San Camp does not take credit cards. Open: end of April to end of October.

Makgadikgadi Camp (5 tents)

Started in 1997, Makgadikgadi Camp stands amongst real fan palms and acacias near the edge of Ntwetwe Pan, south of Gweta. It is run by Reiner Sumerauer, the owner of Gweta Restcamp (see page 428), and marketed by Okavango Tours and Safaris in Maun (see page 178).

The tents have twin beds and en-suite shower, toilet and washbasins. The camp has a main dining area under a thatched roof, with a plunge-pool nearby. Activities include short walks and trips across the pans with 4WDs and quad bikes, and bushcamps are possible.

Rates (2005): US$640 per person sharing/single between July and September; US$375/530 during the rest of the year. Includes all meals, drinks, activities and road transfers from Gweta, but excludes a 10% community levy. Open: March to November, depending on the rains.

NTWETWE PAN & MAKGADIKGADI NATIONAL PARK

Maun

Nxai Pan National Park

Bushman Pits

Makolwane Gate
(for entry into park)

MOTOPI
Labani
Matima

NXAI01

Main Scout
camp
MSCOUT ⊕

Senagom

Ngamisane

LEROOL
Leroo-La-
Tau Lodge

Khumaga
campsite
KHUMAG

⊕ NJUCA
Njuca Hills
campsite

Makgadikgadi Pans National Park

Dikwalo

Boteti River

GPS co-ordinates ⊕

CHAPMA	20° 29.372'S,	25° 14.898'E
GREENS	20° 25.497'S,	25° 13.869'E
GWETA	20° 11.434'S,	25° 15.888'E
KHUMAG	20° 27.350'S,	24° 30.978'E
KUBU-I	20° 53.737'S,	25° 49.421'E
LEROOL	20° 25.240'S,	24° 31.277'E
MMATSH	21° 08.590'S,	25° 39.214'E
MSCOUT	20° 16.963'S,	24° 54.458'E
NXAI01	20° 13.687'S,	24° 38.937'E
PBAOBA	20° 11.344'S,	25° 18.330'E
RAKOPS	21° 02.136'S,	24° 24.432'E
THABAT	20° 42.606'S,	25° 47.476'E
TSHWAG	20° 48.094'S,	25° 45.608'E
TSIVET	20° 58.620'S,	25° 37.178'E
TURNM1	21° 19.468'S,	25° 33.742'E
TURNM2	20° 55.990'S,	25° 40.015'E

Magodi

Sukwane

Tamtiga

Xwatshaa

Xerexwa

RAKOPS
RAKOPS

Gubudaoga

N
Bradt

Toromoja

Dzibui
Pan

Tswanatshae

Xhumo

Boteti River

MOPIPI

Tsokotso
Pan

0 _____ 40km
0 _____ 20 miles

Lake Xau

Txabaka

KEY

Tar road	————————
4WD track	========
National park	– – – ×—× – – –
Veterinary fence with gate	

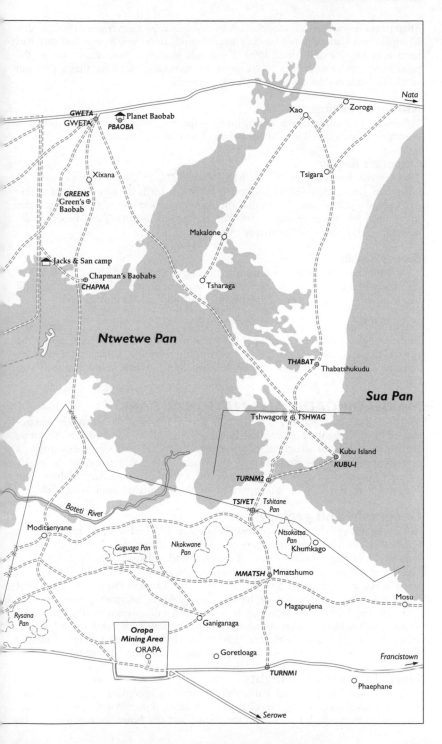

Stop press As my research concluded, I was advised by a government official that Makgadikgadi Camp did not have a current licence to occupy its site, and thus had been operating illegally since 1999. I was told that the government was in the process of getting what it is owed from the company, and after that a decision would be made on the camp's continued existence.

Ntwetwe's landmarks
Ntwetwe Pan doesn't have anything quite so spectacular as Kubu Island, though it does have a few marvellous old Baobabs and an island of its own.

Chapman's Baobab
This famous landmark (✦ CHAPMA 20°29.372'S, 25°14.898'E) was noted by Chapman, when he passed with Thomas Baines in 1861. It's a big tree and visible from some distance away. Note that there are endless tracks to the west of here, many made by nearby private safari camps, and so navigation can be especially difficult – rendering a GPS virtually essential.

Green's Baobab
Less well known than Chapman's, this tree (✦ GREENS 20°25.497'S, 25°13.869'E) is close to the only permanent spring in the area, Gutsha Pan, and still bears the inscription 'Green's Expedition 1858–1859' carved into its bark.

Gabasadi Island
In the middle of Ntwetwe, on the west of the usual north–south route across the pans, Gabasadi Island is a low mound protruding from the surface of the pan. It's actually a fossilised, crescent-shaped barchan dune, which you'll realise if you climb it.

MAKGADIKGADI PANS NATIONAL PARK
Makgadikgadi Pans National Park covers about 3,900km² in a roughly square-shaped block to the west of the pans. It extends from the western edge of Ntwetwe Pan – one corner of which is incorporated within the park, fragmented into a myriad smaller pans – westwards to the Boteti River, which marks the park's western boundary. To the north it meets the southern boundary of Nxai Pan National Park, from which it is separated only by the main Maun-Nata road.

Geography and geology
About one-fifth of the reserve consists of salt pan. The rest is rolling grasslands on Kalahari sands, rising here and there into fossilised dunes and low hills of thicker sand which mark prehistoric limits of the great Makgadikgadi superlake. The great breadth of the sandy Boteti watercourse, and the riverine woodland that lines its steep banks, are evidence of a major river that once carved a channel across central Botswana, carrying the waters of the Okavango into the Makgadikgadi basin.

Today the Boteti only flows at all after good rains, when its thin trickle is dwarfed by the channel that contains it. It hasn't properly flooded for at least ten years. As the dry season advances, this stream dwindles into a chain of rapidly shrinking pools, a few of which retain permanent water throughout the year.

Flora and fauna highlights
Makgadikgadi Pans National Park really contains a spectrum of environments, flora and fauna. Its east side, especially the southeast, is dominated by salt pans and grasslands – very much the same as the rest of Sua and Ntwetwe further east. Its

western border, the Boteti River, is lined by thick riverine forest; here the wildlife has more in common with that found beside the Chobe, the Linyanti or in the Okavango Delta. Between these two very different environments lies the body of the park.

Flora

The vegetation on the east side of the park is very similar pattern to that of the Makgadikgadi Pans (see pages 406–7). Its diversity increases westwards as the saline influence of the pan is left behind; from the bare surface of the pan itself, through rolling grassland and the vegetated dunes of Njuca Hills, into thicker acacia scrub, and eventually to the dense riverine woodland along the banks of the Boteti River. Along the eastern border there are areas of palm-tree woodland, where groves of vegetable ivory palms (*Hyphaene petersiana*) grow among the tracts of tall grassland.

On raised ground between the salt pans, yellowish patches of prickly salt grass (*Odyssea paucinervis*) flourish, contrasting with clumps of the dark succulent *Chenopodiacea* species. Along the pan edges you may also find a cactus-like succulent, *Hoodia lugardii*, which periodically produces striking maroon flowers. The open grasslands are studded with islands of trees and denser vegetation, with such species as the trumpet thorn (*Catophractas alexandri*) and western rhigozum (*Rhigozum brevispinosum*) flowering among the acacia scrub.

Beside the deep sand of the Boteti River, camelthorns (*Acacia erioloba*), blackthorns (*Acacia mellifera*) and silver clusterleaf (*Termilalia sericea*) dominate the riverine forest, interspersed with a few other riverine giants such as sycamore figs (*Ficus sycomorus*) and sausage trees (*Kigelia africana*). Meanwhile for most of the year the 'riverbed' itself consists of a sandy channel carpeted in grasses and punctuated by occasional muddy pools of water.

Mammals

In the wet season, Makgadikgadi Pans National Park boasts good concentrations of grazers that rival those of Nxai Pan to the north, and an aerial view shows the area to be latticed with a dense network of game trails. From about June onwards, herds of Burchell's zebra and blue wildebeest start a westward movement towards the lush grazing of the Boteti region, accompanied by smaller numbers of gemsbok, eland and red hartebeest. (The latter tend to come slightly later, in years when the rains have been exceptionally good.) These herds gradually congregate along the waterfront until, by November, this area becomes jam-packed with game.

In the ecozone between grassland and woodland, browsers such as kudu, bushbuck and grey duiker find a permanent home, while troops of baboons and

OSTRICH BREEDING

Ostriches are particularly common in the eastern grasslands, and can often be seen from the main Nata–Maun road. These huge birds breed before the rains, with several females laying in a single scrape that may hold over 30 eggs. Incubation tends to rotate between the male at night (when his dark plumage is no longer vulnerable to overheating), and the female by day (when her drab plumage provides more effective camouflage). Youngsters from several broods gather together in large crèches, presided over by one adult pair, and can sometimes be seen gathering in the shadow of an adult for shade.

THE LIONS OF MAKGADIKGADI

Makgadikgadi is an erratic and uncertain place for lions. With the first rains, huge herds of zebra and wildebeest move out onto the plains to graze on the succulent grasses and drop their young. In the dry months this pulse of life ebbs back to the Boteti River, 50km to the west, leaving the plains largely deserted by large ungulates. The lions have had to adapt to these huge fluctuations and the unpredictability.

For some the solution is simply tracking the herds back to the Boteti for the dry months, where they must dodge the human residents on the west side of the river. Others stay behind amidst the parched grasses, swirling dust devils and spring hares. This is not the place for huge ungainly prides; rather lionesses pair up and wander over large areas, often in excess of 1,000km², in order to find sufficient food. Males typically spread their time between two or more of these small, efficient prides. They can maintain territories of almost double that, walking up to 50km a night to patrol their vast swathes of baked wasteland.

Water is unavailable for up to seven months a year for these lions, so they must gain all their moisture from their prey. Immediately after killing large prey such as gemsbok they snick open the belly and stomach, slurping up the juices before they soak away into the sand. However large prey is hard to find during the dry season, so they will hunt aardvarks and porcupines, and they increasingly look outside the eastern and western boundaries of the park for sustenance from herds of dopey, slow-moving livestock.

vervet monkeys forage beneath the trees, and small numbers of giraffe and elephant often occur. This area supports a small waterbuck population, resident pairs of bushbuck (locals say the same subspecies/race as the Chobe bushbuck) and there are even a few hippo who have taken up unlikely residence in the permanent pools.

In peak season, from September to November, the area around the Boteti can offer truly outstanding wildlife watching, and the air is filled with the hiccuping calls of the milling zebra herds. However, with the arrival of the rains in December/January, the herds disperse. Some head north towards Nxai Pan, others gather in the grazing grounds of the southeast, where their migration route beyond the park to the Central Kalahari is blocked by a veterinary cordon fence. At this time, zebra and gemsbok may often be seen out on the pans in search of the mineral salts that are lacking on the Kalahari grasslands.

A healthy population of large predators, protected in the park from persecution by ranchers, includes lion, cheetah, leopard, spotted and brown hyena. Lion can be common during peak migration, with prides knocking down more zebra than they can consume and (be warned) sometimes wandering inquisitively through the campsites. Cheetah are less common, but may turn up anywhere where there are springbok, while leopard are permanent residents of the denser bush along the Boteti. Spotted hyena, like lion, follow the dry season herds, while brown hyenas find life more productive (and less competitive) along the park's eastern side.

In the east of the park the two campsites at Njuca Hills offer a panoramic base from which to explore the wildlife of the pans and grasslands. Herds of springbok, well adapted to survive the arid and exposed conditions, are common around the pans, while steenbok – usually found in pairs – are also widespread. Nocturnal predators of the pan fringes include brown hyena, aardwolf, bat-eared fox and striped polecat, while black-backed jackal, African wildcat, honey badger and small spotted genet can occur anywhere in the park. Other small mammals include porcupine, aardvark, spring hare and scrub hare as well as a host of smaller rodents and insectivores (see *General pans fauna*, pages 393–6).

In sandy areas, ground squirrels (here at the northern limit of their Kalahari range), forage by day in small colonies, holding up their tails as parasols against the fierce sun and dashing for their burrows at any hint of danger. These sociable rodents associate amicably with yellow mongooses, who share their burrow systems and help keep a look out for predators.

Reptiles

Perhaps the most bizarre report from this park is of some of the Boteti's larger crocodiles which, when the river drops drastically during the dry season, retreat into holes in the riverbank that they have dug for themselves. One such lair that I saw was a good 4–5m above the level of water even in May, and would have been completely high and dry by October.

Birds

The bird life of Makgadikgadi Pans National Park is largely the same as that elsewhere in the greater Makgadikgadi region (see pages 408–10), with a grading of species according to habitat, and a large summer influx of migrants.

The denser woodland along the Boteti also harbours more cover-loving species such as Myer's parrot, woodland kingfisher, Burchell's coucal and Heuglin's robin. Many raptors cruise the skies over the park, with gabar goshawks hunting the thickets, secretary birds stalking the savannah, and vultures following the game herds in search of carcasses. In summer, storks, bee-eaters, kites, shrikes and other migrants move in and fan out across the grasslands.

Where to stay

Leroo-La-Tau and Xwaraga are both on the western bank of the Boteti, opposite the park. They can be contacted through Traction Safaris, Suite 29 c/o Postnet, P.Bag 114, Maun; tel/fax: 668407; email: 2attract@bushmail.net; web: www.lltlodge.com

Khumaga and Njuca Hills campsites are run by the national parks, and should be booked in advance in Maun (see pages 142–3).

Leroo-La-Tau Lodge (7 tents)
Having opened in 1998, this lodge deserves to be better known. It is situated (◈ LEROOL 20°25.240'S, 24°31.277'E) at the eastern end of a bend in the Boteti River. It is outside the park, yet surrounded by it on three sides.

Accommodation here is in one of seven large Meru-style tents, built on raised wooden platforms. Most are built into the tree line, overlooking the Boteti's channel, whilst a few are set back in the bush.

Each has a large veranda with chairs and table outside, and two double beds inside – complete with high quality down duvets and quilts. These are comfortably furnished with a chair, dressing table and bedside tables, with a torch, and various toiletries and insect repellents provided. At the back of this, still under a shading canvas roof, is a toilet, shower and washbasin area, enclosed within an inner tent of mosquito netting. The hot water is very quick, though the water is mineral water, and so smells slightly of sulphur due to the natural chemicals in the area's ground water.

The main lodge has one side largely made of glass, overlooking a large lawn (with small swimming pool) which leads down to the banks of the Boteti River. At one end of this is a bar, and above that a comfy sitting area with a video recorder (and a library of wildlife videos), and a look-out window. In the centre is a large and rather beautiful wooden dining table, and at the end is a comfy sitting area with a curio shop (which also sells some good books).

Activities centre on game drives and night drives from the lodge. Generally they operate in a relatively narrow neck of land enclosed by a loop of the Boteti. This juts into the park, and is about 10km by 4–5km, though does have lots of riverfront – which is where the game is usually concentrated. This has the advantage of not being liable for park fees. In addition to these, they also run 'cultural trips' to the local villages.

The lodge can also be used as a base for trips into Nxai, Makgadikgadi Pans and the Central Kalahari Game Reserve; expect trips to cost around US$220 for an overnight, two-day/one-night mobile trip, whilst going for longer, or with more people, can prove even better value. Expect to sleep on comfy bed-rolls in dome tents, eat around the campfire and generally get involved. Though safari activities on the west bank of the Boteti are included in the rate, if you want to take a day-trip into the park itself these cost US$85 per person. (If you're going to do this, then I'd do it properly; spend two days there and make an overnight trip of it!)

Leroo-La-Tau is a good-quality lodge in an area that can provide remarkable game spectacles. It's relatively inexpensive for Botswana, largely because it's not well known and without an airstrip it's rarely included in 'fly-in' safari circuits of the country.
Rates: US$190/275 per person sharing/single. Includes all meals, drinks, local activities, laundry. Transfers by road to/from Maun are US$160 per 6-seater vehicle. Open: all year.

Xwaraga Campsite

This lovely bush site is a few minutes' walk from Leroo-La-Tau Lodge. It has five cleared pitches beneath camelthorn (*Acacia erioloba*) trees, each of which used to have an adjacent water standpipe... until the local elephants got wind of them. There are also two simple thatched chalets, each of which has mosquito gauze on the windows, four beds and an en-suite shower and toilet at the back. Each comes supplied with cooking equipment and linen; ideal for self-catering guests.
Rates: P275 per chalet. Open: all year.

Khumaga Campsite

Khumaga, sometimes written 'Xhumaga,' stands within the park near the east bank of the Boteti River (✪ KHUMAG 20°27.350'S, 24°30.978'E), about 4km south of Leroo-La-Tau. This site usually has water available, and sometimes working cold showers and flush toilets. One of the park's two scout camps is here.

Njuca Hills Campsite

Njuca Hills Campsite (✪ NJUCA 20°25.807'S, 24°52.395'E) is located in the heart of the park about 38km east of Khumaga, and it's totally different. It's slightly elevated (no more than about 20m) on one of a series of low, fossilised dunes and here you'll find no water and even less firewood. The campsite is very basic, with just a long-drop toilet surrounded by what looks like a screen sprayed with concrete. Expect the main wildlife here to be barking geckos and perhaps the odd curious yellow mongoose.

Just to emphasise the safety issues raised about travelling in any of the pans, recent visitors Richard and Vikki Threlfall wrote to me: 'We broke down at Njuca Hills Campsite, and were not found until the third morning after discovering the problem! And then it was only pure chance.' Note that this happened at one of only two official campsites in the park, and realise that it would have taken a full-scale air search to find them if they'd been off the main routes. Do take heed of the safety issues detailed in *Getting around*, page 410, before you travel anywhere in the pans area.

What to see and do

Like the bulk of Sua or the rest of Ntwetwe Pan, the Makgadikgadi Pans National Park is really an area for experienced old Africa hands to explore in their own vehicles – though bear in mind my comments on safety under *Getting around* on page 410. That said, in the late dry season you won't be quite so isolated if you stick to the road in the park which runs beside the Boteti and Khumaga Campsite which will then have quite a few visitors.

Alternatively, and much safer, stay at Jack's (or San) Camp for the pans in the eastern side of the park, and at Leroo-La-Tau for the contrasting Boteti Riverfront – exploring each of these areas with their expert local guides.

Getting around

If you're driving yourself here then come armed with copies of both the *Shell* and *Contimap* (see pages 396–7 for details) maps of Botswana, with their wealth of GPS co-ordinates. Then take to heart my caveats in *Getting around*, page 410, and you're ready to explore.

First you'll need to head for one of the scout camps to sign in and pay your park fees. The main game scout camp (⊕ MSCOUT 20°16.963'S, 24°54.458'E) is near the Makolwane Gate, on the Nata–Maun road. The right turn to this is about 23km east of the main turning to Nxai Pans, and about 42km east of Gweta. The scout camp is less than 10km from the road. The alternative is the scout camp at Khumaga (⊕ KHUMAG 20°27.350'S, 24°30.978'E), on the western side near the Boteti.

Note that if you enter the park from the east then you should follow the cut-line north to the main road, and turn left to reach the main scout camp as swiftly as possible; meandering through the park without having paid park fees first is against the rules.

Driving around you'll realise that the more southerly roads, crossing the pans, are particularly hard to locate; arguably they are simply non-existent, washed away with each year's rains. Equally, those around the centre of the eastern side of the park are so numerous that they're totally confusing; complicated by a whole network of tracks used by the camps in the area.

NEARBY TOWNS

The small towns around here tend to be used by visitors driving themselves as simply places to refuel and replenish basic supplies; those flying into the area's camps will probably never see any of these.

Gweta

Gweta (⊕ GWETA 20°11.434'S, 25°15.888'E) is a small, old village about 2km south of the road between Nata and Maun; about 205km from Maun and 100km from Nata. Now it feels quite run-down, but it remains conveniently situated for exploring Makgadikgadi and Nxai Pans. There's a restcamp here, a couple of basic foodstores (including the Maono Restaurant) and even a vehicle workshop for minor repairs. There is often, but *not* always, fuel available here.

Gweta is very clearly signposted south of the main road, in an area of mostly stunted mopane woodlands with the odd small clay pan. Turning off you'll first find a post office on your left, then the fuel station on your right (signposted with little pump signs) and finally the restcamp. Planet Baobab is about 5km east of town, but worth seeking out. If you're arriving by bus, ask them to stop on the road beside the turn-off to Planet Baobab.

Getting there and away

If you're not driving yourself then there are very regular bus services between Maun and Francistown. They usually turn into town and stop in the centre, near the Maono Restaurant. Maun is then about three hours away and costs P20; Francistown is about 4 hours away, costing P25.

Where to stay

The choices here are starkly different: the old and rather run-down Gweta Restcamp or the funky, rustic-trendy Planet Baobab. Both can be used as a base to explore Ntwetwe Pan or the Makgadikgadi National Park, although most visitors to these would probably camp there instead. Both are really best as stopovers, with Planet Baobab doubling as a base for backpackers to take quad-bike excursions onto the pans.

Gweta Restcamp (28 rooms and camping) PO Box 124, Gweta; tel: 612220; email: gweta@info.bw
This old restcamp has been here for years and hasn't, apparently, changed that much. It's still signposted as the 'motel' in the centre of Gweta, and has 28 small and unimpressive rondavels, all with en-suite facilities, and an area where you can pitch a tent with toilets and showers.

In the centre of the restcamp is a cool and generally pleasant thatched bar which serves snacks as well as drinks. This should make a good stop for lunch, though on my last visit it was marred by very loud music and the staff's complete lack of any interest or attention – despite the absence of any other guests.
Rates: P95 per person sharing, P154 single for the room only.

Planet Baobab (18 huts and camping) Contact Uncharted Africa, page 455
This is Uncharted Africa's venture, offering a Makgadikgadi Pans experience to a clientele who can't afford the prices of Jack's Camp, combined with somewhere interesting to stop for people driving past. Set amongst baobabs (✪ PBAOBA 20°11.344'S, 25°18.330'E) about 4km east of Gweta, Planet Baobab is just south of the main Nata–Maun road. If you stay here, there are three choices of accommodation:

The eight **traditional mud huts** are actually brick clad in mud, with a thatched roof on top. Everything inside is rounded as if it's made of mud. There are two beds, one built into each side of the room, each with a mosquito net, and a stylish en-suite washbasin, toilet and shower. These have been very well designed, with glass in the windows and trendy mirrors on the walls.

The ten **Bushman** huts are very basic, rounded shelters built using a frame of thin mopane saplings, and a covering of grasses. There's a door made of sticks and inside are two rustic beds with a cowhide rug on a dung floor, a bedside table and a paraffin lantern. Residents share the same ablutions as the campers. Whilst similar to camping in the dry season, I'd be a little apprehensive sleeping in one during the rains – although I am assured that they're waterproof.

The **campsite** has four showers and toilets built into a large and stylish thatched rondavel – complete with lights set into the walls and clothes-hooks made from branches.

The camp's focus is a funky dining and bar area, dominated by a large, curved bar and lit by two chandeliers made from local beer bottles. This has tables and alcoves and a fine collection of images and interesting things on its walls. A full breakfast here is US$15, lunch is US$10 and a 3-course dinner US$20.

Fly-camping trips to the pans are covered separately, see below. However, there are a variety of optional activities that can be organised out of a base at Planet Baobab, including the following. **Village Tour** which lasts about two hours and includes a visit to the local primary school, Gweta's *kgotla* (traditional court), and a stop at the traditional

LIONS VS LIVESTOCK

Graham Hemson worked as a guide at Jack's Camp, and is studying for a PhD on lion ecology and conservation in the Makgadikgadi area as part of Oxford University's Wildlife Conservation Research Unit. In 1999 he estimated that there were about 39 lions in the Makgadikgadi area, where he investigated their impact on people, and vice versa.

Every year lions kill hundreds of domestic animals in and around the Makgadikgadi Pans National Park, which brings them into conflict with the herders and owners. In retaliation people have, in the past, laid out traps and poison, and hunted lions outside the park with ruthless efficiency. Between November 1999 and May 2000, at least 12 lions were killed here.

However, contrary to common belief, Graham's research indicated that livestock predation does not happen mainly inside the kraal, but rather out in the grazing areas and sometimes inside the park. Although lions will tackle livestock at the villages, often they can simply pick off the many untended stragglers. An interesting ecological response to the predictability of the livestock as prey is that lions that eat livestock have substantially smaller home ranges than those which are dependent on migratory prey, or scarce desert species.

Typically, this livestock predation is only a problem when wild prey is scarce. Lions are forced to change their preferences abruptly as zebra and wildebeest migrate out of their territories.

After surveying the local inhabitants, Graham found that many of the people in charge of the livestock were elderly women; often their husbands were living in town, running more lucrative family businesses. These women were physically unable to keep track of their cattle – hence a large number of stray animals make a veritable man-made buffet for lions.

Following Graham's conclusions, Botswana's Wildlife Dept has lobbied its Veterinary Department to consider re-routing a proposed disease control fence around the Makgadikgadi, to help prevent the wildlife from straying into cattle country. Meanwhile strategies have been developed to help the local people minimise their losses, and to discourage them from killing more lions before the fence is built.

healer. A local guide from the area will lead you, and there's always a chance to stop and sample some of the local sorghum beer. (It's an acquired taste!). **Bushwalk and fireside chat** which is a short guided walk for about two hours through the surrounding bush, concentrating on the environment, the traditional uses of plants and animals, the history of the area and perhaps some local stories. **Traditional meal at the cattlepost** can be arranged in the evening with a local family: typically sorghum, mealie meal, seswaa (beef stew), wild spinach, mopane worms in season, wild beans and perhaps creamy baobab fruit milkshake.

Rates: US$50/75 per person sharing/single for a mud hut, US$25/30 for a bushman hut, and camping is US$4 per person per night.

Kalahari Surf Club

This is the fly-camp of Planet Baobab. It's reached by vehicle from Planet Baobab and is the base for their quad-bike trips around the pans area. 'Accommodation' consists of a bed-roll under the stars, but with minimal dangerous game around, this is all you need and is a great way to sleep.

From here you can explore the northern edge of Ntwetwe with local guides, looking at wildlife, its huge baobabs, the spring at Sweet Water Pan and the stone tools which litter areas of it. Plus learning a lot about the area's geology, archaeology and history.

Rates: A typical 3-day/2-night itinerary including one night in a mud hut at Planet Baobab and one on the pans costs around US$500/650 per person sharing/single, including laundry, meals and activities. For a 4-day/3-night itinerary, with two nights on the pans, expect to pay around US$600/780 per person sharing/single.

Rakops

Useful as a (hand-pumped) refuelling stop and reachable now entirely on tarmac from Maun, Rakops (✪ RAKOPS 21°02.136'S, 24°24.432'E) is notable for a tall radio mast in the centre of town, and as the last outpost passed on many trips into the Central Kalahari Game Reserve. It's also got cellphone coverage.

North of here a new tar road shadows the western side of the Boteti River, to Motopi and thence Maun. East of here, the road passes through Mopopi, around Orapa, and thence splits with one fork heading for Francistown, and the other for Palapye. All of these routes are now tarred and very good quality.

Motopi

A few kilometres south of the main Maun–Nata road, this large village seemed full of road-builders and detours when I was last there. Coming from the south, the main road seemed to go through Motopi and west, although it was possible to take a short cut along a sand track, due north through the riverbed, until about 8km later you reach the main Maun-Nata road. That said – there's probably a smooth, well-signposted alternative by now!

Orapa

This is the heart of Botswana's diamond-mining operations, producing around 12.2 million carats in 2000 – that's around 12% of the world's gem-quality diamonds! This makes it by far the most important town in the country to Botswana's economy, and hence security there is very tight. You're not allowed in, or out, without permission from Debswana, which isn't given easily. Hence it's effectively off-limits to visitors and there's a road that detours around the south side of the mine.

Whilst passing this, consider that there's also a major diamond mine at Letlhakane, about 30km from Orapa, on the Serowe road, and that there's active prospecting continuing throughout the region for more diamond pipes.

The Central Kalahari

Covering about 52,800km², and without a tar road anywhere near it, the Central Kalahari Game Reserve (or the 'CKGR' as it's usually known) is one of the world's largest game reserves. It dominates the centre of Botswana – the wider region that I've referred to in this chapter as simply the 'central Kalahari'. This is Africa at its most remote and esoteric; a vast sandsheet punctuated by a few huge open plains, occasional salt pans, and the fossil remains of ancient riverbeds.

The CKGR isn't a reserve for everybody. The game is often sparse and can seem limited, with no elephants or buffalo; the distances are huge, along bush tracks of variable quality; and the facilities are non-existent. So unless you have a fully equipped vehicle (preferably two) and lots of bush experience, it's probably not the place for you.

The converse is that if you've already experienced enough of Africa to love the feeling of space and the sheer freedom of real wilderness areas, then this reserve is completely magical; it's the ultimate wilderness destination.

Due to limitations of space, this is only a short introduction to the area. It's intended to give you the feel for the central Kalahari and the CKGR (the area of it which most visitors will see) and tell you how to get there and what it's like. I've assumed that most visitors will only be visiting the northern section of the park – Piper's Pan and north – as that's generally regarded as the most interesting area of the park. It's also the obvious part of the reserve to link into a trip with the more popular northern regions of Chobe and the Okavango.

BACKGROUND INFORMATION
History
The Central Kalahari Game Reserve was declared a game park in 1961, on the very eve of independence. At that time, there was increasing international publicity about the San. With the prevalent view of their 'idyllic' hunter/gatherer lifestyle came a growing concern that this was threatened, and that they might become 'extinct'. The British Protectorate of Bechuanaland was the focus for this, so the authorities decided to protect the heart of the Kalahari for the San.

At the time, there was no way to set aside one particular area for an ethnic group. Neither the British authorities nor the Tswana, who were being groomed for government, wanted any discrimination amongst its citizens based on race. This would have set a dangerous precedent, with echoes of the tribal 'bantustans' created by the apartheid regime in South Africa.

Back in the 1960s, legislation to proclaim a separate area for a separate ethnic group didn't exist. Nor was any wanted by a new country anxious to avoid ethnic divisions. Hence the heart of the central Kalahari was protected from further

KEY
4WD track
Veterinary fence

GPS co-ordinates ⊕

CKGATE	21° 09.399'S; 24° 00.417'E
DVLTUR	21° 00.041'S; 23° 39.405'E
JUNCTI	21° 24.301'S; 23° 48.193'E
KUKECO	21° 00.075'S; 23° 53.070'E
TOCKGR	21° 01.718'S; 24° 22.607'E
VETFEN	20° 59.961'S; 22° 25.285'E

CENTRAL KALAHARI

development or agricultural encroachment as a 'game park' – even though it was intended as a place of sanctuary for the San. Thus the Central Kalahari Game Reserve was proclaimed.

(Still to this day the Botswana government has a strict policy of not discriminating – positively or negatively – between any of the ethnic groups in the country. 'We're all Tswana' is their wise approach – designed to minimise any ethnic tensions. However, there lies the nub of a problem. If a group like the San are allowed to live and hunt in a 'game reserve', why shouldn't any other Tswana citizen? Many who are concerned for the San argue that they need positive discrimination, whilst others maintain that such moves would be racist.)

In keeping with its origins, the CKGR remained largely closed for around 30 years; visitors needed special approval and permits, which were not lightly granted. During this time its most famous visitors were probably Mark and Delia Owens. They were a couple of young and idealistic animal researchers from America who lived on a tree island in Deception Valley for about seven years (1974–80), and subsequently wrote a best-selling book, *Cry of the Kalahari* (see *Further Reading*), based on their experiences.

Then in the late 1980s and early '90s the park started to open up more, first allowing in organised groups with tour operators and later, only in recent years, individual travellers in their own vehicles. However, numbers remain very strictly limited by the number of campsites available; so it still feels very much a wilderness destination.

People

When the CKGR was declared as a reserve, a population of around 5,000 San people (see pages 30–2 in *People and culture*) lived within its boundaries. In the last decade or so a borehole had been installed at the small village of Xade, where some of the park's game scouts were based. Research in 1996 estimated that the population in the reserve had fallen below 1,500, a significant proportion of whom had moved to live in the vicinity of Xade, near this fairly reliable source of water.

The government's stated policy is now to encourage relocation of the people to 'New Xade' – a new village which has been created outside the reserve. They maintain that this will make it easier to supply the people with basic health and education services. However, this policy has attracted criticism from international human rights groups, like Survival International, who allege that the San are being forcibly coerced to move outside the reserve.

See page 29 in *People and culture* for more discussion of this issue, and note that this remains a very contentious and political topic.

Geography and landscape

Despite its huge area, the central Kalahari has relatively little scenic variation. The vast majority of it is covered by an enormous, undulating sandsheet. Within the CKGR itself, the north of the park contains the most varied scenery; here you'll find a network of vegetated salt pans and a few fossilised riverbeds.

Flora and fauna

If you're expecting to find stark differences between contrasting environments within this Kalahari reserve, you'll be disappointed. There are subtle changes between its different landscapes, but there isn't the variation here that you'll find around Chobe or the Okavango. Because of this, the animal species found here vary little from area to area – and this is one reason why the central Kalahari is an area for old Africa hands, and not first-time safari-goers.

Flora

People on their first trip trough the Kalahari are often struck by just how green and vegetated it is, often in contrast to their mental image of a 'desert'. In fact most of the Kalahari is covered in a thin, mixed bush with a fairly low canopy height, dotted with occasional larger trees. Beneath this is a rather sparse ground-covering of smaller bushes, grasses and herbs.

To be a little more precise, the central Kalahari's vegetation is dominated by *Terminalia sericea* sandveld (see page 59) standing on deep sand. The most common species within this are the silver terminalia itself, *Terminalia sericea*, the Kalahari apple-leaf, *Lonchocarpus nelsii*, and Kalahari sand acacias, *Acacia luederitzii*, which occasionally form thickets. These vary from bushes to substantial trees, growing to a maximum height of around 10m. (Their flattened canopies are easily confused with the umbrella thorn, *Acacia tortilis*, earning them the alternative name of bastard, or false, umbrella thorn.)

Other common trees include the distinctive purple-pod terminalia, *Terminalia prunioides*, which seem to grow best in areas where there is more clay in the soil; shepherd's trees, *Boscia albitrunca*, with their characteristic whitish bark; and feverberry trees, *Croton megalobotrys*. Bladethorns, *Acacia fleckii,* and their close cousins the bluethorns, *Acacia erubescens*, are common bushes with fine, feathery foliage but keen, curved barbs. Inevitably you'll spot plenty of old, gnarled camelthorn trees, *Acacia erioloba*.

Beneath these you'll commonly find a variety of low bushes and shrubs including wild seringa bushes, *Burkea africana* and bushwillows, *Combretum collinum*. Meanwhile on the ground one of the more common grasses is the lovely silky bushman grass, *Stipagrostis uniplumis*.

Look carefully, perhaps helped by a good guide, and you'll find plenty to interest you here including, during the wetter months of the year, many flowers and herbs. The beautifully curving purple flowers of the cat's tail, *Hermbstaedtia odorata*, form spectacular patches in damper areas. More entertaining are the bright red fruits of the balsam pear, *Momordica balsamina*, which, when ripe, fall to the ground and pop themselves open automatically if disturbed. In *Common wild flowers of the Okavango Delta*, Veronica Roodt (see *Further Reading*) reports that the young leaves of this plant are used as vegetable, and while a few will use the fruits in cooking, many communities treat them as poisonous or use them in medicines.

Fauna
Mammals

Game viewing anywhere in the central Kalahari area can be a stark contrast to the amazing densities of game that can often be seen in the Okavango-Linyanti-Chobe region. To get the best out of the CKGR, you'll require lots of time and patience, often just watching and waiting. The big game is here, but on average it occurs in very low densities – as you'd expect in such a harsh, arid environment. The only way to get around this is, as mentioned below, to visit when it congregates on the open pans in the north.

Springbok are probably the most numerous of the **large herbivores** in the park today. That said, the game populations in the central Kalahari seem to have been fluctuating fairly wildly, at least for the last century, and perhaps longer. In his *Comment on Kalahari Wildlife and the Khukhe Fence* (see *Further Reading*), Alec Campbell suggests that over this period human activities and interference have altered the balance of the wildlife populations in the Kalahari substantially – and led indirectly to population explosions and crashes.

Currently springbok disperse in small herds across the park during the dry season, but congregate in very large numbers on the short grass plains found on pans and fossil riverbeds during and shortly after the rains. (Note that this is exactly the opposite of the usual situation for many mammals, including elephants and buffalo, which gather in larger herds as the dry season progresses, only to disperse during the rains.)

These successful antelope are both browsers and grazers, which can derive all the moisture that they need from their food, provided that the plants that they eat contain at least 10% water. They'll often rest by day and eat at night, thus maximising the moisture content of their fodder by including dew on it.

Springbok populations are very elastic: they are able to reproduce very rapidly when conditions are favourable, allowing them to rapidly repopulate after a bad drought. With good conditions females can produce two calves in 13 months, while even six-month old ewes will conceive, giving birth to their first lamb when they are barely a year old. To maximise the survival of their offspring, the females gather together in maternal herds and synchronise their births, thus presenting predators with a short-term surplus of easily caught young lambs.

The central Kalahari's population of blue wildebeest has, at times within the last century, swelled to enormous proportions. Campbell describes them as peaking in the 1960s when 'herds of 50 and 100 had so accumulated in the Matsheng and Okwa area that they stretched unbroken for many kilometres and numbered hundreds of thousands'. Thane Riney, an ecologist there at the time, was familiar with the vast herds of the Serengeti yet still referred to these as 'the largest herds of plains game left in Africa today'. Wildebeest populations were then estimated at up to 250,000 animals, but within a few years lack of water, grazing and the existence of veterinary cordon fences had conspired to wipe them out from much of the central Kalahari. Today you'll find small groups of wildebeest in the CKGR, but I've never seen them in large numbers here.

Probably the area's most common large antelope are gemsbok (also known as oryx), which can be seen in congregations of hundreds on the short grass plains during the rains, but usually occur in smaller groupings during the rest of the year. These magnificent antelope are supremely adapted for desert-living. They can survive fluctuations of their body temperature which take it to up to 45°C (when 42°C would kill most mammals) because of a series of blood vessels, known as the 'carotid rete', located immediately below their brain. These effectively cool the blood before it reaches the animal's brain – the organ most adversely affected by temperature variations.

Red hartebeest can also be found here in good numbers, as can eland and – an amazing sight – giraffe. Kudu occur, but generally in quite small numbers – either small bachelor groups or family groups consisting of an old male, several females and a number of youngsters. Common duiker are occasionally seen, too, but if you catch a glimpse of a small antelope bounding away from you, it's much more likely to be a steenbok.

The **main predators** here are lion, cheetah, leopard and spotted hyena, which generally occur in a low density, matching their prey species. The lion prides range over large territories and are bonded by loose associations; members spend most of their time apart from each other, living alone or in pairs, and meeting relatively infrequently. Individual lions will often hunt a variety of smaller prey, like bat-eared foxes and porcupines, as well as the larger antelope more commonly thought of as lion fodder.

Similarly the central Kalahari's leopard here have a very catholic diet, ranging from mice and spring hares to ground squirrels and wild cats – plus steenbok, springbok and calves of the larger antelope.

The park's cheetah seem to be more nomadic than the lion or leopard. In other parks, where game densities are higher, cheetah often lose their kills to these larger cats. Thus the CKGR's relatively low density of predators makes it a good place for cheetah. Hence this is one of *sub-Saharan Africa's* better parks for spotting them – at least at times when the springbok concentrate on the pans and river beds.

Amongst the **scavengers and insectivores** found here are the brown hyena (the original object of study for Mark and Delia Owens – see *Further Reading*), black-backed jackal, caracal, Cape fox, bat-eared fox, aardwolf, genet and wild cat. However, as there is no facility for night drives in the reserve, only black-backed jackals are commonly seen as they aren't strictly nocturnal.

Meanwhile the diurnal yellow mongoose is sometimes seen scampering around in search of insects, and families of meerkats (or suricats) are amongst the most entertaining and endearing of all the park's residents.

Birds
The birdlife here is very varied, with Africa's largest bird, the ostrich, doing particularly well. I've never seen more free-roaming ostrich than here, during May, when Deception Valley seemed to be dotted by large flocks of them.

Weighing 14–19kg, kori bustard are the world's heaviest flying birds and are also common, stepping around the plains in search of insects and small reptile and mammals.

Closely related to the kori are the smaller korhaans; here the white-winged black korhaan (or white-quilled korhaan) is one of the area's most obvious birds. The conspicuous black-and-white males have a harsh, raucous call and can be seen flying up and then falling back to the ground in endless display flights. Related red-crested korhaans are a little less obvious, and less common, though equally spectacular when displaying.

Doves are well represented with Cape turtle, laughing doves and, especially, Namaqua doves all being very common. All the species of sandgrouse found in southern Africa – double-banded, Burchell's, yellow-throated and Namaqua – live here. Watch in the mornings as flocks of Namaqua sandgrouse fly to waterholes. They drink and also wade into the water, where each male has specially adapted feathers on his breast, which act like a sponge to soak up water. He then flies up to 80km back to his nest, where the chicks drink from the feathers.

The central Kalahari's most common raptor is the pale-chanting goshawk: a light grey bird, with pink legs and black ends to its wings and tail. It's usually seen hunting from a conspicuous perch, perhaps a fence post beside a track or the top of a small thorn bush, or occasionally hopping about the ground foraging. If disturbed it'll usually fly off low, swooping to land on a similar perch – even if that's another fence post from which it'll shortly be disturbed again.

Black-shouldered kites and rock kestrels, both of which often hunt by hovering in flight, are common here. Bateleurs, black-breasted and brown snake eagles, martial and tawny eagles, and lanner falcons are also around, with the latter making something of a speciality of hunting birds as they come to drink at waterholes.

When to visit
The Kalahari is really unlike any other game area in sub-Saharan Africa in that its game is probably at its most spectacular during and shortly after the rains – from around January to April. Then the animals gather where the best rain has been and the sweetest grazing is, which usually means on the pans. These can be a

TUNNEL VISION

Just below the surface of the Kalahari lies a labyrinth of tunnels excavated by the Damara molerat (*Cryptomis damarensis*), the only member of this endemic African family to occur in the Kalahari. Molerats are rodents, and unlike true moles, which are insectivores, they feed entirely on plant matter – specifically underground storage organs such as bulbs, corms, tubers and desert cucumbers.

They have plump, cylindrical bodies, short, sturdy limbs and formidable projecting incisors for chiselling out the tunnels in which they live their entire lives. Earth excavated by the teeth is shuffled backwards by the forefeet, and when enough has accumulated the molerat reverses up a side tunnel, pushing it to the surface to form a 'molehill'. Digging is easiest when the soil is wet, so the rains prompt a flurry of activity: in one month, one colony of 16 Damara molerats was recorded digging a kilometre of tunnels and shifting 2.5 tonnes of soil to the surface. Not bad for an animal that weighs no more than 300g.

This Herculean effort uncovers enough food to last the colony through the dry season until the next rains. Meanwhile soil is shifted around and burrows modified to create a complex of chambers, passageways and latrines.

Damara molerats are the most sociable of their family. This is a necessary adaptation to the harsh Kalahari environment, where numbers bring more success to a team of blind foragers in search of an erratic, scattered food supply. Their complex societies are more like those of a social insect than a mammal. A colony averages around 15–25 members, occasionally up to 40, but only one pair – the dominant male and female – are reproductive. All others help forage, dig and rear the young, but suppress their fertility, being effectively like sterile worker termites.

The dominant female breeds all year, producing a litter of between one and five pups after a 80-day gestation in a nest chamber two metres below ground. Hierarchies are reinforced aggressively, and each year about 10% of a colony's members leave to breed and found new colonies. Molerats communicate underground with snorts and squeals, and drum with their hind feet on tunnel walls to relay seismic messages to mates or rivals.

Though the casual visitor is unlikely ever to see a molerat, a range of canny predators, notably the mole snake (*Pseudaspis cana*), have learned to watch as a pile of fresh soil accumulates and will snatch the digger just as it approaches the surface.

magnificent sight, with very large herds of springbok and gemsbok, accompanied by good numbers of giraffe and ostrich plus groups of blue wildebeest, hartebeest and eland. Inevitably these attract increased predator activity from lion, cheetah and the odd leopard.

Having said that, this is also the time when the weather, and in particular the driving conditions, can be at their least hospitable. If there has been much rain then the road from Rakops to the scout post and beyond become a series of mudholes lined by black-cotton soil – which is rock hard when dry, but feels like treacle when wet. Meanwhile areas of pans in the park become large, shallow lakes where both navigation and traction present a challenge to any vehicle. Any group coming at this time must be fully prepared for heavy rain, and should expect to have to dig out their vehicle from the mud a number of times.

As a compromise for those who are not fond of endless mud, a favourite time to visit is just after the rains, around March–May – depending on when the rains stop. Then most of the surface water has disappeared, and the black-cotton soil isn't nearly as treacherous as it would have been a few months earlier. The game concentrations will still be good, albeit perhaps not *quite* so spectacular, but your overall experience will probably be much more enjoyable. That is, unless you really enjoy digging your vehicle out of knee-deep mud...

PRACTICAL INFORMATION
Getting there and away
To reach the entrance gate follow the directions below, and note that the small Matswere Scout Camp, where you sign in and pay fees, is a further 8km into the park. From there it's a further 30km to the nearest campsites, those at the north end of Deception Valley.

Driving yourself
Driving yourself into the central Kalahari is only a viable option for experienced and bush-wise adventurers with their own fully equipped 4WDs. Even they need at least two 4WD vehicles and some fail-safe plan for back-up assistance in the event of an emergency. Then there are three usual routes to the park's northern entry gate.

From the Maun-Ghanzi road
About 119km from Ghanzi and 167km from Maun, on the tarred Maun–Ghanzi road, you'll have to stop and pas through the Kuke Veterinary Fence (⊕ VETFEN 20°59.961'S, 22°25.285'E). Immediately north of this, you'll find a good wide gravel road that heads off on a bearing fractionally south of east. After a few kilometres, this thoroughfare bends round to the left, and there's a small turning into the bush on the right. Take this, and you'll find a simple sand track with two clear ruts for your wheels (welcome to the Kalahari!). The veterinary fence will be literally inches from your right side.

Expect only the occasional 4WD to pass you; this isn't a busy track. Beneath your wheels you'll sometimes find patches of hard ground with bands of calcrete rocks. Then there are mud-holes, where thick clay is a sticky hazard during the rains (when this route is perfectly possible, but time-consuming). However, most of the track is good, fairly hard sand on which a reasonably experienced bush driver should be able to average 50km/h.

After about 175km, the taller bush thins out a little, leaving more open grassy areas. At times now you'll find yourself travelling parallel to several fences, and sometimes with one on each side of you. Beware of startling antelope here; they'll run in front of the vehicle with no escape, and become exhausted easily if you drive too fast.

Around 245km after the tar you'll reach a left turning (⊕ DVLTUR 21°00.041'S, 23°39.405'E) which is clearly signposted to Deception Valley Lodge (see page 442 for details). The lodge is about 5.3km as the eagle flies north from here, but a little further using the winding track which leads there, via the lodge's own airstrip at ⊕ DVLAIR 20°58.897'S, 23°39.515'E.

Almost 24km after passing this, you'll reach Kuke Corner (⊕ KUKECO 21°00.075'S, 23°53.070'E). Here a gate marks the junction of several veterinary fences. To the left a straight cut line heads due north, towards the Maun–Nata road. To the right, a well-used track follows the line of the fence, roughly south-southeast (bearing about 143°). This can be quite rutted and tedious driving, but after about 21.5km leads to the main entrance gate to the CKGR (⊕ CKGATE 21°09.399'S, 24°00.417'E).

From Rakops

There is one main track between Rakops and the CKGR's entrance gate at ⊕ CKGATE 21°09.399'S, 24°00.417'E, which is fringed by a few detours and side-tracks. Starting at Rakops, head north out of town towards Motopi, and then turn left off the main road where you see a number of tracks, about 2–3km from the radio mast, around ⊕ TOCKGR 21°01.718'S, 24°22.607'E.

You probably won't find one obvious track until you're a few kilometres from the tar, but if you average a bearing of about 250° then you'll be going in roughly the right direction, and will reach the entrance gate (⊕ CKGATE 21°09.399'S, 24°00.417'E) after around 41km. Even heading roughly in this direction, you can't go wrong, as sooner or later you'll hit the veterinary fence that doubles as the park's boundary.

When wet, during the earliest months of the year, this is one of the muddiest, and hence trickiest, sections of track in the region. I've heard tales of this section alone taking several days to pass, with frequent stops to dig out – so don't tackle it lightly. Later in the year, the track hardens to a roller-coaster ride where you bounce in and out of a succession of dry mud-holes; even then it's fairly slow going.

South along the cut line

This cut line follows a veterinary fence. I haven't driven this route, but believe that it's probably the quickest route between Maun and the CKGR, at least until the tarring of the whole road down from Motopi to Rakops is completely finished. You'll find the north end of this at the small village of Makalamabedi, west of Motopi. Simply follow this due south (driving on the eastern side of the veterinary fence) to Kuke Corner (⊕ KUKECO 21°00.075'S, 23°53.070'E), and from then continue for 21.5km to the main entrance gate at ⊕ CKGATE 21°09.399'S, 24°00.417'E.

Without your own vehicle

If, like most visitors to Botswana, you don't have the knowledge, experience, or equipment for this kind of a trip, then to visit the CKGR you'll need to take a 'mobile safari' to the area. There are several ways to approach this.

Join a group

A few of Botswana's larger safari companies have scheduled group trips, leaving on specific pre-planned dates, which include time camping within the CKGR. See the main listings on pages 96–7, *Planning and preparation*, 167–77, *Maun operators,* and 192–3, *Kasane operators*. Check out what they have running and read between the lines to make sure you understand exactly how much of their time is within the CKGR – often, quite long trips will spend far too short a time in the actual park. Many of these trips will also feature Deception Valley Lodge, or even a private campsite on Deception Valley's reserve. Some of the better ones include a flight one-way, probably best done out of the park at the end of your trip. Expect a return charter on a six-seater plane (up to five passengers) to Deception Valley to cost around US$300.

Organise a private mobile trip

If you have a fairly generous budget, then the same operators (and many of the smaller ones also) will be delighted to organise a private trip for you, for which you'll

NORTHERN CKGR

↑ *Makalamabedi*

0 ━━━━━━ 10km
0 ━━━━━━ 5 miles

Kuke Fence

KUKECO gate
Kuke Corner

Rakops

CKGATE Manganga gate

Veterinary fence

MATSWE
Matswee Game
Scout Post

CKA1

Leopard Pan

LEFORK

CKL1

CKS2,3

Sunday Pan

CKS1

CKD4,5,6

JUNCT1

CKK1,2,3,4

Deception Valley

Deception Pan
DECPAN

CKL2

○ Letiahau
Waterhole

*Central Kalahari
Game Reserve*

KEY

4WD track	═════
Veterinary fence	───────
Salt pan	

GPS co-ordinates ⊕

CKA1	21° 13.844'S;	23° 37.308'E
CKA2	21° 16.157'S;	23° 28.666'E
CKA3	21° 19.965'S;	23° 20.319'E
CKD4	21° 24.213'S;	23° 46.287'E
CKGATE	21° 09.399'S;	24° 00.417'E
CKK1	21° 25.699'S;	23° 47.921'E
CKK4	21° 25.006'S;	23° 47.433'E
CKL2	21° 35.401'S;	23° 44.755'E
CKL3	21° 36.447'S;	23° 33.407'E
CKP1	21° 46.063'S;	23° 11.975'E
CKP2	21° 47.565'S;	23° 12.882'E
CKS1	21° 21.104'S;	23° 40.285'E
CKS2-3	21° 20.071'S;	23° 40.893'E
DECPAN	21° 24.291'S;	23° 46.434'E
DVLTUR	21° 00.041'S;	23° 39.405'E
JUNCT1	21° 24.301'S;	23° 48.193'E
KUKECO	21° 00.075'S;	23° 53.070'E
LEFORK	21° 17.287'S;	23° 41.938'E
LETIAH	21° 38.380'S;	23° 25.023'E
MATSWE	21° 11.892'S;	23° 56.369'E
PATURN	21° 23.924'S;	23° 15.136'E
PUMP1	21° 24.676'S;	23° 13.718'E

Molapo ↙

be able to specify the departure date and the timings. Expect the costs to be high though – in the region of US$200–350 per person per night. (Larger groups and longer expeditions are generally less expensive than smaller groups and shorter trips.)

Book a short trip from a lodge

If you just want a few days in the park, then it's worth checking with Leroo-La-Tau, and perhaps also Deception Valley Lodge (see below for details). They will sometimes organise short, simple, guided camping expeditions into the park. Typically these come as part of a few nights spent either side at their lodge.

Getting organised

A visit to the CKGR requires a lot of organisation before you even start to drive there. You must book a place to stay and make arrangements to bring all your water, food, equipment and supplies. Brackish water is sometimes available at the Matswere Scout Post, near the entrance, but it isn't to drink or to be relied upon. Note that the land outside the park all falls into private farms and concessions, and so camping 'outside the gate' is not a practical option.

Where to stay

You have two choices in this area: either stay within the park, using the park's demarcated campsites mentioned below, or stay at one of the two lodges which are both a few hours' drive from the entrance. However, these lodges are so far from the park that they're really only useful either as destinations in their own right, or as comfortable stops at the start and end of trips into the park. Neither is close enough to the CKGR to be used as a base for day-trips.

Campsites inside the park

The only places to stay inside the park are campsites. All of these are totally undeveloped; they're just cleared patches of ground with no water, toilets or showers. You must bring all the water you need, all your food, and a spade to dig your own toilets. (Don't forget matches to burn any tissue paper before burying it!)

As for the rest of Botswana's parks, it's essential that you book and pay for these campsites in advance, or you will not be allowed in through the gate. See pages 142–3 for how to do this, and details of the costs. Each of the CKGR's campsites has a unique code, eg: CKK1, CKK2, CKL1, CKP1, etc. In *What to see and do*, below, I've made notes on some of these, identifying most with comments and GPS locations.

Lodges outside the park

There is only one lodge really close to the park: Deception Valley Lodge. This must be booked in advance, as if full there are no nearby alternative options. Note that it is at least two hours' drive from the scout gate camp, and over three from the area known as Deception Valley within the CKGR.

One other place should be mentioned, as a convenient stopover en route to/from the park: Leroo-La-Tau (see pages 425–6) and its adjacent campsite, Xwarga. This stands beside the western border of Makgadikgadi Pans National Park, so is at least three hours' drive from the park's entrance gate.

Deception Valley Lodge (5 chalets) PO Box 1315, Pretoria 0001, South Africa; tel: 27 11 663 6948/9; fax: 27 11 663 6947; email: res@deceptionvalley.co.za; web: www.deceptionvalley.co.za

The quality of construction and furnishing used at Deception Valley Lodge ranks it as one of Botswana's top lodges. However, it is also in one of the country's more remote locations, and its relative lack of big game suits old Africa hands more than first-time visitors. Because of these factors, its prices aren't (yet) as high as you might expect.

The lodge has five chalets, each containing a separate large lounge and bedroom, and a smaller bathroom between them. Everything is under thatch. The focus of the lounge is a large, glass coffee-table and a very comfortable sofa. Its walls are dotted with framed Bushman artefacts, whilst lovely rugs are spread across the floors. A constant 220V electricity powers a ceiling fan in each room, a well-stocked fridge/minibar in the lounge and any number of lamps and lights, including some particularly beautiful ones which use ostrich eggshells as shades.

The bedroom has heavy teak furniture, copious wardrobe space and a couple of adjacent twin beds (or a king-size double) with mosquito nets. Sublimely comfortable mattresses are covered with notably high-quality cotton sheets and Botswana's best down quilts – which you'll need as the Kalahari's temperatures plummet at night. Everything is monogrammed with the lodge's own brown hyena logo. The 'blanket box' doubles as a lockable safety-deposit box.

Between these two main rooms is the equally stylish bathroom, with a flush toilet and a washbasin. A free-standing old-style claw-footed iron bath and an outside shower both derive hot water from an efficient gas geyser.

All around the chalet large sliding doors (with brass fittings) can be opened by day, and closed at night for warmth. These lead outside on to a shaded area of polished wooden decking, furnished with leather chairs and a table. Each of the bungalows is widely separated from the next, and linked by natural walkways lit by cute, gecko-shaped lights.

The lodge's main reception, lounge and dining areas are furnished in similar style, with equally careful attention to detail, and there's a small curio shop which sells a fairly unremarkable range of T-shirts as well as quilted warm jackets – handy if you misjudged just how cold it can get here.

Activities centre around drives and walks on the lodge's own area, which shares its southern boundary with the CKGR. (Note that drives don't normally visit the game reserve, which is too far for a comfortable day-trip.) The landscape, flora and fauna here is exactly the same as in the main reserve, although being much smaller and fenced it doesn't get the large wet-season congregations which are a major attraction of the CKGR.

That said, the lodge's private area encompasses a number of natural pans surrounded by larger trees, and there's a bird-hide beside one. Despite the relative lack of big game, there's plenty to look at, although this is an environment in which you would probably miss many of the smaller attractions without a good guide.. The walks are often led by the lodge's San guides, and sometimes incorporate demonstrations of their traditional skills staged in a small village which has been recreated for the purpose.

Rates (2005): US$360/415 per person per night sharing/single. Transfer flights between Maun and the lodge cost around US$95 per person each way (for a minimum of two). Open: all year.

Leroo-La-Tau Lodge (7 tents)
Situated at the eastern end of a bend in the Boteti River (✪ LEROOL 20°25.240'S, 24°31.277'E), Leroo-La-Tau has very comfortable chalets and a choice of activities. See pages 425–6 for full details.

Xwaraga campsite
This bush campsite is a few minutes walk from Leroo-La-Tau Lodge; it is contactable through the lodge and there are more details on page 426.

Getting around
Just over 8km southwest of the entrance into the CKGR you'll find the small Matswere Scout Post at ✪ MATSWE 21°11.892'S, 23°56.369'E. Here you can sign in and, if you ask the scouts politely, it's sometimes possible to fill up with brackish

A CAUTIONARY TALE

On one morning's game-viewing, driving slowly north into the end of Deception Valley, we spotted something unfamiliar moving in the distance. Training our binoculars, we could see the top half of a woman, waving. We signalled that we'd seen her and continued, eventually taking a right track to head in her direction.

Approaching with some trepidation, we found a distressed Tswana woman on her own. She'd been standing on the roof of the 4WD all morning, trying to attract attention. In fact she was one of the park's staff who, together with a few colleagues, had been driving from the Matswere Scout Post to Xade. (I never learnt why they were on a side-track off the main route!)

It seems that late the previous day the fuel filter in their old Land Rover had sprung a bad leak, marooning them there. They'd slept overnight, but with little water or food, her colleagues had set off to walk the 50km or so back to Matswere, and perhaps find visitors on the way who could help.

I spent a petrol-soaked hour under the vehicle, attempting a bush repair with no success, before offering her a lift back to the park's office. However, it transpired that this was the scout camp's only vehicle, so they wouldn't be able to do much. Hours later a better-equipped modern Land Rover approached; it carried a bush-wise South African couple who travelled with what seemed like a garage full of spares and tools. Her colleagues had managed to flag this vehicle down, and enlist the couple's help.

They were lucky. The park's other staff would have been virtually powerless to help – even if they'd known about the breakdown. Fortunately these visitors had the right tools and spare parts, so a repair was soon made. All set off again to Xade in their clapped-out Land Rover with few supplies. I hope they got there.

The morals of this story are simple:

- Don't expect any help from the parks staff; they probably won't have the vehicles or resources.
- Don't come to the CKGR without some basic spares, a simple tool kit, and another vehicle to help you out.
- A satellite phone isn't totally necessary, but is a wise back-up; so bring one if possible.
- Ample food and water are absolutely essential; bring more than you expect to need.

water – which is fine for showers, but not suitable for drinking. (You should have arrived with all your own water, but if you didn't then make the most of this. There are no other waterpoints north of Xade.)

Driving conditions

Visiting in the dry season, the general quality of the tracks in the park is surprising. Many of them, particularly those which follow the valleys, are really very good. You might have expected to be constantly ploughing through deep sand, but it's not like that. Of course there are patches of deep and tricky sand, and also stretches of black-cotton soil (rock hard when dry; virtually impassable if very wet), but many of the road surfaces are easy and hard when it's dry.

What to see and do

Being in a pristine area which is as remote as the CKGR is, for most visitors, an end in itself. Just being able to camp, move around, and watch the wildlife at leisure in such a beautiful wilderness, with the certainty that you'll see very few other vehicles, is the real attraction here. So don't rush around looking for 'sights', as there really aren't any. Just take time to enjoy where you are!

That said, detailed here are some of the areas that you may visit, including a few notes on some of the various campsites, with their names (and booking codes). Your permit for camping in the CKGR will specify the precise campsites booked for you on each night – and these can't be changed when you're here.

If you're entering and leaving via the Matswere Scout Post then a lovely week's circuit can be made by starting around Sunday and Leopard pans, then heading north and west along Passarge Valley, south via the western link to Piper's Pan, and then returning northeast through Letiahau and Deception valleys. This is the order in which I've described these areas.

Sunday and Leopard pans

Just north of Deception Valley, Sunday and Leopard are two fairly large pans. When there are other vehicles in Deception Valley, these are often more deserted. Their campsites make a good first stop if you enter the park via Matswere, and plan on heading around Passarge Valley.

The more southerly of the pair is Sunday Pan, which has three campsites. The first is slightly left of the track when you're driving north, at ✪ CKS1 21°21.104'S; 23°40.285'E. Further on, the turn-off to the second and third sites is to the right at ✪ CKS2-3 21°20.071'S; 23°40.893'E. All are pleasant, in the edge off the bush close to the main open area of the pan. Leopard Pan is about 5km further north, and has one campsite there: CKL1.

Passarge Valley

This is a long valley with many pans and several campsites. Approaching from the east, it's easily reached from Leopard Pan by finding the junction of tracks to the north of the pan (✪ LEFORK 21°17.287'S; 23°41.938'E), and heading north from there.

Initially the landscape is quite a thick mixture of small trees and bushes; typical Kalahari sandveld. Then after about 13km you'll find an old green sign saying: 'Passarge Valley. Help keep this valley pristine by staying on the track', and gradually you descend into a valley with a more open landscape of more grassland – now heading southwest.

About 9.5km further there's a turning south to Manong Campsite at ✪ CKA1 21°13.844'S; 23°37.308'E, which is a lovely campsite set very much on its own.

Continuing in the valley for another 18km you'll then find a track to the north signposted to Kgokong Campsite at ✪ CKA2 21°16.157'S; 23°28.666'E. Here the valley is really stunning: open grassland dotted with a few small tree islands. The campsite is in the thickets just off to the side, slightly above the floor of the valley.

Further southwest, the third of Passarge's campsites is Kukama Campsite at ✪ CKA3 21°19.965'S; 23°20.319'E, which is in a small group of trees beside a fairly scrubby pan. This is about 12km northeast of the junction with the park's main east–west cut-line track at ✪ PATURN 21°23.924'S; 23°15.136'E.

Passarge Pan and the track to Motopi

A little beyond the southwest end of Passarge Valley track, Passarge Pan is on the south side of the track which leads to a water pump, ✪ PUMP1 21°24.676'S;

23°13.718'E. North of here a track leads through some lovely country dotted with small pans to Motopi Pan, and ultimately to the double fence which is the northern boundary of the reserve. Note that there is no open gate here, and no way in or out of the reserve by this road. However, when you reach the fence you can take a right and follow a decent track that runs east beside the fence, and then southeast from Kuke Corner (still confined within the park's boundary fence) to the main entrance.

The western link

On the northeast side of Passarge Pan, the track south towards Phukwi, Tau, San and Phokoje pans starts at ⊕ PATURN 21°23.924'S; 23°15.136'E. This track is the start of the 'western link', which eventually heads south towards Piper's Pan.

You'll see from the map here that this track seems to zig-zag, always heading either north–south or east–west. This is because the inter-dune valleys (with their string of pans) run east–west, and these usually make the best game-viewing areas. These valleys are linked by tracks running north–south, across the top of the dunes.

Note that on this track, the first few kilometres south of the main cut line track (⊕ PATURN) is very boggy; I'd expect this to be exceedingly challenging during the rains.

For an alternative route south, you can enter the western link via Tau Pan. To do this, first turn east along the cut line towards the north end of Deception Valley. About 18km from ⊕ PATURN, there's a track which heads almost due south to Phukwi Pan. There is a campsite on this route at Tau Pan, code CKT1.

The only other campsite on this side is CKT2 which is roughly half way along the track which follows Phokoje Pan, at ⊕ CKT2 21°35.278'S; 23°16.332'E. Heading east along this, the track splits off southeast from Phokoje Pan about 18km before its junction (⊕ LETIAH 21°38.380'S; 23°25.023'E) with the main track from the Letiahau Valley to Piper's Pan.

Piper's Pan

Piper's Pan is as far south as most people visit in the northern section of the park, and as far as I'll describe in this chapter. If you are wondering if it's worth the effort to get here, the answer is a resounding 'Yes'. And that's despite a badly corrugated section of road just north of this area.

Piper's Pan is only a few kilometres across, but it's a stunning stretch of perfectly flat grass. In the rains it's green, and often covered with springbok and gemsbok. By as early as May, it has usually turned a beautiful gold, like a field of ripe barley.

There are two campsites here. CKP1 is slightly further north (⊕ CKP1 21°46.063'S; 23°11.975'E) and in a grove of rather lovely trees on the west side of the track, but close to the edge of the pan.

The second site, CKP2 (⊕ CKP2 21°47.565'S; 23°12.882'E), is further south, up higher on a low fossilised dune. This is just beyond a prominent green water tank (⊕ WATANK 21°47.045'S; 23°12.755'E) which stands at the top of a fossilised dune, beside the track which leads, around 72km later, to Xade.

Around the outside edge of the pan itself there's a 7km circular track that is well worth exploring, although probably impassable during the rains. The eastern side of this (around ⊕ PIPERE 21°46.336'S; 23°15.039'E) is particularly treacherous black-cotton soil, while it often seems to disappear on the southern side. It's a lovely circuit, but very slow driving even when dry, as the hardened earth is very uneven.

Letiahau Valley

Approaching from the south and Piper's Pan, the road to Matswere leads first through Letiahau and then Deception Valley. About 12km northeast of the junction (⊕ LETIAH 21°38.380'S; 23°25.023'E), which is the turning north for the western link, the track enters the picturesque Letiahau Valley. A further 4km on there's a small turning south from the road which, after about 100m, leads to a group of trees in a bushy plain where the Letiahau Campsite (⊕ CKL3 21°36.447'S; 23°33.407'E) is situated. Around 6km further east, a tiny loop takes a closer look at the permanent Letiahau Waterhole.

About 20km east of the first campsite is a second called Lekhubu (code CKL2). This is off on the south side of the road at ⊕ CKL2 21°35.401'S; 23°44.755'E. Continuing east from this, the track backs around to take a more northerly line, as it approaches Deception Valley.

Deception Pan

This open pan (⊕ DECPAN 21°24.291'S; 23°46.434'E) at the southern end of the valley is found by taking a short detour, about 1.5km from the main track. It fills with water during the rains, but for the rest of the year it's flat, cracked mud tinged by a vivid red colour – caused by a small red water plant which flourishes when it's full.

Deception Valley

This is a long, broad inter-dune valley running roughly north–south; it's thought to be the bed of a fossil river. During and after good rains this is carpeted in luscious green grass that attracts dense concentrations of game. It's the park's most famous location, and where Mark and Delia Owens (see *Further Reading*) lived. If you are visiting the northern section of the park for five to six days, then my advice is for you to save this as a highlight for your last couple of days.

Because it is the park's most famous area, and relatively close (35km) to the Matswere Scout Post entrance, this is the place where you're most likely to see other visitors. It's also the area with the most campsites.

Towards the northern end of Deception Valley, on the west side, a track splits off to pass beside the four Kori campsites (codes CKK1 to CKK4), which are about 500m apart. The most southerly one is located at ✪ CKK1 21°25.699'S; 23°47.921'E and the most northerly at ✪ CKK4 21°25.006'S; 23°47.433'E. They're in fairly sparse bush on the edge of the main pan, and very generally close to any animal action there – though bushes obstruct their views.

Deception Valley's other six campsites are all set north of the pan, higher up in fairly thick woodlands. There are six of these (codes CKD1 to CKD6); the first three on the south side of the cut-line road, and then three on the north side. (The middle one of these is found at ✪ CKD4 21°24.213'S; 23°46.287'E.) It consists of a roughly circular area that has been cleared of trees and bushes. Each is separated from its neighbours by a few hundred metres, making them very secluded and private.

If you're heading out of the park then, to find your way out, simply drive towards the north of Deception Valley. There you'll find several small junctions with signposts, as the tracks along the valley are intersected by the straight cut-line road. Head east to ✪ JUNCT1 21°24.301'S; 23°48.193'E, and continue on to sign out at the Matswere Scout Post at ✪ MATSWE 21°11.892'S, 23°56.369'E.

RAKOPS

Rakops is a small town that makes a very useful staging post on the way to the CKGR. It has telephones, cellphone coverage and a range of shops selling most necessities. The fuel station here is generally reliable and has marvellous old hand-cranked fuel pumps. (Marvellous, that is, provided there's someone there to help you physically pump the fuel!) Within 2003 it's likely to be linked by tar to both the north and the east.

Francistown

The eastern edge of Botswana is an area that lies outside the sands of the Kalahari Desert, and looks and feels more like neighbouring Zimbabwe than parts of the rest of the country. There are rivers and readily available ground water, giving a fertile environment that can support fair numbers of people – in fact, some 80% of Botswana's population lives in this region today. When Rhodes' British South Africa Company was looking for ways to get the rich mineral resources of the northern territories out to the sea, the railway was built through eastern Bechuanaland, as Botswana was then called, connecting Zimbabwe with the Cape. Along this route, many small settlements sprung up, feeding off the meagre amount of wealth that was imparted by the rich railway corridor. One of these was Francistown.

Botswana's second largest town – now officially a city – is one of the oldest settlements in the country. Traditionally it had close cultural and trading links with Bulawayo in Zimbabwe before the artificial international boundaries were drawn up. Today, a good tarred road and a railway line links Francistown with Bulawayo, which is only three hours away by car. Francistown has a bit of a Zimbabwean feel to it, except for the very well-stocked shops and stores. It's a popular shopping destination for Zimbabweans looking for hard-to-get imported luxuries and spare parts – if they can lay their hands on some foreign currency. Francistown's initial prosperity derived from acting as a service town to the gold, copper and nickel mining industry – now overshadowed by the diamond mine at Orapa and the soda ash plant being constructed on Sowa Pan. The town and its surrounding area are traditionally the home of Botswana's second largest group of people, the Bakalanga.

As the gateway for travel north to Kasane and Maun, the Okavango, Chobe and the spectacular salt pans of Nxai and Makgadikgadi, Francistown has become a main stopover for travellers and overlanders. Here you'll be able to pick up any supplies or vehicle spare parts that you might need for your trip, get yourself organised and prepare yourself for exploring the interior. Other main roads radiating from Francistown link it with the capital, Gaborone, in the southeast of the country.

GETTING THERE AND GETTING AROUND
The town itself is very compact, with the railway station at the northern end and the bus station at the southern end – both just a few minutes' walk from the centre. The airport is a few kilometres away to the southeast of town and, unless you're hiring a car, you'll need to get a taxi – there's no public transport.

By air
Air Botswana has daily services during the week between Francistown and Gaborone. These take an hour and typically cost about US$85 one-way per person.

Plumtree (Zimbabwe)

N

Bradt

Ntshe River

0 _____ 1km
0 _____ 1 mile

MONARCH

GOVERNMENT
VILLAGE

see page 453

Nata, Airport

BLUE TOWN

Railway station

CENTRAL

TATITOWN

● University

SOMERSET
EAST

RIVERSIDE

Tati River

SOMERSET
WEST

PHASE 4

↓ Gaborone

FRANCISTOWN OVERVIEW

The Air Botswana office is in the Cresta Thapama Lodge on Blue Jacket Street in the centre of town (tel: 241 2393; fax: 241 3834; web: www.airbotswana.co.bw). There is also an office at the airport (tel: 241 2394).

By train

Botswana's railway runs along the eastern edge of the country, linking Ramtlabama in the south to Ramokgwebane to the northeast of Francistown. Botswana Railways (tel: 241 3444)has daily services linking Francistown with Gaborone. Trains depart from both Francistown and Gaborone at 10.00 every day except Friday, when departures are at 08.00 and 14.30. A one-way ticket is approximately P35/20 for first/second class. There is also a night service linking Francistown with Gaborone (and ultimately Lobatse in the south). This takes almost nine hours and costs P120/100/25 for first/second/third class.

By road
By bus

Buses and minibuses link Francistown with Gaborone (433km), Maun (492km) and Kasane (490km). Most buses run in the morning, and then only when they're full enough! The main bus station is to the south of the city centre, beside the railway line. It's best to get there by 09.00, or try to check the latest times the day before departure. In general, buses run as follows:

To Gaborone At least one each day, and as many as five spread throughout the morning. Costs around P35.

To Kasane Mondays, Wednesdays and Fridays – though small, crowded combies will ply this route every day, costing around P45.

To Maun Lots of buses, up to one an hour in the morning and early afternoon. Costs around P45.

To Bulawayo and Harare There are services, but they're much less regular. Check locally.

Bus companies include the following:

Mahube Express Tel: 241 2074
Motswere Express Tel: 240 1605
Seabelo's Express Tel: 241 4199
Sesennye Bus Service Tel: 241 2112
Tjemoyo Bus Services Tel: 241 0898

Car hire

Both Avis and Imperial have offices at Francistown airport, to the southeast of town:

Avis PO Box 222, Francistown; tel: 241 3901 (after hours 241 5867); fax: 241 2867; web: www.avis.com
Imperial Tel: 240 4771/2; fax: 304773; web: www.imperialcarrental.co.za

Hitching

If you take a taxi out of town, you'll find it relatively easy to hitchhike along the main tar arteries, including to Maun via Nata. Frequently, hitching is a faster option than taking the bus, though it's not advisable for single women, or even two women travelling together. You should expect to pay for your lift, at slightly more than the going bus fare. So pay perhaps around P50 to Maun or Kasane, and slightly less to Gaborone.

WHERE TO STAY

Francistown has a surprisingly good range of accommodation both in and around the town, with a choice from guesthouses and budget hotels to the more upmarket facilities offered by the centrally located Thapama. The town's location on the River Tati also makes camping a pleasant option. Alternatively, as in any of Botswana's larger towns, asking a taxi driver for 'private accommodation' should find you a cheap and hospitable roof over your head. And if you have a car, and you're desperate, then you can drive a few kilometres out of town and camp in the bush.

Category B

Cresta Thapama Hotel and Casino (96 rooms) Blue Jacket St, P Bag 31, Francistown; tel: 241 3872; fax: 241 3766; email: thapama@global.bw;
web: www.cresta-hospitality.com/hotels/thapama.htm
Near the centre of town and the bus station, this is probably Francistown's best-known hotel, though it's somewhat lacking in character. Centrally located, near the southern end of town by the roundabout, the Thapama is a four-star business hotel, complete with air conditioning and TVs in the en-suite rooms, and – as the name suggests – a casino for guests. Popular with visitors is the health and sports centre, which features air-conditioned squash courts and a gym, while outside there is a swimming pool, and facilities for golf and tennis. The hotel boasts two bars, of which the pool bar serves light meals as well as drinks, and the Ivory Grill, with both buffet and à la carte meals. Transfers from the airport just 3km away are complimentary.
Rates: single P464.75, double P575.85, including breakfast.

Marang Hotel and Casino (57 rooms and camping) PO Box 807, Francistown; tel: 241 3991; fax: 241 2130; email: marang@info.bw;
web: www.cresta-hospitality.com/hotels/marang.htm
Situated 5km from the centre of town – head south from the town centre to the main roundabout and take a left turn – the hotel is 4km further along past the golf course, on the right. Now a member of the Cresta group, the Marang features a number of attractive thatched chalets built on stilts along the Tati River amongst the acacia trees and mown lawns. There are also chalets, executive rooms and a cottage, all of which have air conditioning and TV. In addition, there are eight budget rooms that lack these facilities, and a campsite (see *Campsites*, below). Further facilities include an à la carte restaurant and swimming pool, as well as the casino, which is open 11.00 till late (though for 'casino' read 'amusement arcade'). Outside, there is secure parking.
Rates: single P435, double 502.70. Breakfast P43.45 per person.

Tati River Lodge (32 rooms) P Bag F333, Francistown; tel: 240 6000; fax: 240 6080; email: trl@info.bw; web: www.info.bw/~trl
This new hotel right on the Tati River features both rondavels and 'executive rooms', respectively aimed at tourists and business travellers, and there are also studios with a small kitchenette that are ideal for a family of four. Each room is comfortably appointed with satellite TV, telephone, and tea- and coffee-making facilities. Breakfast is served in the restaurant, which is also open for buffet lunch and à la carte dinner. There is even an English-style pub. The landscaped grounds have a swimming pool, and nearby is the lodge's campsite, complete with water and electricity hook-ups.
Rates: single P358.50, double P431.00, including breakfast. Camping P27.50 per person.

Modumela Lodge (9 chalets) PO Box 10324, Tatitown, Francistown; tel: 71 302791 or 72 111407; fax: 214644 or 71591178; mobile: 71 635830; email: modumela@botsnet.bw
Though about an hour's drive from Francistown, this friendly lodge, run by Dale and Debbie Green, is a useful stop if you're driving to/from Zimbabwe, and has some attractions in its own right. Hence I've included a mention of it here.

To reach Modumela, take the road to Zimbabwe from Francistown for about 65km until just after the village of Tshesebe. About 5km after this you'll find a signpost to the right (east) for the village of Batale. The lodge is also signposted here (big sign), so take this right turning and follow the road for 7km to reach the lodge.

Each of the chalets here sleeps two adults and two children, and inside you'll find tea/coffee-making facilities and a cooling overhead fan. All have an en-suite bathroom with a shower, toilet and washbasin – except the honeymoon chalet, which also has a bath. There's a bar and small restaurant here, which serves a full breakfast for P46, lunch for P72 and a three-course dinner for P85.

If you have time to stop then there are quite a few activities possible in the vicinity, including rock climbing, abseiling and horse-riding trips. Game is being gradually reintroduced onto the farm, which now boasts impala, kudu, black-backed jackal, civet, steenbok, duiker, zebra, reedbuck, spring hare, scrubhare, wildebeest, eland and hartebeest – as well as ostrich and warthog which are particularly relaxed with visitors. There's also a number of cultural excursions with local villages which can also introduce you to local potters, carpenters and other craftsmen; these are best arranged in advance.
Rates: P330 per chalet. Open all year.

Town Lodge (10 rooms) Plot 1450/52, Leeba St, Minestone, PO Box 50, Francistown; tel: 241 5747/241 8802/3/4; fax: 241 8805; email: jog@info.bw. The en-suite rooms of this small lodge are well equipped with air conditioning, satellite TV, telephone and facilities for making tea or coffee. Lunch and dinner are also available.
Rates: single P198, double P258.50. Breakfast P25 per person.

Grand Lodge (15 rooms) Matsiloje Rd, PO Box 713, Francistown; tel: 241 2300; fax: 241 2309. In the town centre, opposite the railway station, the Grand is cheap but a really very

basic old town hotel. Depending on which rooms you get, it can be a bit dark and run down, and sometimes they don't even serve food.
Rates: single P161, double P187.

YMCA Teema Drive Tel: 241 3046. Opposite the Nyangabgwe Hospital, the YMCA offers standard dormitory accommodation. It's fairly clean but not spacious.
Rates: P95 for a dorm bed.

Satellite Guesthouse Tel: 241 4665; fax: 240 2115. This small guesthouse is clearly signposted in Satellite Town, a few kilometres beyond the Cresta Thapama roundabout. There's secure parking next to the rooms which are arranged around a courtyard. It's clean and comfortable, but don't expect any inspired touches of original design. Use the fax for bookings if nobody answers the phone!
Rates: single P200, double P260.

Camping
Woodlands 4x4 Stop (4 chalets, 8 campsites) PO Box 11193, Tatitown, Francistown; tel: 244 0131/2, cell: 71302906/71302466; fax; 241 6927; email: riverbend@botsnet.bw; web: www.woodlandscamping.com
This new campsite, with swimming pool, grassy sites, electrical points, toilet blocks and barbecue facilities, is right on the river, about 10km north of the town. To get there, take the Nata road. Exactly 1.8km after passing the Orapa turn-off, turn right at the large signboard and follow the notices to the site. As an alternative to camping, visitors may stay at one of four two-bed chalets (no catering facilities). There are plenty of opportunities for birdwatching along the river, and several animals may also be seen on one of the river walks.
Rates: chalets P85 per person, camping P40 per person. Children under 12 half price.

Marang Motel Campsite PO Box 807, Francistown; tel: 241 3991; fax: 241 2130; email: marang@info.bw
The 'in place' for most travellers, and at only P27.50 per person, inclusive of use of the swimming pool, it's not hard to see why. The campsite has a beautiful setting near the banks of the Tati River and has a clean shower/toilet block with hot water. This is a good place to meet other travellers and also to look for lifts.

In addition, the Tati River Lodge has facilities for camping. For details, see above.

WHERE TO EAT
There are a number of take-aways in the shopping mall and around the bus station which are reasonable and fairly cheap. Alternatively, there are always women selling shadza (maize porridge) and meat, and cooked maize cobs, around the vegetable market during the day.

If you're looking for somewhere more Western, **Barbara's Bistro** at the Sport Club (tel: 241 3737) is generally agreed to be the town's best restaurant. Its à la carte menu majors in continental cuisine, and it's open Mon–Sat 12.00–14.00 and 19.00–01.00. Alternatively, try **Diggers Pub & Grill** in the Village Mall (tel: 241 6055), or the **Silver Spur** (tel: 241 4290). Otherwise, the **Marang** and **Thapama** hotels and **Tati River Lodge** all have their own restaurants.

For lighter fare, try the **Calabash Coffee Shop** on the corner of Baines and St Patrick (tel: 240 3360), which is open Mon–Fri 07.00–17.00 and Saturday 07.00–14.00, or **Tina's Coffee Shop** on Blue Jacket Street (tel: 241 0472). There's also the Espresso Café (tel: 221495) which is open from 08.00 to 18.00 during the week, and until 14.00 at weekends. If you're heading out of town for the day, **Sycamore Coffee House** (tel: 241 4417) will provide packed lunches. There are even some fast-food outlets, including **Nando's** and **Kentucky Fried Chicken**.

GETTING ORGANISED

Francistown is pretty compact, with most hotels, restaurants and shopping facilities along or just off the oddly named Blue Jacket Street, which runs more or less north–south, parallel to the railway. The street acquired its name from prospector Sam Andersen – or, more specifically, in memory of his jacket! The town has a large hospital, a library, and various shopping malls and markets.

There are branches of the main banks, each with an ATM, on Blue Jacket Street:

Barclays Plot 6142, Blue Jacket St, PO Box 36, Francistown; tel: 241 3439
First National Bank of Botswana Plot 847, Blue Jacket St, P Bag F35, Francistown; tel: 241 3831/2
National Development Bank Tel: 241 2775
Stanbic Bank Botswana Ltd Francistown Mall; tel: 241 0455
Standard Chartered Plot 687/88 Blue Jacket St, PO Box 45 Francistown; tel: 213452

There is an internet café, Ibis Internet (tel: 241 2520), at the Village Mall.

Tourist information is available from the tourist centre at the Supa-Ngwao Museum (tel: 240 3088).

Health

Francistown has a large **hospital** on the left of the airport road leading out of town, and a clinic, the Pana Medical Consultation Clinic (tel: 241 5351) on Monind Street. For **pharmacies**, try Pharma North at Ntote House, Blue Jacket Street (tel: 241 0877/881), or the Phodisong Pharmacy which has branches in both Francistown Mall (tel: 241 3943) and the Millennium Centre (tel: 241 6624).

Tour operators

A handful of tour operators are based in Francistown:

Africa under Canvas PO Box 1241, Francistown; tel: 7130 3411; email: african@info.bw, landa@mweb.co.zw; web: www.africaundercanvas.com. Despite the Francistown address, they operate out of Maun, with luxury safaris into all national parks.
John Chase Safaris PO Box 444, Francistown; tel: 241 3280, mobile: 7130 2400/1; email: johnchase@info.bw
Uncharted Africa Safari Co PO Box 173, Francistown; tel: 241 2277; fax: 241 3458; email: office@unchartedafrica.co.bw; web: www.unchartedafrica.co.bw

SHOPPING

Those looking for **vehicles parts and repairs** can start with the 4X4 Service Centre in the industrial area (tel: 241 3008, cell: 7120 2987; after hours tel: 241 4225), who claim to stock spares for all makes of 2WD and 4WD vehicles, and also offer a 24-hour vehicles rescue and repair service. Southern Motors (tel: 241 4238; fax: 241 4070), also in the industrial area, stocks a wide range of spares and accessories. If your vehicle has developed electrical problems, try either Southern Motors or Diesel-Electric (tel: 241 3980). Fuel stations are to be found throughout the town. **Safari equipment** may be obtained from PAAM (tel: 241 6936).

Fairway's Supermarket in the centre of town carries a good range of most general foods, whilst more specialist camping and dried foods can be obtained in the **Mall Shopping Centre**. There's also a fruit and vegetable market on Baines Avenue up from the railway station.

There's one **craft shop** – Afri-Kraft (tel: 241 0177) with a fair selection of goods across the railway line from the Tati Hotel. However, if you're planning on visiting Maun or Ghanzi, save your money for the excellent craft markets there instead.

MMILILI'S DAY
Phil Deutschle

Mmilili wakes at 05.30 as his sister, Opha, shouts, 'Mmilili, muka! get up!' He shares two blankets on the mud floor with his brother, Knowledge. He pulls on an old shirt and shorts. Then, shivering, he walks out of the compound into the surrounding bush that serves as the family toilet.

Back in the kitchen, he sits by the fire and waits for the water to heat up for washing himself. He carries the basin back to the children's hut and washes his hands and face. He empties the basin into the hedge and trades it in at the kitchen for a cold piece of yesterday's steam bread. Finally, he gets dressed in his blue and grey school uniform and starts off on his three-mile jaunt to school. Before long, he stops to wrench a branch from a thorn-bush. Students are required to bring a stick of firewood to school each day. The bell is rung at seven o'clock. First the classrooms have to be cleaned. Mmilili starts moving the desks to the back, so that the girls can sweep. He knows that he can't get into trouble with the teachers if he's moving desks. At assembly, after a song and a prayer, all the students not wearing full school uniform are told to remain behind. The offenders are going to be beaten.

His class's first subject is Setswana, the national language. Mmilili hates Setswana. The teacher calls them names if they can't answer her questions. And no matter how hard you work on an assignment it always comes back with a bad mark on it. Next comes agriculture, his favourite subject. The teacher, who is from Swaziland, never beats them and they sometimes have a lot of fun in the garden.

Break is over before it really begins. Coming all the way from the garden, they are among the last in line to get their bowl of sweetened milk tea and one thick slice of bread. The last four periods are not so busy. The class still has no social studies teacher, whilst in English they are told to go away and

ENTERTAINMENT AND NIGHTLIFE

Francistown may not have a lot to offer in the way of entertainment, but there is a cinema and a jazz club, the New Yorker. Both the Marangu and the Thapama hotels have bars and casinos.

WHAT TO SEE AND DO

Francistown's **Supa-gwao Museum** (tel: 240 3088) doubles as an information centre. It also features examples of modern art, including sculptures in the surrounding grounds.

Just outside of town is Botswana's only **animal orphanage**, owned by the Uncharted Safari Company. Currently based at Birds and Game Farm, Plot 8, Inchwe, it was started several years ago by Nicky Bousfield with the aim of rehabilitating the animals in order to be able to release them back into the wild. Over the years, elephants, cheetah, leopard, crocodiles, snakes and a variety of rare birds and smaller mammals have found refuge here, but the orphanage is now hoping to raise the money to move to community land in the hills outside Francistown. If the plan is successful, the animals would be cared for in large areas of natural bush, and the project would incorporate a residential educational centre so that children could learn about conservation, ecology, history and geology. The orphanage is open to visitors every day from 10.00 to 13.00 and 14.00 to 16.00. Admission is P5 for adults and P3 for children.

'study hard'. The maths teacher unexpectedly collects the assignment, which Mmilili luckily did during the time they were supposed to have had social studies.

Lunch is the highpoint. Tuesday's fare is *samp* (boiled maize kernels) and soup. Mmilili eats with his fingers, washes his bowl and then puts it away in the locker that he shares with Simisani.

He's sitting and rocking on the edge of the open locker door, when the teacher comes in and shouts, 'Is that a chair?' Mmilili jumps up scared, not knowing what to do. The teacher looks down at Mmilili. 'Do you have a chair at home?'

'Yes,' answers Mmilili in a whisper.

'You have a chair?'

'No,' stutters Mmilili, too flustered to think. Everyone is looking at him and he just wants to cry. The teacher shakes his head and walks away.

Throughout afternoon studies, Mmilili tries to do his homework, but he is still upset. The schoolwork is hard enough as it is, being all in English or Setswana. He has never seen a single book in his own language, Kalanga.

Sports-time is spent kicking a ball around with the other boys who are not on the soccer team. Supper is a bowl of soft porridge. Evening studies gives him a chance to finally do his work, but he is already dreading the long, dark walk home. The lights of the school are nice, even magic. The school also has water, right in the tap, and bread every day, toilets, and you have your own chair. Not like home.

At 19.30 the final bell is rung. Mmilili, Jabulani, Filbert, Moses and Simisani start the trek to their homes. They talk loudly to chase away the fear of the dark. For the last section, Mmilili has to walk alone.

Opha has saved some *shadza* (maize porridge) for him. Then he crawls under the blankets with Knowledge and quickly shivers himself to sleep.

Visitors should tel: 241 2277 for directions, or ask almost anyone how to get to 'Birds and Game'.

Birdwatching trips can be arranged with Mike West of Woodlands 4X4 Campsite (tel: 241 4708/4713; cell: 7130 2906; email: riverbend@botsnet.bw); you may be lucky enough to see the migrant woodland kingfisher, which nests here in the summer. And if you're at the campsite, you'll find the **Selolwe Ruins**, designated a national monument, within walking distance.

458

Livingstone

I've included a chapter here on Livingstone and Victoria Falls as many visitors to northern Botswana will either start or end their trips here. The Victoria Falls are a magnificent sight, and few can resist a couple of nights here in addition to time on safari.

Livingstone, in particular, is very popular with visitors to Botswana. Its riverside lodges are close to the Falls, and yet a perfect complement to Botswana's small camps. Zimbabwe's small town of Victoria Falls is also lovely, though its popularity has waned over the last few years due to the country's troubled politics. Given this, most visitors stay on the northern (Livingstone) side.

Many still venture across the border to see the waterfall from the Zimbabwean side for an afternoon. Both sides have different views, as they have different attractions for visitors. Just as it is worth seeing the two aspects of the Falls to appreciate the whole waterfall, if Zimbabwe's politics have settled down when you read this, then it's worth venturing south to the Zimbabwean town.

This chapter aims to give brief details of where to stay in and around Livingstone, what to do and how to get organised. For much more comprehensive details, see the latest edition of my *Zambia: The Bradt Travel Guide*.

BACKGROUND INFORMATION
History

We can be sure that the Falls were well known to the native peoples of southern Africa well before any European 'discovered' them. After the San/bushmen hunter-gatherers, the Tokaleya people inhabited the area, and it was probably they who christened the Falls 'Shongwe'. Later, the Ndebele knew the Falls as the 'aManza Thunqayo', and after that the Makololo referred to them as 'Mosi-oa-Tunya'.

However, their first written description comes to us from Dr David Livingstone, who approached them in November 1855 from the west – from Linyanti, along the Chobe and Zambezi rivers. Livingstone already knew of their existence from the locals, and wrote:

> I resolved on the following day to visit the falls of Victoria, called by the natives Mosioatunya, or more anciently Shongwe. Of these we had often heard since we came into the country: indeed one of the questions asked by Sebituane [the chief of the Makololo tribe] travelling was, 'Have you the smoke that sounds in your country?' They did not go near enough to examine them, but, viewing them with awe at a distance, said, in reference to the vapour and noise, 'Mosi oa tunya' (smoke does sound there). It was previously called Shongwe, the meaning of which I could not ascertain. The word for a 'pot' resembles this, and it may mean a seething caldron; but I am not certain of it.

Livingstone continues to describe the river above the Falls, its islands and their lush vegetation, before making his most famous comment about sightseeing angels, now abused and misquoted by those who write tourist brochures to the area:

> Some trees resemble the great spreading oak, others assume the character of our own elms and chestnuts; but no one can imagine the beauty of the view from anything witnessed in England. It had never been seen before by European eyes; but scenes so lovely must have been gazed upon by angels in their flight. The only want felt is that of mountains in the background. The falls are bounded on three sides by ridges 300 or 400 feet in height, which are covered in forest, with the red soil appearing amongst the trees. When about half a mile from the falls, I left the canoe by which we had come down this far, and embarked in a lighter one, with men well acquainted with the rapids, who, by passing down the centre of the stream in the eddies and still places caused by many jutting rocks, brought me to an island situated in the middle of the river, on the edge of the lip over which the water rolls.
>
> from the autobiographical *Journeys in Southern Africa*

Those who bemoan the area's emphasis on tourism should note that there must have been sightseeing boat trips ever since David Livingstone came this way.

Being the most eastern point reachable by boat from the Chobe or Upper Zambezi rivers, the area of the Falls was a natural place for European settlement. Soon more traders, hunters and missionaries came into the area, and by the late 1800s a small European settlement had formed around a ferry crossing called the Old Drift, about 10km upstream from the Falls. However, this was built on low-lying marshy ground near the river, buzzing with mosquitoes, so malaria took many lives.

By 1905 the spectacular Victoria Falls bridge had been completed, linking the copper deposits of the Copperbelt and the coal deposits at Wankie (now Hwange) with a railway line. This, and the malaria, encouraged the settlers to transfer to a site on higher ground, next to the railway line at a place called Constitution Hill. It became the centre of present-day Livingstone, and many of its original buildings are still standing. A small cemetery, the poignant remains of Old Drift, can still be seen on the northern bank of the Zambezi within the Mosi-oa-Tunya National Park.

In 1911 Livingstone became the capital of Northern Rhodesia (now Zambia), which it remained until 1935, when the administration was transferred to Lusaka.

Geology

The Falls are, geologically speaking, probably a very recent formation. About a million years ago, the Zambezi's course is thought to have been down a wide valley over a plateau dating from the karoo period, until it met the Middle Zambezi rift – where the Matetsi River mouth is now.

Here it fell about 250m over an escarpment. However, that fast-falling water would have eroded the lip of the waterfall and gouged out a deeper channel within the basalt rock of the escarpment plateau – and so the original falls steadily retreated upstream. These channels tended to follow some existing fissure – a crack or weakness, formed when the lava first cooled at the end of the karoo period. At around the Batoka Gorge these fissures naturally run east–west in the rock, parallel to the course of the valley.

By around the Middle Pleistocene period, between 35,000 and 40,000 years ago, this process had formed the Batoka Gorge, carving it out to within about 90km of the present falls.

However, as water eroded away the lip of the falls, its valley gradually turned north, until it was almost at right-angles to the basalt fault lines which run east–west. Then the water began to erode the fissures and turn them into walls of

Lusaka

Livingstone Airport

GREAT NORTH ROAD

LUSAKA NORTH ROAD

see pages 464–5

LIBALA DRIVE

HILLCREST

NORTH END

MARAMBA

LIVINGSTONE

MALOTA

DAMBWA NORTH

Sesheke & West

NAKATINDI ROAD

FALLSVIEW

LIBUYU

KASHITU

DAMBWA

LINDA

Pilgrim's Tea Room

Mosi-oa-Tunya National Park

Maramba

Old Drift Cemetery

Tunya Lodge

Nyala Lodge

Game Park gate

Livingstone Overnight

The Boat Club
The Waterfront

Zambezi

Maramba Cultural Centre

Maramba River Lodge

Siloka Island

Songwe Point, Taita Falcon Lodge

0 — 1km
0 — 1 mile

ZIMBABWE

Kingdom Hotel

Curios

Zambezi Sun & Royal Livingstone

local airstrip

Victoria Falls Hotel

Bungee-jumping from bridge

Mosi-oa-Tunya National Park

N

Bradt

Zambezi

Songwe

Hwange, Bulawayo

LIVINGSTONE & VICTORIA FALLS

rock stretching across the valley, perpendicular to it, over which gushed broad curtains of water.

Once such a wall had formed, the water would wear down the rock until it found a fault line behind the wall, along which the water would erode and cause the rock subsequently to collapse. Thus the new fault line would become the wall of the new falls, behind the old one. This process resulted in the eight gorges that now form the river's slalom course after it has passed over the present Falls. Each gorge was once a great waterfall.

Today, on the eastern side of the Devil's Cataract, you can see this pattern starting again. The water is eroding away the rock of another fault line, behind the line of the present falls, which geologists expect will form a new waterfall a few thousand years from now.

PRACTICAL INFORMATION
Orientation
Livingstone town itself is compact, and surrounded by several small township suburbs just a few kilometres from its centre. Navigation is easy, even without a map, though signposts are often missing.

Livingstone's main street is the important Mosi-oa-Tunya Road. Sections of this are lined with classic colonial buildings – corrugated iron roofs and wide wooden verandas. Drive north on the main street out of the city, and it becomes Lusaka Road leading to the capital.

Head south for about 10km and you reach the Zambezi River and Victoria Falls themselves and the border post to cross into Zimbabwe via the Victoria Falls Bridge. On the Zambian side, you'll find a small museum and a well-stocked curio market selling locally produced souvenirs.

Travel west from town on Nakatindi/Kazungula Road and you soon find yourself parallel to the Zambezi, following its north bank upstream towards Kazungula and the ferry to Botswana. Signposts point left, to small, exclusive lodges, perched at picturesque spots on the river's bank.

Getting there and away
By *air*
Livingstone's international airport is just 5km northwest of the town centre on Libala Drive. Thanks to the new Sun hotel developments, it has recently been refurbished and now has pleasant waiting rooms, bar and cafeteria, plus curio shops for last-minute purchases.

It is served by two domestic carriers, Zambian Skyways (formerly Eastern Air) and Zambian Airways (formerly Roan Air), who offer scheduled flights around Zambia. Flights to Lusaka cost about US$160 one way. There are also several new international airlines, including Nationwide, linking Livingstone with Jo'burg and Harare. However, their timetables are very changeable.

The main charter companies with bases in Livingstone are Proflight and Del Air, who offer flight charters to/from Livingstone and around the region. However, for two or three people it's cost-effective to privately charter pilot Ben Parker and his four-seater plane, which are based out of Tongabezi (see page 476 for contact details). Ben flies between Livingstone and most destinations in northern Botswana (or indeed the region), costing only a little more than normal transfers. However, it's a lot more fun as Ben can easily include a flight of angels over the Falls, or even some low-level 'game-spotting' flying, as part of your transfer.

If you are trying to fly into the Falls area, then landing at Livingstone Airport is just as convenient as the Victoria Falls airport on the Zimbabwean side. Remember

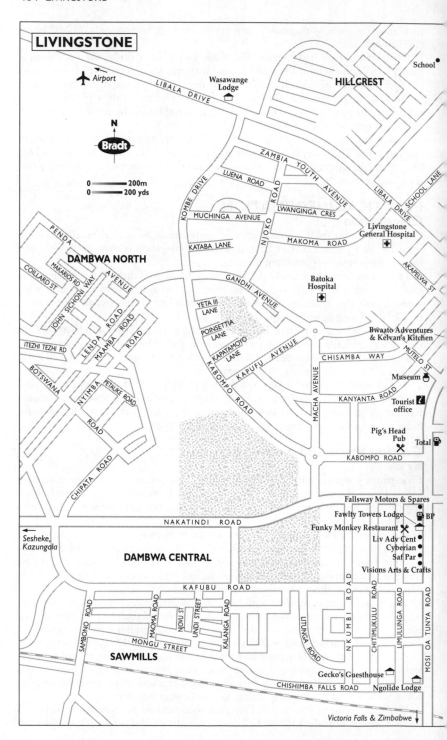

LIVINGSTONE

✈ Airport

LIBALA DRIVE

Wasawange Lodge

HILLCREST

School

N

Bradt

0 ————— 200m
0 ————— 200 yds

ZAMBIA YOUTH AVENUE

LIBALA DRIVE

SCHOOL LANE

KOMBE DRIVE

LUENA ROAD

NJOKO ROAD

LWANGINGA CRES

MUCHINGA AVENUE

MAKOMA ROAD

Livingstone General Hospital ✚

AKAPELWA ST

DAMBWA NORTH

PENDA AVENUE

MAKARIOS RD

COILLARD ST

JOHN SICHONI WAY

KATABA LANE

GANDHI AVENUE

Batoka Hospital ✚

ITEZHI TEZHI RD

LENDA ROAD

MAAMBA ROAD

YETA III LANE

POINSETTIA LANE

KAPATAMOYO LANE

KABOMPO ROAD

KAPUFU AVENUE

Bwaato Adventures & Kelvan's Kitchen

MUTELO ST

CHISAMBA WAY

Museum ☕

BOTSWANA ROAD

NYIMBA ROAD

PETAUKE ROAD

MACHA AVENUE

KANYANTA ROAD

Tourist office ℹ

CHIPATA ROAD

Pig's Head Pub ✗

Total ⛽

KABOMPO ROAD

Fallsway Motors & Spares

NAKATINDI ROAD

Fawlty Towers Lodge 🏨 BP

Funky Monkey Restaurant ✗

Liv Adv Cent ●
Cyberian ●
Saf Par ●

←
Sesheke, Kazungula

DAMBWA CENTRAL

Visions Arts & Crafts

KAFUBU ROAD

NKUMBI ROAD

CHITIMUKULU ROAD

LIMULUNGA ROAD

MOSI OA TUNYA ROAD

SAMBONO ROAD

MAOMA ROAD

NJOVU ST

UNDI STREET

KALANGA ROAD

LITUNGA ROAD

MONGU STREET

SAWMILLS

Gecko's Guesthouse 🏠

CHISHIMBA FALLS ROAD

Ngolide Lodge 🏠

Victoria Falls & Zimbabwe ↓

that if you're leaving Livingstone then you must pay airport departure taxes locally of US$20/5 per person for international/domestic departures.

By bus

The main terminus for local buses is Akapelwa Street, just on Mosi-oa-Tunya Road, opposite Barclay's Bank. (Some may also leave from around the post office, including the popular post bus to Lusaka.) Here a range of buses gather in the early morning. Most head towards Lusaka, though one or two will go west to Sesheke. Expect the first to leave around 06.30, and the last around 11.00, depending upon demand. A seat to Lusaka on a large bus costs around Kw14,000, on a small minibus around Kw17,000. If you are backpacking, then expect the attentions of bus touts.

There is a EuroAfrica coach service that goes from Livingstone to Lusaka and onwards to Kitwe or Ndola. It costs around US$6 per leg and tickets can be bought (in advance) at Bwaato Adventure's office. It normally leaves about 07.00–07.30, but check when you book.

By train

The railway station (reservations: tel: 03 321001 ext 336) is well signposted and is about 1km south of the centre on the way to the Falls, on the eastern side of the Mosi-oa-Tunya Road.

The Zambezi Express train is scheduled to go from Livingstone to Lusaka on Tuesdays, Thursdays, and Saturdays at 18.30, arriving the next morning around 07.00. Bookings can only be made on the day of departure at the railway station, and can only be confirmed by payment – thus you must go in person. Economy class is US$5, first class US$10 and two- or four-berth first-class sleeper compartments are US$14 per person. There is an onward train service up to the Copperbelt or down to Johannesburg from Lusaka.

If you are heading south to Bulawayo or Johannesburg, then it would be best to go across the border (walk or taxi) to Victoria Falls, from where there is an excellent overnight train to Bulawayo. (This makes much more sense than a long diversion via Lusaka.) There are no longer any train services between Livingstone and Victoria Falls.

Steam train

For those with more flexible budgets, Train de Luxe offers the 'Zambezi Express Steam Train' service between Victoria Falls and Hwange, in both directions three times weekly. Departure times allow for morning and afternoon game drives at Hwange. Contact: Railway Safaris, PO Box 2536, Bulawayo; tel/fax: (2639) 75575/64466; email: res@traindeluxe .co.zw.

Alternatively, the Victoria Falls Safari Express runs day-trips on a luxury steam train. These leave Victoria Falls heading north, stop on the bridge over the border for lunch (or a sundowner, depending on the time) and then head back to Victoria Falls. Unfortunately, you can't join the train in Zambia. They have an office in Victoria Falls station; tel: (26313) 4682 or email: fallsexp@mail.pci.co.zw.

Driving west

If you have a vehicle and intend to head west, into Namibia's Caprivi Strip, Botswana, or Western Zambia, then Nakatindi Road continues past the lodges by the river and, after about 60km, to Kazungula – where Namibia, Botswana, Zimbabwe and Zambia all meet at a notional point. Here you can continue northwest, within Zambia to Sesheke, or take the ferry across the Zambezi into Botswana, near Kasane. The road from Kazungula to Sesheke is about 130km, and has been in a very bad state of repair for years, with large, frequent potholes making the drive very slow and uncomfortable.

As an aside, Kazungula is said to take its name from the tree known locally as the Muzungula tree (aka sausage tree, *Kigelia africana*) on which David Livingstone is reported to have carved his name when he passed.

Important note on visas

In recent years both Zambia and Zimbabwe have started to change their rules on visas, requiring more payments for crossing the borders. Zambia's visas proved the major problem, seeming excessive to the operators in the Falls area, who relied for their livelihood on a free-flow of people across the border. (Visitors may stay on one side, but would want to take part in activities on both sides.)

Now a deal has been reached whereby you can legally pop across the border, from Zimbabwe to Zambia, to do an activity or even to stay, without buying a visa – provided that the operator you are going to gives at least 24 hours' notice to the immigration authorities. They basically just need to put your name on a list down at the border post, and you pass through free.

So remember to book your Zambian accommodation or activity in advance by a few days, and you generally won't need to pay.

Zambian operators with a base in Livingstone

By the time you read this, this list won't be exhaustive – new operators are starting up all the time. However, I hope that it proves a useful reference for you to work out who does what. Note that virtually all the operators will book virtually anything (as they receive a commission). Here I've tried to list companies that actually run the specified activities, and don't merely act as booking agents:

Abseil Africa PO Box 61023, Livingstone; tel: 03 323454; email: abseil@outpost.co.zm. Located in the Livingstone Adventure Centre, they are the first company to operate abseiling, high-wire trips, and a cable slide out over the gorges.

African Horizons (see also Fawlty Towers) Tel/fax: 03 323432; email: ahorizon@zamnet.zm or Zimbabwe cell: 011 708 184. Their offices are in Fawlty Towers, and they run the Botswana Bus.

Bundu Adventures PO Box 60773, Livingstone; tel: 03 324407; fax: 324406; email: zambezi@zamnet.zm. Their main office and headquarters is off Mosi-oa-Tunya Road, on the Industrial Road, near the railway crossing – look for the sign. They are one of Zambia's larger companies which operate rafting and canoeing trips. Many of their rafting guides have a good level of experience.

Bwaato Adventures PO Box 60672, Livingstone; tel: 03 324227; fax: 321490 Several offices, one in Livingstone's town centre in the post office complex, another in the New Fairmount Hotel, and a third upstairs in Soper's Arcade, in Victoria Falls. Bwaato operates the full range of river cruises – breakfast, barbecue lunch, sunset booze and dinner – from their jetty near the Boat Club in Livingstone. They also conduct day tours through the MOT National Park and excursions to Chobe. Most useful are the Euro-Africa coaches which depart daily for Lusaka, at about 07.30–08.00. These are modern, fast coaches that can be booked and paid for in advance, and run on time. They take about six hours to arrive in Lusaka, where their office is behind Findeco House. One-way costs about US$15.

Chundukwa Adventure Trails PO Box 61160; tel: 03 324006; fax: 324006; tlx: ZA 24043. Owned and run by Doug Evans, this has its base at Chundukwa River Camp. Doug is an experienced old Africa hand, with professional hunting and guiding licences in both Zambia and Zimbabwe: just the kind of chap to have on your side when the going gets tough. He organises and guides safaris from horseback, canoe and foot. When canoeing he concentrates on two- or three-day trips (covering about 90km) on the upper Zambezi, usually ending at Chundukwa. Horse-riding is usually just one or two days in the region around Chundukwa, though longer trails are possible for experienced riders.

Del Air/Batoka Sky Ltd Maramba Aerodome, off Sichango Road, PO Box 60971, Livingstone; tel/fax: 03 320058; email: reservations@batokasky.co.za. Del Air is signposted from the Mosi-oa-Tunya Road (turn at Tunya Lodge) and operates flights over the Falls in microlights, helicopters and fixed-wing aircraft. Also offers flight charters, air transfers, and is starting tandem parachuting.

Kalai Safaris Beside Livingstone Adventure Centre, 215 Mosi-oa-Tunya Road, PO Box 61075, Livingstone; tel: 03 321103; email: safaris@kalai.co.zw or PO Box 112, Victoria Falls. Tel: (26313) 5842; fax: 5843. Operates a variety of full- and half-day trips in Livingstone and Victoria Falls including village tours, game parks and scenic tours. Also runs transfers and offers extended trips to Zimbabwe's Hwange National Park.

Livingstone Safaris PO Box 60007; tel/fax: 03 322267; email: gecko@zamnet.zm. Run by Dave Lewis, Livingstone Safaris is based at Gecko's Guesthouse on Limulunga Road. Dave runs three-hour tours of the Mosi-oa-Tunya National Park or the Mokuni Village and Zambian side of the Falls. Both cost US$25 per person, minimum of two people. He will also run much longer impromptu trips anywhere else in Zambia (in the dry season), on request for small groups of people. He's been in Zambia for several years and spent ten months in the Bangweulu Wetlands area.

Makora Quest Office in the Livingstone Adventure Centre, PO Box 60420, Livingstone; tel: 03 324253/321679; fax: 302732; email: quest@zamnet.zm. Run by Colin Lowe, Makora Quest was started in 1985 and has a base just downstream from Kubu Cabins. He was the first canoe operator on the Upper Zambezi, and still runs by far the best guided half- and full-day canoe trips there. Compare Colin's knowledge and experience with that of some of the newer guides; the difference is stark. Makora Quest also conducts excellent tours of the MOT National Park and the local area, as well as organising reliable transfers.

Raft Extreme PO Box 61105, Livingstone; tel: 03 324024; tel/fax: 322370; email: grotto@zamnet.zm. Run from a base at Grubby's Grotto (see page 470), Raft Extreme caters almost exclusively for white-water rafting groups on overland trucks, most of whom stay at the Grotto. Only if there's a truck group already scheduled will they take bookings from individuals. They also operate canoe trips, and have a combination trip including full breakfast, followed by a half-day canoe trip to the MOT National Park, a game drive and a booze cruise with barbecue dinner and free drinks (cost US$95 per person).

Serious Fun office is in the Livingstone Adventure Centre, 216 Mosi-oa-Tunya Rd. Tel: 03 323912; fax: 321850; Zimbabwe cell: 011 210 422; email: tloxton@zamnet.zm This company pioneered river-boarding trips on the Zambezi, and that's what they do. For a full day they will collect you at 08.30, go as far as rapid 13, and charge S$95. Half-day trips run from 06.00 to 13.30 and cost US$90.

Shungu Mufu Tours Office at Pilgrim's Tea Room, PO Box 60403, Livingstone; tel: 03 322692; (home) fax: 324094. Run by Cilla and Graham Young, Shungu Mufu are probably the best, and certainly the most established, operators of day trips on the Livingstone side. They run an excellent full-day trip encompassing the Falls, a local village, lunch and a game drive around the MOT National Park – costing around US$80 per person (US$50 for a half day). These tours have been run for years, and part of their beauty is that a small percentage of their cost is automatically paid to the Nakatindi village. Thus the villagers are happy to see strangers strolling around, accompanied by a local guide, and you will not encounter any begging or hassle.

Taonga Safaris Tel/fax: 03 324081. Run by Andrew Simpson, Taonga is based on the riverbank next to the boat club, on Sichanga Road (turn off Mosi-oa-Tunya Road at the Tunya Lodge). They offer breakfast, lunch and sunset cruises; game drives in the MOT

National Park; and canoeing on the Upper Zambezi using three-person Canadian-style canoes.

Wild Side Tours & Safaris Liso House (in Livingstone centre), tel: 03 323726; fax: 323765; email: wild@zamnet.zm or in Victoria Falls at PO Box CT 450, Victoria Falls. Zimbabwe cell: 011 211 103. This owner-operated company, run by Peter and Karin Kermer (who speak English, Dutch and German), offers a wide range of camping safaris to Zambian and regional national parks – all tailor-made to suit each client. They also operate the Okavango Mama bus which runs between Victoria Falls and Windhoek.

Where to stay
There is no lack of accommodation in Livingstone, or across the river in Victoria Falls. In both there's a very wide range of options from campsites and backpackers' hostels to guesthouses, hotels and luxury lodges. The choice is overwhelming, though knowing the options in advance will make finding good value much easier. The Zambian side of the Falls is quieter, but has many bush lodges with lovely situations on the Zambezi River, a short distance from town. Zimbabwe has very few equivalents. Most have a true 'bush' location, whilst being close enough to enjoy the attractions and activities of the Falls.

In town
In alphabetical order:

Asanti Guesthouse (6 rooms)
Signposted from the main Mosi-oa-Tunya Road, opposite Nakatindi Road, Asanti Guesthouse is actually at the intersection in the middle of Nyasa Road. It has six very basic rooms, linked by nicely painted (but rather dark and gloomy) corridors. Five share a couple of separate showers, bathrooms and toilets. The sixth has an en-suite shower and toilet, as well as a more secure lock on the door than the others. It is clean but its atmosphere was less than welcoming when the author last visited, despite the presence of two helpful staff. *Rates: Kw30,000 per en-suite room, Kw20,000 for the other. Breakfast not included.*

Chanter's Guesthouse (3 rooms) Lukulu Crescent, PO Box 60623; tel: 03 323412. (Manager tel: 323850)
Run by former Lusaka hotelier, Richard Chanter, this is more of a restaurant than a dedicated guesthouse. However, it has three guest rooms and plans to expand to a total of seven. It stands in a leafy residential area on the northern side of Livingstone, perhaps 2km from the centre. To reach it leave the centre on Mosi-oa-Tunya Road, towards Lusaka, and turn left on to Obote Avenue, just before the road bends to the left. Chanter's is on Lukulu Crescent, the fourth right turn. This is not named on some maps.

All three rooms have wooden parquet floors, twin beds, satellite TV (all showing the same station) and a bath with shower attachment in the tiled, en-suite bathroom. Two rooms have ceiling fans and one is air-conditioned. They're pleasant but unremarkable. Its public rooms are more stylish, the tables and chairs extending on to a patio and garden at the back. Meals are served all day at this popular local dining spot, and the food is excellent. *Rates: US$40 per room per night, including basic continental breakfast. A la carte options for breakfast are available, but cost extra.*

Fawlty Towers Lodge & International Backpackers 216 Mosi-oa-Tunya Rd, Livingstone; tel/fax: 03 323432; email: ahorizon@zamnet.zm
Located on the Mosi-oa-Tunya Road, just south of the turn-off to Nakatindi/Kazungula Road, you can't miss this popular international backpackers' place. Look for the colourful wrought-iron burglar bars shaped like African faces. Enter through the large gates covered by straw mats, and you come to the lively bar, which has a pool table, comfortable sitting areas... and also serves as reception.

Upstairs, in the main building, are four dorms, each sleeping six, and one separate double room. The rooms are basic, but do have colourful curtains and (a very welcome rarity) air conditioning. There are two comfortable lounges with a TV/video each, and a kitchen, a large dining room, toilets and showers.

Behind this you'll find a spacious private garden area with an inviting swimming pool surrounded by lawns. Campers here on the lawns have toilets and showers, all clean with hot and cold running water. Also in the garden area is a bungalow housing two double rooms and a dorm (which sleeps six). This has a communal lounge, two showers and toilets, and a shared kitchen (all accessories provided). Everything is neat and clean and showers have both hot and cold running water. There are plans to build a further nine (en-suite) chalets in this garden area.

Bed linen and mosquito nets are provided free of charge, as is unlimited coffee and tea. Meals are available at Hippo's restaurant, just at the back of the garden. There is also a comprehensive workshop in the back of the garden, where you can service your vehicle, if necessary. Phone, fax and internet service are also available here, and you can rent a mountain bike for US$8 per day, or US$5 for a half-day.

If you're backpacking without your own transport, then Fawlty Towers is clean, well run and tremendously convenient for the centre of Livingstone. Vibrant colours and ethnic touches help to give it fun atmosphere and it runs daily transfers to and from Victoria Falls.

Rates: US$10 per person for the bungalows, US$6 for a dorm bed. Camping is US$3 per person. At 24 hours' notice, the 'Backpacker's Special' transfers you from the Falls, gives you a dorm bed for the night, a drink in the bar and a meal at the Funky Monkey – all for US$10.

Gecko's Guesthouse PO Box 60007; tel/fax: 03 322267; email: gecko@ zamnet.zm
Run by Dave Lewis, and the base for Livingstone Safaris, Gecko's is on the south side of Livingstone, on Limulunga Road. Travelling from Livingstone to the Falls, passing the railways station on your left, take a right turn beside Ngolide Lodge and then first right again. Gecko's is then on the left, perhaps 10 minutes' walk from the centre. Recognise it by its green gates and white walls with railings.

It's a lovely residential place to stay, a little quieter than the backpackers' places in the centre of town. It has one dorm sleeping six, which is airy and light. There are also four private rooms for two people each and endless space for camping. All guests share well-kept showers and toilets. There's a kitchen for cooking (implements provided), as well as a comfy lounge and lots of useful notice boards. A cook comes in daily and will prepare an evening meal for you, on request. Bedding and fans are provided free, as is tea and coffee. There's secure parking, a safe place to leave luggage and Dave's team will arrange any activities for you during your stay.

Rates: US$6 for a dorm bed, US$10 per person sharing a private room, US$12 for a single room. Camping is US$4 per tent

Grubby's Grotto Tel: 03 324024; tel/fax: 322370
Run by the indomitable Grubby, this is used only by overland trucks. It can be difficult to find, as most maps don't show the section of road it is on. The easiest way to get there is to turn north from Mosi-oa-Tunya Road for three blocks, and then turn right on to Maambo Way (some maps still show a very old name of Northway for this road). Follow this past Kashitu Street, and Grubby's is behind a large set of gates on the left, just before Obote Avenue.

Once inside you'll find a huge old colonial house, which is largely empty. The lawns around the house are used for camping; there's a large swimming pool and a bar at the front which opens on to the veranda. Food isn't normally provided, though with advance notice, a sheep on a spit can be arranged for large truck parties. The overland groups staying here form the basis of the trips for Raft Extreme.

Rates: US$3 per person camping, except the crew who get free rooms

Jolly Boys' Hostel PO Box 61088, Plot No. 559 Mokambo Way; tel/fax: 03 324299; email: jboys@zamnet.zm
Mokambo Way (or *Road*, on some maps) runs parallel to Mosi-oa-Tunya Road, on its eastern side, and Jolly Boys' is easy to find just south of Mutelo Street. This is a quintessential backpackers' lodge, run by the friendly Paul Quinn (with occasional help from his Mum, Val) in a large old residential building with a substantial garden.

It has a total of 24 beds, including two in a private room. All share toilets and showers. The dorms each have 6 beds (3 bunks) and are clean and well kept. A cook organises a simple set menu for breakfast and evening meals, costing Kw4,500 for English breakfast (Kw3,000 for the veggie option), and Kw5,000 for dinner. Friday nights are often sociable affairs with dinner outside from a barbecue. As usual, there's a bar at the back for drinks.

Jolly Boys' facilities are good, with a telephone, fax, pool, fridge, and kitchen. The atmosphere is relaxed and unpretentious, though sometimes too busy to allow much peace and quiet. Paul and the staff arrange activities for you in the Falls, and know the area well.
Rates: Dorm beds are US$6, camping US$3 per person per night

Living Inn PO Box 60853, 25 John Hunt Way; tel: 03 324203-5 or 324182/3; fax: 324206; tlx: 24380 SHAR ZA
This is a small, basic hostel with a central open-air quadrangle surrounded by two storeys of small rooms. Those upstairs are slightly different from those below. All have air conditioning, a fan and TV with Mnet. They are carpeted and each has a couple of easy chairs, a table, a double bed and a bathroom with a shower.

Downstairs the rooms have no TV and are tiled, not carpeted, but they do have both double and single beds. All have telephones, though none is direct dial (all rely on an operator). Living Inn seems to do well from hosting small workshops and conferences for Zambians, but few visitors stay here. If you are stuck for somewhere in the centre of town, then it might be worth trying.
Rates: Kw60,000 for a twin, Kw45,000 for a single.

Maramba River Lodge (5 chalets, tree platform and camping) PO Box 60957; tel: 03 324189; fax: 324266
Between the border post and Livingstone town, about 5km from each, lies this well established campsite just off Mosi-oa-Tunya Road. It's open and grassy with occasional thickets and trees. Near the river are a good swimming pool and a large bar that's open all day. Firewood is available.

Maramba River has five A-frame chalets for rent, all with ceiling fans and en-suite shower and toilet. Three of them take two people, and the other two will accommodate four (two single beds and two bunk beds). Windows are made of netting, with reed mats for blinds. Chalets feel new and basic, and probably get very hot in the summer, but they're very good value. Activities and excursions can be booked from the lodge.

The showers and toilets are clean and security guards patrol during the night. The site is within the Mosi-oa-Tunya National Park, so expect hippos, crocodiles, antelope and the occasional elephant to be around. It's a good campsite, and the chalets are very good value when compared with rooms in town or Victoria Falls.
Rates: US$25 for a 2-bed chalet. The larger chalets are US$35 for 3 people, US$45 for 4 people. US$5 per person camping.

New Fairmount Hotel (73 twin rooms) PO Box 60096; tel: 03 320723-8; fax: 321490; email: nfhc@zamnet.zm
In the centre of town, on Mosi-oa-Tunya Road between Mose and Mwela Streets, the New Fairmount is a large, old hotel that was once the town's focal point. Its rooms have en-suite facilities and air-conditioning and are clean, but all are ordinary and lacklustre. They are in need of updating and refurbishing. All are set around white-painted concrete courtyards at the back, where there's a good swimming pool and plenty of shady sitting places.

A desk for Bwaato Adventures occupies a corner of the New Fairmount's cavernous entrance lobby, while a small shopping arcade hides in a courtyard behind. There you'll discover a video library, a clothes shop, a hair salon and even an office where you can send emails (if you are a hotel resident!).

Rates: Kw103,400 for a twin, Kw84,100 for a single, including breakfast.

Ngolide Lodge (16 rooms) 110 Mosi-oa-Tunya Rd; tel: 03 321092; fax: 321113.
Opened in October '98, this is found on the south side of town, as Mosi-oa-Tunya Road leaves Livingstone for the Falls. It has a large thatch roof and small gardens in front. It's more of a hotel than a lodge, well-built and compact, yet somewhat lacking in atmosphere when I last visited.

Its rooms all lead off a central quadrangle. Each has a high thatched ceiling, polished floors, and twin or double beds with mossie nets. The stone bathrooms should keep you cool in the heat, aided by a free-standing fan. Rooms are very comfortable, and each has its own tea/coffee maker and satellite TV.

Rates: Kw90,000 for a twin/double, Kw80,000 for a single, including full breakfast

Nyala Lodge (10 tented chalets plus camping) PO Box 60774; tel: 03 322446; fax: 321248
email: nyala@zamnet.zm
Nyala Lodge is new and about 5km from town near the entrance to the Mosi-oa-Tunya National Park. From town, head toward the border and look for the well-signposted turn on the right (beside Tunya Lodge). Nyala is run by Moyra and Matthew Wayte and has ten nicely appointed, Meru-style tents under thatched roofs.

All have en-suite showers and toilets, and individual verandas. They are comfortably furnished complete with curtains, cement-tiled floors and nice linen. The roomy bathrooms are uniquely designed – the shower is surrounded by potted plants and rock walls, from where water cascades off a small ledge that serves as the shower tap.

The main lodge area is well designed and maintained, and has satellite TV, a lovely swimming pool, large bar/lounge and a restaurant. Breakfast, lunch, and dinner are served daily with lots of choices on the menu. Snacks are always available.

Nyala also has about ten acres for campers in designated sites with braai stands and separate ablutions. There is another swimming pool and bar under construction, which will cater solely for campers when complete.

Approaching Nyala it would be easy to be discouraged by the ominous electric fence surrounding the property. But once inside, Nyala has a bush-like feel with many indigenous trees, shrubs and small gardens, and it's very good value.

Rates: US$30 per person sharing, US$60 single, including breakfast. Camping US$5 per person.

Red Cross Hostel Mokambo Road; tel: 03 322473
Next to Jolly Boys', on its right, this basic hostel charges the same as Jolly Boys' for a bed. It is slightly run down but is convenient if next door is full.

Rates: Beds in the hostel dormitories are US$5 per night.

Tunya Lodge (32 twin rooms) PO Box 60700; tel/fax: 03 321511
Just south of Livingstone, on the way to Victoria Falls, this used to be called the Zambezi Motel. It's well located on the Mosi-oa-Tunya Road and is reasonably priced, but hasn't changed in years and is in serious need of refurbishment. Motel-style rooms are laid out in small blocks, with parking spaces dotted around. It does have a restaurant and a bar, but with so many new and interesting places to stay, this uninspiring motel with its pale green exterior and depressing rooms has little to recommend it.

Rates: Kw25,000 single, Kw40,000 double, including a light breakfast.

Thompson's Guest House (5 rooms) Lusaka Rd, Livingstone; tel: 03 320565/324100; fax: 322122
Thompson's is beside the main road as you approach Livingstone from Lusaka. It has three double rooms and two singles, a lounge where you can watch videos and self-catering

facilities. This basic guesthouse is away from the centre of town, but it is an inexpensive alternative for budget travellers if other places are full.
Rates: Double rooms are US$12, singles $8.

Wasawange Lodge (19 rooms) PO Box 60278; tel: 03 324066 or 324077/8; fax: 324067 Situated 3km along Libala Road – the way to the airport – just on the edge of town, Wasawange Lodge is a comfortable small hotel with a few ethnic touches. Its rooms are individual rondavels with en-suite facilities, air-conditioning, a fridge/mini-bar and satellite TV. The rooms are well cleaned and serviced, with high wooden ceilings, large mirrors and rugs to cover nice stone floors. Wasawange's popular with business visitors and has a good restaurant, a pool, sauna and jacuzzi, and even a small conference room. Because of its popularity and small size, you will often need to book in advance to get a room.
Rates: US$85 single, US$105 double, bed and breakfast.

Beside the Zambezi
For many years, property in Zambia's prime site closest to the Victoria Falls was the large, and gradually deteriorating, Mosi-O-Tunya Intercontinental Hotel. Even visitors from the relatively developed metropolis of Zimbabwe's Victoria Falls would stop for a drink beside the pool here at what was affectionately known as the 'Intercon'. Next door the Rainbow Lodge was even more dilapidated.

In the mid-1990s these ground to a halt and finally, in 1998, Sun International (the large South African hotel chain which owns much of Sun City) planned to take over both sites.

It took years to finalise the negotiations, but the hotels eventually opened in 2001. This is by far the largest hotel project that Livingstone, or Zambia, has ever seen – and judging by a swift first visit, they have made a first-class job of it. What's more, part of the deal was that Sun International would improve Livingstone's infrastructure, including a welcome renovation of its airport.

Including a brief comment on the Sun's properties, the lodges by the river, going from west (up-river) to east (below the Falls), are:

Jungle Junction (10 huts plus camping) Tel: 03 324127; email: jungle@zamnet.zm
Jungle Junction stands on a small, lush island on the Zambezi. Transfers to the island are arranged by their office in Livingstone, but the launch site is reached via the same turn-off as Zambezi Royal Chundu, about an hour's drive from Livingstone. Facilities here are rustic and basic, but the setting is splendid: palm trees and beaches. Jungle Junction has a well-earned reputation for a hippie atmosphere, attracting visitors to 'party' in paradise. Allegedly, hippos aren't the only ones to snort a lot here.

Visitors can camp or stay in one of ten Fisherman's Huts – tents with mosquito-screening, encircled by reeds. These have mattresses, bedding, linen and mosquito nets. Open-air ablutions (flush toilets and bucket showers) are shared.

Facilities include a large kitchen, a bar, a fire area, a restaurant, several small tables and a shop. The shop has basic essentials, but bring your own food if you plan to cook. The restaurant serves meals for US$3–4 from a set menu.

Activities available include fishing, boat trips, sunset/booze cruises and nature walks. Transfers to/from the island and some activities use mekoro (dugout canoes), which are fun but perilous as some of the river's crocodiles have become habituated to the island's activity. Venturing too near to the river is dangerous, and you would need to be drugged into oblivion before swimming here seemed safe.
Rates: US$50 is the 'cover charge', including transfers to and from Livingstone and all island-based activities. Fisherman's Huts are US$10 per person sharing, or US$15 for singles. Camping is US$5 per person. Everything else is extra.

Zambezi Royal Chundu Safari & Fishing Lodge (6 chalets) PO Box 60889, Livingstone. Tel/fax: 03 321772; email: chundu@icon.co.za. Alternatively book with their South African agents on tel/fax: (2711) 953 3224.

Zambezi Royal Chundu is the furthest lodge from Livingstone on the river bank (a little further than Kubu), and is about 11km off the main road. Owned by Adam and Lynne Morze, and opened in 1996, in some ways Royal Chundu still feels new. Adam grew up in the area, speaks the local language, and has a good relationship with the local Toka-Leya people (a sub-group of the Lozi people).

Most activities are included when you stay here. You can drive to the Falls and take a tour around, visit the Mosi-oa-Tunya game park or one of the local villages, or go walking or horse riding around the local area. On the river you can take a guided mokoro or canoe trip, or try your luck at tiger or bream fishing. Even day trips to Chobe in Botswana are included (and using the ferry at Kazungula, Royal Chundu is only 22km from Botswana).

Royal Chundu has just six brick-under-thatch chalets, all set back from the river next to one another, with a lawn in front of them. These are solidly and compactly built, with four-poster twin beds under mossie netting and en-suite bathroom. Each chalet has gauze windows, electricity and nice fabrics.

The main building of the lodge has plenty of space, comfy chairs and tables. In one direction there's a walkway out on to a deck overlooking the river, in the other lies the swimming pool. Royal Chundu is a comfortable lodge, where no effort will be spared to look after you. It's perfect for visitors who just want to fish, but too far from the Falls for a short stop.

Rates (2005): US$145/175 per person per night, including all meals, excursions and laundry for the brick chalets. Transfers to/from Livingstone are free. Those to/from Vic Falls or Kasane are free if you stay three or more nights at Royal Chundu.

Treetops (3 twin-bed chalets) Contact via Zambezi Royal Chundu, above.

Treetops is immediately adjacent to its sister-property, Zambezi Royal Chundu, and is also run by the Morze Family. It shares facilities like the pool, bar, restaurant, boats, etc with Chundu. Here you'll find three private chalets, built on wooden decks raised on stilts above the Zambezi under an enormous canopy of waterberry trees. Walkways link the chalets to their land-locked bathrooms. Treetops offers a full range of activities, like Royal Chundu, though all are at extra cost.

These chalets aim to be a simpler and more economical alternative to the luxury lodge for visitors who are driving themselves, fishing or simply relaxing by the river.

Rates (2005): US$95/124 per person, including dinner, bed and breakfast.

Siankaba Lodge (6 tented chalets) PO Box 60845, Livingstone; tel/fax: 03 324490; email: siankaba@zamnet.zm

Between Kubu Cabins and Royal Chundu is a new lodge, set on two forested islands in the Zambezi. To get there, follow the signs from the main Livingstone--Sesheke road along 5km of sand track to the lodge's base on the Zambian mainland. It's a 10-minute motorboat transfer to the lodge, best arranged in advance.

Run by its owners, Bonnie and Simon, the lodge is split between two islands, linked by a rope bridge and a winding wooden walkway through the tree canopy. The larger island has the bar and dining room under canvas, a secluded swimming pool and an informative nature trail. The stilted chalets have river views and are all spread around the edge of the smaller island. These are beautifully furnished with en-suite bathrooms (even the ball and claw bathtubs have a great view), ceiling fans, mosquito nets, minibars and private balconies. The décor has lots of vibrant earthy colours contrasting well with the tangle of vines and vegetation surrounding the main lodge and chalets.

Activities from the lodge centre on the river, and include sunset cruises, fishing trips and mokoro trips to the Siansimba rapids. Guided walks beside the river on the mainland are available, and are a great way to see a Zambian village and the local school, as well as the riverside environment.

The lodge arranges transfers to and from airports in the area and guided trips into the Mosi-O-Tunya National Park and the Zambian side of the Falls. Chobe day trips can also be arranged easily, as the Botswana border is only 30km away.

Rates (2005): US$342/414 per person per night, including drinks, transfers and most activities.

Mawala Lodge (2 rondavels) PO Box 60273, Livingstone; tel/fax: 03 324455; email: mawala@zamnet.zm

Opened in July 1999, the lodge stands on the Zambezi, about 30km from Livingstone. To get here, follow the directions to the Kubu Cabins turn-off from the main Kazungula Road, and look for Mawala's signpost there. It shares the same driveway towards the river as Kubu. That takes roughly ten minutes from the main road, down a winding sandy track through the bush.

Mawala is run by Mike and Susan Walsh, long-time residents of the area. It has a small dam for fishing, and a swimming pool surrounded by nice green lawns, but set slightly away from the river. A playground for children is also planned. The main building is solidly constructed of poles and thatch with some beautiful hardwoods. There is an upstairs bar and restaurant, with a lovely view of the river and Zambezi National Park beyond. Mawala's bar and restaurant is open to the public, offering a nice place to have a riverside meal, if a bit far from town. However, some guests may find a flow of outside visitors intrusive.

Accommodation is in one of two thatched rondavels. One is beside the river and the other is right next to the main building. The riverfront rondavel, or honeymoon chalet, is reached across a small footbridge. It has a bedroom with a small double bed, a dressing area, en-suite shower and toilet and a river view. The other rondavel is larger, double-storey and better for families. Downstairs is a small lounge/sitting area, a double room and a small bathroom painted in blue; upstairs are two twins. Both rondavels are basic, but lack decorative flair or charm. The bright, off-white paint used on the lodge's exterior walls doesn't help at all. Activities like sunset/booze cruises, fishing, and vehicle tours into town are all inclusive. Other excursions can be booked at extra cost.

Rates: US$140 per person sharing, US$150 single, including full board, transfers and activities. Children under 5 are free; those aged 6–12 years cost US$45; 13–17 years cost US$85. Overnight stay (dinner, bed and breakfast) cost US$70 per person.

Kubu Cabins – The Livingstone Explorers' Club (5 chalets, 6 tents and a campsite) PO Box 60748, Livingstone; tel/fax: 03 324091

Usually known simply as 'Kubu Cabins', this is well signposted. Leave town on the Nakatindi Road and continue for about 25km, until the camp is indicated off to the left. Follow the signs, and the lodge will appear after a further 5km of sandy track. (This last 5km needs careful driving with a low-slung car.)

The cabins have a beautiful site, opposite the Zambezi National Park in Zimbabwe. Kubu's bar-lounge area is friendly and comfortable – built under thatch, on a wooden deck overlooking the river. 'Kubu' means hippo, which are common here, and there is an extensive collection of drums and xylophones if you wish to accompany their nocturnal grunts.

Kubu's chalets are solid wood-and-thatch structures, thoroughly mosquito-proofed, with twin beds, en-suite facilities, mains lights and electricity. There is also a more spacious honeymoon suite that has a double bed, sunken bath and one side open to the river. The Meru-style tents are further from the main lodge, near the riverbank in a thicket of vegetation. Each has its own en-suite shower and toilet.

As well as its chalets and tents, downstream Kubu has a good grass campsite set under false ebony, marula and teak trees by the river. There is a kitchen area, clean toilets and hot showers.

Activities cost extra, apart from a complementary birding walk along the bank. Kubu run their own sunset and birdwatching boat trips, and short mountain bike trails, but organise other activities with the local operators. Canoeing is usually with Makora Quest, who are less than a kilometre downstream, and horse riding is available through nearby Chundukwa. Kubu is a good place to relax and the food is delicious, however if you wish to make a lot of trips into the falls, for sightseeing or activities, then the transfer costs can begin to add up.

Rates: US$96 per person sharing for dinner, bed and breakfast (US$135 in the honeymoon suite). Transfers to Livingstone Airport are free, to/from town they cost US$15 per vehicle plus US$5 per person. To/from Vic. Falls they cost US$25 per vehicle, plus US$5 per person. Camping is US$10 per person, including firewood.

Chundukwa River Camp (4 chalets) PO Box 61160; tel/fax: 03 324452 at the camp. (Town office is tel/fax: 324006.)

Owned and run by Doug Evans, this is perfect if you want to do some activities, but not the right place if you just want a place to sleep for a few nights.

The camp is roughly 22km out of Livingstone, on the Kazungula Road, before Kubu Cabins. It has three twin-bedded chalets, and one larger for honeymoon or family use. Each is divided in two: the thatched, wooden bedroom with balcony perches on stilts amongst the waterberry trees above the river, whilst the private toilets and showers are just a few yards away (over a wooden walkway) on the riverbank. A novel design, using rustic beams and branches, it's simple but well done.

There is a small thatch *boma* and lounge area next to the river where meals are served, a peaceful spot to relax and enjoy the atmosphere and a swimming pool overlooking the river.

Activities include canoeing (using 2-man kayak-type canoes, accompanied by a guide in a single kayak), horse riding (using McLelen-type, American saddles and a stable of 12 horses), boat trips and island excursions. Doug is an experienced guide of some repute, so the activities that Chundukwa offers are done well.

Rates: US$170 per person sharing, US$215 single, including all meals, bar, boat trips, canoeing, horse trails, transfers (on the Zambian side) and trips to see the Falls.

Tongabezi (5 cottages and 4 houses) P Bag 31; tel: 097770917/18 (res) or 03 324450/68 (for the lodge); fax: 097 840920; email: tonga@zamnet.zm

Set on a sweeping bend of the Zambezi, Tongabezi has set the region's standard for innovative camp design since it opened over a decade ago. It remains one of the most exclusive places to stay on the north side of the Zambezi, and after a few years of mediocrity has recently gained a new and positive air of direction.

It has made a conscious move to invest and train more first-class local Zambian staff, and it is actively supporting some of the local communities and even running a school for local children. It has also re-built and re-furbished many its rooms, and changed the small tented chalets into rather beautiful cottages overlooking the river. Three have king-size beds; all have double-size baths and the services of a private valet dedicated solely to looking after the guests in that room

Now the choice is between stylish twin-bedded cottages or one of the four suites (or houses): the Bird House, the Tree House, the Dog House or the Honeymoon Suite (once cited as 'worth getting married for'). Each suite is well designed, with a king-size double bed, impressive bath, and one side completely open on to the river. They are more private than they might appear.

There is a lovely riverside thatched bar and spacious lounge area. The swimming pool is set against a rock wall, under a tumbling waterfall, while sun-loungers wait on a large wooden deck over the Zambezi.

Guided sunrise and sunset boat trips, canoeing, birdwatching trips, fishing, game drives (to Mosi-oa-Tunya National Park), museum tours, transfers (in Zambia) and even tennis are included. Very few of the guests here are local, so it is best to arrange your stay from overseas before you arrive. There are also options to sleep on Sindabezi, one of the islands in the river, and have a champagne breakfast on Livingstone Island, beside the falls. These should also be booked well in advance.

Rates (2005): US$329–400 per person per night sharing for a chalet, US$389–498 for a house, including drinks, transfers and most activities

Sindabezi Island (3 twin-bed and one double tents) contact via Tongabezi
Sindabezi Island is a short boat trip downstream from its parent lodge, Tongabezi. This small island has just four thatched chalets, each accommodating two people. It's all wonderfully private and designed as an island hideaway from which you can explore the river and surrounding islands. Elephants and hippos are frequent visitors to the island, and activities include canoeing, boating, walking, fishing, birdwatching and also the use of a vehicle on the Zambian side.

Rates (2005): US$329 per person per night, including drinks, transfers and most activities

The River Club (10 luxury chalets including Honeymoon Suite) Book through Wilderness Safaris, PO Box 288, Victoria Falls, Zimbabwe; tel: (26313) 3371/2/3; fax: 4224/2020
Designed to reflect the colonial era, the River Club was opened in 1998, perched on a rise beside the Zambezi, next to Tongabezi. Guests are usually driven from town to a launch site, and then brought up-river by boat to the lodge, a short ten-minute ride. If you are driving, then the turn-off to River Club from the Nakatindi/Kazungula road is well signposted; the same turning is also used to reach Tongabezi.

The lodge has ten thatched, en-suite chalets which are cleverly designed and constructed on stilts, amidst indigenous riverside trees. All are high up with their entirely open fronts, facing over the Zambezi below. Two chalets, including the more secluded Honeymoon Suite, have double beds. The other eight have two singles. All are large with good decoration, quality fabrics and many nice touches (like the claw-foot bathtubs). Each is also named after an explorer or colonial figure, like Stanley and Livingstone.

The main lodge building is also constructed in the colonial style with tin roof and wide verandas (which looks better than it sounds). Inside is the reception, a small gift shop, a formal dining room (with a magnificent teak table), a comfortable lounge, a massive double-sided fireplace and a well-stocked library. Antiques, colonial pictures and many decorator touches add to the lodge's ambience.

Meals are elegant affairs of a high standard. The entire atmosphere, decor and service are all reminiscent of the colonial era. Even the staff dress in white uniforms, red sashes and matching fezes to pamper the guests (perhaps reminding some that the 'good old colonial days' were not so good for most black Africans!?).

Overlooking the river is also a large swimming pool, with sweeping lawns. Croquet is an optional activity, but there's also the choice of fishing, canoeing, sundowner boat trips, game park drives, museum visits, and trips to local villages, stone-age sites and Livingstone town.

Rates: US$285 per person per night, including drinks, transfers and most activities

Thorn Tree Lodge (7 twin-bed tents, 2 honeymoon suites) PO Box 60403, Livingstone; tel: 03 324480; fax: 321320 or contact Safari Par Excellence (see The Waterfront, below)
Thorn Tree Lodge is owned and run by Safari Par Excellence, who have offices in Livingstone and Victoria Falls. To drive there take the main Nakatindi Road, and turn left at the signpost (also indicating to Melrose Farm). This is well before Chundukwa, so if you get that far, turn back.

Thorn Tree's accommodation is in large meru-style tents – built on a brick base under a thatched roof, with en-suite electricity and showers. Two are honeymoon suites, raised up on teak decking with open sides overlooking the river. All have well furnished interiors, and their hot water is heated by traditional Rhodesian boilers.

There's a very comfortable bar and dining area, from which you can watch elephants hopping between the islands in the Zambezi. Also a figure-of-eight swimming pool, one end of which is under thatch for shade. Watch for a barman serving drinks in the centre. On the other side of camp is a shaded sitting area that overlooks a waterhole. Buffalo, elephants, hippo, waterbuck and bushbuck are regular visitors.

Rates: US$260 per person, including full board, activities, drinks and transfers. This reduces to US$210 from mid-January to mid-June.

Susi & Chuma Lodge (10 chalets) Star of Africa, P Bag 6, Hillside, Zimbabwe; tel: (2639) 243954/246433/246430 or (2639) 11 213345; fax: (2639) 246436

Built in 2001, this is ten minutes' drive from Livingstone and within the (unfenced area of) the Mosi-oa-Tunya National Park – at a highly prized site which, historically, was known as 'Fairyland'. The lodge's name has been taken from the two Zambian bearers who carried David Livingstone's body from Zambia to the British Embassy at Dar es Salaam: Susi and Chuma.

Set amongst the riverine forest, Susi & Chuma's chalets command fabulous views over the Zambezi – each consisting of ten large and almost round luxury 'tree-houses' on raised platforms with walkways. Many of their walls are large glass windows, and outside is a sizeable balcony. Furnishings are stylish and tasteful – lots of fabrics and a walk-in mosquito net around the bed(s). Each en-suite bathroom houses a bath with a view.

The raised walkways between the chalets are quite high. They lead to a double-storey dining/lounge area, swimming pool and riverside deck. This main building has a historical significance (and a preservation order), though it has been extensively and tastefully refurbished.

Rates: US$275/355 per person sharing/single, including all meals and guided activities. Open all year.

The Waterfront (20 tents on platforms, 24 rooms in chalets, plus camping) near the Boat Club. Contact Safari Par Excellence; tel: 03 320606–8; fax: 03 320609, or via Victoria Falls; tel: (26313) 44726; email: waterfront@zamnet.zm

This is a large riverside complex, incorporating a 'camping village' and 'adventure centre', which was built in '99 by Safari Par Excellence on a beautiful spot, formerly known as the Makumbi launch site. To get here leave Livingstone towards the Falls, on the Mosi-oa-Tunya Road, then turn right at Tunya Lodge towards the river and Mosi-oa-Tunya Game Park. The Waterfront is adjacent to the old Zambezi Boat Club, and you'll see a sign to it pointing left as you approach the boat club.

The Waterfront aims to offer affordable riverside accommodation very close to the Falls. It has a stunning setting within the Mosi-oa-Tunya National Park – which was one of the best places to view spectacular Zambezi sunsets and enjoy the hippos and birdlife before this development.

The main thatch-and-pole building has a lovely view over the river and contains the reception and booking office, a spacious bar, a lounge and the restaurant on the ground floor. Upstairs an internet café is planned. Outside, amongst palm trees, are sitting areas and a lovely pool.

Sprawling to the left of the main building are 20 permanent tents perched on wooden platforms along the river. These each have two beds; all bedding and linen is supplied. Nearby ablutions are clean and spacious and contain flush toilets and hot and cold showers. A separate grassed camping area can take about 60 campers, and this also has similar toilets and showers.

There are plans to add eight large A-frame style chalets, each containing three separate double rooms (with their own en-suite showers and toilets). This is planned to be on the right of the main building, separate from the tents or camping area.

The Waterfront is intended by Saf Par as a one-stop-shop, where their own 'Adventure Centre' will offer a full range of activities and excursions – many of which will doubtless be operated by themselves. Among these will be two boats offering sunset cruises directly from the Waterfront's own jetty. The *Makumbi*, currently being refurbished, is a larger boat and will offer upmarket cruises. The smaller *Jambezi* will offer a more normal booze cruise.

Rates (2005): Tents are US$15/33 per person, rooms in chalets US$44/99 per person, camping US$5 per person.

The Royal Livingstone Sun International Zambia, PO Box 60151, Livingstone; tel: 03 321122; fax: 03 324 558; email: sunintzam@zamnet.zm; web: www.suninternational.com Opened by the president in July 2001, this opulent five-star hotel situated in extensive grounds is owned by the 'Sun International' group, based in South Africa, and is sister-hotel of the Zambezi Sun, below. As part of the agreement with gave Sun International Livingstone's (and indeed one of Africa's) prime locations, the group has done a lot of work improving the town's infrastructure – including refurbishing the town's airport.

All of the Royal Livingstone's air-conditioned rooms have private balconies and are fitted with satellite TV, radio, video, minibar, mini-safe and telephone. That said, the rooms aren't quite as large as one might expect for a hotel of this standard. Outside there's a boma, crafted in the traditional Zambian manner with seating for up to 350 people.

There is an excellent à la carte restaurant, large verandas and a general air of luxury. There's also a travel agent who can organise your itinerary of activities, from whitewater rafting to bicycle excursions. That said, although the Royal Livingstone's a nice hotel, you've got to wonder if it's really worth the extra over and above its neighbour, the Zambezi Sun. *Rates: US$210/403 per person sharing/single including breakfast. Open: all year.*

Zambezi Sun (212 rooms) see the Royal Livingstone, above, for contact details. This is the colourful and fun 4-star sibling of the Royal Livingstone, which has fast become the obvious place to stay in the Falls if you want somewhere that's convenient and reasonably-priced. All of the air-conditioned rooms are fitted out with satellite TV, radio, video, minibar, mini-safe and telephone and each also features a private balcony.

The rooms are very comfortable: the standard of a good international business hotel, but with rather more flashes of colour and individuality. The hotel complex has a buffet restaurant, and a relaxed al fresco grill beside its extensive, curving pools. (You can always book into the posh restaurant next door if you want to feel more formal for a while.)

Everything here blends well together with a generally fun and unpretentious style. The hotel's location, a few hundred metres' walk from the lip of the Falls and the curio market, simply can't be beaten.

As with the Royal Livingstone hotel, the usual range of Falls-related activities are on offer. So if this is more your style than one of the quieter, more exclusive spots upriver, it is very good and good value for a few nights. *Rates: US$140/269 per person sharing/single including breakfast. Open: all year.*

Songwe Point Village (8 rustic huts) Contact via Victoria Falls Safari Lodge, Zimbabwe; tel: (26313) 3211; fax: 3205/3207; email: saflodge@saflodge.co.zw Songwe Point Village is a joint venture between the local community and Victoria Falls Safari Lodge. It promises the cultural experience of staying in an African village-style setting with local people and an enhanced high level of comfort. The 'village' is poised on the edge of one of the gorges downstream of the Falls, 100m above the Zambezi. It's a breathtaking location.

As the crow flies, it's only 5km downstream from the Falls, but the road winding through the bush, small villages and out to the gorge is a 30-minute drive. (See the directions to Taita Falcon Lodge, below.) Accommodation is in rustic, but comfortable, thatched huts. Each has its own bathroom (toilet and washbasin). Showers and baths, positioned on the edge of the gorge, are memorable.

The hosts welcome visitors into the 'village family' and explain local customs and beliefs. Meals are served in the traditional style and in a central thatched enclosure, called a 'Ntantaala'. There is traditional singing and dancing in the evenings and guests are encouraged to participate if the mood strikes them. Everything tries hard to be authentic, right down to an ox-wagon journey to a small field museum displaying Stone-Age artefacts, some more than 700,000 years old.

The area is seeped in archaeological history and the emphasis is on sharing African culture with visitors. Guided visits are offered to early Stone-Age sites, the 700-year old

Mukuni Village, the tree where David Livingstone first met the local Chief, and various other local historical and cultural sites.

Rates: US$145 per person sharing, including full board, activities, drinks and transfers

Taita Falcon Lodge (6 chalets) PO Box 60012, Livingstone; tel/fax: 03 321850; cell: (26311) 208387

This lodge, opened in 1996, is perched overlooking rapid number 17 in the Batoka Gorge, downstream of the Falls. It is a 45-minute drive from Livingstone, along the road normally used to bring rafters back from the river. To get there, take the main road from town towards the Falls, and then take the well-signposted left just before you arrive. From here it's about 11km of long, winding track through the Mokuni Village area. Near the end, you'll pass a turn on the right to Songwe Point. You'll want a 4WD for this trip during the rains.

The lodge is named after a rare falcon which frequents cliffs and gorges, especially in the Zambezi Valley. (Look for these especially in the evenings, perhaps trying to catch swallows or bats on the wing. Taita falcons are small (less than 30cm long) with cream to brown underparts – no bars or markings – and a strong, fast style of flight. This area is one of the best in Africa for spotting them.)

Run by Faan and Anna-Marie Fourie, the lodge is a pleasant, friendly place. Its six chalets use stone, reeds and local furnishings throughout. All have en-suite facilities, but are rustic and quite simple – thatched ceiling with beams, the odd stone wall, and spaces between the walls and roof for light and flow-through ventilation. Most are doubles/twins, but one is larger, having four beds.

The camp's particularly notable for a lovely deck beside the bar, overlooking the gorges and river below. It's a great place to watch rafters from a very safe distance. Despite the fact that the chalets have been set back from the precipice, I'd be very wary of bringing children here because of the cliffs nearby. The lodge's electricity is from a generator, and there's a nice small pool for a dip.

Taita Falcon's a good place if you want a remote spot away from it all, at which to relax and rest. However, if you want to pop in and out of the Falls for activities, then Taita can feel cut off from the epicentre of things

Rates: US$165 per person sharing, US$215 single, including full board and airport transfers on arrival and departure. Camping at new 'Eagle's Nest' campsite here is US$10.

Where to eat
Take-aways

There are several take-aways in town, including Megabite, Shambas, Eat Rite and the large Hungry Lion. For a few thousand kwacha, these serve the usual fare of pre-packaged chips, burgers, samosas, sandwiches and soft drinks. They are all in the centre of town, along Mosi-oa-Tunya Road. The intersection of Kapondo Street and Mosi-oa-Tunya Road is also particularly good; here you'll find the marvellously titled 'Rave Stone Pub and Nightclub' as well as the more palatable offerings from Eat Rite – a clean and efficient (if generic) fast-food joint – and Bakerite. Just down Kapondo Street is Livingstone's Shoprite/Checkers, the town's outpost of the large South African supermarket chain. Its bakery counter is a good place to look for a quick bite to eat.

If you prefer to sit down, then the Insaka Bar & Restaurant is inside Bwaato Adventures, to the right of the main post office. This offers basic lunches and dinners.

If you're travelling between the border and town, then try **Pilgrim's Tearoom,** on the west side of the road just south of town (1.2km south of the railway station). It's open daily from 07.30 to 17.00, and very occasionally in the evening for special events. It's large, airy, and serves great food, often on individual wooden boards with a side salad. Note that this place sometimes caters to large coach groups, in which case the service can be outrageously slow.

Restaurants

For a long time most of Livingstone's best places to eat were in the better lodges and hotels. However, recently more dedicated restaurants have opened up, some with small guesthouses attached. Here's a small selection of the current favourites:

Hippos (located in the old premises of 'Funky Munky') Tel: 03 323432. Located on the Fawlty Towers site (see page 469), Hippos is a popular spot for residents and visitors alike. Get there either through Fawlty Towers, or by going around the corner to the road behind – there are signs for it at the corner of the Mosi-oa-Tunya and Kazungula roads. Hippos has a thatched bar and tables scattered around a secluded, walled courtyard. Its atmosphere is friendly, and the menu changes daily but usually is based around a set dinner. Expect a meal and a few drinks to cost around US$10 per person.

Funky Munky Pizza Bistro #214 Mosi-oa-Tunya Rd (beside 217 area, near the Adventure Centre); tel: 03 320120. Funky Munky used to be behind Fawlty Towers, where Hippos is now. However, now it's moved slightly and changed completely. It's still a lot of fun and serves great pizzas (eat in or take-away), salads, fish and chips, breakfast rolls, sandwiches, and a variety of very reasonably priced snacks and quick bites. It's open 07.30–21.00 daily.

Zig Zag Coffee House Tel: 03 324081. On Mosi-oa-Tunya Road, in the centre of town opposite Associated Stores – you can't miss Zig Zag. It's a great place for coffee, cappuccino, fresh orange juice, lunch, snacks, cakes and just to 'hang out' and meet people. It's been well designed, despite its busy location, and you can sit inside or outside at one of a number of small teak tables under quaint shady parasols. Prices are very reasonable and there is also a small booking office here for organising activities around the Falls. Open Mon–Sat 08.00–17.00.

Laughing Dragon Tel: 097 846919. On Mutelo Road (turn beside the museum), between the Hungry Lion and Pete's Steakhouse, this is a super fairly new place serving authentic Szechuan Chinese food. It has a full alcohol licence and will also do take-aways. Laughing Dragon is run by a family of Chinese origin and they have a detailed menu, though much of this does depend on what ingredients are available for them to buy on the day in Livingstone. However, what they do cook is very good, and the quantities are generous. Their chow mein is delicious, and one very reliable correspondent described their deep-fried oyster mushrooms as 'too yummy for words'. Expect dinner with several dishes to share to be around US$10–15 each, which is good value for the quantity and quality of the food. Laughing Dragon is open daily 11.00–23.00.

Mr Pete's Steakhouse Tel: 03 323390. On Mutelo Street, next to Laughing Dragon, Pete's is now a favourite amongst locals in the tourism industry. Its interior is a little dim, with large plank tables and no frills. It's not the place for a romantic dinner, but does do a first-rate job of good, hearty meals. They serve great steaks, ribs and hamburgers, all with a selection from small salad bar. Costs around US$10–15 each for dinner, and there's an extensive bar available too.

LOCAL LINGO

Judi Helmholz

Arthur needed a new disposable razor. After enquiring at nearly every shop in town, he was astounded that he couldn't find a single one in all of Livingstone. The clerks merely shook their heads and tried to sell him razor blades instead. After being told again that there were no disposable razors, Arthur noticed an entire display rack full of them, right next to the cashier. 'I thought you said you don't have disposable razors,' said Arthur, pointing to the display. 'Those are not disposal razors,' replied the clerk, 'those are shaving sticks.'

UTSAV Restaurant & Exciting Biting Takeaway Tel: 03 322259. Opposite the post office, on MOT Road near the Mini-Market, this is a small, family-run restaurant/take-away. It serves good curries, naan breads, samosas, a particularly good tandoori chicken, and also pies. It is pleasantly air-conditioned, and usually has special meals designed to suit impecunious backpackers. Open 10.00 until late.

Squire's Grillhouse & Action Bar Located inside the casino in the Falls Convention Centre (part of Sun International's new hotel complex), right off Mosi-oa-Tunya Road, Squire's is a South African restaurant chain serving fairly standard fare, mostly grilled meat and fish. It's not terribly cheap, though they have a 'happy hour' in the early evening, and some lunch 'specials', which are better value. It's very close to the Falls and unfortunately gets noise from the nearby road. Open daily, 11.00–22.00.

Zambezi Sun This has a good restaurant, though it's (unusual for Livingstone) priced in US$ so not cheap. The best value is probably its buffet brunch/lunch – which offers a huge selection of breakfasts, grilled kebabs, burgers, omelettes to order, salads and desserts. It has a fun atmosphere, especially in the afternoons, and tables are set inside and out around a large pool. There's often live music here – making this good value for an evening out. Expect lunch to be about US$12 per person, dinner US$15–20.

Royal Livingstone Sun's flagship hotel has a fabulous restaurant, with correspondingly high prices. The setting is lovely, the service excellent, and the food certainly the best in town. Some of the dishes have a Moroccan theme, but there are many other choices also. Dinner costs about US$15–25 each, excluding drinks. (The hotel also does a very genteel afternoon tea (US$8) which includes lovely finger sandwiches and tea cakes, if you feel like a bit of luxurious civility.

Nightlife
Local Livingstone nightlife centres largely around dancing and drinking, although the bars at various restaurants offer a nice atmosphere if one simply wants to relax and chat. Those wishing to dance should try Eat Rite on Kapondo Street, which moonlights as a night-club – Steprite Sounds – on Fridays and Saturdays. Dress code is 'no shorts, no tropicals and no vests' and entry is free.

Rave Stone, across the street, can also be a fun night-spot. The New Fairmount Hotel has a popular disco/dance club, generally jam-packed on weekend nights. In all of these places, you can dance until you drop and, because they can become rowdy later in the evenings, it's probably advisable to venture out in a group.

Getting around
By taxi
Livingstone town is small enough to walk around, as is the Falls area. However if you are travelling between the two, or going to the airport, or in a hurry, then use one of the plentiful taxis. A taxi between town and either the border or the airport will cost around Kw5,000/US$2 per person depending upon number of passengers. From the airport to the border is about Kw12,500/US$5 or more.

You can also negotiate to hire a taxi for the day to take you around town, to the Falls and into the game park, but for a more informative trip it's better to go with the licensed, more knowledgeable tour operators. Most drivers are unfamiliar with the riverside lodges, and will be reluctant to take you there cheaply, as they will not find a passenger for the return journey.

Banks and money
Livingstone has several major banks and various bureaux de change. There are also freelance 'money changers' around Eat Rite and at the border. Unless you are *very* savvy or desperate, avoid the money changers. They always take advantage of unsuspecting (and even suspicious) tourists by short-changing them somehow.

Banks generally offer a better exchange rate than bureaux de change, but can take more time and hassle. You can also often change money at many of the lodges and hotels. This is the least favourable exchange rate, but most convenient method. The major banks are situated around the post office area, parallel to the main road. Most open Mon–Fri 08.00–14.00, but get there early if you want to avoid long queues. The main ones include:

Barclay's Bank Tel: 03 32114; fax: 322317
Zambia National Commercial Bank Tel: 03 321901
Union Bank Tel: 03 321385; fax: 320695
Finance Bank Tel: 03 323305 (next to Liso House, opposite Pemube Crafts)

Alternatively the larger bureaux de change include:

Falls Bureau de Change Tel: 03 322088. In post office complex, next to Zamtel Telecom Centre, this is open Mon–Fri, 09.00–13.00 and 14.00–17.00, Sat 09.00–13.00
Mo Money situated on the main road between Kubu Crafts and Capital Theatre
Southend Bureau de Change Tel: 03 320241/320773; fax: 322128. In Liso House, almost opposite Pemube Crafts.

Shopping
Food and drink
There is no shortage of grocers and shops in Livingstone and you can find most things, although imported gourmet items might be hard to come by. Mini Market and RiteShop, across the corner from each other, stock the best supply of fresh fruits and vegetables in addition to all the basics like eggs, milk, cheese, chickens, meats and dry goods.

Shoprite Checkers, on Kapondo Street, is a large South African supermarket chain with a wider variety of goods, but at generally higher prices. They have a good meat section. The fruits and vegetables at Checkers are not very fresh since most have travelled up from South Africa via Lusaka and down to Livingstone. Zambian open-air markets and wheel-barrow marketeers, positioned around town, also have fresh tomatoes, onions and other basic fruits and vegetables, generally at less cost.

Other supplies
For cosmetics, toiletries or medicines Livingstone has several well-stocked **chemists/pharmacies**. Both those below have an excellent selection of these items as well as insect repellents, sun creams, medical supplies, batteries, film and more. Each has a trained pharmacist, who can also offer advice on medications and fill prescriptions if on duty.

LF Moore Chemists Tel/fax: 03 321640. Located on Akapelwa Street, across from the High Court and bus depot, LF Moore was established in 1936 and remains the best-stocked chemist in town. It is open every day: Mon–Fri 08.00–12.30 and 14.00–18.00, Sat 08.00–13.00, and Sun/Public Holidays 09.30–12.30
LM Pharmacy Tel: 03 324486. Next to Zambia National Commercial Bank, near the post office, this pharmacy is also open every day: Mon–Fri 08.00–13.00 and 14.00–17.30, Sat 08.00–14.00, Sun/Public Holidays: 08.30–12.00.

For **books** try Pemube on the main road. They have probably the best selection of wildlife reference books and regional travel guides as well as a book exchange and new paperback novels.

Basic **camera supplies** can be found at either LF Moore Chemists (see above), on Akapelwa Street, or better still at the Konica Film Centre on the main road.

Konica does one-hour photo processing and stocks film, photo albums and related supplies.

For **cassette tapes of popular music** including many African selections, try the open-air local market down at the bottom of Kapondo Street. They have a wide selection of cheap (probably bootlegged!) cassette tapes. Follow your ears for blaring music and you'll find a kiosk selling tapes!

Chitenje, the colourful lengths of traditional African cloth, can be found at most of the small Indian shops on the main road and on Kuta Way, one block down, parallel to the main road. These make lovely souvenirs and nice sarongs.

If you need **car repairs**, try Fallsway Motors (tel: 03 321049) at the corner of Nakatindi Road or Channa's Motors (tel: 03 320468) on the main road just across the railway line. Their facilities are somewhat limited, but they should be able to get you on the road again at least temporarily.

The best workshop in town is Foley's Africa (PO Box 60525, tel/fax: 03 320888), but they cater mainly for Land Rovers. In an emergency they might be able to help, or at least advise on who could repair your vehicle. They are located on the Mosi-oa-Tunya Road, next to BP and across from the Total fuel station; you can't miss their big sign. For **punctures and tyre repairs** try the Total fuel station.

Souvenirs and curios

If you like bargaining and have lots of patience, try the **Curio and Craft Centre** in Mukuni Park where local artisans, craftsmen and carvers sell their wares. They have a great selection of wooden carvings and crafts, but expect to be bombarded with vendors vying for your attention and business.

Similarly, there is the **curio village** at the Zambian side of the Falls (beside the Falls Museum) with a wider selection of items and even more aggressive salesmen! It can be fun if you have time and enjoy haggling over prices, but frustrating if you are in a hurry. Failing those, one of the following might suit you much better:

Kubu Crafts Tel: 03 324093. On left of the old Capitol Cinema is this lovely shop, which is really geared more towards interior design than passing visitors. It stocks teak furniture, jewellery, pottery, plates, paintings by local artists, glasses and beautiful hand-made cards amongst other things. In case you're wondering, it's owned and run by Lucy and Roelf, from Kubu Cabins!

Livingstone Museum The museum has a small craft shop in the back with generally a nice selection of locally produced baskets, carvings and other curios. They tend to have the lowest prices in town, but whether it's well stocked or not is hit or miss. You don't need to pay museum entry to visit the curio shop, just tell them where you are going.

African Visions Located on Mosi-oa-Tunya Road, in the Livingstone Adventure Centre complex, you'll recognise this shop by its distinctive burglar bars of African faces. It is the best stocked (and most expensive) curio shop in town. Visions is a lovely shop with a wide selection of textiles, baskets, carvings, artefacts and many Zambian-produced souvenirs. Worth a visit.

Out of Africa & Studio Africa Tel 03 324458; fax: 03 324454; email: judi@zamnet.zm. Out of Africa are the top wholesalers of fine-quality African textiles (like Kuba cloths), artefacts, basketwork and hand-made products. They have a wonderful selection of innovative and quality products – all at affordable prices. They actively participate in community development, having established rural craft groups to make one-of-a-kind products. Because they are the suppliers to lodge shops, designers/decorators and export markets, they unfortunately don't have a shop in town. However, serious buyers can make an appointment to view their wide selection of merchandise. Studio Africa, the sister-company, provides design and sourcing of quality furnishings and interior décor for safari lodges, hotels, retails shops and home interiors. If you are a serious collector of, or interested in, textiles or artefacts from the DRC and Zambia, or interior design, then contact this company.

Information and addresses
Tourist information
Both Livingstone and Victoria Falls have tourist information offices. You can expect pleasant, friendly staff with little useful information.

Livingstone's is situated next to the main Museum, where Mosi-oa-Tunya Road bends into the centre of town. The Victoria Falls office is a small bungalow opposite the Wimpy on Park Way.

Car hire
If you don't have a vehicle and wish to explore the area at your own pace, you can hire a car with or without a driver. Alternatively, you can hire a 4WD with full kit if you wish to do self-drive safaris.

Foley Hire Limited Tel/fax: 03 320888. Newly established, Foley Hire is a sister-company of Foley Africa, Livingstone's local Land Rover specialist. They offer all sorts of options, from vehicles just for the day to fully-kitted-out expedition-ready multi-day hires. All vehicles are Land Rovers with choice ranging from basic 110 Defenders to fully equipped 110 and 130 Defenders. Other models are planned to follow, including Land Rover Discoverys. A fully outfitted vehicle could include: roof and ground tents, awning, table and chairs, additional fuel and water tanks, sand ladders, hi-lift jack, jerry cans, gas cooker, fridge, power winch, water filtration unit and shower, ropes, shovel, axe, camp lights, bedding (duvets and pillows), cooler box, kitchen equipment, books, maps, etc. The list goes on and on! One-way drop-offs are sometimes possible, at a cost. A basic 110 Defender, without extras, costs around US$100 per day, inclusive of insurance and with unlimited mileage. An equipped vehicle is more like US$200 per day.

AJ Car Hire & Tours PO Box 60192; tel/fax: 03 322090. Located in Liso House (room 306), on Mosi-oa-Tunya Rd. This small local hire company has vehicles for self-drive or chauffeured hire as well as transfers, tours and activity bookings. They have two 5-seater Toyota Saloon cars (US$40/day plus 50¢/km), one 8-seater Toyota Hiace mini van (US$55/day plus 50¢/km) and one 26-seater Mitsubishi bus (US$100/day plus US$1/km). These current prices are subject to various taxes and possible extra charges. All vehicles have an air-conditioning unit.

Emergencies
Medical facilities are limited in Livingstone, and the local hospitals are not up to the standard of those in the developed world. However, there are a couple of very good small medical clinics in town. They can do malaria and other routine tests and also make house-calls:

Health Point (Dr Shanks) Office tel: 03 322170; fax: 03 322922; email: shanks@zamnet.zm Zimbabwe cellphone: (011) 212602; Zambian cellphone: 01 794 888. Located on Mushili Way off the Lusaka Road, the clinic is usually open Mon–Fri 08.00–17.00, Sat 09.00–12.00, Sun 11.00–12.00, public holidays 10.00–12.00. In addition to standard care, they are very familiar with malaria and various tropical ailments, and can offer vaccinations, including yellow fever. They will also respond in an emergency with swift first aid.

Dr Shafik's Clinic & Surgery Tel: 03 321130 (24 hours a day); Zambian cell: (097) 784804. Dr Shafik is very good and can be recommended without hesitation. His clinic is located on the Hospital Road on the right side, between John Hunt Way and Maambo Way.

Post and communications

You can't miss the **Livingstone post office** (tel: 03 321400) in the centre of town in a sprawling complex of banks and shops, adjacent to the main road. It's open Mon–Fri 08.00–17.00, Sat 08.00–13.00, and closed Sun.

Zambia has some lovely stamps for sale, a favourite of stamp collectors. The best way to send mail quickly within Zambia is via EMS (Expedited Mail Service). It is a reasonably priced service where letters are hand delivered. It is also available to overseas destinations and is generally less expensive than a courier company.

One reliable courier is **DHL** (Tel: 03 320044), located inside Pemube on Mosi-oa-Tunya Road. Here you can send letters, parcels and small packets via this international express mail service to destinations within Zambia and worldwide. This is costly but reliable. If you need important documents sent from overseas, DHL is one of the quickest ways to be assured of them reaching you safely. It takes about a week from Europe or the USA.

Another good alternative is to use the **Mercury Mail** service; you'll find their office just next to Living Inn.

If you need to make phone calls or send/receive faxes, and can't do so where you are staying, then there are several places in town.

The **Zamtel Public Telecommunications Centre** is conveniently next to the post office. It opens Mon–Fri 08.00–13.00 and 14.00–17.30; Sat 08.00–12.30. Phone calls within Livingstone are about US20¢ per minute, but about US$1.20 per minute to elsewhere in Zambia.

International calls to Europe, USA and Australia average US$12 for three minutes. Incoming faxes cost about US15¢ per page and should be marked for your attention and faxed to tel: 03 320068. Strangely, Zamtel has no incoming public telephone line to inquire about faxes or other information, so you need to go there personally. (I wouldn't rely on this route for any vital faxes.)

Nearby, upstairs in the Zambia State Insurance Building, are the **Moono Secretarial Services** (tel: 03 320517) who offer the same telecom services at comparable rates to Zamtel (keeping the same hours as Zamtel) as well as typing. Also there are **Timeroll Enterprises** (tel: 03 321609) who offer the same but also telegrams and telex. Timeroll are open all day on Sunday but closed on Saturday. The offices are rather run down and the building poorly maintained, but the facilities are there if you need them.

Telephones

By a convenient arrangement, callers in Livingstone or Victoria Falls can telephone the other side using a local, rather than an international, telephone code. From Zambia just dial '6' before a Victoria Falls number; from Victoria Falls dial '8' before a Livingstone number. This makes huge savings on international call charges, but the few lines available are often busy. Just keep re-dialling – you will get through.

Internet cafés

There's only one internet café in Livingstone so far, although residents of Fawlty Towers can use their facilities, for a price.

Cyberian Outpost PO Box 60352; tel/fax: 03 324440; email: cyberian@ outpost.co.zm. Unlikely though it may seem, there's an internet café in the heart of Livingstone, between the Livingstone Adventure Centre and Safari Par Excellence, on Mosi-ao-Tunya Road, just south of the turn-off to Nakatindi Road. This was started in November '98 by the helpful Jen Cowie. Ten minutes at the terminal for internet access (eg: accessing hotmail accounts!), including sending or receiving emails, costs US$2. If you don't have your own email address, then friends can send messages to you at traveller@outpost.co.zm. This costs just US$0.50 per email. You can also make international calls cheaply here (US and UK, for example, are both US$3.70 per minute to call), and sending faxes costs the call time plus US$1. The outpost is also a convenient agent for Mercury Mail (see page 486), which is a reliable way to send things abroad. They've also a useful notice board and make great filter coffee. So drop in and log on!

WHAT TO SEE AND DO

The Falls area has been a major crossroads for travellers for the past hundred years. From the early missionaries and traders, to the backpackers, overland trucks and package tourists of the last few decades – virtually everyone passing through the region from overseas has stopped here. Recently this has created a thriving tourism industry, mostly based south of the river. Apart from simply marvelling at one of the world's greatest waterfalls, there are now lots of ways to occupy yourself. Some are easily booked after you arrive; one or two are better pre-arranged.

The last decade has witnessed a gradual shift in the town's atmosphere. Visitors used to be from Southern Africa, with perhaps the odd intrepid backpacker and the fortunate few who could afford an upmarket safari. Now the sheer volume of visitors to the Falls has increased massively. This increase, especially noticeable in the proportion of younger visitors, has fuelled the rise of more active, adventurous pursuits like white-water rafting, bungee-jumping, and other thrill-based pastimes.

A genteel cocktail at the Victoria Falls Hotel is no longer the high point of a visit for most people. You are more likely to return home with vivid memories of the adrenaline rush of shooting rapids in a raft, or the buzz of accelerating head-first towards the Zambezi with only a piece of elastic to save you.

The Falls

The Falls are 1,688m wide and average just over 100m in height. Around 550 million litres (750 at peak) cascades over the lip every minute, making this one of the world's greatest waterfalls.

Closer inspection shows that this immense curtain of water is interrupted by gaps, where small islands stand on the lip of the falls. These effectively split the Falls into smaller waterfalls, which are known as (from west to east) the Devil's Cataract, the Main Falls, the Horseshoe Falls, the Rainbow Falls and the Eastern Cataract.

Around the Falls is a genuinely important and interesting rainforest, with plant species (especially ferns) rarely found elsewhere in Zimbabwe or Zambia. These are sustained by the clouds of spray, which blanket the immediate vicinity of the Falls. You'll also find various small antelope, monkeys and baboons here, whilst the lush canopy shelters Livingstone's lourie amongst other birds.

The flow, and hence the spray, is greatest just after the end of the rainy season – around March or April, depending upon the rains. It then decreases gradually until about December, when the rains in western Zambia will start to replenish the river. During low water, a light raincoat (available for rent!) is very useful for wandering between the viewpoints. However, in high water a raincoat is largely ineffective as the spray blows all around and soaks you in seconds. Anything that you want to keep dry must be wrapped in several layers of plastic or, even better, zip-lock plastic bags.

The Falls never seem the same twice, so try to visit several times, under different light conditions. At sunrise, both Danger Point and Knife-edge Point are fascinating – position yourself carefully to see your shadow in the mists, with three concentric rainbows appearing as halos. (Photographers will find polarising filters invaluable in capturing the rainbows on film – as the light from the rainbows at any time of day is polarised.)

Moonlight is another fascinating time, when the Falls take on an ethereal glow and the waters blend into one smooth mass which seems frozen over the rocks.

On the Zambian side, viewing the Falls (entrance fee US$10 per person) could not be easier. Simply follow the signs and your nose along the paths from in front of the field museum and curio stalls. One track leads upstream for a while. This is best explored in the late afternoon (take your own snacks and drinks) and you may catch a stunning sunset.

If you visit when the river is at its lowest, towards the end of the dry season, then the channels on the Zambian side may have dried up. Whilst the Falls will be less spectacular then, you can sometimes walk across the bed of the Zambezi as far as Livingstone Island, before you are stopped by a channel which is actually flowing. Looking down on the Falls from their lip does afford a totally different perspective – just don't slip!

The main path leads along the cliff opposite the Falls, then across the swaying knife-edge bridge, via scenic points, photo stops and a good vantage point from which to watch bungee-jumpers. This finishes at the farthest west of the Zambian viewpoints.

A third path descends right down to the water's edge at the Boiling Pot, which is often used as a raft launch-site. It is a beautiful (but steep) hike down through palm-fringed forest – well worth the long, hot climb back. Take a picnic and relax by the river if you've time.

Viewing the Falls by moonlight is not restricted, though elephants wander about occasionally and it is best not to go alone. If you can visit during a full moon then watch for a lunar rainbow, an amazing sight.

From the Zimbabwean side, viewing the Falls is more regulated. There is now a small ticket booth and display at the entrance gate to the Falls, which is a few hundred yards from the Zimbabwean border post. A ticket costs US$20 per person, and you can return for no extra cost during the same day.

Technically this area is within the Victoria Falls National Park – and you will find a map of the paths at the entrance. Start at the western end, by Livingstone's statue – inscribed with 'Explorer, Missionary and Liberator', and overlooking the Devil's Cataract.

Visiting the viewpoints in order, next is the Cataract View. If water levels are low, and the spray not too strong, after clambering down quite a steep stairway you will be greeted by views along the canyon of the Falls. Climbing back up, wander from one viewpoint to the next, eastwards, and you will eventually reach the slippery-smooth rocks at Danger Point.

Few of these viewpoints have anything more than brushwood fences and low railings to guard the edges – so going close to the edge is not for those with vertigo. Viewing the Falls by moonlight is possible by special arrangement.

Birding

Birdwatching isn't normally regarded as an adrenaline sport, but with the outstanding avifauna to be found in and around the Falls, serious 'twitchers' (as keen bird-watchers are known) might disagree.

Even the casual visitor with little interest will often see fish eagles, Egyptian geese, lots of kingfishers, numerous different bee-eaters, ibis (including sacred), and various other storks, egrets and herons. Meanwhile, avid twitchers will be seeking the more elusive rarities like Taita falcon, as they occur only rarely and this is certainly one of the best sites to look for them. Rock pratincoles have almost as restricted a distribution (just following the Zambezi), but can often be seen here balancing on boulders by the water's edge and hawking for insects. Look in the riverine forest around the Falls and you may spot a collared palmthrush rummaging around, and again these are really quite rare birds recorded in only a few areas.

In contrast, African finfoot occur throughout the subcontinent, but are always shy. They prefer slow water, overhung with leafy branches, and they find the upper sections of the Zambezi perfect, so are often seen there if you look when it's quiet.

Museums

Given its history, it is no surprise that Livingstone has several good museums. The main Livingstone Museum is the most important of these, and certainly one of the best in the country.

Livingstone Museum

In a prime position on the crest of Mosi-oa-Tunya Road, in the middle of town, this museum is worth exploring for a few hours. There are exhibits on the Stone Age, and features on more recent history, animals and traditional village life in the area. There is also a unique collection of Livingstone's personal possessions and the museum often has special exhibits.

The staff are friendly and knowledgeable and guided tours are included. It is worth a visit, if only to familiarise yourself with the area and culture.

Rates: entry fee US$2, (US$1 for a child)

Railway Museum

This specialist museum (PO Box 60927; tel: 321820; fax: 324509) is situated about 1km along Chishimba Falls Road, towards the southwest side of town. There's a collection of old steam locomotives and memorabilia, and displays on railway history – appropriate for a town where the railway was built in 1905. However, if you're not a railway enthusiast, give it a miss.

Rates: entry fee US$5. Open: 08.30–16.30 every day

Field Museum

Much smaller than the main museum in town, this is next to the curio stands by the border and concentrates on the origin of the Falls, and the development of man in the area. Snacks and cold drinks are now available here also.

Rates: entry fee US$2, (US$1 for a child)

Local culture

On the Zimbabwean side, you will find practised (and very commercial) tribal dances held, usually just before dinner, at various venues including Elephant Hills Hotel, the Boma (at Victoria Falls Safari Lodge) and the Falls Craft Village. If you want something more sensitive to the local cultures, not to mention authentic, then look north, to Livingstone.

Cultural day trips

There are several companies offering tours around Livingstone and its environs, often including visits to traditional villages, the Mosi-oa-Tunya National Park, Livingstone's museums and historical sites around the Falls. Makora Quest and Shungu Mufu are the two best operators of these trips on the Livingstone side. These are small companies, both are run by people who have lived in Livingstone for years. They understand the place well and its nuances, far better than a new guide from one of the larger companies who has learnt to give a handful of set speeches from a training manual.

A typical trip may begin with a guided walk around the Zambian side of the Falls, followed by a fascinating visit to the Nakatindi village just east of the Falls.

This typical Zambian settlement is home to 6–7,000 people and a guide who lives here will take you around. This is probably the closest you will get to an insight into the life of normal Zambians – an excellent chance to see how the local people live, and to talk with them.

Lunch is offered, followed by a short safari around the Mosi-oa-Tunya National Park. These tours have been run for years, and part of their beauty is that a small percentage of their cost is automatically paid to the Nakatindi village. Thus the villagers are happy to see strangers strolling around, accompanied by a local guide, and you will not encounter any begging or hassle.

Rates: roughly US$80 per person for a full day, or US$50 for a half day

Curio stalls

Just inside the Zambian border, next to the field museum, is an outstanding curio stand. The carvers and traders come mostly from Mukuni village, though the goods come from as far afield as Zaire and Malawi. Mukuni Park in the centre of town has a similar area of curio vendors, but not as wide a selection of goods.

Both are excellent places to buy wooden and stone carvings, chess boards, drums, malachite bangles and the like. Similar carvings are for sale in Zimbabwe, but often at twice the price, so visitors to Zimbabwe who just cross the border to shop here are common enough for this to have become known as 'the best place in Zimbabwe for curios'.

There are usually about 20 or 30 separate traders, laying their wares out separately. All compete with one another and vie for your business. The best buys are heavy wooden carvings: hippos, rhinos and smaller statues, often made out of excellent quality, heavy wood. However, you should consider the ethics of encouraging *any* further exploitation of hardwoods.

This is a place to bargain hard and expect to hear all sorts of pre-fabricated stories as to why you should pay more. When you start to pay, you will realise how sophisticated the traders are about their currency conversions, reminding you to double-check any exchange rates. Traders will accept most currencies and sometimes credit cards.

Victoria Falls Craft Village

Behind the main post office on Livingstone Way, this is Zimbabwe's more regulated answer to Zambia's curio stalls. Amongst this complex are well-built curio shops as well as traders on the surrounding ground. Within the shops you'll find some excellent pieces and if you are shopping for high quality pieces of art, then this may be the place for you. Alternatively, try the new Elephant's Walk Shopping Complex.

But if you're simply seeking good-value curios then look to the carvers and vendors outside, who will bargain hard for your business. Zimbabwe's currency regulations means that they can only accept Zimbabwe dollars for payment, but there are several bureaux de change nearby.

Thrills and spills

The Falls has become the adventure capital of southern Africa in the last few years. There is an amazing variety of ways to get your shot of adrenaline: white-water rafting, canoeing, bungee-jumping, abseiling, river boarding or simply a flight over the Falls.

None comes cheaply. Most are in the US$50–150 range per activity. There are also choices of operator for most of these – so if you book locally, shop around to find something that suits you before you decide. Prices won't vary much – but you will find the true range of what's available. Whatever you plan, expect to sign an indemnity form before your activity starts.

Flight of Angels

Named after Livingstone's famous comments, the 'Flight of Angels' is a sightseeing trip over the Falls by small aircraft, microlight, helicopter or ultra-light aircraft. This is a good way to get a feel for the geography of the area, and is surprisingly worthwhile if you want to really appreciate the Falls. Any of these can be readily booked from agents in the area, including:

Light aircraft

Del Air offers daily scenic flights over the Falls, departing from Livingstone Airport. They use a Cessna 206; every seat is a window seat and the high mounted wing allows maximum photo opportunities. The flight offers stunning views of the Falls and gorges and takes visitors upstream over the Mosi-oa-Tunya National Park for game viewing. Tour operators in Victoria Falls offer comparable flights using the small runway near the town (not the main airport).
Rates: US$50 per person for 25 minutes, US$70 per person for 40 minutes, including transfers to/from your accommodation on either side of the border

Microlight

This is a totally different experience from a light aircraft: essentially sightseeing from a propeller-powered armchair 500m above the ground. It is only available on the Zambian side and is operated by Batoka Sky/Del Air. The microlights take two people: one pilot, one passenger. Because the passenger sits next to the propeller, cameras cannot be carried. However, you can arrange to be photographed, or even pictured on video, above the Falls from a camera fixed to the wing. This is the closest you can come to soaring like a bird over the Falls.

The microlights are affected by the slightest turbulence so, when you book a flight in advance, it's best to specify the early morning or late afternoon. Transport between their Maramba Aerodrome (about a five-minute drive from the border) and Livingstone or Victoria Falls hotels is provided.
Rates: US$70 per person for 15 minutes including circuits over the Falls and a flight over the game park; US$105 for 30 minutes, including mini-safari up-river

Helicopter

This is the most expensive way to see the Falls, but it is tremendous fun. Del Air use a five-seat Squirrel helicopter, based at their Maramba Aerodrome, which is designed to give all passengers a good view. The front seats are on a 'first come, first served' basis. The Zambezi Helicopter Company, based at Elephant Hills, offer similar trips from the Zimbabwe side.
Rates: typically US$70 per person for 15 minutes, US$130 per person for 30 minutes. Prices include all transfers, from either Livingstone or Victoria Falls

Ultra-lights

Another way to get a bird's eye view of the Falls is with an ultra-light (which feels like a cross between a microlight and small plane). As with the microlight, you are completely exposed with the wind in your hair and they take only one passenger at a time. The craft flies more like a small plane and you can carry your camera with you, making for good photographic opportunities without the confines of a small plane. It is also much quieter than a small plane.

These trips are based out of the Victoria Falls main airport (look for them on the tarmac if you fly in here) and run by Bush Birds Flying Safaris. Being so far out of town does make them slightly inconvenient, but they are the closest option to a microlight on the Zimbabwean side. On balance, the microlight is more fun, though you do get a nice view of the gorges as you fly up to the Falls.

Rates: US$100 per person for 35 minutes, US$150 per person for 55 minutes

Upper Zambezi canoeing

Canoeing down the upper Zambezi is a cool occupation on hot days, and the best way to explore the upper river, its islands and channels. The silence of canoes make them ideal for floating up to antelope drinking, elephants feeding, or crocodiles basking. Hippos provide the excitement, and are treated with respect and given lots of space.

There are a variety of options available, from half-day excursions to full days ending with a game drive in the Mosi-oa-Tunya National Park, and even overnight camping trips. You'll find any of them generally relaxing, although paddling becomes a bit more strenuous if it's windy. All canoe trips must be accompanied by a qualified river guide. Canoes range from two-seater open-decked kayaks to inflatable 'crocodiles'.

There are some sections of choppy water if you'd like a little more excitement, though it's possible to avoid most of these easily if you wish. Trips concentrating on these are sometimes sold as white-water kayaking – which shouldn't be confused with the white-water rafting mentioned below.

Once you are used to the water, the better guides will encourage you to concentrate on the wildlife. Trips on the Zambian side have long been run by Makora Quest and Chundukwa Adventure Trails – both are owner-operated and run by very experience guides.

Newer (and more commercial) entrants on the Zambian side include Raft Extreme, Bundu and Safari Par Excellence, whilst on the Zimbabwean side the main operators are both very large: Shearwater and Kandahar.

Zambian rates: around US$75 for a half day, including lunch, or US$85 for a full day. Two-day fully-inclusive camping trips are about US$235 per person. Zimbabwean rates are around US$70 for a half day or US90 for a full day.

Jet-boats

Jet-Extreme, on the Zambian side, runs 30-minute jet-boat trips between rapids 23 and 27. These have been widely criticised as very noisy and damaging the river's tranquil ambience as well as frightening its wildlife. Readers should think twice about these allegations before embarking on such a trip.

Bungee-jumping

There's only one company organising bungee-jumping – African Extreme, an offshoot of the original pioneers from New Zealand, Kiwi Extreme. You jump from the middle of the main bridge between Zambia and Zimbabwe, where the Zambezi is around 111m below you. It is the highest commercial bungee-jump in the world, and not for the nervous.

Masochists can do a 'gruesome twosome' where they jump and are then lowered directly on to a white-water rafting trip rather than being brought back up on to the bridge. Alternatively, 'tandem' bungee-jumps are possible for two people.

You can book in advance, through any of the agencies, or simply turn up at the bridge and pay there. Pictures and videos of your jump are available at extra charge.

Rates: US$90 for one jump (no refunds if you change your mind)

White-water rafting

The Zambezi below the Falls is one of the world's most renowned stretches of white water. It was the venue for the 1995 World Rafting Championships, and rafting is now very big business here with keen competition for tourist dollars. (About 50,000 people now go down the river every year, paying about US$80–100 each. You can do the sums.)

Experienced rafters grade rivers from I to VI, according to difficulty. Elsewhere in the world, a normal view of this scale would be:

* Class I   No rapids, flat water.
* Class II   Easy rapids, a float trip. No rafting experience required.
* Class III Intermediate to advanced rapids. No rafting experience required.
* Class IV   Very difficult rapids. Prior rafting experience highly recommended. No children.
* Class V   For experts only. High chance of flips or swims. No children or beginners.
* Class VI   Impossible to run.

The rapids below the Falls are mostly graded IV and V. This isn't surprising when you realise that all the water coming slowly up the Zambezi's 1.7km width is being squeezed through a number of rocky gorges that are often just 50–60m wide.

Fortunately for the rafting companies, most of the rapids here may be very large, but the vast majority of them are not 'technical' to run. This means that they don't need skill to manoeuvre the boat whilst it is *within* the rapids, they just require the rafts to be positioned properly *before* entering each rapid. Hence, despite the grading of these rapids, they allow absolute beginners into virtually all of the rafts.

A MATTER OF PERSPECTIVE
Judi Helmholz

Spanning the border between Zambia and Zimbabwe is the dramatic Victoria Falls Bridge. Built close to the mighty Falls so railroad carriages could be doused in spray, this famous bridge is becoming renowned for another attraction – the highest bungee-jump in the world: a daunting 110m. It is not unusual for hordes of spectators to gather at the jump site to watch daring individuals test their courage on the elastic line.

Over the course of a week, the Jump Master noticed the same two Zambian men at the bridge each day, closely observing the jump activities. This was unusual. Following each jump, the gentlemen engaged in seemingly heated discussion, gesturing and shaking their heads. After eight straight days of this, the two Zambians approached the Jump Master. 'We have been here many days trying to get up our courage. Although we are very scared, we have no jobs and need money. How much will you pay us to jump?'

When the Jump Master delicately informed them that in actual fact one must pay for the privilege of jumping, the men were confounded. Surely, no one in his or her right mind would actually pay to jump. There must be some misunderstanding. 'Ah, you have failed to understand. We are prepared to jump... FOR MONEY!' the men exclaimed in unison. Further clarification by the Jump Master left the two Zambians incredulously shaking their heads and seeking alternative means of employment. They were last seen heading toward one of the rafting companies.

High or low water, and which side of the river?

Rafting is offered from both sides of the river by a wide range of companies. Some operate on both sides, like Safari Par Excellence. The Zambian side offers a far more spectacular entry, just at the base of the Falls; whereas on the Zimbabwean side you miss this entirely and start off at Rapid Number Four.

During high water this might be partially obscured by spray, but you should try to go from the Zambian side during low-water months (roughly from August to January) so as not to miss such a stunning place to start below the Falls. These low-water months are probably the best time to experience the Zambezi's full glory, as then its waves and troughs (or 'drops') are more pronounced.

In high-water months (February to July), only half-day trips are offered. These start below Rapid Number 9 on both sides. Note that when the river is highest its rapids may seem less dramatic, but it is probably more dangerous – due to the strong whirlpools and undercurrents. At that time, the water is sometimes too high and rafting should then be stopped until it recedes to a safer level.

The trips

A typical rafting trip will start with a briefing, covering safety/health issues, giving the plan for the day and answering any questions. Once you reach the 'put-in' at the river, you will be given a short safety/practice session to familiarise yourself with the raft and techniques that will be used to run the rapids. Half-day trips will run about half of the rapids, but a full day is needed to get through all the rapids from one to twenty-three. Lunch and cool drinks are included. Note that the climb up and out of the gorge at the end can be steep and tiring.

A trained river guide pilots every raft, but you need to decide whether you want to go in an oar boat or in a paddle boat. In an **oar boat** expect to cling on for dear life, and throw your weight around the raft on demand – but nothing more. Oar boats are generally easier and safer because you rely on the skills of the oarsmen to negotiate the rapids, and you can hang on to the raft at all times. Only occasionally will you have to 'highside' (throw your weight forward) when punching through a big wave.

In a **paddle boat** the participants provide the power by paddling, while a trained rafting guide positions the boat and yells out commands instructing you what to do. You'll have to listen, and also paddle like crazy through the rapids, remembering when and if you are supposed to be paddling. You can't just hang on! In paddle boats you are an active participant and thus are largely responsible for how successfully you run the rapids. The rafting guide calls commands and positions the boat, but then it's up to you. If your fellow paddlers are not up to it, then expect a difficult ride. Paddle boats have a higher tendency to flip and/or have 'swimmers' (someone thrown out of the boat).

Originally, only oar boats were run on the Zambezi. However in recent years paddleboats have become more popular as rafting companies compete to outdo each other in offering the most exciting rides. There is, of course, a very fine line between striving to be more exciting, and actually becoming more dangerous.

With either option, remember that people often fall out and rafts do capsize. Despite this, safety records are usually cited as excellent. Serious injuries are said to be uncommon and fatalities rare. (Curiously for an industry that claims such a good safety record, none of the larger companies seem to keep transparent records of injuries or fatalities.)

The operators

All rafting companies offer broadly similar experiences at prices that are invariably identical. Videos and photos of your trip are offered at additional cost. The rapids are numbered starting from the boiling pot, from one to twenty-three, so it's easy to make a rough comparison of the trips on offer.

In addition to day trips, there are four-day expeditions that go as far as the Batoka Gorge, while seven-day expeditions reach the mouth of the Matetsi River. These offer more than the adrenaline of white water, and are the best way of seeing the remote Batoka Gorge. Adrift and Shearwater offer these longer trips out of the Zimbabwean Side. A new company, Zambezi Elite, also from the Zimbabwean side, offers smaller, more upmarket trips at a higher cost (US$150 per person).

Rates: half-day trips are around US$85, full day trips around US$95 per person. Both include transfers as well as breakfast and snacks or lunch and cool drinks.

River-boarding
For a more up-close and personal encounter with the Zambezi rapids, adrenaline junkies can try their hand at river-boarding (also known as boogie-boarding). Serious Fun and Safari Par Excellence both offer daily trips down the Zambezi from Zambia.

After donning your flippers, life jacket and helmet, you and your foam board (the size of a small surfboard) will have an opportunity to 'surf' the big waves of the Zambezi, after being taught basic skills in a calmer section of the river. A raft accompanies each trip and takes you downstream to the best surfing spots of the day. Here you can try your hand at finding the best 'standing waves' where you can stay still and surf as the water rushes beneath you. Experts can stand, but most will surf on their stomachs.

Thrilling for the fit who swim strongly, but not for the faint of heart. Trips are fully inclusive of transfers, a light breakfast, lunch and sundowners.

Rates: US$95–125 per person, fully inclusive.

Abseiling and swinging
The newest additions to the adventure menu are a highwire, a cable slide, abseiling, and 'Rap' jumps (rappelling forwards) down the side of the gorge from the Zambian side. These are currently only offered by Abseil Africa. It's a full day's activity starting with a light breakfast and a basic abseiling course. It continues with a day of highwiring, abseiling and cable sliding to your heart's content. Lunch and cool drinks are included and sundowners are offered. The site is a short drive from the Falls, in a scenic spot on the edge of the Gorge.

Rates: US$95 per person for a full day fully inclusive of transfers and meals.

Tandem parachuting
For an adrenaline rush 8,000 feet high, try tandem parachuting. Here you will be securely strapped to an instructor and free-fall at 200km/per hour for 30 seconds before safely drifting back to earth, some four minutes later, underneath a parachute.

This is currently being offered by Tandemania in Victoria Falls, and is being started by Batoka Sky/Del Air in Livingstone as this goes to press.

Rates: US$160–180 per person inclusive of transfers

Horse-riding
There are two operators offering horse-back safaris in the Falls area: in Zambia, Chundukwa Adventure Trails, and in Zimbabwe, Zambezi Horse Trails. Both can offer day trips for novices in search of game, as well as longer sojourns with overnight camps for more experienced riders.

Rates: US$45–65 per person

Elephant-riding

For an elephant encounter, The Elephant Company in Victoria Falls offer morning, lunchtime or afternoon elephant-back safaris. They are only 15 minutes' drive from Victoria Falls, at the Nakavango Estate adjacent to Zambezi National Park. Here you and your 'Nduna' (the elephant pilot) will have an opportunity to ride African elephants through the bush accompanied by the professional guide on foot.

There is game in the area – including kudu, buffalo, bushbuck and impala – which are sometimes seen. All the elephants were originally orphaned and raised on family farms, and so are comfortable being around people. You will have a chance to interact with them close up – a memorable and moving experience. You will also hear about elephant issues and conservation efforts in Africa. Breakfast, lunch or sundowners and all transfers are included from Victoria Falls. It's a worthwhile experience, especially if you can't afford to stay at the Elephant Camp, just outside the Falls.
Rates: US$118 per person

Booze cruises

These used to be strictly at sundown, and the drinks were free. Now, sadly, the river is full of booze cruise boats operating round the clock (you can now choose from breakfast, lunch, sunset or dinner cruises!), and they are often less generous – with drinks bought from a bar on board. Nostalgia aside, floating on the upper Zambezi with a glass in one hand, and a pair of binoculars in the other, is still a pleasant way to watch the sun go down. Meanwhile you take a gentle look around the Zambezi's islands, surrounded by national parks on both sides of the river. You may even spot the odd hippo, crocodile, or elephant.

On the Zambian side these are organised by Safari Par Excellence, Bwaato Adventures and Taonga Safaris. (Saf Par and Bwaato also have offices on the Zimbabwean side.)

In Zimbabwe, boats leave from several different jetties and there is a wider range of trips to choose from – from upmarket cruises to more basic ones. Book in advance through one of the agents in town, who can advise what best suits you, and will also arrange for you to be picked up about half an hour before the cruise.
Rates: US$20–40 per person inclusive of drinks and perhaps a meal

Livingstone Island lunch

Livingstone Island stands in the middle of the great waterfall, and is the island from which Dr Livingstone first viewed the falls. Only Tongabezi runs these trips and you will be transferred over to the island by banana boat (a long, almost cylindrical design of motorboat) from a launch site fairly near to the waterfall. There you'll spend a few hours gazing over the edge, perhaps bathing in a few small pools, and having a delicious gourmet lunch, usually complete with sparkling wine (French champagne at considerable extra cost). It's a lovely spot and makes an amazing experience.

During the months of very highest water the spray is too intense, so these trips don't operate. When the water's at its lowest, around October and November, you can sometimes walk to the island – and so it loses some of its appeal. But for the rest of the year it's a great trip and well worth the cost.

These can be arranged by tour operators and travel agents as well as directly with Tongabezi, and you must book in advance.
Rates: about US$65 per person

Appendix 1

WILDLIFE GUIDE

This wildlife guide is designed in a manner that should allow you to name most large mammals that you are likely to see in Botswana. For much more detailed information, see the *Visitor's Guide to Southern African Wildlife* by Mike Unwin, also published by Bradt Travel Guides. Less common species are featured under the heading *Similar species* beneath the animal to which they are most closely allied, or bear the strongest resemblance.

Cats and dogs

Lion *Panthera leo* Shoulder height 100–120cm. Weight 150–220kg.

Africa's largest predator, the lion is the animal that everybody hopes to see on safari. It is a sociable creature, living in prides of five to over 20 animals and defending a territory of between 20 and 200km². Lions often hunt at night, and their favoured prey is large or medium antelope such as wildebeest and impala. Most of the hunting is done by females, but dominant males normally feed first after a kill. Rivalry between males is intense and take-over battles are frequently fought to the death, so two or more males often form a coalition. Young males are forced out of their home pride at three years of age, and cubs are usually killed after a successful take-over.

When not feeding or fighting, lions are remarkably indolent – they spend up to 23 hours of any given day at rest – so the anticipation of a lion sighting is often more exciting than the real thing. Lions naturally occur in any habitat, except desert or rainforest. They once ranged across much of the Old World, but these days they are all but restricted to the larger conservation areas in sub-Saharan Africa (one residual population exists in India).

Lions occur throughout Botswana, and are very common in the main northern areas of Chobe, Linyanti-Kwando and the Okavango. They also range across the Kalahari, in the Nxai/Makgadikgadi areas, and the Central Kalahari Game Reserve, though the relative scarcity of prey leads to small, dissociated pride structures which have vast territories.

In the northern reserves, where food is plentiful, the converse is the case. Large prides are the norm and some, like those currently around North Gate and Savuti, have become so big that they make a speciality of killing young and juvenile elephants in order to have enough meat to go around. Even visiting these prolific reserves for just a few days, you're unlikely to not to see at least some lion!

Leopard *Panthera pardus* Shoulder height 70cm. Weight 60–80kg.

The powerful leopard is the most solitary and secretive of Africa's big cats. It hunts at night, using stealth and power, often getting to within 5m of its intended prey before pouncing. If there are hyenas and lions around then leopards habitually move their kills up into trees to safeguard them. The leopard can be distinguished from the cheetah by its rosette-like spots, lack of black 'tearmarks' and more compact, low-slung, powerful build.

The leopard is the most common of Africa's large felines. Some of Botswana's bush is perfect for leopard, which like plenty of thickets, cover and big trees. The riverine woodlands found throughout the Chobe, Linyanti-Kwando and Okavango areas are firm favourites with them. Here they're quite often seen during the by sharp-eyed observers who scan low-hanging branches for these lounging felines. Meanwhile drives around dusk and early evening in the private concessions will sometimes yield good sightings of leopard going out on hunting forays as the light fades. Remarkably, leopard often seem unperturbed by the presence of a vehicle and spotlight, and will often continue whatever they are doing regardless of an audience. Watching a leopard stalk is captivating viewing.

Leopard are very adaptable. There are many records of individuals living for years undetected in close proximity to humans, for example in the suburbs of major African cities like Nairobi, where they prey on domestic dogs. Given this, it's no surprise that they're also found throughout the Kalahari, though in lower densities commensurate with the relative lack of prey.

Cheetah *Acynonix jubatus* Shoulder height 70–80cm. Weight 50–60kg.
This remarkable spotted cat has a greyhound-like build, and is capable of running at 70km per hour in bursts, making it the world's fastest land animal. Despite superficial similarities, you can easily tell a cheetah from a leopard by the former's simple spots, disproportionately small head, streamlined build, diagnostic black tearmarks, and preference for relatively open habitats. It is often seen pacing the plains restlessly, either on its own or in a small family group consisting of a mother and her offspring. Diurnal hunters, cheetah favour the cooler hours of the day to hunt smaller antelope, like springbok, steenbok and duiker; plus young wildebeest, tsessebe and zebra, and also warthog, large birds, and small mammals, such as scrub hares.

Given that cheetah never occur in high densities, Botswana is a better place than most to see them. In areas of dense game, they often lose their prey to lion or spotted hyena, so the relative scarcity of competition in areas like Nxai, Makgadigadi, and the Central Kalahari make these ideal. These also harbour large populations of springbok – a cheetah's ideal prey – and their ability to go for long periods without water gives them

flexibility to move far from waterholes. Although cheetah are often thought of as animals of the open savannah, they do need some cover from which to sprint – so the Kalahari's thin scrub is ideal for them.

Having said that, all of my sightings of cheetah in Botswana have been in some of the central Okavango's areas of densest game – on Mboma Island and in the Mombo Concession! Looking through the sightings records at the camps, it's certainly notable that many of these cats move further into the Delta as the waters recede, and then move back out into the surrounding Kalahari to avoid the floods.

Estimates suggest that there are about 4,000–6,000 cheetah left in southern Africa, plus a few in Iran, Pakistan and the near East. (They did occur throughout India, but are now extinct there.) Scientists noting an amazing lack of genetic diversity amongst all living cheetah have suggested that the species must have gone through a 'genetic bottleneck' in the past – thus perhaps all living cheetah are descended from one female. This goes some way to explain why they are very susceptible to disease.

Serval *Felis serval* Shoulder height 60cm. Weight 9–18kg.
This long-legged cat is the tallest of Africa's 'small cats'. It has a similar build to a leopard, but black-on-gold spots giving way to streaking near the head. Seldom seen, it is widespread and quite common in moist grassland, reedbeds and riverine habitats throughout Africa, including northern Botswana. They're largely absent from the drier areas of the Kalahari.

Serval do particularly well in wetter areas where there is lots of long grass – and are common throughout the Okavango and Linyanti-Kwando area. Although they're relatively rarely seen, there have been consistent reports of good sightings from night drives along the channel from Savuti Camp. Serval prey on mice, rats, small mammals, birds, snakes, lizards and will sometimes even take fish or the young of small antelope. They use their big ears to locate their prey precisely by sound, and their long legs to see over tall grass, and to help them jump high as they pounce.

Caracal *(Felis caracal)* Shoulder height 40cm. Weight 15–20kg.
Smaller but heavier than the serval, caracal resemble European lynx with their uniform tan coat and tufted ears. They are solitary, mainly nocturnal hunters which feed on birds, small antelope and young livestock. Caracal are remarkable hunters for their size, and will often take prey as large or even larger than they are. Their style is very much like small leopards; they normally stalk their prey as closely as possible, before springing with surprise. They also take many of the same species, even caching their prey in trees to return and feed later, and can be quite acrobatic hunters: they have been known to 'bat' birds out of the air as they fly.

Caracal occur throughout sub-Saharan Africa, easily adapting to a variety of environments. They're found throughout Botswana and whilst night drives in the early evening provide your best chance of a glimpse of them, they're still very rarely seen.

Similar species The smaller **African wild cat** *(Felis sylvestris)* ranges from the Mediterranean to the Cape of Good Hope, and is similar in appearance to the domestic tabby cat. It has a ringed tail, a reddish-brown tinge to the back of its ears and an unspotted torso – which should preclude confusion with the even smaller **small spotted cat** *(Felis nigripes)*, a relatively rare resident of the central and southern Kalahari which has a more distinctively marked coat. Both species are generally solitary and nocturnal, often utilising burrows or termite mounds as daytime shelters. They prey upon reptiles, amphibians and birds as well as small mammals.

Wild dog *Lycaon pictus* Shoulder height 70cm. Weight 25kg.
Also known as the painted hunting dog, the wild dog is distinguished from other African dogs by its large size and mottled black, brown and cream coat. Highly sociable, living in packs of up to 20 animals, wild dogs are ferocious hunters that literally tear apart their prey on the run. The most endangered of Africa's great predators, they are now threatened with extinction. This is the result both of relentless persecution by farmers, who often view the dogs as dangerous vermin, and of their susceptibility to diseases spread by domestic dogs. Wild dogs are now extinct in many areas where

they were formerly abundant, like the Serengeti, and they are common nowhere. The global population of fewer than 3,000 is concentrated in southern Tanzania, Zambia, Zimbabwe, Botswana, South Africa and Namibia.

Wild dogs prefer open savannah with only sparse tree cover, if any, and packs have enormous territories, typically covering 400km² or more. They travel huge distances in search of prey, so few parks are large enough to contain them. Northern Botswana has one of the healthiest and most prolific populations in Africa, and Botswana is the best place on the continent to see them. These range right across Chobe, the Kwando-Linyanti and Okavango areas, and spreading out beyond these into Namibia and the northwest areas of the Kalahari.

They generally den around July to early October, and this is the only time when you can be fairly sure of seeing them in any given area. Sometimes they'll den in the same area for several years running, whilst at other times they'll change from year to year. For the best chances of seeing them – and a possibility of following a pack as they hunt (an amazing, exhilarating experience), choose a mainly dry reserve with plenty of open ground. Make sure that off-road driving is permitted, or you'll never be able to follow them, and ideally night drives should be allowed. Selinda, southern Kwando, Kwara and Vumbura would all currently be high on my list – and I've seen dogs in all of these. Better still, ask someone who knows the delta and the reserves well where specific packs have denned the previous season, and go there.

Given that dogs will take most antelope and always run down their prey, the only strategy that their prey can adopt to avoid death is to run as far, and as fast, as they can. They will do this as soon as they realise that dogs are in the area. Thus if you ever see game seriously sprinting with a purpose, and just not stopping, then look hard: maybe there's a pack of dogs behind them!

Black-backed jackal *Canis mesomelas* Shoulder height 35–45cm. Weight 8–12kg.

The black-backed jackal is an opportunistic feeder capable of adapting to most habitats. Most often seen singly or in pairs at dusk or dawn, it is ochre in colour with a prominent black saddle flecked by a varying amount of white or gold. It is probably the most frequently observed small predator in Africa south of the Zambezi, and its eerie call is a characteristic sound of the bush at night. It is found throughout Botswana, with the exception of the far north of the country around the Chobe and Linyanti-Kwando, and is fairly common in the drier areas of the Kalahari.

Side-striped jackal *Canis adustus* Shoulder height 35–40cm. Weight 8–12kg.
Despite its prevalence in other areas of Africa, the side-striped jackal is common nowhere in Botswana. It occurs in the far north of the country, including Chobe, the Linyanti-Kwando area, and the Okavango. It is about the same size as the previous species, but greyish in colour, with an indistinct pale horizontal stripe on each flank and often a white-tipped tail. These jackals are also usually seen singly or in pairs, at dusk or dawn. Both the side-striped and the black-backed jackal are opportunistic feeders, taking rats, mice, birds, insects, carrion, wild fruits and even termites.

Bat-eared fox *Otocyon megalotis* Shoulder height 30–35cm. Weight 3–5kg.
This endearing small, silver-grey insectivore is unmistakable, with its huge ears and black eye-mask. It can be found throughout Botswana, anywhere that the

harvester termite (*Hodotermes mossambicus*) occurs. The best areas are usually short grass plains that receive relatively low rainfall – Savuti Marsh is certainly a favourite habitat.

It is mostly nocturnal, but can sometimes be seen in pairs or small family groups during the cooler hours of the day, usually in dry open country. It digs well, and if seen foraging then it will often 'listen' to the ground (its ears operating like a radio-dish) whilst wandering around, before stopping to dig with its forepaws. As well as the termites, bat-eared foxes will eat lizards, gerbils, small birds, scorpions, beetle larvae and other insects.

Insect populations vary with the seasons and bat-eared foxes will move with them, but when conditions allow some areas will have very high densities of individuals.

Similar species The **Cape fox** (*Vulpes chama*) is an infrequently seen dry country predator which occurs throughout central and western Botswana, but is absent from Chobe and the north side of the Okavango. The Cape fox lacks the prominent ears and mask of the bat-eared fox, and its coat is a uniform sandy-grey colour. I once had a Cape fox approach me cautiously, after dusk, whilst camping in Namibia's Namib-Naukluft Park, but have never seen another.

Spotted hyena *Crocuta crocuta* Shoulder height 85cm. Weight 70kg.
Hyenas are characterised by their bulky build, sloping back (lower hindquarters), rough brownish coat, powerful jaws and dog-like expression. Contrary to popular myth, spotted hyenas are not exclusively scavengers; they are also adept hunters, which hunt in groups and kill animals as large as wildebeests. Nor are they hermaphroditic, an ancient belief that stems from the false scrotum and penis covering the female hyena's vagina.

Sociable animals, hyenas live in loosely structured clans of about ten animals, led by females who are stronger and larger than males, and based in a communal den.

Hyenas utilise their kills far better than most predators, digesting the bones, skin and even teeth of antelope. This results in the distinctive white colour attained by their faeces when dry – which is an easily identified sign of them living in an area.

The spotted hyena is the largest hyena, identified by its light-brown, blotchily spotted coat. It is found throughout most of Botswana, only absent from the eastern areas around Ghanzi, and perhaps the country's furthest southern edge. They are a common predator throughout the north, and will frequently scavenge around camps and campsites at night. Savuti's campsite was, for years, completely plagued by them, whilst few camps in the Delta are without a story of hyena breaking into kitchens or eating their way through larders.

Although mainly nocturnal, spotted hyenas can often be seen around dusk and dawn, and their distinctive, whooping calls are one of the most wonderful, yet spine-chilling, sounds of the African night.

Brown hyena *Hyena brunnea* Shoulder height 75–85cm. Weight 40–47kg.
This secretive, apparently solitary hyena occurs in the most arid parts of Namibia, and throughout Botswana; it is absent only from the far north. It is unmistakable with a shaggy, dark brown coat – not unlike a large, long-haired German shepherd dog – with faint black stripes and sloping back. In contrast to the spotted hyena, brown hyenas do tend to scavenge rather than hunt, and are generally solitary whilst doing so.

They are the dominant carnivore in the drier areas of the Namib and Kalahari, where clans (typically containing 2–10 animals) will defend enormous territories against neighbouring clans. Individuals normally forage on their own and will eat whatever they can, from small birds and mammals to the remains of kill, as well as fruit and vegetables. They can go without water for long periods in the Kalahari, gaining moisture from tsama melons as well as their other food.

Brown hyena are very rarely seen on game drives, although in the last few years researchers based at Jack's Camp have habituated a small clan of hyena to their presence – making this probably the best place in Africa to see them. See *The Clans of Makgadikgadi* on page 418 for more information on brown hyena.

Aardwolf *Proteles cristatus* Shoulder height 45–50cm. Weight 7–11g.
With a tawny brown coat and dark, vertical stripes, this insectivorous hyena is not much bigger than a jackal and occurs in low numbers in most parts of Botswana. It is active mainly at night, gathering harvester termites (specifically those of the genus *Trinervitermes*), its principle food, with its wide, sticky tongue. These termites live underground (not in castle-like termite mounds) and come out at night to cut grass, and drag it back down with them. Occasionally it'll also take other insects, mice, birds and carrion.

Thus open grassland or lightly wooded areas form the typical habitat for aardwolves, which can sometimes be spotted around dusk, dawn, or on very overcast days, especially during the colder months. The *Trinervitermes* often thrive on overgrazed land, which means that aardwolf are often more common on farmland than in national parks – and I don't know of anywhere in central or northern Botswana where they're seen frequently.

Chacma baboon *Papio cynocaphalus ursinus* Shoulder height 50–75cm. Weight 25–45kg.
This powerful terrestrial primate, distinguished from any other monkey by its much larger size, inverted 'U' shaped tail and distinctive dog-like head, is fascinating to watch from a behavioural perspective. It lives in large troops that boast a complex, rigid social structure characterised by a matriarchal lineage and plenty of inter-troop movement by males seeking social dominance. Omnivorous and at home in almost any habitat, the baboon is the most widespread primate in Africa, frequently seen in most of Botswana. The centre of the Kalahari (including the CKGR) is the only area from which they are absent.

There are three African races, regarded by some authorities as full species. The chacma baboon (*P. c. ursinus*) is grey and confined largely to areas south of the Zambezi. The yellow baboon (*P. c. cynocephalus*) is the yellow-brown race occurring in Zambia, northern Mozambique, Malawi, southern and eastern Tanzania and eastern Kenya. The olive or anubis baboon (*P. c. anubis*) is a hairy green-to-brown baboon found in Ethiopia, Uganda, northern Tanzania and Kenya.

With a highly organised defence system, the only predator that seriously affects them is the leopard, which will try to pick them off at night, whilst they are roosting in trees or cliffs. Campers in Chobe and Moremi should treat these animals with respect; long exposure to humans has taught them to steal, and not to be afraid.

Vervet monkey *Cercopithecus aethiops* Length (excluding tail) 40–55cm. Weight 4–6kg.
Also known as the green or grivet monkey, the vervet is probably the world's most numerous monkey and certainly the most common and widespread representative of the *Cercopithecus* guenons, a taxonomically controversial genus associated with African forests. An atypical guenon in that it inhabits savannah and woodland rather than true forest, the vervet spends a high proportion of its time on the ground. It occurs throughout the northern and eastern parts of the country, but is absent from the drier areas of central, western and southern Botswana. Vervets like belts of tall trees with thick vegetation within easy reach of water, and much of northern Chobe, the Kwando-Linyanti area and the Okavango are ideal for them.

The vervet's light grey coat, black face and white forehead band are distinctive – as are the male's garish blue genitals. Vervet monkeys live in troops averaging about 25 animals; they are active during the day and roost in trees at night. They eat mainly fruit and vegetables, though are opportunistic and will take insects and young birds, and even raid tents at campsites (usually where ill-informed visitors have previously tempted them into human contact by offering food).

Lesser bushbaby *Galago senegalensis* Length (without tail) 17cm. Weight 150g.
The lesser bushbaby is the most widespread and common member of a group of small and generally indistinguishable nocturnal primates, distantly related to the lemurs of Madagascar. In Botswana they occur throughout the northern half of the country, including Nxai and Makgadikgadi.

More often heard than seen, the lesser bushbaby is nocturnal but can sometimes be picked out by tracing a cry to a tree and shining a torch into the branches; its eyes reflect as two red dots. These eyes are designed to function in what we would describe as total darkness, and they feed on insects – some of which are caught in the air by jumping – and also eating sap from trees, especially acacia gum.

They inhabit wooded areas, and prefer acacia trees or riverine forests. I remember being startled by a small family of bushbabies once; they raced through the trees above us, bouncing from branch to branch whilst chattering and screaming out of all proportion to their size.

Large antelope
Sable antelope *Hippotragus niger* Shoulder height 135cm. Weight 230kg.
The striking male sable is jet black with a distinct white face, underbelly and rump, and long decurved horns – a strong contender for the title of Africa's most beautiful antelope. The female is chestnut brown and has shorter horns, whilst the young are a lighter red-brown colour. Sable are found throughout the wetter areas of southern and East Africa, but are common nowhere.

In Botswana they occur in the north of Botswana, as far west as the central Okavango. The Chobe riverfront is a good place to look for them, usually between the Kasane and Chobe Game Lodge as there's a herd that frequently comes down to drink there. Similarly, they're occasionally seen near the Kwando and Linyanti rivers. They're not common in the Delta region, but are seen periodically. Good sightings have recently been recorded around the Gomoti River (near Starling's Camp), and in NG20 and NG21. The Vumbura Concession, NG22, probably offer the highest density of sable in the Delta, whilst they're generally absent from NG26, NG27, NG30 and further west.

Sable are normally seen in small herds: either bachelor herds of males, or breeding herds of females and young, which are often accompanied by the dominant bull in that territory. The breeding females give birth around February or March; the calves remain hidden, away from the herd, for their first few weeks. Sable are mostly grazers, though will browse, especially when food is scarce. They need to drink at least every other day, and seem especially fond of low-lying dewy vleis in wetter areas.

Roan antelope *Hippotragus equinus* Shoulder height 120–150cm. Weight 250–300kg.
This handsome horse-like antelope is uniform fawn-grey with a pale belly, short decurved horns and a light mane. It could be mistaken for the female sable antelope, but this has a well-defined white belly, and lacks the roan's distinctive black-and-white facial markings. The roan is a relatively rare antelope; common almost nowhere in Africa (Malawi's Nyika Plateau

being the obvious exception to this rule). In Botswana, small groups of roan are found in the Chobe and Kwando-Linyanti areas, and occasionally some will wander as far as the drier parts of the Okavango Delta – but they're always something of a rarity. Ngwezumba Pans is probably the best location to search for them, but they're not seen regularly even there.

Roan need lots of space if they are to thrive and breed; they don't generally do well where game densities are high. This alone precludes them from success in most of the Delta. Game farms prize them as one of the most valuable antelope. They need access to drinking water, but are well adapted to subsist on relatively high plateaux with poor soils.

Oryx or **gemsbok** *Oryx gazella* Shoulder height 120cm. Weight 230kg.
This is the quintessential desert antelope, unmistakable with its ash-grey coat, bold black facial marks and flank strip, and unique long, straight horns. Of the three races of oryx in Africa, the gemsbok is the largest and most striking. It occurs throughout the Kalahari and Namib and is widespread all over central and western Botswana. They are the dominant large antelope in the CKGR, where they can be seen in large numbers during the early months of the year.

As you might expect, gemsbok are very adaptable. They range widely and are found in areas of dunes, alkaline pans, open savannah and even woodlands. Along with the much smaller springbok, they can sometimes even be seen tracking across open plains with only dust-devils and mirages for company. Gemsbok can endure extremes of temperature, helped by specially adapted blood capillaries in their nasal passages that can cool their blood before it reaches their brains. Thus although their body temperature can rise by up to 6°C, their brains remain cool and they survive. They do not need drinking water and will eat wild melons and dig for roots, bulbs and tubers when grazing or browsing becomes difficult.

Waterbuck *Kobus ellipsiprymnus* Shoulder height 130cm. Weight 250–270kg.
The waterbuck is easily recognised by its shaggy brown coat and the male's large, lyre-shaped horns. The common race of southern Africa (*K. e. ellipsiprymnus*) and areas east of the Rift Valley has a distinctive white ring around its rump, seen on the right of the sketch. The defassa race (known as *K. e. defassa* or *K. e. crawshayi*) of the Rift Valley and areas further west has a full white rump, as indicated on the left.

Only the common waterbuck are found in Botswana, and they're restricted to the Chobe, Kwando-Linyanti and eastern sides of the Delta. Favourite areas include the northern side of the Linyanti (NG15) Concession, and also Vumbura (NG22), but they're relatively uncommon elsewhere. They certainly used to occur at Savuti when the channel flowed, but they deserted the area when the marsh dried up.

Waterbuck need to drink very regularly, so usually stay within a few kilometres of water, where they like to graze on short, nutritious grasses. At night they may take cover in adjacent woodlands. It is often asserted that waterbuck flesh is oily and smelly, which may discourage predators.

Blue wildebeest *Connochaetes taurinus* Shoulder height 130–150cm. Weight 180–250kg.
This ungainly antelope, also called the brindled gnu, is easily identified by its dark coat and bovine appearance. The superficially similar buffalo is far more heavily built. When they have enough space and conditions are right, blue wildebeest can multiply rapidly and form immense herds – as perhaps a million do for their annual migration from Tanzania's Serengeti Plains into Kenya's Masai Mara.

In Botswana during the middle of the 20th century they were probably the most numerous large herbivore, forming herds estimated at a quarter of a million individuals. Although they are still found throughout Botswana, these numbers have reduced drastically. (See the CKGR's *Fauna* section, page 435, for further discussion of this.)

Wildebeest are best adapted to take large mouthfuls of short, nutritious grasses, and they need access to drinking water every two or three days. This limits them to remain relatively close to a source of water, and if that dries up they will journey as far as necessary to find another.

Hartebeest *Alcelaphus buselaphus* Shoulder height 125cm. Weight 120–150kg.
Hartebeests are ungainly antelopes, readily identified by the combination of large shoulders, a sloping back, a glossy, red-brown coat and smallish horns in both sexes. Numerous subspecies are recognised, all of which are generally seen in small family groups in reasonably open country. Though once hartebeest were found from the Mediterranean to the Cape, only isolated populations still survive.

The only one native to Botswana is the red hartebeest, which is found throughout the arid central, southern and western areas of the country. They can be seen in Nxai and Makgadikgadi, and they're one of the more numerous large mammals in the CKGR. Hartebeest may occur in the drier, southwestern corners of the Delta, or in the drier parts of southern Chobe, but I've no records of them being seen in either location.

Hartebeests are more-or-less exclusively grazers, and although they like access to water they will eat melons, tubers and rhizomes when necessary. In the central Kalahari they'll range widely, often with wildebeest, following thunderstorms in search of fresh, green shoots.

Tsessebe *Damaliscus lunatus* Shoulder height 120cm. Weight 125–140kg.
Tsessebe are basically a slightly smaller, darker version of hartebeest, coloured red-brown with an almost purple sheen, though their lower legs are distinctly paler. (A closely related subspecies is known as topi in East Africa.) They look similar in profile or at a distance, although often in the field you can make a good guess from the environment which antelope you're looking at long before you're close enough to examine its colouring.

Tsessebe are found in northern Botswana, and are one of the most common antelope in some parts of the Okavango Delta. (One study claimed 70% of lion kills in the Delta are tsessebe.)

Its favourite habitat is open grassland, where it is a selective grazer, eating the younger, more nutritious grasses. This makes it efficient in pastures where some grasses are old and some fresh, or in more broken country, but less efficient than, say, wildebeest where the pasture is uniformly short, good grass. The tsessebe is one of the fastest antelope species, and jumps very well.

Kudu *Tragelaphus strepsiceros* Shoulder height 140–155cm. Weight 180–250kg.
The kudu (or, more properly, the greater kudu) is the most frequently observed member of the genus *Tragelaphus*. These medium-sized to large antelopes are characterised by their grey-brown coats and up to ten stripes on each side. The male has magnificent double-spiralled corkscrew horns. Occurring throughout Mozambique, Zimbabwe, Zambia and Namibia, kudu are found all over Botswana with the exception of the Kgalagadi Transfrontier Park, in the extreme southwest.

Kudu are particularly common in the well-wooded areas of Chobe, the Kwando-Linyanti area and the Okavango, though they also occur throughout the drier areas of the Kalahari. They are browsers that thrive in areas with mixed tree savannah and thickets, and the males will sometimes use their horns to pull down the lower branches of trees to eat.

Wherever they occur, kudu are normally seen in small herds, consisting of a couple of females and their offspring, usually accompanied by a male. Otherwise the males occur either singly, or in small bachelor groups.

Sitatunga *Tragelaphus spekei* Shoulder height 85–90cm. Weight 105–115kg.
This semi-aquatic antelope is a widespread but infrequently observed inhabitant of west and central African papyrus swamps, from the Okavango in Botswana to the Sudd in Sudan. In Botswana they're concentrated in the Okavango – which has a strong population – though they're also seen periodically in the Kwando-Linyanti and Chobe systems. The best places to go and spot them are the deep-water areas with plenty of papyrus – including Moremi and NG21, 22, 23, 24 and 25.

Because of their preferred habitat, sitatunga are elusive and seldom seen, even in areas where they are relatively common. They are also less easy to hunt/poach than many other species, although they are exceedingly vulnerable to habitat destruction. Sitatunga are noted for an ability to submerse themselves completely, with just their nostrils showing, when pursued by a predator.

Eland *Taurotragus oryx* Shoulder height 150–175cm. Weight 450–900kg.
Africa's largest antelope, the eland is light brown in colour, sometimes with a few faint white vertical stripes. Relatively short horns and a large dewlap accentuate its somewhat bovine appearance. It was once widely distributed in East and southern Africa, though the population has now been severely depleted. Small herds of eland frequent grasslands and light woodlands, often fleeing at the slightest provocation. (They have long been hunted for their excellent meat, so perhaps this is not surprising.)

Eland are very rare in the Okavango area and although they probably occur throughout Chobe, they are seldom seen. Better areas to see them are in the Kalahari's salt pans or, better still, the central Kalahari. They are opportunist browsers and grazers, eating fruit, berries, seed pods and leaves as well as green grass after the rains, and roots and tubers when times are lean.

They run slowly, though can trot for great distances and jump exceedingly well. Eland have a very special significance for the San people – illustrated by the highlight of the famous 'van der Post panel' at the Tsodilo Hills (see page 376), which is a painting of a particularly magnificent eland bull.

Medium and small antelope

Bushbuck *Tragelaphus scriptus* Shoulder height 70–80cm. Weight 30–45kg.
This attractive antelope, a member of the same genus as the kudu, is widespread throughout Africa and shows great regional variation in its colouring. (The animals found in sub-saharan Africa are often claimed to be a subspecies, the 'Chobe bushbuck' – though it seems likely that they're simply a colour variation of the main species.)

They occur in forest and riverine woodland, where they are normally seen singly or in pairs. The male is dark brown or chestnut, while the much smaller female is generally a pale reddish brown. The male has relatively small, straight horns and both sexes are marked with white spots and sometimes stripes, though the stripes are often indistinct.

Bushbuck tend to be secretive and very skittish, except when used to people – when they relax and become almost tame. They depend on cover and camouflage to avoid predators, and are often found in the thick, herby vegetation around rivers – and are the only solitary antelope in Africa which do not defend a territory. They will freeze if disturbed, before dashing off into the undergrowth.

Bushbuck are both browsers and grazers, choosing the more succulent grass shoots, fruit and flowers. In Botswana they have a limited distribution around the Okavango, beside the Kwando-Linyanti and the Chobe. Look for them slowly picking their way through the thick bush near the water. (Serondella used to be a favourite spot, and the island on which Kwetsani stands had several fairly relaxed resident pairs when I last visited.)

Impala *Aepeceros melampus* Shoulder height 90cm. Weight 45kg.

This slender, handsome antelope is superficially similar to the springbok, but in fact belongs to its own separate family. Chestnut in colour, and lighter underneath than above, the impala has diagnostic black and white stripes running down its rump and tail, and the male has large lyre-shaped horns. The impala is one of the most widespread and successful antelope species in East and southern Africa. It is often the most common antelope in wooded savannah habitats, including most of Chobe and the drier, more forested parts of the Okavango Delta – though is rarely seen west of the Okavango, or south of Nxai Pan. Although they can survive without drinking, impala prefer to live near water and are largely absent from the Kalahari.

As expected of such a successful species, it both grazes and browses, depending on what fodder is available. Despite some people's tendency to overlook them as common, take a close look and you'll realise that they're exceptionally beautiful animals. Socially you'll normally see large herds of females and young, lorded over by a dominant male, and small bachelor groups of males.

Springbok *Antidorcas marsupilis* Shoulder height 60cm. Weight 20–25kg.

Springbok are graceful herbivores, similar in size to impala, which generally occur in large herds. Visitors from East Africa noticing their passing resemblance to Thomson's gazelle (*Gazella thomsonii*) will not be surprised that they're southern Africa's only member of the gazelle family.

Even from a distance, springbok are unlikely to be confused with anything else; their finely marked short coats have fawn-brown upper parts and a white belly, separated by a dark brown band. Springbok favour dry, open country, preferring plains or savannah, and avoiding thick woodlands and mountains. They can subsist without water for long periods, provided that there is moisture (minimum of 10%) in the vegetation that they graze or browse.

Since springbok are more dependent on food than water, they congregate in huge numbers during the rains on areas where they can find fresh, green shoots – like the pans of the CKGR. In contrast, during the dry season they spread out across the vast arid parks of the Kalahari. This is exactly the opposite pattern to that followed by most water-dependent antelope, which typically congregate during the dry season (around rivers to remaining pans), whilst spreading out during the rains. Thus explaining why the Kalahari's game is at its densest during the rains, whereas the game in Chobe and the Okavango is at its most prolific during the dry season.

Springbok occur throughout central and southern Botswana, where they are usually the most common small antelope by far; they number in the thousands in Nxai, Makgadikgadi and the CKGR.

Reedbuck *Redunca arundinum* Shoulder height 80–90cm. Weight 45–65kg.

Sometimes referred to as the southern reedbuck (as distinct from mountain and Bohor reedbucks, found further east), these delicate antelope are uniformly fawn or grey in colour, and lighter below than above. They are generally found in reedbeds and tall grasslands, often beside rivers, and are easily identified by their loud, whistling alarm call and distinctive bounding running style.

In Botswana they are only found where there is close access to water in the north: in northern Chobe, the Kwando-Linyanti region, and throughout the Delta. They live in monogamous pairs that defend a territory. You'll often see just a pair together, and they have a distinctive rocking gate as they take flight by bounding away through tall reedbeds.

Klipspringer *Oreotragus oreotragus* Shoulder height 60cm. Weight 13kg.

The klipspringer is a strongly built little antelope, normally seen in pairs, and easily identified by its dark, bristly grey-yellow coat, slightly speckled appearance and unique habitat preference. Klipspringer means 'rockjumper' in Afrikaans and it is an apt name for an antelope which occurs exclusively in mountainous areas and rocky outcrops from Cape Town to the Red Sea. Klipspringers are mainly browsers, though they do eat a little new grass. When spotted they will freeze, or bound at great speed across the steepest of slopes.

Though often thought to be absent from all but the extreme southeast corner of Botswana, there were several reliable reports of sightings of them on Qumxhwaa Hill, near Savuti Marsh, at the end of the 1970s. Given that they only live rocky hills and kopjes, and that most of Botswana is amazingly flat (or gently rolling at best), then it's no surprise that only the odd isolated population exists. It's the same in other parts of their range. I've no reports of them at the Tsodilo Hills, but it would be a perfect habitat for them!

Red lechwe *Kobus leche* Shoulder height 90–100cm. Weight 80–100kg.

Red lechwe are sturdy, shaggy antelope with a chestnut-red coat, paler underneath than on top, and beautiful lyre-shaped horns. They need dry land on which to rest, but otherwise are adapted for life in the seasonal floodplains that border lakes and rivers. They will spend much of their time grazing on grasses and sedges, standing in water if necessary. Their hooves are splayed, adapted to bounding through their muddy environment when fleeing from the lion, hyena and wild dog that hunt them, making them the most aquatic of antelope after sitatunga.

Lechwe reach the southern limit of their distribution in the Okavango and Linyanti areas. They are also found in the DRC, Angola, Namibia's Caprivi Strip, and in Zambia, their stronghold. Wherever they occur, the males are generally larger and darker than the females. When conditions are right, they can be found in huge numbers, and they are the most numerous antelope in the shallow-water environments of the Delta.

Puku *Kobus vardonii* Shoulder height 80cm. Weight 60–75kg.
Easily confused with the lechwe at a glance, the puku has an orange-red colour overall, which is lighter underneath than above. Its legs are uniformly red, and its tail is a lighter yellow. Puku are smaller and slightly shaggier than lechwe, and the males have smaller, stouter, lyre-shaped horns when compared with the lechwe.

Puku are found all over East and central Africa, and are one of the most common antelopes in Zambia. Typically they inhabit open areas near rivers and marshes, though in Zambia are found in a wide variety of habitats. In Botswana their distribution is restricted to the floodplain areas of the Chobe riverfront, and often virtually the only place that you'll see them is the aptly named Puku Flats, just west of Chobe Game Lodge and east of the of campsite at Serondella.

Steenbok *Raphicerus cempestris* Shoulder height 50cm. Weight 11kg.
This rather nondescript small antelope has red-brown upper parts and clear white underparts, and the male has short straight horns. It is one of the most commonly observed small antelope, especially on farmland; if you see antelope fleeing from you across grassland, then it is likely to be a steenbok. Like most other small antelopes, the steenbok is normally encountered singly or in pairs and tends to 'freeze' when disturbed, before taking flight.

Similar species The **Oribi** (*Ourebia ourebi*) is a relatively widespread but generally uncommon antelope, which occurs in very localised areas throughout sub-Saharan Africa. It is usually found only in large, open stretches of dry grassland, where there are also patches of taller grass for cover. It looks much like a steenbok but stands about 10cm higher at the shoulder and has an altogether more upright bearing. In Botswana it is thought to occur in Chobe, and specifically in the Ngwezumba Pans area – although sightings of it even there are not common. **Sharpe's grysbok** (*Raphicerus sharpei*) is similar in size and appearance, though it has a distinctive white-flecked coat. It occurs alongside the steenbok in the far northeastern corner of Botswana, around northern Chobe and the Kasane area, but is almost entirely nocturnal in its habits and so very seldom seen.

Common duiker *Sylvicapra grimmia* Shoulder height 50cm. Weight 20kg.
This anomalous duiker holds itself more like a steenbok or grysbok and is the only member of its (large) family to occur outside of forests. Generally grey in colour, the common duiker can most easily be separated from other small antelopes by the black tuft of hair that sticks up between its horns. It occurs throughout Botswana, and across virtually the whole of southern Africa, with the exception of the Namib Desert. Common duikers tolerate most habitats except for true forest and very open country, and are tolerant of nearby human settlements. They are opportunist feeders, taking fruit, seeds and leaves, as well as crops, small reptiles and amphibians. Despite its widespread occurrence, duiker are relatively rarely seen.

Other large herbivores

African elephant *Loxodonta africana* Shoulder height 2.3–3.4m. Weight up to 6,000kg.
The world's largest land animal, the African elephant is intelligent, social and often very entertaining to watch. Female elephants live in closely knit clans in which the eldest female

plays matriarch over her sisters, daughters and granddaughters. Their life spans are comparable with those of humans, and mother-daughter bonds are strong and may last for up to 50 years. Males generally leave the family group at around 12 years to roam singly or form bachelor herds. Under normal circumstances, elephants range widely in search of food and water, but when concentrated populations are forced to live in conservation areas their habit of uprooting trees can cause serious environmental damage.

Elephants are widespread and common in habitats ranging from the deserts to rainforest; but they require trees and access to drinking water. They are very common in the north of Botswana.

The Chobe, Kwando-Linyanti and Okavango areas have one of Africa's strongest populations of elephants. During the rains, from December onwards, these disperse in the interior of the country, into the vast expanses of mopane forest and into the drier areas of the northern Kalahari. They split up into smaller family groups and spread out as they can then find water all over the place (the clay pans of the mopane woodlands are especially valuable as sources).

Despite their range having become more restricted by human expansion over the years, individuals will often wander widely, turning up in locations from which they have been absent for years.

However, as the dry season progresses and the water holes dry up, they gradually coalesce into larger herds, and head for the permanent sources: the rivers and the Delta. Thus by September and October you can normally see huge herds of elephants along the Chobe, Kwando and Linyanti rivers. The number and size of herds in the Okavango increases also.

In many areas elephants have no natural predators (the huge prides of lion in the Savuti and North Gate areas are an exception to this rule); they are generally constrained by lack of suitable habitat (ie: trees and water) and by man. Thus in many confined national parks in southern Africa, there are programmes to cull elephants to restrict their numbers. This is controversial, even amongst ardent conservationists. Botswana has no such policy. The result, some argue, is an over-population of elephants here, and the severe environmental degradation to be seen around the riverfront in Chobe – where the riverine forests have been decimated. Whilst not denying the observation, it's well worth remembering that there was a sawmill in this area, and extensive logging during the 1930s and early 1940s – so humans should take part of the blame for this.

Black rhinoceros *Diceros bicornis* Shoulder height 160cm. Weight 1,000kg. This is the more widespread of Africa's two rhino species, an imposing and rather temperamental creature. Black rhino were once found all over northern Botswana, but were thought to have been poached to extinction in Botswana, whilst becoming highly endangered in many other countries within their range.

Black rhino exploit a wide range of habitats from dense woodlands and bush, and are generally solitary animals. They can survive without drinking for 4–5 days. However, their territorial behaviour and regular patterns of movement make them an easy target for poachers. Black rhino can be very aggressive when disturbed and will charge with minimal provocation. Their hearing and sense of smell are acute, whilst their eyesight is poor (so they often miss if you keep a low profile and don't move).

Now, following the successful reintroduction of white rhino to Chief's Island, there are plans to reintroduce black rhino here also. The environment is very suitable, and the island is effectively isolated within a large area devoted to wildlife; so it is hoped that poaching them from here would be difficult. Watch this space, and see the comments on page 280; and if you want to help with this work, then see *Giving something back* on pages 42–3.

White rhinoceros *Ceratotherium simum* Shoulder height 180cm. Weight 1,500–2,000kg.

The white rhino is in fact no paler in colour than the black rhino – the 'white' derives from the Afrikaans *weit* (wide) and refers to its flattened mouth, an ideal shape for cropping grass. This is the best way to tell the two rhino species apart, since the mouth of the black rhino, a browser in most parts of its range, is more rounded with a hooked upper lip. (Note that there is *no colour difference at all* between these two species of rhino; 'white' and 'black' are *not* literal descriptions.)

Unlike their smaller cousins, white rhino are generally placid grazing animals which are very rarely aggressive. They prefer open grassy plains and are often seen in small groups. In the accounts of the first trips across Africa by the early white explorers, rhino were found (and shot) in huge numbers.

As with the black rhino, hunting and poaching reduced the population of African white rhinos drastically, reaching a crisis in the 1980s – when only a few South African reserves remained with really strong populations (notably Umfolozi and Hluhluwe). Amongst other countries, Zimbabwe retained remnants whilst Botswana, Zambia and others were effectively poached out.

Since then those parks which effectively saved the species have been used as reservoirs, to slowly re-populate a few protected areas. Recently some have been reintroduced into the Chief's Island area of Moremi, with encouraging success. It's hoped that this will continue, and that once again Botswana will be able to boast at least one area where rhino are prolific.

Hippopotamus *Hippopotamus amphibius* Shoulder height 150cm. Weight 2,000kg.

Characteristic of Africa's large rivers and lakes, this large, lumbering animal spends most of the day submerged but emerges at night to graze. Strongly territorial, herds of ten or more animals are presided over by a dominant male who will readily defend his patriarchy to the death. Hippos are abundant in most protected rivers and water bodies and are still quite common outside of reserves.

They are widely credited with killing more people than any other African mammal. They are clearly very, very dangerous – but I know of no statistics to support this, and many reliable sources suggest that that crocodile, elephant and lion could all vie for this dubious title. So, whilst undoubtedly dangerous, perhaps they don't quite deserve their reputation.

In Botswana you'll find hippo in good numbers in all of the major river systems: Chobe, Kwando-Linyanti and the Okavango. It'd be difficult to go on safari in any of the wetter areas of northern Botswana without seeing large numbers of hippo.

Buffalo *Syncerus caffer* Shoulder height 140cm. Weight 700kg.

Frequently and erroneously referred to as a water buffalo (which is actually an Asian species), the Cape, or African, buffalo is a distinctive, highly social, ox-like animal that lives as part of a herd. It prefers well-watered savannah, though also occurs in forested areas. Buffalo are primarily grazers and need regular access to water, where they swim readily. Lion often follow herds of buffalo, their favourite prey.

Huge herds are generally fairly peaceful, and experienced guides will often walk straight through them on walking safaris. However, small bachelor herds, and especially single old bulls, can be very nervous and aggressive. They have a reputation for charging at the slightest provocation, often in the midst of thick bush, and are exceedingly dangerous when wounded.

Buffalo smell and hear well, but it's often claimed that they have poor eyesight. This isn't true, though when encountered during a walking safari, if you keep still and the wind is right they won't be able to discern your presence.

Common and widespread in sub-Saharan Africa, in Botswana the buffalo is limited to the north of the country, largely by the absence of sufficient water in the rest of the country. Their annual movements mirror those of elephants in general terms. During the rains, from December onwards, they disperse into the mopane forests and into the drier areas of the northern Kalahari, splitting up into smaller groups and spreading out.

However, as the dry season progresses, they gather together into larger herds, and congregate near permanent sources of water: along the Chobe, Kwando and Linyanti rivers – and throughout the Okavango Delta. Then you'll see them in most reserves with water, though the open plains of NG23 (Duba Plains) seem to have particularly high concentrations of buffalo.

Giraffe *Giraffa camelopardis* Shoulder height 250–350cm. Weight 1,000–1,400kg.
The world's tallest and longest-necked land animal, a fully grown giraffe can measure up to 5.5m high. Quite unmistakable, giraffe live in loosely structured herds of up to 15 head, though herd members often disperse when they are seen singly or in smaller groups. Formerly distributed throughout East and southern Africa, in Botswana these great browsers are now found only in the centre and north of the country. The CKGR has a very healthy population, as do Makgadikgadi and Nxai, and they are also found through the Chobe, Kwando-Linyanti and Okavango areas.

Giraffe are adapted to browse vegetation that is beyond the reach of all the other large herbivores, with the exception of elephant. They prefer *Acacia* and *Combretum* species, and an 18-inch tongue ensures that they can extract the leaves from the most thorny of branches.

Burchell's zebra *Equus burchelli* Shoulder height 130cm. Weight 300–340kg.
Also known as common or plains zebra, this attractive striped horse is common and widespread throughout most of East and southern Africa, where it is often seen in large herds alongside wildebeest. There are many subspecies of zebra in Africa, and most southern races, including those in Botswana, have paler brownish 'shadow stripes' between the bold black stripes (which are present in all races).

Zebra are common in most conservation areas, from northern South Africa, Namibia and all the way up to the southeast of Ethiopia. In Botswana they occur in Makgadikgadi, Nxai and to the north– but I don't believe that they still occur within the CKGR. If the rains have been good in the Makgadikgadi Pans area, then during the first few months of the year you can witness huge herds of zebra roaming across the open plains in search of the freshest new grass.

Warthog *Phacochoreus africanus* Shoulder height 60–70cm. Weight up to 100kg.
This widespread and often conspicuously abundant resident of the African savannah is grey in colour with a thin covering of hairs, wart-like bumps on its face, and rather large, upward-curving tusks. Africa's only diurnal swine, the warthog is often seen in family groups, trotting around with its tail raised stiffly (a diagnostic trait) and a determinedly nonchalant air.

They occur throughout Botswana with the exception of the far south, although they don't usually fare well near settlements, as they are very susceptible to subsistence hunting/poaching. Wherever they occur, you'll often see them grazing beside the road, on bended knee.

Similar species Bulkier, hairier and browner, the **bushpig** (*Potomochoerus larvatus*) only occurs in the wetter areas of northern Botswana – northern Chobe, the Kwando-Linyanti and the Okavango. Like the warthog, they don't survive well near settlements: they damage crops and so are persistently hunted. That said, even where they do occur, they are rarely seen due to their nocturnal habits and preference for living in dense vegetation.

Small mammals

African civet *Civettictis civetta* Shoulder height 40cm. Weight 10–15kg.

This bulky, long-haired, rather feline creature of the African night is primarily carnivorous, feeding on small animals and carrion, but will also eat fruit. It has a similarly coloured coat to a leopard, which is densely blotched with large black spots becoming stripes towards the head. Civets are widespread and common throughout a band across northern Botswana, including Chobe, the Kwando-Linyanti and Okavango areas. They occur in many habitats, and make frequent cameo appearances on night drives.

Note that although they are occasionally referred to as 'civet cats', this is misleading. They are more closely related to the mongooses than the felines.

Similar species The **small-spotted genet** (*Genetta genetta*) and **large-spotted genet** (*Genetta tigrina*) are two members of a large group of similar small predators found in Botswana. As even experts often can't tell the various species apart without examining their skins by hand, precise identification of genets is difficult. All the genets are slender and rather feline in appearance (though they are *not* cats), with a grey to gold-brown coat marked with black spots (perhaps combining into short bars) and a long ringed tail.

You're most likely to see genets on nocturnal game drives or occasionally scavenging around game reserve lodges. The small-spotted genet is found all over Botswana, whereas its larger cousin is thought to be restricted to the northern areas of Chobe, Kwando-Linyanti and Okavango. Genets are excellent climbers and opportunists, eating fruit, small birds, termites and even scorpions.

Banded mongoose *Mungos mungo* Shoulder height 20cm. Weight around 1kg.

The banded mongoose is probably the most commonly observed member of a group of small, slender, terrestrial carnivores. Uniform dark grey-brown except for a dozen black stripes across its back, it is a diurnal mongoose occurring in playful family groups, or troops, in most habitats throughout northern and northwestern Botswana. It feeds on insects, scorpions, amphibians, reptiles and even carrion and bird's eggs, and can move through the bush at quite a pace.

Similar species Another six or so mongoose species occur in Botswana. Some are social and gather in troops; others are solitary. Several are too scarce and nocturnal to be seen by most visitors.

The water or **marsh mongoose** (*Atilax paludinosus*) is large, normally solitary and has a very scruffy brown coat; it's widespread in the Chobe, Kwando-Linyanti and Okavango regions.

The **white-tailed mongoose** (*Ichneumia albicauda*), or white-tailed ichneumon, is a solitary, large brown mongoose with long, coarse, woolly hair. It is nocturnal and easily identified by its bushy white tail if seen crossing roads at night. It has a similar distribution, where it can also be found in a few cattle-ranching areas, where it eats the beetle-grubs found in manure.

The **slender mongoose** (*Galerella sanguinea*) is also widespread throughout Botswana where there is lots of cover for it. It, too, is solitary, but it is very much smaller (shoulder height 10cm) and has a uniform brown or reddish coat and blackish tail tip. Its tail is held up when it runs.

The **large grey mongoose** (*Herpestes ichneumon*), also called the Egyptian mongoose, is a large mongoose with coarse, grey-speckled body hair, black lower legs and feet, and a black tip to its tail. It's found in the same northern areas of Botswana, but is common nowhere. It is generally diurnal and is either solitary, or lives in pairs. Large grey mongooses eat small rodents, reptiles, birds and also snakes – generally killing rather than scavenging.

Selous's mongoose (*Paracynictis selousi*) is smaller, with fine, speckled grey fur, and a white tip at the end of its tail. It likes open country and woodlands, occurring in many areas of northern and the further eastern areas of Botswana. It is nocturnal and solitary, eating mainly insects, grubs, small reptiles and amphibians – it seems especially fond of the larvae of dung beetles, and so is sometime found in cattle country.

The **yellow mongoose** (*Cynitis penicillata*) is a small, sociable mongoose with a tawny or yellow coat, and is commonly found across most of Botswana – even in the drier areas of the central Kalahari. It normally forages alone and is easily identified by the white tip on the end of its tail.

Finally, **the dwarf mongoose** (*Helogate parvula*) is a diminutive (shoulder height 7cm), highly sociable light brown mongoose often seen in the vicinity of the termite mounds where it nests. This is Africa's smallest carnivore, occurring in a higher density than any other, it is widespread throughout the Chobe, Kwando-Linyanti and Okavango areas and often seen. Groups of 20–30 are not unknown, consisting of a breeding pair and subordinate others. These inquisitive little animals can be very entertaining to watch.

Meerkat or **suricate** *Suricata suricatta* Shoulder height 25–35cm. Weight 650–950g.
Found throughout central and southwest Botswana, and much of neighbouring Namibia, meerkats are absent from Makgadikgadi and further north. The best places to see them are the CKGR and further towards the southwest corner of Botswana (eg: the KD1 concession, south of Ghanzi, and the Kgalagadi Transfrontier Park).

These small animals are sandy to silvery-grey in colour, with dark bands running across their backs. They are exclusively diurnal and have a distinctive habit of sitting upright on their hind legs. They do this when they first emerge in the morning, to sun themselves, and throughout the day.

Living in complex social groups, meerkats are usually seen scratching around for insects, beetles and small reptiles in dry, open, grassy areas. Whilst the rest forage, one or two of the group will use the highest mound around as a sentry-post – looking out for predators using their remarkable eyesight. Meerkats' social behaviour is very complex: they squeak constantly to communicate and even use different alarm calls for different types of predators. Because of their photogenic poses and fascinating social behaviour, they have been the subject of several successful television documentaries filmed in the southern Kalahari.

Honey badger *Mellivora capensis* Shoulder height 30cm. Weight 12kg.
Also known as the ratel, the honey badger is black with a puppyish face and grey-white back. It is an opportunistic feeder best known for its allegedly symbiotic relationship with a bird called the honeyguide which leads it to a bee hive, waits for it to tear it open, then feeds on the scraps. The honey badger is among the most widespread of African carnivores, and also amongst the most powerful and aggressive for its size. It occurs all over Botswana, but is thinly distributed and infrequently seen, except when it has lost its fear of people and started to scavenge from safari camps.

Similar species Other mustelids occurring in the region include the **striped polecat** (*Ictonyx striatus*), a common but rarely seen nocturnal creature with black underparts and a bushy white back.

Cape clawless otter *Aonyx capensis* Shoulder height 20–30cm. Weight 3–5kg.
This is the larger of the two species of otter that occur in southern Africa. It has a chocolate-brown coat with a pale creme-to-white chin and throat. In Botswana, it is restricted to the northern river systems of Chobe, Kwando-Linyanti and the Okavango (it's not found in broad, tropical rivers like the Zambezi), though will occasionally move away from there, across dry land, in search of other pools and waterways.

Cape clawless otters are active mostly around dusk and dawn, although they will sometimes be seen in broad daylight or at night. Rough skin on their paws gives excellent grip, and with this they prey mostly on frogs and fish. They'll also take freshwater mussels, and will use rocks to help them crack these open.

Although very shy (they'll usually flee when approached by a boat or people), they're delightful to watch; seeming very playful with a variety of aquatic acrobatics and cleaning their face and paws scrupulously after every meal. Visiting Botswana, you're most likely to see otters in the shallow floodplain areas of the Okavango when on a quiet mokoro trip.

Similar species The smaller **spotted-necked otter** (*Lutra maculicollis*) is darker with light white spots on its throat – though difficult to distinguish from its larger cousin unless you're familiar with them both. Their distribution and habits are similar to the Cape clawless, though they are more diurnal, and more tied to bodies of water.

Aardvark *Orycteropus afer* Shoulder height 60cm. Weight up to 70kg.
This singularly bizarre nocturnal insectivore is unmistakable with its long snout, huge ears and powerful legs, adapted to dig up the nests of termites, on which it feeds. Aardvarks occur throughout southern Africa, except the driest western areas of the Namib. Though their distinctive three-toed tracks are often seen, and they are not uncommon animals, sightings of them are rare.

Aardvarks prefer areas of grassland and sparse scrub, rather than dense woodlands, so much of Botswana's bush suits them well. You're most likely to see them on a late-night game drive, and many guides say that they are seen more often during the rainy season, from December to March.

Pangolin *Manis temmincki* Total length 70–100cm. Weight 8–15kg.
Sharing the aardvaak's diet of termites and ants, the pangolin is another very unusual nocturnal insectivore – with distinctive armour plating and a tendency to roll up in a ball when disturbed. (Then it can swipe its tail from side to side – inflicting serious damage on its aggressor.) Sometimes known as Temminck's pangolins, or scaly anteaters, these strange animals walk on their hindlegs, using their tail and front legs for balance. They are both nocturnal and rare, and their distribution is uncertain, although they are thought to occur throughout Botswana. Sightings are exceedingly rare; thus an average of three sightings of pangolin per year in NG31 Reserve counts as a remarkably prolific record by the standards of most areas in Africa!

In some areas further south, particularly Zimbabwe, local custom is to make a present of any pangolin found to the paramount chief (often taken to mean the president). This has caused great damage to their population.

Porcupine *Hystrix africaeaustralis* Total length 80–100cm. Weight 15–25kg.
This is the largest rodent found in the region, and occurs all over southern Africa, except for the western reaches of the Namib Desert. It easily identified by its black-and-white striped quills, generally black hair, and shambolic gait. If heard in the dark, then the rustle of its foraging is augmented by the slight rattle of its quills. These drop off fairly regularly, and are often found in the bush.

The porcupine's diet is varied, and they are fairly opportunistic when it comes to food. Roots and tubers are favourites, as is the bark of cetain trees; they will also eat meat and small reptiles or birds if they have the chance. You're most likely to see porcupines on night drives, as individuals, pairs or small family groups.

Similar species Also spiky, the **Southern African hedgehog** (*Erinaceus frontalis*) has been recorded in eastern and southeastern areas of Botswana, though it is small and nocturnal, so rarely seen even where it does occur. Hedgehogs are about 20cm long (much smaller than porcupines), omnivorous and uncommon.

Rock hyrax *Procavia capensis* Shoulder height 35–30cm. Weight 4kg. Rodent-like in appearance, hyraxes (also known as dassies) are claimed to be the closest living relative of elephants. The rock hyrax and similar **Yellow-spotted rock hyrax** (*Heterohyrax brucei)* are often seen sunning themselves in rocky habitats, and become tame when used to people.

They are social animals, living in large groups, and are largely herbivores, eating leaves, grasses and fruits. Where you see lots of dassies, watch out for black eagles and other raptors which prey extensively on them. In Botswana they're restricted to the southeast of the country, although places like the Tsodilo Hills would seem like an ideal habitat for them.

Scrub hare *Lepus saxatilis* Shoulder height 45–60cm. Weight 1–4.5kg.
This is the largest and most common African hare or rabbit, occurring everywhere in Botswana. In some areas a short walk at dusk or after nightfall might reveal three or four scrub hares. They tend to freeze when disturbed.

Similar species Very similar, the **Cape hare** (*Lepus capensis*) has been recorded in Botswana, both in the southwest and in an area to the north of the great salt pans. However, distinguishing between these two similar species at night, when they are most likely to be seen, would be very difficult.

Ground squirrel *Xerus inauris* Shoulder height 20–30cm. Weight 400–700g.
This terrestrial rodent is common in the more arid parts of Botswana, including the central Kalahari, and southeastern areas. The ground squirrel is grey to grey-brown with a prominent white eye ring and silver-black tail. Within its range, it might be confused with the meerkat, which also spends much time on its hind legs. Unlike the meerkat, the ground squirrels has a characteristic squirrel mannerism of holding food in its forepaws.

The ground squirrel is a social animal; large groups share one communal burrow. It can often be spotted searching for vegetation, seeds, roots and small insects, whilst holding its tail aloft as a sunshade.

Bush squirrel *Paraxerus cepapi* Total length 35cm. Weight 100–250g.
This common rodent is a uniform grey or buff colour, with a long tail that is furry but not bushy. It's widely distributed all over southern and East Africa, and occurs throughout northern Botswana in most woodland habitats, although not wet evergreen or montane forests. Bush squirrels are so numerous in mopane woodlands that it can be difficult to avoid seeing it, hence its other common name – the mopane squirrel.

Bush squirrels live alone, in pairs, or in small groups, usually nesting in a drey of dry leaves, in a hole in a tree. They are diurnal and venture to the ground to feed on seeds, fruit, nuts, vegetable matter and small insects. When alarmed they often bolt up the nearest tree, keeping on the side of the trunk away from the threat, out of sight as much as possible. If they can find a safe vantage point with a view of the threat, then they'll sometimes make a loud clicking alarm call.

Appendix 2

LANGUAGE
Based on an original compiled by Phil Deutschle

Setswana is the national language of Botswana, while English is the official language. In practice this means that though many people speak other languages at home, most will be able to converse in Setswana. English will be spoken by those who have been to school, or who have been outside the country. This means most people, with the exception of the older generation in rural areas.

Learning to speak a little Setswana is easy and, even in educated circles, trying to speak a few words of the language will mark you out as showing respect for the country's culture. It will open many doors, and really make a difference to how you are received. Carry the most important phrases on a slip of paper, and practise whenever you can.

Pronunciation

The only difficult sound is the g, pronounced like ch in the Scottish 'loch' or German 'Ich'. If you have trouble with that, just say the g like an ordinary h. The r is often rolled. Vowels are pronounced as follows:

a	like a in China
e	like ay in day
i	like ee in see
o	like o in go
u	like oo in too

Greetings

Greetings are relatively easy to master, as you can practise them with everyone you meet. They'll also get you instant results; using them is almost guaranteed to bring a smile to the face of those you greet – whilst sending out the message that you're not an arrogant foreigner who can't be bothered to learn a word of Setswana. So even if you never learn anything else in Setswana – do learn the basic greetings and it'll make your trip so much easier and more pleasant.

English	Setswana
Words in underlined italics are optional	
Hello (literally 'Greetings Sir/Madam')	*Dumela Rra/Mma*
How did you rise?	*O tsogile jang?*
I have risen *well*	*Ke tsogile sentle*
How did you spend the day?	*O tlhotse jang?*
I spent the day *well*	*Ke tlhotse sentle*
How are you? (Informal)	*O kae?*
I'm fine (Literally, 'I'm here')	*Ke teng*
It's OK	*Go siame*

517

I am going	*Ke a tsamaya*
Stay well (said to someone staying)	*Sala sentle*
Go well (said to someone going)	*Tsamaya sentle*
Sleep well	*Robala sentle*

Basic phrases

What's your name? (formal)	*Leina la gago ke mang?*
My name is ...	*Leina la me ke ...*
Who are you? (informal)	*O mang?*
I'm ...	*Ke ...*
Where are you from? or	
Where are you coming from?	*O tswa kee?*
I'm (coming) from ...	*Ke tswa kwa ...*
Yes	*Ee*
No	*Nnyaa*
I don't know _Setswana_	*Ga ke itse _Setswana_*
What is this _in Setswana_?	*Se ke eng ka Setswana?*
How goes it?	*Wa reng?*
It goes OK	*Ga ke bue*
Thank you	*Ke itumetse*
What's the time?	*Nako ke mang?*
Excuse me!	*Sorry!*
I'm asking for money/tobacco	*Ke kopa madi/motsoko*
I have no money/tobacco	*Ga ke na madi/motsoko*

Shopping

Numbers are unusually said in English.

Where's the shop?	*Shopo e kae?*
What do you want?	*O batla eng?*
I want ...	*Ke batla/kopa ...*
There is none	*Ga go na*
How much?	*Ke bokae?*
It's expensive/cheap	*Go a tura/tshipi*
Sugar	*Sukiri*
Meali meal	*Dupr*
Tea/coffee	*Tee/kofee*
Meat	*Fnama*
Milk	*Mashi*
Water	*Metse*

Travelling phrases

Where are you going?	*O ya kae?*
I'm going to ...	*Ke ya ...*
Where are you coming from?	*O tswa kae?*
I'm coming from ...	*Ke tswa kwa ...*
Far/near	*Kgakala/gaufi*
I'm satisfied (regarding food)	*Ke kgotshe*
It tastes good	*Go monate*
Men/Women (written on toilets)	*Banna/Basadi*
What do you do? (your job)	*O dira eng?*

Appendix

FURTHER READING
Coffee-table picture books

Chobe – Africa's Untamed Wilderness by Daryl and Sharna Balfour. ISBN 1-86812-692-7
Published in 1997 by Southern Book Publishers (Pty) Ltd, PO Box 3103, Halfway
House 1685, South Africa. An almost day-by-day account of a year that this renowned
couple spent in Chobe and Selinda. Good pictures and a readable diary-format style give
a fair picture of the changing seasons and the wildlife.

Okavango – Africa's Last Eden by Frans Lanting. ISBN 0-8118-0527-1. Published in 1993 by
Chronicle Books, 275 Fifth Street, San Francisco, CA 94103. Probably the ultimate in
coffee-table books includes minimal text but many impressive and beautiful images that
were originally commissioned for the *National Geographic* magazine.

The Swamp Book – A View of the Okavango by Bob Forester, Mike Murray-Hudson and
Lance Cherry. ISBN 1-86812-154-2. Published 1989 by Southern Book Publishers Ltd,
PO Box 548, Bergvlei 2012, Jo'burg. This interesting and quirky coffee-table book
includes highly readable sections on the Okavango Delta, and some of its more common
flora and fauna, as well as comments on a few interesting historical accounts of travel
there. Photographs include several taken under water.

Okavango – Africa's Wetland Wilderness by Adrian Bailey. ISBN 1-86872-041-1. Published
1998 by Struik Publishers Ltd., Cornelis Struik House, 80 McKenzie Street, Cape Town
8001, South Africa. Bright colour plates and a generally informative text make this a
good coffee-table overview of the Delta.

The Miracle Rivers – The Okavango and Chobe of Botswana by Peter and Beverly Pickford.
ISBN 1-86812-755-9. Published 1999 by Southern Books, PO Box 3103, Halfway
House, 1685 Jo'burg. A coffee-table book with some colour plates and grainy black-and-
white shots. Text is a mixture of quotes and travelogue with attention (and almost
homage) paid to various hunting operations.

Savuti – The Vanishing River by Clive Walker. ISBN 1-86812-365-1. Published in 1991 by
Southern Book Publishers (Pty) Ltd, PO Box 3103, Halfway House 1685, South Africa.
Using many simple line drawings, and just a sprinkling of generally impressive
photographs, this is less pictorial than most coffee-table books. It concentrates mainly on
Walker's personal experiences in Savuti, where he spent time with Lloyd Wilmot,
amongst others, and witnessed the final drying out of the Savuti Channel. It's a good
read, though too large to easily travel with.

Okavango: Jewel of the Kalahari by Karen Ross. ISBN 0-563-20545-8. Published in 1987 by
BBC Books, BBC Enterprises Ltd, Woodlands, 80 Wood Lane, London W12 0TT,
England. Written by Karen Ross in parallel with her research for a short series of films,
produced by Partridge Films for the BBC. The film series is stunning, and certainly
raised the UK's awareness of the Okavango Delta considerably when it was first shown.
The book's also first class. Its photography is good, though not exceptional, but the
depth of its text raises it well above the normal standard of coffee-table books. Though
perhaps slightly dated now, it's still well worth getting hold of.

Running Wild: Dispelling the Myths of the African Wild Dog. Text by John McNutt and Lesley Boggs Ross; photography by Hélène Heldring and Dave Hamman. ISBN 1-86812-717-6. Published in 1996 by Southern Book Publishers, PO Box 3103, Halfway House, 1685, South Africa. Some beautiful pictures of dogs in the Delta (the 'Mombo Pack' in the early 1990s) plus informative text about their behaviour and group dynamics – put into the context of observations made throughout northern Botswana.

The Lion Children by Angus, Maisie and Travers McNeice. ISBN 0-75284-160-2. First published in 2001 by Orion Books Ltd, 5 Upper St. Martin's Lane, London. Taken from the UK to live in the Okavango (around NG34) by their parents, who moved there to research lions, this an entertaining scrapbook written by the children about life in the bush. Whilst basically a children's book, it's a lot of fun to read and occasionally quite insightful.

Botswana notes and records

The Botswana Society (see page 149) has published an annual journal since 1969. It contains 'scientific, and semi-scientific articles and notes, written by amateur as well as professional experts on subjects of permanent interest relating to Botswana'. This is an amazing archive of reliable information, which I've only scratched the surface of here – it's a real treasure trove for anyone interested in Botswana. During my researches I've read many articles and made reference to some of them, including the main ones, which are mentioned here:

A Preliminary Report on the Number, Distribution and Movement of Elephants in the Chobe National Park with Notes on Browse Utilisation by M W L Sommerlatte. Volume 7 (1975), pages 121–9.

Clan sized of Spotted Hyenas in the Savuti Region of Chobe National Park, Botswana by Dr S M Cooper. Volume 21 (1989), pages 121–33.

The Depression Rock Shelter Site, Tsodilo Hills by L H Robbins and A C Campbell. Volume 20 (1989), pages 1–3.

Excavations at the Tsodilo Hills Rhino Cave by L H Robbins, M L Murphy, A C Campbell and G A Brook. Volume 28 (1996), pages 23–45.

The Caves of Ngamiland: An Interim Report on Explorations and Fieldwork 1972–74 by H J Cooke and T Baillieul. Volume 6 (1974), pages 147–56.

A Terminal Pleistocen Assemblage from Drotsky's Cave, Western Ngamiland by J E Yellen, A S Brooks, R Stuckenrath and R Welbourne. Volume 19 (1987), pages 1–6.

Discovery and Preliminary Exploration of a New Cave in the Gcwihaba Valley by R C Ritter and R A Garner. Volume 26 (1994), pages 55–65.

Resurvey of Gcwihaba Cave and Exploration of the Aha Sinkhole Caves by R A Garner and R C Ritter. Volume 26 (1994), pages 183–8.

Further Exploration and Resurvey of !WaDoum Cave by P M Mann and R C Ritter. Volume 27 (1995), pages 13–20.

New Locality Record for the Klipspinger by P C Viljoen. Volume 12 (1980), page 169.

A Comment on Kalahari Wildlife and the Khukhe Fence by Alec Campbell. Volume 13 (1981), pages 111–18.

Some Edible Wild Cucumbers of Botswana by Audrey Renew. Volume 1 (1968), pages 5–8.

The Middle Stone Age of Kudiakam Pan by Lawrence H Robbins. Volume 20 (1989), pages 41–50.

The Riddle of the Stone Walls by Alec Campbell. Volume 23 (1991), pages 243–50.

Discovery and Exploration of Two New Caves in the Northwest District by Ron Ritter and Paul Mann. Volume 27 (1995), pages 1–12.

Modelling of Surface Outflow from the Okavango Delta by A Gieske. Volume 28 (1996), pages 165–92.

Putting the Bushmen on the Map of Botswana by Cornelis VanderPost. Volume 32 (2000), pages 107–15.

Franz or Klikko, the Wild Dancing Bushmen: A Case Study in Khoisan Stereotyping by Q N Parsons. Volume 20 (1989), pages 71–6.

A Chronology of Major Events Relating to the Central Kalahari Game Reserve by Robert Hitchcock. Volume 31 (1999), pages 105–17.

Some Notes on the Colonial Era History of the Central Kalahari Game Reserve Region by Jeff Ramsay. Volume 20 (1989), pages 91–4.

The Climate of Botswana in Histograms by J Andringa. Volume 16 (1984), pages 117–26.

An Assessment of the Impact of Fences on Large Herbivore Biomass in the Kalahari by D T & J E Williamson. Volume 13 (1981), pages 107–10.

A Comment on Kalahari Wildlife and the Khukhe Fence by Alec Campbell. Volume 13 (1981), pages 111–18.

Other useful guides

The Guide to Botswana by Alec Campbell. ISBN 0-620-04579-5. First published in 1968 by Winchester Press (Pty) Limited, PO Box 41490, Craighall, Johannesburg, South Africa. Alec Campbell is perhaps the leading authority on Botswana's natural areas and history, having not only lived in Botswana for most of his life, but also held posts as the Director of National Parks and later as the Director of the National Museum of Botswana. There were several very substantial editions to this early guide which give insights into what Botswana was like decades ago. It's also fascinating to contrast and compare his guides with more contemporary guidebooks.

Life and Work of Thomas Baines by Jane Carruthers & Marion Arnold. ISBN 1-874950-12-1. Published by Fernwood Press PO Box 1534, 8081 Vlaeberg, South Africa. Published 1995, reprinted 1996.

An Explorer's Handbook – Travel, Survival and Bush Cookery by Christina Dodwell. 1984. Hodder and Stoughton, 47 Bedford Square, London, WC1B 3DP. ISBN 0-340-34937-9. Over 170 pages of both practical and amusing anecdotes, including chapters on 'unusual eatables', 'building an open fire', and 'tested exits from tight corners'. Practical advice for both possible and most unlikely eventualities – and it's a great read.

Bugs, Bites & Bowels by Dr Jane Wilson-Howarth. Published in the UK by Cadogan Books Plc, London House, Parkgate Road, London SW11 4NQ. Distributed in the US by Globe Pequot Press. ISBN 0-86011-045-2. An amusing and erudite overview of the hazards of tropical travel which is small enough to take with you.

Your Child's Health Abroad: A Manual for Travelling Parents by Dr Jane Wilson-Howarth and Dr Matthew Ellis. Published 1998 in the UK by Bradt Publications and in the US by Globe Pequot Press. ISBN 1-898323-63-1. Full of practical first-hand advice from two leading medical experts. An indispensable guide if you plan to travel abroad with young children.

Discovering Southern Africa by T V Bulpin. Published in South Africa by Discovering Southern Africa Productions, distributed by Book Sales. ISBN 0-9583130-1-6. Part guidebook and part history book, Bulpin covers mainly South Africa but also extends into Namibia and Zimbabwe. A weighty tome with useful background views and information, written from a South African perspective.

East and Southern Africa: The Backpacker's Manual by Philip Briggs. Published in 1998 by Bradt Publications, UK and Globe Pequot Press, USA. ISBN 1-898323-60-7. If you are venturing into Southern Africa for a long budget trip, buy this book. It won't spoon-feed you with all the nitty-gritty details, but it will guide you to make your own discoveries and offer help when you really need it. An excellent manual.

The Lost World of the Kalahari by Laurens van der Post. First published by the Hogarth Press in 1958, subsequently many reprints published by Penguin. Laurens van der Post's classic account of how he journeyed into the heart of the Kalahari Desert in search of a 'pure' Bushman group – eventually found at the Tsodilo Hills. His almost mystical description of the Bushmen is fascinating, so long as you can cope with the rather dated turgid prose. You then need to read Robert J Gordon's very different book, *The Bushman Myth* (see below), to put it in perspective.

The Visitor's Guide to Botswana by Mike Main. The third edition was published in South Africa in 1996 by Southern Book Publishers (Pty) Ltd, PO Box 3103, Halfway House 1685, South Africa. ISBN 1 86812 657 9. Mike Main is a leading authority on all things to do with Botswana, and especially its wilder areas. This book is aimed mostly at readers who are resident in, or very familiar with, Southern Africa. It features route descriptions for some very offbeat 4WD trips, including a few GPS points and schematic maps of the routes.

Top Birding Spots of Southern Africa compiled by Hugh Chittenden. Published in 1992 by Southern Book Publishers (Pty) Ltd, PO Box 3103, Halfway House 1685, South Africa. ISBN 1 86812 419 3. This useful, practical book details about 400 sites for keen birdwatchers, listing local specialities and endemic species with a checklist of key species for each site. Some of its simple maps are now out of date, though I'm not aware of it being reprinted in the last decade.

Field guides

Newman's Birds of Southern Africa by Kenneth Newman. Southern Book Publishers, PO Box 3103, Halfway House 1685, South Africa. ISBN 1-86812-623-4. This has been re-published numerous times since its first edition in 1988 and has become the standard field guide to birds in southern Africa, south of the Kunene and Zambezi rivers. It also covers most species found in Zambia.

Trees & Shrubs of the Okavango Delta by Veronica Roodt. Published in 1998 by Shell Oil Botswana, Queen's Road, The Mall, Gaborone. ISBN 99912-0-241-2. This first book in Shell Publication's 'Field Guide' series isn't just about trees or shrubs, and doesn't restrict its comments rigidly to the Okavango – but it is a masterpiece. Veronica Roodt has lived and worked in Moremi for many years, researching the plants of the area. This book is ostensibly just a field guide to slightly over sixty of the more common trees and shrubs in the area, but in reality it's a fascinating treatise on the insects and animals associated with all of them, plus the medicinal uses and local superstitions attached to each. It's well worth buying a copy as soon as you get to Botswana, even if you're not that interested in trees; it reads very well!

Common Wild Flowers of the Okavango Delta by Veronica Roodt. Published in 1998 by Shell Oil Botswana, Queen's Road, The Mall, Gaborone. ISBN 99912-0-242-0. The second book in Shell's 'Field Guide' series is a little more specialist than the first book on trees, but still manages to comment on diverse topics from the formulae for gunpowder to the treatment of scorpion stings. Like its companion book on trees, it's well worth getting.

The Safari Companion by Richard Estes. ISBN: 0-9583223-3-3. Co-published in 1993 by Russell Friedman Books CC, PO Box 73, Halfway House 1685, South Africa. (Also co-published in Zimbabwe by Tutorial Press, and in Vermont by Chelsea Green Publishing.). Whilst slightly too thick to be an ideal travelling companion, this is a real treasure-chest of information on animal behaviour. It covers all the main animal species found on mainland Africa, from duikers and dwarf antelope to cats, dogs and the great apes. For each it includes a brief description of their social systems and forms of communication, with helpful outlines of body postures and diagrams to explain their typical forms of behaviour. If you've longed to decipher the language of animals, and have the time to stop and watch rather than simply tick game off a list, then you must bring this book.

Historical interest

Serowe: Village of the Rain Wind by Bessie Head offers a fascinating collection of oral history transcripts recording the villagers' memories of their past, and especially the deeds of their enlightened leaders, Khama the Great who ruled from 1875 to 1923, Tshekedi

Khama (1926–59), his son from a late second marriage, and finally Sir Seretse Khama, Khama's grandson, by his first born son Segkoma II (1923–25), who became first president of the independent Botswana.

Africa: A Biography of the Continent by John Reader. 1997. Penguin Books Ltd, 27 Wrights Lane, London W8 5TZ, England. ISBN 0-241-13047-6. Over 700 pages of highly readable history, interwoven with facts and statistics, to make a remarkable overview of Africa's past. Given that Botswana's boundaries were imposed from Europe, its history must be looked at from a pan-African context to be understood. This book can show you that wider view; it is compelling and essential reading. (Chapter 41 and 42 deal with the early settlers in the Cape, and is largely devoted to the Lozi people.)

The Archaeology of Botswana edited by Paul Lane, Andrew Reid and Alinah Segobya. Co-published in 1998 by The Botswana Society, PO Box 71, Gaborone, Botswana. ISBN 99912 60 39 0. This is a detailed and academic overview of the archaeology of Botswana, as well as how archaeology has progressed in the country to date. It's an excellent reference, but not a light read.

Travels and Researches in Southern Africa by David Livingstone. 1857. This classic is fascinating reading, over a century after it was written.

The Bushman Myth: The Making of a Namibian Underclass by Robert J Gordon. Published in 1992 by Westview Press Inc, 5500 Central Ave, Boulder, Colorado, 80301-2847. Also in the UK by Westview Press, 36 Lonsdale Road, Summertown, Oxford. ISBN 0-8133-1381-3. If you, like me, had accepted the received wisdom that Bushmen are the last descendants of stone-age man, pushed to living in splendid isolation in the Kalahari, then you must read this. It places the Bushmen in an accurate historical context and deconstructs many of the myths we have created about them. Despite being mainly based on facts about the San in Namibia, it's still well worth reading for an understanding of their position in contemporary Botswana.

Lake Ngami and the River Okavango by Charles John Andersson. Originally published in the late 1850s, but republished as a facsimile reprint by C Struik of Cape Town in 1967. These two fascinating books record Namibia and Botswana in the 1850s through the eyes of one of the first traders and hunters in the area.

Explorations in South-West Africa by Thomas Baines. Published 1864 in London. Although linked more with the countries further east, the travels of Baines, as he accompanied Livingstone and others, makes good reading and is well illustrated by the author.

The Road to Independence by Peter Fawcus and Alan Tilbury. Co-published in 2000 by the Botswana Society, PO Box 71, Gaborone. ISBN 99912 6040 4. The authors of this were two of Britain's most senior administrators during the final decade that led to Botswana's independence. Their book paints a rare picture (quite densely-packed with detail) of a country's smooth transition from a colonial protectorate to an independent state – and has a particularly interesting foreword by Sir Ketumile Masire, one of Botswana's former presidents.

The Mammals of South West Africa by G.C. Shortridge. Published 1934 in London. This is more of historical interest than a practical field guide.

Other useful references

Article: *Why gossip is good for you* by R I M Dunbar. Published in *New Scientist* November 21 1992.

Article in *Science* magazine, November 10 issue, by Ronald Davis, Professor of Biochemistry and Genetics, and director of the Stanford Genome Technology Center.

USEFUL WEBSITES

A selection of the web's most interesting resources on Botswana might include, in alphabetical order:

http://dmoz.org/Regional/Africa/Botswana is the open directory's page on Botswana, which leads to a number of useful links. (The dmoz.org is a useful start point for links to information on any country.)

http://ubh.tripod.com/bw/bhp1.htm is run by a part of the University of Botswana and includes an impressive section on Botswana's history written by Neil Parsons. This links to a number of other relevant web pages covering many topics, from tourism and the media, to history, geography and Botswana's literature. (The university's official site, www.ub.bw, has much less of interest!)

www.advertiser.bw is a site full of commercial and classified advertisements, as found in the *Botswana Advertiser* paper. If you want to buy or sell something in Botswana, or check the latest TV schedules, try here.

www.bidpa.bw is home for the Botswana Institute for Development Policy Analysis (BIDPA). It's a fairly slow-loading, dry NGO site but includes some quite detailed papers of Botswana economic development.

www.cbnrm.bw is the home page of the Community Based Natural Resource Management Support Programme in Botswana. This is an extensive site used as a noticeboard for communities involved in managing areas. It has lots of information about concessions and community developments, if you're prepared to spend time digging through it, and some real gems.

www.chobeguide.com is a fairly impressive and fast-loading directory for the Chobe area – though judging by the inclusion of the long-closed Lloyd's Camp in Savuti, not everything here is up to date.

www.columbia.edu/cu/lweb/indiv/africa/cuvl/Botswana.html is the home page of Botswana at Columbia University's department for African studies. It's a good starting place for information with basic summaries and lots of good links.

www.info.bw is a fast-loading site from one of the country's main ISPs. It includes a listing of virtually every Botswana website (no comments, just an alphabetical list), a useful page of links to the media on the web, and even weather forecasts for Botswana's various towns.

www.gov.bw/home.html is the home page of Botswana's government. It has links to a huge variety of sites from the official tourist information site (which is good) to the various government departments. If you want to email a minister, download the latest customs regulations, or read the latest budget speech – this is the place.

www.mindspring.com/~okavango is a site by the Okavango researcher, John Bock, which focuses on the peoples of the Okavango area – though it also includes numerous links to other sites of interest concerning Botswana.

www.newafrica.com/history is a general pan-African site, but also has good coverage of Botswana's history.

www.okavango-delta.net is a small site with a useful links page, a few photos, a couple of scanned-in maps and a little general information.

www.stud.ntnu.no/~skjetnep/opwt is the site of the Okavango People's Wildlife Trust, an organisation representing some of the Okavango's local communities.

www-sul.stanford.edu/depts/ssrg/africa/bots.html has a long page of links to sites relating to Botswana – some useful, others not – but a useful starting point if you're surfing around seeking information.

www.sunvil.co.uk/africa is the home page for Sunvil Africa, run by the author, which includes a web-based version of most of this book, together with copies of my other guidebooks to Namibia and Zambia. UK residents can order maps from here, and in future there may be downloads of GPS points within Botswana.

www.wits.ac.za/science/geology/okavango is home for the Okavango Study Group within the Geology Department of Wits University, South Africa.

Newspapers on the web

www.gazette.bw is home to the *Botswana Gazette*, an independent paper which is updated every Wednesday. Sadly, the site is limited and there is not yet a proper archive of past editions (though clearly one has been started).

www.gov.bw/cgi-bin/news.cgi is home to the online version of the *Daily News*, the free, government-sponsored paper. There's a good archive going back to the start of January 1999.

www.mmegi.bw has an online version of the substantial Mmegi weekly newspaper which, judging by its website, started an archive in January 2002 but only finally started recording them regularly in April 2002.

Index

Page numbers in bold indicate major entries; those in italic indicate maps or charts.